The Greek Nation, 1453–1669

Bakalopoulos, Apostolos Euangeleu
(1)

The Greek Nation, 1453–1669

The Cultural and Economic Background of Modern Greek Society

By APOSTOLOS E. VACALOPOULOS

Translated from the Greek by Ian and Phania Moles

Rutgers University Press
New Brunswick, New Jersey

DF
801
B3313

Library of Congress Cataloging in Publication Data

Bakalopoulos, Apostolos Euangelou, 1909–
  The Greek nation, 1453–1669.

  Translation of v. 2 of Historia tou neou Hellēnismou.
  Bibliography: p. 417
  Includes index.
  1. Greece, Modern—History—1453–1821.
I. Title.
DF801.B3313   949.5'05   75-23273
ISBN: 0-8135-0810-X

Contents

Maps by Dorothy deFontaine, following index

Illustrations

Maps, by Dorothy deFontaine, following index

```
𝕝𝕝𝕝𝕝𝕝𝕝𝕝𝕝𝕝𝕝𝕝𝕝𝕝𝕝𝕝𝕝𝕝𝕝𝕝𝕝𝕝𝕝𝕝𝕝𝕝𝕝𝕝𝕝𝕝𝕝𝕝𝕝𝕝𝕝𝕝𝕝𝕝𝕝𝕝𝕝
```

ABBREVIATIONS

AAEEG	*Annuaire de l'Association pour l'Encouragement des Études Grecques en France*
AE	Ἀρχαιολογικὴ Ἐφημερίς
AEAΣ	Ἀρχεῖον Ἑταιρείας Αἰτωλοακαρνανικῶν Σπουδῶν
AΠ	Ἀρχεῖον Πόντου
AΘΓΛΘ	Ἀρχεῖον Θρακικοῦ Γλωσσικοῦ Λαογραφικοῦ Θησαυροῦ
AX	Ἀνδριακὰ Χρονικά
BNJ	*Byzantinische Neugriechische Jahrbücher*
BSA	*Annual of the British School of Athens*
BSOAS	*Bulletin of the School of Oriental and African Studies*
Byz.-Sl.	Byzantinoslavica
BZ	Byzantinische Zeitschrift
ΔΙΕΕ	Δελτίον Ἱστορικῆς καὶ Ἐθνολογικῆς Ἑταιρείας
DOP	*Dumbarton Oaks Papers*
ΔΧΑΕ	Δελτίον Χριστιανικῆς Ἀρχαιολογικῆς Ἑταιρείας
ΕΕΒΣ	Ἐπετηρὶς Ἑταιρείας Βυζαντινῶν Σπουδῶν
ΕΕΦΣΠΑ	Ἐπιστημονικὴ Ἐπετηρὶς Φιλοσοφικῆς Σχολῆς Πανεπιστημίου Ἀθηνῶν
ΕΕΦΣΠΘ	Ἐπιστημονικὴ Ἐπετηρὶς Φιλοσοφικῆς Σχολῆς Πανεπιστημίου Θεσσαλονίκης
EMA	Ἐπετηρὶς Μεσαιωνικοῦ Ἀρχείου
Hell. Contemp.	*L'Hellénisme Contemporain*
HME	Ἡμερολόγιον Μεγάλης Ἑλλάδος
HX	Ἠπειρωτικὰ Χρονικά

JHS   *The Journal of Hellenic Studies*
JÖBG   *Jahrbuch der Österreichischen Byzantinischen Gesellschaft*

KX   Κρητικά Χρονικά

ΛΑ   Λαογραφικόν 'Αρχεῖον

MEE   Μεγάλη 'Ελληνική 'Εγκυκλοπαιδεία
MOG   *Mitteilungen zur Osmanischen Geschichte*
MX   Μικρασιατικά Χρονικά

NE   Νέος 'Ελληνομνήμων
NJKA   *Neue Jahrbücher für das Klassische Altertum, Geschichte und*
                       Deutsche Literatur

OCP   *Orientalia Christiana Periodica*

ΠΑΑ   Πρακτικά 'Ακαδημίας 'Αθηνῶν
PG   *Patrologia Graeca*, ed. Jacques Migne

RE   *Real Encyklopädie Pauly-Wissowa*
REB   *Revue des Etudes Byzantines*
REG   *Revue des Etudes Grecques*

SBN   *Studi Bizantini e Neoellenici*

Viz. Vrem.   *Vizantiiskii Vremennik*

ZDMG   *Zeitschrift der Deutschen Morgenländischen Gesellschaft*

INTRODUCTION

In my book *Origins of the Greek Nation: The Byzantine Period, 1204–1461*, I attempted to uncover the roots of modern Hellenism and to trace its development, especially during the fourteenth and fifteenth centuries, through the fall of Constantinople in 1453 and of Trebizond in 1461.

In this volume I continue the story from those two crucial dates up to the time of Crete's submission to the Ottoman Empire in 1669. The period 1453–1669 forms a distinct political and cultural entity. In it the Turkish conquest of the Hellenic world, except for the Ionian Islands, was finally completed. Especially from the beginning of the seventeenth century, there were encouraging signs of economic and intellectual recuperation which led ultimately to the political rebirth of the modern Greek nation.

This volume concentrates on the recovery of the Hellenic world after the capture of Constantinople. It looks at those lands and social classes which took the lead in the process of national revival. It examines the composition of pre-Independence Hellenic society, and it explains how the elements of that society were differentiated from one another. We are here concerned with the social and economic foundations of modern Hellenic society.

Contrary to the belief still held by many, the date 1453 does not mark the beginning of modern Hellenism. The idea of continuity, basic to all history, utterly rejects the notion that on 29 May 1453 the sun set on the Greek Middle Ages and rose next day on the modern era. So far as the history of modern Hellenism is concerned the Capture merely slowed down a development that had already begun and influenced its ultimate shape.

The period covered by this book is really Greece's "Dark Ages." If it were not for the two institutions of Church and Community, into which Greeks withdrew for self-preservation, the nation would no doubt have lost its bearings. But the sufferings of the people drove them to search for better economic and political conditions—abroad, if necessary. In the crucible of daily hardship and spiritual suffering, the metal of Greek nationalism was forged.

Yet the Greeks of today are far from fully conscious of the extent of their forbears' sufferings. The complete picture has not been generally known because, until now, histories of the Greek nation have tended to skip lightly over, or even avoid altogether, the first centuries of Turkish domination. They have taken up the story in the period of modern Hellenism's economic and intellectual flowering, that is, around the middle of the seventeenth century, or even later, during the Enlightenment. Much of what has been written is either out of date or inexact—unsystematic efforts based on inconclusive evidence. Yet it is in these two dark centuries that we find the social and economic foundations of modern Hellenic society and that the hitherto amorphous elements of modern Hellenism began to take shape. The Greeks erected the framework of their modern economy and began a uniform advance along a wide front—economic, intellectual, and political.

I began my research by inspecting those elements of the ancient world which remained strong: elements of a continuing intellectual, economic, military, and political life. The nuclei of future nationhood—clergy, scholars, merchants, simple copyists, soldiers, and others—were found both in occupied Greece and abroad. Many Greeks migrated to Italy, the Balkan countries, especially central and western Europe, and even to the heartland of Russia. In many cases men of considerable personal stature, they not only preserved the thousand-year-old intellectual tradition of the Byzantine Empire, but also contributed in many greater or lesser ways to the development of modern European civilization.

The role of scholars in the process of national rejuvenation was a vital one. Ever vociferous advocates of freedom and the restoration of Greek rule, they guided the progress of modern Hellenism. They represented a dual tradition: on the one hand, the rich written and oral heritage of antiquity, Roman Byzantine law, the whole fabric of Byzantine institutions, traditions, manners, and customs; and on the other, the Orthodox Church with its own distinctive organization and world of ideas. Indeed the Church was the only institution which remained intact and vital from ancient to modern times, a mirror of the Byzantine world. Its powerful ecclesiastical traditions, which were of the essence of Byzantinism, subsumed the intellectual life of Greece and other Balkan nations until almost the end of the eighteenth century. In the early years of the Captivity, the most notable forms of Greek intellectual activity were theological and liturgical works, which signalize the culture of the period. The Church also monitored, as it were, all other Greek intellectual activity, and thus exercised profound historical influence on the general civilization of the day.

Since there was no longer a Greek state, the history of Hellenism under Ottoman rule must be the history of Greeks wherever they lived, both in

Greece proper and outside it. It must be a history of the problems, undertakings, movements, vicissitudes, and readjustments of Greeks. Because the Greek nation was drained and dispersed by Turkish conquest and persecution, Greeks were forced to rehabilitate themselves not only in the territories that were historically their own but also in others. They thus became even more dispersed, especially throughout the Balkan peninsula, where they exerted a considerable influence on the economic, intellectual, and cultural development of their host countries. A knowledge of Greek history under Ottoman rule is therefore prerequisite to a complete understanding of the histories of other Balkan peoples. Conversely, a knowledge of Balkan history and Turkish history is an essential background to the study of Greek history, for many of these peoples shared the same historical experiences—the taxing of Christian raias, mass migrations from the plains to the security of the mountains, conversion to Islam, and the impressment of children, to mention only a few.

The environment in which Greeks had lived and moved from time immemorial—the Greek peninsula, its surrounding islands, and Asia Minor—was one of abrupt physical change. As in ancient times, too, this physical diversity corresponded with just as many variations in ways of life, artistic forms, traditions, manners, and customs. Given such baffling variety the researcher can but hope that with his few historical tools he may be able to offer some insight into the whole or perhaps fit the pieces together. The mosaic will never be complete, but a coherent picture may form if he starts by selecting those pieces which obviously highlight, both spatially and temporally, the principal segments of the whole. Proceeding in this way, he first notices the emergence of a new society in the mountains of continental Greece and in the islands and learns that in order to understand contemporary Greek life it is first necessary to go back to its roots.

Our study of the period of Ottoman rule will therefore involve some reflection upon Frankish rule, Byzantine rule, even antiquity. At a number of points, we shall allude to *Origins of the Greek Nation: The Byzantine Period, 1204–1461* in order to orient the continuing narrative and to demonstrate the essential contiguity of certain historical events. But we shall constantly adduce new evidence.

The problems and adventures of the nation that we recount here help to explain not only its composition but also its ethos, an ethos reflected in its music, its architecture, its painting and other plastic arts, its folk songs and tales, its literature, its manners and customs, its everyday speech. Hundreds of words and expressions commonly employed in conversation and in literature reflect the hardships of Greeks during the Captivity. Such exclamations as "He makes me furious as if I saw a Turk in front of me" or "He changed his faith" (which means that he was tortured so much that he wanted to change his faith) obviously can only be explained by reference to the past. Indeed, the Greeks of today will never become fully attuned to their environment until they become familiar with their history, with the history of modern Hellenism. Without that familiarity, they will have only an imperfect knowledge of their compatriots and even of themselves. Only a systematic study of the past produces an awareness of important events and turning points that rule our lives.

It is quite impossible to arrive at an understanding of modern Greek civilization without a knowledge of particular periods, places, and events that are reflected in it. For example, the klephtic song may be heard but not truly relished without a knowledge of the difficult conditions under which the klephts lived and the natural surroundings in which they moved. By the same token, the poignancy of expatriate songs has little meaning for the listener who knows nothing of the travels of the expatriate, the perils he faced on land and sea, the vast distances which separated him from his homeland, his adventures and misadventures. Finally, to contemplate the imposing homes of many returned expatriates and the remains of their libraries is to apprehend the importance of travel abroad to their owners, but only deeper study reveals the great importance of those travels to the economic and intellectual character of the Greek nation. The period of Turkish rule was for Greeks a calamity. Yet it was also in a way a salutary experience because the blood and tears of successive generations made Greeks forever conscious of the priceless value of freedom.

Since it is all men that make up the material of history—not just the unique man, the hero, nor even the anonymous masses in action—the historian must aim as far as possible at the reconstruction of history in its totality. History is filled with men who were both lesser and greater than these: men more or less distinguished, often anonymous to us, but men whose ideas influenced heroes; and the little men, the simple folk, those who stood aloof from the mob and who acted on their own initiative, who moved, worked, believed, doubted, suffered, made their way, or despaired. Surely there is no more legitimate form of historical inquiry than that about those who make up by far the larger part of humanity.

Presumably history's highest goal may one day be attained: that of bringing men closer together and facilitating their communication with one another, by helping humanity understand itself and each man himself, even if only those parts inherited from the past. And what, after all, is history if it is not this perpetual search for individual and social self-knowledge to the end of achieving a better tomorrow?

The Greek Nation, 1453–1669

THE RAIAS UNDER
OTTOMAN RULE

My book entitled *Origins of the Greek Nation: The Byzantine Period, 1204–1461* told of the vicissitudes of Hellenism as the Ottoman state supplanted the Byzantine Empire, the way in which it adjusted to the new conditions, and how a shift occurred in its center of gravity from East to West. As we saw, the story did not end with the fall of Constantinople and the last remaining vestiges of the Byzantine Empire, but continued until Byzantine civilization was almost totally blotted out.

While the Byzantines struggled to hold on to their religion and national identity, the Turks, adopting an expedient traditional to Islam,[1] fell back on the aid and experience of many Christian and Jewish raias in the task of completing the work of conquest and organizing their rapidly expanding state. Precisely what these former Byzantines—apostates, or advisers to the sultans who remained loyal Christians, Greeks, Italians, and others—brought to the Ottoman Empire from the end of the fifteenth century is a crucial, if often insoluble, problem.

Its solution is not made easier by the fact that its many elements have scarcely been examined in any scrupulous and impartial manner until the present time. Such evidence as has survived convinces us that the administrative organization of the Ottoman state owed a great deal to the Byzantine experience in practically all branches of the state's jurisdiction. Most of all, perhaps, the Ottomans were indebted to that band of Christian advisers and secretaries who were never far from the sultan's side, even on military expeditions.[2] They comprised accountants in the service of the Sublime Porte's exchequer,[3] as well as editors of the diplomatic correspondence, which was dispatched, in the Greek language, to the foreign states of Christendom.

Christian secretaries, scribes (both of letters and treaties) were used by
Moslem rulers, perhaps from the very earliest of times, when relations
were first established between Arab and Byzantine. The language they
used was closer to the everyday spoken tongue than to the written Attic
officially in use. As the years passed, the Moslems used Greek in writing
not only to Byzantines but also to the Frankish rulers of Greek lands, as
the latter also did in reply.[4] This use of the Greek language for treaties
and diplomatic correspondence became a tradition continued by the Seljuks, the Mameluke sultans, and later the Ottomans. Very few of the earlier examples of this usage still exist.[5] The earliest is a firman by Bayezid I
which is preserved in the monastery of St. Paul at Mt. Athos. Another,
the earliest of Mohammed II's, dates from the period of his first ascent to
the throne and deals with privileges conceded to Venice in 1446.[6]

It was Mohammed II (1451–1481) who, in his determined reorganization of the Ottoman state, chiefly after the capture of Constantinople,
made more use of the counsel of Christian raias than any other sultan.
One of his secretaries was Thomas Katavolenos,[7] a Greek, though he
relied in the main on Italians, from whom he solicited information on the
situation in the West and the state of its dynasties, military power, and
technological skills. The most important of these was Ciriaco de Pizzicolli,
the humanist and merchant from Ancona (1391–1452), who was well-
known for having travelled extensively throughout the Greek world. On
his advice the sultan built up a library of classical and theological manuscripts which he regarded as an important resource from which to improve the government of raias[8] and his empire as a whole.

In their relations with the Venetians, the Knights of St. John, and other
Christian states of the West up to the end of the sixteenth century, the
Turks continued to use the Greek language in its demotic form, interlard-
ing it heavily with Turkish and other foreign words. The Latin and Slavic
languages were scarcely used. In the prolific archives of Venice there are
preserved and resurrected from time to time a great many originals and
copies of Greek texts,[9] letters, and treaties between the sultan or other
official Ottoman personages and Venice which were compiled during the
reigns of Mohammed II and his heirs, Bayezid II (1481–1512), Selim I
(1512–1520), Suleiman I (1520–1566)[10] and Selim II (1566–1574).[11]

The Venetian Republic also employed Greek secretaries who copied
into the *Libri commemoriali* letters written in Greek by the sultans and other
Turkish officials. Translations of these letters into Latin or the Venetian
dialect, which are sometimes found adjacent to the originals in the *Commemoriali*,[12] were probably also made by the Greek secretaries. From the
large number of spelling mistakes which occurred in transcription, their
education was apparently deficient; but at least there would have been no
shortage of such men among the sizable Greek population in Venice.

Although there were always Turkish noblemen in the Greek world who continued to use Greek in their letters and decrees (for instance, the nobles of the Peloponnese and Naupactus in their correspondence with the proveditor of Zacynthus), [13] a difficulty persists in determining exactly when the official use of Greek in the diplomatic correspondence between the Turkish sultan and the West came to an end. [14]

This reliance upon raias, whether Greek or not, as partners in the organization of the Ottoman state did not however imply any *rapprochement*, still less amalgamation, between conquerors and conquered. Whether their services were voluntary or involuntary, the military and administrative auxiliaries of the Turks generally stood outside the regular civil service hierarchy. Of course the first great and unbridgeable chasm between them was that brought about by religious differences. The Koran explicitly forbade the engagement and employment of non-Moslems in public service positions, though the facts suggest that this was an injunction honored more in the breach than in the observance. [15] On the whole, however, the Moslem conquerors and non-Moslem raias (Jew as well as Christian) formed two separate and distinct worlds. The Greek raias too, though scattered more or less evenly throughout the length and breadth of the Ottoman dominion and consisting of the largest non-Moslem group, were nevertheless kept at a contemptuous distance by their conquerors.

In his book *Le Statut légal des non-Musulmans en pays d'Islam* (Beirut, 1958), Antoine Fattal shows how sharply the position of the foreigner (*cimmi*) was delineated within the world of Islam: "The foreigner, we might say, is a second-class citizen. If they tolerate him it is a calculated step, whether because they cherish the hope of converting him or for material reasons, because they force him to shoulder virtually the entire burden of taxation. They provide a place for him in the state, but not without reminding him continually of his inferior status. They prevent him from occupying high positions in society, and if by merit or intrigue he manages to climb to such places everything conspires to relegate him once again to obscurity. If the *cimmi* acquires an independent legal status or privileges associated with personal position, if he is permitted even his own courts, it is only because he cannot share with the Faithful the advantages of their own justice, which is essentially religious. In no case is the *cimmi* the equal of a Moslem. He is condemned to social inequality and forms part of a despised caste: inequality so far as his personal rights are concerned, inequality in taxation, and inequality before the law, since his testimony is neither accepted by the Moslem courts of justice nor even, for the same minor crime, is the punishment the same." [16]

Differences in religion and civilization were not the only ones to enlarge the gulf between conquerors and conquered. Economic disparity also widened it. And there was the imperious attitude and harsh treatment which the one displayed towards the other; even the superficial contrasts in dress and appearances; and, finally, the myriad dispensations circumscribing the life of the raia. These last we will recount presently.

First, however, let me sketch the more humdrum but vital account of the economic relations and differences between conqueror and conquered by considering the position of that section of Ottoman society which was in fact the largest—the Christian peasant raias.

Unfortunately it is not always easy to unravel those arrangements in force in the Ottoman state for the disposal of property, particularly in the fields of land tenure and ownership and the taxation of Moslem and Christian peasants. Disagreements abound not only among European writers but among the Moslem writers themselves[17] on such matters as the correct categorization of forms of land tenure, the origins of agrarian imposts and the criteria of their determination, even the social status of the peasant. There is a vast area of research largely untouched by scholars, and this is being constantly expanded by the addition of new material from Turkish archives. It is an area in which the historian must move cautiously, because of changes in the disposition of land and the condition of peasants which occurred frequently and unexpectedly at different times and in different places.

Disregarding minutiae which really have no place in a general exposition of this kind, we shall attempt to recount as succinctly as possible only those details which best reveal the peasant's relationship with his land, the sultan, and the feudal lords of the Greek Ottoman territories.

Generally speaking, Ottoman domains were deemed to be public or state-owned (mirî). Those appropriated for religious institutions, such as mosques, were called wakfs, while the sultan enfeoffed for life other land,[18] called timars, ziamets, or has, to distinguished soldiers or other specially favored vassals who were obliged to follow him to war on horseback with a certain number of retainers.[19] Turkish landownership was thus transient, at least theoretically, and not alodial, as in the West during feudal times. In a word, the sultan was as a rule the absolute owner of all land, as indeed he was of the raias themselves. Such was the source of the sultan's unlimited power and the blind obedience of his military officers and civil service officials.[20] Only military fief-holders such as the spahis were entitled to hold land separately (hassa çiftlik) and exploit it on their own behalf.[21]

The military organization of the empire and its social organization as well were chiefly based upon the military fief-holders—spahis, janissaries, and others. When each new sultan ascended the throne, fief-holders were obliged to have their grant of fief renewed. Timars and ziamets were revocable, and the fief-holder of a timar or a ziamet possessed no right of

1. Spahis. From Alexander Pallis, *In the Days of the Janissaries*, London, 1951.

2. A Spahi. From Jean-Antoine Guer, *Moeurs et usages des Turcs . . .*, Paris, 1747.

ownership over his land, though he could collect a tithe and certain other taxes.[22] All fief-holders, that is to say, were tax-collectors, whether personally or by proxy; and this was also true of the *mütevellis*, or wardens of wakfs. Peasants who lived on enfeoffed domain or wakf were registered as raias of the *mirî*, wakf, or actual fief-holder. They had no ownership rights in the land, but were entitled to its usufruct (*tasarruf*), which was also heritable.[23] It may be, though there can be no certainty on this point, that lands formerly owned by a peasant but which from the time of his subjection were accounted *arzı* or *haraciye* (that is, subject to the poll tax or state tribute known as *haraç*) continued to remain freehold under his absolute ownership (*mülk*).[24]

In a number of mountain regions where the sultan's authority was never effective, certain forms of tenure apparently prevailed which were *sui generis*. These depended on individual agreements of long standing made between the sultan or his agents and the particular local inhabitants. It is an aspect of the problem, however, which has still to be investigated.

All land was cultivated by Christians or Moslems who fell into the categories of slave,[25] serf (*ortakçı* or *ortakçı kul*), or "free" peasant. The traveller Georgieviz has left this interesting description of the general way of life and particular pursuits of slaves:

Sometimes I saw men pulling the plow harnessed to the yoke. Women were kept continuously confined, and their lot, away from the eyes of men and even conversation with other slaves, is a sorry one. If a man becomes enslaved and has a wife and children, the lord buys him more eagerly. He is placed as overseer on the estate and must look after fields, vineyards, or pastures. All babies born to slaves become slaves too. If the slaves keep their Christian faith, a certain period of slavery is prescribed, after which they become free. However, the children remain slaves unless their freedom is bought. They can all be kept in the same place or moved somewhere else solely at their master's whim. Thus there is no definite abode of slavery. When they buy their freedom they can, if they wish, return to their former homes provided a written travel permit has been issued to them. But for those who give up their religion no period is specified after which a return to the homeland can be made: all hope of deliverance rests on the decision of the master. When they do gain their freedom, they pay the tithe like other Turks, but they are no longer required to pay those other taxes which oppress Christians. The farmer's life is a hard one, but that of the shepherd is worse. These have to live in solitude and spend each day and night with the elements. The man and his wife live alone in a tent and, besides tending the flock, must also pass their spare hours making capotes and rugs. Every month they have to change pastures and move from one mountain to the next. The more generous masters pay their slaves a tiny wage, as we read the Romans once did. This becomes a small purse which they save for travel when they have won their freedom and want to return to their homelands, or else for other necessities of life. But it does not occur everywhere and, even where it does, is no more than a pitiable crumb intended to dissuade

them from making the decision to run away from their life of slavery. On the other
hand, those who have renounced Christ and who have even been circumcised
receive no favors at all because their masters are sure that they will never run
away.[26]

The *ortakçı* (serfs) fell into a distinct category.[27] From the time of
Mohammed II many were to be found working alongside free peasants
on the sultan's domain (*has*), for instance in 110 villages around Constantinople. Others were engaged in agriculture and stock-raising on wakf
estates.[28] Similar domains having whole villages of serfs are also known to
have existed around Adrianople.[29] Again we meet with serfdom in a
number of villages on the Thracian peninsula: Bulayır, Kavak, Demircilü,
Çinger Köyü, Mürefte (Mirafti), Arablu, Kirasiye (Kerasia), which were
either ceded to the wakf of Suleiman Pasha (who made the first landing in
Europe) or else to other wakfs in Eriklice and Malgara. Serfdom in this
region may have followed its inhabitants' submission immediately after
the Turkish landings in Gallipoli,[30] though it is more likely that the serf
population was later transferred there from other districts.

Indeed, serfdom usually resulted from the forcible displacement of
Christian populations originally living within a zone of war. The Turkish
tide washed over their lands and they became, in effect, dislodged prisoners of war. This was certainly how the sultan's domains outside Constantinople and Biga came to be settled.[31] The Christian serf population of the
Biga-Prusa region at the time of Mohammed II was chiefly composed of
cattle-herders (*siğircı kullar*) and shepherds (*koyun kâfirleri*).[32] The
settlement of serfs in isolated parts of the Ottoman dominion took place
primarily on state, rather than private, initiative and was aimed at increasing local populations.[33]

Otherwise, serfdom was without doubt a relic of the Byzantine period.
When Byzantine properties, whether public domain or private estate,
passed under Turkish control, many serfs attached to them must surely
have suffered the same fate. As we have already seen, this happened with
some of the inhabitants of Bulayır, Kavak, Mürefte, and Malgara, which,
after conquest, were thenceforth registered as belonging to the wakf of
Suleiman Pasha.[34]

The conditions of life of these serfs were fixed by custom (or rather,
innumerable customs), which was formalized by firm, written rescript.
Since the legal status of serfs was actually defined, it seems appropriate
before proceeding further to enumerate the general principles on which
this definition was based, even if the very detailed nature of the relevant
enactments precludes full analysis.

Both Moslem and Christian serfs were tied to the land, but otherwise
were at the complete disposal of their master. The children of serfs

retained the status of their parents. Like free peasants they normally worked small holdings, and all necessary tools, seed, and animals were provided by the proprietor or lessor (amil), or his intendant. In other words, their position was very like that of the medieval West European serf.[35] Unless valid reason could be shown, the serf was not permitted to sow less seed than that laid down by the intendant or otherwise to neglect his work. At harvest time, a quantity of seed equal to that originally sown was first set aside, after which the remainder was divided equally between proprietor and serf, less an additional tax on the serf (sâlârlik) of one-fortieth of his own share. If crops other than grain were cultivated, the serf was liable to a one-tenth payment of his share. So far as his beasts were concerned, he could neither rent them, employ them in other work, or neglect them. Tools broken or lost also had to be replaced.[36]

Christian and Moslem both, however, might be released from his bonds of serfdom.[37] Indeed, many of those listed in the State Register of Titles have the notation "freed" (atık) beside their names. In a census taken at the time of Mohammed II, 27 out of 212 Moslem, and 3 out of 67 Christian, families of Bulayır are recorded as "freed." In Malgara, it was 151 out of 938 Moslem families. And families of this kind could be encountered in many villages around Adrianople and Gallipoli.[38] Apparently the number of "freed" serfs also tended to increase in annual volume as the years passed.[39] Certain anomalies existed, however, in the transition from the status of serf to free: sometimes serfs were successful in buying freedom from their overseers with bribes; and sometimes serfs reaped profits from the land which were no less than those a free peasant himself might expect.[40] But it is the position of the serf in law which is of particular interest to explore: his obligations, his hereditary rights, the question of intermarriage, forced labor, and so on.[41]

Besides serfs, there also existed a class of elidji, about whom, unfortunately, we know little more than enough to whet our curiosity.[42] Nor can much more be said of the class of Christian wine-growers (bağbân kâfirler) inhabiting the Asia Minor coast of the Sea of Marmara, who were serfs belonging both to the sultanic domain and wakfs.[43]

It was the duty of the "free" peasant to pay certain stipulated taxes and regularly to cultivate, that is, for two years in every three, those arable lands which he held in tasarruf. If he neglected the cultivation of his land for more than a defined period (which in the case of Samos, for instance, was seven years), his rights in tasarruf became void, and the fief-holder was then entitled to dispose of the land by a grant of tapu (a deed of vassalage[44] ultimately assignable as a title deed) to someone else. In addition, the peasant was required to inform the fief-holder and first obtain his permission before any transaction connected with his tenure, such as sale, could be effected.[45]

3. A Greek villager. From Nicolas de Nicolay, *Les Navigations, pérégrinations, et voyages faicts en la Turquie*, Anvers, 1577.

Peasants could not move from one place to another.[46] The Turkish central government frowned upon any such mobility because of the threat to the livelihood of the spahis which it entailed. Indeed, it was thought that the Sublime Porte's entire system of fief-holding would thereby be undermined. Spahis thus had the right to enforce a peasant's return to his land at any time within a ten-year period. Any peasant seeking the permission of the fief-holder, which was mandatory, to move away could expect this to be withheld unless it were granted in conjunction with the simultaneous exercise of his master's equivalent right to issue a new *tapu* in *tasarruf* to someone else.[47]

But in actual practice the peasant was not quite so securely tied to his land as Gibb and Bowen, for example, tend to think.[48] His dependence on the land was not always absolute; in the sixteenth and seventeenth centuries, at least, his situation was in fact a fluid one. Then, whole villages emptied as peasants refused to tolerate the burden of additional heavy taxes.[49] Spahis found themselves cut off from a prime source of income, and sometimes peasants would even successfully demand the immediate remedy of grievances as a condition of their return.[50]

Many Christian raias were compelled to borrow from the Turks by mortgaging their farms or houses at exorbitant interest rates.[51] By accepting loans at 30% or 40% interest rates, the Albanians of Attica in 1675 lost the farms surrounding their villages.[52] Debtors were put in chains or thrown into prison, or, leaving behind their wives and children as bonds, wandered in search of charity from house to house up and down the land, even occasionally overseas.[53]

Before looking in detail at the imposts on Christian raias and Moslems which had to be furnished to both fief-holders and the sultan himself— before examining, in effect, the entire taxation system of the Ottoman state—it will be helpful to outline some of the general principles on which that system rested. That way, the separate elements of the problem ought the more readily to be understood. The sultan's authority to impose taxes and generally to effect those arrangements for the economic functioning of the Ottoman state derived from the ruler's political and customary right (kanun ve örf) to dispense a separate body of law incorporating his own will. This long-established system had developed in the former Turkish Islamic states, even before Ottoman law first appeared, as supplementary to the Islamic Law or Sheri (şeriat), which sprang from the precepts of the Koran and Sacred Tradition.[54]

The question at once suggests itself: did this system of taxation, indeed the very social organization generally of the Ottoman state, bear any relation at all to those systems which arose in the Byzantine Empire and other Balkan Christian states,[55] or to those of the Ilkhanid (Persian) and the Seljuk empires[56] and other Mussulmanic principalities of the East?[57] There is much discussion and controversy on the subject, but at least it can be said that the Byzantine Empire and other Balkan states did exert a partial influence on the economic organization of the eastern Moslem states, if only in the areas of land registration, system of taxation, and nomenclature. Earlier descriptions of specific economic conditions (for example, use of the word paroikos[58] for the peasant serf) or designations of certain taxes (such as melissonomion)[59] continued under the Turkish occupation along with their equivalent Turkish names. Local tax variations were also probably due, as Inalcik points out, not only to the fact that different laws applied to different classes in Ottoman society but also to the fact that Ottoman tax laws tended merely to follow either local custom or the law of the state which had been supplanted.[60] To that explanation we might also add that local differences stemmed from the manner in which submission to the Ottoman Empire was effected, that is, on peaceable or enforced terms. Thus, one reason why the code (*kanunname*) of Imbros, Lemnos, and Thasos[61] (those islands which, along with Samothrace and Thracian Ainos, were first feudatories of the Gattilusi family and later, in 1460, of Demetrius Palaeologus) prescribed such a light burden of taxation for their peoples was that in 1467 they attached themselves voluntarily to the Ottoman state.[62] More will be said about these arrangements in due course.

Yet another question arises from this sort of consideration of local tax variations. Did those conditions of life for the Christian, particularly the Greek, peasant, which were so deplorable during the last two centuries of the medieval period, show any improvement under Turkish rule? Did they perhaps remain unchanged, or did they grow steadily worse? Unfortunately, the scarcity of evidence prevents us from giving a definite answer. Not only that, but new questions continually arise to complicate the problem. How is it possible to compare conditions in different lands comprising the Ottoman state when they did not enjoy the same political and religious status? How is it possible to compare conditions before the Turkish conquest with those after it, even in the same land, when there is no evidence on which to base such a comparison? Thus the problem is one of explaining both geographical and chronological differences. Even after the Turkish conquest, the conditions of life of Christian raias varied according to whether they lived in the fourteenth and fifteenth centuries, when the Ottoman state was organized in a simple and even beneficent way, or in the sixteenth and seventeenth centuries, when its visible decomposition resulted in vigorous onslaughts on Christians. Of course, in this latter sense, there is clearly no question of any improvement in the lot of raias.

Inalcik is of the opinion that the Ottoman state brought substantial social benefit to Christian peasants[63] by confiscating most aristocratic and monastic properties and thus effectively abolishing the *corvée*. If social change of this kind was in fact accomplished—and perhaps we can at least discern movement in that direction during the initial stages of Ottoman control—it was still partial or local rather than universal in character. How else explain the codices which expressly forbade spahis to exact unpaid labor?[64] Of course the problem merits more comprehensive analysis than we can give it here; but it is a fact that compulsory labor continued in force through the fifteenth century and even came to be included in that system of extraordinary taxation (*avarızı divaniye ve tekâlifi örfiye*) which had

evolved over the years, first as a temporary expedient but eventually as a
series of regular annual taxes arbitrarily imposed and collected at the
raias' expense.[65] So, for example, in Cyprus in 1572 the serfs (*parikoz*)
were required to work two days each week on the estates of beys and
spahis, or one day in the state sugar-warehouses or granaries (*ekinlik-
lere*).[66] Similarly, the entire panoply of Frankish feudal rule remained in
force in Naxos and the rest of the Cyclades for many years after the Turks
took over in 1537. It was only gradually abolished following successive
uprisings by the peasants—which we shall look at in the appropriate
chapter.

On the other hand, it is true that various categories of Christian raias
were exempt from the *corvée* and other extraordinary taxation because of
services they rendered to the Ottoman state.[67] We shall also examine a few
examples of these exemptions later on.

Our knowledge of the tax liabilities and general economic condition of
Moslems and Christian raias comes from a variety of sources. The most
important of these are the Turkish Registers of Titles (*tahrir defterleri*) and
Codices (*kanunname*), which applied both to the whole empire and specific
parts of it. Two codices promulgated by Mohammed II in an attempt to
consolidate the laws of his predecessors deserve particular attention since
they are indicative of his efforts to reorganize the state. The first (*teşkilât
kanunu*) dealt with the setting up of state machinery, defining such matters as court protocol and the functions of higher officials; the second
touched on matters affecting Moslems and Christian raias in common
(*reaya kanunu*).[68] Both codices embodied previous law, and from the
second in particular we are able to form some estimate of the range of
imposts falling upon the peoples of the Ottoman state—at least for the
fifteenth century.

However, a difficulty arises in interpreting the information contained
in the Turkish codices. In the first place, both of Mohammed II's innova-
tions were concerned more with the actual methods of tax collection than
with the construction of new taxes. In the second place, the codes often
give no more than a partial picture of the economic life of the Ottoman
state as a whole or of the particular district to which they refer. In order to
determine if their provisions actually became effective, it is first necessary
to compare the relevant sections of the codices with corresponding civil
service documentation or other local sources.[69] To marshal all this evidence is a perhaps unattainable goal, which, however, the investigator
must constantly seek. Again, the paucity of historical material dealing
with the original advance and settlement of the Turks in Greek territories,
especially during the fourteenth and fifteenth centuries, precludes any
definite assessment of the initial range of tax levies on peasants generally
and Christians in particular. However, it does seem that from this early

period Christians were required to pay (in consideration of land actually held by them at the time of conquest) a land tax, or *haracı mukaseme,* which was a proportional tax amounting to one-eighth, one-seventh, one-sixth, or even one-half of the income from the produce of their land. In addition, a compulsory annual tax (*haracı muvazzaf*)[70] levied directly on the land but not on the crop was also payable to the amount of a specified number of *akçes.* This tax was an annual distraint only and could not, like the *mukaseme,* be reimposed if the land yielded further crops.[71] When the *haracı mukaseme* amounted to one-tenth of the income it was known as the *ösür* (tithe).[72] All land belonging to Christians was subject to the state tribute or vassalage tax known as *haraç* and accordingly designated *arzı haracıye.* This kind of land also continued to be referred to as *mülk.*[73]

After the conquest of the Balkans and the extension of the boundaries of the Ottoman dominion, the state, particularly its military arm, found itself constantly in need of increased financial support. Accordingly, in the fifteenth century, sultans were persuaded to impose various extraordinary taxes, some of which may, however, have been traditional to the Byzantine and other medieval Balkan states.[74]

From the latter half of the fifteenth century the records of the Ottoman taxation system improve. On the whole, Mohammed II's dispensations affecting the lot of peasant raias show that he was quite favorably disposed towards them; so, too, do his words of caution to the spahis warning them against oppressive acts or any untoward persecution.[75] His decrees concerning woodcutters, coachmen, carters, muleteers, carpenters, and other craftsmen[76] similarly manifest the benevolent stamp of his rule: those who were impoverished or disabled by old age paid no taxes at all.[77] There is, however, little value in attempting to compare the numerous detailed provisions of Mohammed II's codices. Frequently it is impossible to ascertain if they were applicable throughout all Greek territories or, as was the case during the sixteenth and seventeenth centuries, if special laws applied locally. In only a few cases is it possible to say with certainty that some of Mohammed II's dispensations had their counterparts in the enactments of sixteenth century sultans: levies on beehives and must and the two-month monopoly of spahis on the sale of a tenth part of their peasants' produce[78] are both pertinent examples.

Unquestionably, too, many of the tax burdens of Christian raias were less onerous during the fourteenth and fifteenth centuries than in later centuries. According to one of Mohammed II's codices, the raia had to pay 15 *akçes* for the tax *ispence,*[79] whereas the corresponding figure in the following century, at least in Greek territories, was 25 *akçes.* Only for widows did the tax remain unchanged at 6 *akçes.* Similarly, a tax levied on raias at the rate of 1 *akçe* for every three sheep became in the next century 1 *akçe* for every two sheep. But an examination of the general economic situation of Greek peasants during the sixteenth and seventeenth centuries, together with their specific tax liabilities, can now follow separately since much more extensive and reliable evidence is available for that period.

In the great codices of Suleiman I (1520–1566)[80] which were applicable throughout all his dominions, a good deal of useful and detailed information can be found on the agrarian situation and the tax burdens of raias in the sixteenth century. Since our frame, however, properly excludes all that which is not germane to the history of modern Hellenism, we shall look only at those lesser codices which were directed specifically at certain Greek territories. These may nonetheless be taken as generally representative.

Typical were those for Lamia, Trikkalà, Naupactus, Euboea, Larissa, and Pharsala which are still extant and which, though dating from the sixteenth century, probably incorporate a considerable number of earlier provisions. They have many features in common, enabling us to form a general impression of the tax liabilities of peasants in central Greece at this time. From the codex of Lamia we learn that the peasant first had to surrender to his lord (his spahi fief-holder or the like) one-tenth of the return from his land, his apiaries (the tax *resmi kovan*, or the Byzantine *melissonomion*) and his must. Moslems in towns were required to give up precisely one-tenth of their grain crop (*öşri gallat*),[81] while Moslems in the countryside had to pay an additional 2½% (the so-called *salariye* or pasture fee). The latter's Christian counterpart, however, was taxed at the rate of 13.3%, and that impost was also levied on the peasant's return from his cultivation of cotton and must. According to the codices of Euboea, Trikkala, and the others, a tithe was also payable on such agricultural produce as cumin, saffron, beans, peas, wàlnuts, almonds, hemp, and fruit. In the codices of Lamia and Trikkala we find that raias were also held liable for taxes on sheep (*âdeti agnâm*) and goats to the amount of 1 *akçe* for every two animals.

Besides these principal levies in kind and other cash liabilities affecting both Moslem and Christian (the right to betrothal, for example, the *resmi arus* or, in the Athens codex,[82] the *gerdek resmi*, which imposed 30 *akçes* on maidens and 15 on widows), there was also a variety of cash imposts, which only Christian raias had to pay. Among these, a land tax or *ispence* of 25 *akçes* yearly was levied on each adult raia capable of work, including widows if they had farms (or 6 *akçes* only if they did not). Married men were required to pay 6 *akçes* for pasture rights (*resmi otlak*, the Byzantine *ennomion*) but this did not fall on widows or unmarried men. Finally, Christians paid spahis a pig tax (*resmi hınzır*, the Byzantine *choirodekatia*) at the rate of 1 *akçe* for every two pigs when these were pastured on wasteland, or 1 *akçe* per head on pigs raised for personal domestic consumption. In Euboea, Christians paid twice as much as Moslems for the use of each acre of grassland and vegetable garden during the grain season, that is, 8 *akçes* instead of 4.

If a Christian peasant absconded from his land, thus forfeiting his rights in *tasarruf* (the codex of Lamia referred to this by its Slavic name, *baştina,* meaning inherited landownership by a peasant), his spahi had the right to exact from him, if he were found, a penalty (*çift bozan akçesi*) of 75 *akçes.* If he were not caught, the peasant was still obliged to pay the tithe in his new village; and if he was not a cultivator he still had to pay a domicile tax (*resmi duhan,* the Byzantine *kapnikon*).[83] When it was time for the collection of *ispence,* and again at harvest time,[84] each married man had to provide the spahi with a chicken and a cake (*bougatsa*). The Moslem was exempt from all these taxes, but actually his situation, even up to the Greek Revolution of 1821,[85] was not much better.

Indeed Moslem and Christian both writhed under the oppression of fief-holders. The codices, for instance, gave the spahi a monopoly of sale lasting two months over the must which he took as part of his tithe. Peasants could only sell their own must[86] after the expiration of this period. Naturally, the lord's right to prior sale brought him premium prices.

Such were the taxes in cash and kind which went to the spahi. But any picture of the full range of the raia's disabilities would be incomplete without mention of those additional taxes paid directly into the imperial exchequer—the extraordinary taxes, and those levied only on Christians, beginning of course with the poll tax (*cizye,* to use the exact Islamic legal term),[87] which was determined on the basis of the raia's capacity to pay. Thus, Christians were classified as *sahib-i mal* (wealthy), *mütevasit ül-halet* (average means) or *fakir-i mütemel* (poor).[88] Even so, sultans from the end of the sixteenth century increased the poll tax.[89] In the islands, 4 *akçes* were payable by males over twenty years of age, while those between the ages of fifteen and twenty paid half that sum.[90]

Not much is known of the agrarian situation in Epirus and the Peloponnese during the sixteenth century except that there were quite a number of Christian fief-holders. Of course this did not necessarily mean that peasants there were better off than elsewhere. In Ioannina, only Christian spahis were to be found in the citadel.[91] In Epirus and the Peloponnese, Christian spahis were required to follow the sultan to war. There was the Christian spahi Tsernota Bey from the Peloponnese, for example, who with a number of others accompanied Selim I on his expedition against Egypt in 1517. This was the same Tsernota Bey who interceded with Selim I on behalf of the monks of Sinai.[92] However, when Suleiman I ascended the throne in 1520, he apparently stripped the Christians in the Peloponnese of their fiefs.[93]

What of those peasants living on the Turkish-controlled islands? There, taxes were distributed proportionately to the amount of property that had been registered and given a valuation. Artisans were taxed on the basis of their profits.[94] In the larger islands, or those which were so close to the coast as to be regarded merely as a continuation of the mainland, the situation was less bearable. From a new codex promulgated for Euboea in 1569, for instance, we learn that the local Turkish authorities indulged in the collection of illegal taxes both in cash and kind;[95] and they were reprimanded for their reprehensible behavior. From another undated codex,[96] we gather that arbitrary practices of this sort were also prevalent on the island of Thasos.

In Aegina during the seventeenth century, according to Giraud, the French consul in Athens, the voivode extracted from the Turks precisely a tenth of their wheat, barley, vegetables, cotton, flax, and the like, while from Greeks he demanded two-fifteenths, as well as one-eighth of their oil. In the case of honey and wax, he took 15–20 okes per colony; and wine and must were taxed an *ambeliatiko* per acre. Having first exacted this tribute, the voivode then attempted to dispose of it by compelling the Greek raias in various ways to buy back large quantities of grain and oil at high prices. Acorn-pickers were similarly exploited: the voivode paid little and sold dearly to European merchants. In addition, there were customs duties levied on Turks at the rate of 4 per cent; for Christians the rate was 5 per cent. Only those who enjoyed trading privileges (*capitulations*) paid a mere 3 per cent. Many other taxes were also imposed, and generally speaking the voivode had ample opportunity to play fast and loose with Greek and Turkish subjects. Naturally, it was the Greeks who bore the major brunt of any oppression.[97] In Samos, too, the people suffered at the hands of agas and cadis[98] who were given to acts of capricious, if spasmodic, lawlessness.

Rather less distasteful was the position of Greek peasants who lived in places remote from the coastal littorals facing Turkish-controlled islands or on islands which had negotiated their surrender. In these latter places, Turks subsequently showed a marked disinclination to move in as settlers. A codex of 1519, for instance, prescribed a relatively easy lot for the inhabitants of Imbros. Its terms provided that the people of Imbros should be exempt from payment of both poll tax and *ispence* (*matakaddemden haraç ve ispenç virmezler*) after capitulation. Where normally only Moslems paid *resmi çift* (the Byzantine *zevgaratikion*), the codex expressly stipulated a payment of 70 *akçes* in this category by those on the slopes of Balabanlu who enjoyed full property rights and 35 *akçes* by those who shared them. Again, all cultivators paid an amount of *mukata 'ai zemin* proportional to the share of the land which they worked, but were exempt from the usual tithe. By virtue of the fact that the holdings of those at

4. Ioannina. From Henry Holland, *Travels in the Ionian Isles, Albania, Thessaly, Macedonia, etc., during the years 1812 and 1813*, London, 1815.

Iskender were particularly large, the tithe was levied on the produce of their land (including olives), but in this event they were exempt from the *mukata'ai zemin*.[99] In general, too, the stock-raising tax and customs duties were far from onerous.[100] From the example of Imbros, we may fairly conclude that the tax imposition on raias varied considerably. Probably the only historical explanation for this is the peaceable manner by which the island became attached to the Ottoman state; or it may perhaps be attributed to the personal efforts made by Kritoboulos[101] and other nobles to ensure the favorable disposition of their island and lands.

Equally deserving of notice is the system in Lemnos whereby certain groups paid some taxes at the normal rate but others at a reduced rate in consideration of various services which they traditionally rendered. Field garrisons and *müsellem*,[102] for example, paid 15 *akçes* as poll tax and 10 *akçes* as *ispence*, while night garrisons and *keşti-banlar* (?) (sailors who provided certain services, perhaps as pilots)[103] paid 12 *akçes* and 10 *akçes* respectively. Other taxes prescribed by Sacred Law or sultanic decree were paid in accordance with custom.[104] The lenient treatment accorded these groups ought not, however, arouse too much surprise because we have already had occasion to notice elsewhere the existence of privileged groups—Christian spahis, *voynuks*, and others.[105]

The villagers of Lemnos were also exempt from payment of the extraordinary taxes,[106] since by tradition they also carried out garrison duties around the coast of the island. Any levy of the tax *oturak âdeti*,[107] which serviced disabled or superannuated janissaries,[108] was accordingly forbidden.

It is perhaps curious that the inhabitants of Thasos who possessed land (*çift*) paid 50 *akçes resmi çift* in lieu of the tithe when *resmi çift*, as previously noted, was normally paid only by Moslems. All cultivators, small or large, were liable to the *resmi çift*. The codex also stipulated that the tax should be collected from the inhabitants by the notable in each Christian village. A tithe was levied on beans, lentils, onions, garlic, and other vegetables, as well as on pomegranates, figs, almonds, and walnuts. There was a maximum of 30 *akçes* payable for *haraç* and 25 for *ispence*; 30 *akçes* for the betrothal right, payable by maidens and widows; 1 *akçe* per head stock-raising tax on goats, sheep, and pigs; and 1 *akçe* for each hive of bees. Penalties (*cürüm ve cinayet*) were laid down for crime according to degree. In the port of Thasos, customs duties on the export or import of animals and agricultural produce were light.[109] In Rhodes and Kos, the inhabitants paid customs duties at the rate of 3 per cent until 1650, after which a 4 per cent rate was fixed by Sacred Law.[110]

In the Cyclades' Duchy of the Aegean, the situation after the Turkish conquest was in many ways unique. Feudalism there, though eroded by time, had not yet collapsed. Frankish feudal families continued to cling to

5. Street of the Knights on the Island of Rhodes. From Louis Lacroix, *Iles de la Grèce,* Paris, 1853.

the largest and most productive tracts of land.[111] Officially feudalism had been abolished, but feudal ties, though looser, still survived, and so did the intolerable burdens of peasants. Of course the people of those islands were spared the constant presence of the Turk among them, but they were still subjected to the brutalities of Turkish sailors when the fleet made its annual tax-collecting visit to the Aegean. Nor could they escape the tax levy of the Venetian fleet, persecution by Venetian troops, or the forcible requisitioning of food. Naturally it was the Greek peasant, not the Frankish feudal lord,[112] who was forced to deliver. And, above all, there were the perpetual depredations of pirates to contend with—but we shall describe these in a more appropriate place.

The provisions of the codices constitute, of course, an official and reliable resource for the historian who, however, must deal with the necessarily uninformative style in which they are set forth. If he is to understand the real predicament of peasants and serfs, if he is fully to comprehend the depth of economic hardship, he must go beyond those sources to the credible eyewitness accounts of travellers.[113] Gerlach reports that in 1576 the Turks of Asia Minor were an indolent people who did their work "through Christians," and these Christians toiled night and day in order to sustain their masters.[114] He also mentions that spahi fief-holders and janissaries in the Bithynian villages were fed by means of the exertions of raias, from whom not merely the tithe, but one-sixth or even one-seventh of their produce[115] was extorted. Schweigger cites the oft-quoted adage: "wherever an Ottoman treads, there nothing grows."[116]

An obligation to part with a proportion of his produce and to perform the *corvée* —duties reminiscent of the medieval West European serf's—is probably further indication of the fact that most of these Bithynian peasants were not "free" peasants, but serfs. They probably moved to Bithynia, whether under duress or of their own volition, to work on sultanic or wakf estates as farmers or shepherds.[117] Indeed that is an inference which we have already made.[118]

The wise and prudent fief-holder was one who knew how to extract the maximum amount of work without, however, going to the kinds of extremes[119] which would cause villagers to abscond. There were some, on the other hand, whose malevolence towards peasants left them with scarcely enough food to sustain life. They simply took everything— money, chickens, fruit. If remote from the seat of government in Constantinople, sometimes the wives and children of peasants might be molested. And the miserable peasant could only suffer in silence. If close to the capital, however, where complaints could readily be laid against his vagaries, the lord might be punished if he had not first offered a bribe to the Pasha.[120] As Gerlach reports: "In Turkey, everything can be arranged with money; without *akçes* you will achieve nothing."[121]

THE RAIAS UNDER OTTOMAN RULE

By and large, the Turk's rapacity and cupidity (referring here, of course, mainly to officials, spahis and other state functionaries) were legendary: "See a Turk and he will want *akçes;* see another and he will want more."[122] So numerous are such sayings that any attempt to collate them all would be futile.[123] This rapacity was evident in the practice of compulsory hard labor that continued despite its express proscription by sultans.[124] In some places, Ophis in the Pontus, for example, it lasted until the very end of the nineteenth century.[125] Even today in Epirus the word in Greek for spahi (*spais*) connotes viciousness, barbarity, and tyranny.[126] No less tyrannical were the agents of great fief-holders (such as the pashas)—the bailiffs or voivodes who collected more taxes than the law prescribed. The excess they applied to their own personal uses, to the economic ruin of the peasant. Even the peasant on the sultanic domain (*has*) was not immune from depredations of this kind[127] since the estates were leased to various wealthy Turks.[128] On the whole, conditions in the towns were incomparably better than those in the countryside,[129] which explains the peasant's propensity for absconding. In the process, whole villages fell into decay.

To begin with, most spahi fiefs were small, and fief-holders consequently soon found themselves without adequate means of support. They therefore set about improving their income by various means: plunder during successful military expeditions was one; moving to a more lucrative fief as a reward for the performance of some meritorious deed was another. Then, whenever plunder and victorious exploits seemed wanting, anger and frustration mounted. The spahis compared their lot with that of those outside the military caste upon whom the sultan bestowed special favors—big landowners, officials of the Porte, foreign interlopers in their society, all of whom contrived to enlarge their properties or otherwise augment their fortunes by such means as subletting tax franchises.[130] Among these foreigners were Greeks, Armenians,[131] and especially Jews.[132]

When the persecution of Jews in various European countries (Hungary, Germany, Spain, Portugal, and others) began in 1478, thousands sought refuge in the Ottoman state, where they found the conditions of life more congenial.[133] Many settled down in Mademochoria, where silver mines are known to have been in operation, as well as in Adrianople, Thessalonica, Skoplje, and Monastir (all of which were part of the sultan's domains at the time of Suleiman I[134]), in Sofia and Constantinople.[135] In general, it was the Jews who were mainly responsible for the movement of goods and money throughout the empire, many becoming powerful capitalists and bankers.[136] Joseph Nazi, Duke of Naxos, was a striking example.

From as early as the middle of the sixteenth century and the beginning of the seventeenth century, foreign visitors to the Ottoman state began to

6. Tower of the Castle of Naxos, built in the thirteenth or fourteenth century. Photo by the author, taken in 1967.

7. A medieval country house at Naxos. Photo by the author, taken in 1967.

comment on the industrial and commercial activities of the Jews and on
the extent of their control and general economic penetration of the
country. They took advantage of Turkish lethargy, dominated trade, and
gained a significant hold on provincial revenues through the purchase of
salt-tax franchises and the like.[137] They were chiefly distinguished for
their mutual interdependence and solidarity[138] and as incorrigible
speculators.[139] The Turks treated them disdainfully, as indeed they did
all European peoples, calling them *çifut*[140] (vile, avaricious). The Jews
were polyglot, shrewd moneylenders, masters of the commerce of Thessalonica and Constantinople, and owners of the largest and greatest
number of merchant establishments. They were also splendid artisans
and spread many mechanical arts and inventions, particularly printing
and the manufacture of munitions and firearms, throughout the whole of
the East. The traveller Nicolay commented on the great damage to Christianity which the arrival of Jews in Turkey had brought about.[141] So far,
historians on the whole have overlooked the importance of their influence
on the commercial and economic development of the state. Here is a
subject for fruitful research.

The Jews also infiltrated the Porte itself—its cliques and the sultan's
private chambers and domain. Their role was essentially that of managers
of the personal affairs of ministers of state; and they proved indispensable
advisers on all matters involving purchase or sale—economics in general.[142] They therefore wielded considerable political influence and
power. Large amounts of capital were deployed to make profits, in almost
every case by hiring the collection of customs duties.[143] In 1553 the
German traveller Dernschwam observed that the Jews, like the Turks,
were conspicuous for their inactivity[144] because they had others, their
slaves, to do all their work.[145] On the whole, Jews looked on Constantinople as the Promised Land, though by the end of that century discrimination was being practiced against them.[146] Despite persecution, however, they were still to be found in all commercial undertakings, influenc-
ing the state's political economy, and retaining in their hands the hiring of
tax collections and other economic enterprises. Their intrusion upon
affairs of state was so persistent that in 1612 the Venetian S. Contarini
was moved to write: *"benchè vi siano discacciati per una via s'introducon per
altra* [even though they are chased off in one way they return in
another]."[147]

Capitalist growth in the state eventually wrought momentous economic
and social changes on its feudal organization. An urban class emerged
and the old conservative imperial structure disintegrated. Economic
influences of this kind, with a variety of other broad impulses (the inflow
of precious metals following the discovery of the New World, devaluation
of the *akçe*, economic disarray within the Ottoman state, to mention a few)

8. Two Constantinopolitan houses. From Salomon Schweigger, *Ein newe Reyss-beschreibung aus Teutschland nach Constantinopel und Jerusalem*, Nuremberg, 1608.

eventually led to the dislocation of the entire economic framework of empire. Spahis and janissaries became impoverished and the military system declined.[148] Penury and the prostitution of their women[149] were but two symptoms of the decadence of the military caste. Later, polygamy and consequent need to support many children by having more slaves rapidly exhausted even the largest incomes and produced serious financial insolvency.[150] Turkish fief-holders therefore became more importunate towards Christians, whether in collecting taxes or as a result of subletting their country estates or town establishments.[151]

Cadis and other officials who received no salary but only the return from fines, together with certain other perquisites connected with their position and circumstances, rarely proved either conscientious or just.[152] Various officials who were entitled to make use of the mails' horses extorted food and drink from local peasants commissioned with servicing the post-stages; more than that, they drove off the peasants' archpriests, took away their horses and forced them to flee into the desert.[153]

Simultaneously with these novel campaigns of intimidation and oppression, general corruption and paralysis of the government machine gradually debilitated the State. In Constantinople, sancakbeys, pashas,

and beylerbeys engaged in trading provincial offices, which was facilitated
by pandering to the magnates of the Turkish Divan. They would arrive in
the provinces, far from the sultan's eye and beyond his reach, with
enormous and expensive retinues in train, and then set about the exploitation of local inhabitants, Turks but especially Greeks, in order to rec-
ompense themselves for money already spent, further enrich themselves,
and live a life of grandeur. Pashas comported themselves like independent petty despots.[154] Charges against them on account of the injustices
they perpetrated, whether true or calumnious, merely provided the occasion for notables, particularly the Grand Vizier himself, to remove one
incumbent only to instal another eager candidate.[155] It is hardly too much
to say that the fabled wealth of the Turks was wrung from the blood and
sweat of raias.[156]

Thus the economic structure of the Ottoman state, gradually but
methodically built up during the fourteenth and fifteenth centuries,
began to falter in the sixteenth century under the economic abuses directed against both Moslems and Christians, but mainly the latter. The
turmoil was immediately reflected in the general social condition of the
Ottoman Turks: laxness replaced discipline, particularly among the governing class, whose example in turn prompted the masses to new heights
of fanaticism, rage, and obduracy towards Christians. Servitude became
more and more intolerable. Characteristically, people in the Pontus still
use the verb *tourkopaidevo* in a metaphorical sense to denote "infliction of
severe punishment."[157]

From the sixteenth century onwards, the attitude of travellers towards
the Turks was no longer favorable as it had generally been during the
fifteenth century. They tended to condemn the Turks out of hand[158]
(though, naturally, there were exceptions) and in particular to accuse
them of loving money too much, making promises that were never
kept,[159] dealing in lies,[160] leaving behind nothing but desert wherever
they trod.[161]

If one considers the variety and severity of imposts upon Christians
(again, notably, the Greeks), the inconstancy of the political climate both
local and imperial, the unproductiveness of the land, the stock diseases,
the epidemics, and so on, it is not hard to understand the depths of
desolation into which individual peasants and whole communities were
plunged, or how they fell into the clutches of usurious fief-holders,
forever contracting debts (the so-called *borçs*), or how they finally met with
economic ruin. Usury dealt the final blow to the peasant.[162] The im-
poverishment of Greeks, both those of the countryside and, with a few
exceptions,[163] those of the towns, was obviously complete.[164] Apart from
the few in towns who had chairs to sit on and tables to eat from, the rest
crouched on the floor and crossed their legs after the fashion of the
Turks. And their utensils were of clay.[165]

As with all Christian raias, Greeks not only labored under certain specific political and economic disabilities but also suffered the consequences of a more general Moslem, and particularly Ottoman, attitude towards them which was contemptuous and uncompromising. This attitude was the byproduct of a tradition based on the cumulative weight of opinions delivered by Arab jurists and the successive decrees of sultans.

Moslem *hauteur* towards those of another faith was calculated to impress even at the level of enforced distinctions in dress. From as early as the eighth century, the Arab caliphs prescribed that Christians and Jews wear clothing peculiar to themselves.[166] As a general rule, Christian subjects of the Ottoman state might dress similarly to Turks,[167] except that their turbans had to be made of blue or striped blue cloth, not white. Greeks usually wore a black or red tarboosh that sat upon the head and around which the approved colored turban was wound, a waistcoat open at the front, simple trousers (the *potouria*, as they were called until recently) and a long black gown over all.[168] There were, however, local differences of detail in the type of apparel worn, and these might also vary according to the social class to which the raia belonged; that is, whether he were a peasant, an artisan, a burgher, or a nobleman. It is probably true, as Belon observed, that only peasant costume preserved any semblance of ancient styles. In places under Frankish control, Greek dress was naturally influenced by Frankish fashions.[169]

Wherever Moslem populations predominated, any form of conversation or public utterance in Greek was frowned upon. The Turkish language was an essential medium of commercial intercourse and provided the only entree to a more bearable existence.[170] Thus, the hegemony of spoken Turkish in some Greek parts of Asia Minor and Europe became complete. No Christian could with impunity engage in casual conversation with a Turkish woman. It might cost him his life.[171] Sexual relations were punishable by death, except if the man apostasized to Islam or expiated his crime through the payment of a considerable cash sum.[172] Moslem intolerance and arrogance and the abrasive formal prescriptions of Moslem society, religious as well as secular, inhibited the amalgamation of the two races—but also preserved the conquered from oblivion.

As the Turkish governmental machine fell into decay, there was a corresponding deterioration in the behavior of the conquerors. But at least they were capable of extending pity towards dogs and cats.[173] The degree of suffering was not everywhere the same, and there might even have been some mitigation of it in individual cases or particular circumstances. But on the whole the vindictiveness of the Turks was a source of profound humiliation to the proud and sensitive raias who were denied all means of retaliation.[174] Resentment festered; only fear restrained them. Yet anger and hostility were stored up layer upon layer in the souls of the raias[175] until in the end nothing could contain them. Every favorable circumstance was seized, and simmering anguish manifested itself in passive resistance or even on occasion explosive violence. Youthful raias in particular often found it difficult to await the most opportune moment and, casting caution to the winds, spontaneously stood up to the oppressor.[176] Obviously, however, discretion was in most cases the better part of valor, and raias could but move away disgustedly to some other place in the hope of finding milder treatment. But in the direst extremity of despair nothing, as we soon shall see, could restrain the impulse to freedom.

The weapons most commonly used to combat the conqueror were therefore equivocation, subterfuge, dissimulation, and outright mendacity. Indeed they were the only weapons which could ensure survival in this atmosphere of terror, torment, and persecution. The spirit was shackled. It was an environment which bred a new sort of *graeculus,* the raia, a pitiful creature who trembled before the conqueror and who was always eager to serve, flatter, or curry favor with him. This was the type, branded with infamy, bereft of any trace of manliness or dignity, which the Greek still vividly calls to mind. The word raia acquired a new, slightly bitter flavor, and something of a residual aftertaste from these darkest days of Turkish rule remains today.

The depth of adversity was described by educated Greeks. John Zygomalas, "Grand Rhetor" of the Oecumenical Patriarchate, remarked to Gerlach that the Greeks generally had become prevaricators; they lived under the yoke of ruthless men who cheated daily, and Greeks merely returned deceit for deceit. Accordingly with them lies were no cause for reproach. No doubt in search of his own self-justification, Zygomalas went on to quote Psalm 18: "With the pure thou dost show thyself pure, and with the crooked thou dost show thyself perverse."[177] This characterization did not necessarily apply to mountain and island folk, whose general lot was a far better one.

Foreign visitors used various epithets to describe the Greeks, but because many were deficient both in education and powers of observation or else possessed by passion and prejudice, their generalizations are frequently of dubious worth. It is hard to find a particular recital of Greek virtues and vices that is not contradicted in almost every respect by another, although there is a fairly steady consensus on the Greek proclivity towards guile, his changeableness, self-esteem, craftiness, as well as ingenuity, verve, natural eloquence, and deft mimicry.[178] And there were always foreign visitors who bore witness to the innocence and blamelessness of many Greeks: "I met many in the Aegean," said the Jesuit Sauger, "who were honest and sincere men of rare wisdom; they possessed all the national virtues and none at all of the vices."[179]

Conversion to Islam

The Ottoman state never officially enforced religious conformity,[1] nor did it pursue a policy of individual conversion under duress.[2] But conversion to Islam, which was often the only avenue of escape from the afflictions of the conquered, was always tempting. By the simple act of acknowledging Islam,[3] the Christian could hope to pull himself out of the mire, perhaps even with a welcoming hand from the conqueror.

A catastrophic event like the rape of a village, the seizure of a city, or the capture of whole populations immediately reaped its crop of apostates. In the case of Constantinople, the Capture brought a windfall of voluntary converts to Islam. And these came not only from the city itself but also from other Greek territories which till then had always looked to the capital as the last remaining source of hope. Gennadius, first patriarch after the Capture, spoke deprecatingly of the large numbers of Christians who turned their backs on Christianity or tortured themselves with the thought of apostasy.[4] By then, the full impact of the monk Joseph Bryennios' remarks some thirty-five years before was realized: stressing the importance of the city as a rock of the Christian faith, Bryennios had said, "For as long as Constantinople has existed, the City and the Faith have remained constant; if she is ever captured or laid low, which God forbid, what soul is there whose faith would not be shaken?"[5] When Constantinople fell, the reality of occupation[6] seemed all the more devastating to Christians. The feeble in faith and the opportunists were tempted. Christian society and the Church found themselves in disarray.[7]

In Epirus and Albania the stream of apostates assumed the dimensions of a torrent, so much so that Moslem authorities found themselves unable to cope with the new converts. The observance of proper initiation rites as defined by Sacred Law became increasingly perfunctory. By special decree of 1474 Mohammed II accordingly ordered strict and punctilious compliance with the appropriate provisions of law on pain of death to violators. Perhaps he was acting out of concern that, if the rate of conversion in Epirus and Albania were not checked, the state would be deprived of one of its most important sources of revenue—the taxes payable by Christian raias. From the time of the Capture to the Treaty of Kioutsouk Kaïnartzi (1774), the flow of dispatches from the Grand Mufti, muftis, cadis, and imams throughout Epirus and Albania on the need to eradicate this anomaly never ceased.[8] Nor did this concern manifest itself only in those two provinces; it appeared after the Capture throughout the length and breadth of the country as a recurring aspect of the phenomenon of conversion to Islam for as long as this took place.

We may confidently assume that the fall of Trebizond was attended by similar conversions in that city and its environs, even though the little evidence available to support this supposition is based mainly on unsafe oral tradition. According to such tradition, the first apostates in the Pontus after 1461 were the Lazi, a Caucasian people, who forgot their language but retained Christian customs and manners.[9] On the other hand it is quite possible, as Dositheos, Patriarch of Jerusalem, points out, that the Lazi, at least those between Trebizond and the River Tsorochi,[10] may have converted to Islam as late as the middle of the seventeenth century.

Other converts to Islam came from the numerous villages around Nicopolis (Siapin Kara Hisar) and Kolonia, the most important of which were Zaapa, Agoutmous, Ortakioï and Parou. Their inhabitants, as almost invariably happened with converts, became in matters of religion *plus royaliste que le roi*. Apparently the only exceptions to this rule were the people of Zaapa, who kept the Turks at a distance, refused to intermarry with them and continued on friendly terms with the Greeks.[11] The Christians of Nicopolis and several of its villages had lost their mother Greek tongue before the Ottoman conquest. This accounts for the survival here of "pitiable remnants of the once flourishing and dense Christian population of the region around which the barbarian flood lapped but which it never wholly swamped, though it did obliterate every Christian monument and indeed the entire ancient civilization of middle Asia Minor." The inhabitants of these districts later began to learn Greek again from the inhabitants of Chaldea in the Pontus after the reopening of alum mines there in the sixteenth century.[12]

Conversions to Islam continued after the sixteenth century, but our knowledge of these is sketchy since it derives chiefly from traditions which have persisted down to the present day. These can hardly do more than hint at the total dimensions of the tragedy. Most of them relate how spiritual tenacity was slowly eroded and how the people eventually gave in to despair. Nor were ecclesiastical prelates of much help in stopping the apostasy. The same traditions tell of the prevalence of rigid dogmatism and obtuse conservatism on the part of clerics as, for example, when the villagers of Moudzour, near Kirsehir, accepted Islam towards the end of the seventeenth century only because their metropolitan forbade them to break the Church's August fast, when all they wanted in this month of frenetic activity in the fields was to refresh themselves with sour milk.[13]

The whole of the former ecclesiastical province of Myron in 1577, except for two or three villages which still had a scattering of Christians, had long succumbed to Islam.[14] Along virtually the entire length of the southern shores of Anatolia, the only evidence remaining of the existence of former Christian communities there consisted of crumbling monuments and deserted churches and monasteries.[15] It is almost impossible to determine the exact time when Islam took hold in the various districts of the Pontus or to ascertain whether or not the phenomenon of crypto-Christianity was still present. Since the evidence surviving from a later period is, however, much more comprehensive, a detailed discussion of crypto-Christianity (whose practitioners were known as *klostoi*) and other related matters is best left to another context.

As for southeastern Europe, Bosnians, Croats, Albanians,[16] and Greeks[17] continued to become converts to Islam. In the middle of the sixteenth century, the traveller Georgieviz had already noted pessimistically that "the new generation of Christians was unlearning its faith, and Christianity would soon be completely forgotten. The same must happen in Croatia, Hungary, and Sclavonia, which have recently been added to the growing Turkish Empire."[18] Mass conversions also occurred frequently among the captive peoples of the northern Balkans and central Europe, who hoped thereby that misfortune could be forestalled. Rarely, however, was it an expedient which brought liberation.[19]

Writing in 1508 Janus Lascaris called attention to the number of Greek parents, undoubtedly crypto-Christian, who were still secretly baptizing their children in the faith, but he foresaw only mass conversions to Islam in the future if the West did not swiftly liberate the people of the Balkan peninsula.[20] By 1586 there were indeed "innumerable Moslem Christians"[21] in Gallipoli and Thrace.

With the passage of time Greek and Albanian spahis gradually became converted to Islam;[22] it is uncertain that all Christian spahis had disappeared by the sixteenth century.[23] As late as the end of the eighteenth century, many spahis of Epirus remained crypto-Christian after their forcible initiation into Islam.[24] Clearly, contrary to Gerlach's opinion, Greeks did not become Moslem without some demur.[25] All the same, from the very moment when they became converts or pretended converts the spahis of Epirus displayed a fanatical, tyrannical attitude—more so even than that of the Turks.[26]

We can perhaps gain some inkling of the agony of conversion from contemporary accounts[27] and by considering the extent of the Church's and religion's overshadowing influence in the lives of simple peasants. It is plain that as the centuries rolled on living conditions and increasing tax burdens became more and more obnoxious until they constituted a significant cause of conversions to Islam.[28] Having precisely this in mind, Nicodemus the Haghiorite towards the end of the eighteenth century advised Christians in these terms: "We say unto you, brothers, that for no other end do they inflict heavy taxes and other misfortunes upon you than to make you tired and fed up so that you will renounce your faith and accept their religion; and knowing that this is their aim, our dear brothers, you must therefore be constantly on your guard."[29] As so many others had done in the century before the capture, Nicodemus, too, urged the virtue of patience. Patience was the essential quality which would ensure victory in this struggle for the soul; and anything less than supreme patience was not enough. As the Bible exhorted: "But let patience have her perfect work" (Epistle of James 1:4). Nicodemus then went on in his own words to define perfect patience, adding embellishments from various other biblical passages and ending with the well-known: "But he that shall endure unto the end, the same shall be saved" (Matthew 24:13).[30]

In addition to the mass conversions there were countless individuals and family groups who made their own private journeys to Islam, especially girls and young women. To take a typical instance, the Jesuit Carayon observed in the middle of the seventeenth century that quite a few Turks in Chalcis spoke Greek because they were the children of Greek mothers.[31] Not infrequently we also encounter apostate clergymen—monks, priests, and bishops[32]—who, commonly for personal reasons such as having had a quarrel with a superior, threw away their cassocks and caps and donned the turban instead. The names of these converts—Papaz Moustapha, Kesis Mouhamet, and the like—betray their priestly origins.[33] From the first until the last years of Turkish dominion the stream of defectors never dried up. The life-blood of Hellenism was being continuously sapped. Some idea of the gravity of the loss may be gained from the extensive lists of converts which appear in certain official Turkish archives and which refer not to the early period of conquest when the religious toll exacted was heaviest but to the later centuries when it was comparatively slight.[34] It is of course possible that certain apostates remained Christian throughout their lives while pretending to be Moslem (a fairly common phenomenon earlier),[35] but sooner or later over successive generations the profession of Islam tended to become sincere. Greeks, particularly refugees from Asia Minor, still tell harrowing tales of crypto-Christianity.

For the Moslem, the voluntary conversion of a Christian to Islam was an occasion to be celebrated as a notable victory.[36] The neophyte, for his part, characteristically affirmed his new faith by abusing and bullying his former countrymen.[37] He was the type of renegade of whom the Venetian Matteo Zane spoke: "gli più arroganti e scellerati uomini che si possa imaginare, avendo insieme con la vera fede perduta ogni umanità [they are more arrogant and wicked men than one could imagine, having lost all humanity when they lost the true faith]."

Along with the phenomenon of voluntary abjuration, there also existed a system of child recruitment whereby long after the capture children were forcibly converted to Islam.

At first, children appear to have been recruited at intervals of five years, when one-fifth of the total number were taken.[39] The system may have developed from the sultan's prerogative of taking one-fifth of all booty in addition to the tax *pencik* or *ispence*. Later, however, recruitment was stepped up to four-, three-, and two-year intervals, or even annually, depending on the needs of war.[40] Some places were exempt from this "blood" tax, whether by reason of special treaty or privilege (Ioannina in 1430,[41] Galata on 1 June 1453,[42] and Rhodes in 1522), or because they happened to be situated on main trunk routes and were already subject to the arbitrary depredations of troops and imperial functionaries.[43]

From evidence which consists mainly in the testimony of contemporary Byzantine writers such as Ducas, Chalcocondyles, and Sphrantzes, as well as the official dispensations made by successive firmans throughout the sixteenth and seventeenth centuries, we learn that children were liable to recruitment between the ages of fourteen to twenty. Children of more tender age than that were also impressed into Ottoman service, though they were destined not for the janissary corps but for the sultan's court and the higher echelons of the administration. They were called *iç oğlan*, and we shall meet them again presently.[44]

Beginning at the end of the fifteenth century, child recruitment was gradually extended throughout the East. Plenary authority to carry out the operation was vested in the *yeniçeri ağası* and *acemi ocağı ağası* (Istanbul *ağası*). Methods of recruitment varied slightly from time to time. After the fifteenth century, a janissary officer (*devsirme ağası*), accompanied by a secretary and an escort of several other janissaries, would be sent into the province where the recruiting was to be done bearing the relevant firman authorizing recruitment. He also took with him a letter (written by the *yeniçeri ağası*) whose contents bore the same purport as the firman but which was specifically addressed to the cadis of the region from which the children were to be recruited. The powers of this officer were absolute; none, not even the civil or military authorities of the local beylerbeylik had the right to interfere with him in the discharge of his duties.

The janissary officer merely presented himself to the local cadi, where-upon his arrival in the village would be at once announced by the crier. In each place, he completed his arrangements by direct consultation with the cadi and the local notable or priest and then confirmed his course of action both by a careful check of the local church's birth records and a personal inspection of those youths eligible for the corps of janissaries. A selection of the young men qualifying for military service would then be made on the basis of their physical appearance, robustness, and apparent intelligence. According to law, such youths were to be selected from among the children of priests and nobles. Only one candidate could be selected from the families of raias having two or more children. Where there was only one son, exemption was granted on the grounds of the family's need. Others falling into ineligible categories were orphans, those who were either too short or too tall, the "beardless," and those already married.[45] Indeed, many Greek, Bulgarian, and Albanian parents pre-ferred to see their children married at eight, nine, or ten years of age[46] rather than drafted.

The officer with power to recruit made out duplicate lists on which the physical characteristics of both the impressed youths and their escort were noted. He retained one list and sent the other to Constantinople by special courier (*sürücü*), where it would be later compared with the original. This was in order to prevent the substitution of one person for another. Money sufficient to pay for the janissary's uniform—his distinctive red head-dress and coat made by the Jews of Thessalonica—was an additional responsibility of the local raias. Finally, the raias were required to reim-burse the recruiting party for all other expenses incurred, even the legally prescribed salaries, or "bounties,"[47] of the janissary officer, his secretary, and aides.

From the sixteenth century, however, recruiting agents began to trans-gress even the limits of this legal extortion. Although they faced severe punishment, even death, for doing so, every opportunity to intimidate and fleece Christians was seized. Two or more sons might be taken from families with many children, and the exemption which had previously applied to families with only one son was no longer automatically applied; but he might be returned to his family in consideration of a bribe of perhaps sixty, seventy, or more gold pieces.[48] While wealthy families could buy back their sons, any supernumerary recruits from less fortu-nate families[49] could be sold as slaves. And even the wealthy could suffer the same fate if they were not prepared to sacrifice their entire fortunes to buy their child's freedom.

In Epirus there was, and perhaps still is, a song:

Be damned, O Emperor, thrice be damned
For the evil you have done and the evil you do.

You catch and shackle the old and the archpriests
In order to take children as janissaries.
Their parents weep, their sisters and brothers, too
And I cry until it pains me;
As long as I live I shall cry,
For last year it was my son and this year my brother.[50]

The raias occasionally rose up against the Turkish agents, hacking them to pieces. But if two such incidents in Albania (1565)[51] and Naousa (1705)[52] can be taken as exemplary, the only outcome of spontaneous uprising was vindictive reprisal.

On the other hand, there were instances, though rare ones, of parents crushed by degrading poverty and lacking in moral fibre who were only too eager to hand over their children to the Turkish plenipotentiaries so as to be rid of the burden of feeding them. Also, there were young men who became "slaves" of the sultan[53] by choice, seeing this as the only avenue of escape from a life of grinding poverty.

After recruitment, the youths were sent to Constantinople in groups under the surveillance of responsible escorts. Once there they were allowed to rest for two or three days before being presented for inspection to the Aga of Janissaries. If in his opinion the recruitment had been carried out in accordance with the law, the names and essential details of every recruit were recorded in a register. Circumcision then followed. If on the other hand, someone in the group had been recruited illegally, the whole detachment was at once separated from the rest of the janissaries and sent to the *tophane* (arms factory) or *cebehane* (munitions factory). The agent responsible for the delivery of the detachment was severely punished.

To minimize the danger of absconding, officers of the *acemi ocağı* were later delegated to take children recruited in Rumelia to Anatolia, and those from Anatolia to Rumelia. But in every case they were delivered into the charge of fief-holders and other Turkish farmers who were required to pay 25 *akçes* for each recruit and who treated them like slaves.

While the grim Turkish regimen no doubt brutalized the recruits, they were eager to adapt to it quickly—to learn the language and adopt the religion, customs, and manners of their masters—since only by those means could they hope to better themselves. To display eagerness meant the possible reward of selection for retransfer back to Constantinople by an officer who made visits of inspection at intervals of about two years. An assignment to one of the companies (*ortas*) of *acem* awaited those selected in the capital. There they lived in groups of twenty-five to thirty men under the orders of the *bulukbaşı*. Each man did his own cooking and had to pay a certain amount for the food each month. From then on he was known as *acem oğlan* and worked on various manual tasks (government

building projects, naval construction, and the like), for which he received
1 *akçe* daily. Those working in the precincts of the palace under the
supervision of the *bostancı başı* got 2 *akçes* daily and had better chances of
promotion. Their new life was not an easy one, but of course it did
represent a considerable amelioration of their previous one because of
the salary and opportunity for advancement that went with it.

The numbers of *acem oğlan* were never fixed, fluctuating in accordance
with the state's immediate and temporary needs. At the beginning of the
sixteenth century, for example, they averaged 3,000, but that figure had
risen to 16,400 by the middle of the same century. The ranks of the
janissaries were replenished from those of *acem oğlan*. Usually, however,
even at the height of Ottoman power, an *acem oğlan* could not expect to
become a janissary before about twenty-four or twenty-five years of age—
not until, that is, his requisite military training had been completed.[54]

By the time of his eventual admission into the corps of janissaries, the
recruit had been so buffeted by hardships and afflictions that even his
most tender remembrances of childhood, family and country must have
grown dim. Such resistance to assimilation as he may originally have had
was slowly but surely eroded by a combination of influences: he was, for a
start, very likely a person of low intellectual caliber; he suffered protracted hardships and privations; his already malleable mind was then
subjected to the constant bombardment of a myriad influences from the
Moslem society which enveloped him. At the same time, there were
apparently many *acem oğlan* and janissaries whose memory of their origin
and ancestral religion remained sharp; they were the men who would
have given eager support to a crusade against the Turk[55] by the states of
the West. We shall eschew a detailed description of the organization of the
janissary corps[56] since this properly falls within the framework of Ottoman history.

Besides those children recruited between the ages of fourteen and
twenty, there was apparently a parallel system of recruitment for children
aged between six and ten years for service in the seraglios of the sultans.
These were the *iç oğlan*. Historians have usually failed to distinguish the *iç
oğlan*, probably because both categories were composed of children.
Their respective ages and duties were, however, quite distinct.

The institution of *iç oğlan* seems to have originated from the Turkish
custom of presenting young, good-looking slaves as gifts to state dignitaries. It was not, as Joseph von Hammer believes, an offshoot of the
acem oğlan, though certainly the idea of systematic recruitment and training for a specific future role germinated under the influence of the *acem
oğlan* system.

The little ones were distinguished not only by their comely appearance,
but by their fine physique and promising intelligence. Following presen-

9. A typical *acem oğlan*.|From Nicolas de Nicolay, *Les Navigations, pérégrinations, et voyages, faicts en la Turquie*, Anvers, 1577.

10. Iç oğlan. From Paul Ricaut, *Histoire de l'état présent de l'empire ottoman*, Paris, 1670.

tation to the sultan, some were sent to the seraglios of Galata and others to the seraglio of Adrianople and to the Great Seraglio in Constantinople. They were well looked after in all three, though those in the Great Seraglio were more fortunately placed, since selection for high office was made first from their ranks.

The *iç oğlan* were supervised by the *Kapı Aga,* who was also overseer of white eunuchs. Eunuchs were cruel to the children, often punishing them severely for even the tiniest peccadilloes. Common punishments were stripes on the soles of the feet, no food, or enforced wakefulness.

The *iç oğlan* lived in four different chambers in the seraglio. In the first, the *küçük oda,* they spent six years, and here the muezzin taught them silence and humility (heads bowed, arms folded across the stomach), as well as reading, writing, and the rudiments of Islamic law. In the second, the *kiler oda,* they spent four years, during which the regimen emphasized physical training and the use of the bow, spear, and other arms; here, too, they perfected their knowledge of the Turkish language and even learned Arabic and Persian. In the third, the *hazinedar oda,* again for a further four years, they learned horseback-riding and were generally expected to become proficient for their age in all other skills. At this time, too, they began occasionally to attend the sultan personally in his dressing room or bathroom. All communication with trainees in the first two chambers was strictly forbidden, except by special permission of the *Kapı Aga.*

After fourteen years of rigorous training and testing, the forty adjudged most capable were finally admitted to the *has oda,* where they received their first real experience of personal freedom. Now they were permitted to consort with any member of the seraglio and to come into personal contact with the sultan. The *iç oğlan* were thus immured in the seraglio between the ages of six and twenty; longer, if they were recruited after the age of six.

By graduation, they had built up a considerable fund of experience and patience. Not only were they capable of endurance to the last limits of fatigue, but mentally they were inured to execute any order blindly and exactly. It was from the ranks of such youth as this that the highest offices of the state and the court were filled. These were the pashas, beys, the *kapıcı başıs,* as well as the masters of the sultan's household: his sword-bearer (*Silâhdar Ağa*), chamberlain (*Cuhadar Ağa*), tax collector (*Resimdar Ağa*), valet of the Turban (*Tulbentdar Ağa*), and eight other personal attendants.[57] The future of these young men was so bright that in 1576 Moustapha Pasha complained to the German ambassador, David Ungnad, that while Moslem children were being thrust aside and ignored, Christian children were attaining the highest offices in the land.[58]

It is clear that the question as to when the system of child recruitment was abolished must be in two parts: when did the collective recruitment of candidates for the *acem oğlan* last take place; and when did the impressment of small children for the class of *iç oğlan* finally come to an end?

So far as the first aspect of the problem is concerned, it is apparent that from as early as the reigns of Suleiman I (1520–1566) and Murad III (1574–1595) the institution of *acem oğlan* became progressively adulterated by the admission into its ranks of more and more Turks, as well as the sons of janissaries (*ocak zade*). The Turks wanted for their children a future no less assured than that of Christians, so many persuaded Christian families covertly to take their sons for eventual presentation as candidates for recruitment. This stratagem became even more popular after Suleiman I granted janissaries the right to marry; for what this signified was that the janissaries, at a single stroke, had been accorded all the honors of a privileged class, including the rights to salary and a family life. Interestingly, the beginnings of the decline of the janissaries' power and fighting prowess coincided with its elevation to privileged status.

Nor did the admission of Moslems into the *acem oğlan*[59] lead only to the degeneration of the class of janissaries: it also marked the appearance of indiscipline and decay within the empire as a whole, of which one manifestation was that the recruitment of children was thereafter carried out only sporadically and only in Europe. A firman of 5 February 1666 in fact remarked that the system of child recruitment had been allowed to fall into disuse for too long, even though it was still of crucial importance to the state. The last known attempt to recruit children was at Naousa in 1705, which provoked the people to revolt.[60] Whether or not the Turks on that occasion successfully completed their mission is unknown, but perhaps the resistance encountered did put an end to this most painful of historical episodes.

So far as the second aspect of the problem is concerned, evidence recently brought to light reveals that the impressment of small children for the class of *iç oğlan* continued until the middle of the eighteenth century. Both classes, *acem oğlan* and *iç oğlan*, did not, however, become formally defunct till the abolition of the janissary corps in 1826.[61]

Hammer reckons that about half a million children were lost to Christianity,[62] while Paparrhegopoulos puts the figure closer to one million.[63] However, it must be admitted that all save the most crude approximations are practically unattainable. There is only one certainty: that no calculation of the number of child-converts to Islam is possible at all if it does not embrace a detailed and specialized study of child-recruitment in all its aspects.

Whatever the actual numbers involved, the drain on Hellenism's children was intensive for almost two centuries, from the middle of the fifteenth century to the middle of the seventeenth century. And the magnitude of the loss cannot be fully appreciated unless it is also realized that those children were invariably the most sound in mind and body. The threat to the Hellenic nation was only dissipated, and its degeneration slowly arrested and finally stopped, when the status of the janissary *acem oğlan* was lifted and Turkish opinion generally began to resent the elevation of sons of infidels to the state's highest offices.[64]

Christians saw only two possible avenues of escape from the system of child-recruitment: conversion, actual or feigned, to Islam, or flight with all that could be carried to settlements of expatriates in neighboring Christian states. The first course was the one usually chosen, since it offered the immediate alleviation of a multitude of ever-present, everyday problems; the second was hardly practicable except for those raias who lived along the coast or near the frontiers of the Ottoman state. But it did occur. In the Peloponnese and Albania, to take two cases in point, populations dwindled and sizable chunks of formerly cultivated land became desolate. As slaves searched for sanctuary in the nearest Venetian colony, fiefs correspondingly depreciated in value. Sometimes this flight of population even brought Venice and the Ottoman state into serious conflict with each other.[65]

The moral and material difficulties of adjustment to the hardships which followed conquest were not made easier by the accompanying plethora of slaughter, enslavement, and voluntary or enforced apostasy. We can only assume that the Balkan countries, particularly Greece and Albania, were depopulated as a result. The havoc reached its apogee during the fifteenth century, when, simultaneously with the mass impressment of Christian child-subjects of the Ottoman Empire, an undisciplined and predatory Turkish horde trampled upon countless men, women and children. As Ducas wrote, "the Albanians, though a populous people, were decimated by the Ottomans; as for the Vlachs [Rumanians], the Serbs, and the Romans [Greeks], they were all exterminated."[66] The process of assimilation and conversion to Islam among the Greeks, particularly those of Asia Minor and more particularly those who lived in the plains, proceeded relentlessly. We base this conclusion on the fact that most Greek place-names in the plains of Asia Minor—mountains, rivers, and villages—were displaced by Turkish names and that this happened much less in mountain regions and still less in towns where dense Greek populations were able to sustain their ancient culture. Cities which were formerly centers of Byzantine administration also retained Byzantine traditions.[67] And after successive conquests, the purity of the Turkish race was itself broken down by an infusion of Greek blood, especially after whole populations in Asia Minor and the Balkans went

11. A Janissary marching to war. From Nicolas de Nicolay, *Les Navigations, perégrinations, et voyages faicts en la Turquie*, Anvers, 1577.

12. Janissaries. From Paul Ricaut, *Histoire de l'état présent de l'empire ottoman*, Paris, 1670.

over to Islam. The Turks, except for the Turcomans and Yuruks, lost the predominantly Mongol characteristics of their race. Indeed, the Turks acquired characteristics which resembled those of the peoples of south-eastern Europe more than those of Turkestan. The Turks of the littorals of Asia Minor, among whom Greeks were always interspersed,[68] are in fact the descendants of Greeks. Thus the Turks and Greeks of modern times are often of the same stock.[69] Finally, Christian converts to Islam, particularly Greeks in the fourteenth century, became the highest political and military dignitaries in the state. Spiritually reborn into the Islamic world, they became the state's most disciplined, zealous, and able soldiers. It was they who dealt the Byzantine Empire its final and most decisive death blows. It was they who were the most merciless persecutors of their fellow countrymen and former coreligionists. It was they who contributed most signally to the organization, extension, and consolidation of the Ottoman state.

The Search for Sanctuary

The Greeks never lost their desire to escape from the heavy hand of the Turks, bad government, the impressment of their children, the increasingly heavy taxation, and the sundry caprices of the conqueror. Indeed, anyone studying the last two centuries of Byzantine rule cannot help being struck by the propensity of the Greeks to flee misfortune. The routes they chiefly took were: first, to the predominantly Greek territories, which were either still free or Frankish-controlled (that is to say, the Venetian fortresses in the Despotate of Morea, as well as in the Aegean and Ionian Islands) or else to Italy and the West generally; second, to remote mountain districts in the interior where the conqueror's yoke was not yet felt.[1]

Not for many centuries had Greeks in such large numbers shown so strong a desire to remove themselves to more secure places. But the uprooting and decay of whole settlements began again and gathered momentum after 1400. It is impossible even to guess at the numbers who migrated or moved. All that can be said is that in the process new colonies were founded, the composition of the Greek nation underwent significant changes, and not only new conditions of life but new conceptions and new customs were discovered.

We find that the first route was more and more heavily trodden the closer Byzantium came to collapse,[2] until at the time of the Capture and just after it was all but choked with human traffic. People flooded into the islands and other places where misery awaited them and the local populations off whom they had to live.[3] Those of the old nobility of Constantinople and Mistra who escaped to Venetian-controlled lands spent the rest of their days poor, sullen, insignificant and despised—"an utterly wretched and lugubrious spectacle."[4] Too late, they discovered that a battlefield death on the soil of the motherland would have been far preferable to the agony they suffered in foreign lands. For almost a century thereafter, they and their descendants enlisted as mercenaries and wandered across Europe from one city to another, recalling lost grandeur, bewailing their fate, begging stipends from powerful rulers in the West, and sometimes being persecuted on suspicion of entering into secret dealings with the Turks. Others, incurably nostalgic for their homeland, returned to the Ottoman state until they eventually faded into oblivion along with the way of life and world of ideas of which they themselves were representatives.[5]

After 1460 it was usual for the Christian population of the Peloponnesian countryside to seek refuge in the Venetian-controlled coastal towns, particularly Nauplia. After seven years' residence there, they acquired rights of citizenship. "And when the people came into the fortress," wrote Dorotheos of Monemvasia, "they built magnificent houses inside and outside the walls which we can still see today; and the whole place became filled with houses and churches intertwined by the walls."[6] It is from this time that we must date the appearance of modern Nauplia's streets and the town's general configuration.

In these former Venetian towns, like Modon and Corfu, a kaleidoscope of various peoples—Greek, Albanian, Arvanito-Vlach, Frank, even Gypsy[7]—still jostle one another. The profusion of color evokes in a most picturesque way, comparable to Mazaris' well-known satire on Peloponnesian society, the veritable mosaic of population of which the Peloponnese consisted at the beginning of the fifteenth century.

The Venetian Government also assumed responsibility for the welfare of many Greek refugees from the Peloponnese, Cyprus, and Crete and resettled them in a number of Istrian towns, notably Parenzo and Pola. There they intermixed with the local inhabitants and thus contributed to the eventual recasting of that region's population. An Orthodox church was founded in Pola in 1589.[8]

The torrent of refugees after the Capture and particularly following the death of Skanderbeg (or George Castriota),[9] Albania's national hero, swept Christians from Epirus and Albania, depositing them in the Ionian Islands, mainly Cephalonia and Corfu where they established new villages,[10] and in Italy.

There were not only scholars, whom we described in *Origins of the Greek Nation,* but many others, notably soldiers, as well. Among them, for example, were the Greco-Albanians Demetrius Reres, Nicholas Binderios Lascaris, Constantine Mazrekios Castriota and others belonging to the family of George Castriota, who, with their families, abandoned their villages and regions for sanctuary in Italy.[11] Mostly they settled in Calabria (where other Greek colonies from centuries past, including hundreds of practicing Orthodox monks in many monasteries, were still to be found)[12] or in the provinces of Palermo and Messina.[13]

The question of the nature and disposition of these Greco-Albanian colonies in southern Italy is a complex one for a number of reasons. In the first place, the origins of their earliest settlements are shrouded in mystery and controversy, and later evidence concerning them tends to be fragmentary or nonexistent; in the second place, it is extremely difficult, so close are their connections, to distinguish between the Albanians and the Greeks (mainly Greeks from Epirus). As we shall see in further contexts, this sort of problem is not an isolated one in history. Moreover, certain refugee peoples over the centuries began to reject their language, customs, and Orthodox religion so that they were eventually assimilated into the Italian environment. By the middle of the nineteenth century, this process had advanced so far that perhaps as many as two-thirds of the total were completely italianized and had become professing Catholics. Finally, those who have tried to analyze the problem have invariably been hampered by their ignorance of the colonists' dialect and by encountering other peoples in southern Italy of different origins.[14] Confronted with all these difficulties, which have become magnified with the passing of time, the historian cannot help but wish for a monograph on the subject, especially since linguistic studies have already been made. From the earlier history of post-Byzantine Greek colonization in Italy, about which more will be said, at least we know of the abortive negotiations in 1472–1474 between Anna Notara and the Republic of Siena for the settlement of Greeks at Montacuto di Maremma in Tuscany.[15]

But permanent Greek colonies were planted periodically in many other parts of Italy. Naples, capital of the Kingdom of the Two Sicilies, became a most important center of Greek population in southern Italy. In 1487, no fewer than five thousand Orthodox Albanians, Epirotes, and other Greeks were serving in the army of King Ferdinand I (1468–1516). And in order to cater to the religious needs of the Orthodox refugees, the Church of St. Peter and St. Paul was built in Naples in 1518 on the initiative of Thomas, son of Demetrius Asanes, who was related to the royal house of Palaeologus.[16]

In 1534 new settlements were also founded in the southern parts of the Kingdom of Naples with the blessing of Charles V (1500–1558); later they received the blessing of Philip II (1527–1598). Similar immigration took place under the Bourbon Charles III of Naples (1716–1788), who also commissioned in his army a Royal Macedonian Regiment (Reggimento Reale Macedone), granted extensive lands to the refugees in the Abruzzo, and gave his permission in 1736 to the establishment of both a Greek Orthodox diocese and a college for the education of Greek youths.[17] In 1744, seventeen men, three women, and a priest from the Epirote village of Pikerni settled at Badessa in the province of the Abruzzo, where they built an Orthodox church to house the icon of the Madonna of Kremizova, which they had brought with them from Epirus.[18] Descendants of these colonists, as well as others in Greek villages between Brindisi and Lecce,[19] in 1875 petitioned the Greek Government to allow them to return to their historic homeland. Greece, however, could not accede to their request for repatriation at that time. King Ferdinand IV(1751–1825) founded yet another Greek Orthodox diocese in Sicily and also granted lands and privileges for the establishment of a Greek colony in Brindisi itself.[20]

That the colonists of southern Italy preserved their Hellenism to some extent is attested by a variety of sources. During the fifteenth century, for example, Antonio Galateo, an eminent physician of Greek descent, who spoke Greek fluently and had a sound Greek education,[21] described the inhabitants of Kallipoli as still conversing in their original mother tongue when he was a young man. Ascanio Persio also said as much of the villagers of Calimera, Maglie, Martano, and Cape Santa Maria di Leuca in the sixteenth century. Gabriele Barri, the Calabrian geographer, confirmed that the Church of Rossano in Calabria Citeriore still retained the Greek liturgy and dogma in his own time (1600), while the inhabitants of towns and villages in the southernmost extremity of Calabria also spoke Greek.[22]

A century ago, Biondelli wrote that several thousand Greeks were to be found in Calabria Ulteriore—in the towns, mountains, and district of Celso as well as in the Reggio, particularly the environs of Brancaleone above Spartivento, the small towns of Bova, Amygdalia, Lefkopetra and Agatha, and the villages of Misoripha, Gardetum, and Pendedaktylon. Approximately eighteen thousand others, all speaking Greek and mostly professing Orthodoxy, were scattered in large and small colonies throughout the length and breadth of Terra d'Otranto.[23]

It is difficult to verify the dates of settlement of Greek colonists since most colonies are composed of successive layers of immigrants, each equally barren of surviving historical evidence. All that can now be said, and this from the evidence of linguistics alone, is that a great many immigrants after the Capture settled in places which had long supported compact Greek populations stretching back to medieval and ancient times.[24] Biondelli expressed that view, which we still hold, as long ago as the middle of the nineteenth century.[25]

Refugees from the Peloponnese also founded numerous villages in Sicily,[26] among them the celebrated Piana dei Greci outside Palermo.[27] In 1583, Palermo contained no fewer than six Greek Orthodox churches, all of which acknowledged the Oecumenical Patriarch as their head. The King of Spain, indifferent to the Pope's protestations, accorded his protection to this Orthodox congregation.[28] Gerlach in 1573 noted that even in Corsica there were Greeks who paid homage to the Oecumenical Patriarch,[29] confirming that the large body of Maniatai known to have immigrated to Corsica in 1676 settled in the midst of an older Greek colony. More will be said of this influx in another context.

Biondelli says that the Greco-Albanian settlements effected in Sicily after the Capture were established in the following chronological sequence: first, Contessa Entellina, then Messoiuso, Palazzo Adriano, and Piana dei Greci.[30] We are indebted for the present highly satisfactory state of our knowledge about the colonization of Messoiuso to the researches of Onofrio Buccola. According to him, many Greco-Albanian refugees settled in various parts of Sicily but came together at Messoiuso in the region of Baronia del monastero di San Giovanni degli Eremiti, where they restored the old Church of St. Maria, conducted Mass in accordance with the Orthodox rite, and settled there permanently in 1501.[31] In the middle of the seventeenth century, they founded an Orthodox monastery which, in 1648, they manned with Cretan clergy who were refugees from the Turkish-Venetian war. From 1669 this same monastery functioned as a seminary for monks. Many young men of the Greco-Albanian community went there to be educated, later to achieve distinction as scholars and monks. These in turn founded new schools until Messoiuso came to be regarded as the religious and cultural capital of the colonies and the custodian of the Greek religion and local dialect.[32]

The Greco-Albanians, particularly those from Epirus and the Peloponnese, for centuries guarded the manners, customs, traditions, faith, and outlook of their fathers. Though permanently settled on the soil of Sicily, they found it impossible to forget their conquered homelands.[33] On the Feast of Pentecost for generation after generation, the people of Messoiuso, their eyes filled with tears, would climb the hill known as Bringa, face the East, and sing in fervent tones: "Beautiful Morea, whom I have not set eyes on since the moment I left you. There live my father, my lord, and my esteemed mother; there my grandfather and my brother dwell. Beautiful Morea, whom since I left I have never seen again."[34] And they sang in Albanian.

The historian or lover of history who travels in southern Italy and Sicily today cannot help being struck by the Greek names on street signs which everywhere confront him and which by themselves tell a great deal about the fortunes of the Greek nation. He can but reflect how many more of these must exist in the countryside, inviting the joint study of Italian and Greek scholars.[35]

Nothing less than separate treatment can be accorded the place which received the largest confluence of Greeks in the entire West—Venice. After 1400 Venice received not only political and ecclesiastical emissaries and scholars, bringing valuable manuscripts with them, but also shipload after shipload of ordinary refugees and their families—merchants, seamen, and soldiers—subsequently entering into the service of the Venetian

13. The Greek Church of St. George, Venice, built at the end of the sixteenth century. Photo by the author, taken in 1963.

THE SEARCH FOR SANCTUARY

Republic. These people were the founders of what was to become a vast community of Greeks. At the time of the Capture and later, particularly after the fall of Venetian colonies in the Peloponnese, Cyprus (1571) and Crete (1669), they thronged in until by 1585, according to the testimony of the manuscript copyist Andrew Darmarios, their numbers had swollen to 15,000 men, women, and children. And that multitude continued to increase with the arrival of more ships, sometimes as many as fifteen or twenty a month, from Constantinople, Alexandria, Crete, and the other Greek islands.[36]

Following an example set by other communities of foreigners—Slavs, Albanians, Armenians, and others—the Greeks from as early as 1470[37] formed themselves into a "Brotherhood" (*Adelphotis*), and with the money obtained from dues and donations undertook the care of their poorer fellow countrymen, of orphans and widows, and the performance of various other charitable works.[38] At first, they obtained permission to hold religious services in the Roman Catholic Church of St. Vlasius.[39] Finally, by dint of persistent efforts, in which the efficiency of the president of the Brotherhood, Manuel Cantacuzenus, was most conspicuous, and with the aid of gifts and a kind of tax levied on Greek merchants, they succeeded in laying the foundations of their magnificent Church of St. George (based on the designs of Sante Solari detto Lombardo and Zuanantonio Chiona) and some thirty-four years later, in 1573, in watching its completion. With the splendid craftsmanship of its cedar stalls, with its pews and reredos, its marble work, silver votives, and four huge bronze candlesticks, this masterpiece of Alesandro Vittorio's combined exquisite taste with materials of unsurpassed quality.[40]

With but few exceptions and those unidentifiable, the donors were neither members of the great Byzantine families nor Greek scholars in the West: rather they were a cross-section of all the people—sea captains, shipowners, tailors, and generally those engaged in mercantile pursuits. Even their surnames—such as Anyphantis, Varelis, Kalapodas, Chalasiaris, and Pagidas[41]—speak eloquently of very humble origins. What this meant was that the leadership of the old aristocracy was already being replaced by that of the burghers. Among the members of the Orthodox Brotherhood listed in two sixteenth-century manuscripts or "ledgers" (*tameia*) are a considerable number with Italian names—Manolli Buchallano, Vassili Cortelli, Zorzi Falier, Matio Floca, Marco Lonza, and Zorzi Matarangga, for instance—as well as many others identifiable as Greek though of Italian origin, that is to say, belonging to persons Hellenized during the late Byzantine period.[42]

Venice's influence upon captive Hellenism was enormous in every economic, intellectual, and cultural sense.[43] Not only material goods but also ideas from Italy and the West generally found their way to Turkish-

occupied Greece through that city. Venice shone so brightly in the imagination of the Greeks—in their songs, their traditions, their folk tales and
sayings[44]—that something of its aura still remains with them. The name of
the city was perpetuated in the Christian names of many Greek
daughters.

According to the Georgian historian Iosseliane, many inhabitants of the
Kingdom of Trebizond and northeastern Asia Minor fled to Iberia and
Georgia after Trebizond fell, particularly in 1490. Subsequently, with the
Turkish advance into the Caucasus, they withdrew into the interior and
founded various ecclesiastical dioceses. One of these was the Archbishopric of Achtala, which remained intact until 1827, and it was there that the
two Oecumenical Patriarchs Joachim I and Theokletos II journeyed in
1498 and 1585,[45] respectively, in order to solicit contributions to the
Church. At this time, too, Greeks, from the northern coast of Asia Minor
sought refuge among the Tartars of the Crimea; in 1777 they moved to
the district of Marioupolis in the Azov. Some of them (for example, the
villagers of Magous) lost their native tongue and came to speak the
language of the Tartars, without in any other way losing their ethnic
identity.[46] It is possible that the researches of Russian scholars are capable
of filling in many of the gaps in our knowledge of these Greeks, but I have
not had any such work at my disposal.

Of much greater significance is the population flight into Greek territories still remaining free as a prelude to the search for even more secure
sanctuary in the remote, though nominally Turkish-held, interior. Usually this kind of movement was effected en masse and only rarely by
individuals.

Except for those places which offered a degree of security by reason
either of their commercial or strategic importance, such as Thessalonica,
or the special immunities which had been conferred upon them, such as
Ioannina, Tyrnavos,[47] Galata,[48] and the like, the phenomenon we observe
in this context is a true uprooting of population that had the same devastating effects whether in Asia Minor, the Balkan peninsula, or the
islands of the Aegean.[49] It is precisely this phenomenon which accounts
for the great disparity between Moslem and Christian urban populations
that Barkan has established for the period 1520–1530. His figures are
most revealing: 3,338 Moslem families in Adrianople, for example, as
against 522 Christian families; in Prusa (Bursa), 6,165 as against 69; in
Ankara, 2,399 and 277; Tokat, 818 and 701; Skoplje, 630 and 200; Sofia,
471 and 238; Thessalonica, 1,229 as against 989 Christian and 2,645
Jewish families; Serrai (Siroz), 671 and 357; Trikkala, 301 and 343;
Larissa, 693 and 75; and so on. Two striking exceptions were Athens,
with only 11 Turkish families in a community of 2,286 Christian families
and Sivas (Sebastia), with 261 Turkish and 750 Christian.[50]

Since this movement of population continued over many centuries, it was of tremendous importance in the evolution and formation of the modern Hellenic nation. And in terms of the light which a study of this movement is capable of shedding on so many demographic problems associated with the history of modern Hellenism—not least towards dispelling the view generally but erroneously held that Greeks congregated mainly in cities and towns[51]—the subject has not been accorded its proper significance.

Such a study, it is true, certainly for the early centuries when the migrations began, must fall back upon oral tradition that has either been written down or preserved in the memory of local inhabitants, as it has been to this day. The investigator, like the preclassical historian, must in consequence frequently resort to posterior evidence in order to infer, by a process of analogy, such matters as when a village or town was founded or how its population was composed. Only when the evidence so adduced tallies with the oral testimony of the local populace is the investigator then entitled to assume that his conclusions are definite signposts in the labyrinthine history of modern Hellenism.

The very first assumption we are forced to make is that the foundation of refugee settlements in this period was caused by the impulsive search for security. The dictates of climate and terrain which we would normally presume to be overriding were in all such cases only secondary. Despite the transformations subsequently wrought by changing conditions, it is possible for us today to trace both the manner of settlement and the types of habitation set up.

But we must first inject a note of caution: with the evidence we have, not even the greatest possible exertion of our imagination will permit us to capture the full picture of colonization or the vivid details of daily settlement and economic life in the countryside. It could hardly be otherwise since so many settlements were destroyed. Sometimes their ruins are sufficient to evoke for the traveller the ghost of some former flourishing community; but just as often they defy him to plumb their long-vanished secrets.

In Asia Minor, as we have seen, the Greek population disintegrated most quickly. Many Greek centers were either overrun and populated by Turks or utterly devastated, with only the ruins of churches and monasteries left to bear mute witness to their former grandeur.[52] In some districts the Ottomans embarked deliberately on massive programs of resettlement in order to alter the balance of population in their favor. For instance, Moslem communities from Amasya, Tsoroumlou, Tocat, Samsun, and Bafra were transplanted to Trebizond; fiefs there were reapportioned among spahis, who moved in from Ottoman dominions as far away as Albania. A sizable part of the Christian population of Trebizond, on the other hand, as well as many Christian military families (*eski hıristiyan sipahiler*) were deported to Constantinople or to Rumelia (European Turkey).[53] There, they very likely received a pension (*dirlik*).[54] Except for the very few who either joined the Turk or co-operated with him, none of these Christian provincial military kept their properties as fiefs. Only recently, after half a millennium, have a few such exceptions been brought to light from the hitherto unexplored recesses of the Turkish archives: the traitor from the castle of Torul (Ardasa);[55] the nine other military *pronoiarioi* who betrayed David Comnenus and defected to the enemy. They, and three others unspecified, were among the few permitted to retain their properties.[56] Finally, there were those charged with the performance of certain military duties who fell into the category of *müsellem*, but a few names is practically all we know about them.[57] Of all those Christians belonging to the former military of Torul, no more than twenty-one succeeded in maintaining their positions as a result of making a deal with the Turks.[58]

At the sultan's command, many royal and monastic properties in Trebizond were converted into fiefs.[59] One such was the pasturage (*çayır*) belonging to the Metropolitan Antonios, who was deported to Constantinople.[60] The information provided by some travellers that the Turks never touched ecclesiastical property is therefore utterly misleading.[61]

The chief beneficiaries of the redistribution of property were of course the soldiers of the sultan (*kapu kulu*). Twenty-five years after the fall of the Empire of the Grand Comnenus, as many as 101 of the original 207 fiefs of the *liva* (administrative district) of Trebizond had already been parcelled out among janissaries, *cebecis,* and others,[62] that is, among those falling generally into the category of *gulâm-i mîr* or *gulâm-i padişah* (slaves of the Porte) and into the class of *kul-oglu* (children of the slaves of the sultan).[63] It is perhaps also of interest to note that a further twenty-five fief-holders of the *liva* of Trebizond were Albanians, some of them Moslem,[64] who had been moved there from their distant homeland.

After the overthrow of the Trapezuntine Empire, the rigors of occupation brought about a swift decline in commerce, and poverty and ruin crowded in upon the populace.[65] Tradition records that many Greeks from the coast took refuge in the mountains and the forested hinterland, particularly in the region of Chaldea astride the river Kanis.[66] Against all adversity, these remnants of the population of a once-great Empire managed to survive throughout the dark centuries of servitude and even to nourish their cultural heritage in places like the monastic oases of Peristereota and the Madonna of Sumela.[67]

With the aid of an oral tradition which is still current, Philip Papa Apostolos Chimonidis, author of the history of Santa, wrote this of his ancestral compatriots:

Year after year went by, but the people of Santa emerged from the wilderness only on rare occasions and with extreme caution because they feared their refuges would be discovered. Their fears were well founded since confusion and disorder reigned unchecked outside their fastnesses. In a single day, one might see an entire Christian village razed and its inhabitants butchered or driven off. There was no law to spare the weak, to safeguard property or even life itself, or to protect the people from the ferocity and rapacity of those more powerful than they. This brutal situation continued until the Pontus was completely subdued.[68]

From the mountain retreats into which they withdrew, the people of the Pontus continued to resist the Moslem invasion with determination. For an indeterminate period they were successful in clinging to their independence, though the inhabitants in some places eventually despaired and acknowledged or pretended to acknowledge Islam, but most remained loyal to Christianity.[69]

The salvation of the people of Chaldea was assisted by the very considerable wealth which lay beneath the soil. From ancient times, silver, copper, and alum mines in the Chaldean mountains had provided the main source of the local inhabitants' livelihood.[70] It is impossible to establish with any certainty what kind of relationship developed initially between the conquerors and the inhabitants of these lode-bearing districts, but it appears that from the very outset mines were not appropriable by local ruling magnates but were deemed the property of the state from the time of conquest, and thereafter only the state had authority to effect arrangements for their disposal and use.[71] The most important mining center in the district was Gumus Hane (Argyroupolis), which, according to tradition, was peopled during the course of the fifteenth century by former inhabitants of the village of Djaha.[72]

Presented with all this subterranean treasure, the conquerors had no other option than to employ the local inhabitants in the mines since only they knew how to work them. The Turks, a people accustomed for generations to living off the produce of the land or the plunder of war but ignorant of the technology of mining, were unable to carry on the work of local miners; and since any form of compulsion would only have resulted in economic dislocation or ruin, they not only left the miners undisturbed at their labors but made their working conditions more attractive through the granting of various exemptions and privileges.[73]

The people of Santa owed their privileged development entirely to their mining expertise and the services they rendered.[74] According to a firman which was promulgated sometime between twenty and forty years after their arrival in this inhospitable region,

no foreigner, Turk or Christian, shall violate their boundaries; the inhabitants shall remain free and unmolested, each *persona grata* within the State, and the local civil and military authorities shall protect and defend them on every occasion and visit exemplary punishment on anyone who shall contravene the orders of these presents.[75]

In the early period of the history of Santa (from the time of the emigration to 1665),

the inhabitants were engaged in various pursuits. They smelted metallic ores (lithium) and extracted iron of the highest grade;[76] others plied the building trade in and around the villages of Santa-Sourmena, Gemouran, and so on; many also worked in the mines of Argyroupolis, which supplied them with all their needs for a frugal yet comfortable life. Some, too, were farmers, but this probably brought them very little return because of the cold and damp climate.[77]

The privileges accorded Santa and its situation ("the villages of Santa were between two high mountain ranges so precipitous as to be impassable for most of the year"),[78] encouraged rapid population growth during the latter part of her history, particularly after an influx of new refugees[79] during a time of anarchy in the Pontus around the middle of the seventeenth century.[80]

On the whole, miners in the Ottoman Empire formed a separate, specially privileged class of raias, who were really a subcategory of the class of *mu'af ve müsellem* (Christians exempt from taxes). A unique body of legislation, based on that of old Saxony but also influenced by the medieval law of Serbia and Bosnia, dealt specifically with mining and with the adjustment of relations between the state and miners. In mining the Ottomans found an autonomous sphere of economic activity capable of supporting Moslems as well as Christians and furthering economic and military enterprise without constituting any drain upon the public purse.[81] In this way the mining villages of Chaldea ("these blessed mines," in the words of Chrysanthos Notaras, Patriarch of Jerusalem[82]) became, especially from the seventeenth century on, true havens in which everyone in the Pontus who wished to escape Turkish repression could find shelter. While in other regions, fertile though they were, the Greek population dwindled and sometimes totally disappeared, in these remote mountains it multiplied. From sheer necessity, lands considered infertile till then were nursed into productivity,[83] and a host of villages and small towns sprang up. Murad III (1574–1595) was chiefly responsible for the rationalization and consolidation into a coherent system of those privileges which applied throughout the mining region: the villages he proclaimed collectively as a beylik and their inhabitants as "people of the sultan"; miners were granted virtually total exemption from taxation and compulsory labor or other forms of misuse; the impressment of their children for the janissary corps was outlawed; and in all matters pertaining to mining they were effectively placed beyond the jurisdiction and reach of civil and military functionaries. Murad III even founded a mint in Argyroupolis in which Greeks were employed.[84]

The Turkish functionaries in mining regions which came within the state's jurisdiction were *emins* and cadis (the latter known as nazirs [supervisors] after 1536). *Emins* were also responsible for the municipal government of provincial capitals such as Argyroupolis.[85] Their chief duties were to protect the local inhabitants from exploitation by tax-collectors and civil servants and to prevent emigration, for miners were bonded to their work. Even those who journeyed to a town in order to appeal against some judicial decision were forcibly returned. Redress rested with the *emin* alone.[86] Appalling conditions in the mines took a grim toll of the miners' health. Thus the peoples of the Greek peninsula and islands were at pains to conceal or deny new discoveries of precious metals whenever these were made.[87]

Throughout the Greek peninsula and especially in the Peloponnese, successive invasions by the Turks in the first half of the fifteenth century brought their usual harvest of destruction, plunder, slaughter, and deportation. After the violence of the last invasion, it was as though a giant swathe had cut through the population of the plains. The old and once-great urban centers were not wiped out, but their populace was diminished. The result was economic blight.

Afterwards, there was continuous movement of people away from the vicinity of roads used by Turkish armies and officials who engaged in sporadic despoliation.[88] Some villages of the plains and small towns on or near the major arterial routes were devastated and abandoned; others sprang to life in the relative security afforded by resettlement in remote places. Two examples of wholesale community transplantation were the villages of St. John and St. Nicholas in the district of Zagorion.[89] The mountains, from which surplus population normally migrated to the plains, thus had to support not only the indigenous inhabitants but also refugees from neighboring plains.

This is how Chesneau described the districts through which he passed on the Isthmus-Megara-Thebes-Chalcis road in 1547:

There are also other ruins of towns and castles in the places through which we passed. This country is so desolate that it is virtually impossible for anyone seeing it now to believe that it is the same fertile and famous land described by historians. For my part, I have never seen anything more wild, arid, and choked with forest and ilex than this.[90]

But it was the physical configuration of the Greek land with its mountain fastnesses, barren terrain, jutting peninsulas, and myriad islands which undoubtedly saved a great part of Hellenism from extinction and the Hellenes from moral and physical degeneration and perhaps even total annihilation. Much later, that apostle of modern Hellenism, Kosmas the Aetolian, conveyed as much when he spoke of the towering mountains as "holy" and the people who dwelled at their feet "blessed"[91] and foresaw dreadful misfortunes for those who lived in the plains.[92]

The mountainous and tree-covered bulk of the Pindus and its spurs sprawled over the whole of western Greece: Grammos,[93] Vermion, Pieria, Olympus,[94] Chasia, Pelion, Othrys, as well as the mountains of Achaea and especially Maina loomed protectively over all nearby villages. Kataphygion in Pieria is a village whose name (there are many such throughout Greece) and history typify refugee resettlement throughout the peninsula. According to tradition, its inhabitants once lived in a village called Podari on the luxuriant banks of the river Aliakmon, but withdrew because of Turkish oppression (exactly when we do not know) to the steep wooded slopes of Mt. Phlambouro (Pieria) where they had previously grazed their sheep. There they cleared the dense forest of oak and pine covering the plateau and founded their new village. Each winter, the village was completely buried in snow, but at least they were able to scorn the Turkish authorities and grow into the most independent village in the district.[95]

Tradition also has it that a large number of villages in western Macedonia and northwestern Epirus were founded in this way, among them Siatista, Galatini, Blatsi, Klisura, Vogatsiko, Kostarazi, Selitsa, and Moschopolis.[96]

In the middle of the seventeenth century, Evliya Tschelebi provided information that confirms this flight to the mountains. To the north of Lake Langhada, he said, he encountered absolutely nothing, except perhaps a few villages that had been razed or the ruined walls of houses. These belonged to "brigand" peoples—Greeks, Bulgarians, and Vlachs—who had fled to the mountains to escape (the phrase is his) Turkish oppression.[97]

Not only the Greeks of Thrace and Macedonia[98] but also those of Thessaly (the late Byzantine "Great Vlachia") retreated into the contiguous mountain maze because, as we have seen, Yuruk Turks occupied their arable plains.[99] Again according to tradition, the Yuruks of Thessaly were settled there by Turahan Bey, who became disturbed at the large number of Christian villages and castles around Larissa.[100] The big landholders of the Thessalian plain who still remained Christian either departed voluntarily or were slowly reduced to poverty and squeezed out by powerful Ottoman fief-holders who already had vast and lucrative holdings there.[101] We can only assume that these fief-holders continued to encroach on the properties of other landowners, big and small alike, despite the expanse of public domain which they already occupied. Time, how-

Vne Mosquée

La Ville de Larisse

La Riviere de Penie

14. Larissa. From Edouard Brown, *Relations de plusieurs voyages . . . ,* Paris, 1674.

ever, moderated the initial belligerence of the Turkish settlers: indeed, by the beginning of the nineteenth century, it was the "peaceable" nature of the peasant that drew comment.[102]

It was only to be expected that Larissa, hemmed in by the estates of Turkish feudal lords and so strategically situated, should have become denuded of its Christian population and flooded with Turks. The city still had twenty-seven mosques at the end of the nineteenth century.[103] This predominance of the Moslem element led to the almost unprecedented transfer of its metropolitan seat to Trikkala.[104] Similarly Pharsala (Tsataltza) was transformed into a Turkish city.[105]

A noteworthy feature of the resettlement of refugees was the concentration of Vlach peoples in the mountainous mass of the Pindus and the foundation here and there of numerous communities of families belonging to the same patriarchal clan. These clans, which were distinguished both by the absolute authority their leaders possessed over all other members as well as by their unique social organization and way of life generally (characteristics still to be found among them in some places) felt the need to come together in one village for common protectioñ.[106] From there, population surpluses eventually overflowed into other mountain fastnesses including, from a very early stage, Olympus itself. The Vlach people of the Olympus villages of Neochori, Phteri, Milia, Vlacholivado, and Kokkinoplo have preserved the tradition that they originally came from the mountains (undoubtedly the Pindus) several hundred years before and built the village of Livadi.[107] The reliability of this tradition is attested by a number of similarities between the names, language, pronunciation, manners, customs, and the like, of the Vlachs of Olympus and those of the Pindus (such as those of Samarina).[108]

In Epirus, too, from the very beginning of the Turkish invasions, people sought refuge in remote natural redoubts; for example, from the Palaea Parga to the Nea.[109] Oral tradition still recalls the disorder and anarchy which prevailed for decades in those parts.[110] Tiny villages, always grouped closely together in the mountains, were formed by the addition of one family to another, and each derived only a bare subsistence from its herds. Such were the villages around Tsamantas: Sotiras, Lintizda, Sminetzi, Griazdani, Maltziani, Povla, Achouria, Phatiri, Babouri, Lia, Glousta, Lista, Zitsa, and Kretzounista, as well as others interspersed among these, of which only ruins remain, suggesting that still more may have completely vanished for one reason or another.[111] The distinctiveness of these communities is certainly explained to some extent in terms of the mountainous topography[112] and the unique way of life of their inhabitants, but it was influenced, too, by Turkish pressure from without.[113] No explanation of the protracted settlement of these peoples in such forbidding places can be complete unless it also takes account of the political conditions of the times.

Apart from the mountains, nature also provided splendid hiding places for a persecuted and hard-pressed people in the many peninsulas protruding from the Greek coast. Isolated from all channels of communication, they ranged in prominence from huge mountainous outcrops to puny promontories like Parga. There was Chalcidice, for instance, which was shut off from the rest of Macedonia by the mountainous, tree-covered escarpment of Cholomon. Describing Cholomon, the traveller Esprit Cousinéry remarked that during periods of revolution and conquest it was the forests rather than the scattered castles which provided real security to the inhabitants, with the consequence that some very old families are still to be found there whose ethnic purity has not been adulterated by a single drop. They are a people fiercely proud of their Greek identity, their churches, bishops, and schools, as well as the privileges that they have so jealously guarded.[114]

The region of Cholomon itself terminated in the three even more secure peninsular sanctuaries of Kassandra, Sithonia, and Mt. Athos. This was neither the first nor the last time that the wretched victims of hostile invasion would find refuge there, though at least Kassandra may have escaped the tread of enemy boots until 1821, when several thousand refugees flooded into the peninsula. So, at any rate, the demotic song would seem to convey:

No one defiled Kassandra
Till Lopout came; only he took her.[115]

Other peninsulas of comparable importance were Thessalomagnesia and Maina, which were protected by the Pelion and Taygetus ranges respectively. The region of Thessalomagnesia beginning on even higher ground at Tsagezi (south of the valley of the Tempe),[116] was completely isolated until the declining years of the Byzantine Empire[117] and also avoided conquest by the Turk for quite a long time. The inhabitants of the Tempe valley (perhaps the Byzantine Lycostomion) thrived in their secure environment and became noted as weavers,[118] and especially for their red fabric. Subsequently, as refugees, they moved on to the northern flank of the Kissavos (Ossa), from which they peopled Ambelakia. The town throve in the seventeenth century and even more in the eighteenth century.[119] To the south of the Kissavos, the town of Agia (named after the Church of St. Anne [Hagia Anna] in the western part of the district) similarly flourished during the same period on the basis of the same industry. According to very old tradition, its people were also adept at weaving various other silk and cotton fabrics, which they exported to Smyrna and Constantinople and (through the people of Ambelakia, who gave their assent and co-operation) to Austria and Germany.[120]

The district surrounding Tsagezi is of especial historical and archaeological interest. Various inscriptions dating from the end of the fifteenth century and surviving in the Byzantine monastery of the Madonna and St. Demetrius tell of its restoration and reconstruction in what was apparently, as previously observed,[121] an era of prosperity. This revival was undoubtedly attributable to the number of people who converged upon the district. Under the Turkish rule, the monastery was fortified in order to repel invaders, chiefly pirates;[122] but no more than ten minutes' walk from it are the remains of a medieval town, smothered in dense undergrowth, as well as the ruins of a small church dating from Turkish times. Evidently this city, together with its little port of Phteri, was consumed in the holocaust of some invasion, to be replaced later by the Turkish Tsagezi.[123]

Refugees from Euboea, Phthiotis,[124] and the two medieval Almyroses colonized Platanos and probably, too, the Pelion villages, which no doubt also gave sanctuary to other neighboring peoples. Most of these villages have the same name as the monasteries around which they grew—for example St. Onoufrios, St. Laurentios—and a few of the monasteries themselves still survive.[125] Demetrias remained inhabited until the end of the sixteenth century, while the fortress of Volos has been continuously occupied from ancient times down to the present day.[126]

In Maina, Louis XIII's emissary Chasteaurenault made this revealing comment on the district in 1619: "the country can be likened to *an immense city, unusually sited yet densely populated,* bounded on one side by the sea, into which only a few narrow roads lead between Kalamata and Passavas, the two extremities of Maina. The place has about 700 towns and villages and innumerable monasteries."[127] Another source mentions 300 villages and 60 towns in 1672;[128] but in any case the hinterland of this district was unquestionably populous. After 1460, many families from Mistra and its neighboring cities and towns, noble and otherwise, apparently took refuge in the eastern and western foothills of the Taygetus. Tradition has it that there they founded new settlements and intermixed with the local Albanian or Arvanito-Vlach colonists who immigrated into the area that was known to foreign travellers as *Brazzo di Maina.* From this melting-pot the bellicose population of Maina eventually emerged,[129] though at the beginning of the sixteenth century (1512) the coasts of Maina gave travellers the impression of being deserted and devoid of human habitation. The peasants there lived in extreme poverty.[130]

Euboea, too, was a kind of remote peninsula, but without the advantages of seclusion that others possessed. Its inhabitants were also observed to move to the sanctuary of the mountains where, supporting themselves as shepherds, they retained their freedom and preserved their language and physical features.[131]

Separate mention must also be made of western central Hellas and Acarnania (that region, roughly triangular, enclosed by a line extending

THE SEARCH FOR SANCTUARY

from the Gulf of Ambracia to the Achelous River) and including the Agrafa and Aspropotamos. The rugged and mountainous districts of Valtos and Xeromero in Acarnania formed a substantial refuge for those Greeks who did not choose the sanctuary offered by the Tocco-held Ionian islands of Leukas and Cephalonia just offshore.

In 1856, the French archaeologist Léon Heuzey recorded some arresting data bearing on the human geography of this district. The poor villages of Valtos, hidden and remote, were buried in the depths of thick forest and accessible only by concealed and treacherous paths. They consisted of huts far removed from one another that seemed to merge almost imperceptibly with the forest trees. Only the crowing of cocks and smoke filtering through the foliage betrayed the presence of human beings. Here, in such wilderness, man felt isolated and completely alone. It was not difficult to imagine that you had strayed and become lost, for there is no horizon nor any other means of orientation. You could see no further than a few meters. The heavy and illimitable shadows and the solitude of the forest were worse than night, because affording as they did total secrecy and impenetrable seclusion they bred dark impulses and lured men to wrongdoing.[132]

The inhabitants of Valtos thus lived up to the reputation their neighbors in Xeromero gave them[133] of being wolves and wild beasts. Her young men—strong, silent, hardy, and stubborn—idealized the life of klephts. Their paragon was Christos Milionis, first of the klephts that they could remember; their aim, to become armatoles:

We descend like wolves
To exact swift retribution.[134]

So the Turks were careful not to antagonize them. They organized them into companies of gendarmerie charged with guarding the mountainous districts between Epirus and the Agrafa. But the people of Valtos proved intractable and unreliable allies, especially when payment for their services was tardy in arriving or when on occasion the Venetians incited them to take up arms against the Turks. Nor did they hesitate to change abode and move to some other forest or ravine which was just as secure in the cover it provided. Then, though in vain, the Turks would send Albanian mercenaries to ferret them out and exterminate them. But the people merely set fire to their ramshackle dwellings and, leaving these ablaze, fled deeper into the forest. The enemy found himself dealing with an invisible opponent who watched his every move from hiding places in the forest and suddenly emerged at some opportune moment to ambush him.[135]

The people of Valtos were so inured to this ambiance of duplicity and desultory violence that their weapons were never out of their hands. They scorned normal agricultural pursuits, considering these as fit only for raias. Consequently, they were without the means of even basic subsistence and suffered greatly from the ravages of malnutrition and malarial fever.[136]

By no means so untamed were the inhabitants of Xeromero, who lived in less wild surroundings. But they were still a proud, restless, belligerent, and brave people, whose sense of honor was inordinately strong even among Greeks. A people whose manners had a certain quality of ingenuousness, their features were also handsome and refined, their stature tall and their bearing graceful.[137] Here, too, as in Valtos, those who had not already emigrated to the contiguous Ionian Islands were forced to lead an anxious existence, perpetually armed, as klephts or armatoles for some four hundred years, although the fertility of their land could give them satisfactory sustenance.

Every winter, Xeromero played host to various bands of klephts who came down from the surrounding mountains—Zygos, Kato Aetolia, Valtos, and Agrafa. Its wooded plateaus were decidedly more congenial than the peaks of snow-capped mountains, yet splendid haunts still abounded here. So they held their meetings in places like Varnaka and a few other villages. Sometimes, too, a particular threat of danger in the mountains might cause this egress from them, for Xeromero was a convenient jumping-off point for the much more secure Venetian-held islands of Leukas, Cephalonia, and Kalamos. Indeed, the leaders of the Xeromero bands built their houses not in the mountains, like their counterparts in Valtos, but near the coast—even right on the shores of the straits separating the mainland from the islands. Facing an avenue of evacuation directly was one way of ensuring peace of mind and certainly was as conducive to the growth of a sense of security as living in the mountains.[138]

The opening of channels of communication between the inhabitants of Acarnania and those of the neighboring Venetian colonies explains the Italian influence discernible in the former's language.[139] The fact, too, that refugees from the mainland named their new settlements after the principal Acarnanian villages, Katouna and Aetos, confirms the direction of a population movement which persisted throughout the entire Turkish period.[140] Similarly, Albanian and Epirote peoples took refuge, as is well known, on Corfu.[141] In all these islands, memories of this distant period have still not faded away. Here and there, the researcher encounters obvious foreign influences as well as concrete evidence of the many changes wrought by strangers on life in the Seven Islands.

The mountainous region of the Agrafa and Aspropotamos, really an extension of Acarnania, also provided a refuge for Christians during the declining years of the Byzantine Empire and, in particular, after the Capture. "This place," an eighteenth-century source notes of the Agrafa, "was virtually impassible and unnamed. Not a single road existed through its more inaccessible parts. The truth was that this was a place unfit not only for villages and people but hardly even for animals. However, as a result of the periodic persecution of Christians, some went to hide there and in that way eventually became settlers."[142] Also, in the middle of the sixteenth century, monks built the monastery of Tatarna near the village of Peniana.[143] By the seventeenth century, some villages, such as Phournas and Vraniana, gave signs not only of population increase but of economic and intellectual vitality.[144] It was here, indeed, that overpopulation first became evident and the problem of emigration arose.

The people from various parts of Greece who were either forced by the conqueror or chose of their own volition to seek refuge in the mountains had no option but to stay there for many years. Inevitably they came to think of settling down permanently and making homes of their temporary refuges. Thus is explained the almost simultaneous founding of so many new villages and towns which, according to local traditions still current, suddenly appeared from the end of the fourteenth century.

These new settlements were built either at the bottom of the slopes of mountains or on plateaus. If in the vicinity of the sea, they were established at a distance of from one to three hours' journey from the coast. The villagers usually went down into the fields only at times of sowing, cultivation, and harvest. There they had huts which they lived in until their work was completed. The sites of these settlements suggest the deliberate choice of isolation and inaccessibility. Rarely are there signs of earlier habitation in their midst. As a general rule, therefore, each new settlement resembled a natural redoubt.

If isolation provided at least a temporary solution to the problem of freedom, there still remained, of course, a desperate need for food and water. Never before had the Greeks come so painfully face to face with the problem of survival as they did in these high retreats. More close study will probably show how perilously near oblivion the Greek people came.

Whether or not their hopes for permanent settlement were realized depended on the availability of land, even narrow cultivable strips, forests, pastures, metalliferous ores. "It is possible, though not easy, to live there," wrote Braudel, speaking of the peoples who live on the fringes of the Mediterranean. "How hard the farmer along its shores must work can be gauged from the fact that very little use can be made of domestic animals. He must till by hand a soil which is already sown with stones. He must struggle incessantly to prevent the sliding of the soil. If it slides, he must toil to bring it up again and contain it by building terraces that climb upwards like ladders. This is back-breaking work which has no end. If he stops even for a moment, the mountains will revert to their original form, and everything must be begun again."[145]

Writing about his refugee ancestors in the mountainous district of

Santa, an inhabitant of the Pontus draws on local legends and traditions to give this account of their hardships:

The first concern of these people [the first families settled there] was to investigate their surroundings. Then, when they were sure that the district was completely devoid of other human habitation, they first of all built small stone huts to live in and afterwards cultivated a small plot of land to satisfy their need for food. So far as primary needs were concerned, the wheat grown just sufficed. However, for the rest of their food, they relied in the main on the bark of elm trees, which they first baked in ovens, then ground, and made bread from the flour.[146]

Of course life became indescribably difficult during the winter months. The inhabitants made provision for fuel and food as best they could, for they were invariably compelled, sometimes for months on end, to remain huddled in their homes, weather-bound and completely isolated from the outside world. However, these conditions produced at least one salutary effect: bodies and spirits were toughened.[147]

Not only villagers but also the inhabitants of towns and cities took refuge in settlements of this kind; and since the refugee burghers were adept craftsmen and traders, those settlements which possessed the potentiality for development tended to grow into new centers of economic activity. Indeed, most settlements had from their earliest beginnings the nucleus of a commercial and industrial as well as agricultural and pastoral population. Each, therefore, almost simultaneously began to raise stock, produce handicrafts, and engage in small trading activities.

Both the new natural environment and the exigencies of living in it obviously created new customs, new habits, indeed a whole new way of life. Thus, plainsmen and farmers were transformed in their new mountain habitats into shepherds, and shepherds or artisans into fishermen. The inhabitants of Kataphygion, for instance, traditionally farmers, became foresters, carpenters, and cattle-breeders. The needs of living sent them wherever timber could be found—to Olympus, Kassandra, and Mt. Athos. Often, they travelled as far as Smyrna and Alexandria in order to sell their lumber. These men were absent from their villages except, perhaps, on two occasions a year, when they returned to celebrate the great feast days with their own kith and kin.[148]

Nature dictated the sources of livelihood. Thus, the inhabitants of the Pindus "took stone from the mountains, which local artisans used in the construction of houses and churches. The sawyers of Vovousa and Aspropotamos obtained lumber from huge stands of fir, wild pine, and beech. The forest also provided for the huntsman; and its soft woods became the principal material for a whole range of household kitchen utensils—bottles, gourds, barrels, porringers, spoons. By a system of wooden locks, trout ascending the rivers could be caught. But always the flock remained the traditional base of their economy. The sheep was the chief source of food, clothing, of fertilizer for the legumes and plum trees in their irrigated gardens, and of the wool which the women wove."[149]

Thus stock-raising became the main source of their meager livelihood. Hunger was a constant companion. The rebellious spirit and occasional aggressive outbursts of the raias were surely attributable to the conditions under which they lived and especially to the famine which struck so frequently in those high altitudes.[150] Today, the visitor to those isolated mountain villages which have survived even the ravages of the Second World War is shocked by the prevalence of malnutrition. He enters the villages like a visitor from another age and readily visualizes the past in the sort of environment, which indeed has scarcely undergone change.

The constant stream of migrants to the mountains had the effect of denuding the population of the plains and continually swelling that of the mountains—naturally to the extent that people were capable of being supported and fed at the higher altitudes. Before 1668 the population of Tsakonia, for instance, was distributed over a much larger area than it is even today, occupying not only the mountains but also villages in the Laconian plain.[151] The unceasing movement of the population upset the normal demographic equilibrium not only in Greece but throughout all the occupied countries of the Balkans. The characteristic pattern of settlement became one in which the Turk occupied the plains and the Greek the mountains.

The phenomenon of localism, which had always distinguished Greek history from the time Greeks first set foot on their peninsula, was as we have seen accentuated by the conquest. While this involuntary isolation naturally meant in more than one sense the retrogression of civilization, it also contributed to the growth of a national spirit. Isolation in itself was not inimical, but was even conducive, to the preservation of popular intellectual and artistic traditions, so that under favorable local conditions they actually flowered in many of these mountain villages. A study of individual villages and towns in the mountains can thus reveal various elements of modern Hellenism.

The spirit developed by these mountaineers was in strong contrast with that of the serfs, the *kolligi*, who chose to remain on Turkish estates. These *kolligi* became a degenerate class under the indiscriminate oppression, malnutrition, terrible epidemics, and the maltreatment by undisciplined soldiery which they suffered. In the mountains, on the other hand, a process of natural selection evolved a dynamic Greek physical type who lived under conditions of greater freedom. They differed from the plainsmen (*kambisioi*) in fundamental outlook and way of life. In effect, a subnation emerges among the Greeks—the "mountain men" (*vounisioi*)—which derived not so much from the difference of geographical abode as from an attitude towards the conqueror:

There are slaves in the towns, down on the plains with the Turk,
But brave men live in the country of ravines and isolation,
Preferring the company of wild animals to that of Turks.[152]

The distinction is of considerable historical importance in terms of arriving at a full understanding of the life of Greeks under Turkish rule. Not a single case exists of a village or town in the plains which developed and prospered either economically or intellectually unless, like Tyrnavos,[153] it also enjoyed privileges of a sort guaranteeing the life, honor, and fortune of its inhabitants. The essence of modern Hellenism was distilled in the mountains; there, the seeds of future regeneration were sown. But for later foreign travellers, it was the effete people of the plains who were the sole descendants of the ancient Greeks.

Throughout the entire Turkish occupation, the stream of refugees into the mountains never once dried up. It was particularly strong at times of revolutionary disturbance. At the same time, refuge in the mountains meant no more than temporary escape from the Moslem yoke. No sooner did the Turk consolidate his conquests and establish permanent settlements in various parts of Greece than he determined to finish the task only partially completed by his predecessors and root out the Greek from his last hiding place. By the end of the sixteenth century and the beginning of the seventeenth century, even as incipient decline in the Ottoman Empire became evident, insecurity was more widespread, particularly in the northern parts of Greece. A number of factors contributed to this disorder: increasing forays by plundering bands of Albanian and Greek brigands in Epirus (from whose depredations Zagorochoria especially suffered), high-handed reprisals by pursuing Turkish troops (of a kind that were still common in the twentieth century), arbitrary spoliation by military deserters or soldiers returning from various fronts whether in victory or defeat, the general tendency to insurrection throughout the countryside in times of war, or actual rebellion by various pashas and other petty tyrants. All such occasions were marked by a rising incidence of conversion to Islam among the inhabitants of the mountains, or emigration born of hopelessness to other parts of the Ottoman Empire or overseas.[154] Finally, overpopulation in the sixteenth and seventeenth centuries due to an increasing birth rate (a common phenomenon throughout the Mediterranean)[155] dictated urgent refugee movement elsewhere. The sudden confluence in a given area of Greeks in flight from anarchy or war was a recurrent aspect of this problem. It was how Siatista, Kozane, and Philippopolis were peopled by refugee migrants from Epirus and Thessaly in the seventeenth and eighteenth centuries.[156]

Despite the manifold hardships faced by the raias, however, despite overall population decline,[157] conversion to Islam, displacement by Turkish colonists, Moslems were still in a minority throughout Hellas in the middle of the sixteenth century. Later, of course, their numbers increased, but not to any significant degree and in any case only slowly, and the increase was attributable mainly to conversions which reflected the continually deteriorating conditions of life for the raias. The same pattern manifested itself, only on a much larger scale, all over the Balkan peninsula.[158] Professor Ömer Lûtfi Barkan has compiled this comparative table of Christian and Moslem populations in the Greek peninsula at the beginning of the sixteenth century, based on census figures taken between 1520 and 1538 in the early part of Sultan Suleiman I's reign:[159]

Name of *Liva*	Moslem Families	Christian	Jewish	Total
Pasha	66,684	183,512	2,998	253,194
Çirmen	12,686	1,578		14,264
Vizye (Vizi)	12,193	9,467		21,660
Gallipoli (including Imbros, Thasos, Lemnos)	5,001	3,901	23	8,925
Rhodes and Kos	1,121	5,191		6,312
Mytilene	332	7,327		7,659
Ioannina	613	32,097		32,710
Karleli	7	11,395		11,402
Trikkala	12,347	57,671	387	70,405
Euboea (Agripos)	663	33,065		33,728
Morea	1,065	49,412	464	50,941[160]
	112,712	394,616	3,872	511,200

4

PIRACY AND POPULATION DISPLACEMENT IN THE GREEK ISLANDS

Under Suleiman I (1520–1566) and Selim II (1566–1574), populations were also uprooted throughout the Ionian and particularly the Aegean seas. People were propelled to rocky sun-drenched islands whose sharp outlines and picturesque shores stood out in even starker relief for being transfixed against a luminous sky. Scattered here and there, big islands and small, their isolation into separate worlds was prevented only by an affinity with the sea, difficult and often tempestuous as it was, which made each tiny speck of land seem an integral part of a much larger, even boundless, space. The sea did not stop at continental Greece but stretched on and on to the open seas and oceans. The story we now relate thus unfolds as a part of the whole.

We have seen that after the Capture many inhabitants of the islands of the northwestern Aegean, particularly the wealthier ones, sought to elude the dangers of Turkish conquest by leaving for the more secure Venetian and Frankish possessions, principally the large island colonies. Others as soon as their islands were conquered, were either removed to Constantinople by the Turks or reduced to slavery.[1] Still others were dislodged from their castles to make way for garrisons.[2]

The inhabitants of the smaller islands seemed the more fortunate since Turkish landing parties and settlers did not remain on their shores nor, except on rare occasions, were they afflicted by pestilence.[3] Nevertheless they did have to face (in addition to the periodic persecution and rapaciousness of itinerant Turkish functionaries)[4] indiscriminate looting by Turkish and Venetian sailors; and they had to endure the irruptions of pirates or corsairs (both words having the same connotation in the fifteenth and sixteenth centuries).[5]

In order to evoke the spirit of these times, the historian must try to describe the feelings of islanders as they watched in terror while strange ships bore down upon them from the high seas and the feelings of navigators who, in a perpetual state of fear, anxiously scanned those isolated and alluring shores looking for the hidden bay or inlet whence an ambush might suddenly be sprung. The effect upon seamen of that apparition of cutthroats ready to pounce on them, who then disappeared in the maze of rocky outcrops dotted everywhere in the limitless expanse of sea, can hardly be imagined.

Geography, then, was one factor in the development of piracy, but it was aided by the recurrence of unstable conditions going back as far as ancient times.[6] As I have shown in *Origins of the Greek Nation*, even in late Byzantine times and the early period of Turkish domination, many of the smaller islands, particularly in the northern Sporades, the Cyclades, the southern Sporades and the Dodecanese (Tenedos, Psara, St. Eustratios,[7] Skiathos, Skopelos, Amorgos, Anaphi, Antiparos, Ios, Kimolos, and others) were either nests of pirates (like Scyrus[8] and the Castro of Skiathos, the latter destroyed in 1538 by the admiral of the Turkish fleet, the archpirate Chaïreddin Barbarossa) or targets of successive devastating invasions for varying lengths of time.[9] The inhabitants of these islands, such as those of Icaria (Nikaria) lived in perpetual fear of pirates. Flat low-lying parts of the islands, few though they were, were suitable both for grazing sheep and cultivating wheat, but were never as productive as they should have been because of the omnipresent fear.[10] Stories of the terrifying invasions of Chaïreddin during the middle of the sixteenth century have been handed down to the islanders of this day. Oral traditions as well as pathetic inscriptions on the walls of monasteries and churches still exist as reminders of those years.[11] Coastal villages were razed, and those inhabitants who escaped moved either to more secure villages in the interior[12] or to larger islands. The populations of the small islands, particularly their male inhabitants, suffered constant attrition. Giacomo Rizzardo, in his chronicle of the capture of Chalcis (1470), provides these illuminating figures on island populations about that time: Andros, 2,000 inhabitants; Tenos and Mykonos, a total of 3,000; Amorgos, 200; Antiparos, 100; Paros, 3,000; Siphnos, 1,000; Melos, 2,500; Seriphos, 200; Kea, 300; Aegina, 1,000; Troizenia, 500; Kythera, 500; Santorini, 300; Karpathos, 300; Leros, 200; Astypalaea, 400; Kalymnos and Patmos, a total of 400; Scyrus, 1,200; Lemnos, 6,000; Imbros, 3,000; Samothrace, 200; Skiathos and Skopelos, 1,200 all told.[13]

We can but conclude that significant demographic changes occurred throughout the Aegean, especially during the first two centuries of Turk-

Tenedos.

15. Tenedos. From Pitton de Tournefort, *Relation d'un voyage du Levant*, Amsterdam, 1718.

ARLADENVS BARBARVSSA CIRTHAE, TVNEI
IO REX AC OTOMANICAE CLASS" PRAEF

16. Chaïredden Barbarossa (c. 1483–1546). From an old gravure.

ish rule, though admittedly this is a matter which has not yet been subjected to systematic investigation.[14] For Mytilene alone, it has been estimated that no fewer than thirty villages were destroyed at this time, never to reappear.[15] The Anatolian trade must have suffered severe damage from the spread of piracy. Those chiefly involved in it, the Venetians, were especially hurt but fought in vain against this Hydra-headed monster.[16]

Even the Dodecanese, nestling under the remote shores of southwestern Anatolia, were not immune from attack. Since Turks on the Anatolian mainland could pick out their shapes on the horizon, they constituted particularly tempting prey. Thus, as early as 1456–1457, Nisyros and Kalymnos were plundered by Turkish pirates from Asia Minor, and the

METELIN

Fron. i. pag. 149.

17. Mytilene. From Pitton de Tournefort, *Relation d'un voyage du Levant*, Amsterdam, 1718.

two strongholds of Neratzia and Peripatos near Kos were devastated by the main Turkish fleet from Gallipoli.[17] To the northwest lay other inviting prey: the islands of the Cyclades.

In order to combat the Turkish pirates, among whom the more notorious were Karacasan, Kourtoglou, Kamalis, Karadromis, Kousaglis, and others, the Frankish rulers in the Aegean levied a special tax, the *Turcoteli*.[18] For their part, the Turks were also concerned with the incursions of Venetian and Frankish pirates and accordingly determined to secure at least a few strategically placed islands. To this end, Tenedos and Lemnos both acquired castle fortifications.[19]

Moslem pirate ships, especially from the Barbary and Algerian[20] coasts of northwestern Africa, were ubiquitous in the Mediterranean, Ionian, and Aegean seas and everywhere terrorized their shores. Spaniards, French, Italians and others from the various islands and lands bordering the Mediterranean were among the worst renegades. They daily supplied Algeria with large numbers of Christian slaves for sale to the Barbary chieftains, who in turn resold them to others.[21]

Hardly less predatory were the Christian pirates, among whom the Knights of St. John from Rhodes were probably the most conspicuous. Whether alone or in league with the Venetians, they extended their activities as far as Thessalonica[22] and Kavala.[23] The coast of Kavala, uninhabited during the fifteenth century, was inviting because along it ran the only caravan route between the Morea and Constantinople.[24] Consequently, the shores of the northern Aegean generally were exposed.[25] The principal base of the pirates in that region presumably was Thasos, wooded from end to end, with a conveniently indented coastline.[26]

Striking back at the cavaliers of St. John, the Turks rained blow after blow on the islands around Rhodes.[27] Kos, Kalymnos, Chalki, Leros, Nisyros, and others[28] became the victims of successive attacks and, according to tradition,[29] were thoroughly devastated in the process. When finally dislodged from their base (1522), the Knights of St. John continued to uphold the tradition of their order with relentless onslaughts against the Moslem and Christian peoples.[30]

There were also Greeks, mostly from those islands and parts of the mainland which were barren, among the Christian pirates. They learned much from their mentors and years later, this time acting alone, put those lessons into practice.[31]

On the whole, the Aegean islands were more frequently prey to pirates than those of the Ionian, where not only were there fewer islands, but the presence of Venetian garrisons and local militia, the likely appearance of Venetian ships which were much more numerous there, the care with which the Venetians sought to prevent depopulation or even actively promote repopulation, all militated against its spread. The charming

18. A model ship of the Knights of Malta. Courtesy of the Malta Museum.

island of Odyssea, once devastated, was repopulated as early as 1504. New settlers from central Hellas and Cephalonia arrived to take up residence under inducements which included the grant of land free from all tax for five years.[32]

Piracy seems to have abated in the southern Aegean in the middle of the sixteenth century, when a definite measure of economic recovery accompanied the gradual repopulation of deserted islands.[33] Conditions showed these signs of amelioration because Turkish authority was firmly established throughout the islands by 1566, after which the Turks turned more vigorously to the suppression of piracy,[34] and trade markedly revived. Tenos, which remained Venetian till 1715, was the only Aegean island which did not feel the stern imposition of Turkish rule, but even so the Turks made a number of landings on the island in the sixteenth and seventeenth centuries in an effort to eradicate this base of Venetian operations.[35]

The situation in the region showed still further signs of improvement towards the end of the seventeenth century with the repopulation of a number of deserted islands after the Turkish war with Cyprus and the naval battle of Naupactus (1570–1571). Most of the historical evidence seems to point to a definite causal connection here. However, the sultans' new policy of rehabilitating Aegean islanders can be explained only if placed in its full historical context, for a good deal of the evidence is admittedly inconclusive. The Turkish geographer Hadji Kalpha mentions that in 1570 (a date which perhaps ought to read 1571, that is, after the appearance of the combined Christian fleet off the western coast of Greece and the subsequent Turkish defeat in the naval battle of Naupactus), the island inhabitants rose up against the Turks, but the Vizier Mehmet Socolli dispatched troops among them and succeeded by a mixture of political and diplomatic means in quashing the rebellions. Hasluck suggests that the "new settlers" were in fact no more than the troops sent against the islanders to establish garrisons—Albanians, favored by the Turkish government, who thereby contributed to the consolidation of the Turkish position in the Aegean.[36] However, if Hadji Kalpha's account is inadequate, Hasluck's suggestion is incredible. Leaving aside considerations of the extent to which Hadji Kalpha can be taken as a reliable source, Hasluck's inferences from his statement are unwarranted and insupportable, for we have incontrovertible evidence that in 1571 resettlement took place, or at least population increased, in a number of the Aegean islands. The Greek pilot Antonios of Melos (Antonio di Milo) wrote in his *Isolario* that Psara was repopulated in 1571, Samos in 1572, Ios in 1575, and that in 1571 a few smaller islands were similarly repeopled.[37] Later, possibly sometime after 1577, St. Eustratios was resettled.[38]

In other words, with the aim of consolidating their power and imposing

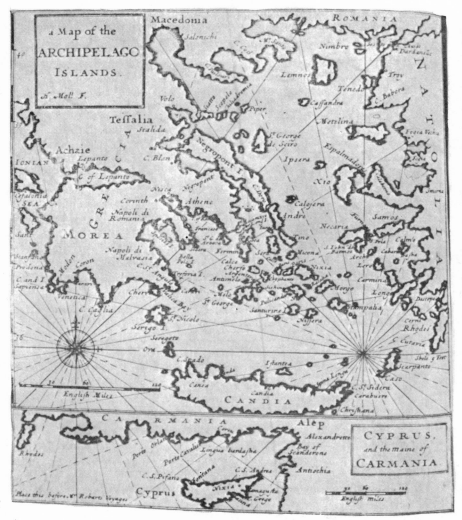

19. A map of the Aegean Archipelago. From William Hack, *Mr. Roberts's Adventures among the Corsairs of the Levant (1692)* . . . , London, 1699.

Turkish sovereignty more effectively throughout the entire Aegean, the sultans pursued a policy of colonization similar to that already applied in Thrace and other imperial territories. The program uniformly adopted was based on the granting of land, together with certain rights of taxation and self-government. Thus, early in his reign, Suleiman I no sooner conquered the Dodecanese than he bestowed privileges of this sort in order to forestall any flight by the inhabitants to Venetian-controlled colonies.[39]

By repopulating deserted but habitable islands, by fleshing out populations that had grown thin—in a word, by the infusion of new, mainly Albanian, settlers into the islands of the Aegean—the sultans hoped to deny local harbors to pirates and Christian fleets, thereby enhancing the security of the region and increasing its agricultural productivity.[40]

The sultans' policy of colonization is clearly exemplified in the repopulation of Samos. Like other island inhabitants during the late Byzantine period, the people of Samos had withdrawn to high ground in various places in the interior, there to build new settlements complete with castles and churches. The ruins of these are still visible today.[41] In time, the wooded character of the island attracted more and more pirates to its shores until it was no longer possible for the inhabitants to live there unmolested. Accordingly, in 1475, they accepted the invitation of the Giustiniani to resettle on Chios, which the people of Icaria had already done.[42]

Yet it is very probable that some Icarians stayed behind on their island,[43] secluded among the woods and forests particularly in the district of Langhada,[44] and that Samos, too, was never completely abandoned. Not only did some remain for several years as coal dealers on the southern part of the island,[45] but tradition generally speaks of the Samians' continuing to occupy the interior of their island.[46] When Belon passed by Samos in the middle of the sixteenth century, he expressed surprise that so large an island and one so renowned from antiquity should appear *almost* deserted. The cause, he suggested, was fear of pirates who frequented those parts: they came to the island to get timber from its forest, which they needed for the construction of their ships.[47]

When and under what circumstances was Samos populated again? The relevant documentary evidence, which may have survived until 1834, probably disappeared along with other interesting records known to have been lost at that time. The Metropolitan Georgirenes was doubtless relying on at least a few of those (particularly the ones affecting the metropolitans of the island)[48] when he wrote that Kilits Ali Pasha landed on the island one day in order to go hunting and was so enchanted by what he saw that he sought the sultan's permission to proceed with its repopulation. He then actually transferred there a number of families from neighboring islands, notably Mytilene.

Thus, overpopulation on other islands was gradually relieved by the transfer of people to semideserted Samos.[49] The name of the present-day village of Mytilenioi on Samos clearly suggests the origins of its inhabitants.[50]

Ingenuous though it may be, Georgirenes' explanation of the resettlement of Samos rings true because it in no way conflicts with the more complete probable explanation of what actually took place: that the Turks, seeking to consolidate their position in the Aegean, were present in the straits of Samos not only to exploit the island's forests[51] but also to guard a vital sea road to Egypt.[52] In order to attract settlers, the Turks accordingly granted them land and various other privileges.[53] Concerning the exact date when recolonization was effected, I am inclined to place most credence in the much travelled Jacob Miloïtis (born in Melos but raised on Patmos), who suggests the year 1577.[54] This would seem to be corroborated by the date of the foundation of the "castle" of Kilits Ali's Christian pilot, Nicholas Sarakinis, also from Patmos, who took up land around Heraeon:[55] the first undertaking of this new proprietor would surely have been to secure his tenancy on the island by erecting a fortified house. Another settler, the priest Athanasios,[56] was the first appointed bishop of Samos.

Colonization of the island proceeded slowly. Its population remained small at the beginning of the seventeenth century due to the atmosphere of apprehension which long prevailed, itself attributable to persistent incursions by pirates who pillaged food and animals.[57]

In 1621, the population of Samos was still not as dense as that of other islands,[58] though by the end of the century a total of seventeen villages and small towns had appeared.[59] According to tradition, the new inhabitants arrived at different times from Chios (descendants of the Samians who had formerly moved there under the Giustiniani), Patmos, Vourla, Mytilene, the Peloponnese, Naxos, other islands of the Cyclades, Rhodes, Cyprus, Euboea, Skopelos, Crete, Kythera, and Aegina.[60] Since Samians today speak a northern Greek dialect, most of them probably had their origins in Mytilene or other northern parts of Greece.[61]

The other deserted or sparsely inhabited islands of the Aegean were settled mainly by Albanians from various parts of Greece, who, besides speaking Albanian, also knew Greek.

Albanian colonization took place most conspicuously on the islands of the Cyclades and the Saronic Gulf. Sizable communities settled on Andros, Hydra, Spetsai, Poros, Salamis (Koulouri), Aegina and Angistri,[62] where their descendants still make up a large proportion of the population and retain their ancient family surnames.[63] Smaller groups went to Kea (Djia), Kythnos (Thermia), and Ios, where they were eventually assimilated and hellenized; only surnames and a few place-names have survived.[64] There were other small groups on Samos (in a little village above Pyrgos, where Albanian was still being spoken in 1677),[65] Psara,[66] Kasos (in today's Arvanitochori)[67] and probably in Skopelos,[68] though in all of these the original or later Hellenic populations absorbed the Albanians. In Samos, the names of such villages as Leca (which had fifty houses at the end of the seventeenth century),[69] Ano, Kato Arvanites,[70] and Morias[71] bear witness to the fact of original Albanian immigration. The inhabitants of these villages spoke Albanian at least until 1677, when Georgirenes' publication noting this appeared.[72] And a tradition which was extant a century ago told of the origin of the place-name Leca: it perpetuated the name of the first colonist from the Peloponnese who followed in the footsteps of the villagers of Morias (deriving from Morea, as Kritikides correctly points out).[73] The obvious importance of this tradition is that it fixes the origins of at least a part of the Aegean Albanian population. What else do we know about them?

Researchers are admittedly still perplexed by the problem of Albanian migration: when the people moved and where from. Hasluck suggests that they were prisoners-of-war captured by the admiral Oulouts or Kilits Ali during the course of his Adriatic operations prior to the battle of Naupactus and following his suppression of a rebellion that the Venetians had stirred up in the region of Drinos and Böiana.[74]

However, even if this hypothesis is sound to the extent that it fixes with reasonable accuracy both the geographical and chronological origins of one or two of the migrant communities, to suggest that it had general validity for all the islands would seem to stretch credulity too far. Albanian colonists were already settled in Attica, Boeotia, Euboea, and Argolis-Corinth as early as the fourteenth and fifteenth centuries, as oral tradition among the settlers themselves confirms. The Albanians of Andros,[75] for instance, especially those from the two villages of Arna and Amolochos (Gabrion not being founded until 1821), say themselves that they came from Karystos in Euboea. Since the people of Amolochos, moreover, speak a dialect similar to that of Poros,[76] we can only conclude, with Sauger,[77] that they came from the Peloponnese. But exactly when they came is not so easily determined. Demetrius Paschalis, the historian of Andros, presumes that the migration took place during the first quarter of the sixteenth century[78] and that it was followed by a second one in the last quarter of the same century.[79] On the other hand, the evidence of the traveller Bordone that the island was almost deserted ("*quasi deserta*") early in the sixteenth century, and of Braconnier in 1701 that Albanian settlers had arrived "about a hundred years previously," would place the migration in the last quarter of the sixteenth century.[80] By 1655, there were 1,200 Albanians living in those villages.[81]

The Albanians, wherever on Andros they settled in large numbers, assimilated the local Greeks and Franks (mainly landowners with their properties on the island). The names of various families leave no doubt about the Greek and Frankish origins of many such cultural converts— for example Veloudos, Vidalis, Gavalias, Decavallas, Exadactylos, Kalognomos, Carlos.[82] As late as 1700 the inhabitants of Arna and Amolochos still wore Albanian dress and followed traditional ways, which were, according to Tournefort, "sans law and sans faith."[83] The Jesuit Portier, who visited Arna at about the same time, reported that its inhabitants were extremely poor and uncouth, but not utter barbarians.[84]

A handful of Albanians probably settled on deserted Psara during the last quarter of the sixteenth century,[85] but they were quickly assimilated, indeed submerged, about a century later (from the middle of the seventeenth century) by a new influx of Greeks from Thessalomagnesia, Euboea, and western Epirus.[86] This is why there is no record that Albanian was ever spoken there, but the similarity in mores between the people of Psara and those of Thessaly and Kyme[87] is striking.

Any attempt to discover the origins of Albanian colonists who settled on the rocky and barren islands of Hydra and Spetsai must again be largely guesswork. André Thevet, travelling in the mid-sixteenth century, notes that Hydra was deserted at that time,[88] and from this we may form the tentative conclusion that the island remained uninhabited until after the battle of Naupactus (1571). The comment of the local historian Antonios A. Miaoulis *grandfils,*[89] a man notable for his researches into the history of the island, that settlement occurred before 1580, lends some support to this conclusion.

But were Hydra and Spetsai totally deserted in Thevet's time? It may well be that a number of Albanian shepherd families occupied the island for, according to Francesco Grassetto, who made a trip through the eastern Mediterranean in 1511 and sailed close to the Dalmatian and Greek coasts as well as many Ionian and Aegean islands:

About 10 o'clock at night, the grand providitor set out from there (Siphnos) and at 6 o'clock the following night he arrived under Hydra (Sidres) at an uninhabited rock towards Spetsai (Specie), where there were about ten other uninhabited outcrops.[90]

If in fact this reference to "uninhabited outcrops" is intended to distinguish them from the islands actually named, which were inhabited, obviously we must look to the end of the fifteenth century, where indeed we do find in popular tradition definite support for the view that settlement took place around that time. The tradition, preserved by Antonios Miaoulis *grandpère,* fixes the time of earliest Albanian settlement at about 1470.[91]

Of course that would not rule out the evidence, which must be considered more reliable, that later settlement was also effected after 1580 by many Albanian-speaking families from various parts of the Peloponnese, Kythnos, Euboea, Parga, Avlona, and Souli. To these were added Greek families from Vourla, Phocaea in Asia Minor and Tenos.[92]

Not until the middle of the seventeenth century, however, do we have the first really substantial proof of settlement of Hydra and Spetsai. Then, Boschini noted that the islands had few houses but that they all enjoyed good fishing.[93] Indeed, fishing was unquestionably the inhabitants' chief means of livelihood, though this was not always so. Oral tradition holds that the first settlers on Hydra led an isolated existence as shepherds, living in huts made of pine, and that they depended for the necessities of life on a crude form of barter (in oil, barley, dry legumes, cheese, and the like); only later did the exigencies of survival and contact with the outside world turn them to fishing and the building of small ships.[94] Such were the humble beginnings of the merchant fleet of Hydra, which became the mainstay of Greek naval superiority during the revolution of 1821.

In 1672 Salamis (Koulouri) had a combined Albanian and Greek population totalling about six hundred,[95] similar to that of Poros at the end of the seventeenth century. Albanian families used Salamis, too, as a stepping-stone to Angistri.[96] Albanians arrived at Kythnos towards the end of the seventeenth century from Euboea, Andros, Attica, and Hydra[97] to settle on the estates of the Roman Catholic bishopric of the island.[98] From the end of the seventeenth century, however, they were known as Greeks.[99] Among the Albanian surnames of the inhabitants were Manesis, Pepizas, Dales, Lalegiannis, Tolias (Togias), Krielas, Maris, Koumis, Goumas, Tountas.[100] Arriving simultaneously with the Albanians were new Greek settlers from Crete, Maina, and other places,[101] who assimilated the last descendants of the Franks of Kythnos. Only a few feudal customs (for example, the delivery of a proportion of produce to the lord) and some vestiges of the spirit of the era lingered on till the end of the nineteenth century. These latter included the survival of various appellations pertaining to class: "nobles" (archontes), "excellencies" (kaloi), "grandees" (megalousianoi), "peasants" (choriates), "serfs" (oxotarides). Also, peasants or serfs in the presence of nobility were always obliged to bare their heads and adopt a stance of humility and submissiveness.[102] The period of Frankish domination on the island is still reflected today in the surnames of a number of families—Agioutantes, Armadoros, Veros, Gasparis, Dallavinias, Domenicas, Kavallieros, Kozadinos, Koronellos, Bastas, and others.[103]

The evidence we have concerning resettlement on Ios is more substantial than that for any other island. At the beginning of the fifteenth century, shortly after the death of his father James, Duke of Naxos, Marcos Krispi invited a number of Albanian families from the Peloponnese to take up residence. He helped establish them as farmers and thus gave a new lease of life to this practically deserted island.[104] In 1558, however, fourteen pirate galleys descended on the island, pillaging it, and enslaving the inhabitants.[105] Following this incident, the island remained unpopulated until about 1579 when "the priest Pothetos, son of the former deacon of Kritiki, arrived bearing 'letters patent' from Oulouts Ali and with God's help resuscitated the island of Nios."[106] Fear of invasion by pirates, however, continued to hang over the island.[107]

Professor I. K. Voyatzides, basing his supposition on the fact that the Albanian language is unknown on the island and all recollection of previous Albanian occupation has disappeared among the inhabitants of today, presumes that the people who accompanied Pothetos were not Albanian but Greek. He further suggests that such remnants of Marcos Krispi's earlier colonization as still remained were assimilated after the priest Pothetos' recolonization of the island.[108] But if this is so, how account for the fact, which Voyatzides himself also notes,[109] that almost all the family names recorded in the register (vrevion)[110] from 1579 till the middle of the seventeenth century were Albanian? A refutation of Voyatzides' hypothesis has been offered by P. G. Zerlentis, who contends that the Albanian settlers, already cognizant of the Greek language through their past exposure to Greek influences, must have succumbed to gradual hellenization.[111] Indeed, we may go further and say that this assimilation would have been rapid after the progressive colonization by Greek settlers which began in the middle of the seventeenth century. At the same time, proof of continuing Albanian settlement is incontrovertible. It is to be found, first, in the remembrance still current among the Sikinos islanders of the derisive name they once gave the people of Ios (Nios) "tsarouchades" on account of the pompon slippers that the latter wore for so long; second, in several linguistic clues which still remain in the pastoral liturgy; and third, in the eight surnames that have survived in the electoral register of the municipality of Ios-Archolekas, Volikakis, Valmas, Gikas, Gikakis, Petzopoullos, Togias, and Chronis.[112]

Thus, the collection and sifting of all the foregoing evidence can throw a good deal of light on our problem, particularly if we begin with the premise that most colonizations of the Aegean generally and the Cyclades especially were effected after Naupactus (1571), when repercussions from the battle spread to the Aegean. In these terms the causal link propounded by Hadji Kalpha, given earlier,[113] appears open to fuller explanation: settlers, consisting mainly of Albanians from the coasts of Euboea, Attica, and Argolis, and not from the Albanian coast as Hasluck maintains, dispersed throughout the Aegean at the instigation of the Turks, who saw population growth and the resettlement of the islands as the best means of consolidating their authority in the region and enhancing its security.

After 1600, as the recolonization of the islands of the Aegean gradually took effect and the imposition of Turkish sovereignty became felt, pirati-cal irruptions on a large scale noticeably abated, particularly on the part of the larger independent corsairs, though it is true that small pirate ships were as ubiquitous as ever. Among the latter, the Maniatai became prom-inent in the seventeenth century.[114] Their barren lands were difficult of access, with precipitous cliffs protecting hazardous little anchorages and villages perched on the top of rocky coastal escarpments. In Maina there was a hornets' nest of pirates. Monks had their hermitages (thyrides) in caverns along the coast, and when a sail appeared far out at sea, the monks gave the alarm, and nearby villagers prepared to pounce on or hide from a possible enemy. Survivors from foreign ships wrecked on the shores of Maina could expect no mercy,[115] though there were Maniatai who also served under the flags of Frankish pirates.[116]

The people of Tenos also indulged in piracy, at least until 1715, concen-trating their enterprise particularly on the islands and shores of western Asia Minor. Among their victims were the inhabitants of Vourla who lived in ancient Klazomenai and who, unable any longer to suffer the continual depredations of pirates from Tenos, withdrew from the coast into the interior, where their small town still exists.[117]

Such examples of persistent anarchy were insignificant, however, in comparison with the incursions of pirates from the West during the seventeenth century; their behavior towards the Orthodox islanders (whom they dubbed "schismatics") was generally abominable.[118] As we shall presently see, the degree of their barbarity often corresponded with variations in the state of tension in Roman Catholic-Orthodox relations throughout the Levant.

In fact, the Archipelago was generally seething with French pirates, many of whom served under the Duke of Tuscany. From the beginning of the seventeenth century, their periodic capture by elements of the Turk-ish fleet created a most delicate situation for the Turkish authorities in their relations with the French Ambassador to the Porte, Jean de Gontaut Biron, who, while officially discountenancing their activities, was none-theless constrained to negotiate their release.[119]

An important factor in the rising intensity of piracy throughout the Aegean was the active engagement of receivers and agents in the islands and coastal towns of Greece who disposed of the pirates' spoils.[120] By the middle of the seventeenth century, the islands around Paros and Delos (including at various times Mykonos, which was despoiled by both pirates and the Turkish authorities) had again become practically uninhab-ited.[121] Along with Gioura[122] and Psara, which were totally deserted by their inhabitants, they had been converted to pirates' nests.[123]

Even the larger islands were not immune from attack. In Thasos, for instance, the populace had withdrawn into the interior and built completely new villages in remote places. From this time, all contact with the outside world was lost, with grievous consequences for her people.[124] Andros, too, paid the price of its prominent location astride the sea-lanes. In 1670 the Frankish pirate Hugues Crevelier pillaged the principal town when its inhabitants refused to pay ransom money, and from that date the character of the island began to change. Throughout the seventeenth century, castles sprouted in the center of the island—high, square, sturdily-built structures with many rooms and underground stores. Entry could be gained only by means of an opening high above the ground, which the occupants approached on a movable wooden staircase.[125]

Alone among the agitated peoples of the Aegean, the inhabitants of Amorgos resisted the attacks of Christian pirates with unexampled courage. Fighting in unison, the islanders withstood attacks with such vehemence and determination that no pirate ever dared make a landing on their shores. Others admired these exploits from afar, but without attempting to emulate such bravery.[126] Indeed, the very success with which they repelled invaders prompted the islanders to try their own hand at piracy, and in the atmosphere of anarchy and strife which infected the coast of Asia Minor[127] none acquired a more fearsome reputation than the people of Amorgos.[128]

Pirates also had their dens on certain islands of the northern Sporades (chiefly Skopelos and Skiathos)[129] and the Cyclades (Melos especially),[130] in fact anywhere they could count on the collaboration of agents among the local population. With Melos as their headquarters, they terrorized neighboring islands. In 1638 Kimolos was plundered and burned and its inhabitants left in a state of desperate poverty.[131] Not until 1646 was a new town, the Castro, built on the initiative of other refugees from Siphnos.[132]

Whatever possessions the islanders had gained over the years and stored away in their houses were vulnerable. All the wealth acquired by dint of scouring the Mediterranean in their little ships might suddenly be lost within the space of hours.

During the second half of the seventeenth century, the people of the Archipelago suffered severely at the hands of pirates from Malta (the Knights of St. John who, after leaving Rhodes in 1522, resumed operations from Malta in 1530), as well as from Livorno (the Knights of St. Stephen, the so-called *Livournezoi* pirates), Majorca, and a number of other places.[133] These Christian pirates found it exceptionally easy to chase and capture the slow-moving ships of the Greeks, the celebrated caïques, whose heavy and high masts protruding from a rounded hull made them especially ponderous craft.[134]

Later, during the Turkish-Venetian wars of 1645–1649, both Turk and Venetian sought the alliance of pirates, whose privateering ferocity made them valued confederates, particularly as corsairs. Like the French armies fighting in Crete, they plundered and maltreated the islanders, who were already obliged to pay taxes to both sides. Not only that, but the islanders were forced to maintain a specified number of galleys manned by their own men for service in the Turkish fleet[135]—one each from Naxos, Mytilene, Samos, Andros, Mykonos, and Seriphos, two from Chios, seven from Euboea, and so on.[136]

The Venetians also impressed the islanders into service, forcing them to row the galleys or perform various other naval tasks;[137] they were no laggards, these Westerners, in any form of persecution.[138]

In addition to the various *ad hoc* war measures devised, the Turks also kept up their annual peregrinations of the Archipelago under the admiral pasha, whose duty was to collect the ordinary taxes due each year. At least on those occasions the Christian pirates were careful to keep out of the way of the Turkish fleet[139] and even the resident populations of the pirates' bases fled like everyone else to the safety of the mountains.[140] In several parts of his poem *The Cretan War,* Marinos Tzane Bounialis graphically evokes the fear which reverberated throughout the entire Aegean: one delegation of islanders appeared before the *kapudan* (admiral) pasha "dishevelled, unrecognizable, and cowering."[141] An episode of singular horror was Kaplan Moustafa Pasha's invasion of Paros in 1668, originally directed against Siphnos but diverted to Paros upon the representations of the Siphnian Notable Kioses,[142]a friend of the Pasha's.

Both 1668 and 1669 were notable for the dire hardships inflicted upon the people of Naxos,[143] Aegina,[144] and the islands generally. In order to evade the Turkish press gangs in search of manpower for the quarries of Crete,[145] the islanders hid in the fields or fled to villages and farms in the interior. But even those efforts were futile: in 1668 a muster on Aegina secured 600 men, which, added to a previous tally of 300, meant that of 3,000 inhabitants on the island more than two-thirds of those remaining were women and girls.[146]

Naturally the islanders complained. It was protested that the *kapudan* pasha collected more than his entitlement,[147] that he stayed for too long on the islands, that his brave cohorts (*leventes*) cruelly oppressed the people and kept them from their affairs.[148] But when, at the turn of the century, the menace of French piracy no longer existed, Turkish demands became even more extortionate.[149]

In certain islands, the number of men left was insufficient to carry on with the work of the land and the sea, and poverty consequently became more widespread. Typically, the commerce of Aegina came almost to a standstill as a result of the forcible impressment of manpower by the Turks, particularly after the piratical seizure in Athens in 1671 of ten or twelve Turkish ships skippered and manned by men from Aegina. The

20. Turkish vessels. From Jacques Dallaway, *Constantinople ancienne et moderne et description des côtes et îles de l'Archipel et de la Troade*, Paris, 1795, Vol. I.

seamen of Aegina were without peer in all the Aegean, and the profits they accumulated from voyages to Constantinople, Chios, Smyrna, and Alexandria had brought a degree of prosperity to their island. After this, however, pirates descended upon the island with such regularity that their houses and stores became empty and animals scarce. The worst moment came in 1673, when the islanders had to sell their household utensils in order to pay taxes to their masters. That year and afterwards, even the pre-Lenten carnival, normally a festive time of meat-eating, was shrouded in gloom: there was meat on Sundays, but otherwise only bread, barley, and a few vegetables to fill hungry bellies.[150] The women were reduced to spinning cotton and making dimities or sails.[151]

Koulouri (Salamis) was yet another island long inured to the privations caused by piracy. At the end of the seventeenth century its Albanian settlers, like most other Albanians scattered throughout Greece, suffered a marginal existence. They had a few products such as wheat, barley, tar, pitch, resin, and fish, which they sold in Athens.[152]

Small or large, the islands of the Aegean were relentlessly stripped of human habitation. Not even the largest—Crete, Cyprus, Rhodes, Chios, Mytilene—were unaffected. In 1672 the *kapudan* pasha asked for reinforcements to repel a threatened invasion, this time by the French.[153]

Disorder throughout the Aegean flared up once again during the Turkish-Venetian war of 1683–1699,[154] in which French pirates participated. Their presence in various pirate havens (for example, Paros, Syros, Melos, Kimolos, Astypalaea, and Episcopi)[155] stretched into an extended sojourn of years, though at least the business dealings necessitated by the length of their stay helped smooth relations with the islanders. In effect, fear and poverty induced the islanders not only to bow to the presence of pirates but also to trade provisions with them. Indeed in some cases (on Kimolos and Melos, for example), there were instances of whole-hearted collaboration and active participation in piratical ventures. It was the experience of sailing acquired on such expeditions that won some of the islanders, those from Melos in particular, considerable renown as pilots on foreign ships.[156]

So, by the end of the seventeenth century, Melos and Kimolos (or Argentiera, as it was known to sixteenth-century travellers) were added to the list of pirates' nests—two more dens of debauchery. The very starkness of the contrast in each of these places between, on the one hand, power and dissipation, and, on the other, impotence and poverty hastened the demoralization of the inhabitants. The dearth of males on Kimolos (many of whose inhabitants, incidentally, were hellenized Italians) helped make prostitution rampant.[157]

On Melos, the process of squandering ill-gotten gains and a flourishing commerce in booty significantly boosted the economy and the population of the island inside fifty years. By the beginning of the eighteenth century, its inhabitants could no longer be described as "few and poor," as the traveller Boschini found them in the middle of the seventeenth century.[158] The people of Melos therefore had reason to remember fondly the French corsairs and their deeds—men such as Beneville de Téméricourt, the knight d'Hocquincourt, Hugues Crevelier (Cruvelier), the knight d'Entrechaut, Poussel, Orange, Lauthier, and others who brought their plunder to this great Aegean bazaar and sold it cheaply. The inhabitants resold the goods at a much better price and benefitted considerably from the transaction. On this island, the good life was no stranger.[159]

At the end of the seventeenth century, Ios' only town was a haven for the pirates of many nations who lived there alongside Albanian settlers (correctly called "Greco-Albanians" by Sauger). With its spacious and beautiful harbor and narrow entrance exposed only to southerly winds, Ios offered a refuge which for security was second to none in the Aegean. Often, as many as twenty to twenty-five ships could be found at anchor there, and in winter no fewer than three to four thousand men-at-arms, mostly French, made it their quarters. A Roman Catholic Church and priest catered to the religious needs of this semipermanent population,[160] and the Turks knew it as "little Malta."

Paros, with its splendid harbors, was also a den of pirates,[161] many of whom married and settled down permanently in the island's principal town, Parikia. Local notables appear to have developed close economic ties with the newcomers. On one occasion in 1676 when the Turks arrived in thirteen galleys to check on commercial consorting with pirates, these notables declined to appear before the *defterci* (financial commissary-general of the province) with the rest of the population. Driven to the utmost extremities of despair by the wanton activities of pirate and Turk, the islanders in a body complained that they were prepared to emigrate somewhere else.[162] Only the notables could have found no cause for grievance in a situation of poverty so crushing that many unhappy women derived their sole support from selling themselves to the seamen who called at the different ports on the island.[163]

The Parians' wish to abandon their homes, which the people of other islands also had, may have been the factor which induced senior officials of the Porte to consider the possible benefits attendant upon resettlement. The security that people would have enjoyed by that means could only have increased their usefulness.[164] However, the more urgent need to impress sailors for the ships of their fleets from any or all islands meant that such projects were never carried very far.

Because of the constant menace of piracy many Turks hesitated to accept the offices of aga or voivode (governor) and cadi on the smaller

21. The harbor of the Island of Ios. Photo by the author, taken in 1967.

islands,[165] particularly since some of these were actually under the *de facto* authority of pirates. In the few cases where appointments proceeded, the "conquerors" merely informed the islanders that in the event of piratical invasion they would be expected to fend for the voivode and the cadi.[166] Usually, though, the islanders were governed by their own compatriots, that is by Greek governors nominated from Constantinople;[167] or else they simply bought immunity from even the most nominal intrusions of Ottoman administration. In this way Salamis, along with Aegina and Poros, acquired their freedom at a cost of 785 piasters paid to the *kapudan* pasha.[168]

The islanders hated Frankish pirates more than any others, and it was only fear that restrained them from demonstrating their hatred. But whenever, as occasionally happened, Franks were chased by Turks, the local inhabitants withheld all assistance from the Franks and let the Turks catch them.[169] Naturally, this kind of behavior only sparked retaliation by other Frankish pirates.[170]

On the other hand, it was by no means rare for Frankish pirates (Italians, Spaniards, and, particularly after 1650, French) and their colleagues who distributed the plunder to settle down permanently at various places throughout the troubled Aegean, notably on certain islands of the Cyclades. They often intermarried with local inhabitants and enjoyed their illicit profits without ever being disturbed.[171] Some French interlopers on Naxos, however, incurred the wrath of the islanders when they had the gall to claim their foreign nationality as an excuse for the nonpayment of the usual resident taxes.[172]

Relations between the pirates and Roman Catholic priests, whether Capuchin or Jesuit, were on the whole friendly. It was very unusual for a priest to accuse a pirate, and then only on grounds of lack of respect.[173] Eager to ingratiate themselves, pirates frequently spent money on the erection or renovation of holy establishments.[174] The pirate Daniel, for instance, donated money, sacred vessels and provisions.[175] The Corsican John Dimarchi undertook the expense of building a Capuchin Church on Paros.[176] The Ligurian John Marias Kardi, who had settled down on Kythnos, built the Church of St. John the Baptist[177] on the island and personally escorted the Roman Catholic Bishop of Tenos, Angelo Venieri, to Naxos and other islands in his own ship. The pirate Paul, who died in the monastery of the Evangelismos of Zoccolanti on Naxos, was buried in its chapel.[178] Similarly Augustine, son of the notorious pirate Hugues Crevelier, was interred in the Church of St. George of Agousa (Naousa) on Paros.[179] An obituary in the Book of Capuchins of Naxos refers to this last incident:

In February 1679 at Agousa, the pirate Augustine, son of the pirate Crevelier, died on his own ship at the age of nineteen. He had received the last sacraments and was buried on the morning of the next day in the nave of the Church of St. George in a crypt never before used and opened by the parish priest Leonard Freri. The pirates paid the funeral expenses and asked the priest to take care of the engraving of the epitaph and arms on the sepulcher. The body was interred with great ceremony, and a catafalque was erected as a repository for the relics. Around this gathered twelve paupers dressed in white carrying candles and twelve wax tapers. The Greek metropolitan and all the clergy were there, and the pirate's chaplain sang the dirge.[180]

So perhaps it is not surprising after all that, over the centuries, piracy should have become exalted in the minds of many Aegean people until it assumed the character almost of Homeric legend, according to which pirates, instead of being vilified for their deeds, were glorified as heroes.[181] The sudden and violent death of a pirate sometimes fired the imaginations of the people of the Archipelago. The capture and execution of the Frankish pirate Beneville de Téméricourt was one example which especially affected Roman Catholics.[182] Another is this:

Monks and often the people as a whole demonstrated feelings of real adoration. Thus, when the corpse of the famous knight d'Hocquincourt was washed up on the shore on Kasos, a Capuchin, aided by a few local fishermen, took it to his little chapel and there, having administered the last rites, buried it next to the altar. A marble slab, not inscribed, covered his remains, and upon it a sacred flame burned night and day. Nearby on the wall hung his long hair, a piteous relic of this prodigal soul and a grim reminder of man's worthlessness—so much so that all who entered the island's harbor, not to say the local Greeks themselves, never failed to visit this Frankish pirate's unpretentious grave and comment on his deeds with mixed feelings of grief and admiration.[183]

Roman Catholic monks often interceded with the pirates on behalf of the Orthodox islanders. Indeed the people of Paros sought to induce Jesuits and Capuchins to settle on their island because they wanted their protection[184] and because there were physicians among them who would render their services free.[185] The priests, of course, were not motivated by considerations of philanthropy alone: a community of disturbed and distraught souls was fertile ground for the assertion of a Roman Catholic spiritual hegemony.[186] Under the circumstances, the temptation to become a convert to Roman Catholicism was difficult to resist.[187] Yet though many islanders opted for Roman Catholicism,[188] the fact remains that many more Roman Catholics embraced Orthodoxy.[189] Western monks, despite great efforts and despite the state of anarchy throughout the Aegean which gave them their opportunity to proselytize, achieved insignificant results. On Naxos, to take one example, despite the intensity of Catholic proselytism, the only practitioners of "Frankism" to be found were those who had a foothold in each faith—the so-called "amphibians" (amphivioi).[190] Capuchins and Jesuits also preached and propagated their faith in schools on Naxos, Paros, Melos, and elsewhere,[191] but their efforts were likewise dissipated, at least in the case of Naxos, by interminable internecine squabbling.[192] All in all, the Orthodox clergy took advantage of this to reinforce the faith of their flock.[193] But the subject of Orthodox-Roman Catholic rivalry should be discussed in a more appropriate place.

The hardships suffered by the slaves of pirates and slaves generally were of course terrible.

The slave was a valuable item of merchandise (and slavery, naturally, a most lucrative commerce)[194] simply because he could be held for lavish ransom or sold as a chattel in one of the many slave markets of the East. His role was that of a laborer assigned to heavy manual tasks or a mere object for the satisfaction of the lusts of his Moslem owner. Slaves arrived in Constantinople both on foot and as entire ships' cargoes and were taken to the bazaars and sold for the highest possible price. Among them were unfortunates of every age from three or four to fifty or fifty-five.[195] This trade in the capital was dominated mainly by Jews, who, in order to enhance their returns, saw to it that the more comely were seductively adorned with frippery and makeup[196] and appropriately tutored in music, dance, and song.[197] The traveller Georgoviz described these bazaars:

At the break of day the slaves are herded together like sheep or goats and taken to the market. The buyers gather and a price is fixed. If the buyers appear pleased, the slaves are stripped of their clothes and displayed in front of their future masters. Each limb is inspected, poked, and probed for possible defects in the articulation of joints. If the buyer is not satisfied, the slave is returned to the merchant in charge. And this will be repeated as many times as there are potential buyers. If the buyer is satisfied, the slave is taken and put to work as a farmer or shepherd or to much harder labor.[198]

The life of oarsmen, whose barracks were part of a huge bath in the port of Constantinople,[199] was especially wretched. There is no dearth of graphic description of the life of a galley slave, but Baron Vegesla Vratislav von Mitrovič's account holds particular interest since it is based on personal experience:

The torment of rowing in a galley is unbelievable in extent. No other work on earth is harder because each prisoner has one of his legs fastened to a chain underneath the seat and can move no further than is necessary for him to reach his rowing place on the bench. The heat is so stifling that it is impossible to row other than in the nude or just a pair of flaxen pants. As soon as the ship passes through the Dardanelles into the open sea, iron handcuffs are clamped on to the hands of each man so that he is able neither to resist the Turk nor defend himself. His hands and legs thus shackled, the captive can do no more than row day and night, except when the sea is rough, until his skin becomes burned like that of a

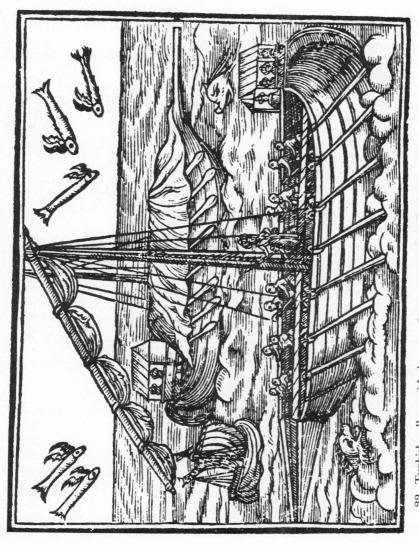

22. Turkish galleys, with slaves rowing. From Salomon Schweigger, *Ein newe Reyssbeschreibung aus Teutschland nach Constantinopel und Jerusalem*, Nuremberg, 1608.

roasted pig and finally cracks from the heat. Sweat runs into his eyes and saturates his body, causing that peculiar agony (which anyone accustomed to an easy life can only find excruciating) of blistered hands. But the ship's speed must not slacken, which is why, whenever the captain notices anyone stopping to draw breath, he lashes out with a slave whip or a rope dripping wet from seawater until the rower's body is covered in blood. Even so, the prisoner must remain quiet, neither turning to look at his tormentor nor emitting a scream of pain, unless he wants the blows to fall doubly hard again and abuse to rain down too: "Dog! Grumble, do you? Answer back! You dare to scowl?"

All the food you get is two small pieces of hardtack. Only when we arrived at islands inhabited by Christians could we sometimes ask for, or buy, if we had any money, a little wine and sometimes a little soup. Whenever we rode at anchor for one, two, three, or more days, we knitted cotton gloves and socks and sold them for a little extra food that we cooked on board. Our benches were not very long, but even so they had to seat five of us chained to them. We even had an abundance of lice and bedbugs, but our skin and bodies were so covered with bites and baked from the heat that they hardly caused any discomfort at all. Each of us had two blue shirts and a red blouse, which we wore only at night, and other clothes simply did not exist. Life on board was so utterly dismal and execrable that it was worse than death.[200]

The majority of Turkish slaves at the end of the seventeenth century were Spaniards, Italians, and French. Most came from the Barbary Coast, which was the annual source of 6,000 slaves. Their endeavors to communicate with one another and with the Turks gave rise to a lingua franca, the so-called "Franco," which was a polyglot mixture of words from each of the neo-Latin languages. Similarly slave-girls, most of whom were Russian, Polish, Georgian, Hungarian, or German, developed "Russiot," which was a sort of bastardized Russian.[201]

Uprisings by slaves on ships were not uncommon.[202] But those who decided to attempt escape, principally the European prisoners-of-war, faced many and varied dangers. Most were eventually recaptured or died trying to escape. If caught, beatings and stripes on the soles of their feet were all they could expect.[203]

Greeks and Armenians were notable for the goodwill and self-sacrifice which they extended towards escapees. They never hesitated to hide them or facilitate their escape by giving them clothes or money and guiding them to Venetian or other Christian ships.[204] A crushing fine, the confiscation of all possessions, or even death awaited those good Samaritans who were caught.[205] On the other hand, wealthy Christians often paid prisoners' ransoms,[206] and priests could always appeal to the people for ransom money.[207]

Generally, however, ransom for a slave was only acceptable from his relatives. Those who could not afford to pay pleaded with ecclesiastical or civil authorities[208] or else borrowed money from their compatriots,[209]

Pl. 23

Sr. Partie page 133

Castellan del et Sculp.

Vue de la Ville de Zante prise de la place.

23. Zacynthus (Zante). From A. L. Castellan, *Lettres sur la Morée et des îles de Cérigo, Hydra et Zante*, Paris, 1808.

sometimes offering their wives and children as pledges of redemption.[210]
Zacynthus had a special fund, set up in 1560, for the ransoming of slaves.
Not until 1787 did it become defunct.[211]Andros, too, had a similar re-
source.[212]

Traces of the period still remain in the traditions of the Greek people.
"May slavery befall you" and "go to Barbary" became two of the worst
possible curses.[213] Many stories about pirates and piratical invasions circulate among some of the older island residents, while a number of demotic
songs evoke the tragic lot of the slave. There is this one from Zacynthus:

Small ships, wherever you are going; small ships return here,
Is the young man you took for sale?
A thousand would I give to see him, a thousand to talk to him,
So would his mother and his sister, too.
And the youth answered, his sweet mouth opened:
"If you have money, spend it. Gold coin? Keep it,
For, my mother, you will have to wait for me
Till the crow becomes a dove."[214]

The diversity of geographical and political conditions in the Aegean
influenced the local architecture as well as the selection of sites for homes
and the type of settlement founded. Thus, the inhabitants of the smaller
and more barren islands took refuge on the highest parts of their islands
where natural fortifications provided maximum security against a pirate
attack. There they built their houses in close proximity to one another so
that external walls, which were doorless, windowless, and only occasionally broken by a highly placed dormer window, formed a kind of continuous circumvallation in the manner of a castle. One or more gates provided
the only direct access for the occupants and other island inhabitants into
what was virtually a fortress.[215]

On the larger islands, as on the coastal littoral of continental Greece, the
inhabitants were forced to withdraw from the sea to the tops of steep
coastal crags or naturally fortified positions further inland. These they
reinforced with artificial ramparts. Such are the well-known Aegean
"castles," which were only gradually abandoned by their occupants over a
period of 140 years after the disappearance of piracy. A number of them
can still be seen by anyone approaching the shores of these islands.
Ringed by crumbling walls and ruins, their somber outlines stand out
starkly against the hillsides. But their narrow little cobbled streets lie
deserted today and only a deep silence reigns where formerly all was life
and movement. The only flashes of light in the gloom of the ruins come
from the tiny white-walled churches which the inhabitants have preserved
as monuments to their devotion. Kalymnos is probably the most striking
example.

Against the time when danger actually threatened, they built towers around the coast (called *castellia* in the Seven Ionian Islands) and garrisoned them.[216] The more usual structure was small, hardly more than an observation post.[217] Sentries were appointed by the local community, often at the behest of Turkish, Frankish, or Venetian authorities, and their job was to observe any suspicious movement of ships and give the alert by bonfire or gunshot as soon as attack appeared imminent.[218] In many places throughout the Aegean and Ionian Seas the ruins of such watchtowers are still to be seen. Where none survive, place-names indicate their former sites.[219]

Thus far, our task has been to describe the vicissitudes and tribulations of the Greek people under the Turkish yoke. We have seen that a new diaspora took place consisting of mass migrations which were both voluntary and involuntary. These interrupted the organic growth of the nation, inhibiting the expression of its fundamental talents but at least ensuring its survival. The aspect of a variegated and fragmented whole which initially emerges arose from the necessity confronting each local component of the nation to cope separately with appalling conditions of life. But this depressing picture, consisting of many pieces in an historical puzzle that the preceding pages have tried to sort out, finally becomes intelligible and whole when we contemplate simultaneously each of its parts—the towns and the villages, the mountains and the plains, the harbors and coastal areas, the islands and the pirate havens. We can then appreciate that the Greeks would never have survived as a nation at all if they had not chosen to congregate together, if they had not determined to deflect, as best they could, the oppressive measures of the conqueror, if they had not attempted to reorganize after defeat and withdrawal. But, by organization and self-discipline, they continued to grow economically and intellectually to reassert the freedom they had lost.

5

ORTHODOXY AFTER THE CAPTURE

The capture of Constantinople was a watershed in the evolution and organization of the Ottoman Empire. A new era begins with Mohammed II's quest for a final and official settlement of his relations with the head of the Eastern Church and his flock, who comprised, after all, the majority of the sultan's subjects. Mohammed II saw the need to assure the Orthodox faithful that they could look forward to the future with hope.[1]

As we now know, a tradition of relative toleration, interrupted from time to time, of the Moslem states towards the Christian Church, was already established within the framework of the Ottoman Empire. This tradition exercised considerable influence. Basically, the Koran adjured indulgence on the part of Moslem leaders towards the "people of the Book," that is, towards Christians and Jews (*ahl al-kitâb*) when they submitted peaceably.[2] What distinguished Mohammed II's policy was that he also chose to behave leniently towards those who opposed him, though it is true that there was some precedent for such a policy. Bayezid I in 1391 and his father Murad II in 1430 had both adopted similar stances in their relations with the people of Thessalonica.[3]

But Mohammed II proposed to follow not merely the prescriptions of Holy Law and the precedents of history. His primary concern was to serve the interests of the state; and he used the Christian raias to supply the everyday needs of the Ottoman Empire, to sustain and promote its industry and trade. The Turks, a nation of warriors, simply could not have managed without the toil, co-operation and, above all, the taxes of the conquered. As the traveller Pierre Belon observed, the Turks were interested in amassing taxes, not souls,[4] and consequently almost the entire fiscal and taxation system of the Ottomans revolved around their non-Moslem subjects.

The hierarchy of the Orthodox Church provided a ready-made machinery for the governance of millions of Christian raias. It was therefore with some reason that the young sultan, fully cognizant of the Church's enormous influence over the public and private lives of Christians, evinced a warm interest in religious matters.

To widen the rift between Eastern and Western Christendom, Mohammed II seized every opportunity to exploit discord and thus took pains to cultivate the anti-Unionist faction. He elevated to the patriarchal throne the monk Gennadius, whose secular name had been George Courtesis Scholarios, a man who combined broad education with a deep religious sense.[5] We shall now dwell in some detail upon this man since, as Oecumenical Patriarch during this period of transition, he played a vital role in the Church-State settlement that so strongly affected the destinies of the Eastern Church and therefore modern Hellenism itself.[6]

George Courtesis Scholarios was born into a wealthy Constantinopolitan family around 1405 and received his first education under the Ephesian Marc Eugenicus, with whom he later developed close ties of friendship and belief. In a number of disciplines—ancient Greek, philosophy, theology and law—he was self-taught; he also taught himself Latin so that he could study the Latin fathers of the Church. His preoccupation with Latin authors, particularly Thomas Aquinas, as well as his connections with many "barbarians" in the West, led to his being accused of "philo-Latin" sentiments, an accusation which he felt constrained to deny over and over again. Immensely proud of his self-acquired erudition,[7] Scholarios was ever lauding his own virtues and promoting himself as an indispensable advisor to powerful men. Since he also disparaged the three or four other distinguished scholars in Constantinople, it might be said that his ambition and amour-propre were inordinate. Although his condescension towards them initially bordered on disdain, he later retracted his criticisms and indeed became almost fulsome in his praise. Altogether, he was a vain and idiosyncratic character.[8]

When he felt that his intellectual prowess had developed to the point of being useful to others, Scholarios opened a school of philosophy, which soon attracted not only Greeks but foreigners, especially Italians, who were eager to study the Greek language and its literature. His aim, like that of a handful of other scholars in the declining years of Byzantium, was to inject new life into a moribund system of education. He particularly chafed at the thought that the Western Europeans, once pupils of the Byzantines, were beginning to excel their teachers and advance to the highest levels of civilization. It was during this period that Scholarios compiled his Greek grammar and also completed a large number of translations and commentaries on Latin writers. But Aristotle, too, commanded his attention.

His most famous students were his nephew Theodore Sophianos, a monk who died in the flower of his youth in the monastery of Vatopediou in 1456, and especially Matthew Kamariotes, who became the dean of intellectuals in the City after its capture. It was for Kamariotes that Scholarios completed his translation and commentary on Thomas Aquinas' *De ente et essentia*.[9]

Scholarios' intellectual gifts were recognized and patronage was showered upon him. Even before the Council of Florence (1439), he held (and retained until 1450) the honorary offices of "Superior Judge of the Romans" and "General Secretary of the Emperor." During this period, though still a layman, he was also official sermonist at court and each Friday preached in the palace before the Senate and the large throng there gathered.[10]

At the time of the Councils of Ferrara and Florence he came to believe that the interests of the state might be threatened and began to advocate the Union of the Churches as the best means of protecting those interests. That is to say, he espoused the philo-Unionist politics of John VIII Palaeologus, as well as the beliefs of Ioannis Bessarion.[11] But the conflict between Unionists and anti-Unionists, which flared up again when he returned from Italy to Constantinople, still filled him with unease. He chose to remain silent and inactive in the midst of all this dissension, an attitude which alarmed Marc Eugenicus.[12] Later, however, his former teacher attempted to justify Scholarios' reticence by suggesting that it was not only his private thoughts which restrained him but certain individuals.[13]

In 1443 the relationship between mentor and pupil was repaired when Scholarios came down flatly on the side of the anti-Unionists. Thereafter he remained steadfast in the "faith of the fathers," that is, in the faith "which was originally transmitted to the Orthodox Church."[14] So reconciled, Marc Eugenicus proclaimed on his deathbed to those around him that Scholarios must become his successor as the official leader of the anti-Unionists' cause. In an emotional scene, his pupil in turn declared that he was now purged of every doubt and hesitation and swore that he would fight unremittingly, "till the last drop of his blood was spilled," for the faith of his fathers and the "purity" of Orthodoxy.[15]

Indeed from this time on Scholarios revealed himself as a fervent defender of the anti-Unionist cause, the self-styled "Exarch of the Congregation of the Orthodox faithful," though in truth he never manifested quite the uncompromising zeal and irrepressible energy that had so characterized Eugenicus. Between 1444 and 1453 he wrote polemics against Roman Catholic dogma concerning the procession of the Holy

Spirit and against the Council of Florence. But his position was undermined by the accession to the throne of Constantine XI, whose philo-Unionist politics were not only well-known but unshakable. In 1450 Scholarios accordingly withdrew to the monastery of Charsianeites to become tonsured as a monk, and under the name Gennadius endeavored from there to direct the anti-Unionist movement with sermons as vehement as before. All the misfortunes of the Byzantine Empire he attributed to desertion from the true faith and the simony and sins of clergy and people. He still thought, however, that God might save the Empire as He had done at the time of the "pious" Manuel, when, "though despairing of any human assistance or friendly power, the City had been saved from the enemy." In general, he suggested, "we have always been happy unless overtaken by self-conceit, impiety, and disrespect towards God, and only then has misfortune befallen us."[16] Even during the actual siege of the City, Scholarios continued to direct the struggle against the Unionists from his cell, thereby exacerbating the confusion and disorder which reigned in Constantinople.

He was captured the day after the City fell and taken to Adrianople. Prisoners were divided up among the captors, and Scholarios fell into the hands of a powerful, though apparently benevolent, Moslem[17] who, out of respect for his education and special qualities, treated him well.[18] Meanwhile the sultan, looking for ways of implementing his plans and hearing a lot of Gennadius' erudition from the Christians around him, became interested in the monk[19] and sought him out.[20] Gennadius himself spoke boastfully of this incident. Returning from Adrianople to Constantinople in the fall of 1453, the sultan took Gennadius with him and installed him in the abbacy of an abandoned monastery, perhaps the monastery of Charsianeites.[21] He was then charged with the welfare of monks, the restoration of churches in ruin or disrepair and the spiritual care of Christians in Constantinople. Later, at the sultan's behest, an episcopal synod assembled from Asia and Europe, elected Scholarios in succession deacon, presbyter, bishop, and patriarch of the Church—all on the same day, 6 January 1454.[22]

Gennadius' ascent to the patriarchal throne of course signified the ascendancy of the anti-Unionist, especially the monastic, viewpoint, one which was generally wedded to tradition and distrustful of scholars and the secular votaries of Greek culture. Such a spirit of conservatism could be expected to have influenced adversely the so-called Macedonian Hellenistic revival of the arts in the thirteen and fourteenth centuries. Thereafter, austere Byzantine traditionalism predominated throughout the entire period of Turkish rule.[23] Of course, this was unquestionably a spirit more attuned to the events of the time, to the eclipse of the Hellenic "race," to the calls for penance and the purging of souls then prevalent.

As patriarch, Gennadius tried to salvage what he could from the wreckage of the Byzantine Empire. Speaking later, in 1460, he insisted that his sole concern, for which he had been prepared by God, was the reestablishment of the patriarchal throne "and everything associated with it."[24] In a sense he had an ally from the start. Mohammed II, moved by the considerations to which we have referred, manifested respect and goodwill in his efforts to regularize relations with the "people of the Book," not only with Gennadius but also with the chief rabbis of the Jewish communities of the Ottoman Empire, Mose Kapsali and the Armenian Chovakim.[25] The historian Kritoboulos of Imbros writes that the sultan restored to the Christians "most of what remained of their Church"[26] and honored Gennadius with his friendship. More than that, "with honorable gifts he acceded to many [of Gennadius'] demands and so met his needs that the power of the Church and the patriarchal authority should become no less than they were under the former emperors."[27] Brief as Kritoboulos' comments are, they nevertheless corroborate events long recognized in oral tradition. The *Political History of Constantinople* elsewhere records such popular memories, as of the occasion immediately after his election when Gennadius was specifically told by the sultan: "Be happy in your reign as patriarch, and have our friendship in all things, as well as all the privileges of your predecessors."[28] The same source also says that the sultan presented Gennadius with a gold-plated bishop's staff, a magnificent horse, and golden coins; and that he listened to all of Gennadius' requests with benevolence and understanding.[29]

What were these "privileges" of the Church? They are defined in general terms in a disputed passage of Sphrantzes' lengthy chronicle as the "inviolable, not taxable and immanent" appurtenances of the patriarch and his successors. Obviously they included such things as the exercise of a definite administrative, as well as judicial, authority by the patriarch and his superior clergy. The same privilege was also accorded all bishops,[30] though no significant innovation was involved here since the episcopal regimen under previous Turkish and other Moslem rulers had been essentially the same. Metropolitans had also been exempt from taxes in former times.[31] Thus the granting of privileges was not so much the result of Gennadius' efforts as it was a legacy of Islamic conventions.[32] But a twofold problem still remains: first, did the sultan actually ratify the election of Gennadius by official proclamation; and second, did such a document, if it existed, actually define, even in a general way, the limits of his jurisdiction—in effect, his privileges?

Sphrantzes' well-known passage, of course, does speak of an official document bestowing the privileges, though it is generally looked upon with suspicion. What is of interest to us here, as others have correctly pointed out, is not whether the passage is rightly attributable to Sphrantzes but whether its contents accord with the facts. To me, it seems likely that they do.[33] In 1464 Gennadius wrote to Theodore Vranas, in sufficiently explicit terms, that the sultan made "many donations"[34] to the Church ("gifts" is the term used by Kritoboulos), a word which in the context can mean nothing other than privileges. The reliability of Sphrantzes' remarks is reinforced, if not proven, by Gennadius' phrase, to which Amantos has previously drawn our attention: "those responsible for the tragedy which has befallen us gave us our freedom in writing."[35]

Thus we may assume that the sultan confirmed both Gennadius' election to the patriarchal throne and the bestowal of privileges by the promulgation of an official berat. We might also add that when Mohammed II favored the patriarch by dispensing specific religious privileges (Gerlach uses the word *Freyheitsbrief*, while Gennadius himself is definite that "freedom" was won), the grant was apparently known to all the people of Constantinople for a hundred or more years after the Capture. Gerlach wrote in 1578.[36] At the same time, it would appear that the document itself was lost very early, perhaps in a fire.

Among the patriarchal berats which have survived, the earliest, dating from 1662, confirms the election of Patriarch Dionysios Vardalis.[37] Berats were also issued on such occasions as the appointment of the patriarchs of Antioch and Jerusalem, as well as of their metropolitans, and these all incorporated similar references to ecclesiastical rights, privileges, and jurisdictions.[38] The oldest of the berats concerning metropolitans affected the Metropolitan of Mt. Athos and was probably promulgated sometime between 1476 and 1482.[39] The earliest berats did not include any precise definition of religious privileges or *imtiyazatı mezhebiye*, which was their official designation in the Turkish language until the end of the nineteenth century.[40]

The lack of research prevents our arriving at any definite conclusions about the growth of privileges, particularly about the extent to which they may have been added to or curtailed over the years.[41] Nonetheless it is true that, without them, the Christian raias would have remained not only politically but religiously leaderless. During this turbulent era of transition it would seem, for example, that many Christians falsely accused by the Turks were only saved from death by Gennadius' personal representations to the sultan.[42] From a later period, we also have the evidence of a firman promulgated by the sultan prescribing dire punishment for those who disturbed or falsely accused Christians.[43] Even today, however, Greeks speak of the fate which frequently befell anyone so accused. In Epirus, people still speak of these foul "calumnies."[44] For Christians under Turkish rule it seemed that conversion to Islam often offered the only avenue of escape from this sort of calumny, which persisted until the very end of the Captivity. Those who resisted the temptation to apostatize, those who chose not to join the ranks of religious renegades[45] became the "new" martyrs of the Orthodox Church.

Mohammed II allowed Gennadius to occupy the Church of the Holy Apostles as his patriarchal church. Shortly afterwards, however, the body of a Turk was found in its precincts and the patriarch, fearful that retribution might fall upon Christians, abandoned it (in the middle, or perhaps towards the end, of 1454). He was not reluctant to take this step since the neighborhood of the church, where so many Byzantine emperors lay buried, was all but uninhabited. Turks were thus left free to pillage the graves of emperors and eventually tore down the church structure. The Turks built in its place the Mosque of Fatih (Conqueror), celebrated to this day. We cannot help wondering if the Greek architect Christodoulos managed to preserve some of the remains of the old imperial church in the foundations of the mosque.

The new patriarchate eventually made its home in the former convent of Pammakaristos, around which lived a community of Christians who had been forcibly moved there from various parts of the Empire.[46] Both Gerlach[47] (1578) and Carlier de Pinon[48] (1579) have left us interesting descriptions of this patriarchal seat. Then, in 1586, the patriarchate was again forced to move to the Church of Theotokos Paramythias in Vlah Seraglio; again, in 1597, to the Church of St. Demetrius in Xyloporta, and finally in 1601 to the little church of St. George in Phanar, which is its present abode.[49] Among the precious relics of the first post-Byzantine Church of Pammakaristos which have survived is the superb mosaic icon of the same name, which is derivative, both in type and technique, of the severe traditionalism of the Comneni (eleventh century).[50]

The income of the patriarchal household was provided by the inhabitants of the ecclesiastical provinces[51] in a variety of forms: dues paid by metropolitans (for which their bishops were obliged to reimburse them),[52] fees for the consecration of property, donations from pious Christians, and payments from priests and archpriests at the time of ordination.[53] Although it is impossible to fix exactly the annual income of the patriarchate, one source in 1621 estimated that it may have come to fifty thousand gold pieces.[54] In his *Manual on the Present Condition of the Greeks,* the seventeenth-century Greek scholar Christophoros Angelos gives us some detailed information about this income:

There are seventy-four metropolitans under the jurisdiction of the patriarch. More than thirty of these have more than one, some as many as three, bishops. In all, there are seventy-two or seventy-three bishops. The fee for a wedding in Constantinople is one gold piece; and each household in the patriarch's own ecclesiastical province is required to furnish twelve denarii [*aspra* (?)]. In addition, deacons and priests make a small donation when he ordains them, after which each priest is then liable to annual dues of one gold piece. Metropolitans similarly

24. The Patriarchate of Constantinople. From Martin Crusius, *Turcograecia*, Basel, 1584.

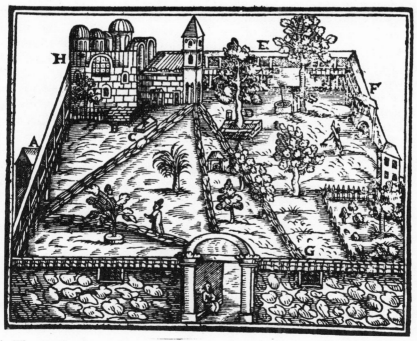

25. The Patriarchate of Constantinople. From Salomon Schweigger, *Ein newe Reyssbeschreibung aus Teutschland nach Constantinopel und Jerusalem*, Nuremberg, 1608.

make a donation when ordained, and their subsequent liabilities annually are twenty, twenty-five, or thirty *mna* [?] to the patriarch, which go towards the sultan's tax—six thousand gold pieces in all. The servants of the patriarch and of the bishops are monks because laymen are not allowed to serve bishops. About seventeen priests and servants sit at the patriarch's table. He also has two parish priests, two deacons, an *ekonomos,* a *sakellarios* who is guardian of the ecclesiastical vestments and attends to other patriarchal matters, two cantors, a janitor, and a stableman. One of the two parish priests, perhaps even both, are eligible to enter the office of *protosynkellos,* which guards the patriarch's seal. There are also three or four others who are responsible for bringing people before the patriarch when he sits in judgment.[55] Bishoprics are organized along the same lines as the patriarchate.[56]

Mohammed II visited the patriarch in the monastery of Pammakaristos on three occasions when their talks ranged widely over Christian theology. By all accounts, he was captivated by the erudition he found there; so much so that later, at the expressed wish of the sultan, Gennadius developed in writing the main points covered in their discussions. Thus appeared his tract *On the Only Means to the Salvation of Mankind (Peri tis monis odou pros tin sotirian ton anthropon),* a small masterpiece of Christian apologetics addressed to Islam. Gennadius' summary of it was translated into Turkish by Ahmet, cadi of Veroia, and then presented to the sultan for his private study.[57] The text proceeds with logical simplicity, without a trace of pedantry or affectation, and is not only the first declaration of Orthodox faith after the Capture but also one of the most memorable.[58]

The sultan's contact with Gennadius, which of course stemmed from political rather than religious concerns, gave rise to many rumors hinting at the sultan's inclination towards Christianity and denial of his own faith.[59] But the young sultan shrewdly understood that the interests of state would be better served by catering to the religious sensibilities of Christians, particularly Greeks. If the attitude of the masses towards him depended on his willingness to nourish an extravagant hope among Christians, then he would certainly do so.

Into the vacuum left by the fall of Constantinople, forces were unleashed which threatened to defame the Eastern Church. "Christians were in such a deplorable condition," wrote Matthew Kamariotes at this time, "that they could hardly be called Christians. All that the name implies they have disavowed. They now dare do only things that cause the wrath of God, and, though punished, most of them do not change their ways, allowing themselves to be led astray by incurable passions."[60] The result was that "the divine and noble aspect of the Church"[61] deteriorated with them.

A study of these critical times, which is essential to any understanding of trends within the Church and the development of modern Hellenism, must lean heavily on the writings of Gennadius. Rich in psychological insight, these take on the aspect of a confession, revealing his total personality.

The supreme leader of Orthodoxy bore heavy responsibilities which seemed to increase with each passing day.[62] The new patriarch had to establish his authority and make clerical discipline effective. "Before the Church and the protector of the Church [here he means the sultan] there must be pious submission and obedience."[63] He had to contend with opposition from all those who took advantage of the disappearance of the state and the accompanying debasement of the Church. Restraints were gone, and infractions and violations of law and authority were endemic. He faced the painful dilemma of "either pardoning virtually everyone who had led an unlawful life and thereby sullying his own character and life, or, by merely trying to guide the sinful back on the path of righteousness, driving them finally over the edge of the precipice of corruption: not only citizens and monks but even those once proud of their episcopal offices seem to prefer going over, or at least threatening to go over, to the enemies of the faith rather than to accept the paternal solicitude which I offer them."[64] These words testified to the numerous conversions to Islam, lay and clerical, which were already taking place and which continued for centuries.[65]

Gennadius met with particular opposition from monks. Their avarice "defamed the clergy and led to ignominious scandals which infected the faithful and even onlookers."[66] It may well be that he incurred the special resentment of those surviving Unionists, whether members of the clergy, the military, or politicians, who never forgave him his policy of collaboration with the sultan.[67] Among these frustrated patriots there may even have been some, as Gennadius alleges, who threatened his life.[68] Perhaps they were the same radical elements that confronted him during the siege. Whatever the case, Gennadius was convinced in 1460 that "he is not happy who sits on the patriarchal throne; no man of his own free will would wish to suffer the hardships that go with it."[69]

The trying conditions under which all Christians lived and the consequent danger of apostasy were responsible for Gennadius' attempt to effect some kind of accommodation with reality. They also moved him to reflect upon some of the basic problems of Christianity itself.

He thought that the Turkish conquest made it necessary to preserve the essence of Christianity, even at the expense of various of its forms which had become established over the centuries. Those who are truly men of the people, he wrote to Maximus and the other monks of the monastery of Sinai (probably towards the end of the first part of his patriarchate, late in 1455), are the ones who believe with all their soul and are always ready to sacrifice themselves for their faith in Christ and "endure ineffable sorrows." Let us not therefore dampen their ardor by expecting a constrict-ing "exactitude and meticulousness in discipline," whether in the sacra-ments, the prelacy, the sacrifices, the psalmodies, the feasts, or monastic regimen. Did it matter that a priest forgot the number of the matutinal Gospel, that he read the ninth, for example, instead of the seventh? For was it not true that the beginnings of Christianity were uncomplicated by such minutiae, and yet its great simplicity did not prevent Christians from being martyred in the hundreds for the sake of Christ? Contemporary circumstances were similar to those which faced the early Christians; the Church was merely passing through a new phase of persecution and testing. All this, he concluded, was because "we are now bereft of an empire, a free church, and outspokenness, as we were before," namely, before the days of the Great Constantine.

Neither Christ nor "those who believe in what Christ stands for" had any use for such trivia. Yet even in these desperate times the man with the courage of his convictions, "who fights to put things right, to restore the customs and laws of the Church, such as they were when Christians were free, is seen as an enemy of Christianity and as trying to achieve the impossible, whereas he who is prepared to compromise in order to pre-serve everything as it is appears as nothing less than a descendant of the Apostles whom God will judge as such."[70]

Any attempt to judge the buying and selling of ecclesiastical offices, Gennadius continued, or even the patriarchal office itself, must neverthe-less take into account this all too prevalent attitude of compromise. The monks of Sinai should not be shocked that money transactions take place in the election of the Patriarch of Jerusalem, nor that after the election he should give money to assist in the functioning of his office; because for some fifty years within the patriarchate of Constantinople itself "the prelacy and the priesthood have also been bought and sold," which is a great sin, and Christians moreover have been the buyers and sellers. Although, Gennadius went on, he had tried in vain as patriarch to extir-pate this evil, he had been finally compelled to turn a blind eye to the "appetites of the religious shepherds of the people in order not to cause perturbation in the souls of men and in order not to shake the faith of the people or possibly make them completely unfaithful." It was necessary to approach similar infringements of canonical rule in the same spirit: "if a shepherd willingly transgress, such transgression will be between him and his conscience; but if it be ignorance or the force of circumstances which lead him to transgress, he will be pardoned by God." Gennadius urged submission, tolerant understanding, and unity if Christianity was to sur-vive.[71]

Thus the Church was forced into making continual *ad hoc* (*kat' oikono-mian*) concessions, and long-accepted traditions underwent various modifications. This *ad hoc* approach was retained by the Church throughout the long era of captivity.[72] Essentially, the Church's policy was to preserve the essence of Christianity and to keep the faithful in her fold; and these ideas Gennadius developed in his *Lament (Thrinos)*, which was completed in the monastery of Timiou Prodromou in Serrai. Created out of the sufferings of Greek Christianity, this work ranks with the best of Byzantine and post-Byzantine literature. In it, while Gennadius is indulgent towards the "sheep," tolerant of their ignorance of religious prescriptions, and content that their religious faith should retain the fervor of self-sacrifice, he castigates the "shepherds of the people":

The workers in the sacred vineyards, the farmers of Christ's earth, must see clearly in their own work the dangers described everywhere in the Bible.[73] It is much better that the folk remain in ignorance of these, as one with an incurable illness ought to remain ignorant of the nature and cause of the disease, else we shall only undermine the hope that the poeple repose in their shepherds; and this is because there exist far worse evils to be feared, which must also be hidden from them. Perhaps God with his infinite mercy will not judge too harshly the present life of Christians, for there is no other form of faith which makes Him so happy as perseverance in the face of gross temptations, and He would surely not withhold the grace of the sacraments from those who hope to be saved by them merely because the clergy is unfit and uneducated, any more than He would want to punish us all a second time for the ignorance of decency that has overtaken us because of previous transgressions.[74]

The patriarch's optimistic belief that he could save Orthodoxy and the "race" under Turkish overlordship was slowly eroded. He never really believed that the heart of Byzantinism would cease to beat despite the amputation of all its limbs. But eventually he had to acknowledge the existence of a completely different world, inconceivably monstrous. Like many other Greeks, he could not adjust to the new reality, to the magnitude of the change that had occurred. More and more, the moral crisis in the Church unnerved him, the nature of his work sapped his strength, and he became unable to cope forcefully with the conditions of servitude, whether these were permanent or merely transitory. The opposition against him, although he never spoke about it in specific terms, apparently continued to gather strength.[75]

Who were his antagonists? At least some of them are identified for us by Theophanes of Medea, also a student of Marc Eugenicus'. Within the patriarch's immediate household there were the self-appointed guardians of strict orthodoxy in the Church who condemned Gennadius for his *ad hoc* policy, maintaining that it went beyond the limits that had been set down by the fathers of the Church. Among these was a certain Strongylos from Thessaly,[76] his Grand Ecclesiarch or Master of the Chapel.

Gennadius reacted impatiently to the interminable squabbling. He began to long for peace and tranquility,[77] perceiving more and more that, however strong his desire to govern the nation, in itself this was not enough. He resolved to resign. The sultan, who still needed him, at first angrily protested; at length, all reasoning exhausted, he gave in.[78]

Gennadius submitted his resignation in the spring of 1456 and retired to the monastery of Vatopediou. After a brief sojourn there, he entered the monastery of Timiou Prodromou. There he devoted his energies to the production of what are now regarded as his best theological works. His own handwritten manuscripts are still extant. It was in Timiou Prodromou that he wrote a refutation of Plethon's *On Law* (*Peri nomon*), which he later burned publicly during a second, or perhaps third, brief interim as patriarch (1463–1465).[79] His subsequent burial place was preserved in oral tradition until 1854, when, at the instigation of Patriarch Anthimos VI, his remains were transferred with great pomp and ceremony to the monastery's second narthex.

Posterity thus remembered the first patriarch after the Capture, though it is true that his philosophical and theological works remained largely unknown. Only in recent years has the major part of his writings been rediscovered and published.[80]

After Gennadius' resignation, the secular and ecclesiastical notables who came into most frequent contact with the conqueror became markedly corrupt. Even Gennadius' opponents, who had formerly berated him for his departure from rigid orthodoxy, themselves made such compromises that Theophanes of Medea rebuked them. Writing to the Grand Ecclesiarch, Theophanes suggested that "the venerable Gennadius had opened the portals of the Church and shepherded the people into verdant valleys because he wanted them to keep their faith and save their souls from contamination. He did not demand this, nor did he expect us to support him, but now other demands are being made by the leaders of the Church, not only that the gates of the Church be kept open, but that they be kept wide open; and in so doing they raise all barriers, wounding the souls of many, stifling the faith and good works of devout people."[81]

Gennadius, in his *Lament* of 1460, is enigmatic in describing the chaos attending the end of the Byzantine world:

And now, as we leave the throne voluntarily, we must confess that we made mistakes, which was not our intention, in all those matters which we set as our aim throughout almost our whole life. And this is because, when we wanted to be a farmer, we were everywhere surrounded by the sea; and, when we wanted to travel, we could not even see the sea; because we associated with some men, thinking that they were fellow-builders, but found that they were only sailors reeling on the land or farmers floundering at sea; and, whenever it happened that everyone had found his proper role, the sailors still drowned because they were not good sailors, and the farmers were equally as bad. Everywhere there was ignorance, lack of judgment, woeful inexperience, and even resentment against those who really did know something or wanted merely to offer advice; and everywhere there were wrongful accusations, insolence, malevolence, and destructiveness. Nought was as it should have been. How could anyone remain sane seeing only wild beasts where once people lived, realizing that no one could be saved . . . when one had no opportunity and got no hearing, when there was neither agreement, desire nor example, when there was no one to provide protection or help, when there was none who loved according to God's will, who had compassion, who knew how to interest himself in anything important, who was able to give advice or even knew how to listen to it?[82]

No one has depicted more graphically than Gennadius, in his *Lament*, the humiliation and degradation of both "shepherds" and "flock" between 1454 and 1460. He not only deplored what had happened to the Church and Hellenism but also predicted much worse for the future:

Alas! Where does one begin to weep? For the physical enslavement of the Greeks, or the spiritual corruption among those who seem to have escaped that enslavement? . . . For the insults which the barbarians have hurled against our faith, or the scandals which have infected the souls of the faithful? For those who every day abjure their faith, or those who merely contemplate doing this?[83] For the Church's sullied image . . . or the mismanagement of those who govern, or rather confound, her affairs? For the general misfortune . . . or the total corruption, visible and invisible? For the irregularities of the clergy everywhere and the frivolous lip service they pay to Christianity, or the deliberate negligence of those who actually dare go up to the altar of God? And which of these two to decry more— involuntary ignorance and illiteracy or the willful infractions of those who know better? Shall we weep for priests because they are so few in number in all the districts of Orthodoxy, or for their rudeness and lack of education? Or shall we weep for the impious way in which the priest is ordained . . . ? Soon it will be impossible to find even such priests as these. . . . Few are the people who are not affected by the priests' casual observance of their religious duties. They perform the holy sacraments not "by reciting in accordance with the rule" but by chanting in a most careless fashion, caring only about the offerings of the poor, which they even go to their homes to collect; and they turn their backs on those who look to them for care, not knowing how to give comfort. Thus deceived by those to whom they turn vainly for salvation, the people come to believe that it is better for Christians not to listen to anyone about obeying the laws of Christ, which they do not in any case know because no one has taught them.[84]

Despite all this the churches, with the chanting and incense-burning, did provide an atmosphere in which the people could find communion with God and at least temporary consolation. For centuries to come, however, they would be tormented, as indeed they already had been, by the question which stretched their faith to the breaking point: "Why did God forsake us and leave us at the mercy of such a cruel tyrant?" Their religious leaders owed them an answer, and Gennadius, drawing upon more or less the same mystical arguments that other prominent clerics had expounded in the past announced that "the end of the world is near."[85] Slavery was the ultimate test which Divine Providence had put to the faithful so that those who met it would be definitely saved at Christ's imminent second coming. "All that can save us," he wrote, "is the strength of our faith in the face of temptation, our knowledge of the struggles of those who never lose hope and of Christ's prophecies regarding tempta- tion, faith and struggle. Then, the nation will not be destroyed or aban- doned but, on the contrary, those who do not yield shall be crowned as the first Christians were crowned."[86]

Gennadius looked upon the fall of Constantinople as the culmination of world history, which therefore placed it at the end of the seventh millen- nium after the Creation. "What we know about the events of the end of the world" we now witness "all around us." According to his calculations, Armageddon would occur in 1493.[87] Gennadius' reputation as a prophet and visionary survived him for more than a century after the Capture.[88]

In the eschatological ambiance within which Gennadius moved, memories of recent events were being constantly refreshed, sharpening the contrasts between new and old conditions of life.[89] Gennadius de- scribed Constantinople as founded by the "two most outstanding races of mankind"; he eulogized the "common Fatherland" of "all those who bear the name of Christ," people "from all over the world, who looked piously and protectively to the City as the source of light and life"; he recalled his relatives, friends, students, most of whom had had an unhappy end; he remembered his books, thrown away, torn, and trampled upon during the Capture, or else scattered throughout the land like a "useless burden" (*achtos mataion*). He called to mind, too, the cut and thrust of public disputation with scholars and his exposition of the Gospel before the Emperor John VIII Palaeologus and an illustrious audience of princes, grandees, bishops, monks, and other inhabitants of the City, foreigners as well as Greeks.[90] The ghost of the "good old days" followed him every- where (though surprisingly he makes no mention of Constantine Palaeo- logus as the heroic fighter whose death so deeply moved the masses).

But now, at every turn, the ugliness of the City was mirrored in the downcast visages of its inhabitants.[91] The people wandered everywhere in rags; ingratitude and false accusation were rife.[92] "Who is there," he wrote, "who would not grieve at such a heart-rending spectacle, at those stooped from the burden of unavoidable miseries, or at others who seem to have lost the feeling of shame, especially when one can remember some of their parents, dear souls, many of whom led utterly blameless lives before God?"[93]

Of course there were other forms of social dislocation as well: the wealthy and the nobility of former times had vanished, entirely new faces reappearing in their places.[94] These were people indifferent to the new conditions except to the extent that the confusion provided a means of climbing to social and economic pinnacles. Their behavior dismayed Gennadius: "It has even come to this, my beautiful country, that such people escape and live while nobles, who represent human order, which in itself is good fortune to those in the midst of other misfortunes, are put out of the way."[95]

The world that emerged from the ruins of the Byzantine Empire was perhaps very different from what he imagined it would be. When he finally saw what it was really like, he regretted many of the attitudes he had held before the Capture, though it is also true that his pride stood in the way of his openly admitting this. But now his feeling for the Greek national consciousness became vivid.[96] He mourned "the destruction of the race by a series of misfortunes"[97] and deplored the enormity of the disaster: "I am terribly sad about the destruction of the race, a race than which there has been none finer on earth, resplendent in its erudition, fortunate in its wisdom, distinguished for its excellent laws, and adorned with all manner of beautiful things. Who is there who will not admit that the Hellenes (Greeks) were the most singular people of all?"[98] The word "Hellene" held a national connotation for him. Indeed, Gennadius' orientation towards Hellenism marked the beginning of the alliance between Orthodoxy and Greek nationalism which remained unbroken in later centuries.

His thoughts went back "to the initial cause of misfortune, the source of these unhappy circumstances," at the time of "the last sunset in Constantinople, the last sunset of all, after which the blackest and most terrible of darknesses descended."[99] Belatedly, he understood how priceless freedom was. He would have preferred poverty, devastation and agony over the City's last years to her present plight, because then, at least, she would still have been free:[100] "O how, glorious land, can we bear living deprived of you, and how do you tolerate us, you who have lost those children who loved you most of all? Indeed, how is it that we are still alive now that you have been lost to us, for truly you are no longer here even though it may seem that you are."[101] He went on to beg his "departed mother" to "take me away from this most evil of mischances, from grief such as I have never known before, contemplating the common misfortunes (my own are less important), from this ugliness of the race that I can not bear to look upon, from a life that I can no longer endure."[102]

Gennadius perceived only one hope for the rebirth of the "race": a return to the path of righteousness, "to holy and paternal love," which alone would move God to restore the freedom of slaves being punished for their sins.[103] This conception gradually gained currency until it became an aspiration common to all Greeks. It predominated throughout all the years of Turkish rule[104] and contributed to the renewal of religion and feeling, of which one manifestation was the reform of manners. In its fulfillment, nothing was more important, according to Gennadius, than the mission of the clergy to awaken and emancipate the faithful: "For if our nation is ever to see the sun shine again, it will only be because the clergy and the monks will have resumed intellectual leadership and, by exercising great power and solicitude, thereby create the great hope that, through charity, our entire nation shall recover completely."[105]

The history of the Church and patriarchate during the early centuries of Turkish rule after Gennadius is not an open book. We do know, however, that the patriarch continued as before to exercise his authority in concert with the metropolitans, who formed a permanent synod (*endimousa synodos*). Without their consent it was impossible to make the larger decisions which affected political and ecclesiastical affairs as a whole.[106] We do not know, on the other hand, just how the first synod after the Capture was constituted; very probably there was no departure from Byzantine tradition.

Closely connected with the problem of the constitution and development of the synod is that concerning the functions of the various Church officials (*offikialoi*).[107] These, too, apparently evolved from Byzantine precedents. On a visit to Constantinople between 1419 and 1421 the Russian deacon Zosimos named the four senior officials in the Church: the Grand Chartophylax, the *Sakellarios,* the *Skevophylax,* and the *Sakelliou.*[108] Thus although it is true that some new officials appeared after the Capture—the Grand Rhetor,[109] for example—it is incorrect to say, as Karolidis does, that they formed a new institution. The patriarch faced the manifold problems of the Church with a generally familiar bureaucracy. One of those problems, however, was a new one: the establishment of harmonious relations with the Porte.[110]

The most important officials, also members of the synod, were the Grand Logothete, the *Grand Skevophylax,* the Grand Ecclesiarch, the *Grand Ekonomos,* The Grand Chartophylax, the *Sakelliou,* the *Grand Sakellarios,* the Grand Rhetor, and the *Protekdikos.* Most of them were clergy, though the highest officials were laymen; and this remained the practice until the very end of Turkish rule.[111] At the same time, all the officials were considered clergy (*"ton ektos tou vimatos"*) even if they did not perform church duties. Those "away from the altar" still assumed office by virtue of a simple ordination (which, in former times, included partial tonsuring) involving the patriarch's blessing in the patriarchal church or chambers.[112] After the Capture, these ecclesiastical nobles sat on the bench of the patriarchal court, which administered the political and religious affairs of the people of Constantinople.[113] In 1577 this court (which also had its provincial counterparts under the bishops of the Church) con-

vened regularly on Mondays, Wednesdays, and Fridays.[114] Later, though
we do not know precisely when, two courts were constituted: a small one
with limited membership, and the "Great Synodical Court" (*Mega dikastir-
ion tis Megalis Synodou*), which reviewed decisions of the synod and served
as a court of appeal from it, though not from the smaller patriarchal
court.[115] Ecclesiastical dignitaries received exarchates by way of compen-
sation for services rendered.[116]

The patriarchal court was also composed of those officials known as
assessors (*axiomatikoi*) or archons. At their head was the Grand Logothete,
who performed the duties of liaison officer between the patriarchate and
the Porte and who accompanied the patriarch whenever he waited upon
the sultan or his officials.[117]

The Church remained relatively free until 1464—"till the time of my
successors," wrote Gennadius to Theodore Vranas—and continued to
enjoy the privileges granted to it by Mohammed II.[118] After the collapse
of the Empire of Trebizond, the last stronghold of free Hellenism, and
after many nobles from Trebizond had been deported to both the Turkish capital and Adrianople, the situation continually deteriorated. The
nobles continued to hold positions of influence for many years after the
disappearance of the Byzantine Empire and brought to the capital many
of the pernicious habits they had acquired as courtiers. Together with the
Peloponnesians and as many of the old Constantinopolitan powerful as
still remained, they sought to capture the only surviving vestige of Byzantine glory—the Oecumenical Patriarchate itself—preserving, it is true,
ecclesiastical tradition and a certain secular power. As Zinkeisen puts it:

After the tempest which had toppled the Byzantine throne subsided, everything
that remained—from the last descendants of the old noble families and what was
left of the sometime grandeur of the Byzantine court to the relics of a decadent
protocol and even dishonorable plotting and intriguing—all still found a broad
field for action within the confines of a satellite court which had become poor and
morally bankrupt. All now congregated round the person of the patriarch and
prospered under the protection of the Cross in a new and peculiar way of life,
which, even during later years of persecution, never showed signs of faltering,
much less dying.[119]

It is highly probable that a number of the newcomers from Trebizond,
as well as Byzantine nobles themselves, were able to appropriate some of
the ecclesiastical offices, which would go a long way towards explaining
their intense preoccupation with patriarchal affairs. In effect, they became the standard-bearers of the first post-Byzantine aristocracy.[120] The
absence of clear evidence, however, makes it difficult to assess their
influence on the formation and organization of the patriarchate during
the early centuries of Turkish rule. But we can be sure that the descendants of this old aristocracy, as well as its new members (often simple raias,

as we shall see, who successfully climbed the rungs of the social ladder by dint of their economic prowess, individual abilities, or skill in personal relationships), followed the patriarchate to its different abodes until it finally settled down in 1601 in the Church of St. George in the Phanar quarter of Constantinople. They were, in other words, the forerunners of the Phanariot class, which gradually emerged, beginning in the seventeenth century.

Among the survivors of the old Byzantine oligarchy was the former chamberlain at the court of Trebizond, George Amiroukes, remembered for his familial ties with the vizier, Mahmoud Pasha, and for his pro-Turkish politics, which certainly favored the Moslem religion if it did not quite descend to the betrayal of his own.[121] With the connivance of Mahmoud, Amiroukes succeeded in convincing the sultan to depose and exile in November 1462 Patriarch Ioasaph I Kokkas, who had vigorously opposed his projected marriage with the comely widow of the last Duke of Athens. This was the first serious blow to the patriarchate and marked the beginning of Turkish interference in its internal affairs.[122] The next patriarch, though only for a very brief period, was very likely Gennadius himself,[123] followed by Sophronios I (1463–1464), who was known to the world as Sylvestros Syropoulos, historian of the Council of Florence. Then came Marcos Xylocaravis (1464?–1465), who met with the opposition and hostility of the clergy when he dared to accuse them of misconduct and cupidity. The corrupt Trapezuntine nobles took advantage of this situation to seek preferment through their own children (who were among the sultan's iç-oğlan and officials of the Porte), and successfully obtained the elevation to the patriarchal throne of one of their own compatriots, Symeon of Trebizond. They offered the sultan a "gift" of 1,000 gold pieces, which he accepted sardonically, not only because this was an entirely unexpected bonus but because he derived contemptuous satisfaction from contemplating the adversity of these successors of the Byzantine Empire and the Orthodox hierarchy. Through the intrigues and plots of the ecclesiastical and secular nobility gathered around the patriarch, each new patriarch thereafter was required to make a large payment to the sultan at the time of his election. Under Dionysios I (1466–1472, 1488–1490), Symeon's successor, the payment was increased to 2,000 gold pieces; and under Raphael the Serb it was legitimized as haraç, that is, as a prescribed annual tax independent of the "gift," fixed initially at 500 gold pieces, but later raised to 1,000 pieces of gold, then 1,500, and so on.[124]

The quarrels among the nobility, in which each faction attempted to win the partisanship of the mob in the capital and its environs, even to the extent of organizing spectacular riots in the streets, provided the sultan and his officials with the opportunity they sought to intervene directly in the internal affairs of the Church. If a patriarch found himself unable to meet his financial obligations, as happened with Raphael the Serb, or if the enemies of the patriarch produced some new ambitious and intriguing candidate who offered much more than the incumbent patriarch, the sultan and his officials did not hesitate to step in.[125] This sort of situation continually recurred during successive centuries.[126]

The new importance which money acquired, to say nothing of the amounts which had to be regularly collected in order to meet the demands of the conquerors and their Christian collaborators, led to the resurgence of simoniacal practices, which had their roots in the past. The assumption and performance of the sacerdotal office became a matter of mercenary commerce. In Constantinople and the provinces, archbishops accepted money or "gifts" from candidates for the episcopacy or the priesthood. Dealings of this kind were economically and morally crippling not only to the postulants themselves but also to the patriarchs, archbishops, and bishops in office; and they also demoralized the people. Candidates for the higher sacerdotal offices devoted themselves not to study but to the accumulation of wealth with which to bribe influential Greeks and Turks.[127] Even a Grand Rhetor himself, in this case Ioannis Zygomalas, confessed to accepting ten gold pieces from rich metropolitans newly appointed to office.[128] This decadence later made a very bad impression on West European Catholics and Protestants.[129]

As Bishop Theophanes of Medea said, simony ate its way into the very vitals of the Church.[130] This same writer also apprised the *Grand Sakellarios* of the disease endemic among the higher clergy: "The high clergy have now lost the most important and exquisite thing of all—God's call. Indeed, instead of becoming free and leaders of the Church, you choose rather to be base and tyrannical. Previously, leadership within the Church was something sacred and beneficial to the souls of all mankind, before whom you stand as arbiters and defenders under God's will; now you betray that leadership."[131] In a similar vein he wrote to the Metropolitan of Ephesus, whom he held in high esteem, on account of certain lapses on the part of that prelate: "Everything decent and honest in the Church has been lost. O Justice! Piety has vanished and, with it, hope in God. I have heard some say that the Church is foundering because of the contrary winds which buffet it; but to my mind it has already sunk to the bottom of the sea. The cause of this calamity is the lust for power among you sapient leaders who constitute the nation of the holy and the kingdom of the religious. What you ignore is the law of simony, which leads to such terrible injustices, and you offer as an excuse the arbitrary will of the conqueror, which does not really exist. Even the important institution of marriage has been shaken, because somebody else has so ordered it."[132]

In 1547, almost a century after the Capture, the patriarch's payment to the sultan had risen to 3,000 gold pieces, while that of Mt. Athos amounted to 4,000 gold pieces.[133] The Turks, aided and abetted by ambitious and avaricious Christians, were draining the life-blood of the patriarchate. According to Gerlach's estimate in 1576, it cost the patriarch merely to remain on good terms with those in power a total of 10,000– 12,000 gold pieces each year, plus 4,000 which was a fixed annual distraint by the sultan.[134] Thus the patriarchal debt never stopped mounting, and the economic outlook of the patriarchate remained dismal.[135]

The economic situation of the Oecumenical Patriarchate, which also had its counterpart in the other Orthodox patriarchates, forced the patriarchs, besides the "dues" (ziteiai) they collected from the predominantly Greek-speaking lands[136] or from Greek communities abroad like Venice,[137] to dispatch patriarchal emissaries, whether high prelates or humble clerics, to other Orthodox countries (mainly the Duchy of Moscow and the principalities of Walachia and Moldavia), for assistance. There are so many instances on record of missions of this kind that they cannot be enumerated here.[138] But the missions were successful despite the general poverty of Christian populations. In some places many priests were unable to support themselves from the donations of their flock and held other jobs as well.[139]

The Church also faced external dangers which seemed likely to subvert not only her mission but her existence. These consisted in sporadic outbursts of hostility on the part of the conquerors. Twice, for example, during the patriarchates of Theoleptos I in 1519 and Jeremiah I in 1539, it would seem that the sultans Selim I (1512–1520) and Suleiman I (1520–1566) embarked on policies of forcible conversion to Islam. These events and the private intentions of the sultans remain largely hidden from us. In the past they have been presented as definite, if isolated and unconnected, occurrences, on the basis of contemporary accounts actually describing a single event or giving secondhand impressions of events as seen by others. However, whether or not the individual incidents do in fact add up to a general policy of forcible conversion can only be determined within the wider context of what is known about secret Turkish diplomacy and the economic crisis that began to paralyze the Ottoman Empire.

Was it really the calculated policy of the sultans to convert to Islam all the Orthodox Christians of this empire, or merely to cow them, to seize some of their great churches for the Porte, and to extort money from them? If forcible conversion was indeed their aim, we may well ask why they stopped short of implementing such a policy upon the patriarchs' protestations that the Porte was bound by treaty to the terms of capitulation and that Mohammed II had granted Gennadius certain privileges including freedom of worship for his flock.[140]

Towards the end of the reign of Suleiman I the advocate of the forcible conversion of Christians and of the expulsion of Jews from the empire was not the sultan, who rather appeared in the role of protector of Christians and Jews, but the Grand Vizier Roustem Pasha.[141] Christians managed to ward off a similar crisis under Murad III (1574–1595) by the payment of money and the intervention of foreign powers.[142]

What all this signifies, it seems to me, is that the sultan's policy was one of intimidating and fleecing Christians and appropriating some of their sacred establishments, but no more than that. It is an interpretation which seems strengthened by consideration of two events: first, the attempt of Selim II to pull down the patriarchal church and erect a mosque in its place (which was thwarted by the offer of considerable "gifts" of money);[143] and second, the seizure in 1568 of the land and property of monasteries on Mt. Athos and throughout the entire empire[144] on the pretext of collecting arrears of tax owed to the Porte.[145]

In 1569, before the naval battle of Naupactus (1571), Selim II again employed his policy of intimidation to the detriment of the Orthodox communities of those two bastions of Hellenism, Serrai and Thessalonica. Some of the churches in these cities he seized;[146] from others, for example St. Menas, Ypomnescon, and St. Angeli (the present-day St. George), he stripped columns to be used in the construction of Turkish buildings.[147]

On the whole, we may say that the religious tenacity of Christians was imperilled throughout the sixteenth century by occasional outbursts of bigotry, provocation, and persecution by the Turkish sultans. Varying in intensity from place to place and time to time, they invariably erupted as sudden and savage bouts of violence in which churches and monasteries were either confiscated or destroyed and property violated. They culminated, around 1540, in specific bans which were placed on the erection of new churches and the renovation of old ones.[148] But it is impossible to catalogue the innumerable disabilities of the Christian Church.[149]

Orthodox Christians were never as free to worship as many West European historians believe. Even during the pre-Ottoman Arab era (622 to 1516–1517), irregularities were by no means unknown.[150] On the other hand, it is equally true that in Constantinople itself many churches functioned unmolested. In 1547 there were sixty-seven in the City and ten in Galata,[151] and people then were in no doubt that Mohammed II had issued to Patriarch Gennadius a document conferring privileges on them. On the occasion of a great feast Christians were free to circulate in the streets and to attend Mass each day and night without let or hindrance. During the first week of Lent—and on feast-days as well—Christians commonly anathematized the Turk as "infidel" and "damned." To be sure, the malediction was pronounced only inside their churches,[152] but the Turks knew what went on without lifting a finger to prevent it.[153]

Things were sometimes different, however, outside the capital, where the religious liberty of Christians depended so much on the volatile dispositions of the local Turkish population and officials. For instance, although the ringing of church bells was forbidden (except for wooden bells),[154] the prohibition was enforced in some places and not in others.[155]

In general, the finest churches were forcibly confiscated and converted into mosques immediately after the Capture or progressively over the years. Christians were left with the smallest and poorest of buildings, in which they had to say Mass secretly and silently. If these churches were ever laid low by earthquake or fire, they could not be rebuilt. For this a special dispensation was needed that often only money could buy. In many places, Christians could not even read the Bible except at grave personal risk.[156] This accounted for the occasional appeals that they made direct to the sultan for permission to read the Bible, if only in muted tones and in the privacy of their own homes and cells, without fear of reprisal by Moslem fanatics.[157] More than once, Moslem mobs actually forced the transfer of a metropolitan seat.[158] The conversion of a Moslem to Christianity was, of course, an impossible occurrence: so heinous was the crime that mere accusation without proof was usually enough to lead to a person's summary execution.[159]

Thus we may conclude that religious "privileges" were often violated, that they were sometimes even totally abolished at the whim of a particular sultan, his official dignitaries, or local functionaries (such as pashas, cadis, and spahis). Similarly well authenticated are the collaboration and interference of powerful Greeks in the City, such as Michael Cantacuzenus, whose meddling in the internal affairs of the Church aimed at securing the appointments of metropolitans, bishops, priests, and the like, and even the enthronement or dethronement of patriarchs.[160] Gerlach comments that in 1577 the members of the bench of the patriarchal court[161] were no more than "*judices personati* or puppets" manipulated by Cantacuzenus.[162]

This situation particularly affected the morale of the clergy. Since illiteracy, crudity, and cupidity were rampant among the higher clergy, they were multiplied among the lower clergy.[163] There was little change for centuries, least of all in remote districts.[164] On the other hand, decent men, scholars, inspired and able clergymen were never wholly absent; their morale and zeal continually lifted the spirits of the people. The Protestant pastor Gerlach, despite the disdain which he ordinarily manifested towards the Orthodox clergy, in 1575 felt obliged to remark on the scholarship of men like the Metropolitan Arsenios of Tyrnavos, the Metropolitan Damascenos of Naupactus and Arta, and the priest-monk Matthew, who was renowned for his Sunday sermons during the September fasting period.[165]

26. The Patriarch of Constantinople. From Salomon Schweigger, *Ein newe Reyssbeschreibung aus Teutschland nach Constantinopel und Jerusalem*, Nuremberg, 1608.

It was inevitable that the confrontation in space and time between the opposing religious camps, Moslem and Christian, should generate ideological exchange. Converts to Islam became carriers of a whole complex of ideas, pagan as well as Christian, that could not easily be eradicated. Precisely what did this exchange consist of? A great deal of research needs to be done on the subject, perhaps with scant hope because the available tools are so few.[166] At least Frederick Hasluck has made a commendable start with his *Christianity and Islam under the Sultans*. But so many Moslem relics in Greece and other Balkan countries (with the partial exception of Yugoslavia), have been destroyed since the revolution of 1821 that research of this kind has been seriously hampered where it has not actually been condemned as ideologically harmful.[167] Nevertheless, the conversion of Christians to Islam unquestionably helps explain many of the distinctive beliefs of the two peoples,[168] their superstitions, their various prophecies,[169] their worship of saints (especially St. George,[170] St. John,[171] and St. Anthony),[172] their rituals (such as the acts of consecration[173] and aspersion of holy water),[174] and their innumerable feasts.[175] An exploration of two areas in particular—public feasts and springs dedicated to saints—could well produce some interesting discoveries.

Certain popular beliefs of the Greeks, which were heterodox in Islamic society not only because they were Christian but because they were to an extent derivative of ancient idolatry, tended to have a common currency among the two peoples, especially in Asia Minor, where for centuries the interchange of religious ideas, rituals, customs, and manners was constant. In times of peace, the chasm between Christian and Moslem seemed somehow wonderfully bridged over. Public feasts and religious rituals assumed an identical pattern in many places, such that it seems impossible to deny that they had a common origin. The influence of one people upon the other is plain, however difficult it is to discern the direction of that influence.[176]

Prerequisite to any understanding of the role and jurisdiction of the patriarch and his ecclesiastical nobility among the Orthodox raias of the Ottoman Empire is the realization that Christians looked up to their leader with trust, veneration, and awe. Attired simply in the usual monastic gown, with a felt crown on which was sewn a cruciform of wide gold ribbon, the patriarch lived modestly in his own ecclesiastical province on a yearly income which, in the middle of the sixteenth century, amounted to two hundred ducats. This was collected from the churches within his own provincial jurisdiction and provided the wherewithal for his clothes, sustenance, and books.[177] Every five years he paid a visit to the outlying ecclesiastical provinces.[178] A characteristic of the Orthodox Church which so often impressed foreigners was the fact that monks in the patriarchal household addressed their superior with respect but without timidity or constraint.[179]

The prestige which the patriarchal office enjoyed under Turkish rule is of course explicable in terms of the privileges that were granted the patriarch immediately after the Capture. According to these, the Turks considered him *millet başı* (leader of a non-Moslem ecclesiastical community, or *millet*). To Greeks he was their ethnarch—the supreme spiritual and political head of Orthodox Christianity. "Religion" and "nation" were still inalienable concepts in Islam, expressed by the single word *millet*.[180]

Since the patriarch was an ethnarch, the authority conferred upon him in former times by late Roman law in all those matters of civil jurisdiction which touched directly or indirectly on the religious life was obviously not only preserved but extended. He was no longer merely the supreme spiritual and political leader of Orthodoxy but also the protector of all Christians and arbiter in all matters not falling specifically within the jurisdiction of the Porte. Marriages, divorces, and devises, as well as a multitude of other concerns, such as petty theft and other offenses,[181] all came within his purview. Whereas previously the Byzantine patriarchs had possessed only spiritual and ecclesiastical authority, the patriarch in Ottoman times was very much a secular figure. This change epitomized the beginning of a new constitution of the Church under which the patriarchs of the Ottoman Empire acquired ever greater powers and prestige in relation to their Christian flock. By the same token, the powers of the metropolitan, the *millet başı* so to speak, of the ecclesiastical province, increased commensurately within the region he governed.[182] The metropolis, at least the greater ones if not all, became a microcosm of the patriarchal court, perpetuating all the customary religious observances of old Byzantium. In Thessalonica, for example, a patriarchal dispensation of 1347 which entitled certain ecclesiastical prelates in the metropolis of the city to wear a cross on their crowns remained in force.[183]

In order to discharge their temporal mission, the patriarch and his metropolitans had the authority to impose various penalties in cases of infringement of the law. Imprisonment and exile were among these.[184] The administration of justice rested, first, on divine, sacred, or canon law; second, on Byzantine statutory law based mainly on Constantine Armenopoulos' *Hexabiblos;* third, on patriarchal covenants, codices, decretals, memoranda, encyclicals, or judicial decisions; and fourth, on local custom.[185]

The patriarch was, of course, responsible to the sultan, who, though content not to circumscribe him in the exercise of his higher spiritual authority, considered him answerable for the overall administration of the Church and the general government of his flock.[186]

The increased responsibilities of the Oecumenical Patriarchate upset an ecclesiastical balance of power according to which the Patriarch of Constantinople, though first in honor, had formerly maintained a position of jurisdictional equality with the three other patriarchs of the East—Antioch, Jerusalem, and Alexandria. Now, however, because he resided in the sultan's capital and was considered the supreme head of the Orthodox *millet*, his prerogatives were no longer coterminous with those of the other patriarchs. He was, for example, able to intercede with the dignitaries of the Porte and the sultan himself on behalf of his compeers. Accordingly, the other patriarchs found themselves obliged to accept not only his recommendations but also his actual selections of candidates for ecclesiastical office within their own patriarchal jurisdictions.[187] The Patriarch of Jerusalem was often in Constantinople, and out of this situation arose a common misunderstanding that identified the Oecumenical Patriarchate with the patriarchates as a whole.[188] Not until 1856 did the separate patriarchates finally receive charters guaranteeing their independence.[189]

The jurisdiction of the Oecumenical Patriarchate encompassed the whole of Asia Minor, the Aegean and Ionian islands, the Balkan countries, Walachia, Moldavia, and Russia.[190] Many metropolitan and episcopal sees in Greek lands, however, having been abandoned by Christians, had completely disappeared. This was particularly so in Asia Minor, where whole districts were inhabited by Moslems. Only six bishoprics remained in the metropolitan see of Athens, where formerly there had been ten; and no more than five out of sixteen remained in Herakleia—Rhaedestos, Panidou, Metron and Athyron, Tyroloë, and Myriophyton.[191]

The extensive and unifying jurisdiction of the Oecumenical Patriarch contributed to a sense of spiritual kinship not only among Greeks in the Ottoman Empire but also among their compatriots abroad, particularly those in Venice and her colonies, Cyprus, Crete, and the Ionian Islands.

The Patriarch of Jerusalem, who ministered to the Orthodox of Palestine, was, in terms of the veneration accorded him, second in importance only to the Oecumenical Patriarch himself, because of his proximity to the holy sepulcher. It was the ambition of all Orthodox faithful to visit the holy places and, whoever did so, was invariably raised in his compatriots' esteem and entitled moreover to prefix his surname with the honorific *chatzi* ("pilgrim").[192] The Patriarch of Alexandria, whose residence in Cairo was as imposing as that of his confrere in Constantinople, led the faithful in Egypt and Arabia; while the Patriarch of Antioch, whose seat was in Damascus, ministered to the Orthodox of Syria, Beirut, Tripoli, Aleppo, and the rest of Asia. All the patriarchs paid taxes to the sultan.[193] Throughout the East generally the language of the Mass was Greek, though in Syria and Egypt sermons were preached in Arabic. In Armenia, the sermon was given in the native language.[194]

We must take note here of a phenomenon peculiar to the Oecumenical Patriarchate that arose from the disappearance of the medieval Orthodox states of the Balkans and Asia Minor. Over the years, national conscious- ness among these peoples atrophied. Among the conquered raias everywhere, the sense of being exclusively Christian supervened, blotting out the development of nationalism.[195] Probably the Greek clergy them- selves were the chief authors of this change, since they wished to have done with the perplexity that use of the word "Hellene" so often caused. Its idolatrous connotations had never quite disappeared and the word enjoyed increasing vogue during the fourteenth and fifteenth centuries. Gennadius himself, for instance, recognized two meanings of the word: though considering himself a "child of the Hellenes"[196] in the sense that he spoke Greek, he also declared that he could never call himself a Hellene because the conceptions of the Hellenes (and here, of course, he is referring mainly to religious conceptions) were utterly foreign to his own. If ever anyone asked him what he was, he would say that he was a Christian because he wished to be identified solely by his religious be- liefs.[197]

This heightened awareness of Christendom naturally made the Or- thodox more conscious of their differences with Islam. By the same token, it served both to bind them more closely together and cement their links with Byzantium. Indeed, the uniformity and unanimity of Orthodox opinion under Turkish rule was such as had not existed even when the Byzantine Empire was at its most glorious peak. Accurately observing this, Constantine Paparrhegopoulos chided the spiritual and political leaders of the Greek nation, especially the patriarchs, for not having taken advan- tage of their enormous prestige during the first two dark centuries of Turkish rule in order to hellenize their coreligionists in Serbia, Bulgaria, Albania, and Armenia.[198] Perhaps he does not give the Orthodox Church her proper due. After all, in pursuit of her oecumenical mission and in conformity with her great ecclesiastical tradition, she set out to preserve and propagate Orthodoxy; and more than that, she interested herself continuously in the religious and moral edification of all the peoples of the Balkan peninsula.[199]

Besides the patriarchates and the lesser metropolitan and episcopal sees, other ecclesiastical centers which exerted a considerable influence on the faithful were the monasteries,[200] chief among which were the exten- sive monastic communities of Mt. Athos and Meteora. Situated in mag- nificent natural surroundings, which conduced not only to seclusion but to an uplifting of the spirit, they enjoyed widespread renown. Mt. Athos, seeming to reach into the vaults of heaven, and Meteora, marvellously perched on its towering thrusts of rock, were perfect symbols of the soul's longing for communion with God; and from both places, particularly the former, the spirit of Orthodoxy emanated in all directions. Monks would

set out, in the direction of the western Greek lands of Macedonia and
Epirus especially, plodding serenely towards "martyrdom" or "seclusion"[201] and in the hope of establishing monasteries and inspiring Christians by their teaching and example. In the Pindus, new monasteries were
still being formed after the middle of the seventeenth century.[202]

A plethora of books and articles has been written about Mt. Athos, but
few are distinguished by the extent or accuracy of their information.[203]
The definitive account, particularly for the period of Turkish rule, has
still to be given. It is unlikely to appear until much more systematic use has
been made of the documentary sources relating to this period (which
remain largely inaccessible to the researcher) and until greater efforts are
made to explain the ethos of monastic life and the spiritual turmoil among
monks which characterized it.

The earliest, and in many ways still the most interesting, accounts of Mt.
Athos come to us from Russian pilgrims. In these truth is often lost in
myth, but they describe in detail such things as the physical surroundings
and histories of the monasteries, the extent of monastic land and property
in Chalcidice and the region of Thessalonica, the treasures which these
harbored, the variety of priceless gifts made by Byzantine emperors, holy
relics and miracles, as well as other fascinating matters that evoke the
pietistic atmosphere of the times.[204] The Russian pilgrim Isaiah mentions
that at the end of the fifteenth century almost half the monasteries were
Slavic or Albanian: Docheiariou, Gregoriou, St. Paul, another—close to
St. Paul—which was dedicated to St. John the Theologian (no doubt he is
referring to Dionysiou), Chilandariou (Serbian), Panteleimonos (Russian), Simon Peter (Bulgarian), Karakallou and Philotheou (Albanian).
He does not identify Zographou, Kastamonitou, Xeropotamou and Koutloumousiou, but Lavra, Vatopediou, Pantokratoros, and Stavronikita are
specified as being unquestionably Greek.[205] The information is probably
reliable since it is entirely consistent with what we know about the voluntary migration of conquered Christian peoples within the Ottoman Empire, especially that of Slavic and Albanian (probably northern Albanian)
peasants and monks to northern Greece, Macedonia, and Epirus. Two
documents in the Synaxis (the Sacred Congregation) also seem to confirm
this view. The one, dated 1399, bears only Slavic signatures of members of
the monasteries of Chilandariou and Dionysiou, while the other, dated
1505 (that is, contemporaneous with the pilgrim Isaiah) has eighteen
signatures, of which eleven are Slavic.[206] In other words, there were a
great many Slavic monks in the monasteries of Mt. Athos during the
fifteenth century, particularly after the Capture. In another context we
shall adduce evidence to show that from the beginning of the sixteenth
century certain Greek monks reacted against this Slavic influence.

In addition to the accounts of Russian pilgrims, there are brief but illuminating descriptions by Pierre Belon.[207] He rhapsodized about the natural surroundings of Mt. Athos, noting that he knew of no other place capable of inducing such feelings of solitude.[208]

If a man who went to Mt. Athos to become a monk had any property, this was bestowed upon the monastery.[209] Monks were normally tonsured without having undergone a novitiate, whereupon they were immediately put to work at various pursuits such as farming, shepherding, and milling. Unfortunately, this lack of proper initiation often produced irresolute souls.[210]

Six thousand monks lived in twenty-four ancient monasteries scattered about the place. All the buildings were solidly constructed, with high fortified walls intended to act as a deterrent to pirates, though pirate or Turk rarely went near them.[211]

The monks dressed humbly and worked hard. In the morning each would set out for work with a haversack stuffed with hardtack and a few onions slung over his shoulders. In his hand he might carry a spade, a hoe, or a pruning hook. Some hoed in the vineyards, some cut wood, others built boats. Still others wove wool or went to work as tailors, shoemakers, builders, or carpenters.[212] They made elegant wooden spoons, back-scratchers, goblets, and multicolored inlaid trays—the making of last a craft which survives even today.[213]

The monks rarely ate meat or even fish, certainly not during Lent. The usual meal consisted of a first course of raw onions and garlic, which was ordinarily followed by a main dish of olives and beans, then greens such as rocket and cress.[214] They offered free hospitality to all visitors. Since Orthodox peoples wherever they lived—in the Balkans, Russia, Poland, the Caucasus, or Mingrelia—were of the opinion that the Mt. Athos monks adhered strictly to the monastic rule,[215] they accorded them much more respect than was generally the case with other monks. Others held in particularly high esteem were monks from Sinai, Lebanon, and the deserts of Syria, who often made long visits to Mt. Athos.[216] A capitation tax of three thalers (usually known as the *haraç*) was levied on each monk, who was also required to buy clothes and farming implements from his own money.[217]

The monasteries, like the patriarchate, derived income from a number of different countries, chiefly Russia and Walachia,[218] to which monks known as "travellers" would often be sent to solicit the charity of Christian peoples. Such journeys ordinarily lasted two or three years and were severely condemned by the more zealous religious, who saw in them a perversion of the austere spirit of monachism.[219] When the monks returned they gave their money to the sacristan of each monastery, who settled the community's more pressing financial commitments but always retained a certain amount to pay the expenses of another "traveller."[220]

The hermit monks awakened the particular curiosity and admiration of people all over the world. Living alone in the desert, they spent their lives in silence and contemplation of the divine, subsisting on no more than two or three meals of bread, vegetables, roots, or chestnuts each week. They often saw visions and made prophecies.[221]

Among later foreign travellers who have left us accounts of Mt. Athos, the most reliable is John Covel, who, in 1677, was in fact the first Englishman to visit it under Turkish rule.[222] Covel (upon whom Ricaut relies)[223] describes the larger monasteries and provides a great deal of valuable information on the organization of Mt. Athos, particularly the government and offices of Lavra. According to him, the Oecumenical Patriarch intervened in the internal government of the monasteries only to the extent of making the traditional appointment of the Metropolitan of Hierissos and Mt. Athos, who was suffragan to the Metropolitan of Thessalonica and resided from time to time in Karyai and Siderokapsa.[224] A berat relating to the appointment of the Metropolitan of Mt. Athos in 1482 is still extant.[225]

The superior ecclesiastic was the *Protos,* whose duties included the inspection of eremitic cells scattered all over the Holy Mountain, as well as the settlement, in conclave with elder monks of the cells in the *Protaton* in Karyai, of disagreements arising among monks or among the monasteries. This office ceased to exist at the end of the sixteenth century.[226]

The *Protos* was then replaced by Elders (*hoi gerontes tis Synaxeos*), or Supervisors (*Epistatai*), who represented their monasteries at meetings in the *Protaton.* In this way, a kind of general council or synod emerged—the present-day Synaxis—which looked into all matters of interest to the monastic community as a whole.[227]

The Turkish aga, in the company of two or three other officials, had his seat in Karyai, the more effectively to protect the monasteries from the incursions of other Turks, especially seamen from the Barbary Coast. Each aga (from the corps of *bostancı*) was appointed by the *bostancı başı* as his representative for a period of two years. His salary was a yearly charge upon the monks. The monasteries invited him to their patronal feasts and, besides feeding him and his retinue, presented him with an additional gift of money, which varied in amount according to the individual monastery's economic circumstances.[228]

So far as internal organization was concerned, certain monasteries during the sixteenth century, notably Lavra and Vatopediou, abandoned the cenobitic regimen mainly for reasons of economy and reverted instead to the loose eremitic system or one which attempted to combine the two. This trend was reinforced under Patriarch Jeremiah II, and it seems that most monasteries followed suit[229] despite the objections of certain ascetics and their efforts to restore the former monastic constitutions.[230]

Some attempts were made to justify this sort of deviation from the strict rule laid down by St. Athanasius. There is this extract, for example, from a statute of the monastery of Lavra dating from the beginning of the eighteenth century:

We shall scarcely be forgiven today (while atheism and the barbarian's sword flourish) for caring not at all about these traditions, as though they were unnecessary to the present circumstances in which the Bible of Grace is being abused and trampled upon and so obviously contradicted by those who are unfaithful. We must preserve the law and order of piety and holiness and not allow the confusion of plunderers outside to move us to abandon them, for then neither rules nor the customs of our fathers will save us. At the same time, we must preserve the security which we enjoy today, if necessary neglecting those things which, while being valuable doctrines and experiments from the past, are not all that relevant to our present predicament.[231]

All monasteries, not only those on Mt. Athos, felt this need for security during the early years of Turkish domination. Otherwise their rights might be violated by neighboring Turkish spahis, or by pirates and robbers,[232] and their strength dissipated by squabbles over property boundaries and so on. In fact, many monasteries did fall into ruins, or into debt and poverty;[233] and they were dealt a particularly heavy blow in 1568 by the state appropriation of all monastic land and property. In a letter of credence of that year, which the monk Daniel Kastrisios as a mendicant carried with him to Western Europe on behalf of the monastery of Iberon, Patriarch Timotheos spoke of its "unbearable" debts and liabilities, to which a further "great loss" had just been added in the previous year when the Turks accused them of supplying food to the Franks.[234]

Greeks abroad helped as best they could.[235] Also, many Orthodox rulers, or simply pious citizens, in places like Russia, Walachia, and Moldavia often sent money to alleviate the distress of the monasteries and help pay their bills. Besides money, they sent votive offerings, donations of embroidered palliums, or printed theological books (fabricated in the presses of Rumanian monasteries or in cities like Jassy, Bucharest, Rymnic, Tîrgoviște, and Snagov). Some became the patrons of certain monasteries or undertook the renovation of individual buildings. In all these ways, people abroad tried to keep in spiritual contact with the monasteries,[236] the relations between Mt. Athos and the Rumanian monasteries being especially close. Many monks from Mt. Athos went to Moldavia and Walachia, while many Rumanians entered various monasteries on the Holy Mountain.[237]

The Phanariots, who in 1711 succeeded the Vlachs and Moldavians as rulers in the Danubian principalities, were not as generous, since they lacked both the wealth and power of their predecessors.[238] Nevertheless, the monasteries of Mt. Athos, as well as other ecclesiastical establishments (for instance, the monasteries of Meteora and the patriarchate of Jerusalem) continued to benefit from donations of land and property by the rulers and people of Walachia and Moldavia. When these countries finally won their independence, the vast tracts of ecclesiastical real estate caused serious problems.

Despite accumulated assets and funds from abroad, the economic condition of the monasteries of Mt. Athos steadily deteriorated under excessive taxes and liabilities, until by 1600 they had incurred a huge debt.[239]

Their situation deteriorated even further between the time of the Cretan war (1645–1669)[240] and the middle of the following century, when the Greek world finally began to stir economically, politically, and intellectually. This revival, which coincided with a renewed outpouring of generosity on the part of the rulers of Walachia and Moldavia, contributed directly to an economic and intellectual recovery on Mt. Athos. This resulted in a spurt of construction that persisted until the eve of the revolution of 1821. The new buildings were solidly constructed in brick or hewn stone and included cloisters and cells.[241] A great storm on 2 September 1820, which caused much damage, provided further incentive to build.[242]

Throughout the eighteenth century and at the beginning of the nineteenth century, especially between 1784 and 1813, eight of the smaller monasteries on Mt. Athos reverted to the cenobitic regimen—Xenophontos, Esphigmenou, Simon Peter, Rossico, Dionysiou, Karakallou, Zographou, and Koutloumousiou.[243]

Commenting on the intellectual life at Mt. Athos, Belon wrote that there were once many and diverse manuscripts there, but that in his time these were confined mainly to theological works.[244] In each monastery, he went on, only two or three monks knew how to read,[245] and this was because none but theological works could be read, at least officially, except on pain of excommunication. Philosophy and poetry were proscribed[246]—by which he meant that the hostility towards philosophy and the absence of a spirit of skepticism in the Church that had dogged Orthodoxy since the time of the Hesychast controversy were still prevalent.

Yet there were many clergy and hierarchs on Mt. Athos who were not without scholarship.[247] Both the variety and richness of musical manuscripts and the large number of precentors and musicians there attest to the persistence of Byzantine musical traditions.[248] It is no exaggeration to say, as Georgirenes, Bishop of Samos, observed, that the Holy Mountain during the period of Turkish rule was the "Great Academy of Orthodox Monachism."[249] If it was not so much a teaching institution, it still remained a repository and symbol of learning. Despite the illiteracy of many monks, their religious fanaticism, and their mercenary excursions abroad, they were responsible, by their preaching, for keeping the faithful within the Orthodox fold. For example, as Roman Catholic priests in the Cyclades knew only too well, the main obstacle to conversion in the islands was the yearly peregrination during Lent of monks from the Holy Mountain, who went around confessing the inhabitants and giving them communion, while simultaneously fomenting disaffection towards the priests of the Roman Church.[250]

Throughout the entire Turkish occupation, the monasteries of Meteora, Thessaly, Southwestern Macedonia, Epirus, and the whole of western Greece were as assiduous as those of Mt. Athos in upholding Orthodoxy. Unfortunately, however, there are considerable gaps in our knowledge about them. Many codices and isolated documents were lost during the early centuries of Turkish rule, while a large amount of material in the archives of the metropolis of Trikkala still remains unpublished. A detailed and systematic history of the monasteries of the region consequently cannot yet be written.[251]

Meteora was Orthodoxy's second Holy Mountain. The monastery of Doupiani, or Meteorou as it is sometimes called, was the seat of the *Protos* in the same way that Karyai was the *protaton* of Mt. Athos,[252] except that in Meteorou he was called abbot (*kathigoumenos*).[253]

27. A Greek priest with Europeans, about 1477. From Ioannis Kallitsounakis, "Ἡ διέλευσις τοῦ πηριυγητοῦ *Arnold von Harff* δι' Ἑλλάδος κατὰ τὸ 1497," ΕΕΒΣ, 23 (1953), 256.

After the conquest of Thessaly by Bayezid I in 1393, relative peace returned to the region, and ecclesiastical authority, such as that of Ioasaph, Metropolitan of Larissa, and other bishops was re-established. In 1401 the Greco-Serbian monk Ioasaph, formerly John Uroš Palaeologus, ruler of western Thessaly, who had taken refuge on Mt. Athos (where he appeared in the monastery of Vatopediou on 17 October 1394), returned as the "father of Meteorou" to the abbacy of that monastery.[254] He died on the same rock on 24 February 1423, and was buried beside his spiritual father, St. Athanasius himself. There is a wonderful story of this king-become-monk, who lived a life of saintliness after the example of St. Athanasius and became the second founder of the monastery of the Metamorphosis. Indeed, popular legend wove many myths around the persons of these two ascetics.[255]

In fact, we do not know if Ioasaph contributed anything to the development and improvement of the monastic state or to the amelioration of the lot of the enslaved people of Thessaly. What evidence we have points to the impressive figure of Larissis Bessarion II (d. 1540) as the founder in 1522 of the large monastery of the Metamorphosis (of Douscou) and the builder of the bridge across the Aspropotamos and other bridges and roads in Thessaly. His fame was widespread throughout western Greece and southeastern Epirus.[256] And it was at this time that the other major monasteries of Meteora were built and monastic life regulated. Thus it would appear that Bessarion made a positive contribution to the monachist institution, the revival of religious feeling, and to the welfare and rehabilitation of the persecuted mountain inhabitants of Thessaly.[257] The evidence for this, admittedly, is inconclusive,[258] but it cannot strain our credulity to imagine that this distinguished hierarch did his utmost to save Christians from the tempest that raged, to establish concord among them, and to save the weak from apostasy. The fact that the Thessalians declared him a saint and cherished him more than any other local saint would seem proof of his popular appeal and influence.[259]

Despite quarrels among the monks[260] and the decline and dissolution of the smaller and poorer monasteries,[261] two brothers from Ioannina, Nectarius and Theophanes Apsarades (or Apsarates) came to Meteora, went up on the rock or monolith of the former monastery of Barlaam, which had been uninhabited for many years, and there in 1542 on the site of the earlier ruins built the cenobitic monastery of St. Panton,[262] which became notable for the austerity of its rule. Two more brothers from Ioannina, Ioasaph and Maximos, built the monastery of Rousanou, possibly in 1545. Their will, which survives in the original, is virtually a replica of that left by the Apsarades brothers from the monastery of Barlaam and contains essentially the same instructions. The constitution of Barlaam was clearly a model for that of the monastery of Rousanou.[263] These two

28. St. Bessarion of Larissa. From N. I. Giannopoulos, "'Ο "Αγιος Βησσαρίων,"
in 'Επετηρὶς Παρνασσοῦ, 7 (1903), opp. p. 224.

monasteries, especially the former, were responsible for the development
of close ties between Meteora and Epirus—ties which remained strong
until very recent times.[264]

Meteora, and very likely the other monasteries of Thessaly as well,
became the center of a definite and not inconsequential movement, some
signs of which were the construction and renovation of churches, chapels,
and the like.[265] The intellectual[266] and artistic[267] ramifications of this
movement, however, are still not fully understood.

The sixteenth and seventeenth centuries were the most trying in the
history of the Orthodox Church after the Capture. Christians, lay and
clergy alike, were impatient for immediate succor, for the direct intervention of God. As Matthew, Bishop of Myreon in southern Asia Minor,
wrote in his *Lament* at the beginning of the seventeenth century:

For our imperfections, Lord, thou didst visit terrible afflictions upon us and
   deliver us into the hands of our enemies; but it was good to test us thus as gold is
   softened in fire before it purifies and hardens.
But pray have pity on us now who are only Thine and acknowledge none other
   as Lord.
How canst Thou bear, Lord, to see us as slaves? Is Thy wrath unrelenting and dost
   Thou regard us as slaves?
How canst Thou bear, Lord, to watch holy monasteries and beautiful churches
   with their sacred images smashed to the last stone of their foundations?
O, soul of charity, I think that Thou dost slumber, no longer having us in mind.
We drown in a sea of slavery and still Thy blessing of freedom is withheld.
Awake, arise. . . .[268]

Not only the Moslems but also Roman Catholics gloated that the Orthodox were merely paying for their shortcomings and their sins.[269]

Theologians of the sixteenth century like Pachomios Rousanos became
concerned at the growing irresolution of the people. They attempted to
arrest the progress of apostasy both by preaching and by written pleas
intended to restore the spiritual equanimity of Christians and convince
them that the Christian religion, despite all they heard and saw, was
superior to Islam:[270]

We know what they say: "if your faith were the true one, your enemies would not
have conquered you; nor would they have made you slaves, creatures of misery
and misfortune only to be despised. But because you are evil—your faith, too—
your kingdom was swiftly lost. And do not hold out any hopes that you will find
another kingdom, for your God is feeble. You crucified him and so he disappeared before your very eyes." Let them go on saying this, publicly or privately,
for they do not know that you shall have eternal life.[271]

Such were the numerous polemics written not only against Moslems,
but also against Roman Catholics, and even Protestants.[272]

The particular sort of hunger that characterized these times explains
the great importance then attached to studies of the lives of holy men and
the different modes of attaining Christian virtue. The sermon remained
the classic means of providing solace for slavery and its attendant hardships, which were seen as afflictions that Christians must suffer in the
interests of moral regeneration.[273] Successive collections of sermons appeared. The works of Damascenos Stouditis of Thessalonica, first published in 1528, were especially notable;[274] but these were soon supplemented by the sermons of Alexios Rartouros,[275] Elias Miniatis (1669–
1714), and others.[276] Not until the nineteenth century were these earlier
anthologies eventually superseded by the *Kyriakodromion* ("Sunday Sermons") of Nikephoros Theotokis (1731–1800).[277]

Of course, this cultivation of the sermon during the period of Turkish
rule was based on a centuries-old tradition of Byzantine rhetoric, though

it was also influenced by an analogous trend in the West. The Western influence, particularly as it was transmitted through the seven Ionian islands,[278] finally became predominant.[279]

The sermon was not the only means of stimulating religious zeal among the faithful. In addition, the pious monk with an arresting personality could offer the example of his own holiness and asceticism, which he strove to model on the traditions of early Christianity. Some of these men, as missionaries of nationalism, were true precursors of Kosmas the Aetolian in the eighteenth century. The holy men would seek out hermitages and perhaps establish a monastic cloister on some remote mountain where the seclusion and majesty of the natural surroundings conduced to metaphysical contemplation.

It would be useful if we could know the activities of the monks, their relations with one another, and the extent to which their fame spread and influenced others, to say nothing of their artistic attainments. We would then come closer to a real understanding of popular tradition, popular psychology, and the prevailing ethos of the times. At least we do know that places like Vermion, Olympus, Kissavos (Ossa), and western Macedonia in the northern parts of Greece were bastions of Orthodox Hellenism. It is in such places that we shall find and hope to preserve those Christian monuments which were as much a part of the movement of religious asceticism as they were of the historical process of Hellenism itself.

Around Veroia in the district of Vermion a vigorous monastic life had persisted from Byzantine times.[280] Probably some time during the fifteenth century a hermit named Anthony left the monastery of Timiou Prodromou and, like another saintly Anthony, lived for fifty years in a cavern in the mountainous wilderness nearby, sustained by nothing more than legumes and his own powerful will. His example led other monks, after his death, to found a cloister named after him, where they lived as he had lived. In Veroia, a church was built which was named after him.[281] The monk Theophanes from the monastery of Docheiariou and his nephew eventually came to the cloister on the mountain and founded the monastery of Asomaton in nearby Naousa.[282] Theophanes lived towards the end of the sixteenth century or the beginning of the seventeenth century.[283]

St. Dionysios also went to the district of Veroia from Sthlatena, near Phanarion in Thessaly, and founded the monastery on Olympus which bears his name. The national evangelism of this monk was apparent from the moment he entered the monastery of Philotheou, then dominated by Bulgarian monks, and transformed it into one which was "Roman" (Greek). For this, he came close to being killed by the Bulgarians.[284] Leaving Philotheou, he went to the monastery of Timiou Prodromou in Veroia and there personally took part in the renovation of its central

29. St. Dionysios of Olympus. From the liturgy of St. Dionysios, Patriarchal edition, Constantinople, 1816.

30. St. Nikanor's rock cave, on the bank of the Aliakmon River. Photo by the author, taken in 1962 near Kozane.

church as well as in the complete reorganization of the monks' way of life.[285] Indeed, he was responsible for reinvigorating the monasticism of this entire district.[286] Later, he withdrew to Olympus to found the monastery of the Holy Trinity, where, apart from a brief sojourn in another monastery in the district of Zagora on Pelion, which he also founded, he spent most of the remainder of his life. He kept in continual touch both with this monastery[287] and Timiou Prodromou.[288] Dionysios also established close intellectual rapport with the monk Nikanor from Thessalonica, who founded the monastery of Zavorda in western Macedonia.[289] The little church of Litochoro in eastern Macedonia, whose walls are covered with frescoes, probably dates from the period of St. Dionysios and may even have had some links with him.

St. Dionysios journeyed to many towns and villages throughout Macedonia (especially Kastoria, Kitros, and Katerini)[290] and Thessaly (Rapsani and Zagora), building churches wherever he went. Their names are unknown,[291] though in the life of the saint published by the Oecumenical Patriarchate in 1816 he is said to have built the Church of the Prophet Elias and the Metamorphosis of Christ on one of the peaks of Olympus, as well as the Church of St. Lazarus in one of the many caves in the vicinity of the monastery. There he died and was buried.[292]

The monastery of Phlamouriou[293] was built in the second half of the sixteenth century by Symeon, who came from Vathyrreuma in Hagia, between Mavrovouni and Pelion.

The efforts of another zealous holy man, Nikanor (1491–1549),[294] bore fruit in the remote regions of western Macedonia. On a journey from his native Thessalonica to western Macedonia, he stopped at one village after another, preaching like an apostle and exhorting Christians "to observe piety in all strictness." His mission to counteract the apostasy following the Capture was rewarded: "by his sweet precepts and the shining example of his virtuous conduct, he was able to hold many in Christ's faith."[295] This was the saintly monk who built the monastery of the Metamorphosis (1534) on Konivo, or Mt. Kallistraton, on the left bank of the Aliakmon, as mentioned in his biography.[296] In his declining years, he withdrew from the world to lead a hermit's life in a cavern on a huge and inaccessible outcrop which rises sheer from the boiling waters of the Aliakmon. Looking at this cloister from a distance, the casual observer gains the impression that it is suspended in midair halfway up a precipice; he cannot help being overcome as much by feelings of admiration for its occupants as by the sense of dizziness which looking at its precarious situation produces.

According to tradition, the monastery of Zavorda eventually overshadowed the older (possibly twelfth- or thirteenth-century) Byzantine monastery of Panagia near Melentsiko (the present-day Melani), because of the powerful influence exerted by the personality of Nikanor. When it went into decline (though its ruins are still visible today), many of its possessions found their way into Nikanor's new monastery.[297] It is possible that among these possessions were a number of manuscripts, including the full text of Photius' lexicon, whose recent discovery has caused such a stir in the literary world.[298]

Various injunctions to cenobites in Nikanor's will, also recently published, reveal his loyalties: he forbade monks to go outside begging alms without the permission of the fathers, to have close contact with those "of another faith" (Turks) or Roman Catholics, or to have any recourse at all to secular justice ("to notables"), and certainly not to seek it from the Turks. He advised them to turn to the monastery of Christ the Savior in Meteora if they could not find a new superior from among their own number.[299] Thus, there was intellectual exchange among the monasteries of Vermion, Olympus, Pelion, Pindus, and Meteora during the sixteenth century.

Holy men of renown from other parts of Greece included the hermit Gerasimos ("the New") in Cephalonia (1509–1579)[300] and his disciple in Zacynthus, Dionysios, Bishop of Aegina (1546 to 17 December 1622).[301] These two men must have contributed to the moral tenacity of the Orthodox in these islands, which lay under Venetian domination. Despite Venice's official proclivity to remain neutral in affairs of religion, she could not escape her predisposition towards the Roman Church.

Large numbers of holy men, not content merely to seek their own sanctity in seclusion, actively strove to transform their monasteries into centers of education and religious art. Just as in Byzantine times, it is possible to discern distinct schools of painting and craftsmanship. To take one example, Ignatius Agallianos, born about 1492 in the village of Pharanga on Lesbos (a village mentioned as late as 1662), dedicated his life to study, prayer, and the copying of manuscripts. In 1526 he founded two monastic institutions, Myrsiniotissis (for women) and Taxiarchis of Limonos, which were set up at his own expense with the aid of donations from rich and poor alike. When Patriarch Jeremiah II made him a metropolitan in 1531, he organized in the monastery of Limonos a school (one of whose teachers was the Zacynthian scholar Pachomios Rousanos) which radiated cultural vitality. Many clergy and copyists received their training there.[302]

A new era of persecution began in this period, and the sacrifices of "these new Martyrs," as Nicodemus the Hagiorite (1749–1809) said, "have renewed the entire Orthodox faith." It is characteristic of this day and age, he continued, that "what is new becomes old, and what is old becomes by a slow process of unfaithfulness and forgetfulness so aged and decrepit that it almost might never have been: 'now that which decayeth and waxeth old is ready to vanish away [Hebrews 8, 13].' "[303]

Popular interest in some of the early martyrs, St. Demetrius for example, was aroused. It was Demetrius who many times saved Thessalonica, the second city of the Byzantine Empire, from its enemies. His deeds were recounted to every Christian, becoming known in every corner of the Greek world through books describing his miracles. In these, numerous Greeks found hope and support; and naturally, the material of the traditional texts of these miracles was reshaped in order to meet their own particular exigencies. That is, the saint reappeared to the Greeks in contemporary guise and in an environment recognizable to them.[304]

Sometime between 1666 and 1669 an anonymous admirer invoked the saint in these terms:

O great martyr of the Lord Christ, Demetrius, where now are the miracles which you once performed daily here in your own country? Why do you not help us? Why do you not reappear to us?[305] Why, St. Demetrius, do you fail us and abandon us completely? Can you not see the multitude of hardships, temptations and debts that crowd in upon us? Can you not see our shame and disgrace as our enemies trample upon us, the impious jeer at us, the Saracens mock us and everybody laughs at us? Why, therefore, O Saint, do you not sympathize with us your compatriots? Do you not hear our sighs? Do you not see our tears? Do you not care about our misfortunes? Can you not help us by interceding with Christ, the King of Kings, begging Him to liberate us from these evils which afflict us? Why do you not entreat Him to have mercy on us? For our part, we know that we are culpable, that we have been disobedient, contumacious, and ungrateful; but it is only He whom we worship, whom we adore, and whom we respect. Accordingly, holy and great martyr of Christ, Demetrius, we implore you to pray for us and intercede for us, your slaves, that your country may be freed from its sufferings by your direct intervention and that we may be released from temptations, lamentations, hideous sufferings, and debts and all manner of such things; to which end we shall henceforth dedicate our lives to your bidding, extol and praise your most holy name, and remain forever thankful for your saintliness.[306]

The sacrifices of the modern martyrs meant that "the world saw again more Georges, more Demetriuses, and more Theodores,"[307] that Christians relived the persecution of Roman times; that faith deepened and Orthodoxy thrived. "These martyrs are young in years, but old in the tortures they have suffered; in time they are the latest to appear in the evolution of the race, but in fame they are the first."[308]

Though mainly Greek, the "new" martyrs came from many different lands throughout the Balkans. Usually, they were simple folk, monks, peasants, merchants, artisans, who shared a common passion to suffer martyrdom.[309] Some were the victims of Turkish calumny,[310] falsely accused of being traitors to the Turkish state[311] or assassins of Turks,[312] agitators,[313] scoffers at the Moslem religion,[314] converts from Islam to Christianity,[315] and the like.[316] Some, like the ex-Patriarch Gabriel II, were put to death because they converted Moslems to Christianity.[317]

Others, like Argyros (1806) from Sochos in Chalcidice or Christodoulos (1777) from Thessalonica, met a similar fate when they persuaded apostates to return to the Christian fold.[318] There were those who had lost their faith in youth but who still did not hesitate to fling their turbans at the feet of Moslems and defiantly proclaim their true faith.[319] Even the Turkish-speaking Zorzis Giourtzis, who was converted to Islam in his youth, assuaged his conscience by shouting aloud his true faith and stoically enduring subsequent torture until he was finally hanged in 1770.[320] Innumerable stories survive of the steadfastness of Christians in their faith.[321] The Bible served to strengthen their ardor: "Whosoever therefore shall confess me before men, him will I confess also before my Father which is in heaven. But whosoever shall deny me before men, him will I also deny before my Father which is in heaven" (Matthew 10, 32–33).[322]

Such martyrdom was a phenomenon that persisted until almost the middle of the nineteenth century.[323] There were so many martyrs that not a single district was without at least one.[324] "We have even seen babies," Nectarius, Patriarch of Jerusalem, wrote between 1660 and 1669, "bow their heads under the executioner's blade."[325] No fewer than ten holy men with the name of Nicholas are known to have finished their lives as hermits or martyrs under the Turkish occupation.[326] Within the space of nine months in 1794, five new martyrs from different places "blossomed in the ineffable paradise of the Church as red and fragrant roses."[327]

Many were considered saints by the people before being officially canonized and even when not canonized at all. Typically, they were called new martyrs, not because their early lives were notable for Christian virtuousness,[328] but because they died for their faith.

Their deaths inspired religious tenacity and a general spirit of resistance to intolerance, duress, and tyranny. In this sense, the fighters for the faith were also fighters for freedom. The people participated vicariously in their martyrdom. Self-sacrifice encouraged further self-sacrifice.

The virtues displayed and the miracles performed by holy men and new martyrs became known far and wide, and the faithful from everywhere flocked to witness them. The fame of some of these martyrs even overshadowed that of their earlier counterparts. The most widely disseminated narratives "of spiritual benefit" were martyrologies. The physical remains or material relics of martyrs, however minuscule, were greatly coveted by Greeks, who venerated them and kept them in the most sacred of places.[329] From time to time, these would be displayed in order to rekindle faith—or perhaps to encourage the loosening of purse strings. They were also used as liturgical accessories, the better to induce saints to save the peasants from plague and other epidemics, to provide cures for the sick, the mentally infirm, or domestic animals,[330] to give protection from the enemy, to bless the harvest, and save it from the depredations of drought and locust.[331]

For every known holy man and martyr,[332] a legion remained unknown or at least unrecognized both by biographers and the Church's official procedure of canonization. The lives of those remembered were customarily set forth by precentors during the divine service, thus perpetuating both the form and substance of an ancient hagiological tradition.[333] Although the biographies of the saints were mainly concerned with their contribution to religion, the accounts sometimes contained information of a general historical nature, which other contemporary written evidence corroborated. The first anthology of lives of the modern martyrs was compiled by Nicodemus the Hagiorite and included both narratives of the martyrs and hymns to them. Most were written by various scholars and ecclesiastical writers of the sixteenth and seventeenth centuries— Nicholas Malaxos, Theophanes of Thessalonica, George Koressios, Meletios Syrigos, Ioannis Karyophyllis, and others. Some were written by Nicodemus himself or translated by him from the Slavonic.[334] A scholarly edition of these lives along the same systematic lines as those which have been carefully worked out for the earlier hagiographies is very much needed to counteract a succession of slovenly publications that compound the historical and literary difficulties facing researchers.

The iconography of these saints is a field deserving assiduous attention from researchers.[335] More studies of movable icons and frescoes are essential if we are ever fully to understand how deeply the people adored their martyrs.

During this period the Church and its representatives became objects almost of awe;[336] and churches became the true focal points of unity among Christians. Greeks everywhere were gripped by a sense of profound religious conviction through which they accepted constraints on their everyday lives and austerity in their customs. As Patriarch Jeremiah II (1572–94) wrote to the Protestant savant David Hytraeus: "Know this, that even though our race is enslaved it is yet courageous in its piety, which it never ceases to preach."[337]

This religious proclivity of Greeks, this acknowledgment of religion as the source of all inspiration led, as we have seen in the case of Mt. Athos, to the construction of new churches and monasteries and the renovation of old ones, despite the severe sanctions the Turks imposed on such activity. The healthy economic upsurge beginning in the sixteenth century promoted this development. Throughout the sixteenth century, and even more in the seventeenth and eighteenth centuries, churches and monasteries all over Greece were renovated and embellished with frescoes, newly consecrated icons, sacred vessels, books, and the like,[338] especially in Epirus, the Pindus, Olympus,[339] central Hellas (including Athens),[340] and the Peloponnese.

The study of monuments, buildings, and frescoes has only just begun (and unfortunately the ravages of time, weather, illiteracy, and indifference have added to the usual difficulties associated with such study), but a good deal can be set down. In contrast to the relatively large, ordered structure of monasteries, new village churches and often those in cities as well were simple and humble, sometimes having such low doorways that it was necessary to bend down in order to enter. From the outside they looked like barns or stables[341] and could only be identified as churches if they happened to be situated on the periphery of a settlement, outside it, or in the complete isolation of the hills. The faint illumination from cracks in the walls or tiny windows created a melancholy atmosphere that was dispelled only by the flickering glow of candles during worship, which made the images of the saints appear to dance.

The congregation was segregated. Women took their places on the right, in the narthex and above the entrance, or on the open floor to the left,[342] in those parts reserved for women even today.

Greek builders were noted for their proficiency.[343] Naturally, Byzantine styles were prominent (both the basilica and the *stavrepistegos,* or cruciform roof), which testified to the survival of a Christian architectural tradition, though some examples were greatly modified.[344] On the whole, however, from the beginning of the sixteenth century there was a definite tendency to eschew Byzantine models even in those churches and monasteries which remained directly dependent on the Oecumenical Patriarchate. By the seventeenth century Byzantine precedents were almost completely forgotten, one reason for this undoubtedly being that post-Byzantine architecture had failed to evolve new styles. The most usual style in the villages and smaller towns was now the long, narrow basilica divided into one or three (more rarely, two) naves, with an arched or gabled roof made of timber. For monasteries, there was the so-called "Hagiorite" (Mt. Athos) cruciform style, which was distinguished by its five cupolas—a large one in the middle surrounded by four smaller ones over the arms of the cross. The other main characteristics of this style were the niches on the northern and southern sides, the choirs (so named because choristers stood in that part of the church), and the large narthex where certain parts of the liturgy were sung.[345]

Construction at ground level, sometimes in brick, became the traditional procedure, though for reasons of economy walls tended more and more frequently to be made of natural stone mortared with lime, windows decreased in number, occasionally disappearing altogether, and doorheads became lower and lower. External surfaces were decorated only in the most frugal of ways: ceramics were almost completely displaced by plates from Kütachya in Asia Minor or Rhodes, or by marble bas reliefs incorporating geometric or floral designs or the figures of saints. Islamic influences, whether architectural or constructional, were notable for their almost total absence.[346]

Where did the craftsmen who worked on the churches come from? A number probably came from northwestern Macedonia and northern Epirus. We know, for instance, that Bithikouki in Epirus was the home of the master-builder responsible for the expertly integrated nave of the monastery of Philosophou (1691) in the district of Demetsana.[347]

Humble little village churches acquired frescoes sometimes composed by the most eminent painters. Regrettably, West European travellers, clergy or lay, have left very few accounts of this form of art; but such as we have are particularly interesting since they not only express personal opinions but also draw attention to the differing religious conceptions of two separate worlds. To the Jesuit Sauger (at the end of the seventeenth century), for instance, the people of the Aegean had no artistic sense and found delight in the most execrable icons; the icons of famous Cretan painters were dreadful. So far as architecture and sculpture were concerned, Greeks were ignorant of even the first principles of these arts.[348]

Sauger's contemporary, the traveller du Mont, was struck both by the large number of icons and the respect that Greeks had for them; but he considered them inferior to those of Western Europe, which were notable for their meticulous design, colorfulness, and deft chiaroscuro. By comparison, they were masterpieces. Greeks, ever conscious of the Byzantine tradition, could only reply that most Western icons were calculated more to arouse desires of the flesh than elevate the soul.[349]

And indeed there was a vast difference between Western and Byzantine, or post-Byzantine, painting, particularly after the austere and conservative Cretan influence came to predominate in the latter. Western styles were permeated by a naturalism which strove to represent nature in realistic forms; Byzantine styles interpreted nature in abstract ways according to a religious tradition that emphasized spiritual reality and attempted to penetrate to its essence rather than to capture its appearance.[350] Thus, the nakedness of a holy man might even create a sense of "nonflesh," the figure appearing ossified, with eyes, ears, nose and hands painted in larger than natural proportions, or the mouth smaller, and so on. In other words, the normal features of the body were of no more interest to the artist than the rules of perspective and chiaroscuro were in depicting them. Paintings were symbolically representational and redolent of the supernatural. The golden background of icons or the treatment of saints' halos were two of the more obvious examples of such symbolism.[351]

Unlike architecture, painting remained faithful to the dual Byzantine artistic tradition, which comprised the so-called Macedonian and Cretan genres. However, from the end of the fourteenth century and the beginning of the fifteenth century the Macedonian influence lost its inspirational strength and became content with lifeless repetition of the works of great masters: decline and disappearance were swift after the Capture simply because the Byzantine assumptions on which it was based no longer existed. What remained degenerated to the level of an inexpert, almost folk, art.[352] The style which became predominant after the Capture is known as Cretan, though it first appeared in Constantinople at the end of the thirteenth century. It is characterized by the application of the technique used in the movable icon to fresco painting in the conservative manner of monks and anti-Unionists, who were intensely attached to the older styles of Orthodox painting.[353]

The Cretan genre spread from Constantinople to those two other centers of Hellenic civilization which had so often maintained political and cultural links with the capital—Thessalonica and Mistra. One of its most beautiful examples, dating from the third quarter of the fourteenth century, is still to be seen in Peribleptos at Mistra and in the later Pantanassa there. From Thessalonica the style spread further in Macedonia and the Balkan countries to the north; and from Mistra it radiated to the rest of the Peloponnese and Greece. From Mistra it also spread to Crete, appearing first at Margarites in 1383 and then at Sclaverochori towards the middle of the fifteenth century. A typical exponent of the style was the painter Xenos Digenis from Mouchlion in Arcadia, who worked in churches in Crete during the second half of the fifteenth century, and later in Aetolia and Epirus.[354] Refugee painters from Constantinople (after 1453) and Mistra (after (1461) reinforced this conservative artistic tradition in Crete so that it became firmly entrenched;[355] and under favorable political and intellectual conditions it continued to develop until, by the beginning of the sixteenth century, it had attained coherence, fully justifying the label of Cretan that modern art historians conventionally attach to it.

It is impossible, however, to discern the stages in the evolution of the style from the middle of the fifteenth century to the beginning of the sixteenth century, mainly because we do not know the dates of monuments in this period. In fact, it is through the great Cretan painters who flourished after 1525 that the elements of the style, by then fully developed, are known to us. From that time the Cretan school exerted its greatest influence through its severe monastic technique. The decline and eventual demise of the school during the course of the seventeenth century was largely due to the intrusion of Western influences.[356]

Two of the most eminent Cretan painters of the sixteenth century were

Theophanes, who perfected the technique of fresco painting, and Damascenos, whose movable icons represented the ultimate in this form of art. The first (1527), so far as is known, of Theophanes' frescoes are to be seen in St. Nicholas of Anapaphsas at Meteora; in the central church of the monastery of Lavra at Mt. Athos (1535) is his most representative work; other frescoes are in the refectory of Lavra (though there is some dispute as to whether Theophanes was in fact the artist responsible for this particular work) and in the central church of the monastery of Stavroniketa (1546). The chief sources of his iconographical inspiration were Palaeologian subjects, representations of which he saw on Mt. Athos, especially the wonderful frescoes of Manuel Panselinos (early fourteenth century) in the Church of the Protaton in Karyai.[357] It is also possible to detect in Theophanes' and Damascenos' work the first definite influences of the great artists of the Italian Renaissance, whose works were becoming known in the East through the spread of chalcography.[358]

An interesting piece of information about Theophanes and his two children, Symeon and Neophytos, has recently been brought to light from the archives of the monastery of Lavra. Here it is recorded that Theophanes appeared before the Synaxis (the Sacred Congregation) in 1536, 1540, 1541, and 1544, when he purchased life properties "for three brotherhoods, two being for his children Symeon and Niphos."[359] In 1552, "Neophytos, son of Theophanes the painter" was working in the monastery of Lavra, which in that year agreed "that he should form one brotherhood" and thereby "take over the grain of the individual members of the order."[360]

The works of Theophanes have excited the admiration both of his contemporaries and those who came after him. His originality, particularly evident in his works in the central church and refectory of Lavra, has been acclaimed; indeed his work is generally hailed as the finest example of the Cretan style.[361] There were also other painters like the Cretan Zorzis (whose work adorns the central church of the monastery of Dionysios), Makarios (who in 1615 completed the frescoes in Dionysios' Chapel of Theotokos),[362] and Frangos Katelanos from Thebes, all of whom attempted to free themselves completely from Theophanes' influence. Katelanos' artistry is to be seen in the Chapel of St. Nicholas in Lavra (1560); and the unsigned decoration of the monastery of Barlaam, which was finished in 1548, is generally attributed to him. In contrast with Theophanes' spare style, Katelanos' scenes tend to be embellished with excessive detail. Particularly in his larger compositions, he owed much to Italian influences.[363]

When Cretan art declined in the seventeenth century it took on a debased or folk character. While seventeenth-century painters in central

Hellas and the Peloponnese continued to emulate the Cretan school, particularly Theophanes, artists in Crete itself turned from frescoes to icons.[364]

The development of fresco painting in the other islands during the seventeenth century has still to be studied in a systematic way. However, not only was the influence of the Cretan school felt[365] but the painters of Crete enjoyed widespread renown.[366]

A number of artistic centers flourished in Epirus (Kapesovo, Kalarites, Chionades),[367] western Macedonia, Thessaly, and other places, where certain forms of folk art developed along with the dominant Cretan genre. We know little about these forms or to what extent they became familiar outside their locale.[368] However, painting was well developed and well-known throughout northern Greece in such Vlach centers as Linotopi[369] and Samarina in the Pindus. Painters from Samarina periodically appeared in the Peloponnese until the very end of the nineteenth century.[370]

Our knowledge of fresco painting in Asia Minor (except that of Trebizond) leaves much to be desired. All that can really be said is that it apparently did not depart from traditional patterns.[371]

Cretan art underwent profound change during the course of the eighteenth century. Folk forms were increasingly in evidence and eventually supplanted all others. The figures and subjects of fresco painting drew not so much on traditional sources of inspiration as on the ordinary experiences of contemporary life.[372]

Unlike the fresco painting of the Cretan school, which had fully evolved by the beginning of the sixteenth century, the artistic development of the movable icon was much slower. Iconographers like Mavrocordato clung to the Palaeologian tradition, though others fell more and more under the aesthetic, as well as technical, influences of the Cretan school.[373]

The work of a number of Greek refugee artists in Ragusa (Dubrovnik), particularly Cretans such as Andreas Ritsos and his son Nicholas (late fifteenth and early sixteenth centuries), also conformed in general with the academic character of Palaeologian art. Another Cretan, Angelos Bizamanos (Bizamanus) worked in the same city between 1518 and 1519, and his work, while remaining faithful to the Byzantine style, revealed definite early Renaissance influences in its backgrounds.[374]

Indeed Western influences were pervasive. Venice was the show place of Western civilization, and it was inevitable that Greeks living there, as well as the seamen, merchants, scholars, and artists who came and went, should fall under her cultural influence. Thus, though Damascenos' iconography unquestionably belonged to the mainstream of the Macedonian school of Palaeologian art, it became impregnated with strong Western influences during the period 1579-1584, when he lived in Venice.

With his constant experimentation and striving to perfect his art, Damascenos' works took on a certain eclectic quality, but at the same time they never entirely lost the austere character of older, traditional styles.[375]

Italian influence was most marked and most disruptive of Orthodox, Byzantine traditions among the later painters of movable icons. Nowhere was this influence more overt than in the icons of the Greek Community in Venice,[376] though none of the new painters of the Cretan school managed to escape it completely. This influence grew stronger in the seventeenth century, as the works of the priest Tzanes[377] and those of Poulakis attest. By the eighteenth century it had become dominant in the works of Tzancarolas (a Corfiot monk), Kallerges, and Nomicos. In the Seven Islands the painter Doxaras used oils exclusively, signifying, of course, the obliteration of Orthodoxy's influence and the complete triumph of the Italian style. His successors, Doxaras *fils,* Koutouzis (1741–1813), and Kantounis (1768–1834), whose works span the Greek Revolution of 1821, showed no awareness at all of the Orthodox, Byzantine tradition in painting. A few memories of the older, traditional styles persisted in folk adaptations that lingered on in continental Greece; but in the Seven Islands the Italian method of painting in oils was the only one practiced.[378]

Examples of movable icons created by post-Byzantine artists, such as Emmanuel Lambardos and Constantine Tzanes, who were both indebted to the Italian style, have been discovered in and around Ragusa. Their presence there is attributable to two factors: a legitimate commerce in icons conducted in the ships of this maritime republic between Greek artists in the Seven Islands and wealthy inhabitants of Ragusa who commissioned the icons; and illicit plunder of Turkish-controlled parts of Greece by the skippers of these same ships. However, the cultural influence of Orthodoxy on Roman Catholic Ragusa represented by these icons was obviously minimal and of brief duration.[379] It was insignificant in comparison with that which had occurred in Byzantine times or with that under Turkish rule, certainly in its early stages, Serbia and present-day Serbian Macedonia.

Then, as in the sixteenth century, Greek artists who had demonstrated their talents in Mt. Athos, Kastoria, and elsewhere, were at work in the churches of Prilep and its environs. It was also a Greek who in 1568 painted the frescoes of the Monastery of the Madonna at Studenica. Greeks working in the Serbian churches of Srem went there from Walachia and Moldavia, while others, probably from Mt. Athos, adorned the monastery of Krušedol on Fruska Gora (sixteenth century). Other Greeks served as mentors of well-known Serbian artists like Georgije Mitrofanović (who in 1621 completed the altar of Chilandariou) and the priest Danilo (who in 1664 painted the frescoes of the Chapel of St. Nicholas in the same monastery, as well as various others).[380] Moreover, the iconography of Serbian painters and goldsmiths from the sixteenth century was modelled on the gravures of Bozidar Vukovič and other Serbian printers whose religious books circulated extensively throughout Slavic lands; and Vukovič in 1520 had been an avid collector of icons created in the Byzantine or post-Byzantine tradition by Greek artists working in Crete and Venice.[381]

The re-establishment of the patriarchate of Pec in 1557 inaugurated a flourishing period of Serbian painting that was essentially "derivative of Byzantine iconography, which by various means penetrated Serbian civilization during the Ottoman period and assumed a position of special importance in the history of art of the Serbs and other Yugoslav peoples."[382]

The supremacy of Greek painting at this time was ensured by the strong reassertion of the Byzantine tradition. The Greek icon became paramount not only in Serbia and the other countries of the Balkan peninsula but also in Russia, the great Orthodox empire to the north.[383]

Also in the sixteenth century the art of ecclesiastical embroidery and decoration of canonicals, especially of those associated with the sacred rites of Christ's burial,[384] achieved similar excellence. Some craftsmen were careful to sign their creations. We know the names of at least ten craftsmen or workshops up to the beginning of the seventeenth century, the most important of them having been established in Constantinople.[385]

During this same period the arts of metalworking (notably goldsmithing and silversmithing) and wood-carving were also highly developed, undoubtedly because of the great variety of social needs they fulfilled.[386] Wood-carving produced probably the most outstanding works of beauty in reredoses, episcopal thrones, crosses, icons, and the like; unfortunately many of these were destroyed by accident or through the negligence of guardians who lacked sufficient aesthetic interest or zeal to preserve them. Few studies of wood-carving have been made, however, and much remains to be learned about its inspirational sources, as well as where, how, and by whom the art was practiced.[387]

6

EDUCATION AFTER THE CAPTURE

Since most scholars and teachers, particularly in the provinces, came from the clergy, the history of education under Turkish rule is inextricably bound up with that of the Church.

As Greek lands fell one after the other before the advance of the conqueror, the most ancient of intellectual centers vanished or decayed. On all sides scholars raised their voices in dismay.[1] Two such men were Ivangos (after 1395)[2] and Andronicus Callistus (after the Capture),[3] who voiced particular concern for youth.

Eight years after the Capture, Patriarch Gennadius pondered the plight of Byzantine intellectual leadership. Some students had died during the siege and assault because they could not bear the prospect of slavery; others had opted for a monastic career since "the epitome of virtue is to end one's life with the peace that comes from God, each one as superbly and faithfully as he could." Indeed, he who followed any other path leading to profane society as it existed after the Capture, would know only a "plenitude of sorrows," in which all opportunity to teach and benefit from both classical knowledge and Christian philosophy would be absent. To youths who had made a similar choice, Gennadius recalled, he had once tried to teach virtue and philosophy through the beautiful medium of Greek in the hope of creating heirs to "wisdom and erudition." But his efforts had been in vain, for his students had been destroyed before they had the chance of attaining any distinction;[4] and as a result schools and academies had had to close their doors.

There is some doubt, however, whether the public elementary schools (*koina scholeia*) did in fact cease to function. Probably not many months went by after Gennadius' election before some families at least from the wealthier strata of society decided that the education of their children could not be neglected. Gennadius himself, formerly founder of a "school of philosophy," was unable to forget his earlier aspirations as a teacher: in the very same year that he became patriarch (1454) he established a "Patriarchal School."

However, the study of philosophy was no longer carried on. As early as the fourteenth century, the predominance of the Hesychast viewpoint meant that the Church had adopted an indifferent, if not proscriptive, attitude towards it. Nor was there likely to be any change in this situation while the conditions of life of the population steadily deteriorated. Scholarios wrote that before the Capture only three or four students had shown any aptitude for Aristotelian philosophy, and they had not been able to give it their undivided attention. "Because of poverty, eternal worry over the necessities of life and the pitiable state of education in our time, learning was a thankless and intimidating task; most young men preferred easier ways to wealth."[5]

The Church's hostility to philosophy was handed down to the clergy and the masses throughout the entire period of Turkish rule.[6]

As cities fell to the armies of the invader, books, the principal means of education, were scattered like people. Many were lost; others were destroyed by the ravages of time and neglect. Ducas, describing the fall of the City, makes this comment:

Innumerable books were dumped into carts and eventually wound up in various Eastern and Western countries. Books by Aristotle, Plato, theological and all kinds of other works, were sold by the dozen for a mere token price. Bibles were sold or discarded after their gold and silver decorations had been removed. Icons were burned; meat was cooked in their flames, and then eaten.

Gennadius, too, groaned over the fate of his books:

Where are the books that we collected for the common needs of the educated? Where are all those long tracts of mine on theology, dialectics, classical philosophy, distinguished for the excellence of both their rhetoric and ideas? Where are the translations and the treatises, all of them the fruit of immense intellectual effort? Some have been destoyed; others, fortunately have found their way to the West. If any still remain in this land, they are doomed to remain unread.[7]

Some of the intellectual treasures not actually destroyed by the conquerors the Byzantines allowed to be lost through indifference and neglect. Indeed some foreigners, Belon for instance, attributed the destruction of manuscripts to nothing more than Eastern indifference and illiteracy,[8] and concluded that the Greeks had become completely degenerate.

In fact, however, there proved to be inexhaustible reserves of manuscripts. For centuries after the Capture, hidden hoards continued to manifest Greek thought to Western intellectuals. At the same time, under

Turkish rule, not only were numerous works of art and other intellectual treasures permanently consigned to oblivion, but close intellectual contact and collaboration between the Greco-Byzantine civilization of the East and the neo-Latin civilization of Western Europe was disrupted. Thus European civilization, instead of emerging as a symmetrical entity based on the fusion of its parts, suffered from a Western cultural hypertrophy. And in the East, Greek education reached such a low point that even the Greek language was threatened with extinction,[9] and the Greek nation gradually lapsed into intellectual torpor. The shame of Greek scholars was apparent: "Who will not agree," lamented Gennadius, "that the Greeks were the most important of all peoples? Who is there, whether he be an Italian or even a barbarian, who does not first refer to the accomplishments of the Greeks? Now, however, it is a disgrace to declare one's origins. Since we are filled with a shame which, to be sure, we deserve, we can only agree with those who say so and indeed by the first, in conscience, to accuse ourselves for the 'deformity' of our race."[10]

Cardinal Bessarion, the so-called Oecumenical Patriarch of the Unionists, also observed that Greece's subjection to "barbarians and lawless men" had led to the disappearance of "the last vestige of wisdom." If hardships continued to multiply at the same rate, he went on, the Orthodox would soon lose their Greek language, their books, whether sacred or profane, even the Bible itself. He wondered what consequences the Capture would have throughout the East, on the Greek peninsula and in the islands, where a noticeable intellectual decline had already set in fifty years earlier in some places and a hundred in others.[11]

It is impossible to gauge with any degree of accuracy the specific levels of education at different places throughout the Turkish Empire. In some parts of Asia Minor, Cappadocia and the Pontus for example, it would appear that the Greek language was constantly disappearing. Popular tradition held that the conquerors cut out the tongues of Greeks.[12]

However, education did not cease entirely. Gennadius' testimony that after the Capture students continued to pursue monastic careers, suggests that various monasteries, perhaps especially at Mt. Athos and Meteora, survived as centers of Byzantine education. Other evidence shows that in the fifteenth and sixteenth centuries certain holy places harbored individual bibliographers and sometimes entire bibliographical workshops.[13] But we are still a long way from any full understanding of the exact contribution which the monasteries made to education during the first century after the Capture.

In the great secular centers of the Ottoman state—Constantinople, Adrianople, Thessalonica, Mistra, and elsewhere—an educational effort, however attenuated, was sustained by individual scholars who remained where they had always lived. It is true that large numbers of Greeks, many of them scholars, fled to Italy after the Capture (among them the Diplovatatzes family trio,[14] Manuel Agallos, M. Iagoupis, N. Trachaniotis, A. Kananos, Michael Chrysoloras Dromachäitis, and others),[15] but some later returned to Constantinople. In 1466 the Italian scholar Francesco Filelfo asked George Trapezountios, who had just arrived from Constantinople, if "the people there, now under barbarian rule for so long, have become barbarians themselves."[16] Of course, that remark was in itself no proof of the absence of intellectual life in Constantinople after the Capture, but unfortunately the perpetual comings and goings of scholars made it impossible to extend such life as there was, particularly when most of them, despite strong feelings of nostalgia, eventually decided that they must remain permanently in Italy, their new and "pure" homeland.[17]

Immediately after the Capture a school for advanced as well as young students functioned in Adrianople under the guidance of two teachers. Nicholas Isidoros, apparently the leader of the Greek community there,[18] followed the students' progress with keen interest. Thessalonica, too, was not devoid of intellectual activity: as early as 1494 its inhabitants had invited the well-known scholar, Ioannis Moschos, to teach in their city.[19] We also learn from Janus Lascaris' visit to the city at the end of the fifteenth century that its scholars were in possession of some remarkable manuscripts.[20] Most scholars and bibliographers fled Mistra when the Peloponnese was conquered in 1461; a few probably remained behind. Various bibliographers, mostly clergy,[21] were to be encountered in the Peloponnese from time to time throughout the entire period of Turkish rule.

Thus, the Byzantine educational tradition, while increasingly weakened, never wholly disappeared, at least in the great centers of Hellenism—Constantinople, Adrianople, Thessalonica, Mistra—or even, perhaps, in a number of the lesser ones. Whether priest,[22] parent, or scholar, there were always teachers ready to impart knowledge to children. Two examples may suffice: D. Raoul Kabakes (Demetrius Ralis Kavakis), who wrote a short history of the Greek nation for his son;[23] and Hierax[24] (sixteenth century), who, incidentally, when recounting the courage of a Byzantine emperor who "became renowned as a Hellene among Hellenes,"[25] used the appellation "Roman" (*Romeos*) and only rarely that of "Greek" (*Grecos*). In the provinces, youths who had been taught the rudiments of Constantine Lascaris' *Grammar* in the elementary schools and who subsequently chose a clerical vocation could, by dint of persistent study, eventually cope with the works of the Church Fathers.[26] In this same period, children were taught ecclesiastical music.[27]

By far the most important center of learning was the Patriarchal School (better known later on as the Patriarchal Academy or the Great School of the Nation), established by Gennadius. This was probably the most significant achievement of the patriarchate, since it became the official source of the propagation of the intellectual traditions of the "race." Hundreds of youths from Greece and other Balkan lands attended this school, particularly after it was reorganized in the seventeenth century by its principal, the philosopher Theophilus Corydalleus. Many of the religious, political, and intellectual leaders of the Greeks and other Balkan nations graduated from it. Its first principal was probably Matthew Kamariotes, son of a priest in Thessalonica. He was also a student of George Scholarios' and a schoolmate of D. Raoul Kabakis'.[28] Kamariotes strongly opposed George Gemistos' ideas, which he found idolatrous and fatalistic. He developed his attack in a philosophical tract. Written two or three years after the Capture, when, as a captive of the Turks, he was travelling from place to place in search of captive relatives,[29] it made no use whatever of other authorities and indeed conveys the impression of having been composed by a distinctly dishevelled mind. Kamariotes returned to Constantinople in 1455 and apparently began to teach in the Patriarchal School at that time; it is not clear whether he served simultaneously as principal.[30] It is unlikely that he was Grand Rhetor of the Great Church of Christ, as Biedl contends.[31] A prolific writer, he died in 1490; his various writings on theology, grammar, rhetoric, and literature, taken as a whole, reveal versatility and learning.[32]

The subjects then taught at the Patriarchal School included Aristotelian philosophy, rhetoric after Hermogenes, theology after Damascenos, and probably grammar after Kamariotes himself.[33]

Among Kamariotes' more distinguished students was Manuel the Corinthian (d. 1530 or 1531), who succeeded him as principal. He was probably the first person upon whom the title of Grand Rhetor was bestowed.[34] Kamariotes and Manuel together managed to pass on the Byzantine intellectual tradition to a few students such as Antonios the monk and Nicholas Malaxos, archpriest of Nauplia (c. 1500–1594[?]).[35]

Up to the middle of the sixteenth century, intellectual activity among teachers appears to have greatly diminished, with the natural consequence of fewer and fewer students. Still, Theodosios Zygomalas, protonotary of the patriarchate, probably exaggerated when he wrote to Martinus Crusius on 7 April 1581 that, twenty-five years earlier, when his father Ioannis left Nauplia to live in Constantinople at the invitation of Patriarch Ioasaph II, "virtually no one there could teach letters."[36] Professor Ioannis K. Voyatzidis adopted this phrase to lend weight to his own theory that the intellectual tradition of the Greeks was disrupted as a result of the Capture.[37] In fact, however, Theodosios Zygomalas may have wished merely to stress the contribution made by his father to the improvement in education in Constantinople following his arrival. That he exaggerated the extent of this contribution is perhaps indicated by the

Tour ou maison de Campagne fortifiée à Napoli de Malvoisie.

Castellan del. et sculp.[t]

31. Country house in Nauplia. From A. L. Castellan, *Lettres sur la Morée et les îles de Cérigo, Hydra et Zante*, Paris, 1808.

efforts of M. Galisiotis, a capable teacher, in the City in the middle of the sixteenth century.[38] Byzantine educational tradition may have been threadbare by the time Ioannis Zygomalas arrived in Constantinople, but it was still functioning. In any case Ioannis Zygomalas had completed his studies in Padua and was therefore representative of a more modern European educational tradition.[39] He had also received part of his initial education in Nauplia when that city was ruled by Venice. Only the very first stage of his education, with Frangiscos Portos as his schoolmate, had been completed under the Greek scholar Arsenios, Archbishop of Monemvasia.[40] And Crusius himself, while quoting from Theodosios Zygomalas' letter, supplies information given him by Gerlach (in a letter of 27 November 1575) that there were Greeks in their homeland who had learned their language from their parents (*per manus quasi traditam*).[41] Others learned the rudiments of Constantine Lascaris' *Grammar* in the elementary schools (*scholae triviales*), while some (for example, metropolitans and a few monks) eventually managed by constant practice to comprehend most of what they read in the writings of the Church Fathers.

Among a number of lesser teachers were some who first studied ancient Greek (*puram linguam*) in Italy and then returned to teach it in their homeland.[42] These included Michael Trivolis from Arta (of the prominent Byzantine family that had taken refuge on Corfu after the Capture), known as Maximos Trivolis after he was tonsured, who studied classical literature and philosophy in Venice, Padua, Ferrara, Florence, and Milan. Maximos Trivolis first spent ten years in seclusion at the monastery of Vatopediou on Mt. Athos (1505/1506–1516) before moving permanently to Russia, where he exerted a notable influence on the intellectual life of that country.[43]

Throughout all the Frankish-controlled territories of the Hellenic world—Cyprus, Corfu, Crete—some level of scholarship was preserved in the persons of those guardians or copyists of codices[44] who earned their living by teaching. In the main, they were refugees from Constantinople or the Morea who, together with other compatriots whose arrival had predated the Capture, carried on the Byzantine traditions of learning and manuscript copying.[45]

Crete was the most receptive to this learning. Many Greeks and Italians,[46] especially Venetians, had settled there permanently as senior military officers or leading Government officials. Avid for knowledge, they spent considerable sums of money on the acquisition of Greek manuscripts.[47] Their interest in the humanities was sharpened by a process of continual intellectual crossfertilization between Crete and Venice and spawned a thriving literary movement. The most renowned of these Greek scholars was Michael Apostolis, a Platonist, a disciple of Gemistos, and a refugee from Constantinople.[48]

Apostolis remained in Crete all his life, at Gortyna, despite the wish he
so often expressed (especially to Cardinal Bessarion) to live in Western
Europe, whether in Italy or somewhere else. Like other scholars, he made
his meager living by copying codices and giving lessons to a few students.[49] But he earned barely enough to survive.[50] He also corresponded
with many scholars of his time, such as Ioannis Moschos and others in
Corfu, most of whom lived in Venetian Greece or in Italy. Intelligent, but
unreconciled to the conditions of life, he was petulant and aggressive;[51]
he shared the restlessness and unease of other refugee scholars on the
island.[52] Devout Orthodox Cretans never forgave him his adherence to
the Unionist dogma.[53] He cursed the Turks for not cutting off his head so
that he might finally have done with all hardships and thereby "die once
and not a thousand times over."[54]

Like other Byzantine scholars, Apostolis venerated his ancestors. Writing after the Capture, he compared West Europeans with those others
"from Asia" and denied that the Westerners were "more refined in all
those things pertaining to philosophy" or that the opinions they held
"about Christ's birth, the procession of the Holy Spirit, and everything
pertaining to theology"[55] were in any sense better. To him, the renown of
both the philosophers of ancient Greece and the early Church Fathers was
proof of the superiority of the East over the West. Athens alone, he wrote,
had produced more philosophers than the whole of Italy.[56]

Troubled by the Turkish advance towards Crete, however, he wrote a
memorandum to scholars in Rome asking for a teaching post there and
promising to instruct youth in the Greek language by a method both
efficient and successful. He would do so—and here he made a new
educational proposal—by giving his lessons in ancient Greek, not in Latin
as the convention hitherto had been. In other words, he would treat
ancient Greek as though it were a living language.[57] His lessons would
proceed from grammar, "the eye of speech," through rhetoric, the ancient authors, logic, physics, and so on. Finally, he went on to stress that
the "fearless and high-minded" Plato, about whom he had been taught
only indifferently before the Capture, would be studied separately.[58]
Apostolis thus showed that he remained constant in his philosophical
allegiance.

If Apostolis lacked the ability and power to match his ambitions and
accordingly fell short of attaining the circle of really prominent
humanists, nevertheless there were some among his students, as well as
other scholars in Crete, who unquestionably did. Indeed, with the gradual
elevation of Greek letters and increasing contact with Venice, Crete began
to figure more and more significantly in the intellectual history of the
nation, exhibiting a brilliance which Cretan literature continued to
radiate. A certain groundswell was already apparent in the works of G.

Choumnos, Ioannis Pikatoros (*Verses of Lamentation*), Stephanos Sachlikis (*Writings, Verses and Commentaries*), Marinos Phalieros (*Love's Dream*), and especially Bergadis (*The Tired One*).[59]

Crete's intellectual renascence began when the Cretans first migrated to Venice and then began to study at Italian universities, mainly Padua. They eventually adopted Italy as their second homeland, settling down permanently, and this intellectual intercourse soon bore fruit.[60]

At this crucial time in the transition of modern Hellenism, two of Apostolis' students, the archpriest Laonicos of Canea and Emmanuel Atrammytinos, achieved special renown. Laonicos, together with an associate, Alexander, in 1486 set up a Greek press in Venice and produced *Frog and Mice Fighting* and a Psalter; Atrammytinos taught Aldus Manutius, the celebrated publisher and votary of ancient Greek literature.[61] Thus, Byzantine learning was perpetuated: first by Apostolis, who took it to Crete, then by his students, who transported it to Venice.

Another of Apostolis' contemporaries, a man renowned both as theologian and copyist, was his compatriot Ioannis Plousiadinos (1429–1500). Appointed Bishop of Methone (Modon) in 1491, he met a violent death at the hands of the Turks during the storming of that city.[62]

As a Greek scholar, Apostolis was outstripped by his son Aristovoulos, known as Arsenios (1468/1469–1535), Archbishop of Monemvasia, one who equalled his father in aggressiveness and in his adulation of powerful men.[63] While still a young man, Aristovoulos worked with Janis Lascaris in Florence as a copyist of Greek manuscripts (1492–1494). His relationship with Niccolò Ridolfi (1501–1550) of the Medici family, who collected hundreds of Greek manuscripts,[64] apparently dates from that time. Arsenios later went to Venice, where he published a number of literary works (1494–1496);[65] he made frequent trips to Crete (1497–1499), probably to collect manuscripts on behalf of Aldus Manutius.[66] For a short period (1519–1520) after Lascaris went to France, he probably taught in the Greek College on the Quirinale in Rome. Later, in 1521, he went to Florence as director of the Greek School, which had been established there as successor to the Rome college.[67] His most distinguished students were the Cretans Marcos Mousouros[68] and Ioannis Grigoropoulos[69] as well as two other expatriates Frangiscos Portos and Ioannis Zygomalas.[70] Arsenios' literary renown rests largely on the *Apothegms of Philosophers, Generals, Orators, and Poets.*[71]

Marcos Mousouros was the most eminent of the Cretan scholars who migrated to Italy, and his contributions to teaching and publishing were matched by his prepossessing manner. Mousouros properly ranks alongside Manuel Chrysoloras, John Argyropoulos, Demetrius Chalcocondyles, and Janus Lascaris, whose company he kept. He arrived in Florence in 1486, at the age of sixteen, when the humanistic studies patronized by Lorenzo de' Medici were at their zenith. From then until 1490 or 1491 he was under the influence of Michael Maroullos Tarhaniotes, Marsiglio Ficino (the neo-Platonist philosopher), Demetrius Chalcocondyles, and Janus Lascaris.

Later, settling in Venice, he became an associate of Aldus Manutius, whose manuscripts he collated and prepared for publication. Under his editorship, successive publications of ancient Greek texts appeared, including Mousaios' *On Hero and Leander* (1494) and the comedies of Aristophanes (1498).[72]

At Manutius' instigation, the New Academy was founded in Venice in 1500 or 1501. It attracted an elite of thirty-six to thirty-nine humanist scholars, twelve of whom were Greeks. Of the Greeks, half were Cretans, including Demetrius Ducas, Ioannis Grigoropoulos, and Marcos Mousouros. The rules of the New Academy stipulated exclusive use of the Greek language and set as their aim the selection of Greek authors for publication and the resolution of any literary problems associated with those works.[73]

In July 1503 Mousouros was appointed professor at the University of Padua, where students and visitors from all over Europe soon gathered to pay homage to his skill as a teacher. The German Johann Konon, the Frenchman Germain de Brie, and Erasmus himself[74] were among those who sat at his feet. Then, in January 1512, he returned to Venice and taught Jean de Pins, the French Ambassador to Venice, Janós Vertessy,[75] the eminent Hungarian humanist, and the young Gelenius from Prague, who settled in Basle in 1524 and there published works by Callimachus, Aristophanes, and others.[76]

In September 1513, again in the publishing house of Manutius, Mousouros brought out the first edition of Plato's *Works,* an epochal event in the dissemination of Platonist philosophy throughout Western Europe. He prefaced this edition with a long and inspired eulogy of Plato in which he expressed the fervent wish that the greatness of the ancient philosopher might move the pope to take the initiative in freeing Constantinople and Greece.[77]

In May 1515 the Venetian senate saw fit to place Bessarion's eight hundred manuscripts in the custody of Mousouros and the Venetian scholar Battista Egnazzio; and in order to house the manuscripts it simultaneously voted funds for the establishment of a library to be erected in St. Mark's Square. Thus the Marciana Library came into existence.[78]

Towards the end of 1516 Mousouros moved to Rome, where, in the previous year, Zachary Kallierges had founded the first Greek press, and Janus Lascaris was directing the Greek College set up by Pope Leo X. Rome then became an important center of Hellenic scholarship. However, Mousouros was able to enjoy neither the new intellectual ferment in Rome, nor the honors showered upon him by the pope (notably his elevation to the archepiscopal see of Monemvasia), nor the income from his ecclesiastical properties in Crete and Cyprus; he died in the Italian capital on 25 October 1517, barely forty-seven years of age. [79]

The Hellenic renascence, which was first sparked in Venice, continued to spread. Cretans especially—writers, proofreaders, the proprietors of printing presses, and their artisans—rendered perhaps the most signal service to their nation by developing Greek printing at such an early stage. As early as the end of the fifteenth century, Marcos Mousouros was voluble in his praise of his compatriots' activities in Venice. [80] From then on, over a period of four centuries, Greek clerics and scholars produced thousands of books in the Greek and Italian publishing houses of Venice [81]—those of Aldus Manutius, Zachary Kallierges (his trademark, the double-headed eagle of the Byzantine Empire, was also the symbol of his hopes), Sabio, Melchiore Sessa, Ravani, Giunta, Zanetti, Scotto, Damiano de Santa Maria, the Farreus brothers, Nicholas Sophianos and associates, Bartholomew Ianninos, and others. Covering a wide range of subjects—literary, ecclesiastical, historical, geographical, scientific, as well as traditional (popular novels and narratives)—these works educated and gave pleasure to Greeks [82] and some of the other captive peoples of the Balkans, particularly the Rumanians. [83]

Scholars and copyists were not only in Italy. Demetrius Ducas, for example, enormously stimulated the growth of Hellenic studies throughout the Iberian peninsula. [84] Another Greek, Nikandros Noukios, was in the service of Hortado de Mendoza, Spanish Ambassador to the Venetian Republic since 1527. [85] In his *Travels,* Noukios has left us an interesting account of the cultivation of humanistic studies in various West European cities. [86]

After the death of Aldus Manutius, humanistic studies, including Latin, diminished throughout Italy. Only the most lucrative arts and sciences continued to prosper. Despite the former strength of the humanistic tradition in Padua, for instance, it became difficult to find any scholars there conversant with the Greek language and its literature. There was even apprehension that classical letters would become completely neglected and that the "old barbarism" would return. [87] Fears of this kind underlay the decision of Pope Gregory XIII in 1576 (who also hoped thereby to propagate Roman Catholicism) to found in Rome the now celebrated Greek College [88] (Collegio Greco), where Greek youths from different lands could study both classical letters and Catholic theology. Its charter was plainly to create an educated nucleus which could be dispersed throughout the Hellenic world in an attempt to raise the intellectual level of Greeks everywhere. Many of its graduates achieved distinction as men of letters or science, among them Leo Allatios and Andreas Rentios, both from Chios; Nicholas Alamannos and Ioannis Pamphilos, both from Andros; the two Cypriot brothers Hilarion and Hieronymos Kigalas; Ioannis Kottounios from Veroia, and others. [89] A significant number were converted to Roman Catholicism and praised not only their alma mater but also the cardinals, who wielded complete authority within it.[90] It was therefore all the more remarkable, not perhaps that most of the college's alumni remained faithful to Orthodoxy, but that they should have become such vehement opponents of Roman Catholicism as soon as they returned home. "Despite every precaution taken," said the Jesuit Sauger, "they invariably became the most bitter enemies of the Roman Church when they returned home, passionately embracing all those teachings anathematized by [Roman] Catholics. As theologians, moreover, they were expert at combative dogmatics and thus became a source of infinite annoyance and embarrassment."[91]

Many Greeks abroad—not only scholars and clerics, but merchants as well—endowed residential "Greek colleges" or hostels to provide food and shelter for students. By the end of the fourteenth century, some young Greeks, mainly from Cyprus, were already subsidized at the University of Padua in this way. After 1400, the number of students from the "glorious nation abroad" increased with new arrivals from the Venetian colonies of Cyprus, Rhodes, Crete, and the Seven Islands. A few of these were noted as coming from the ranks of *nobiles* or *equites*.[92] The most important of the Greek "colleges" in Padua were founded by Iakovos Kokkos, the Roman Catholic Archbishop of Corfu (sixteenth century), for four young Corfiote nobles (possibly from the Kokkos family), and by the Orthodox Bishop Kissamos Gerasimos Palaiokapas (sixteenth century) for twenty-four young men, half of them from the Seven Islands and half from the "Kingdom of Crete."[93] In 1657 the Collegio Cottuniano, founded by Ioannis Kottounios from Veroia (about whom more will be said later), opened in Padua. A few years later the Corfiote Thomas Flangines endowed the Flanginianon College in Venice.[64]

Just as the students in general divided along national lines into various organized national unions (*nazioni*), so the Greeks belonged to the "Overseas Union," with its own committee and insignia. The Greek insignia, bearing the circumscription *Insignia inclitae nationis ultramarinae* (Insignia of the famous nation across the sea),[95] depicted a future emperor of the Greek nation seated upon a throne, and thus was an idealized projection of the students' hopes. Along with the right that many of these "nobles" had to hold office within the overall organizational framework of the university, they were also entitled to engrave their insignia or coats of arms on its walls. The large number of Greek students from Crete is shown by the fact that no fewer than two hundred of these coats of arms can still be seen today in colorful relief on the walls of the university.[96]

In the various colleges and universities of Italy, young men from the

Peloponnese, Crete, Chios, and elsewhere learned ancient Greek, as well as the principles of philosophy and the works of the Church Fathers. When they returned to their homes, they taught their compatriots what they had learned. Some also studied to become doctors of medicine.[97] Thus, the learning that Byzantine and post-Byzantine scholars had first taken to the West was returned to the East.

Padua was the most important university in this process of producing, then dispersing, the hundreds of Greek scholars who reappeared all over the Hellenic world. It has been justly called the alma mater of the entire captive Greek nation.[98] What is very much needed today is a systematic study of its role in the intellectual and political awakening not only of Greece but of all the Balkan nations. Among the Greeks studying in Padua and Venice in 1577, two achieved notable intellectual distinction—Symeon Kavasilas from Acarnania,[99] and Emmanuel Margounios, later the monk Maximos, from Crete.[100] According to Crusius, however, there were others, mostly clergy (*sacrificuli*), who were by no means so well versed even in grammar; indeed, they were "unworthy of their descent, veritable barbarians" (*Nihil in Creta, minus in Corcyra: barbarici plena sunt omnia* [Nothing in Crete, less in Corcyra: both are full of the barbaric]).[101] But the criticism was perhaps too hasty and severe, since only a little later, in 1583, Crusius also refers to other young Greeks studying in Padua whose progress in letters and philosophy was exemplary.[102]

Over the years, Hellenic contact with the West became more intimate and stimulated the Greeks to increasing intellectual and economic efforts. Never once throughout the entire period of Turkish rule did the procession of Greek students into Italy stop. Some reached the highest political or intellectual echelons in their adopted countries. A few even became identified with their second homes: Leonikos Thomaios,[103] Nicholas Sophianos (the author of the first demotic grammar),[104] Antonios Eparchos from Corfu,[105] the philosopher Ioannis Kottounios from Veroia (c. 1577–1658),[106] who succeeded to the chair of philosophy in Padua already made famous by his predecessor Cremonini; Ioannis Synklitikos (1570–1647), who professed law at the same university; his younger colleague and brother-in-law Skipion Gonemios (1605–1700),[107] the versatile Leo Allatios (1588–1669) from Chios, who became one of the leading savants of the seventeenth century;[108] Leonardos Philaras from Athens, who took part in the movement led by the Duke of Nevers aimed at the liberation of Greece;[109] the physician Michael Kontopidis Markellos (1651–1717);[110] and many others.

These successors[111] of Byzantine scholars who either taught or rendered various other intellectual services to their new countries not only contributed much towards the propagation of Hellenic studies but also stimulated the growth of philhellenic sentiments in the West. Unfortu-

32. The University of Padua (now Il Bo). It served as the University from 1493–1552. Photo by the author, taken in 1963.

nately, most of their works remain unknown, or else they have not been analyzed and evaluated in the way those by Leo Allatios, for example, have been. Yet their thoughts and suggestions regarding the improvement of the nation deserve to be studied. A characteristic sample is the letter of Antonios Eparchos to the Oecumenical Patriarch Dionysios II, probably written during his second patriarchate (1545–1555), which is a passionate exhortation to the patriarch to contribute towards lifting the intellectual level of the Greek nation. From the time the "race" became enslaved, its intellectual decline had begun and it had tended more and more towards a vulgar and "pleasure-seeking" way of life which came very close to bestiality. This had resulted in conflict, jealousy, intrigue, avarice, profligacy, and every other evil. Eparchos lauded the value of education and the benefits it conferred. In a series of suggestive questions, he concluded that the Greeks themselves were to blame for their intellectual degeneration: "We have extinguished the divine spark which lit our souls. When we neglect ourselves, can we expect anything else than the loss of humanity?" The duty of parents was to place their children in the hands of learned teachers who would see to their refinement and education. Man was a delicate "spiritual plant, a part of God watching the earthly struggles and Heaven's divine creations; man is not merely human but divine and immortal as well." Previously, Greece had had many such men; and because nothing had since changed, neither the climate, the air, nor the water, it was not really difficult to elevate education again, particularly since the fate of the Church was in the hands of the "great and virtuous" Dionysios, who, "with but a single word," was "capable of leading the Orthodox back on the path of righteousness—the slothful who have lost interest by exhortation and leadership, the weak-kneed by forceful insistence, the contumacious by reproach; with teachers, books, and God's help you can provide all that is needed."[112]

It is likely that a search of the archives of Italian universities and the Vatican will add to our present knowledge of the contribution that scholars made both to the intellectual life of Italy and the renascence of their own nation. The scholars thought constantly about their country's fate. Sometimes, they addressed themselves directly to persons in power (both Protestant and Roman Catholic) in the hope of eliciting their sympathy and support. Ioannis Gemistos, for example, a secretary in Ancona and perhaps the grandson of the philosopher, wrote a poem to the philhellenic Pope Leo X in order to "arm him with foreknowledge" and invite him, as the only possible liberator of the Greeks, to initiate a war of freedom against the Turks. The Turks, he said, abducted and dishonored Greek wives and children, drove them to manual labor, and tortured them. The poet cried out:

Heu, patria infelix, fidei domus inclita quondam,
Heroum genitrix et mater clara decorum,
Heu, ubi nunc proceresque tui sanctusque senatus
Magnanimique duces, populi, regesque potentes!

(Alas, unfortunate motherland, once famous home of our faith, / Bearer of heroes and illustrious mother of decorum, / Alas, where now are thy nobles and sacred senate, / Thy magnanimous leaders, thy people, and powerful kings!)

If, he continued, the renowned heroes and distinguished successors of the Greeks had disappeared forever, nevertheless there still remained one lion (Leo X) who could scatter the Turks and, in alliance with reconciled Christians in the West, give Greece her freedom. This would be a war not only against Turks but also against unbelievers wherever they might be found. And all this would come to pass because Heaven's infallible portents had predicted it.[113]

Similarly, the one dream of Arsenios, son of Apostolis, was the freedom of Greece. "Therefore, arise, arise," he wrote to Pope Clement VII, begging him to prevail upon the two great monarchs of the West, Francis I and Charles V, to launch an expedition against the "Trojans." "Restore to this race, which is everywhere in such disarray, its country; save the Greek women of the cities; listen to the cries of Greeks as they plead with you, most divine of shepherds, for their freedom."[114]

Leo Allatios apostrophized Greece as a suppliant of the heir to the French throne, the future Louis XIV:

Because I am Greece, my child, and Greece was glory
I am an eternal fact whose deeds are only pure.[115]

Antonios Eparchos lamented the fate of Greece in elegiac pentameter:

Now, Muses from Pieria sing mournfully.
Now, Hellicon sighs as tears fall upon her;
Now, the graceful Muses, radiant daughters of Jupiter,
Weep for the final destruction of Greece.[116]

Not content merely with passive regret, however, he wrote on 22 February 1543 to the German scholar Philip Melancthon, "among the most capable men of his time," complaining about the lassitude of leaders in the West who wanted only to fight one another and "who behave like drones, always spending their time wastefully. If ever they remember something they should do, there is still no result because they put matters off from one day to the next—fighting against their fate, as Hesiod would have said—frittering away their hours without solving anything or quarreling among themselves. Though to the tyrant it may seem that he governs irreproachably and praiseworthily, to us who are governed it appears only that he rules with gross indifference: while our affairs become more abysmal each day, our enemies continually advance theirs. What is there for us to do in such depressing circumstances except raise our hands in despair, imploring Heaven's help, as the enemy continues to scoff at us?"[117]

Just as the Unionist scholars of the Byzantine Empire had seen in the Turks a danger greater than any other, so Eparchos emphasized the need to maintain the unity of Christendom as the essential prerequisite of political freedom. He pleaded with Melancthon to intercede with the Germans and convince them that they must make peace with the "Romans" (Italians). Melancthon could accomplish this "as much by the force of such a sublime idea as by the power of his own rhetoric and virtue." For, Eparchos pointed out, a danger menaced the Germans themselves: "Suleiman, I have been informed by men who do not lie, now moves by land and sea to threaten the Germans as he never has before; and whenever he is within striking distance of Christians he first waits, O Heaven and Earth, upon discord among them." Only by reaching a reasonable understanding among themselves could Christians be saved. If the sultan knew that the Germans were united and that they would follow a capable leader, he would not dare to invade their country, for he also knew that of all peoples none was more "strong and warlike" than the Germans.[118]

Finally, we may note the persistent attempts by Maximos the Greek to arouse the Russians against the Turks. After completing a translation of the Psalms, he wrote to Vasily Ivanovich, the Grand Duke of Muscovy, in these characteristic terms: "O, that we could succeed one day, through you, in freeing ourselves from the infidel yoke! New Rome is tossed about by waves of Turks, but let us pray God that she will be freed during your most pious reign and that your paternal throne will be blessed with an heir who, through you, will see the light of freedom shining on us benighted souls." Maximos was determined to incite his coreligionists in Russia to action against the Turks.[119]

The efforts of scholars and others towards this end did not succeed, but they were not without ultimate significance in the advancement of Greek interests. They attracted the attention of foreign scholars and powerful men in the West who encouraged what was to become a swelling stream of philhellenic consciousness. Three German scholars at the University of Tübingen, Johann Reuchlin (1455–1522), better known throughout the Hellenic world as Kapnion, Philip Schwarzerd (1497–1560), or Melancthon, and Martin Kraus (1526–1607), or Crusius, so loved ancient Greece and everything it represented that they established within their university a separate center of Hellenic studies, which became a focal point of philhellenism in the West whose influence extended far beyond the boundaries of Germany. The figure of Crusius is central to an understanding of the intellectual life of Greece during this period.

Martinus Crusius, "teacher of the language of Old and New Rome at the Academy of Tübingen," or, as he described himself, "Greco-Latin teacher of rhetoric,"[120] personally knew and corresponded with many Greek scholars of the time, among them Frangiscos Portos, Symeon Kavasilas, Maximos Margounios, Gabriel Severus, Bishop of Philadelphia, and particularly Ioannis Zygomalas and his son Theodosios, all of whom apprised him of the intellectual situation throughout the Hellenic world after the naval battle of Naupactus (Lepanto) in 1571.

Crusius' main aim was to become proficient in the ancient Greek language and especially the demotic language. On 2 September 1570 he wrote in characteristic vein to the Cretan Frangiscos Portos, professor of Greek Letters in Geneva,[121] that he, a German, would be very happy if he could "make the acquaintance of every Greek, the glorious remains of Greece."[122] Portos replied that tears filled his eyes when he contemplated the spread of Greek education in France, England, and Germany, while Athens "which is Greece's Greece and the light of the world, the sanctuary of the Muses, first of all cities under the sun" remained in bondage to the barbarians. But he consoled himself with the thought that everything in the world was transitory and that "Greece's pure name, honored like a mother's, is much revered" by foreigners and a galaxy of scholars such as Crusius himself.[123] Thus began a correspondence between Crusius, Portos, and Portos' son Aimilios, the last also an Hellenic scholar (d. 1610) whom Crusius once described as "the most comely branch of the very best tree."[124] This correspondence subsequently widened to include other eminent Hellenic scholars, especially Ioannis Zygomalas, Grand Rhetor and Secretary of the Church,[125] and his son Theodosios.[126]

Crusius concerned himself most of all with the collection of Greek manuscripts, which he either bought himself or persuaded the University of Tübingen and the Prince of Württemberg, a patron of letters and the arts, to buy. The manuscripts can still be examined today in the library of the University of Tübingen and the Hof und Staatsbibliothek in Munich.[127]

Crusius prevailed upon clerics and nonclerics to search for books in the demotic dialect, whether handwritten or printed;[128] and the distress he felt in not finding them, not even dictionaries, became all the more acute because of his conviction that proficiency in both forms of the language was indispensable to the successful teaching of ancient Greek: "I study the ancient language in detail in order to be able to connect it with the everyday language in common use."[129] Crusius, in fact, was not only the first foreigner to study the demotic dialect and its literature but also the first to make Western Europe aware of both.[130]

He collected a variety of Greek texts in the Attic, ecclesiastical, and demotic dialects, embracing works of history, literature, and the letters of scholars, with a view to incorporating them all in a book. By such means he hoped to introduce the world of Greek letters to that broadening public with a penchant for the classics. Such people, he hoped, would thereby also become acquainted with the state of Greek education in the Turkish Empire. He hoped that a work of this kind might contribute towards a *rapprochement* between the intellectual leaders of East and West. As he wrote to Gabriel Severus, referring to the impending publication of *Turcograeciae:* "I have translated [the letters] into Latin because I want both the Latin translations and the original Greek texts to appear together in the printed work; in this way Germans and Greeks will become more knowledgeable of one another and concord will grow."[131]

Not only was Crusius the first philhellene to appear in Greece after the Capture,[132] he was the first philhellene in the true sense of the word, since he did not confine his regard to the ancient Greeks: unlike other foreigners, he made no attempt to separate the ancient from the modern Greeks. His feelings went out equally to the ancient Greeks and to their descendants living in captivity. Thus, he used such words as Hellas, Hellene, and philhellene without distinction as to time. An unqualified idealist, he took the lead in propagating Hellenic studies in Germany. "I try by every means in my power," he wrote to Patriarch Jeremiah II, "to preserve the Greek language and disseminate it throughout Germany, just as other highly cultivated men tried to do sixty years ago."[133]

It has indeed been remarked most cogently that philhellenism in all its essential elements originated in sixteenth-century Tübingen in the little state of Württemberg.[134] Crusius was one of the principal instigators, perhaps the most important, of this movement which, by the beginning of the nineteenth century, had become extensive.

Crusius' contemporary fame as a philhellenist led large numbers of Greeks to visit him in Tübingen. From the most humble men of the people to scholars such as the copyist Andreas Darmarios,[135] from plain adventurers to honorable men from all over the Hellenic world—from Constantinople, Athens, Monemvasia, Cyprus, and elsewhere—they came to solicit his moral or material support. Some of them he singled out as protégés whom he wanted to keep with him in order to learn ancient and modern Greek, though insufficient means invariably prevented his doing so. None went away, however, without counsel, comfort, and testimonial.[136] In return, he expected nothing more than information—about the language itself, both its ancient and demotic forms, the geography and demography of Greece, the fate of its noble families, its intellectual life, its scholars—about everything, in fact, connected with Greece under Turkish rule. Possibly he intended to write a history of contemporary Greece, since in 1582 he wrote to the Cretan scholar, Morzenos, asking for historical information about Crete and its adjacent islands. On the other hand, the appearance of *Turcograeciae* only three years later suggests that this was his exclusive concern.[137] All the information gleaned from his meetings and interviews with Greek refugees he noted in *Turcograeciae,* as well as in his diary (the *Diaria*), an encyclopaedia of knowledge and information about persons and events in contemporary Western Europe that he built up over many years.[138]

Greeks in exile, especially the copyists and scholars who wandered all over the West, not only helped revive an awareness of the ancient Greek nation but also made the people of the West aware of the condition of Greece under Turkish rule and thus provided the chief stimulus of philhellenism.

From information supplied to Crusius by the Zygomalas family, particularly Theodosios, as well as by other Greeks, some of them refugees, we are able to construct a picture of the educational condition of Greeks under Ottoman rule. At the end of the sixteenth century,[139] every town, including those of such Aegean islands as Patmos, Samos, and Melos, had a school for boys attached to the local church. There were no grades, and the priest was usually the only teacher. Students acquired little more than an ability to read ecclesiastical books such as the Breviary, the Missal, and the Psalter, and to follow the divine services. Very few, even among the presbyters and monks, acquired any real understanding of what they were taught.[140]

The association of church and school which, even in Byzantine times, had always been a close one,[141] became the accepted norm. Some of the better educated teacher-priests might take their students into a church narthex and there expose them not only to ecclesiastical literature but also to extracts from ancient Greek writers[142]—Aristotle, Plutarch, and so on. Many surviving manuscripts disclose that this kind of education had become common by the eighteenth century.[143] This "crypto-school" of legend could be found even in the most isolated provinces of the Hellenic world until almost the end of the Ottoman era.[144]

The narthex schools were also deemed suitable places in which to paint the images of great pagan scholars alongside those of Christian saints.[145] This, too, was an ancient Byzantine tradition, stemming originally from the proclivity of Greek scholars (and also, later on, of the Slavs) to distinguish between degrees of paganism and to honor those ancients whose thought might be seen as foreshadowing Christianity or even contributory to the later formulation and refinement of Christian dogma.[146] The custom of painting such figures in accordance with surviving memories of the classical Byzantine tradition persisted until the end of Turkish rule. Gerlach, for instance, a Protestant pastor, observed that the Armenian Church of St. George in Constantinople, close to Hagia Sophia, had beautiful frescoes of patriarchs, prophets, apostles, philosophers, orators, and poets, among whom were Aristotle, Josephus, Sophocles, and Philo.[147] Other ancient Greeks like Solon, Plato, Aristotle, and Thucydides were also represented in the frescoes of various churches throughout continental Greece, as for example, the chapel of Portaïtissa in the monastery of Hiviron (1683) and the monastery of St. Nicholas of Spanos in Ioannina (1559–1560). There were others in Asia Minor, in the district of Iconium.[148] Possibly, too, Epirote craftsmen were responsible for similar frescoes over the altar of the monastery of Batskovo (1623) and in the women's section of the Church of the Nativity in Arbanasi,[149] where people from northern Epirus had settled.

Christians were not disturbed by portraits of pre-Christian Greeks on church walls. Indeed, the instructions issued to Dionysios, a painter from Phourna in Acarnania, actually specified definite ways in which Apollonius, Solon, Thucydides, Plutarch, Plato, Aristotle, and others[150] might be depicted. Perhaps the practice throve during the centuries of Turkish rule because it represented a continuing ancestor veneration and an unconscious projection of inchoate nationalist feeling.

Besides the public schools for children (*scholae triviales*) in Constantinople[151] and the provinces, in the narthexes of churches or even monastic cells, there was only the Patriarchal Academy. All schools in Constantinople came under the supervision of the patriarch and his "committees."[152] According to Sauger, very few in the Aegean understood the texts of Homer or Theocritus and were even proud of the fact.[153] Patriarchal officials possessed no more than a mediocre knowledge of the ancient Greek language.[154] A disappointed Crusius wrote: *Nullam in Graecia Graeciam, nullas Athenas Athenis esse* (Greece is no longer Greece, nor is Athens Athens).[155]

In a letter to Crusius, Theodosios Zygomalas, protonotary of the patriarchate, estimated that his father had no more than ten students in Constantinople; there were only four on Chios and about twenty in the Peloponnese and a few other places. If one added to that estimate no more than a dozen or so scattered over the rest of the country,[156] barely fifty students could be counted in all Hellas. Scholars were proportionately rarer, as indeed the Cretan Constantine Servios, who studied in Padua, wrote Crusius in October 1583: the Turkish enslavement had produced a dearth of scholars, and these were principally confined to Crete, the only remaining sanctuary. There was Theodosios Komis from Corinth, a man distinguished for his learning (*humanioribus literis perpolitus*), Ioannis Katélos, or Katelós according to Ninolakis[157] (*summae virtutis juvenis, in politioribus studiis nemini secundus* [a youth of the highest excellence, second to none in the more refined studies]), the lawyer Andreas Spairas, the philosopher-physician Daniel Phourlanos, and a few other physicians.[158]

In Chios, according to Crusius, there were a few Greeks who taught philosophy.[159] He was undoubtedly referring particularly to Michael Hermodoros Listarchos, who taught there at different times between 1533 and 1563[160] and whose students included Iakovos Diassorinos, Iakovos Vasilikos Herakleidis, Ioannis Mindonios, Theodoros Rentios, and Michael Sophianos.[161] Two others may have been Ioannis Koressios and Emmanuel Glyzounios,[162] the latter known to have left a bequest to found and maintain a school on Chios.[163] Somewhat later, during the seventeenth century, George Koressios also opened a school on Chios and taught many students.[164]

However, Crete was the only Greek land where political conditions favored the emergence of writers, lawyers, and physicians, and some distinguished personages appeared. They included George Chortatzis, who wrote the tragedy *Erophile* (c. 1600) and probably the comedy *Katzourbos* (1595–1601) as well, the anonymous poet of *The Little Shepherdess*, and others. Later, during the first half of the seventeenth century, Vitzentzos Kornaros wrote the verse novel *Erotocritus* (*ante* 1650) and probably the tragedy *Abraham's Sacrifice*. There were also Ioannis-Andreas Troilos, author of *King Rodolinos* (1647), and various other writers, some of them anonymous, whose works reflected Frankish influence but at the same time evolved new autocthonous forms. Frankish influence, however, continued to manifest itself in Cretan literary enterprises.[165]

Despite Crete's intellectual vigor, Theodosios Zygomalas wrote in one of the essays that he gave his students to translate into ancient Greek: "to contemplate the apathy of the Greek race towards all that is fine is enough to make one weep."[166] Such despair, though frequently lightened with hope and expectation, was all too common among post-Byzantine scholars.

Theodosios envied Crusius because he lived contentedly in a free city: "with learning as your profession, enlightenment is within your grasp."[167] His students were also impressed with the knowledge of the Germans, who were as fortunate as the students were pitiable, "for although they studied lessons fit for free men, they were prevented from applying them because of their bondage and privation. The real Athens, as we hear, is now where you are."[168] Germany's fame as a center of classical studies had thus spread even to Greece.

According to Theodosios, those who discovered the manuscripts of ancient Greek scholars were even more blessed than those who bought the freedom of slaves. Such discoveries could bring manifold benefits "to the public, as well as to individuals."[169]

Theodosios Zygomalas, like Cardinal Bessarion before him,[170] had faith in the aptitude of Greek children. He observed that, with good teachers, they progressed in their lessons "because of the virtues and qualities of the Greek nation in whatever places, whose God-given advan-

tages are inborn and ineradicable."[171] As we see, the opinion held by
modern Greeks about their unsurpassed climate and geographical situation is matched by the same proud conviction concerning their ancient
and medieval forebears' intellectual superiority. If the sun of education
did not shine, Theodosios went on, and if knowledge lay under a perpetual shadow, this was due to constant misfortune.[172] Poverty and slavery prevented the Greeks from pursuing the "good."[173] So Theodosios
lived vicariously in the past and hoped that "some day God would restore
contentment and freedom to their former abode."[174] The two ideals
commonly shared by scholars during the captivity were to be free and to
be seen as the equals of their ancestors.

Recognizing the need to inculcate these ideals in children, Theodosios,
in one of the letters he used as models for translation by his students,
adapted Cicero (*Letters to His Friends,* II, 5) to show the relevance of his
advice to the situation which the Hellenes faced: "if you have the courage
to do what is best for your country, decide in your own minds what must
be done for the sort of man who, growing up under the old freedoms, was
a worthy defender of his country, but who now under so many adverse
conditions has acquired fatal habits."[175] Writing to Crusius, Theodosios
called freedom "an inestimable thing," and the German professor noted:
"How moved I was to see freedom described as an inestimable thing."[176]

The scholars of the time thought that freedom would be regained only
through the publication and study of the texts of the ancient Greek
writers. Since "scholars are free and slaves are imbeciles,"[177] it was essential that Greeks liberate themselves from ignorance and illiteracy. It is in
these terms that the literary output of post-Byzantine scholars, for example, N. Sophianos' translation of Plutarch's *The Education of Children,*
must be explained. Similarly, the burden of *Travels,* in which the sixteenth
century Corfiote Nikandros Noukios recorded his impressions of various
European countries,[178] was that his compariots should become educated.
Thus a main aim of Greek scholars was to teach children the ancient
Greek language; they were encouraged by the thriving humanist movement of the late Middle Ages that placed so much emphasis on the
classics.[179]

However, the gap between the written and spoken language had
widened over the centuries. Words and phrases quoted by the German
traveller Arnold von Harff in 1477 show that the demotic dialect used by
late Byzantine Greeks[180] differed very little from its present-day form.
Harff considered it "barbaric" and a "hodge-podge of many languages"
because the Greeks were scattered over such a vast area and had consequently incorporated into their many dialects a large number of foreign
words from the languages of neighboring peoples. There was one dialect
in Crete, interlarded with Italian words, another in Athens, and so on.

Nevertheless, Greeks could still understand one another whether they came from Constantinople, Crete, Chios, Nauplia, Epirus, or anywhere else.[181] According to Crusius, Constantinople had the purest speech of all because that city had always been the seat of empire.[182] Athens, on the other hand, possessed the most corrupt version of the language.[183] In Constantinople, the few educated people understood the ancient Greek language and used it with facility, but they also spoke demotic Greek. Women spoke the demotic with great fluency and elegance.[184] There was a greater difference between ancient and demotic Greek than between Latin and Italian.[185]

We learn from other sources in this period that even then Greeks believed that the demotic dialect was very ancient, though they did not know when it was first spoken.[186] In this "vulgar language" they expressed all their joys and sorrows, all their loves and hates.[187] The ecclesiastical form, which mixed "elements of purity and barbarity," was used by clergy and scholars in their correspondence.[188] This form thus became the precursor of the literary form of the language.

Changes in sound and meaning did not escape the notice of scholars, though they attributed these to the differing conceptions and ways of life of peasants and townsmen, as well as to the "scattering of peoples to so many different places."[189]

On the whole, scholars adopted an unfriendly attitude towards the demotic dialect. This could hardly have been otherwise since they were reared on the worship of antiquity and felt a spiritual affinity with the ancients. When in 1577 Gerlach asked Ioannis Zygomalas for a speech or sermon in demotic for Crusius, the Greek scholar replied that he preferred to write the ancient language a hundred times more than the demotic form and that he had no intention of wearing himself out by composing something in "such a barbarous language." At Gerlach's insistence that it would be better if the sermon were to be given in the demotic since otherwise the people would understand nothing, he retorted that it was quite enough if one or two understood and that if Gerlach wanted a change he should first ask the patriarch to set an example. Gerlach attributed Zygomalas' refusal to a lack of books in the demotic.[190] Only two years passed, however, before the patriarch in 1575 gave the first three or four sermons in the demotic dialect, which, naturally, everyone understood.[191]

The traveller Dousa was annoyed that the Greeks not only "knew nothing about the history of their ruined monuments, but also lacked any curiosity or desire to learn anything."[192] Belon detected and himself believed that there was a total absence of enthusiasm for letters and science.[193] Reflecting upon the dearth of educated Greeks and the intellectual decline of the nation, he concluded that they had become a degenerate people.[194]

As we have seen, Greeks themselves felt despondent over the situation. Some, N. Ralis from Chalki in the Dodecanese, for example, a protégé of Jeremiah II, thought the clergy were to blame. They did not want the people to read books, with the consequence that no one knew the Bible or anything else.[195] This was entirely too sweeping a judgment, however, for besides certain idle, uneducated, and refractory clergy, there were those who gave considerable stimulus to the advancement of letters. From the middle of the sixteenth century, a number of the upper clergy showed a very keen interest in the progress of students who attended the so-called "cell schools," that is, those schools directly supported by ecclesiastical establishments. Ioasaph, Archbishop of Adrianople, writing from Constantinople to Ioannis Zygomalas in his metropolitan residence, adjured Zygomalas to teach children "with a clear conscience, assiduously, sparing no effort"; he also promised to send the students the most beautiful of books so that they might study attentively.[196]

Later, as Patriarch Ioasaph II (1555–1565), he contributed much to the revival of education. The Zacynthian Michael Hermodoros Listarchos wrote to Ioannis Zygomalas in 1560: "alone in this fearful chaos he dared light a bright torch at precisely the moment when the voice of the Greeks had been almost stilled; and he tried to revive education by showing the people the virtuous words of Christ, as well as the beauty of God's wisdom, the source of all that is good." When Listarchos again wrote to Zygomalas in 1562, he expressed the hope that God would bless the patriarch with good health so that he might be able, by living a long time, to liberate the miserable race "from illiteracy and such great poverty of intellect."[197]

Patriarch Jeremiah II also showed deep concern for the intellectual advancement of the Greek nation.[198] To this end, he communicated with two of the intellectual leaders of the Greek community permanently resident in Venice: the serene and kind Cretan, Emmanuel Margounios (1549–1602), better known by his monastic name Maximos, who was Bishop of Kythera, and the irascible Gabriel Seviros, Bishop of Philadelphia. Both men were conscious of the "yawning chasm of ignorance" into which the nation had fallen,[199] and both hoped to extricate it from its plight. In an exordium addressed to the patriarch prefacing one of the Gospels, which he published in association with both Margounios and the Chian bibliographer Glyzounios, (or Glytzounis,[200] who also wrote and published the first practical Arithmetic, or *Computation* [*Logariastiki*] as he called it),[201] Seviros remarked that "we have others to publish also . . . for the progress of our race and the glorification of the Church."[202]

Margounios, too, wrote a long letter to the patriarch urging him to "implant" in his flock, clergy and lay alike, "a true reverence for God, a concern for virtue, propriety, and decency. They must preserve all those texts, discarding the inessential ones, which will enable them to live a Christian life, aided by much counsel, much education, much persuasion, much censure, and much ingenuity."[203] A further extract from Margounios' letter apostrophizes the young men of Greece as children, imploring them to emulate their ancestors and not to appear as inferiors of either their own forbears or West Europeans:

What are you waiting for, O children of Greece? Forsake the path of evil and, like good children of good parents, choose that of virtue. Nothing daunts him who really wants to achieve something, and God will even help him overcome. If you wish not to be despised so by others, you must renounce your faults and show forth your faith by good deeds. Do not succumb to the enormity of the misfortune which has befallen us by becoming scared of it, but rather know and convince yourselves that the Divinity leads us much better than we ourselves. How much better it is to become poor honestly than rich dishonestly; and if you covet real wealth, study the virtues as our ancestors themselves studied and decide that you will appear in no wise inferior in virtue to anyone. How shameful to be beaten in knowledge and education by the Latins, you who are Greek children, when they have received everything from us. Why, therefore, when you are really superior, do you choose to be inferior?[204]

Lay scholars, whether living abroad or under tyranny, joined with enlightened clergy in pursuit of the nation's advancement. It is instructive for us to follow them in their quests, to isolate their central ideas, to distill the experiences of long and painful lifetimes. Among the causes of decline, Antonios Eparchos singled out the various manifestations of Greek individualism as deserving special opprobrium.[205] A century later, Patriarch Nektarius of Jerusalem expressed the same opinion in more general terms when he anathematized as "our unique vice" the weakness, egoism, envy, and wickedness lurking in man's soul:

Good and edifying knowledge—the gateway, the handmaiden, the Nestor of intellectual learning—once flourished in the Holy Church and helped her in her struggles with heretics. . . . But the march of time and, most importantly of all, our unique vice little by little eroded it, eventually leaving us bereft of it and much else besides—perhaps not totally bereft, as long as there still remain a few wise and splendid scholars who hold a torch for the race, but we were in imminent danger of losing it completely, to the everlasting dishonor and loss of both Church and nation.[206]

In 1593 Patriarch Jeremiah II the Great called a synod at which the Orthodox archbishops decided to establish schools "for the dissemination of the divine and esoteric scriptures, for the benefit of those who want to teach and learn."[207] From then on the establishment of schools became more general, though not without meeting resistance from ecclesiastical and lay worthies, whose old attitudes, rooted in monastic conservatism, underwent little change from one year to the next. For example, at the beginning of the seventeenth century, the monk Maximos from the Peloponnese who, though conservative in other respects, was at least educated, spoke of the illiteracy of priests and archbishops: "It is absolutely essential that priests and especially archbishops should be knowledgeable, that they should stand at the center of the Church and enlighten others like the lamps which illumine the churches, as indeed they vowed to do when they were consecrated. Just as Peter guarded the sheep because he wanted to become Christ's friend, so, too, should the successors of Peter who have assumed the positions held by both Peter and Christ."[208] According to the scholar monk Pachomios Rousanos,[209] there was indifference towards intellectual pursuits even on Mt. Athos: "almost all scholars suffer from the same defects—never practicing what they preach, and preferring the company of people to solitude in the wilderness, thus only contributing to the general confusion."[210] Maximos also castigated the people of Ioannina, particularly the notables, who showed no interest in those who were "important and wise." He urged them to acquire a basic literacy, but even that they determinedly shunned: "I hoped by suggesting this perhaps to move a few to learn, so that our people, to whom any form of versification is incomprehensible, should not remain forever illiterate. Though they feel ashamed whenever scholars say that they are barbarians, they cultivate barbarism. Whenever anyone suggests that they should turn away from barbarism or that they should correct the wrong they do, they react with anger and vicious hatred. Instead of turning towards wisdom, which is better than light itself, they want nothing more than illiterate wealth."[211] The general poverty of intellectual aspiration among the Greeks continued to chagrin scholars like Matthew, Bishop of Myreon, who evoked the ideal vision of ancient Greece:

Race of Greeks, have you really fallen so,
You have known so many dangers,
You from whom all prudence and wisdom
Came and conquered the universe,
You who showed it arms and letters and
Theology and unsurpassed valor, too.

All the world extolled your wisdom
How has Turkish slavery crushed you so?[212]

Nevertheless, from the middle of the sixteenth century there were signs of a growing interest in intellectual pursuits. Greeks in the major centers of civilization, notably Constantinople, began to recognize value in even the most ordinary of ecclesiastical manuscripts. Monks from Mt. Athos and other places began to compete with foreigners in bidding for the various codices and manuscripts which once belonged to Michael Cantacuzenus and which, together with other of his possessions, were offered for sale at public auction.[213] Since bibliographical workshops were then in operation at Mt. Athos, it is probable that experienced bibliographers among the monks became interested in acquiring model codices for the purpose of copying them and enriching their libraries.[214]

In 1577 Gerlach observed that 150 codices had been thrown higgledy-piggledy into a vault of the Patriarchal Library, where, with not a single person to read them, they merely gathered dust. However, since the patriarch, in accordance with regulations, had denied Gerlach's request to take certain books home on loan, insisting instead that he read them on the spot,[215] it is possible that Gerlach was venting his spleen on the patriarch. Du Fresne's comment only four years earlier that this was a "beautiful" library[216] casts doubt on the veracity of Gerlach's observation.

Those measures taken by various monks and superior clergy to acquire and preserve manuscripts sprang from a concern to prevent the dispersal of this wealth to the West. Western scholars, diplomats, and others, or even Greek scholars and clergy acting as the agents of Western dignitaries (and sometimes at the behest of officials of the Latin Church), bought manuscripts from owners who were often ignorant of their worth.[217] The practice is not unknown in Greece even today. Although manuscripts were commonly acquired by deceiving or bribing their guardians,[218] actual theft was not unusual. The most notorious culprit in this regard was the Cypriote Unionist monk Athanasios "the Orator" (1571–1663), who travelled throughout Greece for ten years in the service of France's Cardinal Mazarin and Chancellor Pierre Séguier, utterly denuding the monasteries of Thessaly (Meteora), Macedonia, and Thrace. The hundreds of manuscripts which he spirited away to France now repose in the Bibliothèque Nationale.[219] Repeated thefts of this kind finally alarmed the monks and owners of codices, particularly the patriarchate, which placed the ban of excommunication on all who sold or stole any manuscript belonging to a monastery.[220]

Foreigners were especially interested in those lesser known ancient Greek or Christian works whose rich contents had not been fully exploited; but they were equally eager to collect recent versions of the better known texts for the purpose of bringing out superior and more up-to-date versions.

Despite this revived philological enthusiasm, the magnificent tradition of copying was not sustained, though it never wholly died out even in the provinces. A bibliographer in Naousa, Macedonia, for example, was copying the works of Bryennios in 1615.[221] The Zygomalases were working, if unsystematically, in Constantinople throughout the whole of the second half of the sixteenth century.[222] Gerlach also mentions that in 1578 Malaxos, then an old man, was about to embark upon copying the history of the patriarchs after the Capture.[223] But, on the whole, copyists were few and inexpert, as indeed Gerlach informed Crusius in 1576 in response to the latter's expression of interest in purchasing manuscripts. It was becoming more and more difficult to find manuscripts, and these were expensive. Gerlach supplied Crusius with a catalogue of books still remaining in Constantinople, pointing out that most were of a theological nature;[224] since the Greeks had no interest in books of any kind, from philosophy to poetry, they would not even know about the existence of these. Greeks superstitiously believed, he continued, that centuries earlier their monks had been forbidden to read books of philosophy or poetry.[225] Ever since then, humanistic studies had been neglected. Most educated people were content to read the Church Fathers and practically nothing else. If works of philosophy or poetry were found, the French and Italians immediately dispatched their librarians to buy them.[226] The emissaries and ambassadors of the German Empire, Venice, and other countries made off with innumerable manuscripts whenever they departed from Constantinople.[227] And indeed, in 1599, the Palatine Library in Heidelberg was filled with so many Greek and Latin manuscripts "that even Italy had cause to be jealous."[228]

This search for manuscripts by foreigners did not go unnoticed in other quarters: when Turkish mobs pillaged the patriarchate on successive occasions throughout the sixteenth and seventeenth centuries, they did not overlook its intellectual treasures, which they knew brought handsome prices in the City's European embassies. Periodic pillaging, fire, and other forms of spoliation also account for the dearth of manuscripts antedating 1680 in the patriarchal archives.[229]

Thus, the flight of Byzantine scholars to the West, the fall of the Empire, and the uninterrupted drain of manuscripts, caused a shift in the center of gravity of Hellenic scholarship from East to West. Theodosios Zygomalas recognized this when he wrote to Crusius on 7 April 1581: "I see now (as I have told you before, and as I never cease telling everyone here, what I say is the truth) that all Greek possessions have gone from here to where you are. These possessions are wisdom and knowledge in letters and the fine arts, fine manners, military technology, wealth, education, and so on."[230]

Despite these vicissitudes, the Greeks gradually began to wake from their torpor. By the end of the sixteenth century and the beginning of the seventeenth century Greek schools had sprouted all over continental Greece (both in Constantinople and the provinces) and in the islands. In his two-volume work on Greek education under Turkish rule from the Capture to Capodistria (Athens, 1936), T. Evangelidis has given us many details about them, particularly the dates when they were established. By 1576 it is likely that a considerable number in Constantinople were in operation: out of forty-four non-Turkish schools[231] (Jewish, Greek, Spanish, Italian, and so on) that had existed before a great fire, more than thirty still remained. The Patriarchal School, which was included in this number, ceased to function around the middle of the seventeenth century, but it was eventually re-established and reorganized through the financial generosity of the national benefactor, Kastorianos Manolakis. It had three teachers, and the elementary education for which one of the teachers was responsible was free. A second teacher gave higher instruction in the arts and sciences, grammar, rhetoric, and logic; and a third taught philosophy and theology. Twelve students in the two upper echelons received bursaries. During this period, however, the Patriarchal School evidently operated on an irregular basis, without a full staff.[232]

Next in importance after the capital were the three former centers of Byzantine civilization, Thessalonica, Ioannina, and Athens. In 1585 there was an Athenian teacher, George, in Thessalonica.[233] A Cretan, Matthew, who had taught many students over a long period, was also in Thessalonica at about the same time.[234] In Ioannina, the Byzantine educational tradition still survived, even if tenuously, despite Turkish rule:[235] oral tradition speaks of the Byzantine Philanthropenos School, which continued to function in the monastery of St. Nicholas on the island of Lake Ioannina.[236] By the end of the sixteenth century, Athens also supported many Greek schools which were attended not only by children but also by "many older notables." Among the large number of teachers there were Loukas, Sebastianos, Germanos, and Karikis.[237] Indeed, the situation had so improved during the course of the seventeenth century that Eugenios Giannoulis, a celebrated teacher, spoke of Athens as "still golden": when "Athens is compared with all the other cities in Greece, the difference is plain; I mean that Athens is the mother of letters and offers humanity so much."[238]

The role of education was not generally understood by the Greek people as a whole. Educators received poor remuneration. Even in Constantinople the teacher's life was a hard one: there were few students, and fees, consequently, were small. In order to supplement his income, the teacher probably had to fall back on the copying of codices.[239] Well-known teachers and scholars like Gabriel Severus, the monk Maximos of the Peloponnese, and Pachomios Rousanos complained bitterly about their lot and the indifferent society in which they lived: "Many have taken great pains," wrote Gabriel Severus to the patriarch, "to print many books that are replete with faith and wisdom, but their books have profited us little because everyone cares for nothing but how to make money."[240] Although there were signs of a growing interest in education among the Greeks, Severus of course was right when he discerned a greater interest in commerce. An acceleration of trade between East and West attracted many to the worship of Hermes. While those with an entrepreneurial bent were certainly the most eager, the god of commerce also seduced many venturesome minds. Of course the denigration of teachers was by no means peculiar to this time and place, "but here," wrote Rousanos, in a typical vein, "things are taken to extremes. On the one hand the educated are very poor and held in contempt; on the other the obsequious and lawless rise to the highest positions, shamelessly amassing useless money on all sides. They do not want even to look at anyone who is a philosopher because they fear that the educated will chastise them for their wrongdoings; so they call all philosophers prattlers, unkempt fellows, and contumacious cowards because the philosophers refuse to condone their stupidities. For such people it is not enough that they live in darkness; they want to drag everyone else down too."[241]

Indeed, the emerging bourgeoisie of the Ottoman Empire were much less enthusiastic than their compatriots abroad for the enlightenment of the "race." Men like Kastorianos Manolakis, who reopened the Patriarchal School and founded other schools in Arta, Anatolikon,[242] and on Chios, were notable exceptions to the general run of their class.

A definite intellectual quickening was also apparent in the islands— Chios,[243] Patmos,[244] the Cyclades (for example, Naxos, Paros, Melos, and others, where Jesuit and Capuchin[245] monks were among the teachers). On Lesbos, two noteworthy events were the foundation of the Limonos School in the monastery of the same name (where Pachomios Rousanos taught briefly between 1532 and 1540), and the establishment of a seminary for female recluses in the monastery of Myrsiniotissis.[246] The teaching of Italian in many of the islands reflected the region's commercial involvement with Venice;[247] in 1593 a school was founded there for the children of expatriate Greeks.[248]

A number of people living a long way from their homes, whether inside the Ottoman Empire or abroad (principally in Venice), made provision in their wills for the establishment and maintenance of schools in their birthplaces.[249] Expatriate Epirotes had a deep interest in promoting education not only in Epirus but throughout the nation and provided numerous legacies for this purpose. Among the Epirote benefactors was the distinguished Corfiote Thomas Flangines (1579–1648), who disposed of a substantial interest in his estate (about 200,000 ducats) to found and maintain in Venice both the Flangines Institute and a hospice for poor Greeks, to ransom captives, to provide dowries for needy Greek women, to subsidize the parishes of the Church of St. George, and to support various other philanthropic causes.[250]

Schools were not always open on a permanent basis; nor were teachers' salaries always assured. "Three years have now gone by," George Sougdouris, a teacher at the Guionma school in Ioannina, wrote his sister Angeliki Glyky in Venice at the end of the seventeenth century, "and no money has arrived at our school. It is for this reason that I want to leave. I therefore beg my cousins to help us. I am unable to work, borrow, or eat, and I therefore ask my cousins to tell Gastaldo [President of the Greek Community in Venice] to send me some money."[251] Confusion, lack of organization, and unco-ordinated labor bedevilled education at this time. They remained as basic deficiencies in the Greek school system even after the attainment of independence.

The Academy of Stravaganti was founded in Canea, Crete, around 1590, the first such institution to appear in the Venetian dependencies. It was followed, sometime before 1637, by the establishment of the Academy of Sterili in Canea; unfortunately the beginning of the Turkish conquest of Crete a few years later stifled its development. The Academy of Stravaganti, whose members included both Greeks and Venetians, evidently played an important part in the cultivation of Cretan letters. Its influence on the growth of the Cretan theater was particularly significant.[252] Although very little is known about the Academy Degli Assicurati on Corfu, founded in 1656, it had a Greek and foreign membership of thirty, among whom were clergy, doctors, and lawyers.[253]

These academies resembled literary clubs, after the style of those that had appeared during the Italian Renaissance, which they consciously imitated. Their membership consisted of votaries of Greek and Latin studies who came together regularly, whether in a closed circle or in public, to discuss science, politics, and especially literature.[254]

During this period, a number of able teachers emerged whose influence on their contemporaries stamped them as forerunners of the later Greek Enlightenment. Two especially stand out. The first, Theophilus Corydalleus, or Skordalos, to give him his real name, was born in 1563 in Athens, where he received his first instruction. Later, he continued his studies in the celebrated Collegio Greco in Rome, as well as at the University of Padua, where he read philosophy and medicine.[255] He completed his studies at a time, generally throughout the West but especially in Padua, when Aristotle was being rediscovered in the original. The inaccurate translations and commentaries of the Arabs, chiefly Averroës (Ibn Raschid, 1126–1198), had distorted the meaning of many passages from Aristotle's works. The principal protagonist in Padua of neo-Aristotelian philosophy was Cremonini, under whom Corydalleus studied. In contrast to the scholastics, who looked upon philosophy as the *ancilla theologiae*, and to Averroism, which, though far removed from the influence of Church dogma, still retained an element of metaphysical speculation, neo-Aristotelian philosophy separated philosophy from theology and regarded metaphysics as too abstruse. Only the harmony of the universe provided grounds for conceiving of God as superior intellect. Neo-Aristotelian philosophy therefore anticipated a goal towards which the physical sciences were also striving—the goal eventually attained by nineteenth-century European philosophy's positivistic conception of the universe. Of course, the dangers of teaching such a philosophy in Corydalleus' time are not hard to imagine.[256]

Following his studies at the University of Padua, Corydalleus taught for four months during 1609 in the Greek Community's school in Venice.[257] Afterwards, he went to Athens, where he taught philosophy and astronomy. Disillusioned by the opposition of his compatriots, however, he left for Cephalonia at the invitation of his student and friend Nikodimos Metaxas.[258] From there he went to Zacynthus (1628) and became an ordained monk, staying there for six years. The notables of Zacynthus considered him an authority on Orthodox dogma, respected him for the breadth of his education, and entrusted their children to him as a teacher without peer.[259] Still later, he was appointed patriarchal exarch; but his fervid temperament, nurtured by his liberal educational background and long exposure to a veritable ferment of ideas, made it difficult for him to become reconciled to monastic life, and after only a few years he divested himself of his habit.[260]

So liberal a spirit nonetheless attracted the attention of Patriarch Cyril Lucaris in Constantinople,[261] and he appointed Corydalleus director of the Patriarchal School. Later, the patriarch bestowed on him the title of Grand Dragoman of the Church. Corydalleus reorganized the school and managed, through his personal efforts as a teacher, to improve its standing.[262] His fame brought numerous students to the school, and his work proved a source of continuing inspiration to his successors—Ioannis Karyophyllis, Alexander Mavrokordatos (also Imperial Privy Councillor), and Sevastos Kyminitis, who later became director fo the Academy of Bucharest.[263]

After the assassination of his patron Cyril Lucaris in 1638, Corydalleus received a number of bitter setbacks. Patriarch Cyril II Contaris, a dupe of the Jesuits, intrigued against him. On 27 October 1639 a former student, the Grand Rhetor Meletios Syrigos, from the pulpit of the patriarchal church, accused Corydalleus of being a Calvinist.[264]

Contaris' successor, Parthenius I, ordained him Archbishop of Naupactus and Arta on 14 November 1640, but the combination of his own theological aberrations and Syrigos' renewed machinations against him, led to his eventual removal from that position by Parthenius II. Finally, at the invitation of his compatriots, he returned to Athens and there found contentment in teaching philosophy to many Greeks and foreigners. Afflicted by arthritis and failing eyesight, he died in Athens in 1646.[265]

Corydalleus' writings on Aristotle continued to be published until almost the end of the eighteenth century,[266] while a large number of them circulated in manuscript form, a fact which suggests that his works were used as manuals of instruction. Thus, Corydalleus' influence prevailed in Greece until modern European philosophers began to have an effect on her intellectual climate.[267] Even in far away Cyprus, his works had an acknowledged impact.[268]

Corydalleus used the rather barren and tedious method of teaching by lecture, which had been developed at the University of Padua a century before. It was for him, however, a necessary technique since he spoke ancient Greek and even used the language and terminology of Aristotle; naturally his students in most cases did not. Only his *On Geography*, or *On the Universe and Its Parts* and most of the *Funeral Orations* were written in a more colloquial language.

Like Aristotle, Corydalleus began by examining physical phenomena. The only means of investigating these was reason itself. The realm of philosophy was thus an autonomous one, having no relation to theology,[269] as was most clearly exemplified by Corydalleus' comments in his *Essay on the Celestial Spaces*. Theological interpretations of Aristotelian texts were accordingly to be rejected. All physical phenomena, whether yet explained or not, had origins that were susceptible of explicit definition. They were not manifestations of some supernatural power. Corydalleus thus scorned mysticism, magic, theosophy, astrology, and so on; nor did he believe in miracles, which he considered merely "accidental" or circumstantial occurrences whose causes were unknown only because they had not been studied.[270] He disclaimed any form of divine intervention either in the creation of the world or in the functioning of natural laws. God was Supreme Being, immanent in, and final cause of, the universe, but not efficient cause.[271] The prime cause which had set the universe in motion was rather a natural one, a need for order in nature, possessing none of the metaphysical characteristics of the God of Christians and neither omnipotent nor omniscient.[272]

Although the propinquity of his position both to Artistotelian philosophy and the materialistic and positivistic conception of the universe is at once apparent,[273] Corydalleus, like Aristotle, did not go so far as to deny the existence of God or a metaphysical world; but he said that neither was capable of being perceived with the senses as nature was.[274]

Perhaps in order to avoid criticism, Corydalleus confined himself to analyzing and developing the thoughts of the great philosopher. He insisted that he was merely arguing the substance of Peripatetic philosophy and that he himself accepted the doctrinal positions of the Eastern Church.

Yet the content of his teaching and the zeal with which he propagated neo-Aristotelian philosophy were bound to bring him into conflict with the Eastern Church. Despite the precautions he took, he became suspect in conservative circles. From time to time, not only Corydalleus himself [275] but also his students and disciples [276] were variously denounced as atheists, Calvinists, or other heretics. Perhaps his Christian faith was not quite as firm as he professed; or perhaps, as his student Eugenios Giannoulis the Aetolian once said, "he never believed the whole truth." [277]

A methodical and disciplined thinker, Corydalleus first analyzed the Aristotelian texts themselves, then discussed and criticized various explications given by different scholars, and finally presented his own original and graceful commentaries. [278] Though he was capable of examining critically the philosophical systems which had been developed up to his time, he lacked the inspiration and creative imagination to develop his own. Nevertheless, his interpretations of Aristotle contributed to the systematic exploration and diffusion of philosophical studies throughout the Near East, and for a century and a half he was considered an authority on philosophical questions. His classes in philosophy were relatively advanced and his audience was always large, comprising rich and poor alike.

His influence was strong in the Danubian principalities, where the confluence of East and West encouraged the cultivation of letters and the arts. There, in the academies of Bucharest and Jassy, which were modelled on the Patriarchal School, Corydalleus' students taught philosophy in accordance with their mentor's system. The first two Rumanian philosophers, Dimitrie Cantémir and Eufrosin Poteca, clearly reflected the influence of Corydalleus' teaching. [279]

Among Corydalleus' Greek students, the most distinguished were Ioannis Karyophyllis, [280] Meletios Syrigos, [281] Païsios Metaxas, Patriarch Nectarius of Jerusalem, and, most outstanding of all, Eugenios Giannoulis. The last, better known as Eugenios the Aetolian, was neither so erudite nor so philosophically adept as his teacher, but he had a virtuous character. Born between 1595 and 1600 of poor peasant parents at Megalo Dendro in Apokouro (in the district of Naupactus), Giannoulis received his education at Mt. Athos, as well as in Trikkala, in Cephalonia (with Païsios Metaxas), Zacynthus (with Theophilus Corydalleus), probably between 1629 and 1637, and then Constantinople. [282] Disappointed by the intrigues and moral infirmity of the upper clergy, he returned to Hellas and taught at Arta (1639–1640), Aetoliko (1640–1641), Missolonghi (1641–1644), and finally in the mountainous region of Agrafa (Karpenision and Vraniana), at a time when its people were just beginning to emerge from isolation and become aware of the need for education. [283] There he remained until his death in 1682. Conscious of "the great dearth and scarcity of educated and wise people," [284] he undertook, particularly in the remoter parts of Aetolia, the very practical task of teaching, founding schools and churches, and generally inculcating in his "thrice barbaric" [285] compatriots the great importance of education.

Eugenios managed to accomplish his mission mainly by virtue of the love he showed towards simple men, his humility, patience, nobility of soul, and deep religious faith. He also had the courage to stand up to the conquerors, the upper clergy, and notables by continually issuing homilies, both oral and written, against them. His many letters, most of them unpublished, to official and nonofficial personages are full of advice, criticism, and comment. All of them, whether written in classical Attic or (only occasionally) in demotic, which his student, Anastasios Gordios, dubbed "semibarbaric," show spontaneity and provide a great deal of information about events and people of the times, as well as about conditions under Turkish rule.[286] Wanton acts, brute force, and anarchy reigned everywhere in western Greece. The Turkish-Venetian wars and the incursions of the "Franks" along the coasts of Aetolia and Acarnania had brutalized the inhabitants. Hunger and "plague" completed the work of destruction. "The struggle of our unfortunate race, it would seem, is connived at both on earth and in heaven, for the deeds of the clergy are cunningly opposed to God."[287] His letters abound with musings on both the "present manifest sufferings"[288] of the race and the "ignorance of those in the Church"[289] who had brought about its decline.[290]

He sought to comfort the people of Agrafa:

And let not your love, I beseech you, give way to grief on account of the evils and misfortunes which presently prevail. The all-powerful grace of God will ensure that some good remains among the elite. The Church and the world have suffered much over the ages, yet they have survived; so let the fear of God remain rooted in your souls, and leave good memories for those who come after you; despise from the bottom of your hearts all deceit, devilry and envy, and never allow the contemplation of God to be absent from your hearts and souls. Always tell the truth; and a most gracious God, seeing your spiritual humility and piety, will exercise compassion towards humanity and free men from the burdens and innumerable evils that afflict them.[291]

Among many students who followed in Giannoulis' footsteps were Anastasios Gordios from Vraniana,[292] another celebrated teacher, and later, in the mid-eighteenth century, Kosmas the Aetolian, who declaimed fervently throughout the Hellenic world on the need for intellectual enlightenment, social solidarity, justice, and freedom.

THE COMMUNITIES

Under Turkish rule every manifestation of Greek culture emanated from individual communities, each one an irreducible unit of social organization. The community began to develop in ancient times as the people's spontaneous response to the problems of everyday life and to threats from the outside world. Like all social organisms, the institution was subject to the protean influences of time, internal evolution, and external change. Any research into the nature of the community under Turkish rule is therefore bound to run into a great many difficulties.

A number of attempts have been made to trace the history of community institutions, fixing their origins, and indicating the various evolutionary stages in their growth.[1] Almost without exception, however, these studies, and indeed the discussions flowing from them, have been unsystematic and inadequate. The debate is still open, and a meticulous re-examination is necessary.

The obstacles confronting anyone who wishes to follow the development of local political institutions and delineate the customs of the Greek *polis* from antiquity to the present are formidable. There are two major pitfalls. The first derives from the nature of the problem itself: while many institutions and customs did not differ from city to town, from continental Greece to the islands, or from one time to another in the same place, there were widespread legal variations corresponding to the variety of geographic and social conditions. The second derives from the paucity of written evidence for the periods of Byzantine and Ottoman rule. On the period from the Capture to the seventeenth century, surviving sources are especially scarce; and although more are available for later centuries, they tend to be restricted to certain, mainly island, communities.[2]

There are at least three major theories of community origins; more, if the partial explanations of some researchers are taken into account.[3]

Constantine Paparrhegopoulos' view was much more an expression of his own intuititve faith in the unbroken continuity of an historical tradition of Hellenism from ancient to modern times than an objective demonstration from the evidence he adduced. Nevertheless, he maintained that the communities under Turkish rule had deep roots in the traditions of the Greek nation, that they had never ceased to exist "in substance," and that those of the Byzantine period were essentially the same as their ancient antecedents: "ancient and autonomous urban institutions," which had merely adjusted to the new circumstances of each passing century. These modifications varied from time to time and from place to place, but usually consisted in no more than a redefinition of the jurisdiction of notables, their titular designation, or perhaps the manner of their election. Thus, when Ottoman rule began, the Turks permitted various communities to continue in operation as an auxiliary arm of government at the local level.[4] Paparrhegopoulos' theory is supported by the lawyer A. Vrekosis, who contends that the historical continuity of free peasant communities was never interrupted. These agrarian organizations resisted attempts by the rural oligarchy to encroach upon their lands.[5]

Then there is the theory of David Urquhart, the English diplomat, who writes that community councils were born solely of the need to collect taxes during the Ottoman period.[6] P. Argyropoulos expresses more or less the same view when he says that the community organizations which developed under Turkish rule were no more than a political and administrative response to the exigencies of that rule.[7]

Moschovakis, who claims to have investigated the matter, though "not systematically," holds that the communities of the Ottoman period were the same as those municipal organizations which began to reappear in Byzantine times, particularly after the Macedonian Dynasty (867–1056). However, they bore no resemblance either internally to one another or externally to the "republics" of ancient Greece and Rome. The new organizations possessed no uniform characteristics simply because they were not legislative creations; on the contrary, they were as varied as the local needs in response to which they had arisen.[8]

Modern research appears to justify and buttress Paparrhegopoulos' theory. Louis Bréhier has distinguished three phases in the growth of community institutions. First, in the large cities of the East which escaped the population upheavals from the third through the sixth centuries, the traditions of the ancient republics were only slightly modified by time.[9] They remained substantially in force until the seventh century. In the West, on the other hand, the migrations of the Germanic peoples resulted in the decline of trade, the reduction of population, the decay of urban centers, and the disappearance of community institutions.[10] Second, although the chaos produced after the seventh century by the invasions of

Arabs, Slavs, Avars, and Bulgarians led to the concentration of governmental authority and a heightening of the state's influence over its subjects that stifled local autonomy, community institutions did not completely disappear but rather contracted to the borders of the Empire. Despite the celebrated forty-sixth Decree of Leo the Wise,[11] whose intention in promulgating it was to demolish self-government,[12] community institutions, in my opinion, persisted not only in the border provinces but probably in many places in the interior as well. Third, from the twelfth century to the fifteenth the people jealously guarded their old community privileges and liberties, exploiting every opportunity to have them confirmed both by Byzantine emperors and foreign rulers. Bréhier believes that during this period the communities lost many of their earlier characteristics because the old class of nobles, or archons, had vanished and been replaced by a new rural aristocracy, the *dynatoi* or "powerful," which dominated town and countryside from the eleventh century on, promoting community freedoms at the expense of central authority.[13] This contention that a new nobility replaced an older one is not wholly convincing; even if true, it would not of course preclude the continuation of community institutions.

One very important point concerning the internal constitution and evolution of the communities needs to be stressed: the character of the old communities was profoundly influenced by the active participation of, and initiatives taken by, the local clergy. During the first centuries of the Christian era a distinctive type of community organization emerged in Greece and the Near East which represented the fusion of ancient Greek polities with the early Christian communities. Though largely uninvestigated, the problem is of great historical interest: the privileged and official position of the bishop or archbishop in the community dates from this time, later to be confirmed and strengthened by the decrees of Justinian. Thus, according to Decree 128.16 the bishop of "each city," together with the "notables," was responsible for seeing that the finances of laborers were sound at the end of each year. This stipulation was not something new, but it was once a reality founded on the long-standing tradition of a bishop's pre-eminent intellectual and moral authority.[14]

We may be fairly sure that, until the final submission of the Eastern Roman-Byzantine Empire to the Turks, isolated communities survived, even if their constitution and functions had undergone some adaptation to changing conditions both local and imperial.[15] One such example was the city of Thessalonica, which had the good fortune not to be sucked into the maelstrom of the great invasions of the Middle Ages. The history of this city's community institutions provides further corroboration of Paparrhegopoulos' theory. Constantine Sathas was the first to adduce detailed historical evidence pertaining to Thessalonica under both Byzantine and Venetian rule; and his view was that the city had acquired substantial privileges in antiquity and had managed to cling to these over the centuries up to the time of her surrender to the Venetians in 1423. Thessalonica accomplished this because of her insistence, whenever submitting to a conqueror, that she remain free and govern herself according to her own laws and customs. Tafrali merely echoes Sathas when he says that the Byzantine emperors and Frankish kings respected all institutions surviving from Hellenistic to Roman times, though naturally with modifications. Finally, when the people of Thessalonica capitulated to the Venetians, they again insisted as the main condition of their surrender that their institutions be respected.[16]

So much oral and written evidence testifies to the ancient lineage of local self-government that, particularly in those places which escaped grave disturbances, it can only be presumed to have had its origins in Byzantine or even (at least in some cases) in ancient institutions.[17] One oral tradition, for example, speaks of Sultan Orchan's granting privileges by firman to the inhabitants of Cyzicus when they surrendered their city. He also permitted the city's clergy to wear a band around their high hats, symbolizing the goodwill be bore towards them. According to this same tradition, the firman remained in force in Cyzicus till the nineteenth century.[18] In my *Origins of the Greek Nation,* it was also argued that both Frankish conquerors (the Venetians, for instance) and Ottoman Turks consistently acknowledged existing privileges or granted new ones when those cities standing in the path of their advance surrendered peaceably. In the case of Thessalonica, the fall of the city to Bayezid I in 1391 and to Murad II in 1430 by no means meant the extinction of community institutions, which, on the contrary, were permitted to adjust to the new conditions.[19] At various times after this, the continuing existence of community notables can be established beyond question.[20]

Not only urban communities but also rural organizations and confederations of free peasant communities can be presumed to have survived up to the period of Turkish rule. The grounds for this belief are simply that the Byzantine emperors from time to time took active steps to protect the peasants who were in danger of disappearing as a class through the predacity of the agrarian *dynatoi.* These rural communities were the basis of the economic life of the Byzantine Empire.[21] Recent research has shown that the terms *omas choriou* (group of villages), *chorion* (village), and *mitrokomia* (small town) which are frequently encountered in Byzantine texts refer to communities of free peasants who were collectively responsible for the payment of land taxes. In other words, the Byzantine Empire adopted an older practice of uniting free smallholders into single units (communities) for the purposes of apportioning and collecting taxes more efficiently. The individual members of the communities, however, remained technically free.[22]

The survival of communities of free peasants is finally proven by the existence of common lands, pastures, and forests during Byzantine times and afterwards.[23] Even if such communities and confederations of communities were confined to isolated regions, they nevertheless existed.

How was authority generally constituted in the Greek communities of the Ottoman Empire? How many persons and which ones normally exercised it? How were they chosen and to what extent was their authority circumscribed? That there are no pat answers to these and similar questions is evident from the kind of source which describes Nicholas Isidoros as a "judge and *emin* of the grand seignior"[24] in Adrianople just a few months after the Capture. Since the designation "*emin* of the grand seignior" undoubtedly signifies that this person enjoyed the favor and confidence of the sultan, are we to assume that he alone was responsible for the government of the Christians of Adrianople as the sultan's direct appointee? Or was he the elected president of a community?

The number of community notables under Turkish rule varied considerably from place to place. A committee known as the *Dodekada*[25] (the "Twelve") in Thessalonica had precise numerical counterparts in Serrai in 1614[26] and in Tsamanta (the *Dodekara*).[27] But in other cities and islands, for example, Athens,[28] Aegina, and in most of the Aegean, four *epitropoi* (commissioners) were elected annually.[29] Chios combined both systems with four governors (*governatori*)[30] at the head of a committee of twelve members.

Some interesting information is available regarding the social origins and method of election of the twelve members of the Serrai committee at the beginning of the seventeenth century. The entire Christian population assembled before the metropolitan, clergy, and notables, probably in the metropolitan church, thus constituting, as it were, the "full synod." "Twelve just, good, virtuous, God-fearing" men representing each guild were then elected, very likely by voice, to manage communal affairs. Their most important function was to apportion fairly the common expenses of the citadel and city of Serrai. Beginning with the members of the Twelve,[31] the economic burden was distributed in accordance with each individual's capacity to bear it.

The social composition and function of Ioannina's community committee was similar, though nothing is known about its numerical strength or the method of electing members.[32]

Of particular interest in the organization of municipal government was the extent of guild representation which, *mutatis mutandis,* was the same in many Greek urban centers of the Ottoman Empire. Until the very end of the Byzantine Empire, only descendants of old Byzantine families, scholars, and wealthy citizens,[33] had taken part in the conduct of community affairs. The transformation in municipal government whereby representatives of the "mechanical" arts came to dominate councils was due not only to the gradual disappearance of Byzantine families but also to the economic growth of handicraft industry under Turkish rule, during which craftsmen enjoyed a new social prominence because the Turks looked upon them as honorable and "beloved of God." We shall examine this matter in another context.

The "full synod" (*megisti synodos*) of Serrai met only infrequently when it was essential to bring some matter—for instance, concerning weights and measures[34]—to the notice of all the people. Each parish had its notables, who, in the codex of Serrai, were referred to as *kallistevontes tou machala* (leading citizens).[35] In 1614 there was also a *protogeros tou kastrou,* or "Chief Elder" of the walled city.[36] There was a person of similar title and rank in Nauplia under Venetian rule in 1509. Spyridon Lambros considers that the creation of this office marked an advance in local autonomy and that the person concerned was "member, or perhaps president, of a committee of local notables that existed in addition to the Venetian authorities."[37]
· As a rule, notables were elected from the ranks of the richest and most talented.[38] Elections were free, though often tradition, or the very wealth and influence of certain individuals or families, predetermined their outcome. Notables, then, occupied all positions of legislative, executive, and judicial authority within the community. Decisions were framed, at least in theory, with the best interests of the community in mind; once made, they had general force and usually brooked no infringement.[39] The system possessed the great advantage that decisions on urgent matters could be made without delay. Needs were met expeditiously and flexibly as they arose, without the retraints that legislative precedent would have imposed. On the whole, the variety of the notables' work and decisions is impressive.[40]

Community notables also comprised a judicial committee which sat in judgment on issues involving the affairs of their compatriots. A general principle of Islamic law was that those subject to the capitation tax (the Christian and Jewish unfaithful, or *ehli zimmet*), came under the jurisdiction of their own laws.[41] The notables did not always dispense justice impeccably, nor were they incorruptible or without moral stain,[42] but on the whole they were more honest and more merciful than the cadis, the outside judges.

Since the cadi was susceptible to the influence of bribes and often arbitrary in his judgments,[43] almost all Greeks chose to submit their differences to their own notables or bishops. Rarely did they go before the cadi[44] for an "outside judgment,"[45] as they called it, except when they were determined to gain a favorable decision through bribery and false testimony.[46] In such cases, trials involving Greeks proved lucrative sources of income for the cadis. A popular saying in Epirus was: "Greeks quarrel and Turks feast."[47] If ever a Christian and a Moslem were the contending parties in a trial, the Christian could never hope for justice, however just his claims: the testimony of Christian witnesses against Moslems was simply not admissible as evidence.[48]

Many community notables (the *kocabaşıs*, as Turks called them) became more unscrupulous after the establishment of Turkish sovereignty. They connived at injustice and collaboration with the conqueror. Sheltering under the umbrella of Turkish authority, they oppressed those of their compatriots who were poor and weak by apportioning taxes unequally. For this reason, the word *kocabaşı*[49] took on a pejorative meaning in Greek, connoting someone who was "crude," "oppressive," and "despotic." The *kocabaşı* thus became a stereotyped figure in Hellenic society, one branded with infamy as in this popular poem by an anonymous author:

A white eagle sat on Mount Smolika's back
Holding a human head in its talons,
Now pinching it, now saying to it:
O head, mulish head, stupid head,
What evil have you done to let my wings envelop you,
To fall into my clutches, to feel my claws?
I was a *kocabaşı* and notable of the land;
From the rich I demanded money, from the poor as much again,
And from a widow, a very poor widow
With a fine vineyard and an ample farm, five times as much.[50]

Local clergy, metropolitans, and bishops were integral members of the community, exercising distinct authority within it. This active and intimate participation of the clergy in community affairs was evident not only from their clearly defined spiritual, and often political, leadership, but more importantly from their judicial authority in matters of civil law. As we have observed elsewhere, this was a legacy from Byzantine times.[51] The opinion of the archbishop carried especial weight in the field of inheritance law, and, by wielding his ordinary ecclesiastical powers of suspension or, occasionally, excommunication, he could prevent those seeking the redress of grievances from appearing before the cadi.[52]

The districts of Zagora, Malakasi, and Agrafa in the Pindus enjoyed definite privileges. Mostly, our knowledge of these derives from oral tradition,[53] which alludes to various incidents as having been responsible for the bestowal or curtailment of certain privileges.

Without doubt, the granting of privileges can be satisfactorily explained by reference to the special circumstances surrounding the Pindus' initial submission to the Turks. In my *Origins of the Greek Nation* I point out that when the Vlach-speaking inhabitants of the Pindus finally acknowledged the sovereignty of Murad II in the middle of the fifteenth century, they were accorded various privileges conferring, in the main, local autonomy.[54] As was also the case in various other parts of the Ottoman Empire, the local inhabitants of the Pindus were careful to seek the periodic renewal of their immunities. The text of the so-called "Treaty of Tamasi" (signed in the village of Tamasi on 10 May 1525) provides information on this subject. The original document, still extant, set out four agreed upon conditions: the villages of the Agrafa would retain their autonomy; Turks were permitted to live only in Phanarion; intercourse between the mountains and the plains, which was vitally necessary to mountain people in general and the Pindus nomads in particular, could continue; and every community was required to pay the Porte a large sum of money annually, to be conveyed to Constantinople by a trustworthy agent of the local committee. According to tradition, this treaty was signed by the then beylerbey of Rumelia after he made an abortive expedition out of Larissa to subdue the people of the Pindus.[55] Just how much historical truth is contained in this tradition cannot be ascertained; but it is certain that the people of Agrafa were not receiving privileges for the first time. They were merely successful in obtaining a renewal of privileges that the Turks had attempted to curtail or suspend.

The central part of the district of Zagora submitted to Murad II by a treaty between powerful local families and the sultan's plenipotentiaries. However, the eastern part of the district, together with the northern Vlach villages of Malakasi, held out until 1478, which was some forty-eight years after the capitulation of Ioannina. It is not known when the western part came to terms with the Turks, though there is evidence to suggest that it remained autonomous for some time. The district of Zagora formed part of the *valide sultana,* or the domain of the Queen Mother, and its inhabitants paid only three taxes—the *prosopikon,* or head tax (*cizye gerban*), the *provatonomion,* or ship tax, and the *haraç.* Around the middle of the seventeenth century a number of its villages were detached from the *valide sultana* and granted as fiefs to various spahis, thereby losing their properties and self-governing status. Between 1681 and 1684, mainly because of the exertions and material support of notables of Zagora, the villages of the eastern and western parts of the district formed a confederacy of forty-seven villages, which lasted till 1868, or almost two hundred years.[56] A president was elected yearly, sometimes every six months in Ioannina, by majority vote of the notables of each member town or village.

Until the beginning of the seventeenth century, the president or head notable of Zagora usually remained where his home was. He had a spacious house with large open rooms (called *krevvates*) in which he conferred with the other notables on such matters as community welfare, the apportionment of taxes among the villages, community differences or personal conflicts, and the safeguarding of privileges. For a continuous period of seventy years during the sixteenth and seventeenth centuries, a member of the Kontodemos family from the village of Vradeto served as president of the confederation. From the second half of the eighteenth century, the president almost invariably resided in the chief town of Epirus in order to cope more effectively with the constraints of various district governors who were bent upon the annihilation of Zagora's privileges. There, until the fall of Ali Pasha in 1822, the notables would meet in the president's residence to elect a new president or resolve the issues which came before them. After the death of Ali Pasha, when the president no longer had his residence in Ioannina, a special house—the so-called *epistasia*—was rented in the town. Whether or not the president chose to occupy it, it was the permanent residence of the secretary of the confederation, who also carried out the duties of treasurer. Both president and secretary received salaries.[57] A parallel authority to that of the head notable was that of the community notables of each village, who were responsible for the levying and collection of taxes, local security, the maintenance of schools, and so on. These notables were obliged to render an account of their actions either annually or every six months.[58]

The actual privileges enjoyed by the confederation from one period to the next cannot be specified with any great degree of accuracy. Nevertheless it is possible, by piecing together the evidence of oral tradition, local records, and official Turkish directives, to say that, first, Turks were forbidden entry into the district of Zagora; second, the inhabitants had no recourse to litigation in Turkish courts; and third, religious freedom (including the right to ring church bells)[59] was guaranteed.

In order to safeguard its privileges and forearm itself against the threat of persecution, the confederation had no compunctions about frequently offering money to the powerful agas and beys of Argyrokastron, Tepelenë, and Ioannina, or their representatives, for protection.[60]

The district of Malakasi, southeast of Zagora, stretches south of Ioannina as far as Arta. It included the villages of Kalarites, Syraco, Metsovon, Arboresi, and many others. It, too, belonged to the *valide sultana* and paid the same three taxes as Zagora. In time, however, the northern villages of Malakasi, except for Kalarites, lost the protection of the *valide sultana* and became enfeoffed to spahis. From 1635 on they were the objects of continuous depredation.[61]

While the villages of Malakasi lost their privileged status, the district of Metsovon acquired new privileges in 1659 during the reign of Mohammed IV (1648–1687) and managed to have these recognized and renewed by that sultan's successors until the time of Selim III (1789–1807). According to tradition, these new privileges were granted as the favor of a vizier to Kyrgios (or Kyriakos) Phlokas, a shepherd from Metsovon. Sultan Mohammed IV issued a firman proclaiming the district of Metsovon (embracing the villages of Metsovon, Anilio, Malakasi, Voutinos, Milia, and Koutsouphliani) inviolable and self-governing, subject only to inspec-

33. Metsovon, in Epirus. From Henry Holland, *Travels in the Ionian Isles, Albania, Thessaly, Macedonia, etc., during the years 1812 and 1813*, London, 1815.

tion by the imperial corps of *bostançı*. He also abolished spahi fiefs in the district, decreed that it was henceforth "in the lump" an appanage of Mecca and Medina, brought it into association with the fiefs of Langkaza and Mataranga in Thessaly, and exempted it from the most onerous taxes and tributes and from having to quarter Turkish troops or, indeed, any Turk.[62] However, it is my view that this grant of "new" privileges was no more than the confirmation or extension of older, perhaps very much older, ones. There is convincing evidence that Murad II was the first sultan to acknowledge or grant immunities to Metsovon, when its people facilitated the passage of Sinan Pasha's army through the narrow passes of Metsovon leading to Ioannina.[63] Afterwards, the old privileges were retained (perhaps with the addition of new ones) because the people of Metsovon commanded a pass that was strategically vital from every military point of view. Murad II himself justified the granting of those privileges: "the people of Metsovon lived in a place through which many people passed all the year round. In winter, the place was covered with so much snow that travellers were in constant danger of becoming lost; and that was why the local people covered the legs of horses and carried the travellers on their shoulders. In summer, when the danger came from bandits, they protected travellers and saw them safely through the pass."[64]

From that time on Metsovon was governed by a committee of seven, probably one from each neighborhood:[65] a president, the so-called *dimogeron* or *geron* (elder or alderman); the *ephoros* (superintendent of schools); the *phrontistis* (superintendent of water); the *eispraktor* (tax-collector); the *agoranomos* (market inspector); the *epitropos* (church warden); and the *oplarchigos* (commander of militia) of the local garrison. There was also a separate committee of wise old men presided over by the *dimogeron,* which constituted a court of customary law. Until the end of the nineteenth century, the composition of these committees was of an aristocratic nature, and the management of public concerns was therefore always in the hands of those considered notables—the powerful—who were distinguishable by their manner of dress and the grandeur of their homes. By the nineteenth century, this class of the powerful was composed not only of landowners and stockowners, as in the past, but also of townsmen who had amassed mercantile fortunes in Egypt, Russia, Walachia, and Constantinople. As with small communities everywhere, Metsovon was rent by factionalism and bitter disputes.[66] It is highly probable that the conflict was exacerbated by the emergence of townsmen insisting on participating in the management of public affairs.

The regime of privilege in Metsovon attracted families from Agrafa and other parts of Thessaly and Epirus.[67] Added to the district's number of natural births, this influx of immigrants produced a continuous growth in population.

A study of the island communities of the Aegean Sea poses problems of peculiar complexity. The social and political history of the region must be borne constantly in mind, for the continuity of political life was broken by frequent changes of rulers; and the effects of this disruption have therefore to be assessed along with other more usual considerations—whether or not changes in sovereignty were effected forcibly or by treaty, whether or not communities became depopulated in the process, whether or not they were subsequently reinhabited when political conditions permitted.

On certain islands, community institutions under Frankish rule followed Byzantine precedents. For example, the privileges and customs of the people of Tenos under the Ghizi[68] were undoubtedly inherited from Byzantine times, and these were subsequently confirmed as a condition of Tenos' surrender to the Venetians in 1390. It is therefore conceivable that public affairs were carried on under Ottoman rule, at least in some of the islands, more or less as they had been in Byzantine, perhaps even in ancient, times. However, it is far from easy to delineate those elements of government which remained constant. When foreign rulers imposed a feudalistic regimen and placed the islands under the Assizes of Rumania, the new institutions, even if modified, must certainly have overridden and constricted those still lingering on from Byzantine times.[69] Thus we may presume that wherever Greek communal authority in the islands persisted, it was more or less vestigial, depending on the prevailing social and political conditions.

But when the power of the various local Frankish rulers began to weaken at the beginning of the sixteenth century, that of Greek community notables proportionately increased, providing an opportunity for the development of local self-governing institutions. The capitulation of Chios and the last of the Cyclades to the Turks in 1566 hastened this process. By 1719 in Chios, for example, in addition to four elders (*kocabaşıs* or *vekilis*) who apparently owed their election to the influence of the four Genoese governors, there were also the so-called *potestatoi* (possibly corresponding to the twelve-member committee of the Frankish period). Although not recognized by Turkish authority, the *potestatoi* played a definite role in the community affairs of the raias that included the collection of taxes which were not officially sanctioned.[70]

The Greeks of the Cyclades were successful in obtaining various political and judicial privileges.[71] There were even some instances where political and social conditions created quite unique forms of community organization. After 1621, for example, Naxos had three separate communities: Kastron (comprising the descendants of the Franks), Bourgos (comprising notables and artisans of the small town of Bourgos), and Choria (comprising the villages of the island).[72]

The typical form of community government in the Cyclades under

Turkish rule was that of two to four (usually four) *epitropoi,* who resided in the island's chief town. This system, certainly in a number of cases, had its origins in Frankish times; it did not emerge, as Sauger[73] would have us believe, only after the Turkish conquest. (While it is true that the word *epitropos* came into general use during the Ottoman period, it did not displace other local nomenclatures.) When partial Turkish sovereignty was established in 1537 and made complete in 1566, feudalism was not overthrown. It continued to exist in all its forms, with the inhabitants divided into social classes and peasants bound in vassalage to Frankish landowners or their descendants. Since social organization thus underwent no change, we may similarly expect to find that change in the management of public affairs was nonexistent or, at most, minimal. Only slowly, as vassals gradually awoke to their predicament and Turkish authority in the islands became internally more effective, did palpable change occur.

The view that community institutions in some of the Cyclades during Ottoman times were merely extensions of those which had functioned under Frankish rule appears strengthened by a consideration of the particular cases of Tenos, Mykonos, Amorgos, and Naxos. Thus, the *syndichoi* (the community notables of Tenos under Turkish rule,[74] whose very title is evocative of the *syndikoi,* or syndics, of the Venetian period) probably differed in no essential respect from the three *procuratori delle Università* (or *della communità*) of the Venetian period, who were elected annually in accordance with ancient custom: *"giusta l'antiqua consuetudine del luogo con l'intervento cosi delli spettabili cittadini, come delli contadini di Thine*[75] [according to the ancient custom of the place with the assent of the notables of Tenos, from both town and country]." (The title of *procuratori* may also be compared with the designation *ton koinon phrontistai,*[76] referring to the public curators, or procurators, of Thessalonica). A Venetian document of 1561 mentions the position of *protogeros,*[77] which was filled biennially on the nomination of the Venetian rector. In this way, the Venetians adapted a Byzantine tradition and, at least nominally, perpetuated it.

Mykonos was governed by a *gouvernadoros* or *capetanos* from the middle of the fifteenth century until the Turkish conquest in 1537. This situation remained unchanged till the death of the last *capetanos,* Simon Giustiniani, in 1615, when the priests and people assembled in the Church of the Prophet Elias outside the citadel and elected two of their compatriots, Andreas Kalamaras and Manuel Stathis, to replace him for a period of one year. As time passed, the people of the island, making use of privileges won from various *kapudan* pashas (admirals of the Turkish fleet) gradually evolved their famous and unique *koinon,*[78] or municipality; it was adapted to their own particular needs and activities.

Perhaps the office of *capetanos* disappeared, as Zerlentis believes,[79] during the course of this development. Against this view, however, must be set the evidence of the *koinon*'s constitution of 1649, which referred to the *capetanos* and *castellanos*, in addition to elders.[80] Whatever the case, by 1665 only one *epitropos* and judge (*kritis*) was elected for the whole island; his name was Pierros Skoutaris, and he was elected again in 1667. He was assisted by two elected *symvoithoi*, or associates, each with the title "general *capetanos*, *kritis* and *epitropos*," who were empowered "to issue orders to big and little men alike, exercising full and complete authority to requisition and to retain whatever is given to them in the interests of the·betterment of our island's affairs."[81] The history of the development of communal institutions on Mykonos is thus in a number of ways typical of the Aegean as a whole: the end of Venetian rule in 1537 marked the beginning of a period of flux in regard to nomenclature, methods of election, and the numbers of people elected in local government. The situation on Mykonos had its counterparts on other Aegean islands, and was prevented from becoming stable in the years after 1537 mainly because of the dislocation caused by the confused struggles between Venetian and Turk.[82]

Amorgos was governed by a *castellanos* (*gouvernadoros* or *capetanos*), who was backed up by a secretary (*grammatikos*) and judges. An office of *notarios*[83] also existed on the island. Sauger is certainly referring to the judges when he says that three old men held court in the island's small town, no one ever daring to appeal to any higher authority.[84] Together with the *castellanos*, the judges made up the four *epitropoi* of the island.

In 1587 on Naxos, one person held the position of *nountzios* and *castellanos*. Other titles were those of *kyvernitis*, used in connection with the island as a whole (which must surely be the equivalent of *governatore*), *capetanios* (for certain villages), *balis*, *apanokynigaris* and *mantrakouratos*.[85] In that same year, three judges were also elected to hand down judgments consistent with the Assizes on matters in legal dispute.[86]

Our knowledge of self-government in the Aegean islands during the Ottoman period is enhanced by evidence indirectly gathered from the sultan's decrees (*ahtnames*) relating specifically to privileges. The nature of the privileges conferred by these (prohibitng child recruitment, permitting the restoration of ruined churches, recognizing existing notarial arrangements, and so on)[87] again reinforces the view that the social life of the Greeks was already organized in Frankish times. Also, community authorities pledged to secure for the Greeks as many liberties and privileges as possible were already well established.

Of fundamental importance were the *ahtnames* of Chios, which served as models for those later promulgated for the other islands of the Cyclades.[88] Issued in 1580 and 1646 during the reigns of Murad III (1574–

1595) and Ibrahim (1640–1648), respectively, these decrees confirmed privileges that were already in force in Naxos, Andros, Melos, Paros, Santorini, Syros, and Siphnos. They contained references to the fact that, until 1566, these islands had been governed by a Christian bey (the last, Duke Jacob IV Crispo); and that, afterwards, the sultan had appointed a Jewish bey, Joseph Nazi, who ruled in accordance with local custom. When Nazi died, the sultan directed that the *ahtname* of Chios[89] should henceforth apply to the government of the other islands.

Among the various articles of the *ahtname* of Murad III, a number may be singled out for comment. First, the inhabitants would continue to pay the head tax, as they had in the past, but would otherwise be exempt from the "*kapenta, avarız,* and other forced labor." Second, they might repair their churches. Third, a tithe on vineyards, gardens, and fields was stipulated. Fourth, neither bey nor cadi had the right to molest the inhabitants by depriving them or their descendants of any of their belongings. Fifth, the taxes on silk, wine, and food were inapplicable. Sixth, old "customs" were to remain in force, including the right of Greeks to settle grievances legally in accordance with these; at the same time, anyone might have recourse to Turkish justice or become a Moslem if he wished. Seventh, those who had to go to work carrying "torches and lanterns" might circulate freely at night. Eighth, "tax-collectors were not to take more than was prescribed by law and custom, nor forcibly confiscate the fodder of horses." Finally, those who had complaints against the *sancak* bey, cadi, or even against their own people, were to be allowed, if they so wished, to journey to the Sublime Porte itself and seek redress of their grievances there.[90]

Those islands of the Dodecanese, such as Syme, which capitulated either before or after the capture of Rhodes by Suleiman I (1520–1566), were also accorded tax privileges and local autonomy.[91] In the case of Rhodes as well as Megisti[92] the bestowal of privileges appears to have been calculated to stop the flight of refugees to Italy and Crete.[93] It is uncertain whether privileges were granted the rest of the Dodecanese at the same time or later, in 1570 or 1645.[94] Whatever the case, the Dodecanese people were liable to few taxes, and these were paid in lump sums to the mosques, imarets, and medresehs founded by the sultan in Rhodes. For this reason, the islands were designated *wakf,* that is, domain set aside for the support of religious establishments.[95] As a direct consequence of the various immunities which the inhabitants of the barren Dodecanese enjoyed, they were able to cope successfully with quite unfavorable conditions of life. In some cases, they even prospered.[96]

The public affairs of the islands were conducted by two, three or four notables, variously entitled *epitropoi* or *syndikoi,* who came from the ranks of the richest and most respected inhabitants. They were responsible for the apportionment and collection of taxes, the delivery of monies to the *kapudan* pasha and the administration of justice. At the end of what was normally a year's service, they were held accountable for their actions. Elections were held by voice before an assembly of clergy, notables, and laymen, though usually the clergy and notables had reached prior agreement among themselves as to the most suitable of the candidates available. The people could either ratify the continued incumbency of a notable already in office, or suggest alternative names for the coming year.[97]

Besides the *epitropoi* who held office in the chief town of each island, every village normally had its own notable, whose authority locally was virtually unfettered.[98] There were also the offices of *cangellarioi* (*cantzillierides* or *catzilierides*)[99] which, like those of the *epitropoi,* dated from the years of Frankish rule. Then, the *cangellarios* had served as the secretary of the local ruler or governing authority.[100] Various codices and documents which are still extant disclose that, both under Frankish and early Ottoman rule, a well-organized *cangellarios* and notarial system was functioning on Chios[101] and on Naxos, the latter the ducal seat of the Duchy of Naxos. However, with the consolidation of Turkish rule, the class of educated special lawyers gradually died out.[102] There was a *cantzilieris* under Ottoman rule who was subordinate to the *epitropoi* and carried out mainly secretarial duties. In those cases (for example, Melos and Kea) where the separate office of *notarios* had disappeared with the end of Frankish rule, the *cantzilieris* also fulfilled the role of notary. Where a *notarios* did exist, he performed the functions of notary, registrar of mortgages, and coroner.[103] For example, one document refers to an office of "*archigrammateus*" (chief secretary) and "*notarios*" (apparent) on Naxos in 1644, and to that of "*notarios*" and "*cantzellarios*" in 1645.[104]

On Mykonos, the community *cangellarios* was designated variously as "general (*catholikos*) *cansilieris*" or "municipal (*koinos*) *cantzilieris,*" while on Syros he was entitled "community (*koinotitos*) *catzillieris*" or "*cantzelleris* apparent."[105] The addition of agnomens like *phaneros* (apparent), *catholikos* (general), or *koinos* (municipal) was intended to distinguish the community notables from the secretaries of local consulates.[106]

Elsewhere, the *cantzilieris* was responsible to higher authority; that is to say, he was a representative of the sultan and the sultan's officials. On Kythnos, for instance, the *cantzilieris* in conjunction with the Turkish voivode, or tax farmer, and the local notables, clergy and lay, constituted the community's political authority, apportioned taxes, formed a civil and criminal tribunal, and generally made the final decisions on every matter affecting the community. The offices of *epitropos* and *protogeros,* here were scarcely more than sinecures.[107] In most of the islands from the end of the seventeenth century or the beginning of the eighteenth century, the office of voivode (which by then implied the status of governor as well as that of tax farmer) was usually filled by Christians.[108]

As a rule, the *cangellarioi* were elected by vote of the inhabitants in the same way as the community notables. However, there were some variations from place to place and time to time in the manner of electing the *cangellarioi*, prescribing their duties, and fixing their periods of tenure.[109]

Research into the community institutions of Samos has been particularly valuable because it is impossible here to avoid confronting a very basic problem: what kind of political organization was adopted immediately after the island's recolonization in 1577? Samos became a *wakf*, the income from which went to the mosque in Galata built by, and subsequently containing the remains of, the island's colonizer, Kilits Ali.[110] The island was governed by notables, who at first were undoubtedly the preferred appointees of Kilits Pasha and the marine pilot Sarakinis,[111] however ostensibly free their elections were. The incumbents were invariably adventurers ready to truckle to the Turks, advance their own interests by any means, even by betraying their compatriots.[112] Thus, from the very outset, the notables of Samos were hardly more than Turkish lackeys, maintaining for many years thereafter an attitude of habitual servility. With the cadi and other Turkish officials (numbering three or four families), and the aga's retinue of about a dozen Turks, they lived in Megali Chora[113] and constituted an oppressive oligarchy.[114]

On every island with elected notables, an assembly of the people convened from time to time, as circumstances decreed, in order to elect new notables and discuss important matters such as taxation. In addition to village assemblies, some islands (Thasos[115] and Samos, for example) also convoked a general assembly to deliberate on matters of concern to the island as a whole. These general assemblies commonly met just before the regular visits of the imperial official who was empowered to collect the *haraç*.[116]

The Porte was represented on each island by a cadi and a bey or aga. The cadi was the judicial arm of authority, while the bey or aga executed policy and ensured the payment of the various taxes to which the islanders were liable.[117] However, instead of exacting a legal tithe, the aga or cadi might extort one-fifth of the islanders' produce and generally so oppress them that the people of Naxos, for example, preferred to pay sixteen to twenty thousand gold pieces direct to the sultan each year to retain their harvest rather than have an aga on their island.[118] In 1710 the people of Mykonos, enraged by the injustices of their cadi, actually drove him off their island.[119]

However, the position of cadi or aga was a precarious one on the smaller islands since these were frequently prey to pirates.[120] Consequently few candidates offered themselves for office, and Turkish authority, if it never exactly vanished, became nominal. Thus the inhabitants of these islands had the opportunity to develop their own institutions and customs. By the seventeenth century the activities of local authorities had significantly expanded. The constitution of the Municipality of Mykonos, which still survives, dates from this time (26 October 1649).[121]

From the foregoing analysis of the community institutions of the Hellenic world, it is possible now to draw a number of fairly reliable conclusions.

To the question of alien influence on the development of community institutions, the degree to which the Slavs, Franks, Albanians, and Turks who invaded Hellas and settled down among the Hellenes imposed their own conceptions and institutions, only a partial answer is possible. Many aspects of the problem still remain obscure, because it is difficult to discern, let alone delineate, any changes in modern Greek society wrought by people who in some cases lived alongside Greeks for centuries.[122] Frankish influence in the islands is undeniable; perhaps, too, Albanians and Arvanito-Vlachs left their imprint in the Pindus.

By the same token, it is possible to make the general assertion that community institutions in many parts of the islands, continental Greece, and the rural interior derived from the Byzantine Empire and antiquity. Although in most cases these institutions were debilitated, in some instances vanishing entirely, for varying lengths of time because of war or other political exigencies, they later revived under the influence of remembered traditions or still living institutions in neighboring towns and districts. Historical continuity from ancient to Ottoman times was thus preserved locally. The idea of self-government never faded, even under Turkish rule.

Did the communities then undergo change with the coming of Turkish rule? From the analysis given earlier, it appears that this question must be answered in the affirmative. At the same time, pending further research, no clear-cut answer is possible. For example, public affairs in the cities of continental Greece and Asia Minor continued to be conducted by the representatives of guilds (*rufetia*). Was a Turkish influence perhaps manifest here? Again, the answer to that question has already been given:[123] what we observe is merely the adaptation of a Byzantine tradition to the conditions of Turkish rule. That the internal structure of community institutions always ran the risk of being subverted by Turkish or Moslem influences cannot be disputed; but the Greeks were saved from that mischance by the great tradition of law, both written and oral, that persisted among them.

Under Ottoman rule the Greek clergy, as we have seen, especially the superior clergy, administered justice alongside community notables. Indeed, this exercise of judicial authority by the clergy remained an integral facet of community autonomy throughout the entire Captivity.

The principal source of law during the Ottoman period, again mainly

for the upper clergy, continued to be Roman law, especially as sum-
marized in the *Procheiron* or *Hexabiblos* of Constantine Armenopoulos,
who lived in Thessalonica during that city's golden age, the fourteenth
century. This compendium was used frequently, gradually displacing
other similar sources until it came to be regarded as almost the only
written law of the Greek nation in captivity. In a very real sense, Armenopoulos had ensured "national autonomy by preserving the nation's
immortal laws."

The *Hexabiblos*, however, like other compilations in use during the
Captivity, was not regarded as absolutely authoritative in the sense that no
deviation from the literal and universal applicability of its laws could ever
be sanctioned. In fact, it was usually consulted only as a guide. The reason
for this was that no written law could be followed scrupulously when on so
many occasions it conflicted with the spirit of local custom and local
customary law. In such cases, public opinion and customary law overrode
written law.[124]

The variety of local customary laws was infinite and it is extremely
difficult to establish their origins. Only in recent years has legal scholarship begun systematically to deal with this most basic of problems.[125]
Research done so far supports the generalization that local customary law
stemmed in some cases from ancient Greek or Byzantine law, while in
others it took shape under Frankish and Ottoman rule.[126]

The Turkish sultans looked upon communities as convenient instruments for collecting taxes and governing the millions of raias in their
empire and tolerated them throughout the Balkans. Byzantine institutions, suitably adapted, thus met the needs of a new era, the needs of raias,
and the needs of the Moslem Empire. The survival of these political
institutions constituted an auspicious prospect for modern Hellenism,
for, with the preservation of local political organization throughout Hellas, the future development of popular culture (including not only customs and traditions, but also painting and architecture) was assured.

Indeed, since the community remained the only political organization
of the Greeks, its influence and durability were enhanced, especially as the
people generally withdrew from the coastal plains to the safe seclusion of
the mountains. Even in the few settlements on the plains and in the cities,
Greeks withdrew into separate neighborhoods and thus remained more
or less isolated. This trend became more and more pronounced with the
gradual disappearance of most of the old Byzantine families and the final
demise of Byzantine central authority. The process was conducive to the
development of community life, a spirit of self-government, and the
hegemony of local notables. Servitude also contributed not only to the
preservation of the family unit but also to the reinforcement of a patriarchal way of life. Individual members of the family became more and more

respectful of their leader, who imposed his will absolutely. This was found to be the most efficacious means of contending with the unpredictable behavior of local Turkish authorities. The modern Hellenic community thus acquired greater cohesion, though without necessarily broadening the base of its earlier political and judicial authority: it was already admirably suited to the needs of a community living within narrow territorial confines and to the execution of such actions as its limited framework imposed. Only when the Greek community was particularly isolated or where the conqueror's rule became particularly lax did conditions favor communal institutions and their expansion into unaccustomed spheres.

Within the larger concourse of each more advanced and civilized community, a number of smaller groups were distinguishable—the unions of artisans. Bound by the common interests of their trade, craftsmen formed themselves into the so-called *rufetia* or *isnafia* (guilds). Such professional organizations existed in ancient Greece at extremely refined levels of development. They continued to exist in medieval times,[127] their organization modified in the light of changing conditions until the end of the Byzantine Empire. Naturally, some disappeared completely, either as a result of the general decline of crafts or the demise of some highly localized craft.[128]

Craftsmen were not only the guardians of centuries-old traditions, but also the creators and teachers of new elements in these traditions. They were the founders of the popular mechanical arts. It is regrettable that no systematic attempt[129] has been made to study their influence locally. Since corporate guilds sprang from the very heart of each community, they both express and explain the innermost intellectual and artistic impulses of the folk.

The Byzantine guild tradition[130] was handed down to a society whose spiritual and material capacities were less robust than they had been. Nevertheless when converts among the Greeks entered the new Moslem society, they took with them the fundaments of their technical knowledge and initiated the conquerors into the secrets of their professions. Of course, the Turks—first the Seljuks and later the Ottomans—also brought with them their own technology and institutional conceptions, both of which were permeated by moral and religious principles and oriented towards equivalent goals.[131] It is thus enormously difficult, in a situation of perpetual interaction between conqueror and conquered,[132] to disentangle the reciprocal influences at work. But it can be asserted on the basis of travellers' observations that craftsmen converts made a notable contribution to the advance of Turkish technical knowledge and thereby also to the Turks' understanding of guild organization. Travellers differed only in their clearly opinionated assessments of Turkish technical ability.

Georgieviz, for instance, found Turkish artisans less competent than those of the West;[133] but other contemporaries praised the Turks for their fine workmanship, regardless of whether the particular artisan was a complete novice in his craft or perhaps not a Turk at all but a Christian apostate.[134] However, the Turks were always eager to assimilate the knowledge and experience of other peoples.[135] Nor was it only Christians whom they imitated. As we shall see later, Jews who suffered persecution in different countries of Western Europe began from the end of the fifteenth century to seek refuge in Turkey, where they, too, became teachers of the Turks.[136] Greeks, Turks, Jews, and Armenians formed separate guilds only when it was intended that these should be composed exclusively of members of the same nationality. Otherwise, they were mixed, such as that of the furriers of Constantinople, which included both Greeks and Turks.[137]

The Greeks naturally felt the need to protect their special skills and to make the best of their common disabilities by defining more rigidly both the composition and aims of their traditional co-operative guilds. Since these were only loosely controlled by the state, they acquired under conditions of steady economic growth considerable opportunity for internal development. Personal initiative was not wholly proscribed, but it was held rigorously in check, confined within the framework of guild and community organization by a multitude of special regulations. Each craftsman was subject to collective controls, and competition was nonexistent. Workshops were clustered together, in accordance with ancient tradition, in a single area of the city or town, a fact which made a particular impression on foreign travellers.[138]

It is impossible to determine the immediate effects of the Capture on the organization of guilds since the evidence no longer exists. However, many of the old ones must have survived in their traditional Byzantine forms.

Guilds of a rather unique type existed in the Venetian-controlled territories, particularly on the Seven Islands. Their organization was much influenced by that of the guilds of the Venetian Republic.[139]

Documents from the Metropolis of Trikki reveal that in the seventeenth century a women's guild, whose members made soap, functioned in Trikkala. It helped maintain not only the Metropolis itself, but also the Turks and Jews of the city.[140]

Membership in guilds was restricted to the *mastoroi* (masters), that is, the artisans who owned workshops. The master artisan might employ, again in accordance with unwritten ancient custom, a journeyman assistant (*kalphas*) and an apprentice (*mathitoudi* or *tsiraki*), each of whom possessed clearly defined rights and obligations. At the head of the guild was the *protomaïstor*, or grand master, who was elected either by acclamation or secret ballot at a general meeting of the masters.[141] The organization and government of each guild, the scope of the grand master's duties, and the relationships among individual members are all worthwhile subjects for future research.[142] In addition to the differences between those guilds professing different crafts, local variations abounded. Yet differences were subsumed in each guild by an unwritten code of customs and regulations which sometimes, particularly in later centuries, crystallized into a written constitution.[143]

Each guild had its patron saint whose feast was celebrated, as it still is, in a church or monastery.[144]

Some guilds throve conspicuously, when other circumstances were also favorable, by producing specialized goods that satisfied traditional demands. Those that enjoyed such good fortune included the furriers of Kastoria, the wood-carvers of Athens[145] and Tournovo (Epirus),[146] the masons (known as *koudaraioi*) of Pyrsogianni and Vourbiani (both Epirus), the silversmiths and gold-embroiderers of Kalarrytai (Epirus),[147] the aba tailors of Philippopolis.[148] The level of guild activity was also regulated by the state of commerce throughout the Near East.

The social reputation which any profession came to enjoy depended on its economic prominence. Accordingly, as the old noble families became impoverished and died out, those possessing economic means were successful in obtaining guild representation on local community authorities. For example, in Serrai,[149] Ioannina,[150] Thessalonica, and Chios, to name just a few, one representative from each guild was eventually to be found in local government. One hallmark of this change which had occurred in local and community life was the Athenian expression "he is cast in the same mold as the twelve" (*kratei apo tous dodeka*), which, when applied to a particular person, meant that he was supremely arrogant. Here, the word *dodeka* ("twelve") was meant to refer to the presidents of the guilds, the grand masters.[151]

The hegemony of guild representatives in local government became more and more complete as time passed; artisans acquired control of civic affairs and also shouldered concomitant economic burdens. For instance, in the Historical Archives of Macedonia there is still to be seen a ledger of the Municipality of Thessalonica, dating from 15 September 1792,[152] which records that city arrears (*mukadem borç*) were met by large numbers of artisans and tradesmen—shoemakers, cooks, coopers, quarry-workers, bakers, millers, cake-vendors, ropemakers, furriers, grocers, painters, tailors, butchers, masons, and many others.

The activities of some guilds, particularly those in the larger urban centers, sometimes became more than local in scope. In Constantinople,[153] for example, the economic vitality of guilds led to an increasing influence in civic affairs which was directed towards assisting their less

34. An eighteenth-century house in Kastoria. Courtesy of the Greek National Tourism Organization.

fortunate compatriots.[154] Besides supervising churches, schools, and hospitals, the guild representatives of Constantinople even took part in the election of the patriarch till the middle of the nineteenth century.[155] Up to that time, when their powers were considerably reduced, the guilds of the City, whose combined membership was greater than that of all others in the Ottoman Empire, were actually looked upon by the Porte as legal representatives not only of the Hellenes but of other Orthodox Christians—Bulgarians and Albanians,[156] as well as Greeks. These craft representatives, together with leading merchants, the Phanariot nobility, the twelve-member Synod, and the patriarch, made up a kind of national assembly of Orthodox Christians, which was, of course, basically Greek in character.[157]

Of all the Constantinopolitan guilds, the most powerful economically and politically was that of the furriers. Since fur denoted wealth and high social status, to be a furrier was to be assured both of handsome profits and important social contacts. Certain citizens of Constantinople and Kastoria, such as the benefactor Kastorianos Manolakis, President of the furriers' guild, thus acquired notable power and influence. The furriers of the City even had their own treasury, "the furriers' casket," which funded charitable and educational objectives like the building of schools and the care of widows and orphans.[158] By 1683 the furriers' and other guilds of Constantinople—of silk-workers, wool-workers, painters, aba-makers, goldsmiths, tavernkeepers, and others—were also maintaining "caskets" for the subvention of the Holy Sepulcher.[159]

Besides guilds, Greek Christian communities also supported "brother-hoods" (*adelphotites* or *adelphata*), such as the "Brotherhood of Venice," which were mainly sources of moral and financial aid to needy members, or patrons of charity generally (for example, the building of schools and churches). However, very little information about brotherhoods is avail-able for the early period of Ottoman rule.[160] The aims of these societies, whose members were drawn from both sexes, coincided with those of the Church, with which they maintained close institutional ties. They ought therefore to be considered more properly as socioreligious organiza-tions.[161]

8

THE ARMATOLES AND KLEPHTS

In a number of mountainous districts throughout Greece, the institution of the community was interwoven with that of the armatoles. As we shall see, the armatoles so invigorated the spirit of independence in western Greece that a state of near autonomy was attained. An analysis of the institution of the armatoles is a necessary prerequisite to a full understanding of political conditions in Greece under Turkish rule and an appreciation of the fighting qualities of the Greek nation. Through the armatoles, the Greeks received their military education and their preparation for the struggle for national liberation.

The earliest origins of the armatoles are lost in the murk of history. However, in my *Origins of the Greek Nation,* an analysis of various sources not previously sifted in any thorough way suggested that the institution first appeared in Thessaly during the reign of Murad II (1421–1451),[1] specifically in the Agrafa, Thessaly. From there, it subsequently spread to other parts of the Hellenic world, though not to the Peloponnese.[2]

Throughout Greece and the Balkans[3] generally, the sultans found themselves faced with the problem of subduing mountain populations swollen by the influx of refugees from the plains. This problem had not been urgent in Asia Minor because there the Turkish peoples advanced in successive waves and spread out gradually. Conquest was achieved by a process of slaughter, enslavement, and innumerable conversions to Islam, or else by the granting of various religious and economic immunities. In the Balkans, on the other hand, the Turks were far from their bases of operation, among hostile peoples. In particular, they had to contend with mountain folk who refused to come to any kind of terms with the conqueror and remained unsubjugated. These were the klephts, who lived in villages known as *klephtochoria,* many of which still survive by the same name.[4]

Turkish colonists who settled down permanently, mainly in the fertile plains of Thessaly and Macedonia, found that they were equally impotent to impose their will. Frustrated, they cast around for an effective method of defending their districts. It would therefore seem that the institution of the armatolés arose principally from the need to establish order and security in those places where mountain populations, stirred up by intrepid young men, not to say bandits, among them, became the bane of Turkish administration.[5]

As in the rest of the Balkans,[6] so in Greece the sultans tried to tempt mountain people with the promise of privileges, particularly those who would undertake the defense of strategic passes through the mountains where they lived. Mohammed II, for example, followed up his conquest of the Peloponnese by granting the Dervenochorites various immunities on condition that they kept open the lines of communication through their district. These privileges remained intact until the time of the Greek Revolution in 1821.[7] Similarly, Mohammed II's father before him had permitted the establishment of the institution of armatoles in the Agrafa. By the fifteenth century, the armatoles throughout the Balkans generally had emerged as an auxiliary fighting arm of the Turkish forces, which they accompanied on military expeditions against the enemies of the Ottoman Empire. They were not paid, and their cruelty and rapaciousness early became legendary.[8]

Most of what we know about the organization of these corps of armatoles comes from a prerevolutionary oral tradition which survived as late as 1821. Such tradition probably retains much that is historically reliable, though by now it has become difficult to disentangle old traditions from later additions and thus to trace with certainty the evolution of the armatoles. According to tradition, whenever the inhabitants of the mountains, that is to say, klephts, submitted to the Turks, they formed a local gendarmerie called *armatoloi,* or in Turkish *martoloz* (from *armatologos, -oos, -os,* according to M. Philintas),[9] and thereby entered into the service of the Ottoman Empire. The district over which the armatoles' authority extended was called an *armatoliki.* Commanders were known as *capetanos* or *capetanios* (from the Italian *capitano*), the rank and file as *pallikaria* (from the ancient Greek *pallix, -ikos*), and section leaders as *protopallikara.*[10] In later centuries, the armatoles comprised not merely former klephts, but also those village stalwarts who had taken up arms against the klephts in the defense of their district and who, following their appointment as armatoles, demanded payment for their services.[11]

Groups of resistance thus were formed by defiant young men and former klephts. There were a number of reasons why they opted for this way of life. One wonders how many times was the cry "I shall join the klephts" actually uttered as a threat to unjust Turkish provincial governors, agas, or local tyrants.[12] Every man cherished freedom, if only for himself, and indeed he was prepared to live by robbing others, even Greeks, if necessary. As for the real robbers, those who had practiced brigandage for many years, they found a rich new field for their endeavors, and one, moreover, which ennobled their profession and eventually made them heroes. They even presented themselves as protèctors and avengers of their oppressed and persecuted countrymen—Robin Hoods who gave only to the poor.

The struggle of the klephts was a campaign of active resistance against the conqueror and his acts of oppression. For example, in 1669 the traveller Edouard Brown, speaking of the Thessalians (and undoubtedly referring also to the Macedonians), noted that they wore little caps similar to those worn in France at the same time, that they were brave and daring, and that if the Turks did them the least harm they invariably retaliated. They had actually captured and killed many Turks.[13]

However, during the early period of Turkish rule, the klephts obviously did not feel that they were engaged in a struggle for national liberation. All that distinguished them from common brigands was a strong hatred of the conqueror and his collaborators, as well as sympathy towards those who were persecuted. But this was precisely why the people began to idolize them. What eventually became a whole complex of myth and legend surrounding the klephts began to take shape from the very beginning of Turkish rule. Slowly, the years of Turkish occupation engendered a tradition which lasted until the death of the last of the brigands, many years after the foundation of the modern Greek state: resistance on the part of the Greek people was first aroused by the klephts, who personified the popular will to resist the conqueror and his Christian collaborators. In this tradition, the klephts regarded the poverty of the people as their ally and the affluence of the enemy their provocation.

Innumerable peaks in the mountain ramparts of Greece sheltered villages of restive Christian raias—Vermion, Pieria, Olympus, Chasia, Pindus, and many more—as though beckoning young men to discover the arcane wonders which they concealed: bottomless ravines, dark crevasses, verdant forests of pine, oak, and fir, wild beasts, bands of renowned klephts. Identifying themselves closely with their environment, the klephts led a primitive existence, wholly rooted in nature:

"Hail, O mountains with your precipices, ravines, and hoary frosts;
And thou, worthy child, brave man, welcome!"[14]

Thus was the arrival of a would-be klepht greeted.

The importance of the mountains of continental Greece as places of refuge must be stressed. Both in medieval and modern times they were traversed by vital lines of communication. The whole subject has so far been thoroughly neglected, even though as long as a century ago the traveller Esprit Cousinéry observed that the mountains of southern Macedonia had surely provided sanctuary for the Greeks on many occasions since the time of the Bulgarian invasions.[15] Cousinéry was attempting to explain why the population of the region remained authentically Greek. He wrote that the Bulgarians who had settled down in the Middle Ages as farmers in the plains of Macedonia and a few mountainous districts[16] never penetrated the forests of Vermion and Pieria, which formed natural ramparts and places of refuge for the Greek population.[17]

Under the Turkish occupation, the mountains continued to shield Greek populations. The irregularities of terrain, far from impeding communications among the inhabitants, facilitated them. The paths, or rather goat-tracks, which crossed the mountains of Vermion, Pieria, Olympus, and Chasia, as well as over the Grammos and the Pindus to Agrafa, enabled the inhabitants to communicate with one another in security and obtain news practically without hindrance. At the time of the 1821 Revolution, news of fighting on the fronts of the Aspropotamos and the Agrafa quickly reached the chieftains of Macedonia.[18] Just as the Bulgarian *chaïdout* (klephts) could cross his country freely from the Black Sea to Serbia by taking advantage of the security of his snow-capped mountains, so the Greek armatoles or klephts had no trouble finding refuge anywhere between Macedonia and western central Hellas. In much more recent times, during the German and Italian occupation, guerrilla bands operated almost with impunity within the same mountainous confines. It was thus no coincidence that the boundaries of the *armatolikia* were conterminous with the various mountain ranges of continental Greece.

The mountainous configuration of the Greek peninsula was the salvation of the Greek people at many critical times in their history. As Kosmas the Aetolian said in the eighteenth century, the mountains had saved the Greeks from total destruction in the past and would do so again in the future. They would also nurture a race of free men quite different from the indolent inhabitants of the plains. We must agree wholeheartedly with the French traveller Lauvergne who visited Greece in 1825: "La Grèce entière, par ses nombreuses montagnes, les gorges effrayantes qui les séparent, les accidents multipliés de son sol déchiré de toutes parts, semble avoir été prédestinée par la nature à être le berceau des hommes libres. [The whole of Greece, with its numerous mountains, the frightful gorges which separate them, the accidents multiplied by its ubiquitously rent terrain, seems to have been predestined by nature to be the cradle of free men.]"[19]

Of the many mountains which served as sentinels of Greek freedom, two must be singled out for special mention: the Olympus-Chasia complex, which cuts laterally across the Greek peninsula, and the Pindus, especially the Agrafa, which cleaves the peninsula perpendicularly. It must have been Koziakas (Kozjak) in the Pindus that was the starting-point of those klephts who descended upon Meteora and threatened the monks during the second half of the fourteenth century.[20]

The first *armatoliki* was established in the inaccessible and naturally fortified district of Agrafa bestriding western central Hellas and Thessaly.[21] Perhaps the second to appear was that on Olympus. Practically nothing is known about Kara Michael,[22] the leader of the Olympus armatoles, but the Turkish word, Kara (black), suggests that he struck terror into the hearts of the Turks with his frequent attacks upon them. Agrafa and Olympus set a pattern for the establishment of successive *armatolikia:* one after the other they appeared in mountainous and unsubjugated districts.[23] The *armatoliki* thus was a product of the peculiar conditions of Turkish rule.[24]

The klephts of Olympus are mentioned in the *Life* of St. Dionysios. When the saint was building the monastery of the Holy Trinity and establishing its cells, tenements, and mills, a few inhabitants of Litochoron denounced him to the local Turkish overlord. According to the accusers, a hermit was building a monastery on Olympus without first having obtained permission, and his intention was to make it a headquarters for klephts. This would constitute a grave danger to the local populace.[25] Were there any grounds for making such an accusation? Probably there were: a monk with such strong Greek sentiments, who had chosen to live a hermit's life in a wild and remote place, would expect his establishment to be frequented by Greek klephts.

Olympus was for Macedonia and Thessaly what the Agrafa was for western central Hellas. Its long klepht tradition and ancient fame ensured Olympus' subsequent role as a symbol of freedom and the "sacred mountain of the klephts." In the popular imagination, the nimbus surrounding Olympus shone even brighter. The klephts ascribed miraculous qualities to its bracing air, crisp snows, and crystalline springs. To them, Olympus was a sort of Elysium where they recuperated after their encounters with the Turks. Here wounds healed themselves:[26]

Klepht, if you want to get well, if you want your wounds to heal
Come up high upon Olympus, to this sublime place.
Up there the brave will not fall sick, the sick will regain their strength.
There live many klephts in four areas.[27]

It is certain that many klephts and armatoles, about whom nothing is known today, lived in northern Greece. So much is proven from the recent publication of *Military Memoirs,* in which Nicholas Kasomoulis from

Kozane describes the military situation in northern Greece during the last two centuries of Ottoman rule. In this work we are introduced to innumerable freedom fighters, among whom the Greeks of Macedonia were pre-eminent.

However, little definite is known about the organization of the klephts (their customs, the relations among commanders and the rank and file, and similar matters) during the early centuries of Turkish rule. It is really only for the later centuries that oral tradition has given us some understanding of their unwritten codes of behavior. But before attempting some discussion of these, it is appropriate to set forth the evidence relating to the organization and development of the armatoles, about whom much more is known.

According to Aravantinos, though he nowhere discloses the source of his information, a large number of *armatolikia* were created in Greece in 1537 during the reign of Suleiman I. At that time, Epirus and Aetolia-Acarnania were divided into five *armatolikia* (Malakasi, Tzoumerka, Xeromero, Lidorikion, and Venetiko), Thessaly into five (Olympus, Agrafa, Chasia, Mavrovouni, and Patratziki), and Macedonia southwest of the Axios River, also into five (Veroia, Servia, Elasson, Grevena, and Milia).[28] Naturally, until written proof is found, this list cannot be taken as authoritative.

It would appear that there was no connection between the *armatoliki* and the Turkish administrative division, or *liva*. An analysis of the administrative organization of Greek territories under Suleiman I (1520–1566) shows that there were some quite small *livas* containing only one town and its environs, for example, Phlorina[29] and Karleli, the latter remaining a small unit even though it embraced Angelokastro (producing an income of 21,002 *akçes*), Vonitsa (18,484 *akçes*), and Saint Maura (26,221 *akçes*).[30] On the other hand, there were also much larger *livas* such as Trikkala (the Turkish Tîrhala, with an income of 131,019 *akçes*, incorporating many towns and districts, as well as estates belonging to the crown and various Turkish officials), Epachto (the Turkish Inebacht, with 212,837 *akçes*), Patratziki (or Batracık, with 107,293 *akçes*), Elasson (or Alasonya, with 38,021), Pharsala (Çatalca, with 39,912), Domokos (Dömöke, 60,323), Larissa (Yenişehir, 113,079), Phanarion (Fener, 60,945), and Agrafa (Ağrafa, 42,994).[31] Perhaps, as Gökbilgin has observed,[32] the smaller *livas* were constituted primarily to meet military needs, that is, to confront the possible threat not merely of an external enemy but also of their unwilling subjects.

It is not easy to find out what the armatoles' obligations towards their Turkish suzerains were, either in Greece or the rest of the Balkans. It is scarcely less difficult to discern what kind of relationship the armatoles had with local inhabitants. So far as is known, however, the conditions which governed the administration of an *armatoliki* were laid down by a competent central authority in Constantinople acting upon the advice of local authorities.[33]

Armatoles formed a separate class whose privileges (consisting mainly of tax exemptions and revocable land grants) and special obligations towards the Porte varied from place to place.[34] From a firman of 1710, it would seem that Orthodox armatoles were also exempt from patriarchal taxes.[35] It is noteworthy that in contemporary records both the brothers and children of armatoles were registered not as raias but as *mu'af*, or "exempt from taxation."[36] Armatoles and their commanders might be appointed either by local authorities (that is to say, Moslem notables, or *ayan*, and other raias)[37] or by local tribunals which then assigned them a particular task, for example, the garrisoning of a *derveni* (mountain pass) in the district.[38] Again, however, neither the rights nor duties of local armatoles can be specified precisely.

The question arises: what prompted Suleiman to set up so many *armatolikia* in continental Greece? One reason consists in the prevalence of disorder in the sixteenth century throughout the Ottoman Empire. In Greece and the other Balkan countries, klephts and brigands infested the countryside.[39] For example, in 1583 Gabriel Kallonas, a Corinthian who served as priest in a village near Philippi, Macedonia, said that robbers were ubiquitous in the mountains and forests outside Athens, "though it is true that a man poorly dressed and without money was safe from even a thousand thieves because he had nothing worth taking."[40]

These "thieves" were the descendants of Christian Albanians, or Arvanito-Vlachs, who had settled in Attica towards the end of the fourteenth century and at the beginning of the fifteenth century. They were fiercely independent, living together in clans and grazing their flocks or robbing and killing travellers in dangerous mountain passes, particularly those of the Parnes range. Of heavier and taller build than the Greeks, they also differed in their dress and spoke Albanian.[41]

In 1621 the mountain-scarred terrain of western Greece harbored so many klephts that any traveller between the western coast (opposite Corfu) and Thessalonica was bound to fall into their hands.[42] This was the period of insecurity which followed Dionysios Skylosophos' revolt in Epirus in 1611.

The incidence of robberies, burnings, and indiscriminate violence in Greece, particularly around Olympus, Pieria, and Vermion,[43] increased during the course of the seventeenth century. In 1639–1640, the inhabitants of Dranista abandoned their village because of excessive taxes and the demands of brigands.[44] Disorder was also rife in the districts of Grevena, Sarigöl, Kastoria, Phlorina, and Prespa. Moslem and Bulgarian klephts (*chaïdout*)[45] operated mainly around Monastir, Perlepe (Prilep),

Veles, and Skóplje, outside the borders of present-day Greece. Banditry reigned not only in the Greek provinces of Thessaly, Macedonia, and Thrace but also in the Balkan countries to the north. Cadis and other *sancak* officials received repeated instructions to take steps against the klephts.[46] The phenomenon of brigandage in these regions was contemporaneous with similar, if less virulent, outbreaks in other Mediterranean countries.[47] Local populations immediately withdrew into the mountains upon the approach of strangers.[48]

The traveller Brown testifies that the klephts remained numerous even though they were severely punished when caught. In some of the more dangerous mountain passes, communities would station lookouts with drums on commanding heights, and a tatoo meant that it was safe for nervous travellers to proceed on their journey through the narrow defiles.[49]

The armatoles were sometimes successful in apprehending klephts,[50] though the fact that they never effectively controlled the situation suggests perhaps that they were less than conscientious in the performance of their duties. They often collaborated with their former comrades. This was undoubtedly why in 1627 Murad IV attempted to abolish completely the system of *armatolikia*. He rescinded the commission of the armatoles to protect narrow passes and defiles, ordering the provincial Turkish governors to replace them with Turkish garrisons. However, the armatoles responded by driving off any Turkish intruders, and Murad's experiment failed.[51] Evliya Tschelebi refers to armatoles' continuing to perform military service in Thessalonica and Elasson. There were also armatoles garrisoning Canea; and in Larissa some two hundred of them mounted guard each night.[52]

Brigands often operated on horseback. They became as brazen as they did because of the weakening of the Ottoman Empire. However, it would appear from a document of 1682[53] that frightened Moslems and Christian notables refused to take any action against, and even on occasion actually supported, the klephts. By 1683, "robbers, rebels, and criminals" had become so numerous in the provinces of Rumelia that a special commissioner was appointed to impose order.[54] That part of his official charge which placed robbers, rebels, and criminals in separate categories is particularly interesting.

Even Mt. Athos felt the repercussions of this ferment. In November 1692 a resolution of the Synaxis read in part: "at a time when the holy monasteries were enjoying peace and prosperity, suddenly the confusion of war descended upon Mt. Athos, and noise and disarray were all about, such that this spiritual haven became practically a refuge for robbers."[55]

In 1699 a new attempt was made to replace Greek and Albanian armatoles by Moslems, at least in the districts of Ioannina, Larissa, Servia,

Grevena, Genitsa, Doïrani, Thessalonica, Veroia, Stromnitsa, Monastir, Perlepe, and Kiouproulou. However, this limited experiment met with no more success than the earlier attempt by Murad IV, which was intended to have universal application. The latest sultanic decree incorporated reasons for the intended reorganization: armatoles in the specified districts who had been appointed by the Moslem notables (ayan) of the vilayets were never satisfied with the salaries paid them by the local inhabitants. They had accordingly begun to exact tolls from travellers and merchants, both raias and nonraias, in the narrow passes through the mountains and to engage in many other forms of illicit activity.[56]

The predacity of Albanian armatoles led to the dismissal in 1704, again by sultanic decree, of Albanian armatoles everywhere. They were to be replaced by other armatoles under a single commander, and the local authorities who appointed them were also to be responsible for their actions. However, the decree was not to apply to the sancak of Trikkala, where the services of armatoles were much needed.[57] Here, geographical conditions were conducive to klepht activity, and the Pindus' reputation as a focal point of Greek resistance was thus already receiving acknowledgment. The same year also saw the appearance of "robbers and criminals" on the banks of the Danube from Adrianople to Belgrade and from Thessalonica to Larissa.[58] These eruptions could not have occurred without the active support, or at least passive acquiescence, of armatoles.

Eventually, the institution of the armatoles was abolished by a firman of Ahmed III in 1721,[59] though it is uncertain whether this decree was designed to have universal application. Possibly it was intended to apply only in northeastern Macedonia beyond the Axios River and in the northern Balkan countries, for the Greek territories from the west bank of the Axios to the Isthmus of Corinth retained their armatoles until the Revolution of 1821.

The Turks entrusted Greek armatoles with the preservation of order only out of sheer necessity. They always recognized the value of the Albanians, as a necessary counterpoise to the Greeks. Thus, from the moment when Albanians were first appointed as derven-ağas and derven-başıs, Greek klephts faced formidable opponents. Albanians had no compunctions about persecuting the local Greek populations, and demotic songs often recounted the clashes that occurred between corps of Greek klephts and Albanian armatoles.[60]

The number of armatolikia in Greece fluctuated in accordance with the needs of changing times and circumstances. Immediately before the 1821 Revolution there were seventeen, of which ten were concentrated in Thessaly and Levadia, four in Aetolia, Acarnania, and Epirus, and the remainder in Macedonia south of the Axios.[61] Between 1537 and 1821 the creation of armatolikia had also been confined more or less to the same regions. Epirus, Aetolia-Acarnania, part of eastern central Hellas, and the adjoining mountain regions of Thessaly and central western Macedonia were thus like the sides of a tinderbox in which the Greek fighting spirit was contained.

Armatoles were paid by the Greek inhabitants of the district they defended.[62] Usually, the title and office of *capetanios* of armatoles, as well as the profession itself, were handed down from father to son. The *capetanios* and some of his men usually lived in the chief town of the *armatoliki*, while the rest, under the command of his lieutenants (*kolidjis*), were scattered throughout the district in a series of small bands.[63] The dress and arms of the armatoles were the same as those of the Albanians: gun, yataghan, and dagger.[64]

Though the institution of the armatoles helped prop up the Ottoman Empire, it also served as a source of inspiration and consolation to the raias. The Greeks retained the illusion that they were conducting their own community affairs and that they themselves were maintaining law and order in the *armatolikia*, the towns, the villages, and throughout the countryside. While it is true that the Turks were mostly out of sight and rarely interfered in the internal affairs of the Greeks, they were yet always ready to abrogate privileges or withdraw dispensations that favored the raias. "In this way the conquest which, so to speak, had ended," wrote Fauriel, "really had no more than paused. In a word, for as long as the Greeks had something to lose, the Turks had something to gain. The pashas undertook to complete the job that the early conquerors left half-finished. Their main aim in governing was slowly to strip the conquered of their remaining material possessions and rights. The armatoles were an obstacle to the realization of such a goal. That is why their history, from its earliest known beginnings, was neither more nor less than a continuous and courageous struggle against the pashas."[65]

The conciliatory attitude of the Turks towards the klephts and armatoles was the product of necessity, an involuntary and temporary capitulation, an armistice in war. Accordingly, whenever the Turks saw an opportunity they tried to curtail their power or exterminate them entirely; whereupon the armatoles might choose to become klephts and the bane of the Turks (not to say, sometimes, the Greeks). Their perpetual irruptions and depredations would then force the Ottoman authorities to return to a policy of toleration.[66]

Armatoles thus became klephts, and vice versa, with understandable frequency. Naturally, the facility with which this transition was effected gave rise to confusion: armatoles and klephts were increasingly identified with one another.[67] As we shall now see, this semantic *rapprochement* merely reflected a growing convergence of the interests and ideas of the two institutions.

From the unique confluence of irregular physiographical and political conditions which locally produced klephts and armatoles, a class of warriors both exemplifying and arousing the fighting qualities of the Greek nation, there emerged a new Greek society, permeated by the attitudes and preoccupations of war. So thoroughly had these become woven into the warp and woof of the everyday lives of the inhabitants that it is impossible for us today to separate them from other threads in the social fabric. Yet they formed part of an unmistakable complex of ideas, customs, manners, and social organization for which parallels were to be found in other parts of the Balkans.

We are chiefly indebted to Fauriel for such knowledge as we have of the life of Greek klephts. This information, however, is based on early nineteenth-century oral tradition and may not faithfully reflect the klepht way of life even at that time. The ideas and customs of Fauriel's day were the result of a long evolutionary development, and their roots have to be traced back much further—to the beginnings of Turkish rule, or even earlier.

The life of a klepht was precarious and dangerous. In their legendary haunts (limeria), wrote Theodore Kolokotrones, the freedom fighter of 1821, "they were free; but what a life they lived, what people they were—tormented, exhausted, living like savages in caves, or like beasts in the mountains and snow, a life which we then shared."[68] However, life on the mountain tops so close to nature was not without its attractions and compensations. Klephts shared the scented and bracing air with wild animals and birds. Their songs particularly dwelt upon the birds that followed them wherever they went, suffered with them, and carried tidings of them to the Greek people everywhere. They therefore did not look upon their existence as a wholly disagreeable one.

They ate spit-roasted lamb, and amused themselves drinking wine and singing songs—often about the earlier or contemporary exploits of some famous klepht. These were almost Homeric scenes.[69] They never forgot to take the precaution of posting guards (karaoulia) at strategic points around the camp. And when night fell, they slept in the branches of trees under a heavy fleece coat. Their movements and sorties were confined to the hours of night.[70]

When winter came, a fierce season in the high mountains of continental Greece, thick snow obliterating the footpaths chased all forms of life down to the plains. And the klephts would spend the winter among friends in the villages, who shielded them from the Turks and their Christian collaborators.[71]

Klepht bands varied in size. The number of individual members might depend on the fame of the leader, the local political situation, the band's sphere of operations, or the military and administrative abilities of the

Turkish district pasha. But usually there were never more than forty or fifty men. Any band with as many as a hundred members was thought extremely powerful.[72]

Klephts were renowned not only for their bravery but also for their extraordinary imperviousness to fatigue, hunger, and thirst.[73] Their physical strength and prowess were enhanced by athletic feats, such as discus-throwing, jumping, and running, in which they, like the ancient Greeks, excelled. One klepht, Nikos Tsaras, set some kind of athletic record by jumping over seven horses standing side by side.[74]

The klephts were famous for their forced marches enabling them to pounce suddenly on an enemy or evade capture. Deadly accurate as sharpshooters, they practiced shooting through a ring from a considerable distance or by aiming at the momentary flash from some hostile gun fired in the night—"feeding fire with fire," as they called it. They were thus expert in ambushing enemies in the dark.[75]

When captured, they displayed great stoicism in the hands of Turkish torturers. It was a question of honor with them to endure all suffering in silence.[76] There is not a single known case of a klepht whose courage failed him or who surrendered his faith in order to save himself from death by torture.[77] The prospect of such a lingering death made them salute their fellows with the words "May the bullet be sure!"[78] If a klepht was so badly wounded that he could not be saved, he implored his comrades—and the request was always honored as though it were sacrosanct—to cut off his head and take it with them so that the enemy could not impale it on a spike and subsequently parade it through the towns and villages.[79]

Klepht tactics were to avoid contact with the enemy on the plains, where cavalry could be deployed, and surprise him in the mountains, where the advantages of familiar terrain canceled out the enemy's superiority in numbers.[80] Such tactics were admirably suited to the physiography of Rumelia, especially western central Hellas, which was pocked with mountains and shrouded in dense vegetation. Even today, in central Hellas, the saying can be heard: "the brave young man is the one who lies in wait."[81] It is no coincidence that Greek resistance against the Italians and Germans in World War II was mainly organized in central and western Greece.

Klephts developed their own guerrilla tactics, which hinged on the successful ambush, and called them *klephtopolemos*—klepht warfare. Each man fought independently, in no battle order, standing or kneeling behind whatever cover was available to him—a wall, tree, rock, even enemy corpses. These protective shields were called *meterizia*. If he was surrounded and had no possible avenue of escape, he would leap forward, yataghan in hand, and flail his way through the enemy. This was the celebrated "sally of desperation," the *giourousi*,[82] which was used on such a large scale and with such great effect at Missolonghi in 1826. Violent death on the field of honor was even preferable to death by natural causes.[83] By these tactics, the klephts hoped to force the enemy into granting them an *armatoliki.*

Klephtopolemos was the only traditional military tactic surviving in Greece at the time of the 1821 Revolution. Without an understanding of it, it is impossible to explain the continual struggles of the Greek people against the Turks. It was not surprising that they should eventually emerge as the natural leaders of the nation, the defenders and very "yeast" of freedom, to use Makrigiannis' phrase.[84] They tried to exploit every opportunity of breaking the Turkish yoke. They were always ready to offer their services to any Christian country at war with Turkey. They expunged the shame of the raias and contributed to the moral rebirth of the Greek nation. They were living examples that could be emulated. Greek children in the mountains and throughout Greece were reared under this inspiration. One of their favorite games was to imitate klepht tactics.[85]

Greeks created the myth of the *pallikari* (literally, brave young man), attributing to him those qualities of young manhood which they most admired: manly pride, a sense of justice, compassion for the weak, unflinching opposition to tyranny. The past has not been obliterated in the ideal vision of the present-day Greek. His admiration of the *pallikari* was expressed in heroic ballads known and loved by everyone in every layer of society. The wonderful, virile accents of the klephts' songs seemed to uplift Greek spirits, spreading hope, making captivity appear more and more intolerable.[86] The Greek will to resist, first stimulated by Franks and Albanians, under the Turks became indomitable.[87]

Thus, to the akritic ballads of Asia Minor were added a new cycle of heroic klepht songs from continental Greece. A few of the akritic ballads had already found their way into continental Greece, where they were regularly sung, and these now blended with the newer klephtic strains to produce distinctive forms of the modern demotic song.[88]

We have so far been describing the readjustment, organization and development of modern Hellenism during the first two centuries after the Capture. The Greek people found a rallying point in the Church, a political framework in their communities (or both communities and *armatolikia* in certain parts of Greece), a social and economic organization in their guilds and brotherhoods. They remained attached to their customs, manners, and traditions, devoted to their traditional pursuits, whether agricultural or otherwise, living more or less as they had always lived.

In order to complete this picture of the Greek raias, it is only necessary to compare the testimony of different writers (Orthodox theologians, such as Pachomios Rousanos, or foreign travellers, such as the Protestant Gerlach) to the uniqueness of various local customs:[89] those associated with baptisms[90] and marriages;[91] the striking apparel of women in Macedonia and the Aegean[92] (for example, Samos,[93] Icaria),[94] and elsewhere; the picturesque and ebullient religious festivals;[95] the agricultural fairs;[96] entertainments and dances;[97] musical instruments;[98] funerals[99] (the coin placed in the hand of the departed,[100] the dirges and hired mourners, the pulling of hair and beating of the face,[101] the alms distributed,[102] the materialization of the dead);[103] the Orthodox custom of exploding fireworks at Easter;[104] the many beggars who congregated at the doors of churches;[105] the blind dressed in tatters in Thessalonica and Constantinople,[106] Turkish and Negro as well as Greek.[107] The list by no means exhausts the innumerable customs, prejudices, and superstitions[108] of the Greeks, many of which have been handed down from antiquity to the present day. They serve as reminders of the continuity and uniqueness of Hellenism.

The historian must look for the ways in which the Greeks satisfied their everyday needs and solved the problem of survival. He must follow them on their journeys to the seaports and trace their travels overseas. He will find himself impressed with their enterprising spirit as craftsmen and as traders. He will notice that trade created a new class, an urban bourgeoisie, which gradually transformed the Hellenic nation. And he will turn, as we shall now, to an examination of precisely those economic forces which slowly differentiated the components of modern Hellenic society from one another.

9

RETURN TO THE PLAINS

The discovery of new worlds in the sixteenth and seventeenth centuries began to affect the trade and communications of every land, including those of the Near East.[1] In the case of Greece and the Balkans this was indeed fortuitous, for it helped to drain off a surplus population in the mountains and ultimately provided deliverance from the Turks and economic want.

In the East, the Christian states of Europe found good customers for their products and valuable supplies of raw materials. From the outset, therefore, they attempted to regularize their relations with the Ottoman Empire in order to ensure the unobstructed flow of trade. And commercial interest generated economic competition.

The Greeks, who lived at the crossroads between East and West, benefitted from the development of commercial intercourse. Even in the earliest years of Turkish rule, some extremely wealthy townsmen could be found in a few cities. During the siege of Constantinople, they had deliberately withheld their wealth from Constantine XI Palaeologus.[2] Turkish records show that by 1470 Greeks and Jews controlled the collection of various local revenues (*mukataa*).[3] By then new faces had begun to appear in the cities—emigrants from the rural interior of the Empire, especially from those parts where life, as we have seen, had become increasingly intolerable. They came mainly from the mountains— stockowners, shepherds, workers, and artisans—men not bound as closely to the soil as the plainspeople generally were. Or else they were men driven by extremities of hardship to come down onto the plains and the coast to find work.[4] Some of them found openings in commerce, and by dint of patience, persistence, and adaptability they successfully overcame the obstacles which local Turkish authorities placed in their way or which the insecurity of their new way of life occasioned.[5] They had to compete with privileged and wealthy European merchants, first the Venetians, then the French. Under Francis I (1494–1547) the French contracted their first commercial treaty with the Turks, from which they received many trade privileges. The English, too, had won various economic advantages.

By the time Turkish rule was consolidated at the end of the fifteenth century, the populations of the old centers of Hellenism (for example, Constantinople and Thessalonica), which had thinned out during the declining years of the Byzantine Empire,[6] once again began to increase as a result of immigration, supplemented by urban births.[7] Entirely new centers of commerce gradually appeared. To trace the various stages of their population growth is a problem of historical geography that lies beyond our present scope, but it would seem that the increase was due not merely, as Barkan believes,[8] to the direct efforts of the sultans, but mainly to the influence of the new mercantile economy and society which had arisen in Europe. That is, the Christian peoples who had survived from Byzantine times and Jewish refugees from Europe stimulated commercial growth and strengthened the general economy. During the sixteenth and seventeenth centuries, flourishing suburbs spread out from the confining walls of castles,[9] for example in Adrianople,[10] Parga,[11] Chalcis,[12] and Trebizond.[13]

Looking at those industrial and commercial centers, which increasingly attracted both Moslem and Christian rural inhabitants, we begin, going from south to north, with Methone (Modon) and Korone (Coron). Methone, with 2,000 inhabitants in 1436, was prosperous under the Venetians (1206–1500) because it was an important staging point for the commerce of Venice, Greece, the Black Sea, Egypt, and Syria.[14] It was also the last port of call for European pilgrims going to the Holy Land by ship. The town's export trade (in smoked pork and lard, sausages, wine, skins, and silk) supported a mixed population of Greeks, Franks, Jews, and Gypsies, who crowded its narrow streets lined with little wooden houses.[15] After its capture by the Turks, the Christians were driven outside the walls of the castle and forced to live in huts.[16]

According to official Turkish sources, Mistra's population at the end of the sixteenth century (1583–1585) was 1,000 Christian families and 199 Jewish families; and as part of the domain of the *sancak* (*hası sancak mirliva*) provided a revenue of 113,250 *akçes*.[17] Greek oral sources put Nauplia's population at 40,000,[18] which, because the Venetian occupation was so recent (the city had only surrendered to the Turks in 1540), still spoke Italian and dressed in the Italian manner.[19] Corinth's population may have been in the vicinity of 15,000, if the estimate of 3,000 dwellings from the same oral sources is correct,[20] but both these figures for Nauplia and Corinth are probably inflated: another source suggests that the people of

Corinth, though engaged in commerce, were "completely barbarized."[21] Dropolitsa, today's Tripolis, was first referred to in 1467 as a castle, but since it then had only sixty-two Christian families (apart from the Moslems)[22] it is unlikely that any significant trade moved through the town.[23] Patras exported acorns, wool, cheese, skins, wax, silk, and currants; Korone, wool, wax, silk, skins, and particularly olive oil; and Nauplia, wool, cheese, skins, and silk.[24]

Athens, with a mixed population of Greek and Albanian origin, was an important center of commerce in central Hellas. Its Albanian population was mainly confined to the villages of Mesogia.[25] Athens' trade very likely grew[26] in proportion to its population, which was 12,633 sometime between 1520 and 1530, and 17,616 sometime between 1571 and 1580.[27] By the middle of the sixteenth century, both Greeks and Albanians had moved outside the farthest wall, built in post-Roman times, to the eastern side of the Acropolis in present-day Plaka. Similarly the Turkish population, which had originally settled in the Acropolis, apparently increased over the years until it too spilled over the eastern side.[28] Athenian merchants traded with the Venetians mainly in olive oil. But although many spent their entire youth in Venice, they were not greatly influenced by its culture.[29] As Andreas Darmarios said, few Athenians were fond of letters and the arts; indeed most of them were illiterate.[30]

In the middle of the seventeenth century, French, Venetian, and, more rarely, English ships sailed into the Piraeus, the little port for Athens and Attica.[31] The French even maintained a consul in Athens whose jurisdiction extended to the ports of Corinth, Patras, Korone, Methone, and Nauplia. In exchange for wool, cheese, skins, olive oil, and wax, the French shipped into the Piraeus fabrics and sardines from France; or coffee, rice, and other products from Alexandria, which they were able to buy at favorable prices in Malta or from Aegean pirates. The usual coins in commercial circulation were the piaster and the zecchino. Venetians and Greeks sent out of the Piraeus large quantities of acorns (mainly from Porto Rafti in Attica), as well as wool, cheese, silk, cochineal, rugs, wax,[32] and the honey of Hymettus.[33] From Venice they returned with fabrics, precious stones, a wide range of silk products, velvet materials, multicolored brocades, and sardines.[34] The English were indifferent towards olive oil, even when it was in abundance,[35] but the Greeks found ready markets for it in Constantinople and other cities of the Ottoman Empire.[36]

The economic and social growth of the Greeks of Athens is evident. Of the city's 1,300 houses, no fewer than 1,050 belonged to those who were liable to the capitation tax.[37] "The infidels," observed the Turk Evliya Tschelebi with rueful exaggeration, "are great merchants and have associates even in the most distant parts of western Europe,"[38] but the few,

Pl. 16

2ᵉ Partie. page 47.

Castellan del. et Sculp.ᵗ

Vue de la Citadelle de Coron prise du mouillage.

35. Coron (Korone). From A. L. Castellan, *Lettres sur la Morée et les îles de Cérigo, Hydra et Zante*, Paris, 1808.

the ruling Moslems,[39] who also spoke Greek,[40] "are bereft of position, wealth, and respect, and are of no consequence." The improving economic situation of the Greeks was manifest in the dress of men, women, and children,[41] as well as in their beautiful one- or two-story houses, most of them built in stone salvaged from ancient ruins and then overlaid with tiles. Almost all of them were set in gardens, and few homes were without wells and stoves. The streets were unpaved, but they were generally dry and clean.[42] An urban bourgeoisie had already begun to emerge there and in a few other cities.[43] Some members of this class in Athens were descended from twelve ancient and distinguished families and took pride in their aristocratic or royal origins. They included the Palaeologi, the Chalcocondyles, descendants of the historian, the Benizeloi, the Limponades, the Perouloi, and the Kaballarioi. These were the archons, whose vanity was usually as great as their estates were small.[44]

One source refers to Thebes as a charming and healthy city producing an abundance of food.[45] But it is just possible that Thebes was mistaken for Levadia, since in 1470 a trustworthy eyewitness, Angiolello, described Levadia as a "very commercial" center, "producing much that was useful to man."[46] Naupactus exported wool, cheese, skins, wax, and tobacco from the regions of Thebes and the Gulf of Naupactus.[47]

In Chalcis, where the French had a consul, there were only sporadic exports of wool, cheese, cotton, skins and silk fabrics from Karystos[48] during and immediately after the Turkish-Venetian war of 1645–1669. Presumably this is why Evliya Tschelebi in his *Itinerary* had almost nothing to say about mercantile activity there.[49] There was some movement of goods in Hypate, for which Jewish merchants were responsible.[50]

Sometime between 1520 and 1530 the Thessalian cities of Larissa and Trikkala had populations of 768 families (693 Moslem and 75 Christian) and 644 families (301 and 343), respectively.[51] We have already seen why the Moslem element predominated in Larissa[52] and why it also increased in Trikkala.[53] By 1626 Larissa had become a city of substantial size with a thriving commerce. In that year, its population was larger than that of either Trikkala or Ioannina. Volos was little more than a harbor for the merchants of Larissa and Trikkala.[54]

Ioannina in 1589[55] was the seat of a *sancak* with sixty-two *ziamets* and 345 fiefs,[56] as well as an important center of trade. It had 10,000 dwellings and was by all accounts a strikingly beautiful city.[57] Until 1611 Greeks and Jews lived together inside the citadel, the Turks remaining outside.[58] Its Greek inhabitants were "itinerant traders" with Venice. The people of Ioannina were also noted for their education and gentility,[59] though Maximus the Peloponnesian stigmatized the nobility for their indifference to all that was "important and wise" and their failure to encourage education.[60] Nevertheless, in this period Ioannina was the focus of civilization for the northwestern territories of Greece.

Arta was somewhat smaller, with a population of between six and seven thousand, mainly Greek, but it carried on a lively trade in tobacco, fish roe, and furs.[61] Many Greeks and Orthodox Albanians also lived in Avlona (Valona).[62]

After 1478 the population of Thessalonica grew considerably with the arrival of numerous Jewish refugees[63] from Hungary, Germany, Spain, Portugal, and elsewhere.[64] The Jews, especially those from Spain, shouldered most of the burden of economic progress in Thessalonica, other Macedonian cities (for example, Kastoria), and the Balkan countries to the north. As early as 1507 thousands of Jewish homes in Thessalonica also served as factories, in which large quantities of woollen cloth, gunpowder, and other goods were manufactured.[65] The fabrication of woollen cloth was Thessalonica's only important industry with a long tradition behind it that still existed at the end of the nineteenth century.[66] By the middle of the sixteenth century, it was a most prosperous city with no fewer than eighty synagogues[67] and teeming with wealthy Jewish merchants. The Jewish element thereafter remained preponderant: archival sources give the population of Thessalonica in the year 925 of the Hegira (1519) as 1,374 Moslem families, 1,087 Christian families, and 3,143 Jewish families. The city was part of the sultan's domain *(has)* and brought him an income of 3,506,762 *akçes.*[68] By the end of the century its population had again shown a remarkable increase, though some estimates must be considered excessive.[69] Still, Thessalonica in this period was the "desired city"—a place of fame, beauty, and order.[70] At the end of the sixteenth century the old Byzantine city of Cassandrea (ancient Potidaea) was still an episcopal seat with sixty priests and 2,000 dwellings.[71] References to it were still made in the seventeenth century,[72] but all that remains today are a few traces of its walls.

The cities of eastern Macedonia, such as Serrai and Kavalla, were dominated by a Greek and Greek-speaking population, though there was also a sizable element of Serbian-speaking peasants as well as Greeks around Serrai. The existence of the Serbian language was undoubtedly a legacy of the period of Stephen Dušan's dominion. The cities were also inhabited by Jews, whom the Turks had brought from Buda, Pest, and Alba Regia, that is, Szekersfehervar. When Belon refers to Kavalla as "once deserted and ruined," he undoubtedly means Christoupolis,[73] but it is true that Kavalla's population rose rapidly after the war between Turkey and Hungary. A fine city developed, with a Jewish population of more than five hundred.[74]

The population of Adrianople grew from 22,335 sometime between 1520 and 1530 to 30,140 sometime between 1571 and 1580.[75] Though the homes were unprepossessing,[76] the city had many distinguished churches, mosques, and minarets; there were also arcades (*bezestens*), seraglios,[77] and other assorted shops.[78] This was in fact the largest urban center in Thrace.[79] Many families of nobles and dignitaries of the old Byzantine Empire had settled in Adrianople, and during the following centuries their descendants were still to be found in the city dreaming of their former grandeur.[80]

Similar changes took place in the size of populations throughout the Balkan peninsula. Barkan estimates that between 1525 and 1575 the populations of Athens, Larissa, Trikkala, Adrianople, Monastir, Skoplje, Sofia, and Sarajevo rose by sixty-eight per cent. Whatever the exact figure, the growth of urban populations in the Balkans appears as startling as in the cities of the western Mediterranean.[81] The population of Constantinople fairly exploded—a phenomenon worth examining in rather more detail.

Constantinople was so steeped in history and tradition and so renowned for its beauty that it was known simply as the "City."[82] Greeks and other peoples whom the Turks deported there after the Capture were eventually joined by voluntary migrants from every corner of the Hellenic world—merchants, craftsmen, artisans—all in search of work.[83]

Mohammed II delegated the task of repopulating Constantinople[84] to the City's first *subaşı*[85] (chief constable), Suleiman.[86] The City was so deserted after the Capture that the empty and silent houses induced feelings of melancholy and apprehension.[87] Only the Jewish community, which lived in Balat (Dursunbey), remained virtually intact.[88]

Fully cognizant of its glorious past and incomparable strategic situation, Mohammed II determined to restore it to life and make it his capital.[89] Naturally, these plans could only be implemented with the co-operation of its former inhabitants and other Christian raias, peasants as well as artisans. He therefore freed many captives, gave them back their houses, and granted tax exemptions for a specified number of years. The same privileges were extended to those able to buy their own freedom.[90] Many former inhabitants chose to take advantage of such favorable conditions of residence and returned to Constantinople.[91]

The sultan also ordered the removal to Constantinople of 5,000 families from Anatolia and Rumelia[92] by September of 1453. Many new colonists, mainly Greek Christians[93] but also Turks and a large number of Jews[94] from many cities and provinces of the Empire, were thus resettled in different parts of Constantinople and its environs. Artisans congregated near the walls and the sea, peasants on the outskirts of the City. The new citizens were allotted tenements or houses, and peasants received in addition livestock and farming implements.[95] Most of the peasants had in fact been moved under duress. They came from lands conquered by force

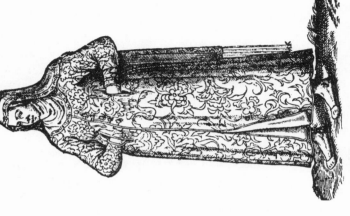

Donna di stato Greca della città d'Andrenopoli. terra di Thracia.

So Femme de Macedoine.

36. A Greek woman of Macedonia. 37. A Greek woman of Adrianople. Both from Nicolas de Nicolay, *Les Navigations, pérégrinations, et voyages faicts en la Turquie,* Anvers, 1577.

of arms and were considered prisoners of war. In effect, they settled in their new homes as serfs (*ortakcı*). Yet they were shortly to transform into fecund gardens[96] the fields that war had left deserted and uncultivated. Their origins are partly revealed by the names of their villages—Bosna, Lazari, Arnavout, and so on.[97] Greek settlers also came from the Peloponnese,[98] Amastris,[99] Thasos, Samothrace,[100] Mytilene,[101] and Argos,[102] from Medea and its villages, Agathopolis (Akhtopol), Mesembria (Nesebar), Selymbria, Herakleia and Panados in Thrace, Orestias,[103] Adrianople, Palea and Nea Phocaea, Kaffa,[104] Trebizond, Sinope, and Argyrocastron.[105]

Such was the basic composition of the population of post-Byzantine Constantinople—mainly Greek and drawn from every direction. However, the Greek dialect which developed in Constantinople shows that the predominant influence was that of southern Greece.[106]

Mohammed II gave to his military dignitaries and relatives[107] the most splendid houses and the finest churches with extensive gardens or vineyards and fields where Greek nobles and wealthy citizens had formerly maintained their country residences. Turkish families and workers associated with the same trade were also assigned specific abodes. For example, fullers of wool or flax were installed in the monastery of Pantokrator and dervishes in the monastery of Mangana[108] in the City.

As Turkish officials, soldiers, and their families became established in the City and as the construction of houses, mosques, inns, bazaars, baths, aquducts, and fountains proceeded, Constantinople began within a few decades of the Capture to take on the appearance of a Turkish city. Yet the survival of many fine examples of Byzantine architecture, both ecclesiastical and secular, as well as its repopulation by Greek colonists in the main, meant that Constantinople also retained much of its Byzantine flavor and way of life.[109] Its magnificent situation, its great historical and civilizing importance, and the generally flourishing state of commerce throughout the Near East contributed to the continual swelling of its population, seriously taxing its supply of food and water. It has been estimated that the population of Constantinople—between three and five hundred thousand at the beginning of the sixteenth century[110]—rose to perhaps seven hundred thousand, counting its suburbs, by the end of that century.[111] Throughout the seventeenth century, the population is believed to have fluctuated between seven and eight hundred thousand inhabitants.[112]

Despite such impressive growth, the City long retained an air of spaciousness. As in almost every city throughout the East, every house had its own garden with trees of various kinds—fig, pomegranate, bitter orange, olive, and so on. It was thus not surprising that in 1573 Gerlach recorded his impression of entering an earthly paradise. The beauty of the City was

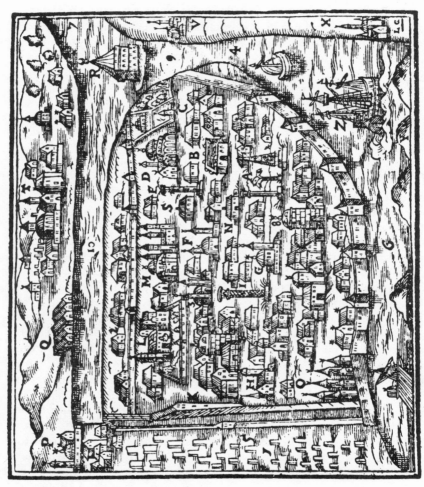

38. Constantinople. From Salomon Schweigger, *Ein neue Reyssbeschreibung aus Teutschland nach Constantinopel und Jerusalem*, Nuremberg, 1608.

LA VILLE ET LE PORT DE CONSTANTINOPLE

Canal de
la Mer
Noire

Le Bosphore de Trace

39. Constantinople in the seventeenth century. From Guillaume Joseph Grelot, *Relation nouvelle d'un voyage de Constantinople*, Paris, 1680.

enhanced by its palaces, grand and stately churches, not to speak of the mosques that the Turks constructed in so many districts.[113] It has been estimated that there were no fewer than three hundred mosques in the City at this time.[114]

The exotic Oriental atmosphere of Constantinople[115] and the renown of its artisans and craftsmen in every field drew comment from foreign travellers.[116] They remarked on its ruined monuments,[117] its symmetrical and spotlessly clean mosques, which stood in striking contrast to low-set houses poorly constructed in timber or inferior brick (for those made of stone were rare).[118] On the other hand, its vermin, bedraggled animals,[119] squalid streets,[120] and fires[121] did not escape notice. Some commented on the night sentries,[122] the water-vendors,[123] the Armenian porters;[124] others were attracted by the covered arcades filled with the workshops of Turks, Greeks, Jews, and Armenians, the variety of other shops, or the tenements of various mosques, such as those of Hagia Sophia, which were *wakf* and included caravansaries and inns.[125] A milling and colorful throng of buyers, merchants and craftsmen crowded the two arcades and displayed their wares from Greece, Italy, and all over the East as far away as India.[126]

40. Greek dancers in the courtyard of a church in Constantinople. From Salomon Schweigger, *Ein newe Reyssbeschreibung aus Teutschland nach Constantinopel und Jerusalem*, Nuremberg, 1608.

Travellers also described the City's various entertainments, which were held in squares like the one facing the Mosque of Sultan Bayezid. There, Turks' performing monkeys and dogs put on their acts; magicians and fortunetellers, both men and women, performed for the curious who gathered spellbound around them every afternoon between three and four o'clock;[127] and in the hippodrome, for a little money, acrobats, jugglers, wrestlers and others performed, accompanied by trained leopards, bears, lions, reptiles, and birds.[128]

Pera, reached by ferry from Constantinople, was inhabited by Greeks and Franks (Italians, French, and others). This was the suburb of ambassadors,[129] commerce and finance, and recreation.[130] Many Catholic residents of Pera were descended from Genoese nobles who had settled there in Byzantine times.[131] Also, scions of the old Byzantine nobility still had houses there.[132]

Wealthy Greek women of Constantinople,[133] particularly those of Pera, enjoyed more freedom than women anywhere else. Foreigners were impressed by the resplendent dress and rich jewellery they wore on festive occasions.[134]

Constantinople was a Babel of races and nations—Turks, Greeks, Syrians, Armenians, and many others. The dominant language was Turkish, followed by Greek, Italian, Croatian, and Hungarian. There were a large number of newcomers from Croatia and Hungary, among them prisoners of war (*propter advenarum et captivorum ex his regionibus multitudinem*). The Jews spoke the language of the European country from which they came.[135] Except for the Turks, the three largest language groups in the city were the Greeks, the Armenians, and the Jews. They also comprised the most active social groups, dominating commerce and the handicraft industries.[136] The bourgeoisie of the City was composed mainly of merchants coming from these groups. Turkish merchants were practically nonexistent.[137]

But the most successful traders were the Jews, who conducted businesses as money-changers, usurers, scrap-dealers, and brokers.[138] Since Jews in Western Europe suffered persecution,[139] foreigners were particularly struck by the extent of liberty and personal wealth which they enjoyed. Some had amassed estates to the value of 100,000 ducats and owned palatial houses and gardens.[140] However, they were reviled by the people[141] because they had also become trusted advisers[142] in the households of the sultan and his officials and were notorious both for their unjust counsel and false accusations.

Jews, as well as some Chians,[143] also practiced medicine in Constantinople and Adrianople.[144] Later, Jewish and Cretan graduates of the University of Padua's School of Medicine became ubiquitous throughout the East.[145]

FILLE D'ESTAT GRECQUE

DE LA VILLE DE PERA

41. A Greek woman of Pera, Constantinople. From Philippe du Fresne-Canaye, *Le Voyage de Levant. Receuil de voyages et de documents*, Paris, 1897.

Greek and foreign sources provide a good deal of information about the composition of the Greek population of Constantinople. All agree, and this is a phenomenon that we shall explore further, that the immigration of Greeks into their famous capital was continuous, even from distant lands. Among these accounts, there is a reference to some freed slaves from the Ottoman naval station (*Tersane*)—Cretans, Ionians, Maniatai, and others—who, in the sixteenth century, were resettled in the delightful and salubrious precinct of Tatavla after their Church of St. Demetrius was converted into a mosque. They brought their saint's icon with them and founded a new church;[146] Greek merchants subsequently congregated there.[147]

What had happened to the old noble families who survived the Capture? In fact, most of them eventually reappeared as merchants in the neighborhood of the Oecumenical Patriarchate. As early as 1476 an official berat referred to some of the Greek descendants of former noble families—Manuel Palaeologus, Palaeologus Quandroz (?), Andreas, son of Chalcocondyles, and Lefteris, son of Galyanoz (Galianos?). These, together with a certain Giakoub, who was probably a renegade Greek official in the palace, were named as customs collectors for the ports of Constantinople, Galata, Gallipoli, Kilid oul-Bahr (on the European shore of the Dardanelles opposite Canakkale), and Mudanya, as well as all the ports of Asia Minor from the fortress of Gioros (at Anatolou Kavak on the Bosphorus) to the two Phocaeas and Cesme.[148]

A century later, in 1586, descendants of the old Byzantine families were still trading in Constantinople, among them the brothers Constantine and Ioannis from the royal house of Palaeologus; Mouzalos (Mouzalon), an extremely wealthy merchant in Moscow, who supplied sables to the sultan's palace; Andreas Ralles from Adrianople, father-in-law of Andronicus, the son of Michael Cantacuzenus of Anchialus; and Eugenicus, "notable of Kontoscali" in Constantinople, whose personal fortune backed his business. Descendants of the Comneni also resided in Constantinople and had their own private incomes.

Other merchants who supplied the sultan's court were Korphinos, an *amil* (a person authorized to let public property and tax franchises); Syrgiangos, "a great lord and merchant"; and Photinos, "the sultan's notable in the fish-market quarter."[149]

In an interesting and discursive letter to Martinus Crusius dated 7 April 1581, Theodosius Zygomalas attempted to apprise him, in response to Crusius' request, of the fate of the Byzantine nobility. He wrote that it was difficult for him to trace the histories of the ten or so families in the City who had aristocratic ancestry—the Mouzalos, the Vatatzes, the Asanes, the Chrysoloras families, and others. However, most of them lived by letting tax franchises. Others were engaged in commerce and a few other vocations. Sometimes they became wealthy; sometimes they were on the edge of poverty. But all of them had to work "like slaves to get whatever they had to live on." Reflecting upon this decline of the old nobility, he went on:

As God is my witness, the nobility can only be really content when they live in their own country and when they are well fed. So is it not amazing that any survive at all after 130 years of occupation? However, little of their former contentment remains; indeed not many names are left. Even such as there are have, I think, lost their nobility and pride, for when the oak tree finally topples over everyone rushes to scavenge some wood. Thus, when the Empire of the Greeks fell, its enemies divided it into many parts. There are many nobles who have even entered into the service of the sultan, and who have received houses, beautiful and fertile estates, and much else besides.[150]

Gentil-homme Grec.

Marchant Grec.

42. A Greek noble.

43. A Greek merchant.

Both from Nicolas de Nicolay, *Les Navigations, pérégrinations, et voyages, faicts en la Turquie,* Anvers, 1577.

Most of the survivors of the old noble families were in fact scattered throughout the Greek cities of the Black Sea—Medea, Sozopolis, Mesembria, Anchialus, and others. Some were in the Peloponnese—the Mamales and Notaras families, for instance.[151] Without exception, they clung tenaciously to Byzantine traditions. The Constantinopolitan families wielded considerable influence in the Christian community of the capital; by their interference in the internal affairs of the patriarchate they were especially influential in the ecclesiastical realm. Gradually, however, they departed for Russia and the neighboring Danubian countries, and by the end of the sixteenth century not many were left. Frequently, too, they intermarried with such *nouveaux riches* as had acquired a certain social prominence.[152] Thus, the new Greek ruling class, the Phanariots, which arose after the Oecumenical Patriarchate moved to Phanar, represented the fusion of the old nobility with the new bourgeoisie. There, in Phanar, where many Jews also lived, their comfortable and spacious homes lined a broad boulevard; and there the Palaeologi, the Cantacuzeni, the Comneni, and others, all proud of their aristocratic or even royal descent, would stroll down the streets like petty satraps wearing their distinctive sable calpacs and yellow shoes. Their ambition was to gain some greater or lesser office in one or other of the principalities of Walachia and Moldavia, where they imagined their fortunes would be made.[153]

Byzantine traditions and the old imperial splendor never entirely vanished. They survived not only among the scions of the nobility, but also among other Greeks, particularly those within the range of Constantinople's influence. Witness the Christian names and surnames of many from such places during the first half of the seventeenth century: on Mytilene, Branas, Ducena and Ducas, Cantacuzenus, Comnene and Comnenus, Lascarina, Palaeologina and Palaeologus; in Trebizond, Gabras, Digenis, Thalassenos, Kalogiannes, Melikes, Palaeologina, Phocas and Chrysococces; in Gallipoli, Agalliane, Theodegina, Cantacuzene, Kalothetos, Comnenus, Kanakes, Lascaris and Lascarina, Logothetes, Mouzakes, Panteugenina, Sgouropoulina, Synodinos; in Rhaedestos, Asanes, Ducas, Lascarina, Mouzalou (from the Byzantine Mouzalos), Sophiane, Synadene, Sphrantzena; on Chios, Vatatzina, Bryony, (Bryennou), Digenis, Ducena, Monobasiotes, Palaeologina, Regena, Chortatzena, Chrysokefalina; in Ainos, Asanina, Apocaucus, Vatatzes, Ducena, Comnenus, Mangaphas, Palaeologina, Regena, Spanopoulos, Philommates, Frangopoulos, Chrysoskoulos.[154] Many of the same names appeared on Samothrace.[155]

Even today, Thasos has families named Lascaris, Comnenus, Skleros, Gabras, Branas, Palaeologus, and so on, perhaps descended from their Byzantine antecedents. Until very recently, the Christian names Loubolina (the feminine of Olobolos), Scamandrane, and others were also given on Thasos.[156] Who could have believed that these Byzantine echoes would still resound, however faintly, in the middle of the twentieth century?

The ever-increasing needs of urban centers encouraged a perpetual ebb and flow of population from the mountains to the plains. Only a limited number of farmers, graziers, and craftsmen could subsist on the mountains, with their infertile soil and rocky slopes, and the surplus population had to go elsewhere. A swelling stream of undernourished and desperate people therefore poured down on to the nearby plains and to distant lowlands. Though their journeys were often long, difficult, and perilous, they made their way hopefully towards the unknown. For reasons of security, travellers (laborers, merchants, and others) in Greece and the other Near Eastern lands preferred to band together in large numbers.[157] As they looked for work, laborers and craftsmen (builders and carpenters, for instance) travelled together on foot, while merchants moved with their personal belongings and wares piled on the backs of pack animals. The beasts of burden were mainly mules,[158] less frequently camels, and they made up the caravans that played such an important part in the development of the trade of the East.

Long distances, inadequate communications, and the hazards of the road made it impossible for most journeys to be completed except in stages. Accordingly, caravansaries and inns that ordinarily belonged to pious Moslems were built as stopping places where a traveller could obtain free meals (each consisting of one plate of rice) and lodging for up to three days. The caravansaries were usually imposing buildings constructed around a spacious courtyard. Fountains and cisterns in the center of the courtyard provided water for men and animals. Guests' quarters and stables occupied the four sides of the building. There were many such caravansaries between Belgrade and Constantinople.

An inn was a plainer and much less prepossessing structure, though it was usually located in high and picturesque surroundings because of the need to have convenient access to cold running water.[159]

Two important sources of emigration were the districts of the Aspropotamos and the Agrafa proper. In 1520 the latter had a population of 332 families and, as part of the domain of Ferhat Pasha, provided an annual revenue of 48,994 *akçes.*[160] Many indigent families came down from the high and isolated mountains to Larissa, most of whose inhabitants were from the Agrafa or Rapsane, despite oppressive administration and high taxation;[161] many went to Kozane,[162] Thessalonica, and elsewhere. By October 1605 there were already so many people from the Agrafa in Thessalonica (called Scourta in official Turkish records), and these so prosperous, that they provided revenue of 70,000 *akçes* annually. This was almost half the amount of 153,280 *akçes* that the Christians of

44. A caravansary. From an old gravure. Reprinted by permission of Christos Spanos.

Thessalonica were required to pay each year for the maintenance of the sixty-nine cannoneers in the fortress.[163]

In this same period, many people settled down on the outskirts of Thessalonica in Asvestochorion (Kirets-Kioï) to the south of a church beside the rill known as Vlachikos Lakkos. Apparently they still spoke Vlach. They were craftsmen—tailors, dyers, jewellers, shoemakers, and so on. They were also more civilized than the local inhabitants, to whom they referred disparagingly as "peasants."[164]

The people of the Agrafa, as we shall see again in a different context, then moved to the east across the Sea of Marmara and colonized villages along the coast of Asia Minor. Others went north and settled in Philip-popolis (now Plovdiv) where there were also Greek immigrants from Epirus, Moschopolis (the exodus from this city was occasioned by its destruction), Rhodes, and the district of Stenemachos.[165] However, most of the migrants from the Agrafa went even further north to the Danubian principalities, where their Latin dialect apparently facilitated intercourse with the indigenous peoples of those lands. During the seventeenth and eighteenth centuries,[166] as evidence of their prosperity, these expatriates built handsome homes and beautiful churches in the Agrafa, the As-propotamos, and generally throughout the Pindus and its spurs. These churches still serve as reminders of the close relations between the Greeks from the Agrafa and the countries to which they migrated, notably Rumania.[167] It is probable that they also colonized the village of Kastania on Samos, despite local tradition that the first colonists came mostly from Epirus.[168]

The migrations from the Agrafa are recorded in their folklore. One demotic song tells the story of a woman of the Agrafa who greeted the return of her expatriate husband.[169] Another laments fathers and sons who were shipwrecked:

Who has a husband and a son abroad?
Tell her not to wait nor to expect their return.
Sixty ships went down and took brave men with them.
Sails filled the sea and bodies the shore.[170]

Groups of poor and hungry men also left Albania and Epirus in search of work to support their families. They ventured down to the estates of beys and sought work as shepherds, laborers, and reapers. Such were the people from Tsamanta, who were hired as shepherds and muleteers in Turkish Konispoli (now Konispol in Albania), or else became itinerant coppersmiths and tinsmiths in neighboring villages, as well as in Nivista near Delvinë.[171] The more venturesome went further afield through the passes of the Pindus[172] to Thessaly and Macedonia, where they settled down on the plains and in the towns and cities of the Ottoman Empire.

Many from northern Epirus, including Arvanito-Vlachs, settled down permanently in eastern Rumelia[173] and Bulgaria. For example, there was the village of Arbanasi, which the Greeks called Arvanitochori. Suleiman the Magnificent (1520-1566) granted them tax exemptions and other privileges which were renewed by later sultans until the beginning of the nineteenth century. Some also settled in Tirnovo.[174]

When Belon was travelling to Constantinople via the ancient Egnatian Way (part of whose pavement he noticed on the plain of Komotine [Gumuljina] near Kypsela [Ypsala]),[175] he encountered large groups of people whom he took to be "Albanians" but who must have been Greeks from northern Epirus,[176] to judge from Belon's remarks: *"Les Albanois ancienement nommez Epirotes sont Chrestiens et parlent une langue à parfoy differente à la Grecque. Il est bien vray qu'ils suyvent la religion des Grecs: et d'autant qu'ilz sont confins de Grece, ils scavent aussi le langage Grec.* [The Albanians formerly called Epirotes are Christians and speak a language that differs at times from Greek. It is true that they practice the Greek religion: more especially as they are in Greece, they also know the Greek language.]"[177] We have only to bear in mind the confusion that has surrounded the words "Albanian" and "Epirote" even in recent years to reach the reasonable conclusion that Belon's "laborers," as they were called, were in fact Greeks from northern Epirus. They were Orthodox Christians, who spoke not only Greek but also another language that differed from Greek in certain respects. They were peasants returning to their homes: seasonal workers who during summer had labored as winnowers and reapers on the estates of Turks in Macedonia, Thrace, and Asia Minor. They were very poor (almost all were barefoot), but they were conscientious and thrifty enough to be able to support their families through the winter on their meager savings. Looking at them, Belon was reminded both of workers from Savoy, who spent their winters destitute in Italy, and others from Lombardy, who went to Germany, France, Flanders, Denmark, and other distant lands to labor as chimney sweeps. We might even go so far as to assert that Belon's "laborers" were masons, that they came not only from Albania and northern Epirus but also from the so-called *mastorochoria*[178] of western Macedonia, and that the language they spoke (according to Belon, somewhat different from Greek) was really no more than their local dialect or perhaps the conventional idiom of masons.[179] We know that for some two thousand years the inhabitants of these districts practiced masonry and were also migratory.[180] It is more than likely that these large groups of travellers were artisans belonging to the same craft on their way to various parts of the Empire, particularly to Constantinople.[181]

Those migratory workers who were fortunate enough eventually brought their families to their place of work and settled down permanently; others presumably married and reared families away from their former homes, if we may reasonably extrapolate from the clear evidence of later centuries. By the end of the nineteenth century, for example, Greco-Vlach strangers and Greco-Albanians who migrated from Thessaly, Epirus, and Albania earlier in the century had settled down with their families of Lakkovikia in Pangaion (Macedonia).[182] At the beginning of the twentieth century the inhabitants of Chalcidice were still hiring seasonal laborers—the so-called *Gekides* from Albania—for farm work.[183]

Peasant laborers also migrated to northern Greece[184] from Bulgaria. Early in the twentieth century, Bulgarian masons and reapers were still regular seasonal workers on the island of Thasos.[185] The people of Chalcidice were also hiring "charcoal workers" and farmhands from Bulgaria and the northern Slav-speaking regions of Macedonia. Those who got married probably never returned to their homelands.

There are a few Slav place-names in Chalcidice that owe their existence to these migrations from the north.[186] The inflow of Bulgarian workers thus had the effect of shoring up the remnants of earlier Slav colonization—a phenomenon not unlike that in the Cyclades, where West European pirates and merchants prevented the disappearance of the Frankish element. Although the movement of populations among the various Balkan countries generally came to an end with the establishment of Ottoman rule, the peaceful infiltration of northern Greece by Slav workers, principally Bulgarians, continued. There was no sudden recrudescence of earlier Slav colonization, but new colonies appeared and the older ones were linguistically and culturally strengthened. Some Byzantinologists and other historians not overly familiar with the history of Turkish rule have ignored or misread the significance of this Slav infusion, mistakenly assuming that it was a result of the earlier Slav incursions.[187]

Many Greeks also travelled north, stopping and eventually settling down in the ancient Greek cities and towns of Bulgaria. There they fortified the existing Greek population or else founded new villages, even as far away as the most northerly of the Danubian principalities. Thus, the Greek communities which had been formed during the last two centuries of Byzantine rule were rejuvenated, and new communities were established. The same process was repeated in the lands of the Yugoslavs.

One example of the growth of Slav toponyms during the Ottoman period is a document of 1640[188] that refers to Novo Selo ("New Village") and other villages around it with Slavic names actually outnumbering those with Greek place-names. This was the district of Mademochoria, with Siderokavsia as its pivot, which received a considerable influx of migrants during the period of Turkish rule. Men of all nations came, but the majority were Bulgarian miners lured by the prospects of the district's mines. The number of workers fluctuated in accordance with the output of the mines, rising in good times and falling in bad. The mines themselves were part of the imperial domain, and at the time of Suleiman I produced a revenue of 155,817 akçes.[189]

The site of Siderokavsia, or Siderokapsa, was not quite that of today's Stratonike, formerly Isvoron, which was famous for its "akçes, gold coins and karagrosia";[190] rather, it was situated in a valley to the north straddling a stream that emptied into Lake Volve (Besikion).[191] The exact location is described by Evliya Tschelebi and Hadji Kalopha (mid-seventeenth century), both of whom visited it. It was a very pleasant, hilly town with a healthy climate some eleven to sixteen kilometers from the sea. At the time, it had one mosque, two baths, and a small market. It fell within the jurisdiction of Thessalonica, and had an army commissariat, a janissary command, and a comptroller of taxes. All of these, however, were subordinate to the emin (superintendent) of the silver mine, who also was a civil and criminal magistrate. The district was verdant and picturesque, with high mountains, forests, and abundant game. The trees in the forests could be cut only for firing the silver-smelting kilns.[192] A good water supply provided hydraulic power for mining installations and also irrigated the vegetable gardens and orchards, as well as the vineyards that surrounded the town.[193]

We learn from a firman of Mohammed II's, which was issued in 1475 or 1476 and confirmed an earlier one promulgated by Murad II, that the miners of Siderokavsia paid an impost of one dram of silver in twelve, but were obliged to sell all of it to the amil (manager) of the mint, whose money-changers bought the silver at a price not below the ruling rate of exchange. Any irregularities in this procedure were punishable by the soubaşı (chief of police) and the cadi in accordance with the seriousness of the fraud. Miners paid the tithe on grain and other produce, but were exempt from the ten per cent military tax, the cask tax, and the postal tax levied on horses. The tithe on vineyards might be paid in must, and there was no levy on those who wished to make charcoal.[194]

From about 1530, when Suleiman I reorganized the mines,[195] Siderokavsia entered upon a new period of prosperity. The town grew rapidly, and two satellite villages, Piavits and Serine, grew up around it near the sea. The attractions of work and various tax exemptions brought Greeks (most of whom apparently became permanent residents) and others from the Balkans who spoke esclavon (Croatian), Bulgarian, Turkish, and Albanian. Most of the miners were Bulgarians. German artisans who had recently begun to work there taught them the German names for ores and mining equipment. By then, the once ramshackle village had begun to assume the character of a small city, reminding Belon of Joachimsthal (now Jachymov) in Bohemia. The marketplace resounded with the din of

Greek and Serbian peasants from the surrounding villages selling their produce. However, the most commonly heard language was that of the many Jews who had flocked to this important silver- and gold-producing center. Work began on Monday and finished on Friday night. The sultan's revenue from the district averaged between eighteen and thirty thousand ducats monthly. Some five to six thousand furnaces throughout the hills, employing more than six thousand Albanians, Greeks, Jews, Vlachs, Circassians, Serbs, and Turks, were kept busy refining the silver and gold. Belon has left us some interesting and detailed information about the mining installations, refining techniques, the separation of lead from gold and silver, and the smelting of silver.[196]

During the next few decades the mines continued in operation, but production apparently declined.[197] However, they were still sufficiently profitable to warrant a ten-day trade fair in Pazarouda (Pazargiach), a Moslem village in the district of Siderokavsia close by the thermal sources of Lake Volve. The fair was held at the same time each year on the feast of St. George (rûz-i hızır Ilyasda) and seems to have been known all over Macedonia (in Thessalonica, Genitsa [Giannitsa], Veroia, Servia, Kastoria, Phlorina, Avret Hisar, Serrai, Drama, Zichna, Monastir, Perlepe, Istib [Stip], Kratovo, Kioustentil, Strumitsa), as well as in certain parts of western Thrace (Gioumoultzina and Kara Genitze) and Thessaly (Elasson, Yenisehir [Larissa], and Chatalja [Pharsala]).[198]

A firman of 1580 addressed to the newly appointed cadi of Siderokavsia (Sidre Kapsi) reveals that at that time production in the mines had virtually come to a halt. The firman stated that, although the cadi had been instructed to resume mining operations and to remit many coins to Constantinople before the new year, time had gone by, another year was already approaching, and still the central government had received no news of what was happening.[199]

By the middle of the seventeenth century, at least the resources of the silver mine were again being exploited by Eboul-Chaïr Ibrahim aga, a steward (kâhya) of the Grand Vizier's. Its production at that time was ten to eleven centners. The city still had its mint, but this was finally closed down by Sultan Ibrahim I (1640–1648).[200] There is at least one further reference to activity by miners in 1779;[201] but by the end of the seventeenth century the mines of Chalcidice had fallen into decay.[202]

By late Byzantine times Thrace was already dry, desolate[203] and denuded of forests.[204] For European travellers on the overland route to Constantinople, this was the first part of Greece they encountered. When Benedict Curipeschitz made the journey from Vienna in 1530, he passed through southern Serbia and eastern Rumelia, with its polyglot population, and entered Greece at Steinen Pruggen (?) and Adrianople.[205]

Everywhere in the towns, markets, and villages of Thrace he met

Greeks with long hair, wearing Turkish clothes and blue hats, who suffered much from the privations of slavery and wondered why their ancestors had not stood up to the Turks.[206]

A degree of mercantile activity was evident in Thrace at this time, notably in the coastal cities. Herakleia, Rhaedestos,[207] and Selymbria were all of some importance, the last for its export trade in goods from Thrace, particularly Adrianople, and Bulgaria.[208] Gallipoli was also an entrepot for the trade between East and West,[209] as it had been in Byzantine times.

The sultans' policy of repopulating deserted or thinly populated areas facilitated the immigration of large numbers of poverty-stricken people into Thrace. New settlers then worked on the estates of Turkish spahi fiefholders[210] or on *wakf* domain.[211] Apparently some of these were free peasants; others were serfs, especially those forcibly deported from conquered Greek territories and resettled among other peasants in the plains of Thrace near Constantinople.[212]

On his way to Constantinople in 1587 the traveller Lubenau passed through the village of Kayali on the left bank of the Hevros (Hebrus), which he found entirely peopled by Albanians from the Peloponnese.[213] This is important information, for it indicates that not all Albanian settlers in Thrace came direct from Albania. The colonization of Kayiali would therefore have occurred under Mohammed II.

In time, many serfs living on *wakf* estates around Adrianople gained their freedom, mixed with free peasants, and thus contributed to population growth in the villages.[214] By the beginning of the twentieth century, in the district of Didymoteikhon alone, no fewer than twelve villages were still inhabited by the descendants of original settlers from the Peloponnese, eleven by Epirotes, and seven by Macedonians.[215]

Suleiman I (1520–1566) and Selim II (1566–1574),[216] were mainly responsible for the colonization of certain districts in Thrace by northern Epirotes and Christian Albanians from Kolonjë, Bithikouki, and thereabouts. They went to villages in the districts of Makra Gephyra, Kessane, and elsewhere,[217] including the islands of the Sea of Marmara—Marmara island itself in 1550, Alone (Pasha-Liman) and Koutale.[218] At the end of the nineteenth century, the village of Aphthoni on Marmara had 280 dwellings and a population of 1,400, mostly sailors of Albanian origin who spoke both Albanian and Greek.[219] Others migrated to the opposite shores of Asia Minor, principally Bithynia;[220] from there they apparently went to the island of Kalolimnos.[221] All of these colonizing ventures were encouraged by the granting of privileges and tax exemptions.[222]

It is therefore most probable that the people who migrated from Gallipoli to Madytos and, finally, to Kallessi (Canakkale) on the Dardanelles, where they settled down as builders,[223] were Epirotes and Albanians originally from the villages of Kessane. Since building was their main vocation, it is likely that they were resettled during the reign of Selim I or Suleiman I for the specific purpose of constructing fortresses. Indeed, the Greeks' whom Gerlach praises as fine builders—of "beautiful churches and caravansaries"[224]—must in many cases also have been northern Epirotes (or western Macedonians).

Besides Albanians, groups of other nationalities settled in Thrace. As early as three or four years after the Capture, Mohammed II had brought to Thrace and the environs of Constantinople a large number of Serbs, Hungarians, and Bulgarians. His motive in doing so was to secure a region that had become deserted and dangerous for travellers.[225] The villages of Yeni Belgrad, Orta Belgrad, and Sultan Belgrad were among those colonized at this time. From the seventeenth century, their inhabitants were exempted from the payment of certain taxes and the impressment of their children on condition that they maintained the aqueducts carrying water to Constantinople.[226] When Belon crossed this flat and treeless land, which reminded him of faraway Picardy,[227] he passed through villages outside Constantinople and elsewhere that were wholly peopled by Bulgarians, Bosnians, Dalmatians, Slavonians, Serbs, and Vlachs, all of them loyal to their own religion. They had been brought there as cultivators of the vacant land.[228]

Another feature of the migrations to Thrace was the annual peregrination of Bulgarian hostlers who came to Constantinople to tend the sultans' and pashas' horses.[229] Their visits continued over the ensuing centuries,[230] and on each occasion some no doubt stayed behind on Turkish farms.

The village of Voulgaro on Alone was also settled by Bulgarians. These peasant newcomers very soon mixed with Greeks and, by the beginning of the nineteenth century, appear to have been completely hellenized. They were responsible for changing the name of their village to Pasha Liman.[231] Other Bulgarians crossed to Asia Minor and settled in the village of Kaber Bachtse on the peninsula of Cyzicus. People from this village founded Kaenourgio Chorio on the same peninsula during the nineteenth century. They supported themselves by farming and making charcoal[232] and at the end of the nineteenth century still spoke Bulgarian.

Thrace's population had been predominantly Greek until the sixteenth century, but colonization by foreigners, to say nothing of the spread of Turkish settlements, gradually altered its character. Although there were several main layers of colonization, it is impossible to date them with any accuracy.

Like the Balkans, Asia Minor also witnessed the unending migratory movement of Greeks from one place to another, from the coasts into the interior and vice versa, from the Greek peninsula and islands to the shores and hinterland of western Asia Minor. They came especially from regions

that were poor, mountainous, and overpopulated, or troubled by civil
agitation and disturbances. To such people the shores of Asia Minor held
out the enticement of greater security as well as the prospects of finding
work, selling produce more readily, and generally improving their
economic lot.

Migrants from European Greece and the islands found in Asia Minor
the survivors of a once large and prosperous Greek population. According to official Turkish records, that population consisted of 78,783
families[233] between 1520 and 1535 and included not only Greeks but also
smaller groups of Orthodox Christians (for example, Armenians).

A little later, in 1575, the Metropolitan of Pisidia told Gerlach that there
were few Christians left in Asia Minor, but he was obviously speaking
mainly on the basis of his knowledge of his own ecclesiastical province,
where only a few churches remained.[234]

How can we distinguish between the descendants of the original Greek
inhabitants of Asia Minor and the new settlers? The problem is not a
simple one, but there is some surviving evidence which at least permits us
to approach it.

Written sources are sparse, but the survival of a local Greek population
in southwestern Asia Minor is proven from the evidence of language and
folklore.[235] New arrivals then clustered around this nucleus, appearing in
large numbers in some places and in smaller numbers at others. During
the seventeenth century, the Greek populations of Side and Attalia (Antalya) in Pamphylia (which enjoyed tax privileges),[236] as well as those of
Myra, Libisi, and Kastellorizo[237] off Lycia, were an amalgam of migrants
and the original local inhabitants,[238] who had spent the difficult years of
captivity "living secretly." From some of these places, a number of new
settlements or villages were subsequently established nearby.[239] The little
town of Attalia, Greek since the days of the Byzantine Empire, finally lost
its mother tongue,[240] apparently because the immigrants were Turkish-
speaking Greeks from Isparta, two-and-a-half-days' journey from Attalia.
However, by the end of the sixteenth century the many Turkish-speaking
Greeks in the area were receiving a Greek education (evidently in a Greek
elementary school) and used Greek books imported from Venice.[241]

Despite the devastation wrought by the invasions of Tamerlane, the
indigenous Greek population of the western littoral of Asia Minor seems
also to have survived. There were Greeks living in Smyrna[242] and other
cities along the coast, for example, Pergamon in Magnesia, Ephesus, and
centers further inland in the region of Philadelphia. The Greeks of
Philadelphia were speaking Turkish by 1577,[243] despite a continuous
influx of Greek immigrants from the fifteenth century on.[244] Between the
Turkish censuses of 1520–1535 and 1570–1580, the Christian population

almost doubled in the *liva* of Aydin (from 451 to 791 families); and similar changes took place in Karası—from 73 to 150—and Menteşe (Mugla)— from 69 to 149. In Sultanönü, the Eskisehir-Sogut region, the Christian population increased twentyfold,[245] which was a most dramatic illustration (however high the local birth rate) of the extent of immigration into these *livas*.

Most migrants, whether from the interior of Asia Minor, the islands (such as Crete, Naxos, Tenos, and Syros),[246] or the Greek peninsula proper, made their way to Smyrna,[247] which, following the conquest of Chios (1566), developed into the major port for the Aegean and Asia Minor generally.[248] Its trade with Constantinople was not then very significant,[249] though its greater volume of trade brought it more foreign merchants than Constantinople had.[250]

During the seventeenth century Smyrna was the destination of a great many overland caravans from the hinterland of Asia Minor, Armenia, Persia, and India. They carried a wide range of merchandise, though silk probably predominated. Merchants of all nationalities came to a particular street jammed with inns and caravansaries to unload their goods.[251] They then shipped their wares to the great ports of the Mediterranean and the Atlantic in English, French, Dutch, Venetian, and Genoese merchantmen. In the city stood a famous market reputed to be one of the richest in the world.[252] Its huge business supported two equally famous bazaars, the larger one established in the seventeenth century and the smaller in the eighteenth.[253]

By 1588 many Venetians and other Italians, as well as Frenchmen, had settled in the city and its environs.[254] The houses of French, English, Dutch, Venetian, Genoese, and other West European merchants lined a long street near the sea-front—the Street of the Franks.[255] This was the "Frankish Quarter" that so many of the later refugees from Smyrna remembered.[256]

The route followed by Greek migrants moving inland from Smyrna lay through the fertile valley of the Hermus (Gediz) to Magnesia, Pergamon, and even further inland.[257] In 1770[258] there was an especially large population movement towards Kasaba (Turgutlu), where, according to the codices in the Ottoman Chancery that date from 1465–1466, a certain Greek, Turgutlu Yiannis, had his estate. The codices refer to him as Turgutlu Yiannis of Kasaba.[259] Was he perhaps a nobleman converted to Islam, or did he remain a Christian with the acquiescence of the Turks?

Still further inland towards Philadelphia,[260] "from Thyra to Koula," lived Turkish-speaking Greeks renowned for their carpet-making.[261] An abundance of wool and dyeing substances had enabled them to preserve their art from ancient times.[262]

The perpetual wanderings of Greeks in search of better conditions not only injected new life into the existing populations of old cities and towns, but also led to the establishment of new settlements. In 1586, for example, two villages at the entrance to the Hellespont, Yenisar and Nichor, were recolonized by Greeks.[263] According to a tradition which the refugee descendants of the first settlers have preserved to this day, Yenisar was founded by forty builders from Yenitsarochori in Ayvalik whom the Turks brought to the Hellespont to construct the fortress of Kumkale. The workmen then sent for their families, felled trees in the densely wooded district, and laid claim to the land they had settled on.[264] Nichor was rebuilt by people from Ayvalik, the Aegean islands, and continental Greece.[265]

Greek populations survived after the Capture in the cities and towns of the Asia Minor coast of the Sea of Marmara. The region maintained frequent communications with Constantinople.[266] All of the inhabitants were Greeks and their language was Greek; most were fishermen, though undoubtedly they also cultivated the soil to a limited extent. The people of Mudanya, for example, were known as excellent vine-growers,[267] and as early as the reign of Mohammed II there were 167 Christian serf vine-growers (bağbân kâfirler) who paid dues of 15,000 akçes annually.[268]

In 1576 the small town of Artaki (Erdek) was the seat of the Metropolitan of Cyzicus. Panormus (Bandirma), inhabited mainly by Greeks, with a few Turks and Italians, was surrounded by vineyards and exported her famous wine to Constantinople. The President of the Community of Panormus was a Venetian.[269] Of all the inhabitants of the Cyzicus peninsula the only migrants were the people of Epano Chorio, who arrived about the year 1700. They came from around Kastoria and became builders, naming their village Yapıcıköy (village of the builders). By 1922, however, their descendants were engaged solely in farming, stock-raising, silk-growing, and charcoal-making.[270]

The district from Biga to Panormus and Prusa (Bursa) was dotted with Turkish villages.[271] Interspersed among these were Christian settlements that had been founded by serfs, mainly from Greek territories, originally brought there as shepherds during the reign of Mohammed II. The sheep were gradually depleted by disease and lack of adequate care.[272] There was little farming at first.

In time, the population of the region increased. When passing through the Sea of Marmara in February 1538, the commander of a French naval squadron, Baron de Saint-Blancard, made an interesting comment on the process of colonization: "Surgimes une nuict du costé de Bithinie en ladicte mer et jusques là estoit Troie, le lieu s'appelle Bugade; lequel pays estait inhabité; le Grand Seigneur y a mis et faict venir d'Esclavons, Albanois et Serviens, quand les eut conquestés: il faict ainsy en plusieurs contrées pour mémoire de ses victoires et pour mesler les langues."[273]

These remarks probably do not refer to colonization by Suleiman the Magnificent, but rather to that by Mohammed II and his successors before Suleiman. They were effected, that is to say, in accordance with the sultans' general policy of repopulating those parts of the Empire which were deserted or only sparsely inhabited. However, Saint-Blancard omitted to make any mention of the local Greek settlers, who in fact comprised, as we shall see, the majority of the population.[274]

Janissaries and spahis were a scourge of the whole region from Panormus to Prusa. In the vicinity of Mihalic, a pretty commercial town, wild Turkish nomads, undoubtedly Yuruks,[275] also grazed their flocks. As a result the sixty Christian families of Olubad (Lopadion), an old city with six churches (three of them official) whose walls were falling into ruins, dared only to cultivate the minimum needed for survival. Gerlach accused them of apathy,[276] apparently not realizing that any further activity would have been fraught with peril.

On the road to Prusa, at the end of Lake Apollonia (Apulyont), was the monastery of St. Constantine, with five or six monks. There was a metropolitan on the island of St. Constantine.[277] Further to the east were the villages of Constantinatoi, Tyrota, and St. Theodore, their clay houses perched on the side of a hill.[278] Prusa itself was situated in delightful surroundings and was renowned for a market stocked with inexpensive silk goods and gold *objets d'art*. Almost all of the city's thousand families attended the Metropolitan Church of the Holy Apostles, since Mass was then rarely said in the Church of St. Nicholas. Two sultans, Osman and Orchan,[279] were buried in one of the old Byzantine churches on the acropolis.

Gerlach, using information supplied to him by the Metropolitan of Nicaea, writes that the Christians of Nicaea (Iznik) had only three churches—the Church of the Madonna, the Church of St. Theodore, and the Church of St. George—though as many as fifty Christian communities in the surrounding district[280] came within the metropolitan's jurisdiction. Such was the melancholy fate of the city where the first oecumenical council of Christians had met, where the Nicaean Creed was born, where Greek nationalism had first been manifested in a determination to resist Franks and other conquerors, and where the flowering of Palaeologian art had initially occurred.

The cities of Nicaea and Nicomedia (Izmit) contained the ruins of ancient and magnificent monuments, both secular and ecclesiastical, which stood in stark contrast to the dilapidated buildings of Ottoman times. They looked like cemeteries of some bygone age.[281]

Most of the Turkish-speaking Greeks in the Bithynian interior—for example, the inhabitants of Vizier Khan, Arsakioï, Peltos, Paboutzak, Devred, and Kizil Kaya—were very likely descended from their local

Byzantine antecedents. The Ottomans of Bilecik (Vilokoma) were probably the descendants of Byzantine Christians who had become converts to Islam.[282]

The Greek population, both Turkish and Greek-speaking, was eventually reinforced by an influx of new settlers. Between the Turkish censuses of 1520–1535 and 1570–1580, the Christian population in the *liva* of Biga increased from 241 to 701, and in the *liva* of Hüdavendigâz in Anatolia from 4,914 to 10,165.[283] Natural increase alone was obviously not sufficient to account for these quite startling differences. Many new villages in Bithynia[284] were founded by immigrants from the Greek peninsula and the interior of Asia Minor. For example, after 1500 Nicomedia received Greek migrants from various inland districts of Asia Minor, as well as from Thrace, Epirus, and a few islands. Among them were many artisans, bakers, and peddlers.[285] A number of villages in the district of Nicaea were also colonized by settlers from the Peloponnese, Epirus, Thrace, and the Aegean islands, as regional similarities in manners, customs, and dialect show.[286] Peloponnesians from Tsakonia colonized the villages of Vatica, or Mousatsa, and Chavoutsi sometime before 1670 (Hasluck mistakenly calls these Albanian settlements);[287] Demerdes in the district of Prusa was settled some time before the middle of the sixteenth century by people from the Agrafa, Peloponnesians, Macedonians, and Epirotes[288] (according to a tradition still current); Neochori on the northern side of Lake Ascanius (Iznik) was colonized around 1650 by Greeks from the Peloponnese and Epirus.[289] This exodus of Epirote and Thessalian emigrants was perhaps not unconnected with the insurrection of Dionysios Skylosophos at the end of the sixteenth century and the beginning of the seventeenth century.

Emigrants from the Agrafa also settled in the Bithynian villages of Tsesnir,[290] Tzampazi, Tzampa, Tzeïneğir, Achtze Pounar, Goulios, Apollonia, and Olubad. As regional similarities in manners and customs again attest, other villages in the same district—Boulgaratoi, or Baskioi, Chorouda, Constantinatoi, Kamariotatoi, Aginatoi, Kydia, Peladatoi, Syriyianni and Primekeri—were colonized around 1600 by Peloponnesian shepherds. These migrants remained serfs until the time of Mahmud II (1807–1839), when they apparently bought their freedom, though remaining shepherds till 1867.[291]

Turkish fiefholders had a vested interest in a program of deportations since they thereby obtained bondsmen (*kolligoi*) for their *çiftliks* or estates.[292] For example, local tradition among the inhabitants of Sari Doğan, a village near Adapazari, held that the spahis of nearby Kaimas instigated their removal from various parts of Epirus and Thessaly in order to work on spahi estates.[293]

Many colonists also came from the Armenian regions of Asia Minor, as well as from Albania and Bulgaria. Villages like Ortakioï and Charta-limi[294] had considerable numbers of Armenian families, while others—for instance, Bachtzetzik, Tengeli, and Ovatzik[295]—were wholly popu-lated by Armenians. In 1608 Armenian refugees fled the persecutions of Shah Abbas the Great of Persia, who temporarily occupied their country, and by the end of the nineteenth century no less than a quarter of the Ottoman province of Nicomedia was Armenian. Settling down mainly in Adapazari and other mercantile centers,[296] they proved capable craftsmen and efficient merchants. Indeed, they were economically the most dynamic element in the province. The Armenian-speaking residents of Adapazari and Geyve were called *Chaïchouroum,* (Helleno-Armenian)[297] because they were completely hellenized and professed Orthodoxy.

The Bithynian villages of Arvanitochori and Kiz Derbent were both in-habited by Albanians. In the middle of the nineteenth century, the inhabitants of the former were engaged in maritime pursuits,[298] while those of the latter were farmers and stockowners. The manner in which Kiz Derbent was originally colonized typifies the general process of re-settlement: the villagers, who spoke an Albanian-Bulgarian dialect, were brought in to guard the major thoroughfares and minor roads which traversed their mountainous district. It is noteworthy, too, that the inhabitants of both villages, like those of other Albanian and Arvanito-Vlach colonies throughout Hellas, were eventually assimilated and even developed a Greek national consciousness.[299]

A continuous stream of Greek emigrants left the hinterland of Asia Minor for other parts of Anatolia and Constantinople. Among these were merchants engaged in fruit trade with Constantinople and other Eastern cities. In Constantinople, fruits concocted into sherbets were a prime source of refreshment during the hot summer months.[300]

Since Prusa was an important stopping place on the way to the capital, its celebrated silk trade attracted other Greeks from Asia Minor. Not only did Prusa produce a large amount of silk, but it also received innumerable shipments of the product from Syria and other lands in the East. It has been estimated that about one thousand camel-loads of silk arrived there each year,[301] and the city became a silk-manufacturing center as well. Its unrivalled importance in both respects led to a near doubling of the city's population between the censuses of 1520–1530 and 1571–1580: from 34,930 to 60,140.[302] The silk was dyed with the fruit of the turpentine tree, which was picked and sold by the people of Thrace and Macedo-nia.[303] Prusa remains proud of its sericulture and silk-manufacturing to this day.[304]

Yet another well-trodden path of Greek emigration was from Karamania, Cappadocia, and the Pontus to other parts of Asia Minor and

to Constantinople through Scutari (Uskudar). It was a route also frequented by Armenian traders.[305] Throughout the entire period of Ottoman rule, Karamania, Cappadocia, and the Pontus remained havens of
Hellenism.

Nevertheless, the poverty of the people, the depredations of neighboring Turks, and the generally uncertain conditions of life induced population movement from these regions as well. Vague local traditions, still
extant, tell of the prevailing insecurity of the times, of ancient cave-
dwellings and refuges[306] (called *kapangia* or *trochia* in Sinasos;[307]
kataphydia or *kereria* in Sylata),[308] of communities, like those around
Nigde,[309] clinging to mountain peaks in the Taurus and totally cut off
from contact with the outside world. From Cappadocia, migrants made
their way mainly to certain districts of the Pontus on the Black Sea (a
region known as Cappadocia in the Pontus), with which they had always
maintained close ties. Contacts between the two regions had produced
marked similarities of dialect, especially between inland Pontus and Cappadocia.[310] Turkish records show that in the sixteenth century the
number of Christian families in the *liva* of Ankara increased from 590 to
1,347, from 570 to 1,889 in Kastamonu, from 81 to 483 in Gangra
(Kangri, now Cankiri), and from 27 to 1,993 in Kotza Ili. In the *liva* of
Bolu, which previously had no Christians, the census of 1570–1580
counted 134 Christian families.[311] The French geographer, V. Cuinet,
using only the evidence of oral tradition, concluded that the Greeks of
Gangra (Cankiri) in recent times were descended partly from the ancient
inhabitants of Paphlagonia and partly from Greek merchants of Caesarea
and Ankara, who migrated to Gangra between 1650 and 1700.[312] However, official Turkish sources now prove beyond doubt that there were
Greek settlers there even earlier, perhaps as early as the first years after
the Capture.

Continuing their journey towards the sea, the migrants eventually
arrived at Partheni (or Parthenia, Turkish Bartin), three hours away from
the Black Sea. At the beginning of the twentieth century, this town had
1,500 Greek inhabitants, originally from Safranbolu, Sinope, Caesarea, Fertek and Procopion in Cappadocia, and elsewhere, out of a total
population of 10,000.[313]

In 1404 most of the inhabitants of Pontoherakleia were Greeks,[314] but
apparently they were dispersed during the course of the fifteenth century: it was then that the city's name disappeared from the list of metropolitan seats.[315] However, a few of its Byzantine inhabitants probably
remained, and at the end of the seventeenth century[316] there was an
infusion of new Turkish-speaking settlers from various parts of Asia
Minor.[317] At first, Turks and Greeks lived side by side, but probably
around the middle of the seventeenth century the Turks moved to the

coast and founded the new village of Eregli. Pontoherakleia then became known as Tepekioï or Giaour Eregli.[318] The bishopric of Pontoherakleia was eventually re-established in 1672, when the city's Christian population was sufficiently large.[319]

At the beginning of the seventeenth century, Amasra (Amastris) was inhabited by Turks, Greeks, and Armenians.[320] Part of its Greek population was undoubtedly of local descent because Mohammed II had accepted the negotiated surrender of the city in 1460.[321]

It is also very likely that Greeks in the districts of Kastamonu and Sinope were at least partially descended from the ancient Greek population.[322] The local Greek population of Sinope was much smaller than it had been and was indeed sunk in misery, but, as in Pontoherakleia, it managed to survive.[323] As time went by, Sinope grew into the largest port of the Pontus, and many Greeks emigrated to it from the west coast of Asia Minor and the islands of the Aegean. The tax privileges which the Turks offered Greek shipbuilders and artisans in the city's important shipyards were a significant enticement. The dialect of these new settlers showed they had come originally from Ionia.[324]

A small nucleus of the Byzantine Greek population survived in Amisus (Samsun),[325] and this was expanded by the immigration of Greeks from the interior of Asia Minor, mainly from the district of Caesarea. The populations of Merzifon and Zile were also derived from this same source.[326] According to oral tradition, the Greeks of Cotyora (Ordu) were not indigenous but had migrated from around Argyroupolis in 1765.[327] However, it is possible that they came much earlier.

By far the largest proportion of emigrants from Cappadocia and Karamania, a people even today renowned for their commercial acumen, went to Constantinople. One source says that in 1466 people from Laranda (Karaman) and Iconium (Konya) were among the many brought to Constantinople after the Capture to repopulate the city.[328] Many of their compatriots, finding life on the barren plateaus of central Asia Minor a continual struggle for survival, later followed in their footsteps. As early as 1477, "the people of Karaman," as the Turks officially described them, occupied 750 dwellings in the City compared with the Turks' 9,000, Greeks' 3,000, Jews' 1,500, Kaffa Christians' 267, and Gypsies' 31.[329] In the same year two Greeks, Kesarioglou and Petraveris (the former name undoubtedly Cappadocian) purchased for 1,000,012 akçes the customs' franchise on all grain imported into Constantinople.[330]

By the sixteenth century, Karamanians were acknowledged as excellent merchants and artisans, especially goldsmiths and locksmiths. Their shops were near the bazaar, and their wives did fine embroidery at home, which they sold in the bazaar and other public places. The less affluent peddled eggs, poultry, milk, cheese, and vegetables.[331] However, most were wealthy and lived in a suburb called Karmania. Their Church of St. Constantine was a most imposing edifice, and their houses were invariably large, gracious, and set in delightful gardens. Although they spoke Turkish and knew little if any Greek, they greatly venerated the patriarch[332] and said their Masses in Greek.[333] The wives of wealthy Karamanians went out only rarely, and then only to church or to the baths.[334] But a visit to church was the occasion for wearing magnificent gold lamé dresses and also for adorning their necks, ears, and hands with jewellery of purest gold and precious stones. This ostentation made a considerable impression on Gerlach: he confessed that in Germany not even a queen would dress so splendidly.[335]

Emigration from Karamania and Cappadocia to Constantinople and other cities in Asia Minor continued until the beginning of the twentieth century. Naturally, this had excellent financial effects on the physical and intellectual resources of both regions:[336] till the very end of the nineteenth century, for example, boys of twelve (or at most fifteen) years of age would be sent to Constantinople by mule train, never to return except for two or three months to find a wife. Employment, sustenance for a family, and security for old age could only be found in the capital.[337] Yet the expatriates never completely severed their ties with the families and homelands they left behind. They continued to hope that, sooner or later, improved financial circumstances might permit a return home before advancing years finally sapped their determination. Not until the end of the nineteenth century did this dream, which remained vivid for centuries, finally grow dim.

Oral tradition preserved to the end of the nineteenth century some interesting recollections of the Cappadocian migrations to other parts of Asia Minor and to Constantinople:

The reason why so many converged on Constantinople was that the soil of Sinasos, indeed the whole of Cappadocia, was rocky and infertile. Except for a few arable patches it was suitable only for vineyards and fruit and vegetable growing, which proved unsaleable for lack of consumers; and so the people of Sinasos and Cappadocia were forced to look elsewhere for the wherewithal to live. At first, the inhabitants of Sinasos went to other parts of Asia Minor and produced linseed oil, returning to their homes for the summer as soon as they had sold it. This is how the people of the Cappadocian plain of Bagdaonitis (Poutak Ova) still live. But after the capture of Constantinople, when the conqueror permitted all of his subjects to trade within the confines of the Empire, the people of Sinasos increasingly took refuge in Constantinople, where they eventually settled down and became successful in commerce.[338] Initially, most of them continued to express linseed and sesame oil, while some were food and fish vendors. Fish not sold were salted and dried, so they soon became vendors of salted fish as well. During fasting periods they also sold caviar, fish roes, and other suitable foods. They gradually developed one of the most influential guilds in Constantinople—the Caviar Mer-

§◦ *Femme de Caramanie.*

45. A Greek woman of Karamania. From Nicolas de Nicolay, *Les Navigations, pérégrinations, et voyages, faicts en la Turquie,* Anvers, 1577.

chants'—which still exists today.[339] From the very beginning, these people were noted for their intense devotion to their homeland, even though the only form of communication with it was by mule over hazardous roads. Undeterred by a journey of twenty-five to thirty days, undaunted by the hardships and sorrows they met along the way, they would nevertheless set out in large caravans meticulously equipped with the picks, shovels, and other impedimenta that were necessary to bury their dead. And they frequently met with death on the road, either from disease or brigands. In that single moment, they would be robbed of everything that long years of hard work and sweat had earned them. If they did not die, they were still unconcerned about jeopardizing both their own lives and all that they carried with them merely in order to enjoy, even if only for six months, their beloved homeland and relatives. Sometimes, they abandoned altogether the gains they had made through years of hard work simply because nostalgia for their homeland completely overcame them after four or five years abroad.[340]

One other vital source of Hellenism was Chaldea in the Pontus, a

mountainous region straddling the Kanis river. From there, too, new
waves of emigrants dispersed to other parts of Asia Minor and its coastal
littorals. There were a number of reasons why people chose to leave their
lands for the coastal towns and elsewhere in the interior: overpopulation,
the unruly dispositions of local beys and *derebeys* (an unmistakable
symptom of decay within the Ottoman Empire), or declining income from
mines, especially those around Argyroupolis. Migrants therefore departed to look for farm work or to discover and exploit new mines. From
Chaldea, particularly Argyroupolis, they trekked in all directions: to
Tripolis, Espien, Kassiope, Cerasus (Giresun), Patlaman, Poulantzake,
Ordu, and Fadisane, or even further west to Oenoe (Unye), Amisus, and
beyond; in the east they founded the Greek-speaking villages around
Alexandroupolis and Tiflis; in the north, new villages in the Caucasus and
the Crimea; and in the south they established new villages and developed
new mines in the interior of Asia Minor, Armenia, Mesopotamia, Cappadocia, Lycaonia, and Bithynia.[341] However, "when the Greeks recov-
ered and reinhabited the lands that they had formerly abandoned or had
had taken away from them," wrote one scholar from the Pontus, "they
found nothing to indicate that those lands had once been Christian; not a
single church, not a single Greek name remained. Only a few towns which
had avoided the tempest and destruction and which on this account never
became entirely bereft of human life retained their original names
though in Turkish versions—Kemach (from Kamachos), Sivas (Sebastia),
Changra (Gangra), and so on. But very rarely today does one encounter a
village or indeed any place with a Greek or Christian name, and the very
few of these have only recently been given."[342]

At first, official instructions were given for the repatriation of miners to
their original jobs. Apparently, however, these were relaxed and the
migrations continued. The Turkish *emins* and Christian *ustabaşis* (mining
overseers) abandoned their attempts to bring back the fugitives simply
because overpopulation provided a ready source of replacements.[343]

This gradual dispersal of the people of the Pontus raises a host of
chronological and demographic problems.

Two new conquests, those of Syria and Egypt, were added to the
Ottoman Empire in 1517, but neither provided an outlet for Greek
colonization at the time. While it is true that the terrible years of persecution of Christians under the Mamelukes had passed, the rule of Selim I
(1512–1520)[344] was hardly less vicious.

At the end of the sixteenth century, Alexandria's only exports were rice
and sugar,[345] and the city itself had only about a hundred dwellings inside
its walls. Moreover, its climate was unhealthy. The economic development
of Alexandria, based on its harbor's convenient location athwart the trade

routes between Europe and India, still lay in the future. Yet there were some merchants in the city, a few of them undoubtedly Greeks. There were also between thirty and fifty-nine Greek merchants in Cairo who lived in the neighborhood of the Patriarchal Church of St. Savvas. Others resided in Rosetti.[346] But the patriarch himself was poor and despised.[347]

10

GREEKS IN CENTRAL EUROPE

When Greeks moved about inside the Ottoman Empire it was, of course, generally because they hoped to find better political and economic conditions in some other region. Similarly, the increasing number of economic contacts between West and East provided more Greeks with the opportunity of travelling abroad, working hard, saving money, perhaps becoming rich, and generally living in much more congenial political and cultural surroundings. As early as 1514 Greek merchants from Arta, Ioannina, and Avlona (Valona) were settled in Ancona. Just like their counterparts under Ottoman rule, they were there accorded various privileges, which included a warehouse and living quarters, in return for supplying the Italians with grain and other produce.[1] Ancona's trade with the East was also stimulated by the activities of Jewish merchants,[2] and from that time on it never faltered. By the middle of the sixteenth century, there were no fewer than two hundred Greek merchant concerns operating in the city,[3] and a Greek community had already been formed. At about the same time, Greeks also settled in other west Mediterranean ports, among them Leghorn;[4] and in 1582 there were Greek traders even in Antwerp.[5]

The proclivity of Greeks to emigrate was often most marked in those regions, cities, towns, or villages whose geographical situation gave them convenient access to the outside world. There were well-established connections, for example, between Epirus and Italy, especially Venice; between western Macedonia and Italy through Durazzo; and between the northern Balkans and central Europe along the valleys of the Aliakmon, the Axios, the Morava, and the Danube. Mountain ranges were no obstacle to migration from continental Greece and the Balkans. On the contrary, their paths, passes, and inhabited slopes provided a certain security. This was true not only of Greece but of all the Turkish-controlled countries of the Balkan peninsula.[6]

After 1600 the traffic of migrants to Serbia, Rumania, and especially Austria and Hungary increased significantly.[7] Large caravans set out from Siatista or Kastoria, loaded with local produce and various wares of the Near East. Passing through Monastir they then followed the Axios and Morava rivers to Belgrade, whose environs, in the middle of the sixteenth century, had a mixed population of Turks, Greeks, Jews, Hungarians, Dalmatians, and others.[8] From there the caravans crossed the Sava River, entering Austria at Zemun[9] and proceeding to Budapest and Vienna.[10] Zemun was a small village at the end of the sixteenth century,[11] but it later grew into an important entrepot. Large numbers of Greeks were already settled in Belgrade and Zemun because of the substantial commercial connections between the two towns and European Turkey, particularly Macedonia.

Thessalonica was the southern terminus of three caravan routes to the Austro-Hungarian dominions. One went through Bosnia, though this was rarely used because of the mountainous nature of the terrain. The second passed through Serrai, Melnik, Sofia, and Vidin, crossing the Austrian frontier at Orsova and continuing to Vienna via Temesvar (Timisoara), Pest, and Raab (Györ). Vidin was also the junction of another route to Moldavia and Walachia.[12] The third followed the same route to Sofia, but branched off there for Nis and Belgrade. The most travelled routes were the two through Sofia.[13]

Albanians, Bulgarians, and Serbs,[14] as well as Greeks, took part in the movements of population and trade, but it is the Greeks who figure most prominently in our discussion. And most prominent among the Greeks were those who lived closest to central Europe—the people of Epirus and Macedonia, closely followed by the Thessalians from a little further south.[15]

It is impossible to know when the first Greek settled in central Europe, but it is likely that the contacts initiated by the Byzantines were never wholly severed, even after the Capture. Many itinerant merchants presumably still crossed the frontiers of the Ottoman Empire and sold a variety of produce in the marketplaces of Europe before returning home with their profits or perhaps other goods for sale. They were tolerated in the Hungarian counties because they contributed to the flow of commerce and thus generated some internal revenue.[16] During the sixteenth century, Greek merchants traded in Reni on the Danube (through which passed a large part of the trade with Moldavia), as well as in other important commercial centers.[17]

By the middle of the sixteenth century Greeks were also settled in various towns and villages throughout Transylvania—Sibiu, Brasov (Stalin), Cluj, Arad, Alba-Iulia, Hunedoara, and others.[18] Indeed, there were Greek merchants in Sibiu and Brasov as early as the fifteenth century.

Around 1545 the Greeks of Sibiu dominated the trade with the East despite various restrictive measures imposed by the local authorities (for example, limiting both the range of merchandise and the number of days on which it could be sold). Greeks also traded in a number of surrounding villages, including Avrig.[19] Local authorities erected barriers to trade mainly because of the hostility of local Saxon and Hungarian merchants towards the Greeks. On 20 November 1581 an edict of the local assembly of Alba-Iulia deplored the unrestricted comings and goings of Greeks in the country. Accordingly, those who had neither "inheritance nor house" within the domains of the Hapsburgs might henceforth enter the country only if they placed their merchandise in bond in warehouses. On the other hand, those whose property and homes were within the Hapsburg Empire would need to go no further than those warehouses in order to purchase goods.[20]

However, the Greeks overcame such opposition, at least to the extent that they were successful in extracting certain privileges, including the right to form commercial "companies,"[21] from the Prince of Transylvania, George I Rakoczy. In 1636 the Prince personally bestowed these privileges on the Greeks of Sibiu, and they were subsequently renewed by the Holy Roman Emperor Leopold I in 1701 and the Dowager Empress Maria Theresa in 1777. Documents in the Rakoczy archives confirm that by 1656 a Greek "company" (*compagnia grecia libiniensis*) was also operating in Libin, Bohemia.[22]

When did the first of these "companies" appear, how were they organized, and what were their aims? A number of answers so far given to these questions are based on pure conjecture,[23] but it would seem that the company—the term itself, *compagnia,* was Italian—was usually a kind of association of small businesses engaged in local, or at least nonmaritime, trade. The limited company of today is probably its lineal descendant.[24] Unfortunately we cannot know much more about the early Greek companies until some very thorough research is done.

There is, however, some suggestive information in the "books of annotations," resembling chronicles, written by Panos Ioannou from Arvanitochori in Bulgaria, who in 1655 was the "notable" (president) of the Sibiu Company. Ioannou says that Prince George Rakoczy conferred the right of *jus judicanti* (the right to judge) on the Greek merchants of Transylvania, and on the feast of the Epiphany in January 1639 the first committee of a company, consisting of twelve members presided over by a "president,"[25] was formally elected.[26] This body managed the affairs of the company and settled differences among Greek merchants, or among the Greek and native merchants. There were also the *capetanoi* (delegates), who provided liaison between the executive committee (the president and his twelve sworn assessors) and the rest of the merchants.

Official tax-collectors gathered fixed assessments (varying from five to a hundred florins) from each Greek merchant in order to pay company tax to the state and to defray various other common expenses. All of these officials—"notables," assessors, *capetanoi,* tax-collectors, as well as church trustees—were required to be sworn in before assuming office.[27]

The company concerned itself not merely with the business affairs of its members, but also with regularizing relations among its own and foreign merchants. Above all, it strove to forge a relationship with the state whose hospitality Greeks enjoyed. To these ends, the company watched over every compartment of its members' lives and their relations with one another. This social role was regarded as being of paramount importance. Perhaps, as an organization of many members, it was realized that the individual's adherence to a strict code of ethics was a necessary prerequisite of the company's survival. Although much more research needs to be done, this peculiar moral cast of the Greek company is plain from the records of the Sibiu Company alone.

From the various Company statutes, which together made up a rudimentary system of law, several examples may be selected to portray the kind of spirit that pervaded those closed circles of Greek merchants. Members of the company were sworn to obey both the laws of the state and the emperor. They might not speak against the emperor even outside the boundaries of the state. They were enjoined to humility when in the presence of the president of the Company. They were to refrain from swearing or quarrelling in the streets. They might have one shop, but not two, in Sibiu. The priest was always to be obeyed, and members were to behave in a quiet and dignified manner in church. Those who were dissatisfied with the rulings of the Company might appeal to the imperial *comornic* (treasury).

Gambling was forbidden so that hard-gotten gains might not be foolishly dissipated. Members might not invite guests to dine or to dance without first obtaining the persmission of the president. Workmen and children would under no circumstances be admitted to such entertainments. Apprentices, working for *tzavala* [a small allowance, or pocket money, sufficient for basic expenses like clothes], would not be paid for the first two months, but after that they would receive a salary starting at three piasters a month for the first three months. Before setting himself up in his own business, the apprentice must have worked under a master for at least five years and accumulated capital of at least 103 piasters. No member of the company might employ local children as apprentices.

The penalties for any violation of company regulations might be money fines or corporal punishment.[28]

Thus, the Greek commercial company in central Europe was evidently a kind of guild not at all unlike the guilds that existed in Greek lands. It was recognized by the state; it looked after the interests of its members[29] and exercised definite control over its members' social lives. Above all, the company wished to ensure the loyalty of each member to the state which extended hospitality to them all.

Greek traders selling grain and animals appeared in Walachia and Moldavia in the sixteenth century. More and more Greeks followed—clerics and courtiers[30]—though they all met with the hostility of the local inhabitants. By the end of the sixteenth century the newcomers included very wealthy men—Greeks who had been abroad for many years and who were temporary or permanent residents in the principalities. Such a person was the "fabulously rich" Patroulas from Serrai, who in 1598 had had his fortune confiscated by the Turks.[31] On the whole, Greeks proved more financially adept than either the natives, the Genoese, or the Armenians, and by 1600 they controlled a large part of the trade of the eastern Balkans.[32] From the time Michael the Brave, Prince of Walachia (1593–1601), undertook to resist the Turk and ally himself with the German emperor, the Orthodox hierarchy looked more and more to the Rumanian rulers as their chief patrons and protectors.[33] Under Matthew Basaraba of Walachia (1632–1654) and Basil the Wolf of Moldavia (1634–1653), relations between Rumanians and Greeks, particularly between the principalities and the Oecumenical Patriarchate, became progressively closer. Both rulers showered gifts on the patriarchates of Constantinople and Jerusalem, as well as on Mt. Athos.[34] Greek neighborhoods, which even today retain their original names, proliferated throughout the cities of Walachia and Moldavia, and (names like *Grec* and *Grecul*) became common.[35]

Greek merchants went even as far north as Poland. Records of the city of Poznan mention the names of two Greeks in 1580; another, Iakovos Barkentine from Cephalonia, was definitely living there at that time.[36] In 1599 there were also Greeks, probably Cretans, as well as Jews and Armenians, in Leopolis (Lvov).[37] This city had grown into a commercial center of some significance because of its trade (for example, in Cretan wines) with the East through the Black Sea. Its inhabitants were indulgent towards foreigners, and the city consequently prospered. Various scholars (in *humanitatis studiis*)[38] had also brought the city considerable intellectual repute. A certain Constantine Korniaktos from Kydoniai in Crete undoubtedly owed his immense wealth to the Cretan wine trade. One source suggests that in 1586 the annual income from his estate, which encompassed more than a hundred villages, amounted to "urns overflowing with taler." Not only did he lend money to the King of Poland, but in Leopolis he had built a castle more opulent even than the archiepiscopal palace. The Greek Church probably owed its existence to his generosity, for, like the Grand Duke of Moscow, he was a lavish benefactor and had made huge donations to the sacred establishments of Constantinople, Alexandria, Mt. Athos, Sinai, and others.[39]

Merchants from Greece and other Balkan countries also ventured into northwestern Europe, to German cities such as Leipzig; but little is known about their movements and activities before the eighteenth century. One fragmentary piece of evidence is that after 1623 Leipzig's *Freundsche Hof* provided lodgings for merchants from eastern and southeastern Europe.[40]

Expatriate Greeks referred to foreign climes as "oppressive, worse even than orphanhood";[41] or, according to another song:

A foreign land, prison, discontent, or the pain of love?
Of all four it is a foreign land that chafes the most.
For there you are buried in a lonely grave
Sans priest, sans incense, sans a mother's tears.[42]

The expatriate's feelings of sorrow and nostalgia were matched in intensity by the joy of his family and relatives when he returned home. The unexpected return of an expatriate to the bosom of his family was always treated as an occasion for great rejoicing both by the family and the whole community. Emotions were often so deeply stirred that a return would be celebrated in song; and some of these songs are among the most beautiful in the demotic repertoire:

I have come from the City, playing the lemon [which means being carefree], enjoying myself, and singing sweetly:
    "All the money I have earned, my love, is for you."
    "O handsome youth, I did not know that it was me for whom you came; but I shall be the earth you tread on, a bridge for you to walk over, a silver chalice offering you wine and shining on the inside as you drink."[43]

But if the expatriate returned home, it was usually only for a brief time. His affairs soon beckoned:

We of Zagora have an unfortunate custom of fetching
water at night and wood in the morning.
On one such occasion when the sun was setting two
women began talking to each other. Said one:
    "How is it, sister, between you and your husband?"
    "Sister, wretched. This husband of mine spends
twelve years in foreign lands and three nights at home;
and one night, hateful night, three hours before dawn
I found the doors open and the horse gone,
I found the mattress and the pillows empty.
O mattress and pillows
Where is the young man who slept with you last night?
—He came with the night and left with the day."[44]

The Epirotes were the most seasoned travellers in the whole of Greece.[45] Political conditions in Epirus and the barrenness of the land invited emigration. Accordingly, the demotic lore there incorporated much more foreign experience than that of Greeks anywhere else. The same themes recur and are expressed with deep and delicate emotion: the sorrow of being apart, the joylessness of living in a foreign land, seduction by foreign women, the return of an expatriate.

Nevertheless, travellers who returned home or merely wrote letters to their kinsmen served to remind their brothers in captivity of what it was like to be politically free. Their long and often dangerous sojourns abroad became the subjects of long narratives which were eagerly solicited, discussed, and absorbed by relatives at home. In this way, certain Greek provinces began visibly to shake off their lethargy from the beginning of the seventeenth century. The intellectual vitality of Hellenism seemed to increase in direct proportion to the number of Greeks who went abroad.

In many parts of Greece remote from the outside world, the peasants tended to become illiterate drudges—morose in their attitudes and laconic in their speech. But there were other parts of Greece where "all was not silence" and where travellers were not strangers. It is no exaggeration to say that they, together with the Greek communities abroad, revived both the Greek language and the Greek nation. A very definite factor in the evolution of the modern, demotic form of the Greek language was the active participation by Greeks in the commerce between East and West. Recognition of the importance of the living language as a medium of communication led to the compilation of the earliest demotic grammars. It was no coincidence that Nicholas Sophianos, who composed the first of these in 1540, lived in Venice, where many Greeks had settled who felt the need to correspond both with one another and their compatriots abroad.

Greek migration abroad had many intellectual, economic, and cultural ramifications. The expatriates' homelands usually experienced a strong surge of economic development. After the return of a money economy at the beginning of the sixteenth century, there was a marked economic revival among the poverty-stricken mountain communities of peninsular Greece. Bigger and better houses were built, churches were renovated or completely rebuilt on more solid foundations, villages grew into towns and cities, and a bourgeois class gradually appeared. Simultaneously, Greeks were successful in obtaining or consolidating various privileges which ensured the unimpeded economic growth of their villages. Such privileges might include exemption from the billeting of Turkish soldiers, or the transference of a village to the jurisdiction of the *valide sultana*. Unfortunately, the state of research so far does not permit us to follow the various stages in the population growth of particular villages, towns, and cities.

It was thus a combination of despair and courage that induced the inhabitants of the mountains to travel abroad. It may have seemed incongruous to foreign visitors that, while mountain villages became more and more affluent, those on the plains and in other fertile places remained economically stagnant.[46] But the explanation for that, of course, was the flow of wealth from travellers abroad to the mountain homes which they had been forced to leave. For example, the villages of Epirus[47] and western Macedonia[48] experienced slow but steady economic progress and even grew into flourishing towns and cities. One was Koziane (today's Kozane) whose name appears for the first time in 1534 in the codex of the monastery of Zaborda: it became a town, a "city" even, because of certain privileges which it enjoyed, an influx of refugees from neighboring villages and towns, and the development of local trade. The sort of evidence which would allow us to plot accurately the stages of urban growth is unfortunately lacking,[49] but the testimony of Charisios Megdanes, a scholar from Kozane, is at least suggestive: he wrote of the great increase from 1662 on in the numbers of those who were engaged in trade with Austria, Hungary, Germany, and Constantinople. Their profits had so multiplied that they had "acquired a taste for luxury, self-indulgence, and the better things of life; and they vied with one another in building and beautifying the most splendid of homes and in the luxury and gentility of their living."[50]

Macedonia and Epirus enjoyed the most favorable geographical advantages in all of continental Greece for initiating contacts with Italy and central Europe. While physical propinquity to Europe was perhaps the most important prerequisite for economic progress, the inhabitants of these regions were also impelled by poverty, hunger, and Turkish harassment to acquire wealth in trade and establish lucrative businesses. As we shall see, their economic tenacity was later matched by an equal determination to meet new political and intellectual challenges. By these means, the captive territories of Hellas gradually revived.

This was therefore a seminal period in the history of modern Hellenism, and undoubtedly change would have been quicker if Turkish control had not been so omnipresent: economic and social reorganization would have gone further, cities would have grown larger, intellectual life would have been much less inhibited. As things were, however, the prevailing anarchy in Macedonia and Epirus deterred the Greek bourgeoisie abroad from permanently returning to their native lands. The development of commerce and industry was therefore continuously held back. Of course, some of the bourgeoisie stayed behind in the cities and towns of Macedonia and Epirus, but they were few in number. It was largely outside the Ottoman Empire, in much more congenial economic, political, and cultural environments, that the urban class of modern Hellas emerged, multiplied, and flourished.

Simultaneously, a class of merchant sea captains arose in the Ionian and Aegean islands as well as on certain parts of the coast of continental Greece. This development took place largely within the Ottoman Empire. These seafarers came from many disparate walks of life, but together they formed yet another distinct component of modern Hellenism.

11

COMMERCE AS CATALYST

If even the inhabitants of isolated mountain districts in continental Greece profited from the growing commercial intercourse between West and East, then obviously the Ionian and Aegean Islanders also shared in it. Those islanders who lived in places with convenient access to the trade routes were particularly conspicuous in the world of commerce as merchants or carriers of the goods of others.

The present state of our knowledge of the history of navigation among the Greek islands is quite satisfactory, based as it is on the manuscripts and printed *portolani* (navigational aids for sea captains) of the sixteenth, seventeenth, and eighteenth centuries, which followed Italian models.[1] Indeed, a subject of no little fascination, but one which we cannot pursue here, concerns Greeks naval technology itself: the shipyards of the time and their whereabouts, the method of building ships, their size, shape, and outfitting,[2] the development of shipbuilding locally, local differences, and the influence of all these factors on the life of the people.

Western Europeans travelling to the East by ship arrived first at the Ionian Islands, where they also made their first contacts with the Hellenic world. On arriving at Zacynthus, one traveller felt that he had entered a different world: the way of life, the language, the dress, the social customs of the people he encountered were all redolent of the East.[3]

The Ionian Islands generally lacked sufficient grain. Corfu had to import wheat from the nearby mainland[4] and occasionally even olive oil from the Peloponnese and wine from Crete.[5] However, from the sixteenth century on, when the raisin grape was first introduced into Zacynthus and, soon afterwards, into Cephalonia and Ithaca,[6] both currants and wine were exported from the islands. By the middle of the sixteenth century, Zacynthus was producing good wine in ever-increasing quantities—the red known as *romania,* and the white known as *robola,* both of which are still produced under the same names. Zacynthus' exports also included olive oil and the famous little black raisin grape of the Corinth variety. This grape, known in Italy as *uva passa* (Latin, *uva corinthiaca*), was much more sought after than the red grape of Cephalonia. It grew so prolifically that the Venetians were able to fill six ships each year merely from the compulsory tithe in grapes. Zacynthus also grew some wheat (enough to last the islanders for about four months), as well as an abundance of fruit—oranges, lemons, figs, almonds, peaches, and pomegranates, to name a few.[7] The English were regular buyers of the island's currants,[8] which they used in Christmas puddings and other confections.[9] The only foreign residents on the island were the Venetian rulers and a few Frankish clerics.[10]

The slopes of the high mountains of Cephalonia are today bare and infertile, but in 1621 they were covered with vines, olive trees, and cotton. The raisin grape, after its introduction, was cultivated in profusion, indeed with such increasing disregard for other crops, that the Venetian Senate was forced to forbid the planting of new vines. However, despite this restriction and also a heavier tax, raisin grape production continued to increase for the simple reason that the financial return to the inhabitants was higher than that for any other crop. Total production figures in fact increased from 400,000 liters in 1576 to 1,500,000 liters in 1593, and 4,000,000 liters in 1603. Foreign merchants, mainly English and Dutch, bought currants direct from the producers and loaded them on their ships in the island's main port, Argostoli, which then had only a few inhabitants. Cephalonia thus became the most important producer of currants in the entire region, and its people enjoyed steady economic progress until the middle of the eighteenth century. Economic decline then gradually set in for a number of reasons: civil insecurity brought about by conflicts among nobles, a fall in the price of currants due to oversupply, neglect in fertilizing, and soil exhaustion.[11] The people of Cephalonia then had to import their grain from Epirus and the Peloponnese.[12] Magnificent stands of forest, particularly fir, might perhaps have provided an alternative source of income, but, as happened in almost every part of Greece, shepherds periodically thinned them out by fire and they eventually disappeared.[13]

The forests of Ithaca's mountains, celebrated by Homer, were destroyed in the same manner during the sixteenth century. Before that, the main export of this picturesque island had been acorns;[14] afterwards, the people turned to the cultivation of vines and olives.

The commerce of the Aegean islands and the eastern Mediterranean as a whole not only throve better than that of the Ionian islands, but also its economic and social effects ran deeper. Economic activity in the region began in the earliest years of Turkish rule. Even before the Capture, Cretans were renowned as excellent sailors.[15] In the years after the

Capture, Crete no longer produced a surplus of grain[16] and was forced to import about half of its yearly requirements. On the other hand, Venetian merchants bought large quantities of olive oil[17] and wine,[18] which they exported from Crete's main port, the wealthy fortified city of Chandax (today's Herakleion).[19] The Cretan wine most sought after in western Europe was the sweet *malvasie* (or *malvoisie*),[20] whose name derives from Monemvasia. There was also a muscatel variety, but this could not be shipped beyond Gibraltar because, unlike the other, it was not chemically treated and did not travel well. There were in fact two varieties of each of the malvasia and muscatel types.[21]

Crete had extensive gardens and orchards, and its inhabitants reaped considerable profits from the sale of almonds, olives, pomegranates, figs, oranges, lemons, apples, and much else besides. Fruit juices were also extracted on the island and exported to Turkey, Constantinople, and elsewhere. Juice was in great demand; it was usually sold in the same shops that purveyed salt fish.[22] Cretans also gathered laudanum, employing an interesting but exceedingly tedious technique. This plant, indigenous to Crete, grew especially at the foot of Mt. Ida in the village of Tsigalinos(?) near Mylopotamos,[23] and was coveted for its medicinal properties.

At the beginning of the sixteenth century, Cyprus produced and exported wheat, the metal used in making both vitriol and *ruzene a medesina de ditto* (the drug was actually manufactured from the rust of the metal), sugar, and various other products. There was ample fresh water in the capital, Leukosia (Nicosia), where nobles had established many productive estates,[24] and by the seventeenth century Leukosia had become an important center of commerce. The island's products, which then included silk, cotton, and salt as well as wine and olive oil,[25] attracted English, French, and Dutch merchants, who even maintained commercial depots in the capital. The population was a mixed one, but the preponderant element was Greek.[26]

In the Dodecanese, the commercial lead was taken by the peoples of Lindos (Rhodes) and Syme, both of whom were famous for their fine fleets of ships[27] (even today, many houses in Rhodes have mosaics, wallplates, and wooden furnishings which are redolent of a maritime past). The people of Syme skimmed from island to island in their sleek and distinctive craft (*foustes*),[28] exchanging their excellent wine for essential foodstuffs.[29] They were then, and indeed remained until very recently, superb divers, collecting sponges from depths of up to twenty-five fathoms and exporting them to Venice.[30] The people of Kastellorizo were barely able to scratch a subsistence from their barren and waterless rock, but a large harbor on the lee of the island afforded them an alternative means of making a livelihood:[31] they imported cotton and honey from

Egypt and Karamania,[32] and then re-exported to Italy. The people of
Icaria traded a fine white wine with their neighbors;[33] and with Chios they
exchanged a wide range of products for the grain they did not have—
timber (fetched from Samos and a number of other places in the East),
sheep, goats, honey, wax, and the little boats which had earned them a
widespread reputation.[34] We learn from Jacob Miloïtis,[35] writing in
1587, that the people of mountainous and unproductive Patmos[36] travelled to Venice and other places in Italy in order to sell products that came
mainly from their own Monastery of St. John the Theologian and its
estates in Crete,[37] Samos, and Tzia (Kea).[38] The elongated island of Kos,
which was extremely productive, sent barrels of lemon and grapefruit
juice to Constantinople, to be made into lemonades and sherbets.[39]

But of all the islands near the coast of Asia Minor none surpassed Chios
in commercial importance. By the middle of the sixteenth century, Chian
merchants were active in Constantinople along with Venetians, Ragusans,
and Florentines.[40] Chios had the only really important port in the entire
region opposite Smyrna. However, after the conquest of Chios by the
Turks (1566) and the expulsion of Frankish families (especially after
1600), the island lost its export trade to Smyrna. More and more Chian
merchants settled in Smyrna[41] and became prominent in the trade in
wool, wax, cotton, and silk. This produce was brought into Smyrna,
instead of to Aleppo as before, mainly by Armenians, who were not taxed
as highly as Greek merchants. Chian merchants therefore found themselves in vigorous competition there with Armenians, as well as with
Venetians, English, and Dutch.[42] Such was the environment in which
Adamantios Koraïs, one of the great founding fathers of the modern
Greek nation, later grew up.

An idyllic island, Chios cast a spell over all who visited it. Its women,
noted for their striking attire, were beautiful, friendly, and cultured;[43] its
people were generally outgoing; its folk dances were colorful; its buildings were handsome; its little rivulets picturesque; and its orchards of
lemons, bitter oranges, pomegranates, and olives lush and verdant.[44] Had
it not been for the occasional sight of a turban (for there were comparatively few Turks on the island), the visitor might well have imagined that
Turkish rule had bypassed the island. More than two hundred churches
and thirty monasteries tolled their bells with impunity. Orthodox and
Roman Catholic lived side by side in harmony, religious feasts were
celebrated without hindrance, and religious processions wound unmolested through the streets.[45] The population of the island in 1621 was
50,000 Orthodox, 4,000 Roman Catholics (with a bishop), and 4,000
Turks.[46] The Turks so liked the Chians (indeed they were considered the
sultan's best subjects)[47] that the islanders enjoyed extensive freedom and

privileges.[48] On the whole, the Turks confined themselves to their castles, where they served as an island garrison. Most of the Roman Catholics were Spaniards, though there were a few French.[49] In 1674 the seven Roman Catholic churches on the island were maintained by local Jesuit and Dominican monks, as well as French Capuchins.[50]

Chios stood apart from neighboring islands because of its rich civilized inheritance, which made an immediate impression on travellers.[51] Not only was the Genoese influence still remembered[52] but it was manifest in the language of the people,[53] their way of life, their secular and ecclesiastical architecture. Many of these monuments remained standing until the earthquake of 1881.[54] Gates and walls were adorned with the images and escutcheons[55] of the Giustiniani.[56] Many families claimed noble ancestry, even in some cases actual descent from the Giustiniani, but to foreigners their education and style of living were disappointing.[57] They dressed after the fashion of their old Frankish (Genoese) forebears in the days before the Turkish occupation,[58] and to contemporary Frankish nobles they appeared ridiculously old-fashioned.[59] Foreigners were astonished and amused to see these quaint, neatly dressed figures (including even notables of the island) strolling quite unself-consciously to the marketplace and returning home laden with provisions.[60]

The Chian ruling class was of mixed Frankish and Hellenic ancestry. When he conquered the island, Sultan Selim II referred to them as the "local Genoachians."[61] However, the Hellenic element, like that in Crete and other Aegean islands, proved culturally the stronger of the two, and the foreign minority was eventually assimilated.

The fabrication of silk and cotton goods on Chios provided plenty of employment. Gloves, stockings, scarfs, silk purses, silk stuffs (serges de soie), damasks (damas),[62] taffetas, and satins[63] were the most beautiful and sought-after in the East.[64] However, the island's main product was mastic,[65] which was exported to all Mediterranean countries and even faraway Germany. The Chians also carried on a flourishing trade with Alexandria.[66] The prosperity of Chios provided a vivid contrast to the poverty of other islands.[67] Almost all the islanders were there to trade.[68]

The people of Andros were famous for the caïques which they built in a number of shipyards on their island and sold to Chios and other islands. The industry was worth some 4,000 akçes annually. Andros was also well-known for its silk goods and white panniers, which were used all over the archipelago.[69] Naxos exported wines and rare cheese to Chios, Alexandria, and Smyrna,[70] as well as emery to Venice and Marseilles.[71] Forests of olive trees covered Naxos, and it supplied many islands with olive oil and fat, tasty olives.[72]

Citrus trees were widely cultivated both on Naxos and Andros. When the orange and lemon trees were in blossom, a sweet scent perfumed the air.[73] The wines of Naxos and Andros were equally distinguished,[74] and Naxos also grew laudanum.[75]

The people of Tenos, like those of Andros,[76] had been engaged in sericulture ever since the days of the Byzantine Empire.[77] The thousands of mulberry trees on Tenos survived until the end of the nineteenth century. At that time, the silkworms succumbed to a disease, and the people were forced to replace their mulberry trees with olive, fig, and citrus.[78]

Among the remaining islands of the Cyclades, Santorini (Thera) exported wines and cloth to Chios, Smyrna, and Alexandria.[79] Its watermelons were also the most succulent in the Aegean.[80] Paros' renown stemmed mainly from its Monastery of Our Lady of the Hundred Gates, but its fertile soil made it probably the most intensively cultivated island in the Aegean.[81] Kythnos (Thermia) was noted for its cloth and thread;[82] so, too, was Siphnos, whose trade was mainly with Ancona in French and Venetian ships.[83] Syra (Syros) exported cotton cloth and wines, Tzia (Kea) acorns (mainly to Venice where they were used in dyeing), Sikinos wheat, and Antiparos stone.[84]

Mykonos, a notorious nest of pirates and hucksters, produced cotton and an excellent wine. However, its inhabitants were in cahoots with the pirates and more often simply bought plundered goods at very low prices, which they then resold at high prices in Constantinople, Italy, and France.[85]

Apart from the produce of its famous salt marshes,[86] a variety of goods flowed out of the spacious harbor of Melos—wheat, wine, sulphur, alum, vitriol,[87] and delicious melons.[88] The inhabitants also manufactured hand mills and exported them to Constantinople, Egypt, the Peloponnese, Zacynthus, Cephalonia, and Ancona.[89] Melos had the further reputation that its people were exceedingly courteous, and its women wore exceedingly short dresses.[90]

The commerce of the Cyclades with the outside world, particularly Venice, permitted its people to indulge a certain taste for luxury goods. Such imports included gilt mirrors and other sumptuous, finely made furnishings. Many of these survived in good condition until very recently and drew favorable comment from visitors.[91]

Of the islands of the northern Aegean, the fertile and densely populated Mytilene was amply endowed with farmlands, orchards, and pastures.[92] In Belon's time, its wines were reputedly the best in the Aegean. Wine and fir timber were exported to Constantinople,[93] and the timber to a number of other places throughout the East.[94] Tenedos was noted for its muscatel wines,[95] Thasos for its orchards and vineyards.[96] At the end of the sixteenth century, Lemnos was cultivated more intensively than at any previous time: the island supported no fewer than seventy-five villages, all except two or three of them Greek. Lemnos was denuded of trees, but it had a fortress, and the people consequently felt reasonably secure from attacks by pirates. Basking in this security, they worked hard and prospered. The island produced peas, beans, chick-peas, lentils, wheat, wine, meat, cheese, wool, and flax.[97] In 1579 Carlier de Pinon noted that the sultan imported from Lemnos large quantities of *terra sigillata* which was used as a panacea.[98]

In the northern Sporades, the "most delightful" Scyrus was inhabited solely by Greeks and produced considerable quantities of wine.[99] The sweet and dry wines of Skopelos were also highly regarded, and certain quantities of both were exported to the Peloponnese and Venice through Thessalonica.[100]

On the whole, the Aegean islands had plentiful supplies of fruit (figs, pomegranates, oranges, and other citrus varieties), choice grapes (Tenedos muscatel, *aïdonia, sirikia, aetonyhia, monemvasiana,* and others),[101] and good wines, all of which were exported to Constantinople.[102] However, the islands were unable to grow enough grain, and therefore had to trade if they were to survive. Unlike the mainlanders, the islanders therefore became less susceptible to the effects of bad harvests and famine, though time was measured "from the great famine," which in 1647 ravaged Naxos and the Cyclades generally.[103]

Arid conditions prevailed on most of the Aegean islands, particularly the smaller ones.[104] Even on fertile islands like Ios, the constant fear of pirates kept the inhabitants from making the fullest use of cultivable areas.[105] Poverty and malnutrition were therefore endemic on the islands, except on Lemnos and Chios.[106] There were frequent outbreaks of tuberculosis.

Despite these difficulties, the 145,000 Aegean islanders (not including Crete) at least enjoyed the boon of relative freedom from Turkish rule. In their songs, dances, and innumerable feasts, men and women alike celebrated this good fortune.[107] They loved their little, poverty-stricken islands and even considered themselves blessed. The most terrible curse that a native of Santorini could call down on a fellow islander was: "die miserably outside Santorini."[108] Notwithstanding its very apparent shortcomings, Santorini was in fact one of the most densely populated of all the islands.[109]

The foreign trade of the Cyclades and the Aegean as a whole was not very significant. In the main, it was confined to the essential provisioning of the islands. The chief mercantile powers, France, England, and the Low Countries, did not consider that the size of their trade warranted the establishment and maintenance of diplomatic posts in the region. On a few rare occasions, the French Ambassador to the Porte appointed a

46. Two women of Melos. From Pitton de Tournefort, *Relation d'un voyage du Levant*, Amsterdam, 1718.

consular representative in the Cyclades, but the post usually went to a Greek because foreigners considered it singularly unrewarding. The only important commercial transactions involving foreigners were with pirates who offered plunder for sale.[110] Melos, as we have seen,[111] figured prominently in these shady transactions, and it was undoubtedly at this time that a bourgeoisie first appeared on the island. Indeed, the economic development of Palaea Chora, Melos' chief town, coincided exactly with the reign of anarchy in the archipelago between 1600 and 1700. Palaea Chora today lies in ruins in a fertile valley.[112]

Many of Melos' ruined churches, as well as the still-intact churches of Portiane and St. Charalampos, date from the seventeenth century; so, too, do most of Melos' more imposing icons.[113] When Tournefort passed through Palaea Chora in 1700, the town was flourishing: it had 5,000 inhabitants living in substantial two-storied houses of pumicelike stone, though it had no sewers and was dirty. The people raised pigs in the ground floors of their houses underneath a semicircular gallery, from which scraps could be conveniently thrown. Melos was also large enough to support both an Orthodox and a Roman Catholic bishop.[114]

So many ships passed through the Aegean and the islanders themselves
so desperately needed trade (both to obtain life's necessities and dispose
of their own meager range of products) that the sea and its beckoning
horizons exerted more and more influence over them. That influence was
a salutary one, for definite economic progress was made, especially after
1600. It manifested itself in the construction of better houses, the importation from abroad of furnishings and other items of domestic use, the
establishment of small private chapels, the erection of much more lavish
churches complete with consecrated vessels and the icons of famous
artists.[115]

Patmos was a striking example of this economic well-being. Although
the island was almost completely barren, it had a spacious open harbor[116]
and—its greatest asset—the Monastery of St. John the Theologian. The
monastery was built on the highest point of the island and, with its high
walls and solid turrets, resembled nothing so much as some stern
medieval castle. In both a physical and spiritual sense, its presence was
overpowering. From its ramparts, where today a yellow flag emblazoned
with the black double-headed eagle of the Byzantine Empire flutters in
the stiff breeze that always blows, it is possible to see the entire coastline of
the island, the two little islands of Chiliomodi and Leipsos, Nikaria (Icaria)
further to the north, Samos towards the coast of Asia Minor, Leros to the
south, and, faintly on the horizon, both Kalymnos and Kos.

The people of Patmos clustered around their monastery, and in this
way the "Chora" of today developed. The monastery was the focus of the
islanders' religious devotions and moral ideals and, more than that, it
became the focus of their economic life. The Roman Catholic rulers
accorded the monastery their protection,[117] and the people of Patmos
were thereby able to develop trade based on the monastery's villages and
properties in Crete,[118] its relations with Rome, and its commercial contacts with Venice[119] and, especially, Ancona.[120] The islanders became
wealthy, exporting stockings (which were considered of better quality
than the Italian product),[121] ceramics,[122] and, most of all, the produce of
their monastery's estates.[123]

Thus the people of Patmos, who had once clung to the walls of their
monastery like oysters, gradually became acquainted with other peoples
and other ways of life, which visibly affected them. Simple colonists, so to
speak, shucked off their parochial shell. And with the money they earned
came a taste for a better way of life, a desire to be well dressed, to replace
their humble dwellings with fine stone houses, to adorn their wives with
jewellery. Eventually, some eight hundred new homes appeared,[124] each
built in stone and of striking appearance, each usually two-storied, all
huddled around the monastery in a maze of narrow and sunless, but
spotlessly clean, streets.[125] Some of these houses still partly survive in their

47. Patmos. From Pitton de Tournefort, *Relation d'un voyage du Levant*, Amsterdam, 1718.

original form, though most were subsequently renovated, altered, and even completely replaced, especially during the course of the nineteenth century. The interiors of the houses were decorated and ornamented with vases, wall-plates, tableaux by Dutch painters,[126] wood-carvings, and stained furniture (for example, magnificent carved chests, tables, and chairs),[127] which were either imported from abroad or made locally. It is only in recent years that the islanders' descendants were reduced by poverty to selling these possessions.

Not even the monastic way of life remained unaffected by economic prosperity, and the monastic rule on Patmos became idiorrythmic, that is, without the stricter discipline of a *coenobium*.[128] Eventually, however, the island was convulsed by a series of revolutions, and economic decline set in. According to Georgirenes, Bishop of Samos, ships of commerce gave way to tiny fishing boats, and the people of Patmos sank into poverty.[129] Unfortunately, Georgirenes does not tell us what these revolutions were about, nor when they occurred. But the chief cause of destruction was probably the Venetian invasion, which was launched on 18 June 1659. A sorry episode, it was probably an explosion of rage on the part of the Venetian general, Francesco Morosini, who had grown impatient with the overtures of the people of Patmos towards the Turks. Until the mid-nineteenth century a demotic song plaintively recalled the disastrous plunder that followed:

The olive oil is ruined, the grain is destroyed,
The roads are crammed with engines of war, the streets crowded with pikes.
In Anemomylos the streets are strewn with bedclothes and pillows,
Arrack and wine flow in the gutters,
And down in Gennadio bowls and pitchers lay strewn all around.[130]

Patmos could not recover from this destruction, the poverty which came in its wake, and the unstable conditions throughout the Aegean generally. However, the full picture of economic and social dislocation on Patmos is one which we are unable, from this distance, to reconstruct.

When Tournefort passed through Patmos at the beginning of the eighteenth century he could not explain why there were such well-built houses—more substantial even than those on islands with a bustling trade—on such a poverty-stricken island. He was particularly astonished at the profusion of churches—some two hundred and fifty of them[131]—representing so many architectural styles: small private chapels with a single gabled roof, others dome-shaped, others arched, some with two or three foundations (that is, with a second or third foundation extending beyond the first but joining it in the interior of the church) and as many altars, dedicated to separate saints. Each church had a beautiful reredos, which was typically carved in wood, as well as icons, which were mostly representative of the Cretan School.[132]

FRANCES: MOROSINI
Caualier, e Procuratore
Cap: Genal da Mar.

48. Francesco Morosini at Venice in 1686. From N. N. (Domenico Rossi), *Successi dell'armi venete in Levante nella campagna 1685*, Venice, 1686.

Those most active in the trade of the Cyclades were feudal lords, Franks or their hellenized descendants. Although they gradually lost many of their old privileges, particularly after the Ottoman conquest, they continued to engage in commerce, selling their goods either through others or on their own financial initiative. They thus became, however slowly, a bourgeois class, and their capital generated the means of support of others. Naxos is a good example of what happened. As Sauger wrote, "among the Aegean nobility, Latin names were Sommaripas, Coronelli, Giustiniani, Grimaldi, Barotzi, Sforza, Girardi, Rogeri, and Ghizi, while

Greeks were represented by the famous names Coccos, Grivia, Malatesta, Dellaroca. Whatever occurred on other islands, *all of these people employed others who handled their money and the income of their estates, often with great profit to themselves.*"[133]

In addition to the nobles who lived in their castles and really formed a closed class (never intermarrying with the people and even dressing differently from them),[134] a lower class comprising former peasants, but particularly seamen and merchants, also began to acquire wealth. Many so improved their economic and social status that the medieval organization of society in the Frankish-held islands, which had begun to crumble with the imposition of Turkish rule, finally broke down. A new class of wealthier peasants and townsmen emerged. The former serfs, or *kolligoi,* slowly acquired their lords' estates, became more and more economically independent, and finally refused, as their confidence grew, to fulfill their one-time obligations to the fiefholders.[135]

Of course, some of the old feudal customs lived on, even after the Greek Revolution of 1821. For example, according to one liberal noblewoman the peasants of Naxos were continuing to offer gifts to the "scabrous nobility" who lived off the sweat of the people. Although the peasants were beginning to withhold these customary offerings, which was making the life of the nobility an increasingly difficult one, conceit was still common: the nobles were obsessed with the idea that they were descended from royal houses. Moreover, they were useless: "interested neither in travel nor in trade, they, their wives, and their children only sat around moping."[136]

Thus, a once insignificant social class became more and more affluent, while a once significant noble class was reduced to the status of small proprietors. By the end of the nineteenth century, the former were the most conspicuously wealthy group in the whole Aegean; the latter could only cling to their traditions, their pride, their gentle breeding, though, because they were often better educated (indeed, in some cases wealthier), they managed to remain the leading class until as late as the middle of the nineteenth century.[137] Certain feudal customs, such as the serfs' offerings of fruit and timber to the lords, persisted until the late nineteenth century and even the early twentieth century.[138] In 1925 Andros' historian, Demetrius Paschalis, wrote:

Even today, the *kolligoi* become entitled to the usufruct of the land only upon the fulfillment of certain conditions. In return for this usufruct, they must make certain offerings to the proprietor, such as cocks at Christmas, a lamb at Easter, one or two rams for the *choerosphagia* of St. Demetrius, as well as a quarter of a calf and one suckling pig in August, a certain quantity of silk if there are mulberry trees on the estate, and depending on the size of the estate, various other things like fish or game (rabbits, partridges, and so on). From February to October, the *kolligoi* are also obliged to supply the lord with milk and yoghurt, as well as vegetables and eggs every fortnight throughout winter. They are sometimes required to provide figs, grapes, beans, maize, and other produce from the estate. In addition, the *kolligoi* have to carry to the proprietor's home, without payment, his requirements of wood for fuel, as well as vine branches after pruning in the vineyards. They also must collect cattle manure, giving a certain amount of it to the lord, and make chaff for fodder. Other compulsory tasks include providing transport for the proprietor to go to the vintage, as well as on some other occasions, washing the wine casks, supplying red clay for lining the rooms of the proprietor's house, and even forgoing a day's wage for some job previously agreed upon. However, it is true that in recent times the number of these obligations has decreased, at least on the smaller properties, or else they are only desultorily fulfilled.[139]

The story of the rise of the bourgeoisie in the islands was by no means one of unobstructed development. Just as in the northern regions of Greece brigandage and the unpredictable attitudes of local Turkish (and especially Albanian) beys had impeded normal economic growth, so in the islands piracy and recurrent warfare remained prevalent. They had also to contend with the sustained efforts of foreign merchants and their governments to eliminate competition and monopolize the trade of the entire Mediterranean.

Greeks sailing their little ships in the Aegean, Ionian, and Mediterranean seas found themselves in direct competition with the great maritime powers of Western Europe, whose ships were as large as their naval and mercantile experience was long. Not only did the Western powers persist in improving their naval technology, but they also extracted favorable trading privileges from the Porte.[140] The Greeks also had to compete with local, Jewish, and Armenian merchants.

Throughout the fifteenth century and the first half of the sixteenth century, the Venetians continued to dominate the trade of the East.[141] By the end of the fifteenth century, various Venetian mercantile houses (Bembo, for example), were established in a number of ports in the eastern Mediterranean—Methone (Modon), Rethymnon, Herakleion, Thessalonica, Chios, and Cyprus. From their agents in Crete the Venetians bought large quantities of wine and cheese,[142] and in Thessalonica and Constantinople they were able to purchase all their requirements of grain.[143] In exchange, they sold soap, exquisite brocades (*étoffes*) from Flanders, metal goods, and various other merchandise.[144] By the middle of the sixteenth century, the Hellespont was crowded with the ships of Venetians, Anconans, Genoese, Neapolitans, and Ragusans.[145]

Since Constantinople was naturally the chief object of Venice's diplomatic attention,[146] an enormous range of produce inevitably entered its harbor in Venetian ships: silk (*damas*), satin, and woollen cloth, copper, pewter, sulphide of arsenic (*réalgar*), efflorescence of mercury (*sublimé*), minimum, arsenic, turpentine, mirrors, glasses, paper, knives, brushes, bells, lutes, comb scabbards, ceruse. Income from the sale of these goods then permitted the purchase of caviar, skins, carpets, wool, especially the fine, long, silklike Angora wool from the district of Ankara. The women of Ankara obtained their yarn by fine-combing the hair of goats and then spinning it. The material known as camlet was made by a special process of pressing the Angora weave and pouring water over it in order to produce waves in the wool. This material was widely used in the manufacture of felts and topcoats.

In Constantinople, apothecaries (*apoticquaires*) sold the period's universal panacea, "soil of Lemnos" (*sigillé*). Foreigners were also interested in a kind of luxury paper (some called it "persian") which was embossed with colorful motifs such as flowers. A single sheet might be used for a poem or a number of leaves for a high quality, handwritten book.[147] Ordinary paper was not produced in the East, at least in the middle of the sixteenth century, but was bought from Italian merchants.[148]

Venetians sold their merchandise in Constantinople through Jewish middlemen, whom they paid a commission of one or two per cent.[149] Belon thought these Jews full of guile; indeed, he had a low opinion of Jews wherever they lived. Quick to learn foreign languages, they were invariably the first to make contact with foreign merchants whenever a ship arrived in Constantinople from Alexandria, Kaffa (Feodosiya), Venice, or anywhere else. As a rule, the intercession of Jews was indispensable to the successful conclusion of all business deals within the Ottoman Empire. Indeed, they were a factor to be reckoned with not only in the economic life of the Ottoman Empire but the entire East—from Egypt north to Syria and Armenia, from Babylonia east to Persia and India. Their influence even extended far into Europe, to Russia, Poland, and Hungary.[150] Jews made particularly handsome profits from the trade in precious stones from Persia.[151] Their skill as jewellers gave them an entrée into every seraglio, and the Turks sought their advice before purchasing anything.[152] Greeks and Armenians were also adept as jewellers, but they were essentially business apprentices of the Jews.[153] Whenever a Jew travelled abroad he wore a white turban rather than the yellow one which was a badge of his nationality, for he knew that foreigners trusted Turks more than they did Jews.[154]

In the sixteenth century the Venetians and Genoese slowly lost their monopoly over the trade of the Mediterranean. Increasing use of the Cape of Good Hope route to India meant that Portugal became northern Europe's entrepot for merchandise from the Far East.[155] New maritime powers—France, England, and the Low Countries—dominated this trade, and the economic life of the Italian cities correspondingly decayed.

Venice tried to stave off the catastrophic consequences of this competition by transforming herself into a hive of industry.[156]

Venice thus lost two of her customers, England and France,[157] during the course of the sixteenth century, especially after the Turkish-Venetian war of 1570. Not only that, but English merchants themselves began to penetrate the eastern Mediterranean early in the sixteenth century, notably between 1511 and 1534. The intrepid sea captains of London, Southampton, and Bristol initiated commercial contacts with a number of islands, including Crete, Chios, and (though to a lesser degree) Cyprus. Crete was probably frequented the most for its wines and oils,[158] and in 1522 the English appointed their first consul in Herakleion (Chandax). English ships also put in at Sicily, Tripoli, and Beirut. The English not only sailed their own ships but also chartered the ships of others—Cretan, Ragusan, Sicilian, Genoese, Venetian, Spanish, and Portuguese. To the ports of the East they brought colorful woollen fabrics, fine woollen cloth, underclothing, cotton, certain materials called "statutes," "cardinal-whites," and "calveskins"; and to the ports of Britain they returned with silk, Angora weave (camlet), various roots which had pharmaceutical uses, malvasia, muscatel, and other wines, oils ("sweet oyles"), woollen and cotton materials, Turkish carpets, and tree sap, which had a variety of uses in dyeing, in medicine, and in the preparation of tannin, pepper, cinnamon, spices, and some other products. Jews, Turks, and other foreigners all participated in this trade with the English.[159]

English commercial activity diminished temporarily after 1534, but revived again in 1575–1578 as a direct result of the representations of English merchants, who deplored this hiatus in so lucrative a trade. England again resumed commercial relations with the East,[160] and in 1579 Queen Elizabeth I and the sultan concluded a treaty defining reciprocal trade rights between the two states. This conferred upon England certain privileges similar to those already enjoyed in the Ottoman Empire by the French, Venetians, Poles, and Germans.[161] By the end of the century, English ships plied all the world's seaways.[162] Wherever English merchants went, their demeanor, the deference they showed towards others (many were of noble descent), and their impeccable honesty in business transactions made them objects of respect and admiration.[163]

In the middle of the sixteenth century, French commerce with the eastern Mediterranean was still at an incipient stage: only five or six ships each year sailed from Marseilles, France's chief port on the Mediterranean. Moreover, France had no consuls, representatives, or agents at any port in the eastern Mediterranean. French commercial activity really began with the Turkish-Venetian war of 1570, when the merchants of Marseilles simply appropriated a good deal of Venice's trade with the East. Marseilles assumed a position of new commercial importance, and many of its citizens acquired new wealth. French merchants, business-men, and artisans also began to settle in the East's major port, Smyrna. The jurisdiction of the French consul in Smyrna (who took diplomatic precedence over all his French colleagues except the Ambassador to the Porte himself) extended to Asia Minor, Chios, Mytilene, and many other Aegean islands, where he made vice-consular appointments. The impor-tance of this office was generally acknowledged throughout the entire eastern Mediterranean.[164]

However, French commercial activity in the East was dealt a severe blow by the restoration of Turkish-Venetian diplomatic relations; and it was virtually paralyzed when religious conflict in France itself led to the persecution of Protestants, among whom were some of the most active merchants of Marseilles.[165] Not until the reign of Henri IV (1589–1610) and the return of civil tranquility to France did the people of Marseilles again begin to profit from trade with the East. On 5 August 1599 an ordinance of Marseilles' *Conseil de Ville* set up a *Bureau du Commerce* which subsequently contributed a great deal to the commercial growth and economic prosperity of the city.[166] France's new monarch interested himself personally in his country's commercial relations with the East, and he accordingly designated as ambassadors to the Porte eminent men like Savary de Brèves and de Gontaut-Biron, who did much to restore France's prestige throughout the Ottoman Empire. In 1604 de Brèves not only successfully obtained the renewal of France's former trading privileges (capitulations), but also extended these to define free trade, tax exemptions, rules for the protection of a merchant's property in case of his death, fishing rights off the coast of North Africa, and the Porte's responsibility to take steps against the Barbary pirates.[167]

In order to restrict the increasing interest and activity of English mer-chants, as well as contain the persistent efforts of their ambassadors to extend England's trading privileges, de Gontaut-Biron also fought for the addition to the capitulations of new articles benefitting France.[168] Not only was he successful in this aim, but he also secured Ottoman recogni-tion of the French ambassador's precedence over the diplomatic envoys of England, Venice, and other European countries.[169] These moves and countermoves inaugurated a period of economic competition among England, Venice, and France, whose bitterness is very evident in the of-ficial dispatches of the various ambassadors.[170]

When the merchants of Marseilles resumed their operations in the East, they found that the Dutch had also settled in Smyrna and that, as com-mercial competitors, the Dutch were no less redoubtable than the En-glish.[171] The Dutch followed others over the same route originally blazed by Vasco da Gama, sought spices and other products of pharmaceutical value in the Moluccas (the "Spice Islands" were the source of the most important goods in the entire Far Eastern trade), then returned to Europe and sold their merchandise all over France, England, and Germany. The commercial center of gravity in Europe thus shifted again from Spain and Portugal to the Ponant region of the Flanders coast. For centuries to come, Amsterdam was to be the principal entrepot for the Far Eastern trade, and merchants from the other towns of the region and from as far away as Rouen and La Rochelle flocked into it in order to buy the coveted spices and pharmaceuticals.

Marseilles was thus faced with a serious threat to her economic survival. Recognizing this, her merchants decided to concentrate all their efforts on the silk trade with the eastern Mediterranean. By the beginning of the seventeenth century, they were satisfied that they had made their city "the principal warehouse for this trade"; and this despite serious obstacles which they had to circumvent—war, piracy, plague, and the various imposts and restrictions imposed on them by the Moslem authorities. The main export terminals for this trade in silk cloth were Alexandretta (Iskenderun) and Sidon.[172]

Commercial rivalry between the French, Portuguese, English, and Dutch was felt in every port of the eastern Mediterranean. On the whole, the English and Dutch gained the upper hand because they enjoyed trading privileges within the Ottoman Empire, they had consuls in the most important ports, they exported goods of superior quality, they also dealt in embargoed merchandise (for example, lead and pewter), their prices were generally low, they were precise and honest in their business transactions, and they honored their agreements. The Dutch were in the ascendant commercially in Smyrna, the English in Aleppo, and both were equally uncompromising adversaries of the French in the markets of Egypt.[173] Indeed the competitiveness of the Dutch was a source of some concern to the English. On 13 March 1660, Winchelsea, the English ambassador to the Porte, wrote that "the Dutch have, within the space of a few years, almost undermined the English trade in this Empire. They have four ships for every one of ours in Ottoman ports."[174]

When Marseilles chose to impose duties on pharmaceuticals and spices, Leghorn soon emerged as a competitor of the French. Disgruntled foreign merchants began to unload their merchandise in Leghorn instead of Marseilles, and the Grand Duke of Tuscany was quick to seize this commercial advantage. He declared Leghorn a free port and offered various other inducements to attract merchants. Greeks were among those who subsequently came to the city, joining their compatriots who had settled there in the middle of the sixteenth century.[175] When Genoa also declared itself a free port in 1656, Marseilles had a second rival.

Yet another category of merchants in competition with the French in a number of ports, though mainly in Turkey, were the so-called *pros-*

tatevomenoi (*protégés*), or French-protected subjects of the Ottoman Empire[176]—some Greeks, but mostly Armenians—who also served as interpreters to the French Ambassador and his councils.[177]

Indeed, of all the merchants in the eastern Mediterranean trading with Venice, Leghorn, Marseilles, Amsterdam, and other cities in Western Europe, none were more active than the Armenians.[178] One estimate placed their numbers at 6,000 in Smyrna alone.[179] They were the strongest competitors of the merchants of Marseilles, particularly in the silk trade. Not only did they convey their merchandise from its sources to the ports of Aleppo and Smyrna, but they also began to engage directly in the promotion and sale of their goods to France. Marseilles resented this intrusion and ascribed the most nefarious qualities to these merchants in the East.[180] A rather more concrete demonstration of their opprobrium was the imposition of a twenty-per-cent tax on Armenian commerce, which in turn prompted the Armenians to forsake Marseilles for Leghorn. Accordingly Leghorn, until then an unprepossessing little town, became the most flourishing entrepot for the Mediterranean silk trade.[181]

Nevertheless, the commerce of the eastern Mediterranean continued to remain Marseilles' chief source of wealth.[182] The ships of Marseilles which travelled to the ports of the East were of considerable tonnage and were always loaded to the gunwales with local produce—fabrics, paper (*papier fin, papier de marine*), bonnets—or the produce of the New World. The latter included Brazilian timber, pepper, cinnamon, ginger, cloves, and other produce of the Indies. The ships from Marseilles unloaded their cargoes in the ports of the eastern Mediterranean and returned home even more heavily laden with other spices and pharmaceuticals, cotton, textiles, flax, coarse blankets, wool, sponges, and especially silk. At the beginning of the seventeenth century, ships from Marseilles called more frequently at the ports of Egypt and Syria than at those of Greece—Chios, Smyrna, Constantinople, Nauplia, the Ionian islands (of which Zacynthus was the most important), and other islands in the Aegean—but Greek ports figured more prominently in this trade towards the middle of the century.[183] France's trade with the eastern Mediterranean continued to expand after 1650.[184]

The French government's interest in extracting new trading privileges from the Sublime Porte did not flag. Indeed, its preoccupation here led to the unpleasant consequences for France of the discovery of the Cape of Good Hope route.[185] But at least the French language rose to a position of pre-eminent importance throughout the eastern Mediterranean.[186] Only recently, after centuries of influence, has it lost this ascendancy.

Hemmed in politically by the Ottoman conqueror and constricted economically by foreigners, the Greeks strove to break down these two confining walls. Peasants, laborers, artisans, and sea captains all played their separate parts in producing the wares of the Ottoman Empire and promoting them in other lands. In doing so, they laid the foundations of the modern Hellenic economy and thus guaranteed not only their own survival but also the future viability of the Greek nation. The growing economic exchange between East and West was also counterpointed by a vigorous cultural and religious colloquy between them. But this forms the basis of another story.

NOTES

Every reference is given in full the first time it appears in the Notes. Because so many languages are involved, foreign language titles, unless the meaning is generally obvious, have also been given in translation the first time the title appears in the Notes. The number in parentheses immediately following the title is the number of the note in the chapter where the full citation occurs; if there is an additional number preceding a colon, that is the number of the chapter where the full citation may be found.

Chapter 1

1. See Antoine Fattal, *Le Statut légal des non-Musulmans en pays d'Islam* (Beirut, 1958), pp. 236 ff.

2. See Ioannis Anagnostes, Διήγησιας περί τῆς τελευταίας ἁλώσεως τῆς Θεσσαλο-νίκης [*Account of the Last Capture of Thessalonica*], ed. Immanuel Bekker (Bonn, 1838), pp. 493–494; Michael Ducas, *Historia byzantina*, ed. Immanuel Bekker (Bonn, 1834), pp. 186–187 (ed. Basile Grecu [Bucharest, 1958], p. 235).

3. "Αὐτοί διοίκουν πᾶσαν τήν βασιλείαν. Οἱ γάρ ἀγαρηνοί ἦσαν ἀγράμματοι καί ἀμαθεῖς πολλά [They governed the entire realm because the Moslems were illiterate and extremely uneducated]" is the rather exaggerated and tautological comment of the anonymous author of the 'Ιστορία Πολιτική Κωνσαταντινουπόλεως [*Political History of Constantinople*], ed. Immanuel Bekker (Bonn, 1849), pp. 26–27.

4. Spyridon Lambros, " 'Η 'Ελληνική ὡς ἐπίσημος γλῶσσα τῶν σουλτάνων [Greek as an Official Language of the Sultans]," NE, 5 (1908), 41–42, 44.

5. *Ibid.*, p. 56; *cf.* Fuad Köprölü, *Alcuni osservazioni intorno all'influenza delle istituzioni bizantine sulle istituzioni ottomane* [*Some Observations on the Influence of Byzantine on Ottoman Institutions*] (Rome, 1953), pp. 115–118.

6. See Alessio Bombaci, "Il 'Liber Graecus,' un cartolario veneziano comprendente inediti documenti in greco (1481–1504) [The 'Liber Graecus,' a Venetian chartulary containing unpublished Greek documents (1481–1504)]," *Westöstliche Abhandlungen* (1954) (*in memoriam* Rudolf Tschudi), pp. 288–289, which contains the relevant bibliography.

7. See Kritoboulos of Imbros, Συγγραφή ἱστοριῶν [Histories], ed. Karl Müller, III, 20 (5); IV, 7 (4) in Fragmenta *historicorum graecorum* Vol. V (Paris, 1883).

8. See Franz Babinger, *Mehmed der Eroberer und seine Zeit* [*Mohammed the Conqueror and His Times*] (Munich, 1953), pp. 120–121.

9. Note the recent discovery by Alessio Bombaci, "Nuovi firmani greci di Maometto II [New Greek Firmans of Mohammed II]," BZ, 47 (1954), 298–319. *Cf.* Lambros, " Ἡ Ἑλληνική" (4), pp. 77–78. These Greek documents deserve comparative study since they hold both linguistic and historical interest—which, of course, varies in proportion to the significance of the events they describe. *Cf.* Köprülü, *Osservazioni* (5), p. 117.

10. Here I follow the Western historiographical convention in referring to Suleiman as the "First" (see A. D. Alderson, *The Structure of the Ottoman Dynasty* (Oxford, 1956), *passim*.

11. See Lambros, " Ἡ Ἑλληνική" (4), pp. 73–74. *Cf.* his " Ἑλληνικά δημόσια γράμματα τοῦ σουλτάνου Βαγιαζίτ Β' [Greek Official Correspondence of Sultan Bayezid II]," NE, 5 (1908), 155 ff.

12. Lambros, " Ἡ Ἑλληνική" (4), pp. 73–74.

13. Spyridon Lambros, " Ἑλληνικά ἔγγραφα ἐν τῷ ἀρχείῳ τῆς Βενετίας, ἐν οἷς καὶ ἔγγραφα Τούρκων ἀρχόντων ἑλληνιστί μετά τινος παραδρομῆς περὶ τοῦ ὀνόματος τοῦ Μορέως [Greek Documents in the Archives of Venice, together with Some Official Turkish Documents Written in Greek Containing an Error in regard to the Name of Morea]," ΔΙΕΕ, 4 (1892–1895), 634–652. *Cf.* Neculai Iorga, *Byzance après Byzance* (Bucharest, 1935), pp. 58–59, which contains the relevant bibliography.

14. See Lambros, " Ἡ Ἑλληνική" (4), p. 77.

15. There are many instances cited by Fattal, *Le Statut légal* (1), pp. 236–263. See p. 236: "O vous qui croyez! Ne prenez pas de confidents en dehors de vous! [Oh you believers! Don't trust anyone but yourselves]."

16. *Ibid.*, pp. 369–370. On the difficulties involved in rendering the word *ḏimmi*, see pp. 71–84.

17. See Demetrios K. Tsopotos, Γῆ καὶ γεωργοὶ τῆς Θεσσαλίας κατὰ τὴν Τουρκο-κρατίαν ἐπὶ τῇ βάσει ἱστορικῶν πηγῶν [*The Land and Farmers of Thessaly during Turkish Rule, according to Historical Sources*] (Volos, 1912), pp. 47 ff.; H. A. R. Gibb and Harold Bowen, *Islamic Society and the West* (London, 1951), I[1], 237. The works of Bulgarian specialists in the Turkish language are most interesting (for a critical survey, see Josef Kabrda, "L'Etude du féodalisme turc-ottoman dans l'historiographie bulgare," *Sbornick praci filosofiské fakulty brněnsté university*, 11 (1962), Rade historické C9, 129–144. See especially the views of Vera P. Mutavčieva in her specialized monograph, Аграрните отношения в османската империя през XV–XVI B [*Agrarian Relations in the Ottoman Empire during the Fifteenth and Sixteenth Centuries*] (Sofia, 1962), which contains the older bibliography. See also the article by Bistra Cvetkova, "Miscellanea. Bibliographie des ouvrages parus dans les pays slaves sur les aspects économiques et sociaux de la domination ottomane [Miscellanea. Bibliography of Works Which Have Appeared in the Slav Countries on Economic and Social Aspects of Ottoman Rule]," *Journal of Economic and Social History of the Orient*, VI, 3 (1963), pp. 319–326, which contains the most up-to-date bibliography.

18. The sultans took these lands away from Christian proprietors (even if they occupied the conquered land), or from monasteries and other ecclesiastical domain if the owners did not appear on the land in seven years. In Thasos, for example, there was the case of St. Anargyri, which belonged to the monastery of Pantokrator (Ömer Lûfti Barkan, *XV ve XVI inci asırlarda osmanlı imparatorluğunda ziraî econominin hukukî ve malî esasları* [*The Legal and Fiscal Principles of the Agrarian Economy in the Ottoman Empire during the Fifteenth and Sixteenth Centuries*] (Istanbul, 1945), p. 346. When fiefs (timars) and *has* were delineated during the fifteenth and sixteenth centuries, the extent of the land and its taxable return (whether from one or more

taxes) were stipulated. The usufruct went to persons favored by the sultan—a custom perhaps stemming from the Byzantine *pronoia* (see Vera P. Mutavčieva, "Sur le caractère du timar ottoman," *Acta Orientalia Hungarica*, 9 (1959), I, 55–61.

19. See Vera P. Mutavčieva, "За състоянието на спахилъка през XV–XVI В. [On the Situation of the *Spahilik* during the Fifteenth and Sixteenth Centuries]," Исторически преглед, XV, 3 (1959), 33, which contains the relevant bibliography.

20. See Hans Dernschwam, *Tagebuch einer Reise nach Konstantinopel und Kleinasien (1553–1555)* [*Diary of a Journey to Constantinople and Asia Minor (1553–1555)*] (Munich-Leipzig, 1923), p. 59.

21. See Ömer Lûtfi Barkan, "Les Formes de l'organisation du travail agricole dans l'empire ottoman aux XVème et XVIème siècles," *Istanbul Üniversitesi Iktisat Fakültesi Mecmuası*, I (1939–1940), 311–312. And see the article "Filâha" by Halil Inalcik in *Encyclopaedia of Islam*. *Cf.* p. 320 of Barkan's article just cited where he observes certain differences between Turkish landholders and the feudal lords of the West. On the *hassa çiftlik*, see the study by Vera Mutavčieva, "Към въпроса за чифлиците в османската империя през XIV–XVII В. [On the *Ciftlik* Problem in the Ottoman Empire during the Fourteenth to the Seventeenth Centuries]," Исторически преглед, XIV (1958), I, 34–57.

22. See Stephan Gerlach, *Tagebuch* (Frankfurt am Main, 1674), p. 129. According to Islamic law, the decrees of a particular sultan (laws, berats, treaties, and so on) did not fundamentally bind successive sultans. In order to have continuing force, it was necessary that they be promulgated again by each succeeding sultan (Halil Inalcik, "Osmanlı hukukuna giriş [An Introduction to Ottoman Law]," *Siyasal Bilgiler Fakültesi Dergisi*, 13 [1958], 13).

23. Gibb and Bowen, *Islamic Society* (17), I^1, pp. 238–239.

24. See François-Alphonse Belin, *Etude sur la propriété foncière en pays musulmans et spécialement en Turquie (rite Hanéfite)* (Paris, 1862), p. 126, where they are regarded as *mülk*. But cf. p. 161, where they are considered *mülk* only when granted by agreement.

25. On the multitude of slaves in the middle of the fifteenth century, see Bartolomeo de Jano, "Epistola de crudelitate Turcarum," PG, CLVIII, col. 1062.

26. See Bartholomew Georgieviz, *De Turcarum moribus epitome* [*A Summary of Turkish Customs*] (Lyons, 1558), pp. 85–89. For interesting comments on prisoners and slaves, see pp. 76–85, 110–111. See also Dernschwam, *Tagebuch* (20), p. 68; and *cf.* the sorcery used by the Turks to prevent slaves from absconding (Gerlach, *Tagebuch* [22], p. 481). The freedom of a slave, whether Christian or Moslem, was conferred by canonical dispensation or holy writ (see the unpublished documents numbered 9, 31, 138, 139, 268, and others *passim*, in the typed résumé of a codex issued by the *serî* (Moslem ecclesiastical court) of Veroia. For further information on the freedom of slaves, see D. C. (Louis Deshayes, Sieur de Courmenin), *Voyage de Levant, etc.* en *année 1621* (Paris, 1632), 2nd ed., pp. 113–114.

27. There is information on this special category in Vera Mutavčieva, "За приложението на робския труд в османското стопанство през XV–XVI В. [Contribution to the Problem of Slavery in the Ottoman Empire during the Fifteenth and Sixteenth Centuries]," Изследвания в част на Марин С. Дринов (*Studia in honorem M. S. Drinov*), (Sofia, 1960), pp. 505–519.

28. See Barkan, "Les Formes" (21), pp. 16–17, fn. 3.

29. Nicoară Beldiceanu, *Actes de Mehmed II et de Bayezid II du Ms. fond turc ancien 39* (Paris, 1960), I, 144–145, has some interesting comments on these villages. *Cf.* p. 166, where he remarks on differentiations in the ranks of the *ortakçi* which were made at the time of Bayezid II.

30. See Barkan, "Les Formes" (21), pp. 297–300; *cf.* pp. 397–403 of the Turkish

text (Ömer Barkan, *Osmanlı imparatorluğunda toprak isçilliğinin organizasyonu sekilleri. I, Kulluklar ve ortakçı kullar. "İktisad Fakültesi Mecmuasi,"* Cilt I, Sayi 1, 2, 3, 4. [Istanbul, 1939]), where there is further information.

31. *Ibid.*, pp. 20–22, 35–37. For interesting details on the serfs of Biga, see pp. 165 ff. For the names of the sultanic villages outside Constantinople, see pp. 61–69 of Barkan's Turkish text (first published in October 1939). On the villages around Biga, see pp. 177–178; their names are on pp. 225–227 of the Turkish text. On the economic relationship between the lessor (*amil*) and the Christian serf, see Beldiceanu (*Actes* [29], pp. 119–124).

32. As for these, see Barkan, "Les Formes" (21), pp. 177–178. The names of the villages are on pp. 225–227 of the Turkish text (Barkan, *Osmanli imperatorluğunda* [30]). On the question of their obligations towards the *subası* (chief of police), there is useful historical evidence at pp. 228–229 of the Turkish text. See pp. 230–233 for additional information on the villages of Susığırlık, Koyun Kâfiri, and others, as well as the names of their inhabitants.

33. Barkan, "Les Formes" (21), p. 302.

34. See *ibid.*, pp. 297–298.

35. *Ibid.*, pp. 17–18, 30, 301–302.

36. *Ibid.*, p. 25. *Cf.* pp. 26–31.

37. *Ibid.*, pp. 22–23.

38. *Ibid.*, pp. 299–300, and especially pp. 397–404 of the Turkish text (Barkan, *Osmanlı imparatorluğunda* [30]), which deal with their obligations, peculiarities, and other relevant problems. *Cf.* pp. 404–416 of the Turkish text for comment on other pertinent cases.

39. For relevant details, as well as the personal views of Barkan, which ought to be treated a little sceptically, see pp. 304–305 of "Les Formes" (21), or pp. 418 ff. of the Turkish text, (Barkan, *Osmanlı imparatorluğunda* [30]), where he puts forth his views at great length.

40. Barkan, *Les Formes* (21), p. 30.

41. For details, see *ibid.*, pp. 24 ff., 31 ff., 308.

42. *Ibid.*, pp. 178–180, and pp. 233–242 of the Turkish text (Barkan, *Osmanlı imparatorluğunda* [30]).

43. Barkan, *Les Formes* (21), p. 180, or in greater detail on pp. 242–244 of his *Osmanlı imparatorluğunda* (30).

44. Belin, *La Propriété foncière* (24), p. 127, fn. 2.

45. See Joseph Georgirenes, *A Description of the Present State of Samos, Nicaria, Patmos and Mount Athos* (London, 1678), pp. 11–12. *Cf.* Gibb and Bowen, *Islamic Society* (17), I^1, 240, 242.

46. See Dernschwam, *Tagebuch* (20), p. 68.

47. See Gibb and Bowen, *Islamic Society* (17), pp. 242–243.

48. *Ibid.*, p. 243.

49. See note 50 below for examples.

50. See the unpublished document of the year 1049 (1639–1640) in the typed resumé of the codex issued by the *şerî* (Moslem ecclesiastical court) of Veroia, which discloses the terms agreed upon for the inhabitants of the village of Dovliani. They were to pay taxes on one derelict building instead of on two, on eight portions of land instead of fourteen, and there was to be no surcharge for a period of five years (see document No. 14 of the typed résumé; and *cf.* document No. 91, which refers to the abandoned village of Dranista).

51. *Cf.* the unpublished documents Nos. 129–130 for the year 1049 (1639–1640) in the typed résumé of the codex issued by the *şerî* of Veroia, where the annual rate

of interest on an amount of 1,000 *akçes* is recorded as being 15%. *Cf.* also document No. 137, where the interest rate mentioned is only 10%. An exception is document No. 137, which mentions a figure of 2,000 *akçes* as the interest on 1,000 *akçes*, though this is apparently a mistake for 200. *Cf.* the mortgage rates detailed in documents Nos. 142, 144, 150, 153, 172, 179, 181, and *passim*.

52. Maxime Collignon, *Le Consul Jean Giraud et sa relation de l'Attique au XVII*ème *siècle* (Paris, 1913), p. 38. This book also discusses the diet of Turks and Greeks (pp. 39–40) and the cost of food in Attica. *Cf.* the unpublished document No. 122 of the year 1049 (1639–1640) in the typed résumé of the codex issued by the *şerî* of Veroia.

53. See Georgieviz, *De Turcarum moribus* (26), p. 99. Also Martinus Crusius, *Turcograeciae libri octo* [*Eight Books on Turkish Greece*] (Basel, 1584), p. 522, where a letter from Gabriel Severus, Metropolitan of Philadelphia, commends to Crusius and others two "Greeks," Luke and Andrew Argyros from Santorini, who, "as Christians and Hellenes," could be entrusted to collect money for the purpose of securing liberation from the "Mohammedans."

54. There are ample details in Inalcik, "Osmanlı hukukuna giriş" (22), pp. 1 ff.

55. In Tsopotos, Γῆ καὶ γεωργοὶ τῆς Θεσσαλίας (17), pp. 47 ff., there is clear proof of the close relationship between the two systems. The appropriate bibliography is in Köprülü, *Osservazioni* (5), pp. 60 ff., which, however, contradicts this. See also the recent work by Bistra Cvetkova, Извънредни данъци и държавни повинности в българските земи под турска власт [*Extraordinary Taxes and Compulsory Public Labor in Bulgarian Regions under Turkish Rule*] (Sofia, 1958), pp. 9, 50, 51, 58, 61, 75–76; and especially the interesting reflections and conclusions in the study by the same author, "Influence exercée par certaines institutions de Byzance et des Balkans du moyen âge sur le système féodal ottoman," *Byzantinobulgarica*, I (Sofia, 1962), 237–257, which contains the most recent bibliography.

56. See Halil Inalcik, "Ottoman Methods of Conquest," *Studia Islamica*, 2 (1954), 110: "Lastly in the *defteri* of 1431 occur many formulas in Persian that might indicate a Persian-Ilkhanid or Seljuk origin of the system." *Cf.* Köprülü, *Osservazioni* (5), pp. 62 ff.

57. See Köprülü, *Osservazioni* (5), pp. 61 ff.

58. See Barkan, *XV ve XVI inci asırlarda esasları* (18), pp. 348, 349.

59. See Apostolos E. Vacalopoulos, *Thasos. Son histoire, son administration de 1453 à 1912* (Paris, 1953), p. 53.

60. These laws (*kanunlar*) were defined following local inquiries that were made immediately after conquest by officials whose job it was to register land holdings (*tahriri memleket*). The laws were then submitted to the sultan for his approval. See Inalcik, "Osmanlı hukukuna giriş" (22), p. 20. *Cf.* Joseph Kabrda, "Les Codes (*kanunname*) ottomans et leur importance pour l'histoire économique et sociale de la Bulgarie," Сборник в чест' на Академик Никола в. Миков (Sofia, 1959), p. 186.

61. See Barkan, *XV ve XVI inci asırlarda esasları* (18), pp. 238–240.

62. See Vacalopoulos, *Thasos* (59), pp. 24–25. *Cf.* his *Origins of the Greek Nation. The Byzantine Period, 1204–1461* (New Brunswick, 1970), pp. 212–213, 221.

63. See Inalcik, "Osmanlı hukukuna giriş" (22), p. 18. *Cf.* Fernand Braudel, *La Méditerranée et le monde méditerranéen à l'époque de Philippe II* (Paris, 1949), p. 510.

64. *Cf.* Gălăb D. Gălăbov, Турски извори за историята на правото в българските земи. [*Turkish Sources on the History of Law in Bulgarian Regions*] (Sofia, 1961), I, 25, Par. 2, 8.

65. See Cvetkova, Извънредни данъци (55), pp. 153 ff.; where examples will be found; and also the paper by the same author, "Contribution à l'étude des impôts

extraordinaires (*avariz-i divanye ve tekâlif-i örfiye*) en Bulgarie sous la domination turque. L'Impôt *nuzul*," *Rocznik Orientalistyczny*, 23 (1959), No. 1, pp. 57–65.

66. For the Cyprus *kanunname*, see Barkan, *XV ve XVI inci asırlarda esasları* (18, pp. 348, 349.

67. For examples and details, see Cvetkova, Извънредни данъци (55), pp. 197–203.

68. Inalcik, "Osmanlı hukukuna giriş" (22), p. 15. There is evidence to suggest that the second *kanunname*, known to us from a copy published by Friedrich Kraelitz-Griefenhorst and dating from the reign of Bayezid II, was framed immediately after the capture of Constantinople. It is the Ottoman Empire's oldest codex. The Bulgarian Academy of Science has recently published Bulgarian translations of these codices, produced as a co-operative venture by several specialists of the Turkish language under the aegis of the well-known Turcologist Gălăb D. Gălăbov (Турски извори [64], pp. 11–26).

69. See Joseph Kabrda, " 'Ο τουρκικός κώδικας (*kanunname*) τῆς Λαμίας [The Turkish Codex (*kanunname*) of Lamia]," Ἑλληνικά, 17 (1962), 203–206, for a rich bibliography of the works based on Turkish documentation produced mainly in Yugoslavia and Bulgaria. Kabrda's work is also in French in the *Annals of the School of Philosophy of the University of Brno*, 10 (1961), Historical Series C, VIII, 174–190. And see especially Cvetkova, Извънредни данъци (55), which also has a bibliography.

70. See *Üsküb-ve Selânik kanuni* in Barkan, *XV ve XVI inci asırlarda esasları* (18), p. 298.

71. On the fixing of these taxes, see Belin, *La Propriété foncière* (24), pp. 20–29. On the *haracı mukaseme* see p. 27; and on the *haracı vazife* or *muvazzaf*, see pp. 28–29.

72. *Ibid.*, p. 126, fn. 3.

73. *Ibid.*, p. 126, fn. 1.

74. Cvetkova, Извънредни данъци (55), pp. 8, 9.

75. Gălăbov, Турски извори (64), p. 22.

76. *Ibid.*, pp. 23–24.

77. *Ibid.*, p. 23.

78. See *ibid.*, p. 25.

79. *Ibid.*, p. 25. On the tax *ispence*, see Bistra Cvetkova, "О религиознонациональной дискриминации в Болгарии во время турецкого владычества [About Religious and Nationality Discrimination in Bulgaria during the Turkish Occupation] Советское Востоковедение, 2 (1957), 79, fn. 4, which contains the bibliography.

80. Gălăbov, Турски извори (64), pp. 28 ff., where there are various other interesting texts.

81. An old measure which varies in volume from place to place (18–22, 30, 33, 44, 50, 66 okes).

82. Is this tax the Byzantine παρθενοφθορία? Was it essentially the counterpart of *jus primae noctis*? Lambridis mentions that before the middle of the seventeenth century in many parts of Thessaly the bride was taken after her wedding to the spahi, then to the *subaşı*, to be collected by her husband after three days. This gross humiliation was still practiced in Thessaly as late as 1803, though in Epirus it lasted no more than a few decades because the spahi was frequently killed. Ioannis Lambridis, Ἠπειρωτικά μελετήματα [*Essays on Epirus*], Τεῦχος 3, Τά Κουρεντιακά καί τά Τσαρκοβιστιακά [*No. 3, On Kourenta and Tsarkovista*] (Athens, 1888), p. 10.

83. See Kabrda, " 'Ο κώδικας τῆς Λαμίας" (69), pp. 208 ff., which contains the relevant bibliography. Almost the same stipulations were made in the codex (*kanunname*) of Amphissa (see Joseph Kabrda, "Законоположение об Амфиссе [The *Kanunname* of Amphissa]," Восточные источники по истории народов Юго-восточной и Центральной Европу, [Moscow, 1964], pp. 222–230).

84. See Barkan, *XV ve XVI inci asırlarda esasları* (18), p. 290.

85. There is an extensive compilation of the range of taxes levied on Moslems early in the nineteenth century in the manuscript by Iakovaky Rizos Néroulos, "Analyse raisonnée de l'ouvrage intitulé 'Charte Turque,' " (Geneva Public Library), pp. 20–21.

86. See Kabrda, " Ὁ κώδικας τῆς Λαμίας" (69), p. 216. *Cf.* the same state of affairs at the time of Mohammed II (Gălăbov, Турски извори (64), p. 25.

87. The *haraç*, as we have seen, was a property tax, but the *cizye* was a head tax (Fattal, *Le Statut légal* [1], p. 266; Belin, *La Propriété foncière* (24), p. 15, and, for details, pp. 44–47).

88. See Franz Babinger, "Beginn der Türkensteuer in den Donaufürstentümern (1394 bzw–1455) [The Beginnings of Turkish Taxation in the Danubian Principalities (1394–1455)]," SOF, 8 (1944), 1, fn. 1. On the collection of *haraç*, there is some information in a document written sometime before 19 December 1476 about the districts of Grevena and Premeti (Beldiceanu, *Actes* [29], pp. 148–158; and Gerlach, *Tagebuch* [22], p. 396).

89. Carlier de Pinon, *Voyage en Orient* (Paris, 1920), p. 109.

90. See Paul Ricaut, *Histoire de l'Eglise Grecque et de l'Eglise Arménienne* (Amsterdam, 1710), trans. Mons. de Rosemond, ed. 2a, pp. 18–19. *Cf.* p. 337. See also Sieur du Mont, *Voyages en France, en Italie, en Allemagne, à Malthe, et en Turquie* (The Hague, 1699), IV, 2–3. On the *haraç* and other relevant evidence, see Pericles Zerlentis and Floros E. Katsouros (eds.), Νησιωτικὴ ἐπετηρίς [*Islands' Almanac*] (Hermopolis on Syros, 1918), I, 23–26. According to Guillaume Joseph Grelot (*Relation nouvelle d'un voyage de Constantinople* [Paris, 1860], p. 203), the *haraç* was paid from the age of fourteen years. In 1700 Pitton de Tournefort said that the poll tax in the islands was 5 *écus* (*Relation d'un voyage du Levant* (Amsterdam, 1718), I, 59.

91. See Nectarius, Patriarch of Jerusalem, Ἐπιτομὴ τῆς ἱεροκοσμικῆς ἱστορίας [*A Survey of Sacred and Political History*] (Venice, 1758), pp. 432–433; also Constantine Sathas, Τουρκοκρατουμένη Ἑλλάς (1453–1821) [*Greece under Turkish Domination 1453–1821*] (Athens, 1869), p. 211, fn. 1.

92. Athanasius Comnenus Ypsilantis, Τὰ μετὰ τὴν Ἅλωσιν [*After the Capture 1453–1789*] (Constantinople, 1870), p. 47.

93. This important piece of information is in Marco Minio, *Relazione di Constantinopoli* (Venice, 1845), p. 18: "Ha etiam molte altre persone particulare le quale sono tutte provisionate da sua excellentia, et in questo numero erano molti cristiani Grechi che abitvano nella Morea, ma al presente per questo signor a tutti ditti cristiani è stato tolto la provisione [There are also many other persons in his employ, all of them paid by His Excellency; among them were many Christian Greeks, established in the Morea, whom, however, the present sultan has deprived of their means of support]."

94. See William Miller, "Lichtle's Description of Naxos," BNJ, 6 (1927–1928), 450. There is information about the collection of the poll tax on Samos as well as other matters in Georgirenes, *Description* (45), pp. 9–12.

95. See Barkan, *XV ve XVI inci asırlarda esasları* (18), pp. 341–343.

96. *Ibid.*, p. 345.

97. For details, see Collignon, *Le Consul Jean Giraud* (52), pp. 16, 30–34. *Cf.* pp. 21–22.

98. See Georgirenes, *Description* (45), pp. 26–27, 30–31.

99. Barkan, *XV ve XVI inci asırlarda esasları* (18), p. 237.

100. For details, see *ibid.*, pp. 237–238.

101. This is discussed in Vacalopoulos, *Origins of the Greek Nation* (62), pp. 216 ff.

102. Kabrda considers the *müsellem* an organized class of military landowners (see "Les Codes ottomans" [60], p. 190.

103. Orally reported by Cyril Mundy.

104. Barkan, *XV ve XVI inci asırlarda esasları* (18), p. 238. Field garrisons and night garrisons were appointed by judicial rescript according to Sacred Law (see the typed résumé of unpublished Turkish documents numbered 22, 26, 110, and 224, for the year 1639 in the historical archives of Veroia).

105. Vacalopoulos, *Origins of the Greek Nation* (62), pp. 152 ff. On the *voynuks*, see Georgieviz, *De Turcarum moribus* (26), p. 49. Many thousands of Bulgarians paid no tax (Gerlach, *Tagebuch* [22], p. 54), undoubtedly because they were *voynuks*.

106. On these taxes, see the specialized study by Cvetkova, Извънредни данъци (55).

107. See Barkan, *XV ve XVI inci asırlarda esasları* (18), p. 239.

108. See Deshayes, *Voyage* (26), p. 198; Charles Schefer (ed.), *Journal d'Antoine Galland pendant son séjour à Constantinople (1672–1673)* (Paris, 1881), I, 168; Sieur du Loir, *Les Voyages du Sieur du Loir* (Paris, 1654), p. 97.

109. See Barkan, *XV ve XVI inci asırlarda esasları* (18), p. 240, and, for other evidence in the codices of Rhodes and Kos, pp. 338–340).

111. See Pericles G. Zerlentis, Φεουδαλική πολιτεία ἐν τῇ νήσῳ Νάξῳ [*A Feudal State on the Island of Naxos*] (Hermopolis on Syros, 1928), pp. 3 ff.; and Antonios Vallindas, Κυθνιακά [*On Kythnos*] (Hermopolis on Syros, 1882), p. 78.

112. See Zerlentis, Φεουδαλική πολιτεία ἐν τῇ νήσῳ Νάξῳ (111), p. 20.

113. For further information on taxes, both of a general and specific nature, see Carlier de Pinon, *Voyage* (89), pp. 107–109.

114. Gerlach, *Tagebuch* (22), p. 481.

115. *Ibid.*, p. 256. *Cf.* p. 215.

116. Salomon Schweigger, *Ein newe Reyssbeschreibung auss Teutschland nach Constantinopel und Jerusalem* [*A New Description of a Voyage from Germany to Constantinople and Jerusalem*] (Nuremburg, 1608), p. 140.

117. See Barkan, "Les Formes" (21), p. 298; also Chapter 9.

118. See above p. 9.

119. See Gerlach, *Tagebuch* (22), pp. 176, and Deshayes, *Voyage* (26), pp. 197–198, for additional information on the spahis.

120. Gerlach, *Tagebuch* (22), pp. 369–370. *Cf.* pp. 52, 129–130.

121. *Ibid.*, p. 370.

122. Demetrius Bikelas, Ἡ Ἑλλάς πρό τοῦ 1821 [*Greece before 1821*] (Athens, 1884), pp. 8–9 of the reprint from No. 8 of the journal Παρνασσός.

123. See, for example, the views of Pierre Belon, *Les Observations de plusieurs singularitéz et choses mémorables, trouvées en Grèce, Asie, Indée, Egypte, Arabie et autres pays estranges* (Paris, 1553), pp. 28a–29b, 64a, 191a; Philippe du Fresne-Canaye, *Le Voyage du Levant (1573)* in the series *Recueil de voyages et de documents pour servir à l'histoire de la géographie depuis le XIIIᵉ jusqu'à la fin du XVIᵉ siècle* (Paris, 1897), XVI, 133: "la cupidité des Turcs à qui l'on ne parle jamais sans quelques présents, n'eût-on leur donner que quelques aspres [the cupidity of the Turks, to whom one never speaks without offering some presents or some aspers]." See also Vegesla Vratislav von Mitrović, Ἡ Κωνσταντινούπολις κατά τόν 16ον αἰῶνα (1591–1596) [*Constantinople in the Sixteenth Century (1591–1596)*] ([n.p.], [n.d.]), tr. Ioannis E. Dryskos, pp. 57–58; Julien Bordier, *Relation d'un voyage en Orient par Julien Bordier, écuyer de Jean Gontaut baron de Salignac, ambassadeur à Constantinople (1604–1612)* (Athens, 1934), V, 29 (a reprint from Volume VI of Ἀρχεῖον Πόντου): "car le naturel des Turcs n'est de donner, sinon que pour mieux prendre [for it is the nature of Turks to give only in order the better to take]."

124. *Cf.* the outlawing of such rapacity in the islands of the Duchy of the Aegean (Pericles G. Zerlentis, Γράμματα τῶν τελευταίων Φράγκων δουκῶν τοῦ Αἰγαίου πελάγους [*Correspondence of the Last Frankish Dukes of the Aegean Sea*] (Hermopolis on Syros, 1924), pp. 103–104). See also Barkan, "Les Formes" (21), p. 312.

125. See I. Parcharides, "Στατιστική τῆς ἐπαρχίας Ὄφεως τοῦ νομοῦ Τραπεζοῦντος [A Statistic Relating to the District of Ophis in the Region of Trebizond]," Παρνασσός, 3 (1879), 232.

126. *Cf.* the expressions "μοῦρθε σπαής (he burst upon me like a spahi)"; χτυπάει τά ποδάρια σάν σπαής (he struts like a spahi)"; τό πῆρε σπαΐλίκι (he is behaving like a spahi)." See K. Lazarides, "Οἱ Τοῦρκοι σπαῆδες [The Turkish Spahis]," Ἠπειρωτική Ἑστία, 1 (1952), 10. On the arbitrariness and oppression which generally prevailed throughout Epirus in the seventeenth century and afterwards, see Lambridis, Ἠπειρωτικά μελετήματα (82), No. 3, pp. 7–13.

127. Gerlach, *Tagebuch* (22), p. 376.

128. See Beldiceanu, *Actes* (29), pp. 142–144.

129. Gerlach, *Tagebuch* (22), p. 376.

130. See Bistra A. Cvetkova, "L'Evolution du régime féodal turc de la fin du XIVe jusqu'au milieu du XVIIIe siècle," *Etudes historiques à l'occasion du XIe Congrès International des Sciences Historiques, Stockholm, Août 1960* (Sofia, 1960), pp. 171–191.

131. Beldiceanu, *Actes* (29), pp. 113, 146, 152.

132. Cvetkova, "L'Evolution du régime féodal turc" (130), p. 184.

133. Apóstolos E. Vacalopoulos, *A History of Thessaloniki* (Thessalonica, 1963), pp. 78–80.

134. M. Tayyîb Gökbilgin, "Kanunı sultan Süleiman devri baslarında Rumeli eyaleti, livaları, sehir ve kasabaları [Vilayet, 'Livas,' Cities and Towns of Rumelia during the First Part of the Reign of Sultan Suleiman the Lawgiver]," *Belleten*, 20 (1956), 251, 253.

135. See I. J. Emanuel, *Histoire des Israélites de Salonique* (Thonon, Switzerland, 1939), I, 66.

136. The evidence is in a book published by the Bulgarian Academy of Science, Ašer Hananel and Eli Eškenazi [eds.], Еврейски извори за обществено-икономическото развитие на Балканските земи [*Jewish Sources on the Social and Economic Evolution of the Balkan States*] (Sofia, 1960), II.

137. See Belon, *Observations* (123), p. 75b.

138. Dernschwam, *Tagebuch* (20), p. 117.

139. *Ibid.*, pp. 109–110.

140. Nicolas Nicolay, *Les Navigations, peregrinations et voyages, faicts en la Turquie* (Anvers, 1577), p. 247; and see Dernschwam, *Tagebuch* (20), p. 107.

141. Nicolay, *Les Navigations* (140), pp. 245–246. See also Jaques Gassot, *Le Discours du voyage de Venise à Constantinople* (Paris, 1550), p. 11a. For a compilation of the different occupations of Jews, see Dernschwam, *Tagebuch* (20), pp. 112–113; *cf.* pp. 112–114.

142. See Eugenio Albèri, *Le relazioni degli ambasciatori Veneti al Senato* [*The Relationship of the Venetian Ambassadors with the Senate*] (Florence, 1855), Series III, Vol. 3, p. 389; Deshayes, *Voyage* (26), p. 121; Cornelio Magni, *Varie lettere scritte in Italia, le quali principalmente includeno l'esame della metropoli di Costantinopli etc.* [*Various Letters Written in Italy, Principally concerning the Study of the Metropolis of Constantinople*] (Parma, 1679), p. 202. And see Iorga, *Byzance après Byzance* (13), pp. 48–50.

143. See Carlier de Pinon, *Voyage* (89), pp. 107–109.

144. Dernschwam, *Tagebuch* (20), pp. 64, 67.

145. *Ibid.*, p. 67.

146. Nicolò Barozzi and Guiglelmo Berchet, *Le relazioni degli stati europei lette al*

Senato dagli ambasciatori veneziani nel secolo decimosettimo [*Papers on European States, Read by the Venetian Ambassadors in the Senate during the Seventeenth Century*] (Venice, 1871), I, 32.

147. *Ibid.*, pp. 165–166.

148. For full details, see Cvetkova, "L'Evolution du régime féodal turc" (130), pp. 189 ff., 171 ff., which contains the relevant bibliography. It has been observed that the sultan's seal was sometimes forged for the purpose of appropriating fiefs, a crime punishable by death (see Gerlach, *Tagebuch* [22], p. 376; and *cf.* Cvetkova, "L'Evolution du régime féodal turc", p. 185). On the arbitrariness of spahis in Epirus, see Lambridis, 'Ηπειρωτικά μελετήματα (82), No. 3, pp. 11–12: "We must agree that the spahis' savagery towards Christians and their barbaric behavior generally were accompaniments of the gradual devaluation of the coin of the empire and increased grain and food costs."

149. Dernschwam, *Tagebuch* (20), pp. 132–133. For a full account of the economic decline of the spahis and its causes, see the specialized study by Mutavčieva, За състоянието на спахилъка" (19), pp. 32–63.

150. *Cf.* the example of the German Embassy guard (Gerlach, *Tagebuch* [22], p. 214).

151. Belon, *Observations* (123), p. 158b.

152. See Michel Febvre, *Théâtre de la Turquie* (Paris, 1688), pp. 69 ff., 143–149, 149–154, 157.

153. Gerlach, *Tagebuch* (22), p. 49; *cf.* p. 423. On these particular afflictions, see Cvetkova, Извънредни данъци (55), pp. 53–59.

154. See Gerlach, *Tagebuch* (22), pp. 49, 93. The public office of teacher could also be bought (p. 94). And see Robert de Dreux, *Voyage en Turquie et en Grèce* (Paris, 1952), p. 36: "ces bachalis sont des gouvernements de province . . . le train d'un tel bacha doit être au moins de cinq à six cent hommes [these pashaliks are the provincial governments . . . . the escort of such a pasha must consist of at least five to six hundred men]."

155. See Gerlach, *Tagebuch* (22), pp. 129–130. *Cf.* p. 450.

156. See du Fresne-Canaye, *Voyage* (123), p. 133.

157. See Pericles Triantaphyllidis, Οἱ φυγάδες, δρᾶμα εἰς πέντε πράξεις μετὰ μακρῶν προλεγομένων περὶ Πόντου ['*The Fugitives,*' *a Drama in Five Acts, with a Long Introduction on the Pontus*] (Athens, 1870), pp. 105–107, where he depicts the lot of the people of the Pontus under Turkish rule.

158. With only rare exceptions (*cf.* du Loir, *Voyages* [108], pp. 166–167, where the simplicity and kindliness of the Turkish people are praised).

159. Gerlach, *Tagebuch* (22), p. 401.

160. *Ibid.*, p. 358.

161. *Ibid.*, p. 215; see Albèri, *Relazioni* (142), Series III, Vol. 1, p. 309.

162. For full details, see Cvetkova, "L'Evolution du régime féodal turc" (130), p. 201, which contains the relevant bibliography.

163. A number of wealthy people in Constantinople lived in magnificently ornamented villas (Gerlach, *Tagebuch* [22], p. 468), proof of which is to be found in their survival till very late in the post-Byzantine period.

164. See Crusius, *Turcograeciae* (53), pp. 487, 492.

165. *Ibid.*, p. 239.

166. See Fattal, *Le Statut légal* (1), pp. 96 ff.

167. For details of Turkish dress, and other matters, see Gerlach, *Tagebuch* (22), pp. 415–416. See also Febvre, *Théâtre* (152), p. 196, where there is a description of the humiliating prescriptions for Christians.

168. The Jews wore a yellow turban, though they were sometimes allowed to wear a blue or blue-striped one (see Carlier de Pinon, *Voyage* [89], p. 123). *Cf.* the proscription against wearing Frankish dress in Dernschwam, *Tagebuch* (20), p. 63. On all these differences between the Turks and the Christian raias, see Ivan Snegarov, Турското владичество пречка за културното развитие на българския народ и другите балкански народи [*Turkish Rule as an Obstacle to the Cultural Evolution of Bulgaria and Other Balkan Nations*] (Sofia, 1958), pp. 27 ff., which contains the relevant bibliography.

169. Belon, *Observations* (123), p. 5b.

170. Crusius, *Turcograeciae* (53), p. 487: "quae discenda est, si quis cum Turcis contrahere, aut commodius vivere velit [which must be learnt, if anyone wishes to deal with the Turks or to live easily]. Under Selim I (1512–1520), thousands of Christians in Egypt had their tongues cut out because they were speaking Greek (see Ypsilantis, Τὰ μετά τήν "Αλωσιν [92], p. 117).

171. Georgii Dousae, *De itinere suo Constantinopolitano epistola* [*Letters from His Constantinopolitan Journey*] (n.p., 1599), pp. 28, 30. Turkish women generally were confined to their homes and not allowed even to look out of their windows. Those who ventured out doors were thought immoral. When going outside could not be avoided, the body was draped in such a way that no part of it could be seen.

172. *Ibid.*, p. 30.

173. See Gerlach, *Tagebuch* (22), pp. 399–400; Vratislav von Mitrović, 'Η Κωνσταντινούπολις (123), p. 86; Albèri, *Relazioni* (142), Series III, Vol. 1, p. 398.

174. See du Mont, *Voyages* (90), IV, 3. The Turks also treated the Jews in the same way (p. 19).

175. *Cf.* the expression which has survived down to the present day: "σάν Τοῦρκο τόν βλέπω μπροστά μου [it is as though the Devil (Turk) himself were standing in front of me]." See Phaedon Koukoules, 'Η νέα ἑλληνική γλῶσσα καί τά βυζαντινά καί μεταβυζαντινά ἔθιμα [*The Modern Greek Language and Byzantine and Post-Byzantine Customs*] (Athens, 1952), pp. 31–32, which records similar expressions.

176. See Petros T. Pennas, Σερραϊκά χρονικά [*Annals from Serrai*] (Athens, 1938), No. 1 (Τό χρονικόν τῶν Σερρῶν [*The Chronicle of Serrai*], written by Papasynadinos, with an introductory study), p. 38, where there are some typical examples of this spontaneity.

177. Gerlach, *Tagebuch* (22), p. 200. *Cf.* his poor opinion of the Greeks of Constantinople (p. 204).

178. See du Loir, *Voyages* (108), p. 166; Grelot, *Relation* (90), pp. 97–98; Père Sauger, 'Η παροῦσα κατάστασις τῶν νήσων τοῦ Αἰγαίου Πελάγους [*The Present State of the Islands of the Aegean Sea*] (Hermopolis on Syros, 1878), p. 14. *Cf.* Abbé della Rocca, *Traité complet sur les abeilles* [*Complete Treatise on Bees*] (Paris, 1790), I, 10–11.

179. Sauger, 'Η παροῦσα κατάστασις (178), p. 14; and *cf.* della Rocca, *Traité complet* (178), I, 11.

Chapter 2

1. Belon, *Observations* (1:123), p. 180a.

2. *Ibid.*, p. 191b. *Cf.* such proscriptive decrees (berats) as there were in Manuel Gedeon, 'Επίσημα γράμματα τουρκικά ἀναφερόμενα εἰς τά ἐκκλησιαστικά ἡμῶν δίκαια [*Turkish Official Correspondence Relating to Our Ecclesiastical Rights*] (Constantinople, 1910), pp. 13, 92.

3. Fattal, *Le Statut légal* (1:1), p. 170.

4. Georgios Scholarios, Ἅπαντα τά εὑρισκόμενα [*The Complete Works*] (Paris, 1928), I, 285–286. For more details see, Chapter 5 of this book.

5. Joseph Bryennios, Τά εὑρεθέντα [*Works Found*] (Leipzig, 1768), II, 277. The possible consequences of the capture were also foreseen by Andronicus Callistus as soon as he learned of the event: " Ἐκκλινοῦσι πάντες καί ἀχρεῖοι γενήσονται, καί οὐδείς ἔσται ποιῶν χρηστότητα οὐδέ μέχρις ἑνός νῦν πράγματα πάντα κατά τόν φάμενον οὕτως ἔσται νυκτομαχία τις δεινή [Everybody will turn towards evil and absolutely no one will show any goodness; everything will now be plunged into darkness; as is often said, it will be like the torment of a night-battle]" (Andronicus Callistus, Μονῳδία ἐπί τῇ δυστυχεῖ Κωνσταντινουπόλει [*Monody on Unfortunate Constantinople*], PG, CLXI, col. 1138).

6. *Cf.* the first occupation of Thessalonica (Basil Laourdas, " Ὁ Γαβριήλ Θεσσαλονίκης [Gabriel of Thessalonica]," Ἀθηνᾶ, 56 (1952), 202.

7. Scholarios, Ἅπαντα (4), LV, 225.

8. Joachim Martinianos, Ἡ Μοσχόπολις 1330–1930 [*Moschopolis 1330–1930*] (Thessalonica, 1957), p. 19.

9. Savas Ioannides, Ἱστορία καί στατιστική Τραπεζοῦντος καί τῆς περί ταύτην χώρας ὡς καί τά περί τῆς ἐνταῦθα ἑλληνικῆς γλώσσης [*The History and Statistics of Trebizond and of the Region around It; and on the Greek Language of the Area*] (Constantinople, 1870), p. 118; *cf.* Triantaphyllidis, Οἱ φυγάδες (1:157), pp. 82–83.

10. See Antonios Papadopoulos-Kerameus, Ἀνάλεκτα ἱεροσολυμιτικῆς σταχυολογίας [*Selections from Collected Documents concerning Jerusalem*] (St. Petersburg, 1894), I, 287.

11. *Cf.* oral tradition among refugees.

12. See Triantaphyllidis, Οἱ φυγάδες (1:157), pp. 64–65.

13. I. Georgiou, " Ἡ ἐν Καππαδοκίᾳ Νεβσεχίρ [Nevsehir in Cappadocia]," MX, 1 (1938), 419.

14. Emile Legrand, *Notice biographique sur Jean et Théodore Zygomalas* (Paris, 1889), p. 130: "ἐξέκλιναν καί ἠχρειώθησαν ἐκ πολλοῦ [they have deviated, long ago choosing the path of evil]."

15. *Ibid.*, pp. 130, 131.

16. Gerlach, *Tagebuch* (1:22), p. 221. On the conversion of the Bulgars to Islam, see the collection of texts apposite to this question in Petar K. Petrov, Асимилаторската политика на турските завоеватели [*The Assimilation Policy of the Turkish Conquerors*] (Sofia, 1962).

17. Gerlach, *Tagebuch* (1:22), p. 379. *Cf.* p. 151, where this tendentious parson writes that Greeks living among the Albanians were always ready to become Turks "for a penny." The inhabitants of the village of Lialovo in eastern Macedonia spoke Greek (George Chatzikyriakou, Σκέψεις καί ἐντυπώσεις ἐκ περιοδείας μετά τοπογραφικῶν ἱστορικῶν καί ἀρχαιολογικῶν σημειώσεων [*Thoughts and Impressions from an Itinerary, with Some Topographical, Historical, and Archaeological Notes*] [Athens, 1906], p. 210), which can probably be explained only by the fact that they were apparently not converted to Islam until at least 1600.

18. Georgieviz, *De Turcarum moribus* (1:26), p. 95.

19. See Gerlach, *Tagebuch* (1:22), *passim*. For an instance when it did, see p. 452.

20. See Iorga, *Byzance après Byzance* (1:13), p. 29.

21. B. A. Mystakidis, "Δύο Ἕλληνες, Κ. Ἀστέλλα καί Μ. Μουζίκιος ἐν Τυβίγγῃ κατ᾿ Αὔγουστον 1586 [Two Greeks, K. Astella and M. Mouzikios, in Tübingen in August 1586]," Πραγματεῖαι Ἀκαδημίας Ἀθηνῶν, 1 (1935), No. 3, p. 9.

22. On conversions to Islam among the Greeks at the time of Mohammed II, see Ömer Lûfti Barkan, "Osmanlı imparatorluğunda bir iskân ve kolonizasyon metodu

olarak wakıflar ve temlikler. I. Istilâ devlerinin kolonizatör Türk dervisleri ve zâvi-yeler [Wakfs and the Conveynance of Property as a Method of Settlement and Colonization in the Ottoman Empire. I. The Turkish Dervishes as Colonizers, and Their Monasteries, during the Period of Ottoman Expansion]," *Vakıflar Dergisi* (Ankara, 1942), II, 345. Regarding the son of a Christian (one Mehmed, son of Theodore) from the district of Angelokastron, a convert to Islam sometime around 1527, see Gökbilgin, "Kanunı sultan Süleiman" (1:134), p. 283.

23. Inalcik, "Ottoman Methods of Conquest" (1:56), p. 116.

24. See François Baron de Tott, *Mémoires du baron de Tott, sur les Turcs et les Tartares* (Amsterdam, 1784), II, 208–209.

25. Gerlach, *Tagebuch* (1:22), p. 379.

26. On the hardships experienced by the Epirots, see Lazarides, Οἱ Τοῦρκοι σπαῆδες (1:126), pp. 13–14.

27. On the spiritual turmoil among Christians, see Georgios T. Zoras, Μαρτυρίαι τινές περί τό παιδομάζωμα [*Some Evidence on Child Recruitment*] (Athens, 1962), pp. 9–11.

28. So tradition attests, though it cannot be dated (see Georgiou, 'Η ἐν Καππα-δοκίᾳ Νέβσεχιρ (2:13), p. 419.

29. Nicodemus the Hagiorite, Νέον μαρτυρολόγιον [*New Martyrology*], 3rd ed. (Athens, 1961), p. 15.

30. *Ibid.*, p. 17.

31. Auguste Carayon, *Relations inédites des missions de la Compagnie de Jésus à Constantinople et dans le Levant au XVIIᵉ siècle* (Poitiers-Paris, 1864), p. 141.

32. For some ready examples, see Pennas, Σερραϊκά χρονικά (1:176), No. 1, p. 31. *Cf.* pp. 36–37 on the conversion to Islam of two priests in 1621 and 1622; and for the apostasy of metropolitans see Georgieviz, *De Turcarum moribus* (1:26), p. 20, and F. H. Marshall, "Two Liturgical Manuscripts Recently Acquired by the British Museum," BNJ, 6 (1928), 58.

33. Grelot, *Relation* (1:90), p. 174.

34. For such lists, see Ioannis K. Vasdravellis, Ἱστορικά ἀρχεῖα Μακεδονίας. Α'. Ἀρχεῖον Θεσσαλονίκης 1695–1912 [*Historical Archives of Macedonia. I. Archives of Thessalonica, 1695–1912*] (Thessalonica, 1952).

35. See Vacalopoulos, *Origins of the Greek Nation* (1:62), pp. 67–68, 89–90. On the baptism of children of crypto-Christians, see Gerlach, *Tagebuch* (1:22), p. 242: "Etliche Türken die zu vor Christen gewesen lassen ihre kinder heimlich taufen [Some Turks who had been Christians baptize their children secretly].

36. See Georgieviz, *De Turcarum moribus* (1:26), pp. 19–20. There are innumerable examples in various other travel texts.

37. See Dernschwam, *Tagebuch* (1:20), p. 70.

38. Albèri, *Le relazioni* (1:142), Series III, Vol. 3, p. 389.

39. The word for "child recruitment," "παιδομάζωμα" dates from 1675 (see Constantine Amantos, Σχέσεις Ἑλλήνων καί Τούρκων ἀπό τοῦ ἐνδεκάτου αἰῶνος μέχρι τοῦ 1821 [*Greek-Turkish Relations from the Eleventh Century to 1821*] (Athens, 1955), I, 1, p. 90, which contains the relevant bibliography). Before that time, the word γιανιτζαρομάζωμα [janissary recruitment]" appeared in Papasynadinos' Τό χρονικόν τῶν Σερρῶν (1:176), where it is recorded that in 1622 and 1636 the first recruitment of children took place in Serrai. On the first occasion six children were taken, and on the second five (Pennas, Σερραϊκά χρονικά; [1:176], No. 1, pp. 36, 54).

40. See Johann Wilhelm Zinkeisen, *Geschichte des osmanischen Reiches in Europa* (Gotha, 1854), III, 216 (and fns. 1 and 2). See also J. A. B. Palmer, "The Origin of the Janissaries," *Bulletin J. Rylands Library*, 25 (1953), 464, 467–468.

41. See Constantine Amantos, " Ἡ ἀναγνώρισις ὑπό τῶν Μωαμεθανῶν θρησκευτικῶν καί πολιτικῶν δικαιωμάτων τῶν Χριστιανῶν καί ὁ ὁρισμός τοῦ Σινάν πασᾶ [The Recognition by the Mohammedans of the Religious and Political Rights of the Christians, and the Order of Sinan Pasha]," HX, 5 (1930), 207–209, which contains the older bibliography.

42. See E. Dallegio d'Alessio, "Le Texte grec du traité conclu par les Génois de Galata avec Mehmed II le 1ᵉʳ juin 1453," Ἑλληνικά, 11 (1939), 118, 124. Cf.·pp. 115–116, where there is a bibliography of early publications.

43. Zinkeisen, Geschichte (40), III, 216.

44. See Apostolos Vacalopoulos, "Προβλήματα τῆς ἱστορίας τοῦ παιδομαζώματος [Some Problems concerning the History of Child Recruitment]," Ἑλληνικά, 13 (1954), 284 ff. See also G. D. Gălăbov, "Един закон и някои други официални документи във връзка с набирането на деца за еничерския корпус [A Law and Some Other Official Documents concerning the Recruitment of Young Children for the Janissary Corps]," годишник на софийския университет (Sofia, 1939), No. 2, pp. 1–36, which contains information on the recruitment and way of life of the janissaries.

45. See Zinkeisen, Geschichte (40), III, 217–220; Ismail H. Uzunçarsılı, Kapukulu ocakları [The Corps of Slaves of the Porte] (Ankara, 1943), I, pp. 14 ff.; J. H. Mordtmann, "Dewshirme," Enzyclopædie des Islam; Ismail H. Uzunçarsılı, "Devsirme," Islâm Ansiklopedisi.

46. See Gerlach, Tagebuch (1:22), p. 306; also p. 314. See also Deshayes, Voyage (1:26), p. 144.

47. For recruitment documents dated 1666, see Ioannis K. Vasdravellis, Ἀρματολοί καί κλέφτες εἰς τήν Μακεδονίαν [Armatoles and Klephts in Macedonia] (Thessalonica, 1970), 2nd ed., pp. 91–93; Uzunçarsılı, "Devsirme" (45).

48. See Gerlach, Tagebuch (1:22), p. 306. Cf. Mordtmann, "Dewshirme" (45).

49. See Zinkeisen, Geschichte (40), III, pp. 217–220; Uzunçarsılı, Kapukulu ocakları (45), I, pp. 14 ff.; Uzunçarsılı, "Devsirme" (45). For supplementary information about the system of child recruitment, see Jaques Gassot, Le Discours du voyage de Venise à Constantinople (Paris, 1550), pp. 20b–21a; Dernschwam, Tagebuch (1:20), pp. 60–68; Crusius, Turcograeciae (1:53), pp. 193–194; Deshayes, Voyage (1:26), pp. 144–145; du Loir, Voyages (1:108), pp. 98–103; Amantos, Σχέσεις Ἑλλήνων καί Τούρκων (39), I, 168–171 (which has the relevant bibliography). Christophoros Angelos, Ἐγχειρίδιον περί τῆς καταστάσεως τῶν σήμερον εὑρισκομένων Ἑλλήνων [A Manual on the Present Condition of the Greeks] (Leipzig, 1676), pp. 60, 62, is inconsequential.

50. Panagiotes A. Aravantinos, Χρονογραφία τῆς Ἠπείρου [The Annals of Epirus] (Athens, 1856), I, 218, fn. 1. See also Constantine Dyovouniotis, "Τό ὑπ᾽ ἀρ. 21 χειρόγραφον τῆς Πανεμιστημιακῆς Βιβλιοθήκης τῆς Τυβίγγης [Manuscript No. 21 of the University Library of Tübingen]," ΠΑΑ, 11 (1936), 275–276.

51. Zinkeisen, Geschichte (40), III, pp. 220–221.

52. See the bibliography in Vacalopoulos, "Προβλήματα" (44), pp. 292–293.

53. Zinkeisen, Geschichte (40), III, pp. 221–222. Cf. the evidence of J. A. B. Palmer, "The Origin of the Janissaries" (40), p. 470, which comes from Idris al-Bitlisi; and Gerlach, Tagebuch (1:22), p. 257.

54. Zinkeisen, Geschichte (40), III, 225, 228–229. On the acem oğlan, see Gerlach, Tagebuch (1:22), pp. 34, 48, 80; Nicolay, Navigations (1:140), pp. 125–130. On the uniform and pay of the janissaries, see Carlier de Pinon, Voyage (1:89), p. 100. On the janissaries at the time of Mohammed II, see Serif Bastav, Ordo Portae. Description grecque de la Porte et de l'armée du sultan Mehmed II (Budapest, 1947), p. 8. See Gălăbov, един закон и някои други официални документи (44), pp. 18–19, on the drastic

measures adopted after the recapture of certain recruits from Caesarea, who, though converted to Islam, escaped from Constantinople and returned to their homeland (28 December 1564). See also another decree on pp. 20–21, probably dating from 1567–1574, whereby the sultan promoted to the ranks of the janissaries seven *acem oğlan*, who worked as ironsmiths in the manufacture of windows for the mosque built in Adrianople by the architect Sinan Pasha.

55. Emile Legrand, *Bibliographie hellénique ou description raisonée des ouvrages publiés en grec par les Grecs au XVᵉ et XVIᵉ siècles* (Paris, 1885), I, cxli, cliv. *Cf.* the janissary Mouhamet Papadatos from Arta, who escaped abroad and was baptized in Tübingen in 1587 at the age of twenty-eight (Pericles Zerlentis, Σημειώματα περὶ Ἑλλήνων ἐκ τῶν Μαρτίνου Κρουσίου σουηκικῶν χρονικῶν [*Some Notes about Greeks in Martinus Crusius' Swabian Chronicles*] [Athens, 1928], pp. 20–21; and Basileios Mystakidis, " Ἠπειρωτικά ἀνάλεκτα [Epirot Analects]," HX, 4 [1929], 87–93).

56. There is a good description of the janissaries and their duties in von Mitrović, Ἡ Κωνσταντινούπολις (1:123), pp. 23–25.

57. On the organization and life of the ἰς oğlan, see Dernschwam, *Tagebuch*(1:20), pp. 139, 246; Deshayes, *Voyage* (1:26). pp. 147–150; Ricaut, *Histoire* (1:90), pp. 82–101, 109–113; Jean Baptiste Tavernier, *Recueil de plusieurs relations et traité singuliers et curieux* (Paris, 1679), pp. 447–449, 505 ff. There are also the articles under "Acem oğlan" by C. Huart and V. L. Ménage (the latter also gives a bibliography) in the latest edition of the *Enzyklopaedie des Islam*. These articles appear in the *Islâm Ansiklopedisi* with the addition of a Turkish bibliography. For further information (of a kind, however, which must be carefully checked), see, *inter alia*, Minio, *Relazione* (1:93), p. 18; Gerlach, *Tagebuch* (1:22), pp. 230, 252–253, 397; du Loir, *Voyages* (1:108), pp. 90–93; Carlier de Pinon, *Voyage* (1:89), pp. 82, 86–87, 97, 98–100; Jean Chesneau, *Le Voyage de Monsieur d'Aramon . . .* (Paris, 1887) in the series Recueil de voyages et de documents pour servir à l'histoire de le géographie depuis le XIIIᵉ jusqu'à la fin du XVIᵉ siècle, VIII, 44–45. See also von Mitrović, Ἡ Κωνσταντινούπολις (1:123), pp. 67–71, for detail concerning the childhood conversions to Islam of higher officials of the Porte. See the sketch of Ibrahim, vizier of Suleiman I, in Constantine Mertzios, "Τό ἐν Βενετίᾳ κρατικόν ἀρχεῖον [The Venetian State Archives]," HX, 15 (1940), 27. On the reaction against child recruitment, see Basilike Papoulia, *Ursprung und Wesen der "Knabenlese" im osmanischen Reich* [*Origin and Nature of "Child Recruitment" in the Ottoman Empire*] (Munich, 1963), pp. 109 ff.

58. Gerlach, *Tagebuch* (1:22), p. 280. *Cf.* the comments of Marcantonio Barbaro in 1672: "E còsa veramente degna di molta considerazione, che le ricchezze, le forze, il governo, ed in somma lo stato tutto dell'impero ottomano sia fondato e posto neile mani di gente tutta nata nella fede di Cristo [It is a circumstance that really deserves much consideration, that the wealth, power, government, indeed the entire Ottoman State was founded only to fall into the hands of those people born in Christ's faith]" (Albèri, Relazioni [1:42], Series III, Vol. 1, p. 315).

59. See Zinkeisen, *Geschichte* (40), III, 222–223, 228, 229–230, 247–261; and Mordtmann, "Dewshirme" (45). On acquiring the right to marry under Suleiman I, see Dernschwam, *Tagebuch* (1:22), p. 133. However, this probably represented no more than official acknowledgement of a *de facto* state of affairs (note one relevant example in Constantine Mertzios, Μνημεῖα μακεδονικῆς ἱστορίας [*Monuments of Macedonian History*] [Thessalonica, 1947], p. 109). Even as late as the beginning of the seventeenth century, married janissaries were not regarded as highly as those who were unmarried (Deshayes, *Voyage* [1:26], p. 199; and *cf.* pp. 303–304, on the substitution of Turkish children for Greek children).

60. See Vacalopoulos, "Προβλήματα" (44), pp. 290–293. On the excess of Turkish

children in the janissary corps as early as 1558, see Georgieviz, *De Turcarum moribus* (1:26), p. 48. On the virtual cessation of child recruitment by the second half of the seventeenth century, see Ricaut, *Histoire* (1:90), p. 19.

61. Uzunçarsılı, *Kapukulu ocakları* (45), I, 66–70.

62. Joseph von Hammer, *Geschichte des osmanischen Reiches* [*History of the Ottoman Empire*] (Pest, 1834), I, 98.

63. Constantine Paparrhegopoulos, 'Ιστορία τοῦ ἑλληνικοῦ ἔθνους [*History of the Greek Nation*] (Athens, 1932), V, part 2, p. 15.

64. Regarding this discontent on the part of Turks, see Albèri, *Relazioni* (1:142), Series III, Vol. 3, pp. 414–415.

65. See Zinkeisen, *Geschichte* (40), III, 220.

66. Ducas, *Historia byzantina* (1:2) [(Bonn), pp. 136–137; (Bucharest), pp. 175–181]. *Cf.* de Jano, "Epistola," PG (1:24), CLVIII, col. 1062: "est patria Dalmatiae, Croatiae, Bosniae, Bulgariae, Albaniae, Wallachiae, regna non parva, in paucis annis habitatoribus spoliata? [Have Dalmatia, Croatia, Bosnia, Bulgaria, Albania, and Walachia—by no means small dominions—been denuded of their inhabitants within the space of a few years?]"

67. Karl Dieterich, *Das Griechentum Kleinasiens* [*Hellenism in Asia Minor*] (Leipzig, 1915), pp. 13–14.

68. See Ioannis K. Voyatzidis, " 'Ιστορικαί μελέται [Historical Studies]," ΕΕΦΣΠΘ, 2 (1932), 150–151, which contains the relevant bibliography; and Georgios Arnakis-Georgiadis, Οἱ πρῶτοι 'Οθωμανοί. Συμβολὴ εἰς τό πρόβλημα τῆς πτώσεως τοῦ ἑλληνισμοῦ τῆς Μ. 'Ασίας (*1282–1337*) [*The First Ottomans. A Contribution to the Problem of the Fall of Hellenism in Asia Minor* (*1282–1337*)] (Athens, 1947), pp. 124–125, fn. 152, for pertinent extracts from special studies and other relevant works. *Cf.*, on the other hand, the cautious view of Ares Poulianos, 'Η προέλευση τῶν 'Ελλήνων [*The Origin of the Greeks*] (Athens, 1960), p. 73; also W. C. Brice, "The Turkish Colonization of Anatolia," *Bulletin of the J. Rylands Library*, Vol. 38, no. 1 (September, 1955), p. 23: "There is also present, especially in the towns and villages of southern Anatolia, an element of the small Mediterranean race, with short stature, delicate skeleton, dark complexion and long head, which may be aboriginal or descended from Macedonian and other colonists of Hellenistic times." *Cf.* p. 22.

69. Ioannis K. Voyatzidis calls them "Greco-Ottomans" (" 'Η ρῆξις τῶν ἑλληνοτουρκικῶν σχέσεων [The Rupture of Greek-Turkish Relations]," ΠΑΑ, XXX [1955], 407).

Chapter 3

1. See Vacalopoulos, *Origins of the Greek Nation* (1:62), *passim*.

2. Thus, at the end of 1452, the monk Gennadius advised a friend to postpone his trip to Italy until they saw what fate awaited the City, which they would know in the spring; if the inevitable occurred, its causes would be found in Italy and every other country (see Georgios Scholarios, "Απαντα [2:4], IV, 500–501).

3. *Ibid.*, I, 280: "Καί τούς μέν ἄλλους πολίτας, τούς μέν ὑπ' ἀνάγκης, τούς δέ πρόφασιν ποιουμένους τήν κοινήν τύχην καί μετά τήν ἰδίαν ἐλευθερίαν, πᾶσαι μέν ἤπειροι, πᾶσαι δέ νῆσοι καθάπερ ἄχθος τι μέγα ἐπαιτοῦντας ἄχρι καί νῦν δέχονται [Of the other citizens, some were obliged to leave their homeland because of poverty, others chose to leave of their own volition because of the common misfortune; and they were received all over the mainland and in the islands as burdensome beggars]." On the attitude of rulers towards Byzantine refugees—a suggestive topic for research—the Genoese archives hold the official correspondence between Genoa and the Giustiniani of Chios (see Aimilia K. Sarou, "Περί μεικτῶν ναῶν ὀρθοδόξων καί

καθολικῶν ἐν Χίῳ [On Mixed Orthodox and Catholic Churches on Chios]," ΕΕΒΣ XIX (1949), 207.

4. Charitonymos Hermonymos, " Ἐπικήδειος εἰς Αἰκατερίνην τὴν Παλαιολογῖναν [Funeral Panegyric for Catherine Palaeologina]," in Spyridon Lambros, "Παλαιολό-γεια καί Πελοποννησιακά [Palaeologian and Peloponnesian Affairs] (Athens, 1930), IV, 268–269.

5. Iorga, Byzance après Byzance (1:13), p. 35.

6. Karl Hopf, Chroniques gréco-romanes inédites ou peu connues (Berlin, 1872), p. 239.

7. Philippe de Voisins, Voyage à Jérusalem (Paris, 1883), p. 23: "Et y habitent au dict pais une grande quantité de nations de gens qui se noment les Chimbres que l'on appelle Boysmes en France, qui sont pouvres gens et mal conditionés [And there live in the said land a great many people named Chimbres, who are called Bohemians in France, and who are poor and in bad condition]."

8. See Giuseppe Stefani, I Greci a Trieste nel settecento [The Greeks at Trieste in the Eighteenth Century] (Trieste, 1960), p. 20.

9. Onofrio Buccola, La colonia greco-albanese di Mezzojuso, origine-vicende e progresso [The Greco-Albanian Colony of Messoiuso, Origins, Vicissitudes, and Progress] (Palermo, 1909), pp. 11–14, 31.

10. There is some interesting material regarding Cephalonia in Antonios Miliara-kis, Γεωγραφία πολιτική νέα καί ἀρχαία τοῦ νομοῦ Κεφαλληνίας [A Political Geography of Modern and Ancient of the Prefecture of Cephalonia] (Athens, 1890), pp. 93 ff.

11. See Buccola, La colonia (9), p. 6, regarding the emigration of Demetrius Reres' family. Cf. Xenophon A. Siderides, " Ἡ ἠπειρῶτις οἰκογένεια Ρερέ [The Reres Family of Epirus]," HX, III (1928), 160–168. Bernardino Biondelli has attempted to catalogue the Albanian peoples in Italy in the middle of the nineteenth century (Studi linguistici [Milan, 1856], p. 60). Cf. Georg J. von Hahn, Albanesische Studien (Jena, 1834), p. 31. See also the manuscript by Antonino Mongitore, "Memoria de'Greci venuti dall'Albania in Sicilia," Bibliotèca Comunale di Palermo, Qq, E32, f. 81.

12. Until almost the middle of the fourteenth century the Orthodox monastic element in Calabria sustained its dogma and reacted vigorously against the efforts of the Roman Catholic clergy to eradicate it (see G. Garitte, "Deux Manuscrits italo-grecs," [Vaticanus graecus 1238 et Barberinus graecus 475], Miscellanea G. Mercati, III [1946], 35–40). We are now able to get a good idea of the distribution of the seventh-eight Orthodox monasteries in Calabria from the very striking map recently published by Marcel-H. Laurent and André Guillou, Le "Liber visitationis" d'Athanase Chalkéopoulos (1457–1458) (Vatican, 1960).

13. Buccola, La colonia (9), p. 14.

14. See Biondelli, Studi linguistici (11), pp. 59, 61, 62–63, which has the earlier basic bibliography. On the question of "Italianization" he writes: "Essendo venuti separatamente in Italia, e in vari tempi, senza beni, non poterono mai formare un corpo nazionale ne abitare un'intera città; ma dispersi per le valli e per le montagne, in piccoli ed appartati villagi, rimasero sempre estranei al progressivo incivilimento [As they arrived in Italy separately and at different times, without fortune, they were never able to form a national unit nor settle in a single city; and, being distributed throughout the valleys and mountains in small and separate villages, they remained forever strangers to the progressive commonalty]." Cf. p. 65. On the proclivity of the Greek Albanians towards Orthodoxy during the nineteenth century, it is interesting to read K. C. Vamvas, "Περί τῶν ἐν Ἰταλίᾳ Ἑλληνοαλβανῶν καί ἰδίως περί τῶν εἰς Ἑλλάδα μεταναστευσάντων [On Greek-Albanian Immigrants in Italy and especially Greece]," Παρνασσός, I (1877), 23.

308   NOTES—CHAPTER 3

15. For details, see the study by Giovanni Cecchini, "Anna Notara Palaeologa: Una principessa greca in Italia e la politica senese di ripopolamento delle Maremma [Anna Notara Palaeologa: A Greek Princess in Italy, and the Politics in Siena concerning the Repopulation of the Maremma]," *Bolletino senese di storia patria*, N.S., IX (1938), 6–13. For a later study of the colonization of Paganica and Sovana by emigrants from Cheimarra and Maina during the time of the Medici, see the article by D. M. del Rosso in *Miscellanea Senese*, IV (1896), 9–11 (referred to by Cecchini, "Anna Notara").

16. See Gian Vincenzo Meola, *Delle istorie della Chiesa Greca in Napoli esistente* (Naples, 1790); and Nikolaos Katramis, Ἡ ἐν Νεαπόλει ἑλληνική ἐκκλησία [*The Greek Church in Naples*] (Zacynthus, 1866), pp. 7, 10, which gives the bibliography. From 1866, continual litigation, buttressed by the tracts of Greek Unionists and Italians, aimed at removing the Church from the jurisdiction of the Greek Orthodox community.

17. See Biondelli, *Studi linguistici* (11), pp. 61–62.

18. Vamvas, "Περί τῶν ἐν Ἰταλίᾳ Ἑλληνοαλβανῶν" (14), p. 24.

19. *Ibid.*, pp. 25–26.

20. Biondelli, *Studi linguistici* (11), pp. 61–62.

21. See Carlo de Frede, *I lettori di Umanità nello studio di Napoli durante il Rinascimento* [*Readers in the Humanities at the University of Naples during the Renaissance*] (Naples, 1960), p. 99.

22. Biondelli, *Studi linguistici* (11), p. 65. *Cf.* similar evidence in Crusius, *Turcograeciae* (1:53), pp. 523, 525, 528, 529, 530, on the Greeks of southern Italy, Sicily, and Malta during the sixteenth century (their language, way of life, churches, and so on) and esp. p. 538: "Habere templa pulcherrima, antiqui operis, tam ruri, quam in civitatibus, per totam Siciliam. In Calabria, sive Magna Graecia, prope Hydruntem habitantes populos, Salentinos nomine, esse Graecos: religione, vestitu, moribus, lingua. Quod est tractus olim Constantinopolitanos Imperatores pertinuerit, nec omnes e Normannis expelli potuisse. Itaque nunc habere plurima oppida et castella Calliopolim ibi ad mare: natura et manu munitissimam mercaturae deditam [They have beautiful churches built in ancient times, in the country as in towns, throughout the whole of Sicily. In Calabria, or Magna Graecia, near Otranto, live people named Salentini who are Greek in religion, dress, customs, and language. This land formerly belonged to the Byzantine emperors, but the Normans could not expel the inhabitants. Therefore they have many towns and fortresses, and there near the sea is Callipolis, fortified by nature and manual labor and dedicated to commerce]."

23. Biondelli, *Studi linguistici* (11), p. 64. There is a bibliography concerning these villages in Vamvas, "Περί τῶν ἐν Ἰταλίᾳ Ἑλληνοαλβανῶν" (14), p. 22, which contains statistical information on some of them. There is also a note by Andreas Darmarios, in 1585, on the Greek churches of St. Anne in Ancona (where "now the Greeks are forced to serve Mass the papal way"), St. Catherine and St. Nicholas of Naples (see Legrand, *Zygomalas* (2:14), pp. 190–191).

24. The bibliography is in Vacalopoulos, *Origins of the Greek Nation* (1:62), p. 358, n. 9. On these Greeks in the fourteenth century, see the further evidence of Hopf, *Chroniques gréco-romanes* (6), pp. 143–144: "Sonovi anco molti Greci in Calabria ed in Terra d'Otranto, che ubbidiscono alla Santa Chiesa Romana, mà forse non così, devotamente, come farianno, se l'imperator sior Michiel Palealogo detto, il patriarcha Constantinopolitano ed il figlio del detto imperatore sior Andronico fossero fermi e ubbidienti alla Chiesa Romana, e non in contumacia, onde ne segue danno immenso [There are also many Greeks in Calabria and the Otranto region

who acknowledge the Holy Roman Church; still, they would be more sincerely devoted if the Emperor Michael Palaeologus, the Patriarch of Constantinople, and Andronicus, his son were staunchly loyal to the Roman Church and not, as they now really are, in willful disobedience, a fact which leads to great havoc]." On earlier layers of Greek population in Sicily, see Tassos D. Neroutsos, " Ὁ ἐν Σικελίᾳ ἑλληνισμός κατά τόν μέσον αἰῶνα [Hellenism in Sicily during the Middle Ages]," Παρνασσός, X (1886), 157–174.

25. See Biondelli, *Studi linguistici* (11), p. 64: "Interrogando gli scrittori e i documenti dei vari tempi, troviamo non dubbie tracce della presenza non mai interrota di colonie greche nella parte più meridionale della nostra penisola [Investigating various writers and documents of different periods, we found incontrovertible evidence of the uninterrupted presence of Greek colonies in the southeastern parts of our peninsula]." *Cf.* p. 65: "Buona parte dei Greci coloni dell'Italia Meridionale sono reliquie d'una molto più numerosa populazione, colà da tempi assai rimoti stabilita, e che, mentre dall'una parte un gran numero coll avvicendarsi delle generazioni, perdette le naturali primitive impronte, adottando la lingua ed i costumi d'Italia, altri invece, nelle parte piu meridionale, formarono, quasi un nocciòlo, intorne a cui molti esuli moderne successivamente si raggrupparomo [A large number of the Greeks of southern Italy are relics of a much more numerous population which established itself there a long time ago; most of these eventually lost their natural primitive character, adopting the language and customs of Italy, and many in the southernmost parts of the region formed a sort of core to which many successive refugees subsequently attached themselves]."

26. See Crusius, *Turcograeciae* (1:53), p. 102; Aravantinos, Χρονογραφία τῆς Ἠπείρου (2:50), I, 180; Buccola, *La colonia* (9), pp. 6, 11, 14 ff., 32. *Cf.* the following extract from the Sicilian historian Tommaso Fazello in his *De rebus siculis*: "Plures Graecorum coloniae in Siciliam sunt deductae, a quibus pagi permulti, qui Graecorum casalia adhuc appelantur, sunt conditi [Many colonies of Greeks have been established in Sicily, where they have founded many villages, until now called the *casalia* of the Greeks]." *Cf.* also Siderides, " Ἡ ἠπειρῶτις οἰκογένεια Ρερέ" (11), p. 163, which is based on Buccola's study. And see Antonios Chatzis, Οἱ Ραούλ, Ράλ, Ράλαι *(1080–1800)* [*The Raoul, Ral, or Rales Family (1080–1800)*] (Kirchhain, Germany, 1909), pp. 40 ff. There is also a review by Nikos A. Bees in Βυζαντίς, II (1911–1912), 250–255.

27. See the manuscript by Mongitore, "Memoria de'Greci venuti dall'Albania in Sicilia" (11), fol. 81.

28. Pericles Zerlentis, Σημειώματα περί Ἑλλήνων (2:55), p. 10. *Cf.* Legrand, *Zygomalas* (2:14), p. 191, where there is a reference to the Church of St. Catherine in 1583.

29. Gerlach, *Tagebuch* (1:22), p. 103.

30. Biondelli, *Studi linguistici* (11), p. 62, fn. 1.

31. Buccola, *La colonia* (9), p. 31.

32. *Ibid.*, p. 47.

33. See Vamvas, "Περί τῶν ἐν Ἰταλίᾳ Ἑλληνοαλβανῶν" (14), p. 20.

34. See Buccola, *La colonia* (9), p. 35.

35. The place-names Pimonoro and Filaca have recently attracted the attention of Italian and Greek nomenclators (see Ioannis A. Thomopoulos, "Κατω-ιταλικά ἑλληνικά τοπωνύμια [Greek Toponyms in Southern Italy]," Ἑλληνικά, XVI [1958–1959], 70–76, which contains the bibliography).

36. See Basileios A. Mystakidis, "Περί τῶν πατριαρχῶν Διονυσίου Β′ καί Μητροφάνους Γ′ καί τῆς καθαιρέσεως αὐτῶν κατά νέα ἀνέκδοτα ἔγγραφα [The Dethrone-

ment of Patriarchs Dionysios II and Metrophanes III according to Hitherto Unpublished Documents]," Ἐκκλησιαστικὴ Ἀλήθεια, X (1890), 182, fn. 12. See also Legrand, *Zygomalas* (2:14), p. 190; and Zerlentis, Σημειώματα περὶ Ἑλλήνων (2:55), p. 12. On the Greek population of Venice in the fifteenth and sixteenth centuries, see Deno J. Geanakoplos, *Greek Scholars in Venice* (Cambridge, Mass., 1962), pp. 60–61), which contains the relevant bibliography.

37. Sophia A. Antoniadis, "Πορίσματα ἀπὸ τὴν μελέτην προχείρων διαχειριστικῶν βιβλίων τῶν ἐτῶν 1544–1547 καί 1549–1554 τῆς παλαιᾶς κοινότητος Βενετίας [Results of a Study of the Books of the Old Community of Venice Covering the Years 1544–1547 and 1549–1554]," ΠΑΑ, XXXIII (1958), 468.

38. Ioannis Veloudis, Ἑλλήνων ὀρθοδόξων ἀποικία ἐν Βενετίᾳ [*A Colony of Orthodox Greeks in Venice*] (Venice, 1872), p. 3.

39. Antoniadis, "Πορίσματα" (37), p. 468. See also Constantine Dimaras, Βενετία: 1477, 1828 [Venice: 1477, 1828]," Θησαυρίσματα, I (1962), 2–3, 8–9.

40. See Sophia A. Antoniadis, "Νέα στοιχεῖα ἀπὸ κατάστιχα τῆς ἑλληνικῆς ἀδελφότητος Βενετίας (16ος αἰ.) [New Evidence from the Registers of the Greek Brotherhood of Venice (Sixteenth Century)]," Ἀφιέρωμα στή μνήμη τοῦ Μανόλη Τριανταφυλλίδη (Thessalonica, 1960), pp. 63–67; and *cf.* the same author's Πορίσματα" (37), pp. 467, 468 ff., 475. See also Manoussos I. Manoussacas, Ἡ πρώτη ἄδεια (1456) τῆς βενετικῆς γερουσίας γιά τό ναό τῶν Ἑλλήνων τῆς Βενετίας καί ὁ καρδινάλιος Ἰσίδωρος [Cardinal Isidore, and the Initial Warrant (1456) of the Venetian Senate for the Erection of the Greek Church in Venice]," Θησαυρίσματα, I (1962), 109–118.

41. Antoniadis, "Πορίσματα" (37), pp. 474, 477. On the different occupations of Greeks in Venice, see the article by the same author, "Πορίσματα ἀπ' τή μελέτη τοῦ βιβλίου Συνοικεσίων τῆς Ἀδελφότητας Ἑλλήνων Βενετίας [Results of a Study of the Marriage Register of the Greek Brotherhood in Venice]," Εἰς μνήμην Κ. Ἀμάντου (Athens, 1960), p. 436.

42. Antoniadis, "Πορίσματα" (37), pp. 476–477. On this aspect of Hellenization, *cf.* Vacalopoulos, *Origins of the Greek Nation* (1:62), p. 235.

43. Veloudis, Ἑλλήνων ἀποικία ἐν Βενετίᾳ (38), pp. 1 ff.

44. Note, for example, the sayings " Ἔχασε ἡ Βενετιά βελόνι [Venice has lost a needle]" (an ironical comment on a loss so insignificant that it ought never to have been mentioned); and "ἔχει μισή Βενετιά [he owns half of Venice]" (a comment on someone's extreme wealth). See Nikolaos Politis, Μελέται περὶ τοῦ βίου καὶ τῆς γλώσσης τοῦ ἑλληνικοῦ λαοῦ, παραδόσεις [*Studies in the Life and language of the Hellenic People; Traditions*] (Athens, 1904), II, 43; III, 96. See Petros P. Kalonaros, Ἡ Βενετία εἰς τοὺς θρύλους καὶ τά τραγούδια τοῦ ἑλληνικοῦ λοῦ [*Venice in the Legends and Songs of the Greek People*] (Athens, 1942).

45. See Demetrius Apostolidis, Ἱστορία τοῦ ἑλληνισμοῦ τοῦ Πόντου [*A History of the Hellenism of the Pontus*] (Thessalonica, 1935), pp. 50–51. *Cf.* Ioannides, Ἱστορία (2:9), pp. 106, 108, 118–119.

46. Poulianos, Ἡ προέλευση τῶν Ἑλλήνων (2:68), pp. 26, 89–90, 127.

47. See Vacalopoulos, *Origins of the Greek Nation* (1:62), pp. 148–150, 166–167.

48. One hundred and twenty-six years after its surrender to the Turks, Galata continued to maintain its privileges and its Greco-Frankish character; there were fewer Turks and Jews than Franks and Greeks. Twice each week, the merchants of Galata gathered in a small plaza which they called *La Logia*—a sort of stock exchange (see Carlier de Pinon, *Voyage* [1:89], p. 88).

49. See Vacalopoulos, *Origins of the Greek Nation* (1:62), *passim.*

50. Ömer Lûtfi Barkan, "Essai sur les données statistiques des registres de recen-

cement dans l'empire ottoman au XV et XVI siècles," *Journal of Economic and Social History of the Orient*, I (August, 1957), 35. By 1454 Larissa already had 355 Moslem families, of which 217 were the families of artisans. Trikkala had 255 families, of which 125 were artisans (*ibid.*)

51. Unfortunately, the earth of geographical knowledge in Greece has meant that these problems have not been studied by Greek geographers and anthropogeographers, as their counterparts in other European lands have done long ago for their own countries.

52. On the district of Pisidia, see Gerlach, *Tagebuch* (1:22), p. 99. *Cf.* Legrand, *Zygomalas* (2:14), pp. 130, 131.

53. See Ömer Lûtfi Barkan, "Osmanlı imperatorluğunda bir iskân ve kolonizasyon metodu olarak sürgünler [The Use of Displaced Persons as a Method of Settlement and Colonization in the Ottoman Empire]," *Iktisat Fakültesi Mecmuası*, vol. XV, nos. 1–4, p. 10 (of the reprint). *Cf.* Vacalopoulos, *Origins of the Greek Nation* (1:62), p. 228. On the Albanian fief-holding families of Mazeraki and Cheïkal, see the articles by Halil Inalcik in the new English edition of the *Encyclopaedia of Islam*, "Arnawutluk," and "Timar."

54. See Barkan, "Osmanlı imparatorluğunda bir iskân ve kolonizasyon metodu olarak sürgünler" (53), p. 11; and Cvetkova, "L'Evolution du régime féodal turc" (1:130), p. 183, fn. 56: "terme générique désignant toute rétribution de l'état (traitement or revenu bu bien feudataire)."

55. Barkan, "Osmanlı imparatorluğunda bir iskân ve kolonizasyon metodu olarak sürgünler" (53), p. 11.

56. *Ibid.*, p. 12.

57. *Ibid.*, p. 11.

58. *Ibid.*, p. 14.

59. *Ibid.*, p. 12.

60. *Ibid.*, p. 12 (fn.).

61. See, for example, Gerlach, *Tagebuch* (1:22), p. 55.

62. The Turkish names were *cebeci*, an armorer, attached to a special military corps; *ulufeci*, a member of the old cavalry corps; *segban*, one of the three janissary corps; and *solak*, a guardsman for the sultan in processions.

63. Barkan, "Osmanlı imparatorluğunda bir iskân ve kolonizasyon metodu olarak sürgünler" (53), p. 13.

64. *Ibid.*, p. 13.

65. See Triantaphyllidis, Οἱ φυγάδες (1:157), pp. 44–45.

66. See *ibid.*, pp. 51–52; and Philip Cheimonidis, Ἱστορία καί στατιστική Σάντας [*History and Statistics of Santa*] (Athens, 1902), p. 63. *Cf.* Georgios T. Kandilaptis, Οἱ ἀρχιμεταλλουργοί τοῦ Πόντου καί τό ἐθνικόν ἔργον αὐτῶν, μετά παραρτήματος. Τά ἀνέκδοτα τῶν Οὐσταπασίδων [*The Chief Metallurgists of the Pontus and their National Endeavors; Including an Appendix. The Anecdotes of the Ustabaşıs*] (Alexandroupolis, 1929), p. 28, fn. 9: "All the villages of the province of Chaldea have an important common historical tradition in that they received an influx of people from the fallen Empire of the Grand Comnenus—Mouzena and Lerion, especially, taking many of the noble families from Trebizond. The names of many of these former governing nobles of the Trapezuntine Empire are still encountered in those parts today—such names as Soutsoi, Karali, Mourouzai, Kalogiannides, to mention a few." *Cf.* the manuscript written by a certain Alexander M. Ioannides from Livadi, near Imera, which is to be seen in the village of Panorama at Thessalonica (1939): "Livadi was first inhabited by three people" (p. 2); "when and where they came from is unknown, but, I searched and learned that after the capture of Constantinople, not only this,

but also that all the other villages—Imera, also, which is so sprawling and with so many outlying habitations that individual families live quite apart from one another, and the woods separating them conduce eventually to their not even knowing one another—all were inhabited by refugees from captivity and they were all scared for our Christian religion and of that other religion of the enemy" (p. 3); "in time they found neighbors in the surrounding villages and lived a pleasant life, and even after the passing of two or more centuries there were still 200 families or so remaining" (p. 4).

67. A firman of Selim I's in 1519 granted tax exemptions to the monastery of Sumela (see Ypsilantis, Τά μετά τήν "Αλωσιν (1:92), p. 50.

68. Cheimonidis, Ἱστορία (66), p. 41.

69. Triantaphyllidis, Οἱ φυγάδες (1:157), pp. 9–10.

70. See Georgios Georgiadis-Arnakis, " 'Η περιήγησις τοῦ "Ιμπν Μπατούτα ἀνά τήν Μ. 'Ασίαν καί ἡ κατάστασις τῶν ἑλληνικῶν πληθυσμῶν κατά τόν ΙΔ' αἰῶνα [Ibn Batouta's Journey through Asia Minor and the Condition of the Greek Population There during the Fourteenth Century]," ΕΕΒΣ, XXII (1952), 143: "Argyropoulis [in the fourteenth century] we know to have been a center of trade for the silver mines, while Erzurum lay for the most part devastated by wars."

71. See Robert Anhegger, *Beitraege zur Geschichte des Bergbaus im Osmanischen Reich. I, Europaeische Türkei* [*Contribution to the History of Metallurgy in the Ottoman Empire. I, European Turkey*]. (Istanbul, 1943), I, p. 5. Perhaps at the outset (see Kandilaptis, Οἱ ἀρχιμεταλλουργοί [66], pp. 24, 25, 26) the mines, or some of them, were exploited by the inhabitants themselves, who rendered a part of their output to the fiefholders called *derebeys* or voivodes, as well as a tithe to the tax farmers, who held the franchise on the taxes *salian* and *salguni*.

72. See Demetrius I. Oikonomides, " 'Αργυρόπολις [Argyropolis]," ΑΠ, III (1931), 146–147.

73. Triantaphyllidis, Οἱ φυγάδες (1:157), pp. 61–62. *Cf.* Anhegger, *Beitraege zur Geschichte des Bergbaus* (71), I, pp. 106–107.

74. Cheimonidis, Ἱστορία (66), pp. 46–47.

75. *Ibid.*

76. Apparently there was a mine at Ishan in the district of Santa, but because a dead Turk was once found nearby the inhabitants were forced to abandon it in lieu of paying a penalty.

77. Cheimonidis, Ἱστορία (66), p. 56.

78. *Ibid.*, p. 59.

79. *Ibid.*, pp. 47–51.

80. *Ibid.*, pp. 58–60, 64.

81. See Anhegger, *Beitraege zur Geschichte des Bergbaus* (71), I, *passim.*; II (1944), *passim. Cf.* I, 8 ff., 90–92.

82. Kandilaptis, Οἱ ἀρχιμεταλλουργοί (66), p. 18.

83. Triantaphyllidis, Οἱ φυγάδες (1:157), p. 62.

84. Kandilaptis, Οἱ ἀρχιμεταλλουργοί (66), pp. 26–27; also Triantaphyllidis, Οἱ φυγάδες (1:157), p. 67.

85. See Anhegger, *Beitraege zur Geschichte des Bergbaus* (71), I, 104. *Cf.* Triantaphyllidis, Οἱ φυγάδες (1:157), p. 62.

86. See Anhegger, *Beitraege zur Geschichte des Bergbaus* (71), pp. 106–107. *Cf.* Triantaphyllidis, Οἱ φυγάδες (1:157), p. 68.

87. See, for example, the attitude of the inhabitants of Telos (Marco Boschini, *L'Arcipelago* [Venice, 1658], p. 16) and of Siphnos (de Tournefort, *Relation* [1:90], p. 67).

88. See Deshayes, *Voyage* (1:26), p. 471: "Les Grecs ne demeurent pas volontiers sur les grands chemins [The Greeks don't tarry willingly on the highways]."

89. Their inhabitants wished to avoid the consequences of the frequent passage of Turks along the so-called "Turkish thoroughfares" (Τουρκοδρόμια) through their communities (see Ioannis Lambridis, Ζαγοριακά [*On Zagora*] [Athens, 1870], p. 37). The length of time monks spent in their monasteries tended to be influenced by the frequency with which Turks passed by. See Ioannis M. Phountoulis, Γαβριήλ μητροπολίτου Μηθύμνης περιγραφή Λέσβου [*Description of Lesbos by Gabriel, Metropolitan of Methymna*] (Athens, 1960), p. 40.

90. Chesneau, *Le Voyage* (2:57), p. 159. *Cf.* Nicolay, *Navigations* (1:140), p. 304 (on Greece as a whole): "La plus déserte, barbare et desolée province de la terre habitable."

91. See Phanis Michalopoulos, Κοσμᾶς ὁ Αἰτωλός [*Kosmas the Aetolian*] (Athens, 1940), pp. 52, 55, 64, 76.

92. *Ibid.*, p. 55.

93. There is a tradition about the flight of certain people to Grammos in the newspaper Μακεδονία (23 September 1955).

94. Esprit Cousinéry, *Voyage dans la Macédoine* (Paris, 1831), I, 68, there expresses the opinion that Vermion, Pieria, and Olympus also provided protection at the time of the Bulgarian invasions during the Middle Ages.

95. Léon Heuzey, *Le Mont Olympe et l'Acarnanie* (Paris, 1860), pp. 205–206.

96. See Apostolos E. Vacalopoulos, Δυτικομακεδόνες ἀπόδημοι ἐπί Τουρκοκρατίας [*Emigrants from West Macedonia under Turkish Rule*] (Thessalonica, 1958), p. 4, where the relevant bibliography is collated.

97. Nicephoros Moschopoulos, " Ἡ Ἑλλάς κατά τόν Ἐβλιά Τσελεμπῆ [Greece according to Evliya Tschelebi]," ΕΕΒΣ, XIV (1938), 503.

98. See Vacalopoulos, *Origins of the Greek Nation* (1:62), pp. 72, 166.

99. See *ibid.*, p. 165. Yuruk Turks settled on the east bank of the Aliakmon in the so-called Tsiarsiaba district. See also Michael Kalinderis, Αἱ συντεχνίαι τῆς Κοζάνης ἐπί Τουρκοκρατίας [*The Guilds of Kozane under Turkish Rule*] (Thessalonica, 1958), pp. 4–5. On population withdrawal into the mountainous parts of Thessaly, see Alfred Philippson and Ernst Kirsten, *Die griechischen Landschaften* [*The Greek Territories*] (Frankfurt am Main, 1950), I, part 1, pp. 281 ff., 296 ff.

100. Léon Heuzey, *Excursion dans la Thessalie turque en 1858* (Paris, 1927), p. 30. On the fertile lands belonging to Turkish villages, see also Jakob Philipp Fallmerayer, *Schriften und Tagebücher* [*Writings and Diaries*] (Munich-Leipzig, 1913), II, 193–194.

101. *Cf.* Tsopotos, Γῆ καί γεωργοί τῆς Θεσσαλίας (1:17), p. 42; also pp. 38 ff., 121–122, 122–123.

102. Iakovaky Rizos Néroulos, *Histoire moderne de la Grèce* (Geneva, 1828), p. 53.

103. On Larissa's appearance, see Epaminondas G. Pharmakidis, Ἡ Λάρισσα [*Larissa*] (Volos, 1926), p. 14.

104. A bibliography of the works of Nikolaos I. Giannopoulos on the metropolitan see of Larissa and its associated bishoprics appears in Panos I. Vasileiou, Ἡ ἐπισκοπή Λιτζᾶς καί Ἀγράφων ἐπί Τουρκοκρατίας [*The Bishopric of Litza and Agrafa under Turkish Rule*] (Athens, 1960), p. 9.

105. Fallmerayer, *Schriften und Tagebücher* (100), p. 193.

106. See Apostolos E. Vacalopoulos, " Ἱστορικαί ἔρευναι ἐν Σαμαρίνη τῆς Δυτ. Μακεδονίας [Historical Investigations in Samarina in Western Macedonia]," Γρηγόριος ὁ Παλαμᾶς, XXI (1937), 11–15 (of the reprint). See also J. B. Wace and M. S. Thompson, *The Nomads of the Balkans* (London, 1914), pp. 144–147.

107. Heuzey, *Le Mont Olympe et l'Acarnanie* (95), pp. 45–48.

108. See Constantine Krystallis, Ἅπαντα [*Complete Works*], ed. George Valetas (Athens, 1959), I, 504.

109. See C. P. de Bosset, *Parga and the Ionian Islands* (London, 1821), pp. 56–57. *Cf.* P. A. S. [Salapantas], Ἡ Πάργα [*Parga*] (Athens, 1861), pp. 66 ff.

110. See, for example, S. Kontonasios, " Ἀπό τήν παλαιότερη ἱστορία τοῦ Βασιλικοῦ "Τσαραπλανῶν" [From the Older History of Basilikon, "Tsaraplana"]," HE, I (1952), 800.

111. Nikolaos Nitsos, Μονογραφία περί τῆς ἐν Ἠπείρῳ κώμης τοῦ Τσαμαντᾶ [*A Monograph on the Village of Tsamanta in Epirus*] (Athens, 1926), p. 18. *Cf.* A. K. Papastavrou, Ἡ Ζίτσα [*Zitsa*] (Athens, 1895), pp. 8, 11, and Nikolaos Patselis, Τό Δελβινάκιον τῆς Ἠπείρου [*Delvinakion in Epirus*] (Athens, 1948), p. 32.

112. See Constantine Stergiopoulos, Παρατήρήδεις εἰς τήν νεωτέραν Γεωγραφίαν τῆς Ἠπείρου [*Remarks on the Geography of Modern Epirus*] (Athens, 1937), pp. 30, 31.

113. Nitsos, Μονογραφία (111), p. 19.

114. See Cousinéry, *Voyage* (94), II, 143.

115. See the historical note in the newspaper Μακεδονία (29 June 1951). *Cf.* the demotic song " Ἡ Ἀναστασιά [Anastasia]," in A. Manolis, "Δημοτικά τραγούδια τῆς Κασσάνδρας [Folk Songs of Kassandra]," Χρονικά Χαλκιδικῆς, IV (1962), 227–228. Fallmerayer's notorious pro-Slavic bias leads him to make the assertion that the western district of Chalcidice, with most of its fifteen larger villages ("*Freidörfer*"), together with Kassandra, remained under Byzantine control, while the eastern, predominantly mining, district was completely Slavicized (*Schriften und Tagebücher* [100], II, 151–152; he also criticizes other travellers who talk about the unadulterated Hellenism of the region.

116. There is a reference to the founding of Keramidi, between Mavrovouni and Pelion, around 1500, in Arist. Papachatzopoulos, "Κεραμίδι [Keramidi]," Θεσσαλικὰ χρονικά, II (1931), 120–121. *Cf.* Giannis K. Kordatos, Ἱστορια τῆς ἐπαρχίας Βόλου καί Ἁγιᾶς [*A History of the Province of Volos and Hagia*] (Athens, 1960), pp. 493 ff.

117. On the extent of the Byzantine Empire in this period, see Apostolos E. Vacalopoulos, "Les Limites de l'empire byzantin depuis la fin du XIVᵉ siècle jusqu'à sa chute (1453)," BZ, LV (1962), 60 ff. For material gathered from travellers and geographers concerning the villages of this region under Turkish rule, see Kordatos, Ἱστορία (116), pp. 493–506.

118. On this traditional pursuit, see Vacalopoulos, *Origins of the Greek Nation* (1:62), p. 167.

119. See Elias P. Georgiou, Ἱστορία καί συνεταιρισμός τῶν Ἀμπελακίων [*A History of the Town and Association of Ampelakia*] (Athens, 1951), p. 10.

120. See Zosimas Esphigmenitis, "Περί Ἁγιᾶς ἤ Ἀγυιᾶς [Concerning Hagia]," Προμηθεύς, I (1889), 48. This writer says that Hagia grew between 1665 and 1680, around the time the Turks destroyed Vathyrreuma, birthplace of St. Symeon, who was the founder of the monastery of Phlamourion.

121. See George Sotiriou, "Βυζαντινά μνημεῖα τῆς Θεσσαλίας ΙΓ' καί ΙΔ' αἰῶνος [Byzantine Monuments in Thessaly (Thirteenth and Fourteenth Centuries)]," ΕΕΒΣ, V (1928), 354–355. On the condition of the monastery in the nineteenth century, see Ioannis Leonardos, Νεωτάτη τῆς Θεσσαλίας χωρογραφία [*A Chorography of Modern Thessaly*] (Pest, 1836), pp. 169–170.

122. Sotiriou, "Βυζαντινά μνημεῖα." (121), p. 353.

123. See *ibid.*, p. 355.

124. Demetrius Sisilianos, Ἡ Μακρυνίτσα καί τό Πήλιον, ἱστορία-μνημεῖα-ἐπι-

γραφαί [*Makrynitsa and Pelion. History, Monuments, Inscriptions*] (Athens, 1939), pp. 59, 69.

125. Nikolaos Giannopoulos, " Ἡ μεσαιωνική Φθιῶτις [Medieval Phthiotis]," ΔΙΕΕ, VIII (1922), 73–74; and see the same author's "Αἱ παρά τήν Δημητριάδα βυζαντιναί μοναί [Byzantine Monasteries near Demetrias]," ΕΕΒΣ, I (1924), 234–237. See also Sisilianos, 'Η Μακρυνίτσα καί τό Πήλιον (124), pp. 56, 69, concerning the refugees from Euboea and Phthiotis.

126. Nikolaos Giannopoulos, Παλαιοχριστιανική ἐπιγραφή καί παλαιοχριστιανικόν νεκροταφεῖον Βόλου [An Early Christian Inscription and the Early Christian Cemetery of Volos]," ΕΕΒΣ, XII (1936), 409. See also the same author's Τό φρούριον τοῦ Βόλου [The Fortress of Volos]," ΕΕΒΣ, VIII (1931), 110–133.

127. Marinos P. Vrettos, " 'Απόπειρα ἀναστατώσεως τῆς Μάνης κατά τόν ΙΖ' αἰῶνα [The Attempt at Disorder in Maina in the Seventeenth Century]," 'Εθνικόν ἡμερολόγιον, VI (1866), 199–200. See also Stephanos I. Papadopoulos, 'Η κίνηση τοῦ δούκα τοῦ Νεβέρ Καρόλου Γονζάγα γιά τήν ἀπελευθέρωση τῶν βαλκανικῶν λαῶν (1603–1625) [*The Movement of Charles Gonzaga, Duke of Nevers, Aimed at the Liberation of the Balkan Peoples (1603–1625)*] (Thessalonica, 1966), pp. 124–133.

128. See Spyridon Lambros, " 'Ο εἰς τήν Τοσκάναν ἐξοικισμός τῶν Μανιατῶν [The Emigration of the Maniatai (Maniotes) to Tuscany]," NE, 11 (1905), 397.

129. There is some interesting material on old bills of sale in Stavros C. Skopeteas, " Ἔγγραφα ἰδιωτικά ἐκ Δ. Μάνης τῶν ἐτῶν 1547–1830 [Private Documents from West Covering the Years 1547–1830]," 'Επετηρίς ἀρχείου ἱστορίας ἑλληνικοῦ δικαίου, III (1950), 63–67; it also provides an excellent bibliography. See pp. 102 ff., where he notes the settlement of virgin mountains in Maina by refugees. See also Eugène Yemeniz, *Scènes et récits des guerres de l'indépendance. Grèce moderne* (Paris, 1869), pp. 257–259.

130. See Domenico Trevisan, *La Relation de l'ambassade de Domenico Trevisan auprès du Soudan d'Egypte, 1512*, in the series *Recueil de Voyages et de Documents* (1:123), V, 162: "Les paysans n'avaient rien dans leurs maisons, ni lits, ni meubles, et ils dormaient sur la terre comme des animaux [The peasants had nothing in their houses, neither beds nor furniture, and they slept on the ground like animals]."

131. See Constantine Gounaropoulos, 'Ιστορία τῆς νήσου Εὐβοίας ἀπό ἀρχαιοτάτων χρόνων μέχρι τῶν καθ' ἡμᾶς [*A History of the Island of Euboea from Antiquity to Our Own Day*] (Thessalonica, 1930), p. 215.

132. Heuzey, *Le Mont Olympe et l'Acarnanie* (95), pp. 243, 257–258.

133. See *ibid.*, p. 259.

134. *Ibid.*, pp. 246–251. *Cf.* Claude Fauriel, *Chants populaires de la Grèce moderne* (Paris, 1824), I, 4–6, 84.

135. Heuzey, *Le Mont Olympe et l'Acarnanie* (95), p. 252. *Cf.* Yemeniz, *Scènes et récits* (129), p. 6.

136. Heuzey, *Le Mont Olympe et l'Acarnanie*, pp. 256–259.

137. *Ibid.*, pp. 259–260.

138. *Ibid.*, pp. 261–262, 406.

139. *Ibid.*, p. 242.

140. *Ibid.*, pp. 257–258, 261.

141. On these emigrants in 1562, 1627, 1628, and 1632, see Mertzios, "Τό ἐν Βενετία κρατικόν ἀρχεῖον (2:57), pp. 31–32, 42, 44.

142. I borrow this from Michalopoulos (Κοσμᾶς ὁ Αἰτωλός [91], p. 9), who in turn refers us to Gregoriou, 'Ιερά διήγησις μονῆς Προυσσοῦ [*A Sacred Narrative concerning the Monastery of Proussou*] (Lamia, 1869), p. 22.

143. See Nikos A. Bees, "Drei Urkunden der Brüderschaft des Tatarnaklosters [Three Documents of the Brotherhood of the Monastery of Tatarna]," BNJ, XVI (1940), 210–224.

144. See Charalambos S. Chatzithanos, Ὁ Φουρνᾶς τῶν Ἀγράφων [Phournas in the Agrafa] (Athens, 1959), p. 8.

145. Braudel, La Méditerranée (1:63), p. 21.

146. See Cheimonidis, Ἱστορία (66), p. 41. Cf. the text of the manuscript by Alexandros M. Ioannides, cited in n. 66 above.

147. Ioannis Philemon, Δοκίμιον ἱστορικόν περί τῆς Φιλικῆς Ἑταιρείας [An Historical Essay on the "Philike Hetaireia"] (Nauplia, 1834), pp. 72–73.

148. Heuzey, Le Mont Olympe et l'Acarnanie (95), pp. 205–206.

149. Sophia Anastasiadou, Πίνδος [Pindus] (Athens, 1955), pp. 29–30.

150. Cf. Pericles Triantaphyllidis, Ἡ ἐν Πόντῳ ἑλληνική φυλή, ἤτοι τά Ποντικά [The Greek Race in the Pontus] (Athens, 1866), pp. 86–87, 112.

151. See T. P. Kostakis, Σύντομη γραμματική τῆς τσακωνικῆς διαλέκτου [A Short Grammar of the Tsakonian Dialect] (Athens, 1951), pp. 154–155.

152. See Fauriel, Chants populaires (134), I, xlix.

153. See Vacalopoulos, Origins of the Greek Nation (1:62), pp. 166–167.

154. Population descent from the mountains to the plains and towns, which arose from overpopulation, was a phenomenon common to the entire Mediterranean throughout the sixteenth century (see Braudel, La Méditerranée [1:63], pp. 380–383). Cf. the hardships suffered by the inhabitants of the district of Zagora, and the emigration of many of them (Lambridis, Ἠπειρωτικά μελετήματα. [1:82] Τεῦχος 9, Ζαγοριακά [No. 9, On Zagora], pp. 37 ff.).

155. Braudel, La Méditerranée (1:63), pp. 50–51, where there are interesting reflections on the various migrations. Cf. p. 358.

156. See Kalinderis, Αἱ συντεχνίαι τῆς Κοζάνης (99), pp. 10–14, which gives the relevant bibliography; Ioannis Apostolou, Ἱστορία τῆς Σιατίστης [History of Siatista] (Athens, 1929), p. 12; and Kosmas Myrtilos Apostolidis, "Δύο ἔγγραφα ἐκ Φιλιππουπόλεως ἀπό τῶν ἀρχῶν τοῦ 19 αἰῶνος [Two Early Nineteenth-Century Documents from Philippopolis]," Θρακικά, II (1929), 347.

157. On the decline of the Christian population and the corresponding increase of the Moslem population from as early as the fifteenth century, Ducas writes vividly (Historia byzantina [1:2], pp. 136–137 [Bonn]; pp. 177–179 [Bucharest]).

158. See Nicolaj Todorov, "За демографското състояние на балканския полуостров през XV–XVI B. [On the Demographic Situation in the Balkan Peninsula during the Fifteenth and Sixteenth Centuries]," годишник на софийския университет. философска-исторически факултет LIII (1959), 224–226, which provides statistical tables. Cf. Petâr Petrov, Асимилаторската политика на турците завоеватели [The Policy of Assimilation of the Turkish Conquerors] (Sofia, 1962).

159. As early as 1502 or 1503, Bayezid II, in a bid to counteract the anti-Ottoman propaganda of the Shiites among the Turcomans of Anatolia, ordered the deportation of a group of Turcoman Shiites (Kızılbaş) from the districts of Teke and Hamit to Modon and Coron (see Ömer Lûtfi Barkan, "Les Déportations comme méthode de peuplement et de colonisation dans l'empire ottoman," Revue de la Faculté des Sciences Economiques de l'Université d'Istanbul, Vol. XI, nos. 1–4 [Istanbul, 1953], p. 55).

160. Barkan, "Déportations" (159), p. 63. Cf. the same author's "Essai sur les données statistiques" (50), p. 32.

Chapter 4

1. See Vacalopoulos, *Origins of the Greek Nation* (1:62), pp. 216, 221; and F. W. Hasluck, "Depopulation in the Aegean Islands and the Turkish Conquest," BSA, XVII (1910–1911), 166.

2. See Anthoine des Barres, *L'Estat présent de l'Archipel* (Paris, 1678), I, 190.

3. Sauger, 'Η παροῦσα κατάστασις (1:178), p. 5. However, there is a reference in the Νησιωτική ἐπετηρίς (1:90), I (1918), 16, to the fact that epidemics did reach Naxos.

4. Ioseph Chatzidakis, 'Η ἱστορία τῆς Μήλου [*History of Melos*] (Athens, 1927), pp. 170–171, 260–263.

5. On the meaning of the two words (in Greek πειρατής and κουρσάρος), and for a discussion of the ways in which men became pirates, see Belon, *Observations* (1:123), pp. 86b–88b.

6. On piracy in ancient times, see Erich Ziebarth, *Beiträge zur Geschichte des Seeraubs und Seehandels im alten Griechenland* [*Contribution to the History of Piracy and Maritime Commerce in Ancient Greece*] (Hamburg, 1929). *Cf.* Lucien Febvre, *La Terre et l'évolution humaine* (Paris, 1922), pp. 226, 267.

7. See Christopher Buondelmonti, *Description des îles de l'Archipel*, ed. Emile Legrand (Paris, 1897), Part 1, where he says that Psara (p. 73), Tenedos (p. 79), and St. Stratis (p. 95) were deserted after 1418.

8. Haji Khalifeh, *The History of the Maritime Wars of the Turks*, tr. James Mitchell (London, 1831), p. 59.

9. See Hasluck's study, "Depopulation" (1), pp. 151–175, which has a bibliography of many rare travel texts. Trevisan says that in 1512 Antikythera was deserted and uncultivated because pirates had plundered it and enslaved its inhabitants; and pirates' ships were always to be seen in the harbor (*Relation* [3:130], p. 163). Also uninhabited in 1544, according to Jerome Maurand (*Itinéraires d'Antibes à Constantinople* (*1544*) [Paris 1901], pp. 155–161), were Kythera, Antimelos, Mykonos, and Delos, the last of which he described for its antiquities. See also p. 173, on the plunder of Mykonos. In 1579 Carlier de Pinon (*Voyage* [1:89]) referred to certain islands around Melos as being uninhabited as well as Sikinos and Pholegandros (p. 55), Kythnos and other islands (pp. 57–58), and Saint Eustratios (p. 63). However, his account is not as reliable as it should be (see Hasluck, "Depopulation" [1], p. 157, fn.). Pholegandros was reinhabited by people from Siphnos in 1577 (see Zapheirios D. Gavalas, 'Η Νῆσος Φολέγανδρος *The Island of Pholegandros* [Athens, 1866], p. 40). During the fifteenth century, the inhabitants of Antiparos left for Paros (Père Sauger, 'Ιστορία τῶν ἀρχαίων δουκῶν καί τῶν λοιπῶν ἡγεμόνων τοῦ Αἰγαίου Πελάγους [*History of the Dukes and other Princes of the Aegean Sea*] [Hermopolis of Syros, 1878], p. 215).

10. Belon, *Observations* (1:123), p. 86a. On the invasion of Icaria by Turkish pirates in the fifteenth and sixteenth centuries, see Ioannis Melas, 'Ιστορία τῆς νήσου 'Ικαρίας [*History of the Island of Icaria*] (Athens, 1955), I, 147, 159–160, which contains the relevant bibliography.

11. See Michael C. Ghitakos, 'Ανέκδοτοι ἐπιγραφαί καί χαράγματα βυζαντινῶν καί μεταβυζαντινῶν μνημείων τῆς 'Ελλάδος [*Unpublished Inscriptions and Engravings on Byzantine and Post-Byzantine Monuments in Greece*] (Athens, 1957), pp. 52, 58–59, 112, 113, 140. On the destruction of Chaïreddin Barbarossa, see Nikolaos Moutsopoulos, 'Η Παληαχώρα τῆς Αἰγίνης [*Palaeochora on Aegina*] (Athens, 1962), pp. 24 ff.

12. For example, there is the case of the inhabitants of Anaphi: "Per l'insolentia de Corsari si risolvero di ruinare affato il Castello, e si ritirorno sopra un monte nel

mezzo del'Isola, dove hora e un Castello ma con poca e povera gente [Because of the brazenness of the corsairs they decided to destroy the citadel and withdraw to a mountain in the middle of the island, where now there is another castle, but with very few and poverty-stricken people]" (Boschini, *L'Arcipelago* [3:87], p. 22).

13. See Giannis Ghikas, "Δύο βενετσιάνικα χρονικά γιά τήν ἄλωση τῆς Χαλκίδας ἀπό τούς Τούρκους στά 1470 [Two Venetian Chronicles concerning the Capture of Chalcis by the Turks in 1470]," Ἀρχεῖον εὐβοϊκῶν μελετῶν, VI (1959), 231. See also Boschini, *L'Arcipelago* (3:87) on the large numbers of unmarried women on Siphnos (p. 30) and Naxos (p. 48).

14. Although the material relating to piracy, both published and unpublished, is profuse, the history of piracy on the Greek seas has still to be written. The study by Denis Zakythinos, *Corsaires et pirates dans les mers grecques au temps de la domination turque* (Athens, 1939), is really no more than a brief sketch.

15. See G. M. Valetas, " Ὁ Ἅγιος Ἰγνάτιος Ἀγαλλιανός καί τό ἐν Λέσβῳ ἀναμορφωτικόν ἔργον του [St. Ignatios Agallianos and his Reformist Work on Lesbos]," Θεολογία, X (1932), 290–291. On the devastation of the villages of the province of Methymna on Mytilene, see Phountoulis, Γαβριήλ (3:89), pp. 31 ff. On various dates in connection with the history of Mytilene during the fifteenth and sixteenth centuries, see Hasluck, "Depopulation" (1), p. 171. See also Boschini, *L'Arcipelago* (3:87), p. 60: "In molti luochi anco è deserta [In many places it is still deserted]."

16. On this point, see Alberto Tenenti's *Piracy and the Decline of Venice 1580–1615*, tr. Janet and Brian Pullan (London, 1967).

17. See Spyridon Lambros, " Ἐνθυμήσεις ἤτοι χρονικῶν σημειωμάτων συλλογή πρώτη, Ἀρ. 1–562 [Memoirs, or, An Initial Collection of Chronological Notes Numbered 1–562]," NE, VII (1910), 162.

18. See Zerlentis, Γράμματα τῶν τελευταίων Φράγκων δουκῶν (1:124), p. 3; and Mertzios, Μνημεῖα μακεδονικῆς ἱστορίας (2:59), pp. 111, 118, 119, 120.

19. See Khalifeh, *History of the Maritime Wars* (8), p. 18.

20. See Leonidas C. Zois, Ἱστορία τῆς Ζακύνθου [*History of Zacynthus*] (Athens, 1955), p. 65.

21. Nicolay, *Navigations* (1:140), pp. 16–17. On the life of slaves in Algeria around the middle of the seventeenth century, see Emmanuel d'Aranda, *Relation de la captivité du sieur Emmanuel d'Aranda, iadis esclave à Alger* (Paris, 1665). At the beginning of the seventeenth century, most pirates were Turks from Nea Phocaea (Deshayes, *Voyage* [1:26], pp. 341–342).

22. See Mertzios, Μνημεῖα μακεδονικῆς ἱστορίας (2:59), pp. 106, 114–115.

23. *Ibid.*, pp. 106, 117.

24. *Ibid.*, pp. 168, 170, 203.

25. See John Vasdravellis, *Piracy on the Macedonian Coast during the Rule of the Turks*, tr. T. F. Carney (Thessalonica, 1970), pp. 8 ff.

26. Vacalopoulos, *Thasos* (1:59), pp. 28–29.

27. Mertzios, Μνημεῖα μακεδονικῆς ἱστορίας (2:59), p. 117.

28. See Hasluck, "Depopulation" (1), p. 163; and the same author's "Albanian Settlements in the Aegean Islands," BSA, XV (1908–1909), 423–428.

29. See Demosthenes Chaviaras, "Σουλτανικά φιρμάνια περί τῶν προνομίων τῆς νήσου Σύμης καί τῶν λοιπῶν νοτίων Σποράδων [Sultanic Firmans concerning Syme and Other Islands of the Southern Sporades]," ΔΙΕΕ, VI (1902–1906), 328.

30. Maurand, *Itinéraire* (9), pp. 162–163, speaks about the misfortunes of the inhabitants of Antila [Tilos?]. See George Valetas, "Οἱ Ἰωαννῖται τῆς Ρόδου καί ἡ πειρατική των δρᾶσις [The Knights of St. John in Rhodes and Their Piratical Acts]," Ἐκκλησία, XIV (1936), 332–333.

31. See Maurand, *Itinéraire* (9), p. 163, concerning Giannis Staphialisis, known as "the Greek," who was a friend of one of the Knights of Malta.

32. See Miliarakis, Γεωγραφία πολιτική (3:10), pp. 153–154, pp. 189–192. *Cf.* Josef Partsch, Κεφαλληνία καέ Ἰθάκη. Γεωγραφική μονογραφία [*Cephalonia and Ithaca. A Geographical Monograph*], tr. L. G. Papandreou (Athens, 1892), pp. 117–118; and Zois, Ἱστορία (20), pp. 65–66.

33. Details of recolonization are in Hasluck, "Depopulation" (1), pp. 156 ff. *Cf.* pp. 172–173. On the resettlement of Pholegandros in 1577 by people from Siphnos, and later by Cretans, see Gavalas, Φολέγανδρος (9), p. 40.

34. In the middle of the sixteenth century, the Turks equipped five armed galleys solely for the prosecution of piracy in the Cyclades, the Sporades, and elsewhere throughout Greece (Belon, *Observations* [1:123], p. 90b). *Cf.* pp. 26a–26b: "Il faut entendre, qu'en toutes les isles de Grèce qui sont en la mer Méditerranée et ou l'on parle grec, les habitants se trouvent en sûreté sous la puissance du Turc, n'entendent sinon à vivre, et n'on aucun soing de garder les forteresses: car les Turcs les ostent de ceste peine. De là vient qu'ils aiment autant demeurer aux champs comme en ville . . . un viellard natif de l'isle disoit, que jamais le pays n'avoit esté si bien cultivé, ne plus riche et n'y a eu plus de peuple qu'il a maintenant. Laquelle chose il fault attribuer à la paix de longue durée, qu'ils ont eue sans estre molestez [It should be understood that, on all the islands of Greece that are in the Mediterranean and where Greek is spoken, the inhabitants feel secure under Turkish sovereignty; they have no other care but living, and no one takes care of the fortresses: the Turks do this task. This is why they prefer to stay in the fields rather than in the cities. . . . An old native of an island said that the land had never been better ·cultivated or the people richer than now. This must be attributed to the fact that peace has lasted for a long time ·and that the inhabitants have not been disturbed]."

35. Marcaky Zallony, *Voyage à Tine* (Paris, 1809), pp. 5–7. A translation of this book by Demetrius Mavromaras was published in Athens in 1888.

36. See Hasluck, "Depopulation" (1), p. 174.

37. *Ibid.*, p. 174. There is a comment about Antonios and the skillfulness of the Melos pilots in Chatzidakis, Μήλου (4), pp. 157–160, which is based on oral tradition.

38. See Mystakidis, Δύο Ἕλληνες ἐν Τυβίγγῃ (2:21), p. 10.

39. See Hasluck, "Depopulation" (1), pp. 173–174 (also fn. 10).

40. See Hasluck, "Albanian Settlements" (28), p. 228; and *cf.* his "Depopulation (1), pp. 169–170.

41. See Emmanuel I. Kritikidis, Πραγματεία περὶ τῆς ἐρημώσεως καὶ τοῦ συνοικισμοῦ τῆς Σάμου [*Essay on the Depopulation and Colonization of Samos*] (Hermopolis on Syros, 1870), pp. 7–8.

42. Hasluck, "Depopulation" (1), pp. 168, 169. For other dates relating to the depopulation of Samos, see p. 169 fn. 4.

43. On the Icarians, see Melas, Ἱστορία Ἰκαρίας (10), I, 161, which has a picture of a typical Icarian house during the period of Turkish rule.

44. *Ibid.*, I, 166–169, where there is a description of the district. See also pp. 170–174, on Icaria's archaic dialect, which is entirely due to its isolation from the outside world. And see p. 161, which deals with the conquest of Icaria by the Knights of St. John between 1481 and 1521. The purity of the Icarian dialect attracted Sauger's attention at the end of the seventeenth century, when he went on to comment: "Even though most of its inhabitants today are coal merchants and woodcutters, they possess illustrious names like Palaeologus, Comnenus, and Cantacuzenus

('Η παροῦσα κατάστασις [1:178], p. 15). Perhaps they were descendants of Byzantine refugees and not exiles as Sauger believes.

45. See Emmanuel I. Kritikidis, Τοπογραφία, ἀρχαία καί σημερινή τῆς Σάμου [A Topography of Ancient and Modern Samos] (Hermopolis on Syros, 1869), p. 8, fn. a. See also Kritikidis's Πραγματεία περί Σάμου (41), p. 12.

46. See Epaminondas I. Stamatiadis, Σαμιακά [On Samos] (Samos, 1881), II, 3–4, 6–7. Stamatiadis's work is based mainly on the summary by I. D. Vakirtzis, Ἱστορία τῆς Σάμου ἀπό τῶν ἀρχαιοτάτων χρόνων μέχρι τοῦ 1834 [History of Samos from Ancient Times to 1834] (Samos, 1912).

47. Belon, Observations (1:123), p. 86b.

48. See Emmanuel I. Kritikidis, Περίβασις εἰς τάς μονάς καί μετόχια τῆς Σάμου κατά τό 1854 [A Journey through the Monasteries and Monastic Domains of Samos in 1854] (Hermopolis on Syros, 1873), pp. 78–79. Cf. his Τοπογραφία Σάμου (45), pp. 8–11.

49. Georgirenes, Description (1:45), pp. 2–3. Cf. p. 18, where the writer gives his views on the inhabitants' last refuge before the Captivity, based on the discovery of human bones in an inaccessible part of the interior near the Madonna Phaneromeni.

50. Orally reported by Mr. Alexander Abatzis (a lawyer).

51. Samos and Thasos are the only densely wooded islands in the Aegean.

52. Cf. Hasluck, "Depopulation" (1), p. 169.

53. These privileges are discussed by Kritikidis, Πραγματεία περί Σάμου (41), pp. 27–28; and Stamatiadis, Σαμιακά (46), II, 7. There is also a legal analysis of the privileges in the study by Alexis D. Sevastakis, Τό δημόσιον δίκαιον ἐν Σάμῳ [Public Law on Samos] (Thessalonica, 1959), pp. 1 ff. However, this study is incomplete because it overlooks the early sources.

54. Zerlentis, Σημειώματα περί Ἑλλήνων (2:55), p. 27. Cf. Mystakidis, "Δύο Ἕλληνες ἐν Τυβίγγῃ" (2:21), p. 10. For other dates that have been suggested, see Hasluck, "Depopulation" (1), pp. 169–170.

55. Kritikidis, Πραγματεία περί Σάμου (41), pp. 23–24; and also the same author's Περίβασις εἰς μονάς Σάμου (48), p. 67. On Sarakinis, see Kritikidis, Τοπογραφία Σάμου (45), p. 13; and Stamatiadis, Σαμιακά (46), II, 9–10.

56. Kritikidis, Πραγματεία περί Σάμου (41), pp. 28–30.

57. Henry de Beauvau, Relation journalière du voyage du Levant (Toul, 1608), p. 106.

58. Deshayes, Voyage (1:26), p. 350.

59. Georgirenes, Description (1:45), p. 3.

60. See Kritikidis, Τοπογραφία Σάμου (45), p. 9 (fn.). See, though guardedly, the same author's compilation of new settlers by origin and date of arrival (Πραγματεία περί Σάμου [41], pp. 19–22). And cf. his much more analytical work, Περίβασις εἰς μονάς Σάμου (48), pp. 8–13. As for the Samians on Chios, see especially Kritikidis, Πραγματεία περί Σάμου (41), pp. 25–28; and also Stamatiadis, Σαμιακά (46), II, 8.

61. See N. I. Zapheiriou, Περί τῆς συγχρόνου σαμιακῆς διαλέκτου [On the Present-Day Dialect of Samos] (Athens, 1914), p. 4.

62. See Demetrius P. Paschalis, "Οἱ Ἀλβανοί εἰς τάς Κυκλάδας [The Albanians in the Cyclades]," HME (1934), 263; and Constantine Biris, Ἀρβανίτες, οἱ Δωριεῖς τοῦ νεωτέρου ἑλληνισμοῦ [Albanians, the Dorians of Modern Greece] (Athens, 1960), pp. 240–245.

63. Note, for example, the Andros surnames, Vlamis, Ghinis, Theodorizas, Isaris, Kaklamanos, Koliatsos, Korovesis, Lempesis, Mazarakis, and others; the given names of men, Zepas, Michas, Biris, and others; the given names of women, Zika, Lougga, Bilia, Pogga, and others (Paschalis, Οἱ Ἀλβανοί [62], pp. 263, 277–278).

64. See ibid., p. 280, regarding Kea, Kythnos, and Ios. Cf. Biris, Ἀρβανίτες (62), pp. 245–247. For various names of the people of Kea, see I. N. Psyllas, Ἱστορία τῆς

νήσου Κέας [*History of the Island of Kea*] (Athens, 1921), p. 213. Sauger errs when he says that Albanian colonists formed the largest parts of the populations of Kea and Kythnos Ἱστορία τῶν ἀρχαίων δουκῶν [9], p. 220). The fact that they were in a minority is clearly proven by the occurrence of surnames, place-names, and words in the dialect which are only occasionally Albanian (see Vallindas, Κυθνιακά [1:111], pp. 78, 139, 149–150).

65. Georgirenes, *Description* (1:45), p. 16.

66. Hasluck, "Albanian Settlements" (28), p. 277. The evidence of Lupazzolo, that all the new immigrants on Psara were Albanian, is quite unreliable (see Hasluck, "Depopulation" [1], pp. 168–169).

67. Hasluck, "Albanian Settlements" (28), p. 277; and see also Paschalis, Οἱ Ἀλβανοί (62), p. 282.

68. The only source in the case of Skopelos is the traveller Antonio di Milo (see Hasluck, "Albanian Settlements" [28], p. 226).

69. Georgirenes, *Description* (1:45), p. 20. *Cf.* Kritikidis, Τοπογραφία Σάμου (45), pp. 104–105.

70. On this village, see Kritikidis, Τοπογραφία Σάμου (45), p. 80. *Cf.* Georgirenes, *Description* (1:45), p. 16.

71. Kritikidis, Τοπογραφία Σάμου (45), p. 104.

72. Georgirenes, *Description* (1:45), p. 16.

73. See Kritikidis, Τοπογραφία Σάμου (45), pp. 104–105; *cf.* Stamatiadis, Σαμιακά (46), II, 8–9.

74. Hasluck, "Depopulation" (1), p. 174.

75. On the sources relating to medieval Andros, as well as the population of the island and its distribution according to the 1920 census, see Ioannis K. Voyatzidis, "Γλῶσσα καί λαογραφία τῆς νήσου Ἄνδρου [Language and Folklore of the Island of Andros]," ΑΧ, IV (1951), Part 1, pp. 16 ff.

76. Hasluck, "Albanian Settlements" (28), p. 225.

77. Sauger, Ἱστορία τῶν ἀρχαίων δουκῶν (9), p. 211.

78. Paschalis, Οἱ Ἀλβανοί (62), p. 267.

79. *Ibid.*, p. 278.

80. On this travellers' testimony, see Hasluck, "Albanian Settlements" (28), p. 225. See also M. L. Aimé-Martin, *Lettres édifiantes et curieuses concernant l'Asie, l'Afrique et l'Amérique* (Paris, 1838), I, 67. And *cf.* Voyatzidis, "Γλῶσσα καί λαογραφία" (75), part 1, pp. 62–63,part 2, p. 135.

81. Jean de Thevenot, *Relation d'un voyage fait au Levant* (Paris, 1665), p. 29.

82. Antonios Miliarakis, Ὑπομνήματα περιγραφικά τῶν Κυκλάδων νήσων κατά μέρος. Ἄνδρος-Κέως [*Descriptive Notes on the Cyclades: Andros-Kea*] (Athens, 1880), pp. 40–43, which gives Albanian as well as Frankish and Greek surnames. See also Paschalis, "Οἱ Ἀλβανοί" (62), p. 277. Note the case of the "Albanization" of the Greek village of Vourkoti (Demetrius Paschalis, "Πειρατεία καί δουλεμπορία ἀνά τάς Κυκλάδας ἐπί τουρκοκρατίας [Piracy and Slave Trading in the Cyclades under Turkish Rule]," ΑΧ, I (1948), 151–152.

83. De Tournefort, *Relation* (1:90), I, 133–134.

84. Aimé-Martin, *Lettres* (80), I, 68.

85. See Hasluck, "Albanian Settlements" (28), pp. 226–227.

86. See K. Nikodemos, Ὑπομνήματα τῆς νήσου Ψαρῶν [*Notes on the Island of Psara*] (Athens, 1826), I, 11–12, 13.

87. *Ibid.*, I, 92.

88. Hasluck, "Albanian Settlements" (28), p. 224. Paschalis presumes that at the beginning of the sixteenth century shepherds from Kranidi went across to the adja-

cent islands of Hydra and Spetsai in search of pastures for their goats; and that others from Damala in Troezen similarly went across to Poros (Οἱ Ἀλβανοί [62], p. 279).

89. Antonios A. Miaoulis, Ἱστορία τῆς νήσου Ὕδρας [History of the Island of Hydra] (Athens, 1874), p. 36.

90. Francesco Grassetto, Viaggio de Francesco Grassetto da Lonigo, lungo le coste dalmate, greco-venete ed italiche nell'anno MDXI e seguenti (Venice, 1886), p. 16. Thus, Hasluck errs when he says that these islands are mentioned for the first time in Thevet's Insulare ("Depopulation" [1], p. 163).

91. See the " Ὑπόμνημα περί τῆς νήσου Ὕδρας [Note on the Island of Hydra]," in Miaoulis, Ἱστορία Ὕδρας (89), p. 35.

92. See G. D. Kriezis, Ἱστορία τῆς νήσου Ὕδρας πρό τῆς Ἐπαναστάσεως τοῦ 1821 [History of the Island of Hydra up to the (Greek) Revolution of 1821] (Patras, 1860), pp. 10 ff.; Miaoulis, Ἱστορία (89), pp. 36–37; Vallindas, Κυθνιακά (1:111), pp. 90–91. Cf. Antonios Vallindas, Ἱστορία τῆς νήσου Κύθνου [History of the Island of Kythnos] (Athens, 1896), pp. 95–97.

93. Boschini, L'Arcipelago (3:87), p. 100.

94. On this point, see Kriezis' interesting remarks (Ἱστορία τῆς Ὕδρας [92], pp. 17–19). And see Miaoulis, Ἱστορία (89), pp. 19, 40–41.

95. Giraud, Relation (1:52), pp. 23, 24. Cf. Hasluck, "Albanian Settlements" (28), p. 224, and Biris' supposition that the Albanians of Salamis were "among those moved by the Turks at the end of the sixteenth century who were descended from the Kampiots of Acronauplia, from whom the Gaggaraioi of Athens are also descended" (Ἀρβανίτες [62], p. 241).

96. Biris, Ἀρβανίτες [62], p. 241.

97. Vallindas, Ἱστορία τῆς Κύθνου (92), p. 41.

98. Hasluck, "Albanian Settlements" (28), pp. 225–226. On these estates, see Vallindas, Ἱστορία τῆς Κύθνου (92), p. 41.

99. Sauger, Ἱστορία τῶν ἀρχαίων δουκῶν (9), p. 220.

100. Vallindas, Κυθνιακά (1:111), p. 78.

101. Vallindas, Ἱστορία τῆς Κύθνου (92), p. 41.

102. Vallindas, Κυθνιακά (1:111), pp. 76, 77–78; and see also his Ἱστορία τῆς Κύθνου (92), pp. 39–40.

103. Vallindas, Κυθνιακά (1:111), p. 77. On Frankish influences in the dialect of Kythnos, see pp. 138–139.

104. Sauger, Ἱστορία τῶν ἀρχαίων δουκῶν (9), p. 137.

105. Hasluck, "Albanian Settlements" (28), p. 225.

106. See Ioannis K. Voyatzidis, Ἀμοργός. Ἱστορικαί ἔρευναι περί τῆς νήσου [Amorgos: Historical Research on the Island] (Athens, 1918), p. 144.

107. Boschini, L'Arcipelago (3:87), p. 42.

108. Voyatzidis, Ἀμοργός (106), pp. 145–146.

109. Ibid., p. 146. Cf. the names listed by Paschalis, Οἱ Ἀλβανοί (62), p. 282.

110. The official register of the movable and immovable property of monasteries, churches, and the like.

111. Pericles G. Zerlentis, "Μετοίκησις Ἀλβανῶν εἰς Ἴον [Albanian Colonization of Ios]," Νησιωτική Ἐπετηρίς (1:90), I (1918), 260–265.

112. Paschalis, Οἱ Ἀλβανοί (62), p. 282.

113. See above, p. 77.

114. See Hasluck, "Depopulation" (1), p. 173. Cf. the landing of Maniotes (Maniatai) in the harbor of Pholegandros (Thevenot, Relation [81], p. 205, and also p. 201).

115. See Zakythinos, *Corsaires et pirates* (14), pp. 23–24, and Thevenot, *Relation* (81), p. 24.

116. See Pericles G. Zerlentis, Ἱστορικά σημειώματα ἐκ τοῦ βιβλίου τῶν ἐν Νάξῳ Καπουκίνων, 1649–1753 [*Historical Notes from the Register of Capuchins on Naxos, 1649–1753*] (Hermopolis on Syros, 1922), p. 89.

117. See Drosos Drosos, Ἱστορία τῆς νήσου Τήνου. Ἀπό τῆς πέμπτης σταυροφορίας μέχρι τῆς Ἑνετικῆς κυριαρχίας καί ἐκεῖθεν μέχρι τοῦ 1821 [*A History of the Island of Tenos from the Fifth Crusade through Venetian Rule to 1821*] (Athens, 1870), p. 6.

118. See Zerlentis, Ἱστορικά σημειώματα (116), pp. 16 ff., which also gives the relevant bibliography, also pp. 34–35, 35–36. *Cf.* Ricaut, *Histoire* (1:90), p. 353. On the behavior of Frankish pirates in the islands, see Guillet de la Guilletière, *Lacédémone ancienne et nouvelle* (Paris, 1676), pp. 60–61.

119. Jean de Gontaut Biron, *Ambassade en Turquie 1605 à 1610. II, correspondance diplomatique et documents inédits* (Paris-Auch, 1888), *passim*. On Florentine pirates, see Mertzios, Μνημεῖα μακεδονικῆς ἱστορίας (2:59), pp. 167, 170.

120. Note the Turkish accusations against English merchants in Thessalonica (Mertzios, Μνημεῖα Μακεδονικῆς ἱστορίας p. 165).

121. Thevenot, *Relation* (81), pp. 26, 196. See also des Barres, *L'Estat présent de l'Archipel* (2), I, 124–125; and Boschini, *L'Arcipelago* (3:87), p. 42. *Cf.* R. P. Pacifique, *Relation d'un voyage de Perse faict par R. P. Pacifique* (Lille, 1932), pp. 9–10.

122. Thevenot, *Relation* (81), p. 204.

123. Boschini, *L'Arcipelago* (3:87), p. 76.

124. Vacalopoulos, *Thasos* (1:59), pp. 29, 38.

125. There is a fine description in Miliarakis, Ἄνδρος–Κέως (82), pp. 66–69. But contrast this with the evidence of the Jesuit J. X. Portier (1701) in Aimé-Martin, *Lettres* (80), I, 67. *Cf.* Demetrius P. Paschalis, " Ὁ βασιλεύς τῆς Μήλου, 1677–1680 [The King of Melos, 1677–1680]," Ἀνδριακόν ἡμερολόγιον, (1927), p. 9 (of the reprint).

126. Sauger, Ἱστορία τῶν ἀρχαίων δουκῶν (9), p. 126: "These islanders are vastly superior to the other Greeks of the Aegean. They are bigger in stature, more courageous and more daring. They thus became such a threat to their Christian assailants that, while these ravaged all the other islands, they never dared land on Amorgos."

127. See Antonios Miliarakis, " Ἀμοργός [Amorgos]," ΔΙΕΕ, I (1883–1884), 587.

128. Alexandre Buchon, *Voyage dans l'Eubée, les îles Ioniennes et les Cyclades en 1841* (Paris, 1911), p. 185.

129. Boschini, *L'Arcipelago* (3:87), p. 94: "Scopoli, è affato dishabitata, e Schiati non nutrisce altro che pochi Greci, la maggior parte religiosi [Skopelos is completely uninhabited, while Skiathos sustains only a few Greeks, most of these religious]."

130. See Bordier, *Relation* (1:123), pp. 32, 33.

131. Thevenot, *Relation* (81), p. 203.

132. Karolos Gion, Ἱστορία τῆς Σίφνου ἀπό τῶν ἀρχαίων χρόνων μέχρι τῶν καθ' ἡμᾶς μετά τῆς περιγραφῆς ἀρχαίων αὐτῆς μεταλλείων χρυσοῦ καί ἀργύρου [*A History of Siphnos from Antiquity down to Our own Day, Including a Description of the Ancient Gold and Silver Mines*] (Hermopolis on Syros, 1876), p. 143.

133. See Ricaut, *Histoire* (1:90), p. 353. There is a reference to the Leghorn Pirates in Nointel's letters of 1673 (see *Journal d'Antoine Galland* [1:80], II, 173, 179, 181).

134. Thevenot, *Relation* (81), p. 205.

135. For various examples confined to the Cyclades, see the article by Demetrius P.

324 NOTES—CHAPTER 4

Paschalis, "Αἰ Κυκλάδες κατά τούς μεταξύ τῶν Τούρκων καί τῶν Βενετῶν πολέμους, 1644–1669 καί 1684–1699 [The Cyclades during the Wars between the Turks and the Venetians, 1644–1669 and 1684–1699]," Εἰς μνήμην Σπυρίδωνος Λάμπρου (Athens, 1935), pp. 132–139, which contains the relevant bibliography. *Cf.* Ricaut, *Histoire* (1:90), pp. 337–338.

136. O. Dapper, *Description exacte des isles de l'Archipel* (Amsterdam, 1703), p. 18. On the seventeenth century, see the comments of various travellers in the Νησιωτική ἐπετηρίς (1:90), I (1918), 34–35.

137. Note the example of the people of Aegina, in Giraud, *Relation* (1:52), p. 20.

138. A number of examples are given in the Νησιωτική ἐπετηρίς (1:90), I (1918), 28–31.

139. Magni, *Lettere* (1:142), pp. 292, 294.

140. *Ibid.*, pp. 292–293.

141. See the Νησιωτική ἐπετηρίς (1:90), I (1918), 28.

142. See Magni, *Lettere* (1:142), pp. 294–295; and Emmanuel Kriaras, Λεηλασία τῆς Παροικίας Πάρου. Κρητικόν ποίημα τοῦ 17ου αἰῶνος [*The Plunder of Paroikia of Paros. A Cretan Poem of the Seventeenth Century*] (Athens, 1938). *Cf.* Gion, Ἰστορία Σίφνου (132), pp. 154–157.

143. Zerlentis, Ἰστορικά σημειώματα (116), p. 37.

144. Giraud, *Relation* (1:52), p. 20.

145. Zerlentis, Ἰστορικά σημειώματα (116), pp. 37–38.

146. See Giraud, *Relation* (1:52), p. 20.

147. Zerlentis, Ἰστορικά σημειώματα (116), p. 102. *Cf.* the complaints of the inhabitants of Melos (de Tournefort, *Relation* [1:90], I, 59).

148. Zerlentis, Ἰστορικά σημειώματα (116), pp. 102–103. *Cf.* the privations of the people of Naousa (Paros) at the time of the pursuit of the pirate, Captain Antoni, in 1677 (Michael I. Markopoli, Τουρκικαί βιαιοπραγίαι ἐν Ναούσῃ τῆς Πάρου. Ἐπεισόδιον τοῦ ἔτους 1677 [*Turkish Outrages in Naousa, Paros: An Incident in 1677*] [Naxos, 1893], pp. 10–23).

149. De Tournefort, *Relation* (1:90), I, 59.

150. Giraud, *Relation* (1:52), pp. 20–21.

151. *Ibid.*, p. 21.

152. Dapper, *Description* (136), p. 283.

153. Galland, *Journal* (1:108), I, 38.

154. In 1687 Kel Mehmed Pasha launched an assault on the monastery of Seriphos (see Tryphon Evangelidis, Ἡ νῆσος Σέριφος καί αἰ περί αὐτήν νησῖδες [*Seriphos and Surrounding Islands*] [Hermopolis on Syros, 1909], p. 132).

155. Magni, *Lettere* (1:142), p. 294; and "Mr. Roberts' Adventures among the Corsairs of the Levant . . ." in William Hacke, ed., *A Collection of Original Voyages* (London, 1699), pp. 8, 25. The latter work contains material on the pirates' way of life and their leaders' profits.

156. De Tournefort, *Relation* (1:90), I, 58. *Cf.* Antonios Miliarakis, "Κίμωλος [Kimolos]," ΔΙΕΕ, VI (1901–1906), 23–24; and Chatzidakis, Ἰστορία Μήλου (4), pp. 157–160.

157. See du Mont, *Voyages* (1:90), IV, 152, 155–157. On the licentiousness of the women of Kimolos and Melos, see also de Tournefort, *Relation* (1:90), I, 68. On the history of Kimolos and Melos, see also Hasluck, "Depopulation" (1), p. 160; and *cf.* Miliarakis, "Κίμωλος" (156), pp. 27–28. On the Frankish origin and surnames of many of the people of Kimolos, see Miliarakis, pp. 25–26, and on the name "Argentiera," pp. 18 ff.

158. Boschini, *L'Arcipelago* (3:87), p. 28.

159. De Tournefort, *Relation* (1:90), I, 58.

160. Sauger, 'Ιστορία τῶν ἀρχαίων δουκῶν (9), p. 137.

161. Zerlentis, 'Ιστορικά σημειώματα (116), pp. 17, 31–32, 60–62. *Cf.* Markopoli, Τουρκικαί βιαιοπραγίαι (148), pp. 3 ff.; and Roberts, *Adventures* (155), pp. 46–47.

162. Zerlentis, 'Ιστορικά σημειώματα (116), pp. 17–18, 88.

163. See des Barres, *L'Estat présent de l'Archipel* (2), I, 151.

164. Ricaut, *Histoire* (1:90), p. 338.

165. See *ibid.*, p. 362; and also Vallindas, Κυθνιακά (1:111), p. 82.

166. See du Loir, *Voyages* (1:108), p. 5. This occurred on Mykonos and Syros in 1711 (see Antonios P. Katsouros, Κουρσάροι καί σκλάβοι. 'Ανέκδοτα μυκονιάτικα καί συριανά ἔγγραφα [*Corsairs and Slaves. Unpublished Documents from Mykonos and Syros*] [Syros, 1948], pp. 34–45). In 1678 the monks of Melos defended and saved the cadi of the island, who had taken refuge in the monastery (Zerlentis, 'Ιστορικά σημειώματα [116], p. 94).

167. See Dapper, *Description* (136), p. 335, for the example of Mykonos at the end of the seventeenth century; and de Tournefort, *Relation* (1:90), I, 58, for the example of Melos at the beginning of the eighteenth century. The Greek governor not only collected the poll tax but also had the right (as did the aga of janissaries in the towns of Turkey) to punish the inhabitants. See, for instance, what Katsouros says about Syros in 1722 (Κουρσάροι καί σκλάβοι [166], pp. 35–36). The main responsibility of the Greek governor, who was appointed by the *kapudan pasha*, was the collection of the tithe and the tax *yemeklik*.

168. Dapper, *Description* (136), p. 283. One source says that the few Turks on Aegina were also afraid to remain on the island (see Constantine Biris, Τά 'Αττικά τοῦ 'Εβλιᾶ Τσελεμπῆ. Αἱ 'Αθῆναι καί τά περίχωρά των κατά τόν 17ον αἰῶνα [*Attica according to Evliya Tschelebi, Athens and Environs in the Seventeenth Century*] [Athens, 1959], p. 68).

169. Zerlentis, 'Ιστορικά σημειώματα (116), pp. 69–70. *Cf.* Febvre, *Théâtre de la Turquie* (1:152), p. 411.

170. Zerlentis, 'Ιστορικά σημειώματα (116), p. 70. Zerlentis describes the plunder and devastation of the bishopric of Telos by Crevelier and others because its inhabitants had failed to come to the assistance of the pirate Daniel.

171. *Ibid.*, p. 16 (on Naxos). See Vallindas, 'Ιστορία τῆς Κύθνου (92), pp. 41, 49, 69.

172. Zerlentis, 'Ιστορικά σημειώματα (116), p. 16.

173. *Ibid.*, pp. 27, 67–68.

174. De Tournefort, *Relation* (1:90), I, 58.

175. Zerlentis, 'Ιστορικά σημειώματα (116), pp. 42–43, 48–49, 50 (concerning the benefactions of the pirate Daniel). *Cf.* p. 53, on the benefactions of the pirate Auger.

176. *Ibid.*, pp. 18–19.

177. See Vallindas, 'Ιστορία τῆς Κύθνου (92), pp. 49–50, on the pirate Kardi, as well as another, Louis Thibaut from Toulon.

178. Zerlentis, 'Ιστορικά σημειώματα (116), pp. 35–36.

179. *Ibid.*, pp. 95–96.

180. *Ibid.*

181. See Thucydides, *The Peloponnesian War* (Teubner edition, Leipzig, 1901) I, part 5, pp. 1–2. And *cf.* Vallindas, 'Ιστορία τῆς Κύθνου (92), p. 49.

182. See des Barres, *L'Estate présent de l'Archipel* (2), II, 142–157, for the strange details about the interference of Panagiotes Nikousios, interpreter of the Sublime Porte, in the execution of Téméricourt.

183. Sauger, Ἡ παροῦσα κατάστασις (1:178), pp. 25–26.

184. *Ibid.*, pp. 17, 31–32, 60–62.

185. *Ibid.*, pp. 23–25.

186. There are some interesting comments in Zerlentis, Ἱστορικά σημειώματα (116), pp. 17–20, and *passim.*

187. See Ricaut, *Histoire* (1:90), pp. 338–340.

188. *Ibid.*, p. 339.

189. See Vacalopoulos, *Origins of the Greek Nation* (1:62), p. 98.

190. See Zerlentis, Ἱστορικά σημειώματα (116), p. 6, which also gives the bibliography.

191. See Georg Hofmann, "Apostolato dei Gesuiti nell'Oriente greco (1583–1773)," OCP, I (1935), 145, 146, 154–156; and Zerlentis, Ἱστορικά σημειώματα (116), pp. 20–23.

192. Zerlentis, Ἱστορικά σημειώματα, *passim.*

193. *Ibid.*, pp. 56–57.

194. For slave prices, which were determined by the factors of sex and age, see Belon, *Observations* (1:123), p. 88b. It is curious to find references to the purchase of Turkish slaves by Greek islanders (see Katsouros, Κουρσάροι καί σκλάβοι [166], pp. 13–14, 18–19; other examples are given by Paschalis, "Πειρατεία" (82), pp. 152–154). *Cf.* the ransom payment in Byzantine times for buying back prisoners: "δι᾽ ἀνδρός ἐπιστέλλω τῆς παρά τῶν ἀσεβῶν πειραθέντα δουλείας καί νῦν ἀδυναμίᾳ τοῦ τό χρέος ἐκτίσαι περιιόντα [I hold command with a man who has suffered slavery under the barbarians and who is now unable to pay off his debt]" (Raymond J. Loenertz, *Correspondance de Manuel Calecas* [Rome, 1950], p. 250).

195. See Robert de Dreux, *Voyage* (1:154), p. 57. *Cf.* Chesneau's comments in the year 1547 (*Le Voyage* [2:57], pp. 34–35), and the cruder but more realistic comments of du Fresne-Canaye in the year 1573 (*Voyage* [1:123], pp. 95–96). Von Mitrović provides similar descriptions (Ἡ Κωνσταντινούπολις [1:123], pp. 109–110). All travellers visiting Constantinople invariably gave accounts of its slave bazaars; it would thus be superfluous to cite more.

196. Magni, *Lettere* (1:142), pp. 205–206.

197. See du Loir, *Voyages* (1:108), p. 58.

198. See Georgieviz, *De Turcarum moribus* (1:26), pp. 85–86. For additional comment on prisoners and slaves, see pp. 76–85; and also Dernsçhwam, *Tagebuch* (1:20), p. 68. *Cf.* magic practiced by the Turks to prevent the escape of slaves (Gerlach, *Tagebuch* [1:22], p. 481, and Gassot, *Discours* [2:49], p. 12a).

199. See de Dreux, *Voyage* (1:154), p. 54. Gerlach provides some interesting detail (*Tagebuch* [1:22], pp. 493–494. See also du Mont, *Voyages* (1:90), II, 372–377.

200. Vratislav von Mitrović, Ἡ Κωνσταντινούπολις (1:123), pp. 143–145. See also Reinhold Lubenau, *Beschreibung der Reisen* (Königsberg, 1912), I, 216–220. There is further comment on the prisoners on pp. 212–221.

201. See du Mont, *Voyages* (1:90), II, 372–373. *Cf.* Deshayes, *Voyage* (1:26), pp. 112–113. On the "Franco," which was known as far as Algeria, see also d'Aranda, *Relation* (21), p. 22. On the national characteristics of slaves physically, see Magni, *Lettere* (1:142), pp. 207–209.

202. See Gerlach, *Tagebuch* (1:22), p. 209.

203. There is much detail in Georgieviz, *De Turcarum moribus* (1:26), pp. 89–92, and Dernschwam, *Tagebuch* (1:20), pp. 68–69, 73. See also Gerlach, *Tagebuch* (1:22), p. 412, on the lives of prisoners in the jails of the sultan and his pashas, as well as their escapes. Galley slaves frequently killed their guards and absconded (Gerlach, *Tagebuch*, p. 491, and *passim*). *Cf.* pp. 335, 373, and elsewhere. For still further detail

concerning escapes by slaves, see p. 501. There is a fifteenth-century Turkish document relating to the recapture of slaves in Beldiceanu, *Actes de Mehmed II* (1:29), I, p. 143.

204. See Georgieviz, *De Turcarum moribus* (1:26), pp. 92–93. Tenos, the only island in the middle of the Aegan under Venetian sovereignty, was one steppingstone on an escape route of Christian slaves to Crete, thence to Italy (see Stergios Spanakis, Μνημεῖα τῆς Κρητικῆς ἱστορίας [*Monuments of Cretan History*] [Herakleion, 1958] IV, 64; for the report of Benedetto Moro, "Relazione, 1602."

205. Georgieviz, *De Turcarum moribus* (1:26), p. 92; Johan Sommers, *Wasser und Land-reyse, gethan nach der Levante* (Amsterdam, 1664), p. 60; Zerlentis, Σημειώματα περί ʽΕλλήνων (2:55), pp. 13–14, 18–28; B. A. Mystakidis, "Οἱ Ράλλαι [The Ralles Family]," ΕΕΒΣ, V (1928), 273–274; and his "Δύο ʽΈλληνες ἐν Τυβίγγῃ" (2:21), pp. 3–6. In 1589 the Athenian nun, Philotheï Venizelou, died a martyr's death because she was found sheltering female Christian slaves in her convent (see Chrysostomos Papadopoulos, Νεομάρτυρες [*The New Martyrs*], 2nd ed. [Athens, 1934], p. 27, which contains the relevant bibliography). See also Constantine D. Mertzios, " ʽΗ ὁσία Φιλοθέη. ʼΑνέκδοτα ἔγγραφα [St. Philotheï: Unpublished Documents]," ʽΕλληνικά, XIII (1954), 122–128. *Cf.* the decapitation or incarceration of Roman Catholic priests for the same reasons (Gerlach, *Tagebuch* [1:22], pp. 40, 45).

206. Crusius, *Turcograeciae* (1:53), pp. 82 ff.

207. See Silvio G. Mercati, "Di Giovanni Simeonachis Protopapa di Candia," *Miscellanea G. Mercati*, III (1946), 329–330, on the appeals of Ioannis Simeonakis, priest and archpriest of Candia.

208. Zakythinos, *Corsaires et pirates* (14), p. 37.

209. See Katsouros, Κουρσάροι καὶ σκλάβοι (166), pp. 12, 16, 27, 30 ff.

210. See Mystakidis, "Οἱ Ράλλαι" (205), p. 277.

211. Leonidas C. Zoïs, "Ταμεῖον ἐξαγορᾶς αἰχμαλώτων [A Fund for the Ransom of Slaves]," ΕΕΒΣ, V (1928), 342–347.

212. Paschalis, "Πειρατεία" (82), p. 159.

213. Koukoules, ʽΗ νέα ἑλληνική γλῶσσα (1:175), pp. 27–28.

214. Nikolaos Katramis, Φιλολογικὰ ἀνάλεκτα Ζακύνθου [*Literary Analects on* (Zacynthus, 1880), p. 56. *Cf.* the song from Amorgos in Miliarakis, " ʼΑμοργός" (127), pp. 645–646. A variant is also sung at table by mountain people from.the Pindus who have travelled at one time or another to different parts of the East and abroad (see Christos M. Enisleidis, ʽΗ Πίνδος καὶ τά χωριά τῆς: Σπήλαιον–Γρεβενά–Σαμαρίνα [*The Pindus and its Villages: Spelaion, Grevena, and Samarina*] (Athens, 1951), p. 110.

215. See Zapheirios D. Gavalas, Περί τῆς νήσου Σικίνου [*Concerning the Island of Sikinos*] (Athens, 1885), p. 39; Gavalas, Φολέγανδρος (9), p. 23; and Miliarakis, " ʼΑμοργός" (127), p. 593. On Kimolos, see du Mont, *Voyages* (1:90), IV, 156. On the castle of Melos, see also Chatzidakis, ʽΙστορία Μήλου (4), pp. 153–157.

216. One of these, dating from the fourteenth century, can be seen on the domain of the monastery of Docheiariou, three-quarters of an hour from Miriophyton in Chalcidice, near ancient Olynthos (see Anastasios Orlandos, "Βυζαντινός πύργος παρά τήν ʼΌλυνθον [A Byzantine Tower near Olynthos]," ΕΕΒΣ, XIII [1937], 393–396). See also Zoïs, Ζάκυνθος (20), p. 65.

217. These watchtowers or observation posts went by various names in different parts of Greece—βιγλοστάσια, βιγλαριά, βίγλες, μεροβίγλια, νυχτοβίγλια, στροβίγλια (and in the Ionian Islands, βαρδιόλες or κοῦλες). Regarding the βιγλαριά (hence βιγλάρηδες or βιγλάτορες meaning watchmen or sentries; and hence, too, the surname Βίγλαρης), see Vacalopoulos, *Thasos* (1:59), pp. 29–30. On Chios, three or

four of the smaller villages, those with populations ranging from thirty or fifty up to a hundred persons, would combine to erect observation posts around the coast of the island at intervals of three or four miles from one another. Each village delegated two men to scan the sea and thus to guard against Turkish invasion from the opposite shore of Asia Minor (Thevenot, *Relation* [81], p. 185). As for the βίγλες, note the toponym Μεγάλη Βίγλα, near the village of Provlakas in Chalcidice (Belon, *Observations* [1:123], p. 37a). On the βιγλοστάσια, see Νησιωτική ἐπετηρίς (1:90), I (1918), 18. And on the κοῦλες, see Zoïs, Ζάκυνθος (20), p. 15, where several examples are mentioned.

218. For details on pirates who sailed the Greek seas in the middle of the sixteenth century, see Belon, *Observations* (1:123), pp. 87a–89a. On the appointment of sentries, see the seventeenth-century *kanunname* of Rhodes and Kos, in Barkan, *XV ve XVI inci asırlarda esasları* (1:18), p. 340. According to an old tradition, the inhabitants of the villages of Lemnos were commissioned as coastal garrisons, in return for which they were exempted from the payment of extraordinary taxes (see p. 239). *Cf.* the sentries in the islands of the Duchy of the Aegean, similarly according to an old family tradition (Zerlentis, Γράμματα Φράγκων δουκῶν [1:124], p. 104). For Tenos, see Constantine Sathas, Μνημεῖα ἑλληνικῆς ἱστορίας [*Monuments of Greek History*] (Paris, 1882), III, 281–282. *Cf.* the *vigliatiko* (garrison tax) in Euboea in 1415 (see Sathas, p. 125). On the lighting of bonfires, see de Gontaut Biron, *Ambassade en Turquie* (119), p. 49. *Cf.* Zakythinos, *Corsaires et pirates* (14), pp. 32–33, which contains a partial bibliography on pirates.

219. See Zoïs, Ζάκυνθος (20), p. 65; Voyatzidis, "Γλῶσσα καί λαογραφία Ἄνδρου" (75), p. 50. *Cf.* the location of the watchtower on Hydra (Miaoulis, Ἱστορία Ὕδρας [89], pp. 17–18).

Chapter 5

1. *Cf.* Ἱστορία πολιτική τῆς Κωνσταντινουπόλεως (1:3), p. 27; and Georgius Sphrantzes, Χρονικόν [*Chronicle*], ed. Immanuel Bekker (Bonn, 1838), p. 308. Similarly, Mohammed II sought to regularize his relations not only with raias but also with Jews and Armenians through their religious leaders, Mose Kapsali and Chovakim respectively (see C. G. Papadopoulos, *Les Privilèges du Patriarcat Oecumenique* [*Communauté Grecque Orthodoxe dans l'empire ottoman*] [Paris, 1924], pp. 83–84; and also Babinger, *Mehmed der Eroberer* [1:8], p. 122).

2. For details of the position of non-Moslem raias in Middle Eastern countries between 622 and 1517, see Fattal, *Le Statut légal* (1:1); and on relations between the Christian Church and the Moslem State, see especially pp. 214 ff. See also Gibb and Bowen, *Islamic Society* (1:17), I¹, 20; and I², 207–208. The section of Gibb and Bowen's study dealing with the position of the *cimmi* ("tolerated infidels"), particularly Orthodox Christians, under the Ottomans (I², 207–261) is not fully documented; it does not rely on all the pertinent sources (this is very obvious at p. 207, fn. 1). On the words *kâfir* and *ahl al-kitâb*, see the appropriate entries in the *Encyclopaedia of Islam*.

3. See Apostolos Vacalopoulos, "Οἱ δημοσιευμένες ὁμιλίες τοῦ ἀρχιεπισκόπου Θεσσαλονίκης Ἰσιδώρου ὡς ἱστορική πηγή γιά τήν γνώση τῆς πρώτης τουρκοκρατίας στήν Θεσσαλονίκη (1387–1402) [The Published Homilies of Isidorus, Archbishop of Thessalonica, as an Historical Source for Knowledge of the First Turkish Dominion in Thessalonica (1387–1402)]," Μακεδονικά, IV (1960), 31–32. *Cf.* N.P. Eleutheriadis, Ἀνατολικαί μελέται. Τά προνόμια τοῦ οἰκουμενικοῦ πατριαρχείου [*Eastern Studies. The Privileges of the Oecumenical Patriarchate*] (Smyrna, 1909), I, 159 ff.

4. Belon, *Observations* (1:123), p. 180a.

5. Various opinions and theories have been advanced in an attempt to explain Mohammed II's attitude towards Christians and his willingness to grant privileges. These are set forth by Papadopoulos, *Les Privilèges* (1), pp. 73–101. On the privileges themselves, see pp. 103 ff. Papadopoulos' book, an excellent one, examines the whole question of privileges mainly from a legal viewpoint. *Cf.* Nicolaos Pantazopoulos, "Τινὰ περὶ τῆς ἐννοίας τῶν "προνομίων" ἐπὶ Τουρκοκρατίας [Some Suggestions concerning the Meaning of 'Privileges' under Turkish Rule]," 'Αρχεῖον ἰδιωτικοῦ δικαίου, 10 (1943), 6–8. See also Papadopoulos, *Les Privilèges* (1), pp. 5–26.

6. We still lack a monograph on George Scholarios. A careful and systematic study of his "Απαντα (2:4) will undoubtedly bring to light much new information. Professor Constantine Bonis' study, "Γεώργιος–Γεννάδιος Κουρτέσης ὁ Σχολάριος (1405–1475) [George-Gennadius Courtesis, Called Scholarios (1405–1475)]," Νέα ἑστία, LIII (1953), 841–858, is limited mainly to those of Scholarios' works which his editors, Louis Petit, Xenophon Siderides, and Martin Jugie, included in "Απαντα [2:4] (*cf.* the relevant article by Martin Jugie in the *Dictionnaire de théologie catholique*, 14 (1941), 1524–1570, which contains the bibliography on Scholarios). The same limitations also apply to the study by Adamantios N. Diamantopoulos, "Γεννάδιος ὁ Σχολάριος ὡς ἱστορικὴ πηγὴ τῶν περὶ τὴν "Αλωσιν χρόνων [Gennadius Scholarios as an Historical Source for the Period of the Capture]," 'Ελληνικά, IX (1936), 285–308. Bonis, in his study, pays tribute to the many and varied intellectual gifts of Gennadius, but condemns him for his opportunism and religious fanaticism at a critical time in the nation's history. However, Nikolaos Tomadakis denies that Gennadius possessed these qualities. See his article, "Γεώργιος ὁ Σχολάριος καὶ αἱ πολιτικαί του ἀντιλήψεις [George Scholarios and his Political Thought]," 'Εκκλησία, 31 (1954), 257–261, 292–295.

7. Scholarios, "Απαντα (2:4), I, lx–x.

8. Diamantopoulos, "Γεννάδιος ὁ Σχολάριος" (6), pp. 287, 290–293.

9. For full details, see Martin Jugie, "George Scholarios, professeur de philosophie," SBN, 5 (1939), 482–494. *Cf.* Scholarios, "Απαντα (2:4), I, x, xiii, and on Theodore Sophianos, 277–283, where there is a panegyric to him.

10. Scholarios, "Απαντα (2:4), I, x–xi.

11. On Gennadius' Unionist proclivities before 1443, see the special chapter by Petit, Siderides, and Jugie, in "Απαντα (2:4), VIII, 33*–47*, particularly pp. 44*– 47* and also the review by Adamantios Diamantopoulos in EEBΣ, 13 (1937), 433–435. On Scholarios' standpoint from just before the councils of Ferrara and Florence up to the Capture, see Diamantopoulos, "Γεννάδιος ὁ Σχολάριος" (6), pp. 294–299.

12. See Martin Jugie, "L'Unionisme de Georges Scholarios," *Echos d'Orient*, 36 (1937), 65–86, where Scholarios' attitude is explained in terms of his fierce national pride. Perhaps the more reliable view is that of Adamantios Diamantopoulos, who suggests that when Scholarios used the phrase πάτριον δόγμα ("faith of our fathers") he was referring to the fathers of the Church, not to the fathers of the nation (see his review in EEBΣ, 13 [1937], 434).

13. See Marc Eugenicus of Ephesus, " 'Επιτελεύτιοι ὁμιλίαι παρούσης τῆς τῶν ὀρθοδόξων συνάξεως καὶ πολλῶν τῆς συγκλήτου καὶ τῆς πολιτείας [Final Sermons before an Assemblage of Orthodox, Senate, and State Dignitaries]," in Lambros, Παλαιολόγεια καὶ Πελοποννησιακά (3:4), I, 37–38.

14. Scholarios, "Απαντα (2:4), VIII, 46*.

15. Lambros, Παλαιολόγεια καὶ Πελοποννησιακά (3:4), I, 40–41.

16. *Ibid.*, p. 103. For Gennadius' views on the calumnies of his enemies, see *ibid.*, II, 106–119. See also Scholarios, "Απαντα (2:4), I, xi–xii; III, xi–xiv; and especially III, xiii–xiv.

17. Scholarios, Ἅπαντα (2:4), I, xii, 280.
18. Kritoboulos of Imbros, Συγγραφή ἱστοριῶν (1:7), II, 2 (1).
19. Scholarios, Ἅπαντα (2:4), IV, 224.
20. Kritoboulos of Imbros, Συγγραφή ἱστοριῶν (1:7), II, 2 (1).
21. Diamantopoulos, "Γεννάδιος ὁ Σχολάριος" (6), p. 300.
22. Scholarios, Ἅπαντα (2:4), I, xii–xiii; IV, 224–225.
23. See Andreas Xyngopoulos, Σχεδίασμα ἱστορίας τῆς θρησκευτικῆς ζωγραφικῆς μετὰ τήν Ἅλωσιν [A Brief History of Religious Painting from the Fall of Constantinople] (Athens, 1957), p. 59.
24. Scholarios, Ἅπαντα (2:4), I, 292.
25. Papadopoulos, Les Privilèges (1), 83–84. A chief rabbi was the recipient of many honors from the sultan, including, so it would seem, that of precedence over the Oecumenical Patriarch. He was responsible for the apportionment of taxes among the various Jewish communities, the actual collection of taxes by means of a system of special agents, and the remission of such monies to the state exchequer (see Babinger, Mehmed der Eroberer [1:8], p. 122). From the time of Arcadius and Honorius the Byzantines had accorded similar privileges to the Jews of the Empire, including the right to maintain their own ecclesiastical courts, where Jewish law, and not the Roman jus civile, applied (see Fattal, Le Statut légal [1:1], p. 345).
26. Kritoboulos of Imbros, Συγγραφή ἱστοριῶν (1:7), II, 2 (3).
27. Ibid., II, 2.
28. Ἱστορία πολιτική τῆς Κωνσταντινουπόλεως (1:3), p. 28.
29. Ibid., pp. 27–28, 30–31. Cf. Phrantzes, Χρονικόν (1), pp. 304–306. On the question of the publication of the Ἱστορία Πολιτική, its relation to other apposite works, and the problem of its authorship, see the brief bibliographical note in Theodore Papadopoullos, Studies and Documents relating to the History of the Greek Church and People under the Turkish Domination (Brussels, 1952), pp. xx–xxi.
30. Phrantzes, Χρονικόν (1), p. 308. The disputed passage itself is discussed by Nikolaos Tomadakis, Περὶ ἀλώσεως τῆς Κωνσταντινουπόλεως (1453). Συναγωγή κειμένων μετὰ προλόγου καὶ βιογραφικῶν μελετημάτων περὶ τῶν τεσσάρων ἱστοριογράφων [On the Fall of Constantinople (1453). A Collection of Texts with a Preface and Biographical Sketches of the Four Historians] (Athens, 1953), pp. 156–157. Cf. Tomadakis' conclusion on the authorship and reliability of this lengthy chronicle (pp. 162–163).
31. See Halil Inalcik, Fatih devrinde üzerinde tetkikler ve vesikalar [Researches and Documents relating to the Period of the Conqueror] (Ankara, 1954), I, 151.
32. Friedrich Giese, "Die geschichtlichen Grundlagen für die Stellung des Christlichen Untertanen im osmanischen Recht [The Historical Background of the Position of Christian Subjects in Ottoman Law]," Islam, 19 (1931), 264–268. Cf. Fattal, Le Statut légal (1:1), pp. 218 ff., 344 ff.
33. See Gunnar Hering, "Das islamische Recht und die Investitur des Gennadios Scholarios (1454) [Moslem Law and the Investiture of Gennadius Scholarios (1454)]," Balkan Studies, 2 (1961), 240, in which he considers the passage authentic because of its striking stylistic similarities with the Chronicon Minus.
34. Scholarios, Ἅπαντα (2:4), IV, 266. Cf. his boast in 1460 in his Θρῆνον [Lamentation], to which we have previously alluded, that the re-establishment of the patriarchal throne was due entirely to his own efforts (Scholarios, Ἅπαντα [2:4], I, 292).
35. Amantos, Σχέσεις Ἑλλήνων καί Τούρκων (2:39), I, 125, fn. 1.
36. See Gerlach, Tagebuch (1:22), p. 469, where he speaks about the behavior of Greeks at their important religious festivals, as well as their freedom of movement, even at night: "darinnen singen, lesen und beten, und ihnen von den Türcken kein

Leyd geschiehet und dessvegen haben sie von dem Sultan Mehmet einen sondern freyheitsbrief [then they sing, read, and pray, entirely unmolested by the Turks, because Sultan Mohammed has granted them a charter of freedom]." *Cf.* Ypsilantis, Τά μετά τήν "Αλωσιν (1:92), p. 52.

37. See the text in Gedeon, 'Επίσημα γράμματα τουρκικά (2:2), pp. 9–14.

38. The relevant documents are in Joseph Kabrda, "Sur les bérats des métropolites orthodoxes dans l'ancien empire ottoman au XVIIIᵉ siècle," Известия на Българското Историческо Дружество, XVI–XVII (Sofia, 1939), 259–268; and also in Panagiotis I. Zepos, "'Ανέκδοτα τουρκικά έγγραφα έκ τῶν ἀρχείων Βεροίας καί Θεσσαλονίκης [Unpublished Turkish Documents from the Archives of Veroia and Thessalonica]," Αρχεῖον 'ιδιωτικοῦ δικαίου, 11 (1944), especially pp. 75–89. Both these studies contain the older, though still comprehensive, bibliography.

39. See Beldiceanu, *Actes de Mehmed II* (1:29), p. 137. *Cf.* Franz Babinger, *Sultanische Urkunden zur Geschichte der osmanischen Wirtschaft und Staatsverwaltung am Ausgang der Herrschaft Mehmeds II des Eroberers* [*Sultanic Documents relating to the History of Ottoman Economics and Administration towards the End of the Reign of Mohammed II the Conqueror*] (Munich, 1956), pp. 229–232, which includes the relevant bibliography. *Cf.* also the interesting text of a berat of 1604 in Gedeon, 'Επίσημα γράμματα τουρκικά (2:2), pp. 87–97.

40. On the official designation of privileges, see Eleutheriadis, 'Ανατολοκαί μελέται (3), I, 214.

41. The relevant bibliography is in Zinkeisen, *Geschichte des osmanischen Reiches* (2:40), II, 13; and also in Constantine Amantos, "Οἱ προνομιακοί ὁρισμοί τοῦ μουσουλμανισμοῦ ὑπέρ τῶν Χριστιανῶν [The Moslem Statutes Conferring Privileges on Christians]," 'Ελληνικά, 9 (1936), 112–115, 143. *Cf.* Papadopoullos, *Studies* (29), p. 5.

42. Scholarios, "Απαντα (2:4), IV, 265.

43. Anonymous, Πατριαρχική ἱστορία Κωνσταντινουπόλεως [*Patriarchal History of Constantinople*], ed. Immanuel Bekker (Bonn, 1849), p. 94.

44. For some typical "calumnies," as well as comment on Turkish justice, see Carlier de Pinon, *Voyage* (1:89), p. 107. *Cf.* the terrible imprecations peculiar to Epirus, where these "calumnies" are wished upon others ("κακή ἀβανιά νά σέ πάρη" or "νά σοῦ ῥθη ἀβανιά" ["the foulest of curses upon you"]). *Cf.* other expressions, as well as the word "ἀβανιοκαμένος" ("accursed"), appearing in Phaedon Koukoules, 'Η νέα ἑλληνική γλῶσσα (1:175), pp. 28–29.

45. *Cf.* the present-day expression "τοῦ ἄλλαξαν τήν πίστη στό ξύλο" ("before I have finished with you, you will want to give up your faith") (Koukoules, 'Η νέα ἑλληνική γλῶσσα (1:175), p. 29).

46. These deportees were known as σουργούνηδες, from the Turkish *sürgün*.

47. Gerlach, *Tagebuch* (1:22), p. 462.

48. Carlier de Pinon, *Voyage* (1:89), p. 85.

49. 'Ιστορία πολιτική τῆς Κωνσταντινουπόλεως (1:3), pp. 28–29. On the transfer of the patriarchate, and a description of the convent of Pammakaristos, see Manuel I. Gedeon, Χρονικά τοῦ πατριαρχικοῦ οἴκου καί ναοῦ [*Chronicles of the Patriarchal Household and Church*] (Constantinople, 1884), pp. 52–62. See also Agathangelos Ninolakis; Μελέτιος ὁ Πηγᾶς, ὁ Κρής πατριάρχης 'Αλεξανδρείας καί ἐπιτηρητής τοῦ οἰκουμενικοῦ θρόνου, 1545–1602 [*Meletios Pegas, Cretan Patriarch of Alexandria and Keeper of the Oecumenical Throne, 1545–1602*] (Canea, 1903), p. 73, fn. 1; and Gennadius (Gennadius Arambatzoglou), Metropolitan of Heliopolis, "Σημειώσεις περί τινων ἐν Κωνσταντινουπόλει ναῶν καί ἰδίως τοῦ Πατριαρχικοῦ μετά τό 1453 [Notes on Some Churches in Constantinople, the Patriarchal Church especially, after 1453]," 'Ορθοδοξία, 11 (1936), 396–403; 12 (1937), 11–20, 51–57. *Cf.* Chrysostomos Papado-

poulos, Ἡ ἐξωτερική κατάστασις τῆς Ἐκκλησίας Κωνσταντινουπόλεως ἀπό τῆς ἁλώσεως μέχρι τοῦ ιη' αἰῶνος [*The External Situation of the Constantinopolitan Church from the Capture up to the Eighteenth Century*], ed. Gregorios Papamichael (Athens, 1950), p. 17 (fn. 2 of the same page contains the relevant bibliography); Pericles Zerlentis, Σημειώματα περί Ἑλλήνων (2:55), p. 29. One of Zerlentis' "notes," on Patriarch Jeremiah, mentions that he ascended the throne on 1 January 1588 and continues: "but his former residence, the convent of Pammakaristos, was confiscated by the sultan." *Cf.* also p. 31, where there is a letter of Iakobos Miloïtis', dated 5 October 1588 in Cracow, in which he says that when he had been in Tübingen the previous year the patriarchate was seized and the patriarch went to Moscow in May in order to solicit funds from the Czar for the construction of a new residence. For a description of the patriarchate in the second half of the seventeenth century, see Gennadius Arambatzoglou, Φωτίειος βιβλιοθήκη [*Photian Library*], part 1 (Constantinople, 1933), 217 ff.

50. See Georgios A. Sotiriou, " Ἡ εἰκών τῆς Παμμακαρίστου. Ψηφιδωτή φορητή εἰκών τῆς Παμμακαρίστου τοῦ πατριαρχικοῦ ναοῦ τῆς Κωνσταντινουπόλεως [The Icon of Pammakaristos. A Portable Mosaic Icon from Pammakaristos Belonging to the Patriarchal Household of Constantinople]," ΠΑΑ, 8 (1933), 359–368.

51. The function of the exarch was to collect this revenue (see Gerlach, *Tagebuch* [1:22], p. 393, where there is a reference to Theodosios Zygomalas' exarchate in the Aegean islands in 1577. See the relevant encyclical letter of Patriarch Jeremiah II in Legrand, *Zygomalas* (2:14), pp. 120–122 and *cf.* pp. 123 ff.

52. B. de Khitrowo, *Itinéraires russes en Orient* (Geneva, 1889), p. 60 (concerning the monk Isaiah of Chilandar).

53. See Gedeon, Χρονικά τοῦ πατριαρχικοῦ οἴκου καί ναοῦ (49), pp. 65–69, 135 ff. There is a bibliography of the financial condition of the patriarchate in Papadopoullos, *Studies* (29), p. 132, fns. 2 and 4. See also the systematic and enlightening analysis by Georg Hofmann, "Das bischöfliche Abgabenwesen im Patriarchat von Konstantinopel vom XI bis zur Mitte des XIX Jahrhunderts [Episcopal Remittances to the Patriarchate of Constantinople from the Eleventh to the Middle of the Nineteenth Century]," OCP, 5 (1939), 434–513 (and, on the period of Turkish rule, pp. 477–513).

54. Deshayes, *Voyage* (1:26), p. 122.

55. Christophoros Angelos, Ἐγχειρίδιον περί τῆς καταστάσεως τῶν σήμερον εὑρισκομένων Ἑλλήνων (2:49), pp. 838–842. On Angelos and his works, see Stephanos Makrymichalos, "Βιβλιογραφία τῶν ἔργων Χριστοφόρου Ἀγγέλου, 1575;—1638 [A Bibliography of the Works of Christophoros Angelos, 1575?—1638]," Βιβλιόφιλος, 7 (1953), 43–51. There are two other relevant studies by Makrymichalos, "Τό χειρόγραφο τῆς "πονήσεως" τοῦ Χριστοφόρου Ἀγγέλου [Christophoros Angelos' Work Manuscript]," Βιβλιόφιλος, 11 (1957), 28–29; and "Χριστόφορος Ἄγγελος ὁ ἑλληνοδιδάσκαλος τῆς Ὀξφόρδης [Christophoros Angelos, Greek teacher in Oxford]," Πελοποννησιακά, 2 (1957), 219–255. There are some interesting remarks on the way of life and income of the clergy in Crusius, *Turcograeciae* (1:53), pp. 486–487.

56. For details, see Angelos, Ἐγχειρίδιον (2:49), pp. 842–844. Regarding priests and deacons, see pp. 844–848.

57. See Kritoboulos of Imbros, Συγγραφή ἱστοριῶν (1:7), II, 2 (3); Scholarios, Ἄπαντα (2:4), III, xxix, 434–452, 453–458; Ἱστορία πολιτική (1:3), pp. 29–30; and Πατριαρχική ἱστορία (43), pp. 83–93. See also Martin Jugie, "Ecrits apologétiques de Gennadios Scholarios à l'adresse des musulmans [The Apologetics of

NOTES—CHAPTER 5 **333**

Gennadius Scholarios Addressed to the Moslems]," *Byzantion*, 5 (1929), 296. On the question as to whether Ahmet, or someone else, a Greek, translated this tract of Gennadius', see Jugie, "Ecrits" p. 309.

58. See W. Gass, *Symbolik der griechischen Kirche* [*Symbolism of the Greek Church*] (Berlin, 1872), p. 40.

59. Ἱστορία πολιτική (1:3), p. 31. See also the ingenuous theory of the anonymous author of the Πατριαρχικὴ ἱστορία (43), pp. 93–94. Regarding Theodoros Spandouginos, see Constantine Sathas, Μνημεῖα ἑλληνικῆς ἱστορίας (4:218), IX, p. 169.

60. See Crusius, *Turcograeciae* (1:53), p. 78, and PG, CLX, col. 1064.

61. Crusius, *Turcograeciae* (1:53), p. 79, and PG, CLX, col. 1065.

62. Scholarios, Ἅπαντα (2:4), IV, xiv–xv, 223, 224–226, 233. *Cf.* pp. 231–233; VIII, 30*–31*, and Πατριαρχικὴ ἱστορία (43), p. 94.

63. Scholarios, Ἅπαντα (2:4), IV, 232.

64. *Ibid.*, 225.

65. Regarding the apostasy of clerics on personal grounds, see Grelot, *Relation* (1:90), p. 174.

66. Scholarios, Ἅπαντα (2:4), IV, 224. Most helpful for our understanding of this crisis in the Church is the study of the letters of Theophanes of Medea by Spyridon Lambros, " Ἐπανέκδοσις ἐπιστολῶν Μηδείας Θεοφάνους [A New Impression of the Letters of Theophanes, Metropolitan of Medea]," NE, 10 (1913), 260 ff.

67. See Diamantopoulos, "Γεννάδιος ὁ Σχολάριος" (6), pp. 289, 303.

68. See Scholarios, Ἅπαντα (2:4), IV, 228, 229, 265.

69. *Cf. ibid.*, I, 292.

70. *Ibid.*, IV, 203–204.

71. *Ibid.*, 202–203.

72. *Cf.* the resolution on matrimony made by the Synod of 1609 during the patriarchate of Neophytos (Ypsilantis, Τὰ μετὰ τὴν Ἅλωσιν [1:92], pp. 124–127).

73. Scholarios, Ἅπαντα (2:4), I, 286–287.

74. *Ibid.*, p. 286.

75. *Ibid.*, IV, 229.

76. Sophronios Eustratiades, Κατάλογος τῶν κωδίκων τῆς Μεγίστης Λαύρας (τῆς ἐν Ἁγίῳ Ὄρει) [A List of the Codices of the Monastery of Megiste Laura on the Holy Mountain] (Paris, 1925), pp. 408 ff.

77. Scholarios, Ἅπαντα (2:4), IV, 229.

78. *Ibid.*, IV, 226.

79. See *ibid.*, I, xiii–xiv; IV, 180–181; VIII, 31*–32*. *Cf.* also Diamantopoulos, "Γεννάδιος ὁ Σχολάριος" (6), pp. 296, 306; and Charles Astruc, "La Fin inédite du 'Contra Plethonem' de Mathieu Camariotes [The Unpublished End of 'Contra Plethonem' of Mathew Camariotes]," *Scriptorium*, 6 (1955), 261–268.

80. Scholarios, Ἅπαντα (2:4), VIII, 32*–33*. On the question of the dates of Gennadius' patriarchates, as well as the reasons for his resignation, see the study by Papadopoulos, Ἡ ἐξωτερικὴ κατάστασις (49), p. 6, fn. 3.

81. Eustratiades, Κατάλογος τῶν κωδίκων (76), pp. 418–419.

82. Scholarios, Ἅπαντα (2:4), I, 292–293.

83. *Cf.* Matthew Kamariotes in Θρῆνον [*Lamentation*] (PG, CLX, cols. 1065, 1968), expatiating upon the Capture: "τό δὲ καὶ πρὸς τὴν ἀσέβειαν ἐλεεινῶς μετατέθειται (and there are those whose faith pitifully disintegrates)." See also Crusius, *Turcograeciae* (1:53), pp. 79, 82: "οἱ δὲ τὴν ἀμώμητον πίστιν ἤμειψαν [they thus changed their pure faith]."

84. Scholarios, Ἅπαντα (2:4), I, 285–286, 291–292.

85. *Ibid.*, pp. 184, 211; III, 288, 383 ff. The study by Alexander Vasiliev, "End of the World," *Byzantion*, 16 (1942–1943), 497–499, is also relevant.

86. Scholarios, Ἅπαντα (2:4), III, 291. These eschatalogical ideas also appeared in Russia at the beginning of the fifteenth century, but they asserted themselves much more vigorously after the Capture (see Vasiliev, "End of the World" [85], pp. 500–502).

87. Scholarios, Ἅπαντα (2:4), IV, 511.

88. See Gerlach, *Tagebuch* (1:22), p. 102, regarding certain letters found on the marble tombstone of Constantine the Great, which, it was said, Gennadius had explained.

89. Scholarios, Ἅπαντα (2:4), I, 290.

90. *Ibid.*, VIII, 30*–31*; and I, 283–294. Crusius published an extract from this letter in *Turcograeciae* (1:53), p. 100. *Cf.* Matthew Kamariotes' Θρῆνον [*Lamentation*] (PG, CLX, cols. 1064–1065): Greeks groaned under the weight of their illustrious past. *Cf.* also Hermonymos, Ἐπικήδειος (3:4), pp. 267 ff.

91. Scholarios, Ἅπαντα (2:4), I, 290.

92. *Ibid.*, I, 290–291.

93. *Ibid.*

94. *Ibid.*

95. *Ibid.*

96. *Cf.* Diamantopoulos, "Γεννάδιος ὁ Σχολάριος" (6), p. 305.

97. Scholarios, Ἅπαντα (2:4), IV, 230.

98. *Ibid.*, I, 285.

99. *Ibid.*, p. 287.

100. *Ibid.* In his Μεσαιωνικὴ βιβλιοθήκη [*Library of the Middle Ages*] (Venice, 1872–1874), VII, l–li, Constantine Sathas criticizes Gennadius bitterly.

101. Scholarios, Ἅπαντα (2:4), I, 287.

102. *Ibid.*, p. 293.

103. *Ibid.*, p. 179.

104. *Cf.* Hermonymos, Ἐπικήδειος (3:4), pp. 272–273.

105. Scholarios, Ἅπαντα (2:4), I, 182.

106. Néroulos, *Histoire moderne* (3:102), pp. 31–32. The Synod of 1673 is described in Magni, *Lettere* (1:142), pp. 620–622.

107. Néroulos, *Histoire moderne* (3:102), pp. 44–45, agrees that Byzantine traditions were perpetuated in Church offices. *Cf.* Papadopoullos, *Studies* (29), pp. 41–42.

108. Khitrovo, *Itinéraires russes* (52), p. 207. On the office and duties of the Chartophylax both before and after the Capture, see the monograph by Manuel Gedeon, Μνεία τῶν πρό ἐμοῦ [*Narrative of Events before My Time*] (Athens, 1934), pp. 7 ff.; and of the *Referendarius*, see Gennadius, Metropolitan of Heliopolis, "Τό ὀφφίκιον τοῦ Μ. Ρεφερενταρίου ἐν τῷ Οἰκουμενικῷ Πατριαρχείῳ [The Office of Grand *Referendarius* in the Oecumenical Patriarchate]," Ὀρθοδοξία, 19 (1944), 245–248.

109. For relevant details, see Gennadius of Heliopolis, "Τό ὀφφίκιον τοῦ Μ. Ρήτορος ἐν τῷ Οἰκουμενικῷ Πατριαρχείῳ. [The Office of Grand Rhetor in the Oecumenical Patriarchate]," Ὀρθοδοξία, 19 (1944), 173–179.

110. Pavlos Karolides, Ἱστορία τῆς Ἑλλάδος, 1453–1862 [*History of Greece, 1453–1862*] (Athens, 1925), pp. 233–234.

111. See Papadopoullos, *Studies* (29), pp. 42 ff. Regarding their separation into two groups of five, and the precedence of the various titles, see Néroulos, *Histoire moderne* (3:102), p. 45. In 1578 the Grand Chartophylax and the Nomophylax were ordained priests (Gerlach, *Tagebuch* [1:22], p. 484). On Manuel Corinthios, student

of Matthew Kamariotes and one of the teachers of the nation (late fifteenth century and early sixteenth century), see Crusius, *Turcograeciae* (1:53), p. 90. See also Christos G. Patrinelis, "Οἱ μεγάλοι ῥήτορες Μανουὴλ Κορίνθιος, Ἀντώνιος, Μανουὴλ Γαλησιώτης καί ὁ χρόνος τῆς ἀκμῆς των [The Grand Rhetors, Manuel Corinthios, Antonios, Manuel Galesiotes, and Their Time]," ΔΙΕΕ, 16 (1962), 17–25. As to officials after the Capture, see Schweigger, *Constantinopel* (1:116), pp. 219–221; and also Gedeon, Μνεία τῶν πρό ἐμοῦ (108), pp. 40 ff. On Ioannis Zygomalas and Gavras, both of whom were laymen and held the office of Grand Rhetor, see Gerlach, *Tagebuch* (1:22), pp. 210–211, and p. 484 respectively. There is a mid-sixteenth century synodical document referring to priests and officials in Legrand, *Zygomalas* (2:14), pp. 89–90. However, the larger problem of the complement and roles of various officials in different periods remains unsolved (*cf.* Gedeon, Μνεία τῶν πρό ἐμοῦ, pp. 179–180).

112. Néroulos, *Histoire moderne* (3:102), p. 45. See also Gedeon, Μνεία τῶν πρό ἐμοῦ (108), p. 14.

113. See du Fresne-Canaye, *Voyage* (1:123), p. 107; and Néroulos, *Histoire moderne* (3:102), p. 45.

114. See Gerlach, *Tagebuch* (1:22), p. 367; and Gennadius of Heliopolis, Φωτίειος βιβλιοθήκη (49), part 2, pp. 14 ff.

115. See Ioannis Philemon, Δοκίμιον ἱστορικόν (3:147), pp. 32–33. Later, Gedeon said that the members of the ecclesiastical court, or court of the *Protosyncellus*, were the Grand Chartophylax and two or three archons of the Patriarchal Court (Μνεία τῶν πρό ἐμοῦ [108], p. 11); but he is obviously referring to the lower court.

116. Néroulos, *Histoire moderne* (3:102), p. 45. *Cf.* Gedeon, Μνεία τῶν πρό ἐμοῦ (108), pp. 11–12.

117. Karolides, Ἱστορία τῆς Ἑλλάδος (110), pp. 233–234. *Cf.* Gerlach, *Tagebuch* (1:22), p. 502.

118. Scholarios, Ἅπαντα (2:4), IV, 266.

119. Zinkeisen, *Geschichte des osmanischen Reiches* (2:40), II, 13–14.

120. *Cf.* also Néroulos' plausible hypothesis (*Histoire moderne* [3:102], p. 46), which is supported by oral tradition.

121. The view that Amiroukes abjured his faith is thought to be incorrect by Nikolaos Tomadakis ("Ἐτούρκευσεν ὁ Γεώργιος Ἀμιρούτζης; [Did George Amiroukes become a Turk?"] ΕΕΒΣ, 18 (1948), 116). Michael Apostolis, an opportunist scholar, justifies Amiroukes' passivity and his pro-Turkish attitude (see Hippolyte Noiret, *Lettres inédites de Michel Apostolis* [Paris, 1889], p. 83). On the deviousness of Amiroukes in his relations with the sultan, see Noiret, *Lettres*, p. 47.

122. Πατριαρχική ἱστορία Κωνσταντινουπόλεως (43), pp. 95–101.

123. Jugie believes (*Dictionnaire de théologie catholique* [6], p. 1525) that Gennadius himself is alluding to this brief patriarchate in Ἅπαντα (2:4), IV, 265–266. *Cf.* Diamantopoulos, "Γεννάδιος ὁ Σχολάριος" (6), p. 307. Tasos A. Gritsopoulos specifies the following sequence of early patriarchs: Gennadius (1454–1456); Isidore II Xanthopoulos (1456–1462); Sophronios I Syropoulos (1463–1464); Ioasaph I Kokkas (1464–1466); Markos II Xylokaravis (1466) ("Ὁ ἀπό Φιλιππουπόλεως οἰκουμ. πατριάρχης Διονύσιος Α' ὁ ἐκ Δημητσάνης, ὁ ἐν ἁγίοις καταλεγόμενος 1466–1472, 1488–1490 [The Oecumenical Patriarch Dionysios I from Dimitsana, Metropolitan of Philippopolis, Regarded as a Saint"], ΑΘΓΛΘ, 20 (1955), 8). If this is the case, when were the second and third patriarchates of Gennadius?

124. See Πατριαρχική ἱστορία Κωνσταντινουπόλεως (43), pp. 101–110, 116, 136, 139; Ἱστορία πολιτική τῆς Κωνσταντινουπόλεως (1:3), pp. 39–44; and Antonios Papadopoulos-Kerameus, "Μάρκος Ξυλοκαράβης, πατριάχης οἰκουμενικός καί εἶτα

πρόεδρος Ἀχριδῶν [Markos Xylokarabis, Oecumenical Patriarch then President of the Ecclesiastical Province of Ochrida]," Viz. Vrem., 10 (1903), nos. 3–4, pp. 5–14 of the reprint. According to the last researcher, Symeon of Trebizond ascended the throne three times (Athanasius Papadopoulos-Kerameus, "Περὶ τῆς τρίτης πατριαρχείας Συμεὼν τοῦ Τραπεζουντίου [On the Third Patriarchate of Symeon of Trebizond]," ΔΙΕΕ, 3 (1890–1891), 478–486). See also Papadopoulos, Ἡ ἐξωτερικὴ κατάστασις (49), pp. 8–10. Cf. Chrysanthos the Metropolitan, " Ἡ Ἐκκλησία τῆς Τραπεζοῦντος [The Church of Trebizond]," ΑΠ, vols. 4 and 5 (1936), 525 ff., which gives the relevant bibliography. On the reliability of the Πατριαρχικὴ ἱστορία Κωνσταντινουπόλεως (43), see the views of Theodosios Zygomalas in Crusius, Turcograeciae (1:53), p. 96: "Προσέξοις δὲ τοῦτο, ὅτι Μαλαξὸς, ἐν οἷς συνέγραψεν, ἐκ πολλῶν ἐρανισάμενος, οὐ πάνυ ἀληθεύει. Ἐνίοτε γὰρ πρὸς χάριν, ἄλλοτε πρὸς ἔχθραν [Mark you, the writings of Malaxos do not always contain the whole truth. He gathers his information from many quarters, sometimes approving of it and sometimes not]." On Dionysios I, who is considered the founder of the monastery of Eikosiphoinissa, see Constantinos K. Theocharis, " Ἡ μονή τῆς Εἰκοσιφοινίσσης καί ὁ οἰκουμενικός πατριάχης Διονύσιος Α' [The Monastery of Eikosiphoinissa and the Oecumenical Patriarch Dionysios I]," Μακεδονικὸν Ἡμερολόγιον (1951), pp. 193–199. See also, more importantly, the systematic study by Gritsopoulos, " Ὁ ἀπό Φιλιππουπόλεως οἰκουμ. πατριάρχης Διονύσιος Α'" (123), pp. 3–37, which contains the relevant bibliography. The Trapezuntine iç-oğlan continued to exercise power under Bayezid II (1481–1512) (see Ypsilantis, Τά μετά τήν Ἅλωσιν [1:92], p. 27).

125. See Πατριαρχικὴ Ἱστορία Κωνσταντινουπόλεως, passim. On the dethronement of patriarchs, see Néroulos, Histoire moderne (3:102), p. 32.

126. Thus, in 1678, the English consul in Smyrna, Ricaut (on whose character and reliability see Magni, Lettere [1:142], p. 51), observed that the Turks had more to do with the election of the patriarch than the Greeks (Ricaut, Histoire [1:90], p. 106). For another example, in 1670, see Constantinos Mertzios, "Μικρός Ἑλληνομνήμων [A Minor Greek Remembrance]," HE, 7 (1958), 739–741, 843 ff. Cf. Magni, Lettere pp. 625–626. In 1691 the traveller du Mont called the Orthodox clergy "venal" (Voyages [1:90], IV, 3). See also the views of the contemporary Roman Catholic, Sauger, Ἱστορία τῶν ἀρχαίων δουκῶν (4:9), pp. 10–12. Cf. Georgios Tertsetis, Ἅπαντα [Works], ed. George Valetas (Athens, 1953), III, 223: " Τά πρωτεῖα ὅσα ἐσυγχωροῦσε τό ὕποπτο τῆς τυραννίας, ὄχι ἀγορασμένα μέ τιμή εἰς τόν ἀνοικτό ἀέρα, ἀλλά μέ δόλο, μέ δωροδοκία, μέ συκοφαντία [The honors of a distrustful tyranny were bestowed neither freely nor openly, but by fraud, bribery, and sycophancy]."

127. Ioannis Zygomalas, Grand Rhetor, in 1576 satirized the patriarch for the laxness of his ways with a droll (and therefore unreliable) description of him having supper with the four to ten monks of the patriarchal household (Gerlach, Tagebuch [1:22], pp. 210–211). The monks served the patriarch for seven or eight years, receiving only their food in return. Their one hope was to be rewarded some day with a metropolitan seat, but that goal proved unattainable unless they bought it from their superiors. Cf. the recipient of the money of a wealthy metropolitan, and the price of the purchase (p. 211). See also the apposite remarks concerning a metropolitan of Athens in the second half of the seventeenth century, in Collignon, Jean Giraud (1:52), pp. 36–37; and George Tsoukalas, Ἱστοριογεωγραφικὴ περιγραφή τῆς ἐπαρχίας Φιλιππουπόλεως [An Historico-geographical Description of the Province of Philippopolis] (Vienna, 1851), p. 41.

128. Gerlach, Tagebuch (1:22), pp. 211–212. For similar evidence, see p. 324. Note Gerlach's intemperate assessment of the Zygomalas family, as well as of Greeks

generally, and especially those of Constantinople (p. 212). There are other such expressions of opinion *passim*. *Cf*. the questioning of Gerlach's reliability and an explanation of his malevolence in Legrand, *Zygomalas* (2:14), pp. 18–12. It is true, however, as Gerlach says (*Tagebuch passim*), that Ioannis Zygomalas became senile. *Cf*. pp. 331, 334, 348, 355–356, 456–457. Gerlach even went into such pettifogging details about the Zygomalas family as the squabbles of its members (pp. 233–234, 371–372).

129. Grelot, *Relation* (1:90), pp. 167 ff. See p. 170: "La pauvre église grecque, qui n'est plus que l'ombre de ce qu'estoit autrefois [The poor Greek Church, which is no more than a shadow of what it was formerly.]"

130. Lambros, Ἐπανέκδοσις ἐπιστολῶν Θεοφάνους (66), p. 260. *Cf. ibid*., pp. 261–262.

131. *Ibid*., p. 268.

132. *Ibid*., p. 270. *Cf*. p. 271, for a characteristic explanation of the violation of sacred institutions and laws. On the disarray caused by simoniacal practices in May 1484, see Spyridon Lambros, "Σύμμεικτα. Συνοδικά σιγίλλια τοῦ πατριάρχου Συμεών [Miscellanea. Synodical Seals of the Patriarch Symeon]," NE, 10 (1913), 349–350.

133. Gregory the Monk, in Khitrovo, *Itinéraires russes* (52), pp. 269–270. Contrast this with evidence relating to the years 1528, 1533, 1549, and 1574, which appears in Ypsilantis, Τά μετά τήν Ἅλωσιν (1:92), pp. 60, 62–63, 96, 108.

134. See Gerlach, *Tagebuch* (1:22), pp. 211, 224. *Cf*. p. 502, where it is mentioned that Jeremiah sent gifts of towels to the grandees of the sultan's household. Gerlach believes that the person responsible for the increase from 4,000 to 12,000 gold pieces was Michael Cantacuzenus, called *seïtan-oğlan*, collaborator of the Turks and opressor of Greeks (p. 224). As Gerlach points out (p. 502), in 1578 the amount of the fixed annual payment was 3,500, and of the "gift" 6,000. See also the remarks of Arambatzoglou, Φωτίειος βιβλιοθήκη (49), pp. 120–121, 146–149.

135. In 1673 the debt amounted to 200,000 *zecchini* (Magni, *Lettere* [1:142], p. 625).

136. See Janus Lascaris' comment on the journey of Patriarch Maximos in the summer of 1491: "'Εξῆλθε ἐκεῖνος ἐν ἀγύρτου καί ἀναιδοῦς παρασίτου μοίρᾳ, τό εἰωθός (φεῦ τῆς τῶν Ἑλλήνων κακοδαιμονίας τε καί ἀθλιότητος) τήν Ἑλλάδα πᾶσαν καί τούς περί αὐτήν τόπους ἐνιαυτόν ὅλον ἐν συνεχεῖ τῇ πλάνῃ περιοδεύσων [For an entire year he wandered all over Greece and neighboring countries like an impudent and brazen beggar (alas, for the misfortune and misery of Greeks)]" (Legrand, *Bibliographie hellénique* [2:55], II, 322–323). On the sixteenth century, see Gerlach, *Tagebuch* (1:22), pp. 33–34. *Cf*. Iorga, *Byzance après Byzance* (1:13), p. 96. On the arbitrary actions of Turkish pashas and their men within the province of the Patriarchate of Jerusalem, see Papadopoulos-Kerameus, Ἀνάλεκτα ἱεροσολυμιτικῆς σταχυολογίας (2:10), IV, 428.

137. See Constantinos D. Mertzios, Θωμᾶς Φλαγγίνης καί ὁ μικρός Ἑλληνομνήμων [Thomas Flangines and the Minor Greek Remembrance] (Athens, 1939), IX, 216–218.

138. See Gerlach, *Tagebuch* (1:22), pp. 396, 401.

139. See Georgievez, *De Turcarum moribus* (1:26), p. 96. *Cf*. Crusius, *Turcograeciae* (1:53), pp. 205, 487. On priests in the Aegean, see Collignon, *Jean Giraud* (1:52), p. 21; and on the expropriation of revenues of the Church in 1577, see Gerlach, *Tagebuch* (1:22), p. 413.

140. For a detailed treatment of these matters, see Ypsilantis, Τά μετά τήν Ἅλωσιν (1:92), pp. 50–53; Papadopoulos, Ἡ ἐξωτερική κατάστασις (49), pp. 12–14; and

Gunnar Hering, "Die Investitur des Gennadios Scholarios," *Balkan Studies*, 2 (1961), 252–256, which contains the relevant bibliography.

141. See Gerlach, *Tagebuch* (1:22), p. 61.

142. Papadopoulos, Ἡ ἐξωτερική κατάστασις (49), p. 15.

143. See Gerlach, *Tagebuch* (1:22), p. 212.

144. Crusius, *Turcograeciae* (1:53), pp. 261–263. *Cf.* Iorga, *Byzance après Byzance* (1:13), pp. 75–76, concerning Mt. Sinai.

145. For the relevant firman and the legal aspects of the question, see Paul Lemerle and Paul Wittek, "Recherches sur l'histoire et le statut des monastères athonites sous la domination turque [Researches in the History and the Rule of the Monasteries of Athos under Turkish Domination]," *Archives d'histoire du droit oriental*, III (Wetteren, 1948), 442–472. *Cf.* George Tsioran, Σχέσεις τῶν ρουμανικῶν χωρῶν μετά τοῦ Ἄθω καί δή τῶν μονῶν Κουτλουμουσίου, Λαύρας, Δοχειαρίου καί Ἁγίου Παντελεήμονος ἤ τῶν Ῥώσων [*Relations of the Rumanian Lands with Mt. Athos, Especially the Monasteries of Koutloumousion, Lavra, Docheiarion, and Agios Panteleimon, or, the Russian*] (Athens, 1938), p. 82, which gives the older bibliography. Undoubtedly it is this period, and not 1534, which gave birth to the tradition among monks that the Turks seized the monastic estates of Mt. Athos on Lemnos and in Asia Minor, plundering and destroying many monasteries (even some on Mt. Athos itself) and slaughtering monks (see Fallmerayer, *Schriften und Tagebücher* [3:100], II, 77–78). That the tradition dates from 1568 also seems verified by specific reference to these events in a brief chronicle (Spyridon Lambros, "Βραχέα χρονικά [Brief Chronicles]," ed. Constantine Amantos, in Μνημεῖα τῆς ἑλληνικῆς ἱστορίας [*Monuments of Greek History*] [Athens, 1932], vol. I, part I, p. 60). On the seizure of monastic estates on Mt. Athos, see also Georgios A. Lavriotis, Τό Ἅγιον Ὄρος μετά τήν ὀθωμανικήν κατάκτησιν [*The Holy Mountain after the Ottoman Conquest*] (Athens, 1963), pp. 9–10.

146. Petros T. Pennas, Ἱστορία τῶν Σερρῶν ἀπό τῆς ἀλώσεως ὑπό τῶν Τούρκων μέχρι τῆς ἀπελευθερώσεως τῶν ὑπό τῶν Ἑλλήνων (1383–1913) [*A History of Serrai from Its Capture by the Turks to its Liberation by the Greeks (1383–1913)*] (Athens, 1938), p. 41.

147. See Apostolos Vacalopoulos, "Ὑπῆρξε ἐπί Τουρκοκρατίας μητροπολιτικός ναός ὁ Ἅγ. Γεώργος (Rotonda) καί πότε; [Does the Cathedral Church of St. George (Rotunda) Date from Turkish Rule, and, If So, When?]," Μακεδονικά, 4 (1960), 549.

148. On the destruction of sacred establishments, even in Constantinople, see Vitalien Laurent, "Les Chrétiens sous les sultans (1553–1592)," *Echos d'Orient*, 28 (1929), 401–403; and in the lands comprising present-day Yugoslavia in 1539, see Benedict Curipeschitz, *Itinerarium der Botschaftsreise des Joseph von Lamberg und Niclas Jurischitz durch Bosnien, Serbien, Bulgarien nach Konstantinopel 1530* [*Itinerary of the Journey of Ambassadors Joseph von Lamberg and Nicholas Jurischitz through Bosnia, Serbia, and Bulgaria to Constantinople in 1530*] (Innsbruck, 1910), p. 36. *Cf.* similar occurrences in Greek lands about the same time, in the διαθηκῷον γράμμα ("Will") of the brothers Nectarios and Theophanes, where they speak about the construction of the small chapel in the monastery of Varlaam (Spyridon Lambros, "Συμβολαί εἰς τήν ἱστορίαν τῶν μονῶν τῶν Μετεώρων [Contribution to a History of the Monasteries of Meteora]," NE, 2 (1905), 108–109, 145). On the imposition of a heavy fine on a priest of Lidorikion for renovating his church, see Zerlentis, Σημειώματα περί Ἑλλήνων (2:55), p. 17.

149. Nevertheless, there are some examples in Papadopoulos, Ἡ ἐξωτερική κατάστασις (49), pp. 15 ff.

150. On this question, see Fattal, *Le Statut légal* (1:1), pp. 174–214.

151. See the narrative of Gregory the Monk (Khitrovo, *Itinéraires russes* [52], p. 269).

152. Gerlach, *Tagebuch* (1:22), p. 469. See also pp. 484 ff. on Mass in the Church of St. George of Karamania. In their writings the clergy often applied abusive language to the Turks (see Phountoulis, Γαβριήλ μητροπολίτου Μηθύμνης [3:89], p. 19, where Gabriel of Methymna refers to the Turkish villagers of Mytilene as "bandits," "tyrants," "devils," and so on). On the hardships suffered by the Mytilene Greeks, see Mystakidis, "Δύο Έλληνες" (2:21), p. 9; and also Vacalopoulos, *Origins of the Greek Nation* (1:62), p. 135.

153. Mystakidis, "Δύο Έλληνες" (2:21), p. 9.

154. See Angelos, Έγχειρίδιον (2:49), in *epistola dedicatoria* (pages not numbered).

155. See Kostas S. Papadopoulos, "'Απαγόρευσις τῆς κωδωνοκρουσίας καί προνομιακή κατά τόπους χρῆσις ἐκκλησιαστικῶν κωδώνων καί σημάντρων ἐπί Τουρκοκρατίας [The Prohibition on Ringing Bells, and, in Some Places, Their Privileged Use, under Turkish Rule]," Γρηγόριος Παλαμᾶς, 42 (1959), 110–118, 204–214, 305–311, which also contains the appropriate bibliography.

156. Georgieviz, *De Turcarum moribus* (1:26), p. 96.

157. *Cf.* the relevant firman of 1604 concerning the Metropolitan of Larissa, and of 1653 dealing with Kasaba (Constantine Amantos, "Σουλτανικός προνομιακός ὁρισμός [A Sultanic Decree Conferring Privilege]," ΠΑΑ, 10 (1935), 48–49. *Cf.* various other sultanic decrees of a similar nature, in Gedeon, 'Επίσημα γράμματα τουρκικά (2:2), pp. 89, 91–92.

158. On the transfer of the metropolitan seat from Methymna to Achyrona on Lesbos, see Phountoulis, Γαβριήλ μητροπολίτου Μηθύμνης (3:89), p. 34. *Cf.* the transfer from Larissa to Trikkala, and others.

159. An old man (Greek) received two hundred lashes because of an allegation that he tried to convert a Turkish boy to Christianity (Gerlach, *Tagebuch* [1:22], p. 389). On the Christianization of Moslem women by St. Philothea, see Mertzios, "'Η ὁσία Φιλοθέη" (4:205), pp. 123, 125, 127. On the execution of Patriarch Gabriel II in 1659, see Nicodemus the Hagiorite, Νέον Μαρτυρολόγιον (2:29), pp. 80–81.

160. See Eustratiadis, Κατάλογος τῶν κωδίκων (76), p. 417. There are examples in Gerlach, *Tagebuch* (1:22), pp. 53, 55–61, 462, 502–504. *Cf.* typical comments by Gerlach, written in 1576 (p. 211). On Cantacuzenus' reprehensible role, see (though guardedly) pp. 267–268, 278–279, 367, 395–396. *Cf.* the examples from the recent history by Chrysostomos Papadopoulos, "Οἱ ἐπίσκοποι ἐν τῇ ἐκκλησίᾳ Κωνσταντινουπόλεως κατά τούς μετά τήν Άλωσιν χρόνους [The Bishops of the Constantinopolitan Church during the Years after the Capture]," ΕΕΒΣ, 17 (1941), 300–302; and his 'Η ἐξωτερική κατάστασις (49), pp. 26–27, 28–29.

161. See above, pp. 116–117.

162. Gerlach, *Tagebuch* (1:22), p. 367.

163. For evidence of this in the year 1553, see Manoussos I. Manoussacas, "'Αρσενίου Μονεμβασίας τοῦ 'Αποστόλη ἐπιστολαί ἀνέκδοτοι (1521–1534) [Apostolis' Unpublished Letters of Arsenios of Monemvasia]," ΕΜΑ, 8–9 (1958–1959), 22. See also Gerlach, *Tagebuch* (1:22), pp. 99, 103, 122, 512. On the situation in 1590, see Zerlentis, Σημειώματα περί Έλλήνων (2:55), p. 34, which is based on information given Crusius by Greek clergy: "Οἱ ἐπίσκοποι καί ὁ ἑλληνικός κλῆρος ἀπαίδευτοι οἱ πλείους καί ἀντέστησαν τῷ πατριάρχῃ 'Ιερεμίᾳ, ὅταν πρό πολλῶν ἐτῶν ἠθέλησε σχολεῖα καί παιδείαν καί τυπογραφίαν νά εἰσαγάγῃ εἰς τήν Έλλάδα· διότι φοβοῦνται μήπως παραγκωνισθοῦν εἶτα διά τήν ἐκπαίδευσιν [The bishops and Greek clergy, most of them uneducated, opposed Patriarch Jeremiah when he wanted to

establish schools, education, and printing in Greece many years ago, because they feared they would be replaced later on as a result of their lack of education]." *Cf.* Grelot, *Relation* (1:90), pp. 183 ff. But we must remain critical of these remarks about the illiteracy and boorishness of priests.

164. See the severe characterizations by Eugenius the Aetolian in the seventeenth century (Sophronios Eustratiadis, "᾽Επιστολαί Εὐγενίου ᾽Ιωαννουλίου τοῦ Αἰτωλοῦ [Letters of Eugenius Ioannoulios the Aetolian], ῾Ελληνικά, VIII (1935), 275).

165. Gerlach, *Tagebuch* (1:22), pp. 119, 470; also pp. 259, 510. *Cf.* Iorga's criticism of Gerlach (*Byzance après Byzance* [1:13], p. 74).

166. There is, however, some interesting material in the book by Febvre, *Théâtre de la Turquie* (1:152), esp. pp. 7–8, 36, 41. See also Olga Vatidis, ῾Η Χριστιανικότητα τῶν Τούρκων καὶ οἱ ῞Ελληνες τῆς Μικρασίας [*The Christianity of the Turks and Greeks of Asia Minor*] (Athens, 1956).

167. *Cf.* Franz Babinger, "Quelques problèmes d'études islamiques dans le Sud-Est Européen [Some Problems in Islamic Studies in the European Southeast]," *Aufsätze*, I, 82–83.

168. See Vatidis, ῾Η Χριστιανικότητα τῶν Τούρκων καὶ οἱ ῞Ελληνες (166), pp. 23–25.

169. *Ibid.*, pp. 64 ff.

170. See, for example, Gerlach, *Tagebuch* (1:22), p. 185, and elsewhere, on Turkish respect for St. George. A Turk in Galata slaughtered a lamb on the feast of St. George (see Ogier Ghiselin de Busbecq, *The Life and Letters* (London, 1881), I, 148–150). See also Vatidis, ῾Η χριστιανικότητα τῶν Τούρκων καὶ οἱ ῞Ελληνες (166), pp. 19–23.

171. See Vatidis, ῾Η Χριστιανικότητα τῶν Τούρκων καὶ οἱ ῞Ελληνες (166), pp. 23–25.

172. Pacifique (*Relation* [4:121], pp. 42–44) also has some interesting comments.

173. De Busbecq, *The Life and Letters* (170), pp. 255–256; also Vatidis, ῾Η Χριστιανικότητα τῶ Τούρκων καὶ οἱ ῞Ελληνες (166), pp. 48–49.

174. Those with fever hung a thread or a small piece of their clothes on a tree near water (Gerlach, *Tagebuch* [1:22], p. 255; also p. 455). On the aspersion considered suitable for women who wanted to get back their milk, see p. 341. Gerlach writes about this ritual: "Diese Aberglauben haben sie von den Griechen gelernt [They learned this superstition from the Greeks]." *Cf.* the beautiful descriptions of other forms of aspersion, pp. 368, 487. See also de Monconys, *Journal des voyages* (Lyon, 1665), part 1, p. 406. On the holy water of the Church of St. Demetrius in Constantinople, also used by the Turks, see Gerlach, *Tagebuch* (1:22), p. 99. See also Vasilios Deligiannis, "Τό ἐν τῇ περιφερείᾳ Προύσης χωρίον Κουβούκλια [The Village of Kouvouklia in the District of Bursa]," Μικρασιατικὰ χρονικά, I (1938), 291–292; and Vatidis, ῾Η Χριστιανικότητα τῶν Τούρκων καὶ οἱ ῞Ελληνες (166), pp. 25–30. *Cf.* the opinions about these aspersions held by Pachomios Rousanos (Odysseus Lampsidis, "῾Ο Παχώμιος Ρουσᾶνος καὶ ὁ βίος τῶν συγχρόνων του [The Life and Times of Pachomios Rousanos]," ΕΕΒΣ, 13 (1937), 389–390.

175. Gerlach, *Tagebuch* (1:22), p. 501. Gedon compares many of the feasts, aspersions, and so on, in places around Constantinople (Μνεία τῶν πρό ἐμοῦ [108], pp. 329–343).

176. See Vatidis, ῾Η Χριστιανικότητα τῶν Τούρκων καὶ οἱ ῞Ελληνες (166), pp. 36 ff.

177. Nicolay, *Navigations* (1:140), p. 302. On the patriarch's broad-brimmed hat and the retinue that accompanied him whenever he ventured outside the patriarchal residence, *cf.* Gerlach, *Tagebuch* (1:22), p. 389; and on the patriarch's vestments, and the saying of Mass in the patriarchal residence, see pp. 83–85, 330–331, and elsewhere (for the years 1575–1577). *Cf.* also du Fresne-Canaye, *Voyages* (1:123), pp. 107, 108.

For a description of Mass in the Church of Chrysopigi in 1608, with Patriarch Neophytos as celebrant, see Bordier, *Relation* (1:123), pp. 112–116. During the patriarchate of Methodios III (1668–1671), the patriarch and clergy were forbidden to wear their broad-brimmed hats and instead wore little caps of red velvet embossed with red crosses. See Papadopoulos, 'Η ἐξωτερική κατάστασις (49), pp. 27–28, which also contains the relevant bibliography; and *cf.* pp. 31–32.

178. See Gerlach, *Tagebuch* (1:22), p. 462; also pp. 489–490. On his return visits to Constantinople, typically bearing gifts from all the people, see p. 500.

179. *Ibid.*, p. 188.

180. Karolidis, 'Ιστορία τῆς 'Ελλάδος, 1453–1862 (110), pp. 214–216.

181. Néroulos, *Histoire moderne* (3:102), pp. 33–34. Greek women who married Turks or Franks were excommunicated by the patriarch (Gerlach, *Tagebuch* [1:22], p. 155). On the legal and other rights of the patriarch, see the study by Chrystomos Papadopoulos, "'Η θέσις τῆς ἐκκλησίας καί τοῦ ἐλληνικοῦ γένους ἐν τῷ τουρκικῷ κράτει μετά τήν ἅλωσιν τῆς Κωνσταντινουπόλεως [The Position of the Greek Church and People in the Turkish State after the Capture of Constantinople]," Θεολογία, 12 (1934), 21–24. However, despite the excellence of Papadopoulos' bibliography, this is in other respects a mediocre study.

182. See Papadopoullos, *Studies* (29), pp. 9–10.

183. See Georgios Theocharidis, "Οἱ σταυροφόροι ἄρχοντες τῆς μητροπόλεως Θεσσαλονίκης [The Cross-bearing Archons of the Cathedral in Thessalonica]," Μακεδονικά, 3 (1955), 379–381. In Constantinople the cross-bearers said Mass and wore crosses on their hats only on the occasion of important feasts; they did not do so normally through fear of the Turks (Gerlach, *Tagebuch* [1:22], p. 249).

184. See Néroulos, *Histoire moderne* (3:102), pp. 34–35. *Cf.* Papadopoullos, *Studies* (29), p. 356 (lines 2889, 2904–2905).

185. See Demetrios Petrakakos, Κοινοβουλευτική ιστορία τῆς 'Ελλάδος [*Parliamentary History of Greece*] (Athens, 1935), I, 214–215.

186. See Papadopoullos, *Studies* (29), p. 38.

187. See Scholarios, "Ἅπαντα (2:4), IV, 198–199; and also Papadopoullos, *Studies* (29), pp. 11–12. The first Greek patriarch to ascend the patriarchal throne of Jerusalem after the Capture was Germanos in 1534 (Ypsilantis, Τά μετά τήν "Αλωσιν [1:92], pp. 63–64). For details of the patriarchate of Alexandria, see Chrysostomos Papadopoulos, "'Ιωακείμ ὁ 'πάνυ' ἐξ 'Αθηνῶν Πάπας καί Πατριάρχης 'Αλεξανδρείας (1487–1567) [Joachim the 'Great' of Athens as Pope and Patriarch of Alexandria (1487–1567)]," ΕΕΒΣ, 7 (1930), 174–175, which also contains the relevant bibliography.

188. Gedeon, Μνεία τῶν πρό ἐμοῦ (108), pp. 322–323.

189. See Papadopoulos, *Les Privilèges* (1), p. 16.

190. See Crusius, *Turcograeciae* (1:53), p. 486.

191. *Ibid.*, p. 292. In 1547 Gregory the Monk of Sinai wrote to Makarios, Metropolitan of Russia, that there were 84 metropolitans (see Khitrovo, *Itinéraires russes* [52], p. 270).

192. Gedeon writes at some length about these pilgrims (Μνεία τῶν πρό ἐμοῦ [108], pp. 322–324).

193. Belon, *Observations* (1:123), p. 35a. This writer is a little at sea when he attempts to define the jurisdiction of the patriarchs. On the patriarchates of Alexandria and Antioch, see also Iorga, *Byzance après Byzance* (1:13), pp. 73–74.

194. Gerlach, *Tagebuch* (1:22), p. 69. Contrast this with the earlier testimony of Georgieviz in 1558 (*De Turcarum moribus* [1:26], p. 178) that in Syria and Palestine the Arabic language prevailed.

195. Charles Diehl, *Byzance. Grandeur et décadence* (Paris, 1919), p. 79.

196. Scholarios, Ἅπαντα (2:4), III, 6, 13.

197. *Ibid.*, p. 253.

198. Paparrhegopoulos, Ἱστορία τοῦ ἑλληνικοῦ ἔθνους (2:63), V, part 2, pp. 78–82. The priests in Albania were Greeks from the Peloponnese (perhaps from the Albanian—speaking districts) and from Ioannina. The Mass and all ceremonials were conducted as they were in Greek lands, that is to say, in Greek (Gerlach, *Tagebuch* [1:22], p. 151).

199. *Cf.* the discussion and bibliography in Michael Lascaris, Τό Ἀνατολικόν Ζήτημα 1800–1923 [*The Eastern Question 1800–1923*] (Thessalonica, 1948), I, 254–255.

200. See the general information about the main category of monks, known as μοναστηριακή ("cenobitic")—their dress, way of life, and the mendicant monks who went abroad soliciting alms, money, and so on—in Angelos, Ἐγχειρίδιον (2:49), pp. 580–586; about the second category, known as ἀναχωρητική ("anchorite"), p. 586; and about the third, known as ἀσκητική ἤ ἐρημητική ("ascetic" or "eremitic"), pp. 598–600. Early in the fifteenth century another form of monastic life appeared, the so-called, idiorhythmic. On the fasts of monks in the first and second categories, see pp. 606–612. On various other aspects of the monastic life, see pp. 614 ff. *Cf.*, though critically, the information given by Crusius, *Turcograeciae* (1:53), p. 487, and Gerlach, *Tagebuch* (1:22), p. 458.

201. Under Turkish rule, Mt. Athos and Meteora both had their saintly hermits and "new" martyrs. See, for example, the blessed martyrs of the monastery of Dionysios (Archimandrite Gabriel, Ἡ ἐν Ἁγίῳ Ὄρει ἱερά μονή τοῦ Ἁγίου Διονυσίου [*The Holy Monastery of St. Dionysios on Mt. Athos*] (Athens, 1959), pp. 154–156. See p. 155 (in manuscript number 619), on the life and martyrdom of St. Christophoros. On Nicodemus, a "new" martyr from Meteora, see Lambros, "Συμβολαί εἰς τήν ἱστορίαν τῶν μονῶν τῶν Μετεώρων (148), pp. 136–137.

202. Ezekiel of Velanidia, Αἱ ἱεραί μοναί τῆς Πίνδου [*The Holy Monasteries of the Pindus*] (Athens, 1929), *passim. Cf.* Vacalopoulos, "Ἔρευναι ἐν Σαμαρίνῃ" (3:106), pp. 7–8, 15–17 of the reprint.

203. Of the early works, that of Manuel Gedeon, Ὁ Ἄθως, ἀναμνήσεις–ἔγγραφα–σημειώσεις [*Mt. Athos. Recollections, Documents, Notes*] (Constantinople, 1885), must be singled out for its importance. See esp. pp. 65 ff. See also Philipp Meyer, *Haupturkunden für die Geschichte der Athosklöster, grösstentheils zum ersten Male hrsg. und mit Einleitungen versehen* [*Select Documents for a History of the Monasteries of Mt. Athos, Edited Mostly for the First Time, and with Introductory Notes*] (Leipzig, 1894), *passim.*

204. See the texts in de Khitrowo's book, *Itinéraires russes* (52). However, the evidence adduced by Khitrovo must be carefully scrutinized. In 1489 Isaiah, a Russian monk of the monastery of Chilandariou, wrote: "Personne n'ose entreprendre le voyage de la Sainte Montagne sans un écrit de l'empereur [No one dares to undertake the voyage to the Holy Mountain without the emperor's writ.]" p. 259).

205. De Khitrowo, *Itinéraires russes* (52), pp. 260–264.

206. See the article by Archimandrite Christophoros Ktenas, "Ὁ πρῶτος τοῦ Ἁγ. Ὄρους Ἄθω καί ἡ 'Μεγάλη Μέση' ἤ 'Σύναξις' [The *Protos* of the Holy Mountain of Athos and the *Megale Mese*, or *Synaxis*]," ΕΕΒΣ, 6 (1929), 275–278.

207. Fallmerayer speaks about Belon in sympathetic terms (*Schriften und Tagebücher* [3:100], II, 78).

208. Belon, *Observations* (1:123), p. 39a.

209. *Ibid.*, pp. 38a–38b.

210. See Lampsidis, " Ὁ Παχώμιος Ρουσάνος" (174), p. 392.

211. See Belon, *Observations* (1:123), pp. 34b, 36a–36b. John Covel's numbers (in 1677) agree more or less with those of Belon, but he is relying on Belon. He

added that 2,000 monks were away as "mendicants" (πρός ζητείαν) (see F. W. Hasluck, "The First English Traveller's Account of Athos," BSA, 17 [1910–1911], 114). In 1578 Gerlach, relying on Metrophanes of Veroia, said that there were 2,500 monks (*Tagebuch* [1:22], p. 448); later, however (pp. 459–460), he mentions a figure of 6,000 supplied to him by the monk Methodios. Gerlach says very little about their organization and way of life, least of all that of the eremitic monks. On the rare incursions by pirates, who usually only asked for wine and bread, and on castle fortifications, see Hasluck, "The First English Traveller's Account" (211), p. 124. *Cf.* the burning of the monastery of Mylopotamos by pirates in 1527 (Lavriotis, Τό "Αγιον "Ορος [145], p. 45).

212. Belon, *Observations* (1:123), pp. 35a–35b, also pp. 38a–38b.

213. See Moschopoulos, "'Η 'Ελλάς" (3:97), p. 501.

214. Belon, *Observations* (1:123), pp. 34b, 39a, 44b.

215. *Ibid.*, p. 38a.

216. See *ibid.*, pp. 34b–35a, 38b–39a.

217. Georgirenes, *Description* (1:45), p. 99. This accords with Gerlach's remark that monks paid the sultan a total of 18,000 thalers, that is, 6,000 monks each paid 3 thalers (*Tagebuch* [1:22], p. 460). *Cf.* the evidence provided by Belon, *Observations* (1:123), p. 35a; and Hasluck, "The First English Traveller's Account" (211), p. 112, where he says that they were paying 12,000 ducats.

218. Belon, *Observations* (1:123), p. 38a. Tsioran gives detailed information (Σχέσεις τῶν ρουμανικῶν χωρῶν μετά τοῦ "Αθω [145], p. 82).

219. Gedeon talks about this (Μνεία τῶν πρό ἐμοῦ [108], p. 115).

220. Georgirenes provides some interesting details (*Description* [1:45], pp. 99–101). On the historical significance of the register of "travellers," or "mendicants," see Manuel Gedeon, "Παριστορήματα ἱστορικῆς σημασίας "Εἰς κεφαλήν γωνίας" [Tales of Historical Importance], EMA, 12 (1962), 35–36.

221. See Gerlach, *Tagebuch* (1:22), pp. 448, 459–460; also Basilike Papoulia, "Die Vita des Heiligen Philotheos vom Athos [The Life Of St. Philotheos of Mt. Athos]," SOF, 22 (1963), 265.

222. The earlier book by William Wey (fifteenth century), as well as books by the Italian Alessandro Ariosto (fifteenth century) and the Frenchman Jean Thenaud (sixteenth century), are accounts by men who never actually visited the Holy Mountain (see Hasluck, "The First English Traveller's Account" [211], p. 104, fn. 7).

223. Hasluck, *The First English Travellers Account* (211), p. 115.

224. *Ibid.*, pp. 112, 113, 122.

225. Babinger, *Sultanische Urkunden* (39), pp. 229–232.

226. See Ktenas, "'Ο πρῶτος τοῦ 'Αγ. "Ορους "Αθω" (206), pp. 234, 236–238, 240, 249.

227. Georgirenes, *Description* (1:45), p. 90. *Cf.* Lavriotis, Τό "Αγιον "Ορος (145), pp. 10–11.

228. Georgirenes, *Description* (1:45), pp. 90–91. *Cf.* Hasluck, "The First English Traveller's Account" (211), pp. 112–122. On the aga and his men, see also Moschopoulos, "'Η 'Ελλάς" (3:97), p. 501. *Cf.* Lavriotis, Τό "Αγιον "Ορος (145), pp. 12, 38–39.

229. Hasluck, "The First English Traveller's Account" (211), p. 128. In the monastery of Dionysios the cenobitic regimen was strictly maintained until the middle of the sixteenth century. At that time, in order to surmount various, mainly economic troubles, a combination of the cenobitic and "idiorhythmic" rule was adopted; that is, each monk, at his own expense, could increase his food beyond that supplied by the common table (see Gabriel, 'Η ἐν 'Αγίῳ "Ορει ἱερά μονή [201],

pp. 74–75). On the reasons why the monks were forced to abandon the cenobitic rule, there is also the view of Tsioran, Σχέσεις τῶν ρουμανικῶν χωρῶν μετά τοῦ Ἄθω (145), pp. 82–83. However, cf. the views of Theodoritos Agiannites (sixteenth and seventeenth centuries), in Gedeon, Μνεία τῶν πρό ἐμοῦ [108], pp. 115–116, 117–119.

230. Lavriotis, Τό Ἅγιον Ὄρος (145), pp. 12–13.

231. Ibid., p. 13.

232. See the various Acta. See also Lemerle and Wittek, "Recherches sur l'histoire et le statut des monastères athonites" (145), pp. 411–472; and also Ioannis K. Vasdravellis, "'Ἀνέκδοτον φιρμάνιον τῆς μονῆς Βλαττάδων τοῦ ἔτους 1486 [An Unpublished Firman from the Monastery of Vlattadon, Dated 1486]," Μακεδονικά, 4 (1960), 533–536.

233. See Gedeon, 'Ο Ἄθως (203), pp. 148 ff., 315–316 (on the destruction of the monastery of Esphigmenou). On these matters, the archives of the monasteries will undoubtedly yield much valuable information about the period following Turkish rule.

234. See Pericles Zerlentis, "Ρωμανοῦ Νικηφόρου καί Δανιήλ Καστρησίου ἐπιστολαί [Correspondence of Romanos Nicephorus and Daniel Kastresios]," Βυζαντίς, 2 (1911–1912), 294.

235. On the collection of funds in Venice between 1604 and 1611, see Mertzios, Θωμᾶς Φλαγγίνης καί ὁ μικρός 'Ελληνομνήμων (137), IX, 216–218.

236. The economic problems of Mt. Athos during the seventeenth and eighteenth centuries are discussed in Lavriotis, Τό Ἅγιον Ὄρος (145), pp. 105 ff. On the monasteries' revenues, and the assistance that came from Moldavia and Wallachia, see pp. 74–104. The generosity of the rulers of Moldavia came to an end in 1821. Skarlatos Kallimaches, last Phanariot ruler of Moldavia, built the entire Russian monastery of Agios Panteleimon between 1812 and 1819 (see Tsioran, Σχέσεις τῶν ρουμανικῶν χωρῶν μετά τοῦ Ἄθω [145], p. 43). On relations between the Rumanian rulers and the Orthodox monasteries generally, see Iorga, Byzance après Byzance (1:13), pp. 126 ff. On the various dates of construction of the monasteries, see Hasluck, "The First English Traveller's Account" (211), p. 129. Gedeon also makes a number of relevant points ('Ο Ἄθως [203], pp. 157–199); so, too, does the Archimandrite Christophoros Ktenas in the appropriate parts of his work, 'Η μονή Δοχειαρίου (963–1921) [The Monastery of Docheiariou (963–1921)] (Athens, 1926). See also Archimandrite Gabriel, 'Η ἐν 'Αγίῳ Ὄρει ἱερά μονή (201), pp. 14, 16 ff.

237. See Tsioran, Σχέσεις τῶν ρουμανικῶν χωρῶν μετά τοῦ Ἄθω (145), pp. 91 ff. and passim.

238. Ibid., p. 117.

239. Ibid., pp. 86–87.

240. Hasluck, "The First English Traveller's Account" (211), p. 128.

241. Gedeon, 'Ο Ἄθως (203), pp. 152, 317; Hasluck, "The First English Traveller's Account" (211), p. 129. Tsioran is not strictly correct when he says that the monasteries gradually extricated themselves from their condition of penury "mainly because of the generosity of the Rumanian people" (Σχέσεις τῶν ρουμανικῶν χωρῶν μετά τοῦ Ἄθω [145], p. 87).

242. The tempest is vividly described in a text cited by Ioannis Mamalakis, "Διήγησις περί 'Αγίου Ὄρους ἐν καιρῷ τῆς ἐπαναστάσεως τοῦ 1821 [An Account of the Holy Mountain during the Revolution of 1821]," ΕΕΦΣΠΘ, 7 (1957), 227–228.

243. Hasluck, "The First English Traveller's Account" (211), p. 128.

244. There were few classical manuscripts, and such as there were had been brought in by scholars withdrawing to the Holy Mountain (see Christos G. Patrinelis, Βιβλιοθῆκαι καί ἀρχεῖα τῶν μονῶν τοῦ 'Αγ. Ὄρους [Libraries and Archives

of the Monasteries of Mt. Athos] (Athens, 1963), pp. 14–15). There is a useful annotated bibliography in Manoussos I. Manoussacas, "Ἑλληνικά χειρόγραφα καί ἔγγραφα τοῦ Ἁγίου Ὄρους [Greek Manuscripts and Documents on the Holy Mountain]," ΕΕΒΣ, 32 (1963), 377–419.

245. See Belon, *Observations* (1:123), p. 37b. See also Gerlach, *Tagebuch* (1:22), p. 448, where he quotes Metrophanes of Veroia as saying that there were no more than a couple of educated monks. *Cf.* the comments on illiteracy and slovenliness in Pachomios Rousanos' letter to Païsios, Bishop of Drama (Andreas Moustoxydis, "Παχώμιος Ρουσάνος [Pachomios Rousanos]," Ἑλληνομνήμων, I (1843–1853), 647).

246. Belon, *Observations* (1:123), p. 38a.

247. Many eminent clergy are listed in Gedeon, Ὁ Ἄθως (203), pp. 205–240, 338–342.

248. *Ibid.*, p. 331. See Eustratiades, Κατάλογος τῶν κωδίκων τῆς Μεγίστης Λαύρας (76), pp. 441–461; and also Nikos A. Bees, "Χειρόγραφα καί παλαιότυπα τοῦ ναοῦ τοῦ Ἁγ. Νικολάου Τρικκάλων [Manuscripts and Incunabula in the Church of St. Nischolas in Trikkala]," EMA, 12 (1962), 5–6.

249. See Georgirenes, *Description* (1:45), at the end of his letter to the reader. According to Belon (*Observations* [1:123], p. 36b), it was what Rome was to the Latins.

250. See Sauger, Ἡ παροῦσα κατάστασις (1:178), pp. 8–9, where he accuses these Mt. Athos monks of being illiterate, impudent, and avaricious.

251. There is a review of the older bibliography of this subject in Lambros, "Συμβολαί εἰς τήν ἱστορίαν τῶν μονῶν τῶν Μετεώρων (148), pp. 49–51. *Cf.* pp. 154–156. See the same author's "Δύο ἀνέκδοτα πατριαρχικά σιγίλλια περί τῆς ἐν Μετεώροις μονῆς τοῦ Σωτῆρος Χριστοῦ καί συμπληρώματα εἰς τά περί Μετεώρων [Two Unpublished Patriarchal Seals from the Monastery of Christ the Redeemer, Meteora, with Supplementary Notes on Meteora]," NE, 4 (1907), 195–205. There is a fairly popularized, but still quite good, history of the district and monasteries of Meteora by Ioannis B. Papasotiriou, Τά Μετέωρα [*Meteora*] (Trikkala, 1934). The old history by the monk Polycarpe (Τά Μετέωρα [Athens, 1882]), is incomplete and full of historical inaccuracies. *Cf.* the small but attractive publications, aimed at the public, by Dionysios, Metropolitan of Trikki and Stagon in Thessaly. The best monograph yet published is by D. M. Nicol, *Meteora: The Rock Monasteries of Thessaly* (London, 1963), which contains the relevant bibliography.

252. See Papasotiriou, Τά Μετέωρα (251), pp. 12, 13.

253. See Lambros, "Συμβολαί εἰς τήν ἱστορίαν τῶν μονῶν τῶν Μετεώρων (148), pp. 108, 148.

254. See Nikos A. Bees, "Geschichtliche Forschungsresultate und Mönschs- und Volkssagen über die Gründer der Meteorenklöster [Results of Historical Research on Monkish and Folk Stories concerning the Founder of the Monasteries of Meteora]," BNJ, 3 (1922), 378.

255. *Ibid.*, pp. 378 ff. On the reason why Ioasaph was referred to as the "father of Meteora," and not as an abbot, see Léon Heuzey, "Discours historique sur les couvents des Meteores [Historical Discourse on the Convents of Meteora]," AAEEG, 9 (1875), 242; *cf.* p. 238.

256. On the character of St. Bessarion, see Nikos A. Bees, "Prosopographisches, Hagiographisches und Kunstgeschichtliches über den Hl. Bessarion, den Metropoliten von Larissa (d. 1540) [Notes concerning St. Bessarion, Metropolitan of Larissa (d. 1540). Prosopography, Hagiography, and Art History]," BNJ, 4 (1923), 351–400, which also contains the relevang bibliography.

257. See Pharmakidis, Ἡ Λάρισσα (3:103), p. 86, note 1, and pp. 86–92. See also Μέγας συναξαριστής (1950), 345 ff.; and the article on Bessarion by Nikolaos I.

Giannopoulos in Θρησκευτική καί χριστιανική ἐγκυκλοπαιδεία, II, 547–548, which also gives the relevant bibliography. For the views of Pachomios Rousanos on Bessarion, see Spyridon Lambros, " ῞Αγιος Βησσαρίων Λαρίσης καί Παχώμιος ὁ Ρουσᾶνος [St. Bessarion of Larissa and Pachomios Rousanos]," NE, 5 (1908), 291, 292–295. This article contains Rousanos' brief account of the life of Bessarion, his panegyric to Bessarion, and Bessarion's will. The will has been published more recently by Nikos A. Bees, ῾Η ἀρχέτυπος κτητορική διαθήκη τοῦ ἐν ἁγίοις πατρός ἡμῶν Βησσαρίωνος Μητροπολίτου Λαρίσης, ἱδρυτοῦ τῆς μονῆς Μεγάλων Πυλῶν [The Original Will of Our Saintly Father, Bessarion, Metropolitan of Larissa and Founder of the Monastery of Megale Pyle] (Athens, 1949).

258. See Rousanos' brief "Life": τίς . . . ἐξαγγελεῖ τάς τῶν αἰχμαλώτων ῥύσεις, τάς εἰς τούς λιμώττοντας καί δεομένους ἐπικουρίας καί χορηγίας, τάς ἐν ποταμοῖς γεφύρας; [Who will proclaim his liberation of slaves, the succor and aid he gave to those who were starving and needed help, the bridges he built over the rivers?] (see Lambros, " ῞Αγιος Βησσαρίων Λαρίσης καί Παχώμιος ὁ Ρουσᾶνος [257], pp. 293, 294–295).

259. There are frescoes depicting Bessarion in a number of churches in Thessaly (see Bees, "Prosopographisches" [256], pp. 396–399).

260. Heuzey, "Discours historique" (255), pp. 232–235, 246.

261. Ibid., p. 244.

262. It is best known as the monastery of Varlaam, after the hermit who lived there during the second half of the fourteenth century (see Lambros, "Συμβολαί εἰς τήν ἱστορίαν τῶν μονῶν τῶν Μετεώρων" (148), pp. 93 ff., esp. pp. 98–107, where Lambros sets down the brief autobiographies of the Apsarades brothers " ῞Ολη ἡμῖν ἡ σπουδή, αὕτη, ἦν τοῦ σωθῆναι καί σῶσαι καί ἄλλους τινάς διά τοῦ παρασείγματος τῆς ἡμετέρας βιοτῆς. Καί ταῦτα ἐπήρκεσεν ἐν ἡμῖν τῆς τριακονταετίας πλείονας, ὡς τό ἀληθές ἔχει [Our only purpose was to achieve salvation for ourselves and others by the example of our lives. The truth is that this took us more than thirty years]," p. 104. Cf. pp. 107–113, which contain the will of the two brothers Nectarios and Theophanes. For a bibliography of the Apsarades brothers, see Athenagoras, " ῾Η Σχολή τῶν Φιλανθρωπηνῶν ἐν ᾿Ιωαννίνοις [The Philanthropeni School in Ioannina]," HX, 4 (1929), p. 57, fn. 2.

263. Lambros, "Συμβολαί εἰς τήν ἱστορίαν τῶν μονῶν τῶν Μετεώρων" (148), pp. 143 ff.

264. Ibid., pp. 88, 94 ff., 135, 145. Cf. Nikos A. Bees, " ῾Ο Χριστόφορος Βαρλαμίτης καί τό βραχύ χρονικόν αὐτοῦ [Christophoros Varlamites and his Brief Chronicle]," HX, 1 (1926), 63–64.

265. Ioannis K. Voyatzides, "Μικρά ἀνέκδοτα ἐκ Μετεώρων [Short Unpublished Texts from Meteora]," ΔΙΕΕ, 7 (1910–1918), 161–177.

266. Cf. the phrase "οἱ φοιτηταί τόν διδάσκαλον [the students to their teacher]" (the latter referring to Theophanes Apsaras), in Lambros, "Συμβολαί εἰς τήν ἱστορίαν τῶν μονῶν τῶν Μετεώρων" (148), p. 119. In the monastic idiom, the word "φοιτητής (student)" also means "monk" and "dependant."

267. There was a workshop producing embroidered paschal canonicals (see Demetrius I. Pallas, " ῾Ο ἐπιτάφιος τῆς Παραμυθιᾶς [The Epitaphios of Paramythia]," ΕΕΒΣ, 27 (1957), 143, 146–148).

268. The Lament is in " ᾿Ετέραν ἱστορίαν τῶν κατά τήν Οὐγγροβλαχίαν τελεσθέντων, ἀπό Σερμπάνου [A Further History of Hungaro-Vlachia from the Time of Şerban]" (Emile Legrand, Bibliothèque grecque vulgaire [Paris, 1881], II, 231–333). There are extracts from the Lament on pp. 319, 320, 321. However, the Lament is not the work of Papasynadinos, the priest from Serrai, as Lambros initially believed (see

the letter by Demetrius Rousos in NE, 6 [1909], 495–499). The *Lament* has been published under Papasynadinos' name by Pennas, Τό χρονικόν τῶν Σερρῶν (1:176), pp. 79–80; and also by Spyridon Lambros, "Μονῳδίαι καί θρῆνοι ἐπί τῇ ἀλώσει τῆς Κωνσταντινουπόλεως [Monodies and Laments on the Fall of Constantinople]," NE, 5 (1908), 254–255.

269. See Nicolay, *Navigations* (1:140), p. 304. *Cf.* Cornelio Magni, *Relazione della città d'Athene* [*Narrative of the City of Athens*] (Parma, 1688), p. 32, where the writer says that, notwithstanding all their sufferings, they still had not been sufficiently humbled.

270. See Ioannis N. Karmiris, Ὁ Παχώμιος Ρουσᾶνος καί τά ἀνέκδοτα δογματικά καί ἄλλα ἔργα αὐτοῦ [*The Unpublished Dogmatics and Other Works of Pachomios Rousanos*] (Athens, 1935), pp. 48–49, 242–265. On sermons generally, as well as the language used in sermons, during the period of Turkish rule, see Basileios A. Mystakidis, "'Ιωάννου Ζυγομαλᾶ λόγος ἐν τῇ Παμμακαρίστῳ Κωνσταντινουπόλεως [Ioannis Zygomalas' Sermon in the Church of Pammakaristos in Constantinople]," Θεολογία, 6 (1928), 274–309.

271. Matthew of Myreon (Legrand, *Bibliothèque grecque vulgaire* [268], II, 325–326).

272. See, for example, Karmiris, Ὁ Παχώμιος Ρουσᾶνος καί τά ἀνέκδοτα δογματικά (270), pp. 49–52, 265 ff.

273. Ioannis N. Karmiris, "Ὁ ἀνέκδοτος λόγος "πρός τούς δυσανασχετοῦντας πρός τάς ἐκ τῶν ἐθνῶν ἐπαγομένας ἡμῖν θλίψεις" τοῦ Παχωμίου Ρουσάνου [The Unpublished Sermon by Pachomios Rousanos, 'To those indignant at the Suffering Caused by Other Peoples']," Ἐκκλησία, 16 (1938), 215–219, 231–235.

274. *N.B.* his Θησαυρός [*Thesaurus*].

275. First published in 1560. Rartouros was presbyter and chartophylax of Corfu.

276. For example, various anthologies of sermons published from the beginning of the eighteenth century include: 'Αποστολικόν δίκτον [*Apostolic Net*]; 'Αποστολική σαγήνη [*Apostolic Seine*]; Πνευματική κιθάρα [*Spiritual Guitar*]; Ρομφαία δίστομος κατά τοῦ διαβόλου [*Double-edged Sword Against the Devil*]; Εὐαγγελική σάλπιγξ [*Evangelical Trumpet*].

277. See Gedeon, Μνεία τῶν πρό ἐμοῦ (108), pp. 146–148, 149–151. See esp. the monograph by Constantine Kourkoulas, 'Η θεωρία τοῦ κηρύγματος κατά τούς χρόνους τῆς Τουρκοκρατίας [*The Theory of Sermonizing under Turkish Rule*] (Athens, 1957), pp. 9–12, 15 ff.; it contains the relevant bibliography.

278. See Constantine Kourkoulas, "'Η ἐκκλησιαστική ῥητορεία εἰς τά 'Επτάνησα ἀπό τοῦ ΙΣΤ' μέχρι τοῦ ΙΘ' αἰῶνος [Ecclesiastical Rhetoric in the Ionian Islands from the Sixteenth Century to the Nineteenth]," Παρνασσός, 6 (1964), 323–340.

279. See Kourkoulas, 'Η θεωρία τοῦ κηρύγματος (277), pp. 30 ff.

280. On this subject, see Georgios Chionidis, Σύντομη ιστορία τοῦ Χριστιανισμοῦ στήν περιοχή τῆς Βεροίας [*A Brief History of Christianity in the Region of Veroia*] (Veroia, 1961), pp. 45 ff.

281. See 'Ακολουθία τοῦ ὁσίου καί θεοφόρου πατρός ἡμῶν 'Αντωνίου τοῦ νέου καί θαυματουργοῦ τοῦ ἐν τῇ σκήτῃ Βεροίας ἀσκήσαντος [*The Divine Service of our Holy and Blessed Father St. Anthony, New Martyr and Worker of Miracles Who Lived in the Hermitage of Veroia*] (Thessalonica, 1894), pp. 13–16. On the controversy over the time when the "new" St. Anthony lived, see Georgios Chionidis, Σύντομη ιστορία τοῦ Χριστιανισμοῦ (280), pp. 37–38; and also his Ὁ ὅσιος 'Αντώνιος ὁ νέος ἐκ τῆς Μακεδονικῆς Βεροίας [*Holy Anthony, the "New" Martyr from Macedonian Veroia*] (Veroia, 1965).

282. 'Ακολουθία ὁσίου Θεοφάνους τοῦ νέου, ἀσκητοῦ καί θαυματουργοῦ, τοῦ ἀσκήσαντος ἐν τῷ ὄρει τῆς περιφήμου πόλεως Ναούσης, τοῦ ἐξ 'Ιωαννίνων [*The Divine Service*

of our Holy and Blessed Father St. Theophanes from Ioannina, "New" Martyr, Ascetic, and Worker of Miracles, Who Lived as a Hermit in the Mountains of the Famous City of Naousa] (Venice, 1764), p. 34.

283. Ibid., p. 33. I have established this period on the basis of what the 'Ακολουθία says in connection with the punishment meted out to a renegade from Veroia, who, in 1681, desecrated the monastery and stole the skull of the saint (pp. 43–46).

284. 'Ακολουθία τοῦ ὁσίου καί θεοφόρου πατρός ἡμῶν Διονυσίου, τοῦ ἐν τῷ 'Ολύμπῳ τῆς Θεσσαλίας ἐκλάμψαντος, τοῦ νέου ἀσκητοῦ [The Divine Service of Our Holy and Blessed Father Dionysios, New Ascetic, Whose Radiance Illumined Mt. Olympus in Thessaly] (Constantinople, 1816), p. 23. In his study, 'Η ἱερά πατριαρχική καί σταυροπηγιακή μονή τοῦ 'Αγ. Διονυσίου τοῦ ἐν 'Ολύμπῳ [The Blessed Patriarchal Stavropegion Monastery of St. Dionysios on Mt. Olympus] (Thessalonica, 1917), p. 18, Gennadius, Metropolitan of Thessalonica, notes that the saint's letters had been kept in the monastery of Phiotheos. As an example of the strong Greek sentiment that existed at this time, we might also note that in May 1501 Patriarch Joachim I instigated a synodical resolution forbidding the Greek monastery of Koutloumousiou to be called "Bulgarian" (Manuel I. Gedeon, Πατριαρχικαί 'Εφημερίδες [Patriarchal Journals] (Athens, 1936), p. 13).

285. 'Ακολουθία ὁσίου Διονυσίου (284), p. 35.

286. Ibid., p. 38.

287. Ibid., pp. 39 ff., 50 ff. The monastery in the district of Zagora, which he built stone by stone, was undoubtedly that of Sourvia on Pelion (see Μέγας Συναξαριστής, 1 (1950), 364–365. Cf. what Sisilianos has to say about it 'Η Μακρυνίτσα καί τό Πήλιον [3:124], pp. 146–149).

288. 'Ακολουθία ὁσίου Διονυσίου (284), pp. 35–39.

289. See Demetrius I. Toliopoulos, ed., 'Ακολουθία τοῦ ὁσίου καί θεοφόρου πατρός ἡμῶν Νικάνορος τοῦ Θαυματουργοῦ, τοῦ ἐν τῷ τοῦ Καλλιστράτου ὄρει ἀσκήσαντος [The Divine Service of our Holy and Blessed Father St. Nikanor, Worker of Miracles, Who Lived in a Hermitage on Mt. Kallistraton] (Kozane, 1953), pp. 36, 39–40.

290. 'Ακολουθία ὁσίου Διονυσίου (284), p. 23.

291. Ibid., Thessalonica, pp. 42 ff.

292. Ibid., Constantinople, p. 24.

293. See Apostolos Konstantinidis, "'Η μονή Φλαμουρίου [The Monastery of Phlamouriou]," Θεσσαλικά Χρονικά 5 (1936), 164–177; and also Sisilianos, 'Η Μακρυνίτσα καί τό Πήλιον (3:124), pp. 153–156. Cf. the activities of the blessed martyr Damianos in the districts of Tempe, Kissavos, Larissa, and Agrafa (Ezekiel of Thessaliotis and Phanariophersalou, "'Ακολουθία τοῦ ὁσιομάρτυρος Δαμιανοῦ τοῦ νέου [The Divine Service of the "new" Holy Martyr Damianos]," ΕΕΒΣ, 7 (1930), 59–60). Cf. Nicodemus the Hagiorite, Νέον μαρτυρολόγιον (2:29), pp. 60–61.

294. On the dates of his birth and death, see Georgios T. Lyritzis, 'Ο ὅσιος Νικάνωρ καί τό μοναστήρι του [The Holy Nikanor and his Monastery] (Kozane, 1962), pp. 6, 14.

295. See Toliopoulos, 'Ακολουθία ὁσίου Νικάνορος (289), p. 32.

296. See Nikolaos P. Delialis, "'Η διαθήκη τοῦ ὁσίου Νικάνορος τοῦ Θεσσαλονικέως [The Will of the Holy Nikanor of Thessalonica]," Μακεδονικά 4 (1960), 416.

297. For a description, see Demetrius Karras, "Τό μοναστήρι τοῦ 'Αγίου Νικάνορα [The Monastery of St. Nikanor]," 'Ο Φάρος τῆς βορείου 'Ελλάδος 2 (1940), 236. There are other details in Lyritzis, 'Ο ὅσιος Νικάνωρ (294), pp. 14 ff.

298. On the collection of these manuscripts, see the article by Linos Politis, "Die Handschriftensammlung des Klosters Zavorda und die Neuaufgefundene Photioshandschrift [The Collection of Manuscripts Belonging to the Monastery of Zavorda,

and the Recently Discovered Manuscript by Photius]," *Philologus*, 105 (1961), 136–144.

299. See Delialis, "Ἡ διαθήκη τοῦ ὁσίου Νικάνορος (296), pp. 418–425, esp. pp. 422, 423, 424.

300. See Chrysostomos Papadopoulos, "Ὁ Ἅγιος Γεράσιμος "ὁ νέος" ἀσκητής Κεφαλληνίας (1509– 15 Αὐγούστου 1579) [The "New" St. Gerasimos, Ascetic of Cephalonia (1509–15 August 1579)]," Θεολογία, 18 (1940), 7–25. On St. Gerasimos' cell and monastery, see Josef Partsch, Κεφαλληνία καί Ἰθάκη (4:32), p. 221.

301. See Georgios Sypandros, Ἀκολουθία τοῦ ἐν ἁγίοις πατρός ἡμῶν Διονυσίου, ἀρχιεπισκόπου Αἰγίνης τοῦ Ζακυνθίου, ψαλλομένη τῇ ιζ' τοῦ Δεκεμβρίου [*The Divine Service of Our Holy and Blessed Father St. Dionysios from Zacynthus, Archbishop of Aegina, Sung on 17 December*] (Venice, 1839). *Cf.* the publication of Chatzipartheniou Kardaris, Ὁ βίος τοῦ ἐν ἁγίοις πατρός ἡμῶν Διονυσίου, ἀρχιεπισκόπου Αἰγίνης τοῦ θαυματουργοῦ [*The Life of the Blessed Father St. Dionysios, Archbishop of Aegina, Worker of Miracles*] (Thessalonica, 1937).

302. See Valetas, "Ὁ Ἅγιος Ἰγνάτιος Ἀγαλλιανός (4:15), pp. 292, 295, 298–385.

303. Nicodemus the Hagiorite, Νέον μαρτυρολόγιον (2:29), p. 10. *Cf.*, on the same page: "Οἱ νεοφανεῖς οὗτοι Μάρτυρες ἐνδυναμώνουσιν ἐν ταυτῷ, καί ἀναθάλλουσι, καί ἀνακαινίζουσι τήν ἀδυνατισμένην, τήν μεμαραμένην καί τήν γηραλέαν πίστιν τῶν τωρινῶν Χριστιανῶν [These new martyrs have grown strong in the struggle; and they have revived the weak, waning, decrepit faith of present-day Christians and made it flourish]." For an historical survey of the "new" martyrs, see Papadopoulos, Νεομάρτυρες (4:205).

304. At this time, "ἔπεσεν τό σκοτεινόν νέφος τῆς εἰδωλολατρίας καί ἐσκέπασεν ὅλην τήν οἰκουμένην. Ἀλλά πάλιν ἐλάμπασιν λαμπρά ἐκεῖνοι ὁπού μαρτυροῦσαν διά τήν ἀγάπην τοῦ Χριστοῦ, ἀπό τούς ὁποίους ἦταν περιβόητος ... [ὁ Ἅγιος Δημήτριος] [The dark cloud of paganism hung over the entire world. But those who suffered for the love of Christ, and among these ... the outstanding [St. Demetrius] shone brilliantly]." The text of this quotation is in Basileios Laourdas, Μεταβυζαντινόν δημῶδες κείμενον περί τοῦ Ἁγ. Δημητρίου [*A Post-Byzantine Demotic Text about St. Demetrius*] (Thessalonica, 1960) (pp. 2–6 of the reprint from Γρηγόριος ὁ Παλαμᾶς).

305. This is an allusion to St. Demetrius' flight from the city.

306. See Basileios Laourdas, "Βυζαντινά καί μεταβυζαντινά ἐγκώμια εἰς τόν Ἁγ. Δημήτριον [Byzantine and Post-Byzantine Encomia of St. Demetrius]," Μακεδονικά, IV (1955–1960), 114.

307. Nicodemus the Hagiorite, Νέον μαρτυρολόγιον (2:29), p. 11.

308. *Ibid.*, pp. 12–13.

309. See *ibid.*, pp. 50–51, 52–57, 59, and elsewhere.

310. See Crusius, *Turcograeciae* (1:53), p. 321; and also Ninolakis, Μελέτιος ὁ Πηγᾶς (49), p. 18. See Dernschwam, *Tagebuch* (1:20), pp. 69, 111–112, on the forcible circumcision and subsequent death of a Greek because he persisted in his faith, and *cf.* pp. 140–142. See Nicodemus the Hagiorite, Νέον μαρτυρολόγιον (2:29), pp. 27–29, on the execution of a Trapezuntine merchant in Asprokastro (Akkerman) in 1646; also pp. 38–44.

311. See Pennas, Τό χρονικόν τῶν Σερρῶν (1:176), p. 27.

312. *Ibid.*, p. 29.

313. *Ibid.*, p. 44.

314. See *ibid.*, pp. 37–38; and also Nicodemus the Hagiorite, Νέον μαρτυρολόγιον (2:29), pp. 58–59.

315. On the martyrdom of Michael Mavroeidis of Adrianople (third quarter of the fifteenth century), based on an account of Ioannis Moschos', see Sophronios, Metropolitan of Leontopolis, "Ὁ νεομάρτυς Μιχαὴλ Μαυροειδὴς ὁ Ἀδριανουπολίτης [The New Martyr Michael Mavroeidis of Adrianople]," Θρακικά, 10 (1938), 7–28. Sophronios distinguishes between this "new" martyr and his namesake, Michael of Granitsa in the Agrafa, who in 1544 also died a martyr in Thessalonica. Cf. the usual traps laid by the Turks, in Dernschwam, Tagebuch (1:20), p. 73; du Loir, Voyage (1:108), pp. 208–209; and Schefer, Journal d'Antoine Galland (1:108), I, 200–201. See also Fattal, Le Statut légal (1:1), p. 170: "Le cimmi devient Musulman en prononcant la profession de foi islamique. S'il est idolâtre, il suffit qu'il prononce la formule suivante—'il n'est de dieu qu'Allah.' [The cimmi become Moslem by pronouncing the confession of the Islamic faith. If they are pagan, it is enough that they pronounce the following phrase—'there is no God but Allah']."

316. See, for example, the sacrifice of the "new" martyr Ioannis of Ioannina in 1526 (Lambros, "Συμβολαί εἰς τὴν ἱστορίαν τῶν μονῶν τῶν Μετεώρων "[148], p. 140). Cf. Nicodemus the Hagiorite, Νέον μαρτυρολόγιον (2:29), pp. 44–50, 58, 67–69, 70–76, and elsewhere.

317. See Nicodemus the Hagiorite, Νέον μαρτυρολόγιον (2:29), pp. 80–81.

318. Μέγας συναξαριστής, 1 (1950), 243–346.

319. On the "new" martyr, Cyril of Thessalonica, who on 6 July 1566 was burnt alive in the Hippodrome first outside the Church of St. Constantine and Helen when he was only twenty-two years of age, see Panagiotis Kastaris, " Ἅγιος Κύριλλος, ἕνας νεομάρτυς Θεσσαλονικεύς [St. Cyril, "New" Martyr of Thessalonica]," Μακεδονία, (6 July 1961). See also Mario Vitti, " Ὁ νεομάρτυρας Μᾶρκος Κυριακόπουλος ποὺ ἀποκεφαλίστηκε στὴ Σμύρνη τό 1643 (μιά δυτική πηγή) [The "New" Martyr Markos Kyriakopoulos, Decapitated in Smyrna in 1643 (a Western Source)]," MX, 10 (1962), 89–103. Cf. Dernschwam, Tagebuch (1:20), p. 73; and Georgios P. Sotiriou, Ὁ νεομάρτυρας Ἅγιος Θεόδωρος ὁ Βυζάντιος πολιοῦχος Μυτιλήνης The "New" Martyr [St. Theodore the Byzantine, Patron Saint of Mytilene] (Mytilene, 1960), passim.

320. Μέγας συναξαριστής, 1 (1950), 53–54. Moslems who apostatized to Orthodoxy also paid with their lives and were venerated as Orthodox "new" martyrs (see Papadopoulos, Νεομάρτυρες [4:205], pp. 41, 68, 70).

321. Such stories can be read in Mitrović, Ἡ Κωνσταντινούπολις κατά τόν 16ον αἰῶνα (1:123), pp. 102–105; and also in Μέγας Συναξαριστής, V (1950), 409–410.

322. See Μέγας Συναξαριστής (257), I (1950), 730.

323. On the "new" martyrs from Albania, Bulgaria, and other lands, see Snegarov, турското владичество пречка за културното развитие (1:168), pp. 72–73; and also Nicodemus the Hagiorite, Νέον μαρτυρολόγιον (2:29), pp. 29–38.

324. On the "new" martyrs of Lesbos, native and others, see Eustratios I. Drakos, Ἱστορία τῆς Εἰκοσιφοινίσσης, μονῆς ἐπί τοῦ Παγγαίου, καί ἀγιολογία τῆς Λέσβου [History of Eikosiphoinissa, Monastery on Mt. Pangeon, and of the Saints of Lesbos] (Drama, 1928), pp. 17–18.

325. Nectarius of Jerusalem, Πρός τάς προσκομισθείας θέσεις τῶν ἐν Ἱεροσολύμοις φρατόρων διά Πέτρου τοῦ αὐτῶν μαΐστορος περί τῆς ἀρχῆς τοῦ Πάπα ἀντίρρησις [Objections to Opinions Held by the Western Monks of Jerusalem, through Their Leader Peter, about the Authority of the Pope] (Jassy, 1682), p. 209. Cf. the execution of a child of twelve in Constantinople (Grelot, Relation [1:90], p. 230), and another in 1673 (Magni, Lettere [1:142], pp. 671–672). See also Nicodemus the Hagiorite, Νέον μαρτυρολόγιον (2:29), pp. 72–73, on the execution of the youthful tailor John of Mariés (on Thasos) in 1652 at the age of fourteen years.

326. Ezekiel, Metropolitan of Thessaliotis and Phanariophersala, " Ὁ νεοφανής

Ἅγ. Νικόλαος ὁ ἐξ Ἰχθύος καί οἱ Ἅγιοι Νικόλαοι τοῦ ὅλου ἐνιαυτοῦ [The "new" St. Nicholas of the Fish, and All the St. Nicholases of the Calendar]," Θεολογία, 8 (1930), 213–227. On the eighteen-year-old Nicholas of Neochori (Thessaly), who also suffered martyrdom on 27 September 1672 in Constantinople, there is the testimony of foreigners (Shefer, *Journal d'Antoine Galland* [1:108], I, pp. 220–221).

327. Nicodemus the Hagiorite, Νέον μαρτυρολόγιον (2:29), p. 13.

328. For an account of the martyrdom of the *Skevophylax* (Sacristan) of Serrai, Manolis Bostantzoglou, in 1604, see Pennas, Τό χρονικόν τῶν Σερρῶν (1:176), p. 29. Those who showed weakness and abjured their faith under torture were despised (p. 31).

329. See Carayon, *Relations* (2:31), p. 191.

330. See, for example, Lyritzis, Ὁ ὅσιος Νικάνωρ (294), p. 58.

331. See St. Nicholas of Metsovon (died 1617), in Μέγας Συναξαριστής, V (1950), 422–424.

332. See "Κατάλογον τῶν ἀπό τῆς ἁλώσεως Κωνσταντινουπόλεως μέχρι τοῦ ἔτους 1821 ὑπέρ τῆς χριστιανικῆς πίστεως μαρτυρησάντων [A List of Those who became Martyrs for the Christian Faith, from the Fall of Constantinople to 1821]," in Sathas, Μεσαιωνική Βιβλιοθήκη (100), III, 605–610.

333. On the sung masses of the "new" martyrs, see Louis Petit, *Bibliographie des acolouthies grecques* (Brussels, 1926); and also Sophronios Eustratiadis, Ἁγιολογικά. Βιβλιογραφία τῶν Ἀκολουθιῶν [*Hagiological Notes. A Bibliography of the Divine Services*] (Athens, 1932).

334. See the Introduction by B. P. Paschos, in Nicodemus the Hagiorite, Νέον μαρτυρολόγιον (2:29), pp. 6–7.

335. See the study by Louisa Syndika-Laourda, "Μιά εἰκόνα τοῦ ὁσίου Νικάνορος [A Picture of Holy Nikanor]," Μακεδονικά, 4 (1960), 426–431.

336. The women of Makra Gephyra stood in the presence of the priest out of respect for him (Gerlach, *Tagebuch* [1:22], p. 507). The Greeks of Prusa wanted more churches, but the Turks forbade any more construction (p. 413).

337. See Constantine Sathas, Βιογραφικόν σχεδίασμα περί τοῦ πατριάρχου Ἱερεμίου Β′ (1572–1594) [*A Biographical Sketch of Patriarch Jeremiah II (1572–1594)*] (Athens, 1870), p. xlii (μβ′).

338. See Panagiotis I. Poulitsas, "Ἐπιγραφαί καί ἐνθυμήσεις ἐκ τῆς Βορείου Ἠπείρου [Inscriptions and Memoirs from Northern Epirus]," ΕΕΒΣ, 5 (1928), 53–99, where there is abundant evidence; and see also Athenagoras, Metropolitan of Paramythia and Parga, "Νέος Κουβαρᾶς, ἤτοι χρονικά σημειώματα ἀναφερόμενα εἰς τήν πόλιν ἰδία τῶν Ἰωαννίνων, εἰς μονάς αὐτῆς καί τάς ἐπαρχίας αὐτῆς [New Kouvaras, or Chronological Notes, Especially concerning the City of Ioannina, Its Monasteries, and Its Districts]," ΗΧ, 4 (1929), 2 ff.

339. Heuzey, *Le Mont Olympe et l'Acarnanie* (3:95), pp. 205–206.

340. See Ioannis N. Travlos, Πολεοδομική ἐξέλιξις τῶν Ἀθηνῶν ἀπό τῶν προϊστορικῶν χρόνων μέχρι τῶν ἀρχῶν τοῦ 19ου αἰῶνος [*Development of the Layout of the City of Athens from Prehistoric Times up to the Beginning of the Nineteenth Century*] (Athens, 1960), pp. 186–190, which contains plans, pictures, and the relevant bibliography.

341. See Gerlach's impressions of the churches of Asia Minor (*Tagebuch* [1:22], p. 259, particularly on the churches of Prusa); also, p. 467.

342. *Ibid.*, p. 469.

343. *Ibid.*, p. 379.

344. Anastasios Orlandos, "Ἡ ἐν Ἑλλάδι ἐκκλησιαστική ἀρχιτεκτονική ἐπί τουρκοκρατίας [Ecclesiastical Architecture in Greece under Turkish Rule]," Hell. Contemp. (commem. vol. 1453–1953), pp. 205–207, 218.

352 NOTES—CHAPTER 5

345. Andreas Xyngopoulos, Ἡ θρησκευτικὴ τέχνη τῆς Τουρκοκρατίας [Religious Art under Turkish Rule], reprint from Νέα Ἑστία (1955), pp. 3–5.
346. See Orlandos, "Ἡ ἐν Ἑλλάδι ἐκκλησιαστικὴ ἀρχιτεκτονική (344), pp. 207–218.
347. See Tasos A. Gritsopoulos, Μονή Φιλοσόφου [Philosopher's Monastery] (Athens, 1960), pp. 32, 34 ff.
348. Sauger, Ἡ παροῦσα κατάστασις (1:178), p. 15. The Frankish or Byzantine statue of the Archangel Michael in the Church of St. Michael in the village of Mantamados on Lesbos, which was laid waste at the beginning of the seventeenth century, provoked the criticism of some Greeks who considered all "sculptured images as idols" (see Phountoulis, Γαβριὴλ μητροπολίτου Μηθύμνης [3:89], p. 38). Regarding this statue, see also S. G. Paraskevaïdes, "Ὁ Ταξιάρχης τοῦ Μανταμάδου [The Michael of Mantamados]," Λεσβιακά, 4 (1962), 91–101.
349. See du Mont, Voyages (1:90), IV, 19–20.
350. Cf. Constantine Kalokyris, Ἡ οὐσία τῆς ὀρθοδόξου ἁγιογραφίας. Ἀρχαιολογική, αἰσθητικὴ καὶ δογματικὴ ἑρμηνεία τῆς βυζαντινῆς ζωγραφικῆς [The Essence of Orthodox Hagiography. Archaeological, Aesthetic, and Dogmatic Interpretation of Byzantine Painting] (Athens, 1960), pp. 40–47, also pp. 12 ff.
351. See ibid., pp. 49 ff.; cf. Demetrius Sisilianos, Ἕλληνες ἁγιογράφοι μετὰ τὴν ἅλωσιν [Greek Hagiographers after the Fall of Constantinople] (Athens, 1935), pp. 14–15.
352. See Xyngopoulos, Σχεδίασμα (23), pp. 61–69.
353. Ibid., pp. 85–86, 90–91.
354. Ibid., pp. 86–87. Cf. other examples in Constantine Kalokyris, Ἄθως [Athos] (Athens, 1963), pp. 60–65. For the names of Cretan painters during the fourteenth and fifteenth centuries, see Spyridon Lambros, "Ἕλληνες ζωγράφοι πρὸ τῆς Ἁλώσεως [Greek Painters before the Fall of Constantinople]," NE, 5 (1908), 270–289.
355. Manolis Chatzidakis, "Τοιχογραφίες στὴν Κρήτη [Frescoes in Crete]," KX, 6 (1952), 79; and also Constantine Kalokyris, Αἱ Βυζαντιναὶ τοιχογραφίαι τῆς Κρήτης [The Byzantine Frescoes of Crete] (Athens, 1957), pp. 174 ff.
356. See Xyngopoulos, Σχεδίασμα (23), pp. 89–92.
357. See Xyngopoulos, Ἡ θρησκευτικὴ τέχνη (345), pp. 5–10. See also the same author's analysis in the relevant section of Σχεδίασμα ἱστορίας (23), pp. 94–112. Cf. Kalokyris, Ἄθως (354), pp. 65–90.
358. See Manolis Chatzidakis, "Ἡ κριτικὴ ζωγραφικὴ καὶ ἡ ἰταλικὴ χαλκογραφία [Cretan Painting and Italian Chalcography]," KX, I (1947), 27–46.
359. Lavriotis, Τὸ Ἅγιον Ὄρος (145), pp. 1–2, fn.
360. Ibid., p. 3, fn.
361. Xyngopoulos, Σχεδίασμα (23), pp. 111–112.
362. Regarding Theophanes' influence on the painters who worked in the monasteries of Dionysiou and Docheiariou, see Kalokyris, Ἄθως (354), pp. 90–96.
363. See Xyngopoulos, Σχεδίασμα (23), pp. 112–126. See also Frangos Katelanos' works in the village of Veltsïsta in Epirus (Stephanos Bettis, "Ὁ ζωγράφος Φράγκος ἐκ τόπου Θήβας [The Painter Frangos from Thebes]," HE, VII (1958), 820–827).
364. Xyngopoulos, Ἡ θρησκευτικὴ τέχνη (345), p. 11.
365. See Constantine Kalokyris, Ἔρευναι χριστιανικῶν μνημείων εἰς τὰς νήσους Νάξον, Ἀμοργόν καὶ Λέσβον [Researches on Christian Monuments on the Islands of Naxos, Amorgos and Lesbos] (Athens, 1960), p. 35 of the reprint; and see Nikolaos Drandakis, "Εἰκόνες κρητικῆς τέχνης εἰς Ἀντίπαρος [Representations of Cretan Art on Antiparos]," Κρητικὴ Πρωτοχρονιά, III (1963), 66–72.
366. Sauger, Ἡ παροῦσα κατάστασις (1:178), p. 15.
367. See Christos I. Soulis, "Ἐπιγραφαὶ καὶ ἐνθυμήσεις ἠπειρωτικαί [Inscriptions and Memoirs of Epirus], HX, IX (1934), 81 ff.

368. On the district of Prespa, see Stylianos Pelekanidis, Βυζαντινά καί μεταβυζαντινά μνημεῖα τῆς Πρέσπας [Byzantine and Post-Byzantine Monuments of Prespa] (Thessalonica, 1960), pp. 136–137. The despot's icons on the reredos of the monastery of Docheiariou were executed by anonymous "Albanian," that is to say, Epirotic, painters. The murals in the narthex of the central church of the same monastery were executed by natives of Ioannina in 1717 (see Gedeon, Ὁ Ἄθως (203), pp. 327–328).

369. The relevant evidence is in Manolis Andronikos, "Κτητορική ἐπιγραφή τοῦ Ἁγίου Δημητρίου τῆς Παλατίτσας [Inscription on the Foundation Stone of the Church of St. Demetrius in Palatitsa, near Veroia]," Μακεδονικά, I (1940), p. 194, fn. 3.

370. There are some interesting details in Krystallis, Ἅπαντα (3:108), pp. 478–479. Cf. Nikolaos I. Giannopoulos, " Τό χωρίον Βοεβόδα (νῦν Βασιλική) ἰδιοκτησία τῆς κυρᾶς Βασιλικῆς τοῦ Ἀλῆ πασᾶ καί ἀνάγλυφον ἐπί μαρμάρου αὐτῆς [The Village of Voevoda (now Vasiliki) Belonging to Ali Pasha's Wife, Vasiliki, and Its Marble Bas-relief]," HX, V (1930), 10 ff.; and Vacalopoulos, " Ἱστορικαί ἔρευναι ἐν Σαμαρίνῃ" (3:106), p. 24 of the reprint.

371. See Manolis Chatzidakis, "Συμβολή στή μελέτη τῆς μεταβυζαντινῆς ζωγραφικῆς. Τά καλλιτεχνικά κέντρα [Contribution to the Study of Post-Byzantine Painting. The Artistic Centers]," Hell. Comtemp. commem. vol. 1453–1953, pp. 235–240.

372. See Tasos A. Gritsopoulos, "Πέτρος καί Μιχαήλ οἱ Πεδιῶται, δύο Κρῆτες τοιχογράφοι ἐν Παλοποννήσῳ κατά τάς ἀρχάς τοῦ ΙΗʹ αἰῶνος [Peter and Michael the Pediotae, Two Cretan Fresco Painters in the Peloponnese at the Beginning of the Eighteenth Century]," KX, II (1948), 436–453. For some details of the life of Ioannis Kornaros, see Nikolaos B. Tomadakis, " Ἰωάννης Κορνάρος, Κρής ζωγράφος (1745–1796?) [Ioannis Kornaros, Cretan Painter (1745–1796?)]," KX, II (1948), 253–264.

373. Xyngopoulos, Σχεδίασμα (23), pp. 127–136.

374. See Vojislav Djurić, Icones de Yougoslavie (Belgrade, 1961), pp. 52, 55–56, which contains the relevant bibliography.

375. Xyngopoulos, Σχεδίασμα (23), pp. 136–159.

376. See Manolis Chatzidakis, " Ἡ συλλογή εἰκόνων τῆς ἑλληνικῆς κοινότητος τῆς Βενετίας [The Icon Collection of the Greek Community in Venice]," KX, III (1949), 574–582, which lists the painters' names.

377. See the informative note on him in Nikolaos B. Tomadakis, " Ἐμμανουήλ, Κωνσταντῖνος καί Μαρῖνος Τζάνε Μπουνιαλῆς (φιλολογικόν καί βιβλιογραφικόν διάγραμμα) [Emmanuel, Constantine and Marinos Tzanes Bounialis (A Literary and Bibliographical Sketch)]," KX, I (1947), 145–150; see also Tomadakis' "Εἰκόνες Ἐμμανουήλ Τζάνε ἐν Κερκύρᾳ [Emmanuel Tzanes' Icons in Corfu]," KX, II (1948), 476. Cf. Manolis Chatzidakis, "Συμπληρωματικά στόν Ἐμμανουήλ Τζάνε [Additional Information about Emmanuel Tzanes]," KX, II (1948), 467–475.

378. Xyngopoulos, Ἡ θρησκευτική τέχνη (345), 10–15. For full detail, see also Xyngopoulos' Σχεδίασμα (23), pp. 159 ff. There is some archival material on Michael Damascenos and later painters who worked in Venice in Mertzios, Θωμᾶς Φλαγγίνης (137), pp. 229–247. On Nikolaos Kantounis, see Spyridon de Viazis, "Οἱ ζωγράφοι τῆς Ζακύνθου. Νικόλαος Καντούνης [The Painters of Zacynthus. Nikolaos Kantounis]," Παρνασσός, XIV (1891–1892), 436–442. For aesthetic opinions and historical data concerning the Doxaras family and their work, see the study by Panagiotis G. Rontogiannis, "Τά ἔργα τοῦ Παναγιώτη Δοξαρᾶ [The Works of Panagiotis Doxaras]," Ἠώς, no. 42 (pp. 32–37), no. 43 (pp. 21–24), no. 44 (pp. 70–72), no. 45 (pp. 14–15), no. 46 (pp. 62–63), no. 47 (pp. 46–49), nos. 48/49, pp. 96–99, all 1961, which provide the relevant bibliography. See also Angelos Prokopiou,

" Ὁ Νικόλαος Δοξαρᾶς στήν Λευκάδα [Nikolaos Doxaras in Leukas]," Παρνασσός, VI (1964), 299–312.

379. Djurić, *Icones de Jougoslavie* (374), pp. 57, 59–60.

380. *Ibid.*, pp. 61–62. On Georgije Mitrofanović, see also pp. 67–68. These and others are discussed by Svetozar Radojčić, Мајстори старог српског сликарства (Belgrade, 1955).

381. Djurić, *Icones de Jougoslavie* (374), pp. 60–61.

382. See *ibid.*, pp. 62 ff. On the patriarchate of Pec in 1578, see Gerlach, *Tagebüch* (1:22), pp. 530–531.

383. See Chatzidakis, "Συμβολή στή μελέτη τῆς μεταβυζαντινῆς ζωγραφικῆς" (371), p. 240.

384. On the techniques associated with these arts, see Angeliki Chatzimichali, "Τά χρυσοκλαβαρικά–συρματεΐνα–συρμακέσικα κεντήματα [The Chrysoklavarika-Syrmateïna-Syrmakesica Embroideries]," *Mélanges offerts à Octave et Melpo Merlier* (Athens, 1956), pp. 447–498.

385. For details, see Eugenia Vei-Chatzidaki, Ἐκκλησιαστικά κεντήματα [*Ecclesiastical Embroidery*] (Athens, 1953); and Pallas, " Ὁ ἐπιτάφιος τῆς Παραμυθιᾶς" (267), p. 142. See also Nikolaos B. Drandakis, " Ὁ ἐπιτάφιος τῆς Ζερμπίτσης [The *Epitaphios* of Zerbitsa in Laconia (1539–1540)]," Εἰς μνήμην Κ. Ἀμάντου, 1874–1960 (Athens, 1960), pp. 454–462. On sixteenth-century vestments, *cf.* Maria S. Theocharis, " Ἐκκλησιατικά ἄμφια τῆς Μονῆς Τατάρνης [Ecclesiastical Vestments of the Monastery of Tatarni]," Θεολογία, XXVII (1956), 123–147; and on eighteenth-century vestments, see Theocharis, " Ἀνέκδοτα ἄμφια τῆς Μονῆς Φανερωμένης τῆς Σαλαμῖνος [First Publication on the Canonicals of the Monastery of Phaneromeni on Salamis]," Θεολογία, XXVII (1956), 325–333. *Cf.* Theocharis' article " Ὑπογραφαί κεντητῶν ἐπί ἀμφίων τοῦ Ἄθω [Embroiderers' Signatures on Canonicals at Mt. Athos]," ΕΕΒΣ, XXXII (1963), 496–503, which contains the older bibliography.

386. See Angeliki Chatzimichali, " Ἡ στάχωσις τοῦ εὐαγγελίου τῆς ὑπεραγίας Θεοτόκου Πωγωνιανῆς Μολυβδοσκεπάστου [The Binding on the Gospel of the Virgin Mary in the Monastery of Molyvdokepastos, Pogoniani]," ΗΧ, XV (1940), 179–182; and Vei-Chatzidali, Ἐκκλησιαστικά κεντήματα (385), p. ιη′ (xviii).

387. Relevant to these questions is the splendid bibliography in Angeliki Chatzimichali, "La Sculpture sur bois," Hell. Contemp., IV (1950), 103–139, 227, 244. There is also a supplementary bibliography in Demetrios I. Constantinidis, " Ἡ ἐκκλησία τῆς Παλατιανῆς χώρας Ἄνδρου [The Church of Palatiani in the Town of Andros]," ΑΧ, XIV (1963), 77–78. *Cf.* the chapter entitled " Ἔρευναι μεταβυζαντινῶν ἁγιορειτικῶν τέμπλων [Researches on the Post-Byzantine Iconostasis of Mt. Athos]," in Kalokyris, Ἄθως (354), pp. 175–216.

Chapter 6

1. See, in this connection, Voyatzidis, " Ἱστορικαί μελέται" (2:68), pp. 242 ff.

2. Emile Legrand, *Lettres de l'empereur Manuel Paléologue* (Paris, 1893), p. 107: ὦ νέων διατριβαί, ὡς ἀποκέκλεισται ὑμῶν ἤδη τό φιλότιμον, καί γενήσεσθε ἀντί λόγων μουσείων χειρωναξιῶν ἐργαστήρια [O the preoccupations of youth! They have forsaken all that is good; instead of becoming educated, they have become common laborers]."

3. Andronicus Callistus, Μονῳδία (2:5), PG, CLXVI, cols. 1137–1138.

4. Scholarios, Ἄπαντα (2:4), I, 288.

5. Lambros, Παλαιολόγεια καί Πελοποννησιακά (5:13), II, 17.

6. See Belon, *Observations* (1:123), p. 37b.

7. Scholarios, Ἄπαντα (2:4), I, 288. *Cf.* Ducas, *Historia* (1:2), p. 312 (Bonn), p. 393 (Grecu).

8. See Belon, *Observations* (1:123), p. 37b.

9. See Noiret, *Apostolis* (5:121), p. 65 (writing to Angelo Vadio in 1462 or 1463): "τῆς Ἑλλάδος ἀπάσης, ὅση τε νῆσος καί ὅση ἤπειρος, κινδυνευούσης ἀποβαλεῖν ὅσον οὐκ ἤδη, μή ὅτι λόγους, ἀλλά καί γλῶτταν αὐτήν [All of Greece, the mainland and the islands, are in danger of losing what is left—not only tradition, but even the language itself]." *Cf.* Gennadius' remarks in ῎Απαντα (2:4), I, 291.

10. Scholarios, ῎Απαντα (2:4), I, 285.

11. Bessarion, Ἐπιστολή καθολική [*Encyclical*], PG, CLXI, cols. 452–453.

12. See Joachim Valavanis, Μικρασιατικά [*On Asia Minor*] (Athens, 1891), pp. 13–14, 59, where there is another bibliography. *Cf.* the example of the waning of the Greek language in Karamania and Cappadocia even as late as the nineteenth century (Symeon M. Pharasopoulos, Τά Σύλατα. Μελέτη τοῦ νομοῦ Ἰκονίου ὑπό γεωγραφικήν, φιλολογικήν καί ἐθνολογικήν ἔποψιν [*Sylata. A Geographical, Literary and Ethnological Study of Iconium*] (Athens, 1895), pp. 22–23).

13. On the bibliographers of the monastery of Eikosiphoinissa see Athanasios Papadopoulos-Kerameus, " ῎Εκθεσις παλαιογραφικῶν καί φιλολογικῶν ἐρευνῶν ἐν Θράκῃ καί Μακεδονίᾳ [A Report on Paleographic and Literary Researches in Thrace and Macedonia]," ΕΦΣΚ, XVII (1886), 31–39 (Appendix). See also Linos Politis, " Ἁγιορεῖτες βιβλιογράφοι τοῦ 16 αἰῶνα [Hagiorite Scribes of the Sixteenth Century]," Ἑλληνικά, XV (1957), 357–384; and also Politis' "Eine Schreiberschule im Kloster τῶν Ὁδηγῶν [A School of Bibliographers in the Monastery of the *Odigoi*]," BZ, LI (1958), 271, 277–278, 281–283.

14. On one of these, Thomas (1468–1541), who became an eminent lawyer, see Giovanni Fabris, "Professori e scolari Greci all'università de Padova," *Archivio Veneto*, XXX (1942), 130–132, which also contains the appropriate bibliography.

15. Crusius, *Turcograeciae* (1:53), pp. 57–58. *Cf.* pp. 90–91. Regarding another, by the name of Agallos, see Spyridon Lambros, "Προσθῆκαι εἰς τούς Λακεδαιμονίους βιβλιογράφους καί κτήτορας κωδίκων [Additional Notes on the Lacedemonian Bibliographers and Owners of Codices]," NE, IV (1907), 493.

16. Emile Legrand, *Cent-Dix Lettres grecques de François Filelfe* (Paris, 1892), p. 127.

17. *Ibid.*, p. 169 (the letter dated 9 November 1473): "You have come back, O Demetrius Zgouropoulos, from among the most impious of barbarians to (as has been said) a pure and beloved land."

18. Jean Darrouzès, "Lettres de 1453," REB, XXII (1964), 100–102.

19. See Andreas Moustoxydis, " Ἰωάννης, Γεώργιος καί Δημήτριος Μόσχοι [Ioannis, Georgios and Demetrios Moschos]," Ἑλληνομνήμων, I (1843), 386. On Ioannis and Georgios Moschos as bibliographers see, Spyridon Lambros, "Λακεδαιμόνιοι βιβλιογράφοι [Lacedemonian Bibliographers]," NE, IV (1907), 347–348, where there is also a bibliography. *Cf.* Legrand, *Bibliographie hellénique* (2:55), I, lxxxviii. It would seem that the Thessalonians invited him to come from Corfu, where he had settled down to spend the rest of his days, and not from Mistra, as Voyatzidis believes (Ἱστορικαί μελέται [2:68], p. 246). *Cf.* Manoussacas, " Ἀρσενίου Ἀποστόλη ἐπιστολαί" (5:163), p. 47, regarding Iustinos Dekadyos (late fifteenth century or early sixteenth century). Manoussacas also provides a bibliography.

20. See Vacalopoulos, *Origins of the Greek Nation* (1:62), p. 251.

21. See Lambros, "Λακεδαιμόνιοι βιβλιογράφοι (19), pp. 312–357, 492–494.

22. Valettas, " ῎Αγιος Ἰγνάτιος Ἀγαλλιανός" (4:15), p. 293.

23. Sathas, Μεσαιωνική βιβλιοθήκη (5:100), I, ρκστ' (cxxxvi).

24. *Ibid.*

25. *Ibid.*, p. 246. On Hierax's work, see Gyula Moravcsik, "Zur Quellenfrage des historischen Gedichtes von Hierax [Contribution on the Origins of the Historical Poem by Hierax]," BNJ, X (1934), 413–416.

26. Crusius, *Turcograeciae* (1:53), p. 494. *Cf.* Valettas, " "Άγιος 'Ιγνάτιος 'Αγαλλιανός" (22), pp. 293, 296.

27. See Spyridon Lambros, " 'Αμοιβαί διδασκάλων καί ρητόρων ἐπί Τουρκρατίας [The Emoluments of Teachers and Orators under Turkish Rule]," NE, IX (1912), 196–198.

28. A. Biedl, "Matthaeus Camariotes. Specimen prosographiae byzantinae," BZ, XXV (1935), 337. See the recent notable work by Tasos A. Gritsopoulos, Πατριαρχική Μεγάλη τοῦ Γένους Σχολή [*The Great Patriarchal School of the Nation*] (Athens, 1966), I, 74 ff.

29. See Astruc, "La Fin inédite" (5:79), pp. 254, 258, 260.

30. *Ibid.*, p. 261.

31. *Ibid.*, p. 248 (also fn. 12).

32. Biedl, "Camariotes" (28), pp. 337–339. Biedl's reference on p. 337 to the Grand Rhetor "*Scholae Patriarchicae*" is incorrect. *Cf.*, though also with reservations, Manuel I. Gedeon, Χρονικά τῆς πατριαρχικῆς 'Ακαδημίας. 'Ιστορικαί εἰδήσεις περί τῆς Μεγάλης τοῦ Γένους Σχολῆς, 1454–1830 [*Chronicles of the Patriarchal Academy. Historical Evidence on the Great School of the Nation*] (Constantinople, 1883), pp. 30–35. One noteworthy piece of "historical evidence" is Matthew Kamariotis' comment in his Θρῆνος (5:83) on the Capture of Constantinople (PG, CLX, cols. 1060–1069).

33. See Gedeon, Χρονικά τῆς πατριαρχικῆς 'Ακαδημίας (32), p. 44. *Cf.* Biedl, "Camariotes" (28), p. 338.

34. See Sophronios of Leontopolis, " 'Ο νεομάρτυς Μαυροειδής (5:315), p. 13; and Christos Patrinelis, "Οἱ μεγάλοι ρήτορες Μανουήλ Κορίνθιος, 'Αντώνιος, Μανουήλ Γαλησιώτης καί ὁ χρόνος τῆς ἀκμῆς των [Manuel the Corinthian, Anthony, Manuel Galisiotes and the Period when They Flourished]," ΔΙΕΕ, XVI (1962), 20, for the relevant bibliography.

35. See Sophronios of Leontopolis, " 'Ο νεομάρτυς Μαυροειδής" (5:315), p. 13; and Petros P. Petris, "Νικόλαος Μαλαξός, πρωτοπαπάς Ναυπλίου (c. 1500–1594) [Nikolaos Malaxos, archpriest of Nauplia (c. 1500–1594)]," Πελοποννησιακά, III–IV (1958–1959), 348–375, for the relevant bibliography, and pp. 32–33 for a note on Antonios Karmalikis, another of Manuel's students.

36. Crusius, *Turcograeciae* (1:53), p. 92. At the time Ioannis Zygomalas was teaching Greek language and civilization to fifteen students.

37. See Voyatzidis, " 'Ιστορικαί μελέται" (2:68), p. 241, which contains the early bibliography.

38. See Patrinelis, "Οἱ μεγάλοι ρήτορες" (34), pp. 34–37.

39. See also Gedeon, Χρονικά πατριαρχικῆς 'Ακαδημίας; (32), p. 56. As to when Ioannis Zygomalas arrived in Constantinople, see Constantine Dyovouniotis, "Θεοδόσιος Ζυγομαλᾶς [Theodosios Zygomalas]," Θεολογία, I (1923), 24.

40. Legrand, *Zygomalas* (2:14), pp. 71, 104.

41. Crusius, *Turcograeciae* (1:53), p. 494.

42. *Ibid.*

43. See Gregorios Papamichael, Μάξιμος ὁ Γραικός [*Maximos the Greek*] (Athens, 1950), pp. 13 ff., 398 ff. See also the monograph by Elie Denissof, *Maxime le Grec et l'Occident* (Louvain, 1943).

44. See Noiret, *Apostolis* (5:121), pp. 96–97, and *passim*. *Cf.* Politis, "Eine Schreiberschule" (13), pp. 279, 282, 283; and Patrinelis, "Οἱ μεγάλοι ρήτορες" (34), p. 22, for the bibliography.

45. Hermonymos, 'Επικήδειος εἰς Αἰκατερίνην τήν Παλαιολογῖναν (3:4), p. 271 [in Corfu]: " 'Ω δυστυχεῖς ἡμεῖς εἰς οἷον ἄρα καιρόν γεγόναμεν. Οἷα καθ' ἑκάστην ὁρῶμέν. Οἷα μέν νῦν πάσχομεν, οἷα δέ πείσεσθαι προσδοκῶμεν. Τί ποτε ἄρ' ἡμῖν ἔσται

πέρας τῶν πικροτάτων τουτωνί ἐπί ξένης συμφορῶν; [O, what misfortune to be born at such a time. What terrible things we witness each day. What calamities we suffer now and shall continue to suffer. Will there ever be an end to all our anguish and afflictions in foreign climes?"]. See also Apostolos Vacalopulos, "Die Frage der Glaubwürdigkeit der *Leichenrede auf L. Notaras von J. Moschos* (15 Jh.) [The Problem of the Authenticity of Ioannis Moschos' *Lament for L. Notaras* (Fifteenth Century)]," BZ, LII (1959), 14 ff.

46. See Noiret, *Apostolis* (5:121), *passim.*

47. See Geanakoplos, *Greek Scholars in Venice* (3:36), pp. 49–50.

48. See Vacalopoulos, *Origins of the Greek Nation* (1:62), pp. 184–185, 241, 254, 260. There is a recent bibliography on him in Geanakoplos, *Greek Scholars in Venice* (3:36), pp. 73–110.

49. Legrand, *Bibliographie hellénique* (2:55), II, *passim*; Noiret, *Apostolis* (5:121), *passim*, and p. 113; Basileios Laourdas, "Κρητικά παλαιογραφικά [Cretan Palaeographs]," KX, IV (1950), 240 ff., 251 ff., on Gortyna as a center for the copying of codices.

50. Noiret, *Apostolis* (5:121), p. 74: "κοινή τοῖς ἐρῶσι λόγων ἡ κάκιστ' ἀπολουμένη πενία [abject poverty is common among those fond of letters]."

51. See how Noiret characterizes him (*ibid.*, p. 24).

52. *Ibid.*, p. 54.

53. Legrand, *Bibliographie hellénique* (2:55), II, 234.

54. Noiret, *Apostolis* (5:121), p. 58.

55. Basileios Laourdas, "Μιχαήλ 'Αποστόλη λόγος [A Speech of Michael Apostolis']," ΕΕΒΣ, XIX (1949), *passim.*

56. *Ibid.*, p. 243: " Τίς τῶν Εὐρωπαίων Σωκράτους, Τιμαίου καί Πυθαγόρου σοφώτερος; Τίς Πλάτωνος καί 'Αριστοτέλους καί Ζήνωνος; [Which Europeans are wiser than Socrates, Timon and Pythagoras? Who wiser than Plato, Aristotle or Zeno?].

57. Noiret, *Apostolis* (5:121), p. 150. See Geanakoplos, *Greek Scholars in Venice* (3:36), pp. 101–107, for an English translation of most of the memorandum, a bibliography, and relevant comments by the writer.

58. Noiret, *Apostolis* (5:121), p. 153.

59. See Stylianos Alexiou, " 'Η Κρητική λογοτεχνία καί ἡ ἐποχή της [An Epoch in Cretan Literature]," KX, VIII (1954), 76–108; Manoussos I. Manoussacas, 'Η Κρητική λογοτεχνία κατά τήν ἐποχή τῆς Βενετοκρατίας [Cretan Literature under Venetian Rule] (Thessalonica, 1965); and Constantine Dimaras, 'Ιστορία τῆς νεοελληνικῆς λογοτεχνίας [History of Modern Greek Literature] (Athens, 1954), pp. 76–80.

60. On intercourse between Crete and Venice, there is a useful study entitled "Les Crétois hors de Crète," which is Chapter 4 in Henri Pernot, *Etudes de littérature grecque moderne* (Paris, 1916), pp. 129–294. On the importance of Venice as a center for the dissemination of Greece's intellectual heritage, see W.-Th. Elwert, "Venedigs Literarische Bedeutung. Ein Bibliographischer Versuch," *Archive für Kulturgeschichte*, XXXVI (1954), 261–300. Cf. Christos G. Patrinelis, " "Ελληνες κωδικογράφοι τῶν χρόνων τῆς 'Αναγεννήσεως [Greek Copyists during the Renaissance]," EMA, VIII–IX (1958–1959), 63–225. And see the emendations and additions of Paul Speck in BZ, LV (1962), 320–324.

61. Geanakoplos, *Greek Scholars in Venice* (3:36), p. 108, also p. 58.

62. For details of his life, and the relevant bibliography, see Manoussos I. Manoussacas, "Recherches sur la vie de Plousiadènos," REB, XVII (1959), 28–51; and also Manoussacas' " 'Αρχιερεῖς Μεθώνης, Κορώνης [Archbishops of Modon and Coron]," Πελοποννησιακά, III (1959), 97–100. Nor should we omit mention of Georgios Kalyvas who, after 1522, was priest, teacher, and copyist of codices on his island of

Crete (see Constantine I. Dyovouniotis, "Γεώργιος Καλύβας [Georgios Kalyvas,"
ΕΕΒΣ, VI (1929), 80–99). Kalyvas concerned himself mainly with theological subjects, but he also studied the classical authors. It is interesting to read his correspondence with a student, Iakovos, through whom Iakovos became involved with the
ancient Greek writers (Laourdas, "Κρητικά παλαιογραφικά" [49], ΚΧ, V (1951),
p. 331: "Σπούδασον δή παντί σθένει καί τοῖς αὐτόθι σοφοῖς ὁμίλει καί γραμ-
ματικοῖς ἀκροῶ, ἐξ ὧν καί τ' ἄλλα μαθεῖν εὐχερές [Study with all resolution, associate
with the wise men around you, and listen to educated people, from whom you will
readily learn all things]."

63. See Manoussacas, " 'Αρχιερεῖς Μεθώνης, Κορώνης" (62), p. 106, fn. 2. See also
pp. 105–135, esp. pp. 105–106. For details of his life, see the recent work by Geanakoplos, *Greek Scholars in Venice* (3:36), pp. 167–200, which contains a complete bibliography of relevant works. On the period of his prelacy in Monemvasia, see Manoussacas, " 'Αρχιερεῖς Μεθώνης, Κορώνης pp. 105–121; and Geanakoplos, *Greek Scholars
in Venice*, pp. 177–182.

64. See Manoussacas, " 'Αρσενίου τοῦ 'Αποστόλη ἐπιστολαί (5:163), pp. 5, 45,
54–55.

65. Geanakoplos, *Greek Scholars in Venice* (3:36), p. 172.

66. *Ibid.*, p. 173.

67. Manoussacas, " 'Αρχιερεῖς Μεθώνης, Κορώνης" (62), pp. 126–127, 133; and
also Manoussacas' " 'Αρσενίου τοῦ 'Αποστόλη ἐπιστολαί" (5:163), pp. 32, 35, 53.

68. See Manoussos I. Manoussacas, " 'Η ἀλληλογραφία τῶν Γρηγοροπούλων χρονολογουμένη (1493–1501) [The Correspondence of the Grigoropoulos Family (1493–
1501)]," EMA, VI (1957), 193, fn. 3. On Ioannis Grigoropoulos and the Grigoropoulos family surroundings, see pp. 156–209.

69. *Ibid.*, p. 179. See also Manoussos I. Manoussacas-Christos Patrinelis, " 'Η ἀλ-
ληλογραφία τοῦ 'Ιωάννου Γρηγοροπούλου μετά τοῦ Μ. Μουσούρου, Α. 'Αποστόλη,
Ζ. Καλλιέργη καί ἄλλων λογίων τῆς 'Αναγεννήσεως χρονολογουμένη (1494–1503)
[The Correspondence of Ioannis Grigoropoulos with M. Mousouros, A. Apostolis,
Z. Kallierges and other Renaissance Scholars (1494–1503)]," EMA, X (1960),
163–201.

70. Gerlach, *Tagebuch* (1:22), p. 304. *Cf.* p. 274; and Legrand, *Zygomalas* (2:14),
pp. 71, 104.

71. Manoussacas, " 'Αρχιερεῖς Μεθώνης, Κορώνης" (62), p. 124. *Cf.* Geanakoplos,
Greek Scholars in Venice (3:36), pp. 184–186.

72. Geanakoplos, *Greek Scholars in Venice*, pp. 110 ff.

73. *Ibid.*, pp. 128–132. On Demetrius Ducas, who worked in Spain for the dissemination of Greek studies there, see pp. 223–255; *cf.* Geanakoplos' *Byzantine East
and Latin West* (New York, 1966), pp. 126, 148–149. There was also the Corfiote,
Nikandros Noukios, an associate of Diego Hurtado de Mendoza, Spanish ambassador
to Venice from 1520 (see I. A. Foucault, *Nicandre de Corcyre, Voyages* [Paris, 1962],
pp. 10–11, 12–13). In his *Travels*, Nikandros Noukios writes about the cultivation of
humanistic studies in a number of cities in the West (pp. 21 and *passim*).

74. Geanakoplos, *Greek Scholars in Venice* (3:36), pp. 133–142.

75. *Ibid.*, pp. 144–145.

76. *Ibid.*, p. 145.

77. *Ibid.*, pp. 149–154. *Cf.* Iorga, *Byzance après Byzance* (1:13), pp. 37–38. On the
eulogy and its influence, see the study by Gregorios M. Siphakis, "Μάρκου Μουσούρου
τοῦ Κρητός ποίημα εἰς τόν Πλάτωνα [A Poem to Plato by Marcos Mousouros the
Cretan]," ΚΧ, VIII (1954), 366–388.

78. Geanakoplos, *Greek Scholars in Venice* (3:36), p. 145.

79. *Ibid.*, pp. 155–162. See also Mousouros' preface to Pausanias' work for its eulogistic remarks about Janus Lascaris' contribution to the education of young Greeks through his founding of the Greek College in Rome (Legrand, *Bibliographie hellénique* [2:55], I, 148). On the exact date of Mousouros' death, see Manoussos Manoussacas, "La Date de la mort de Marc Musurus," *Studi Veneziani*, XII (1950), 459–463. On Zachary Kallierges, see Legrand, *Bibliographie hellénique*, pp. cxx ff.

80. See Marcos Mousouros' forward and epigram in the Τὸ μέγα ἐτυμολογικόν [*The Great Etymological* (Lexicon)] published by Zachary Kallierges (Venice, 1499).

81. Because the printers were foreigners, the books were filled with typographical mistakes. On these printers' errors, see Spyridon Lambros, "Αἱ κατὰ τῶν τυπογράφων τῆς Βενετίας αἰτιάσεις τοῦ Καισαρίου Δαπόντε καὶ τοῦ Παχωμίου Ρουσάνου [Complaints against the Printers of Venice by Kaesarios Dapontes and Pachomios Rousanos]," NE, II (1905), 337–349. The need to employ scholarly Greek editors, especially for religious works, the demand for which grew yearly, was soon recognized. A list of such editors is given by Nikolaos G. Kontosopoulos, "Τά ἐν Βενετίᾳ τυπογραφεῖα ἑλληνικῶν βιβλίων κατὰ τὴν τουρκοκρατίαν [The Printeries for Greek Books in Venice during the Period of Turkish Rule in Greece]," Ἀθηνᾶ, LVIII (1954), 310–337, 339–340.

82. For extensive details, see Kontosopoulos, "Τά ἐν Βενετίᾳ τυπογραφεῖα" (81), pp. 286–310, 337–339, which contains the relevant bibliography. In 1551 the Cretan Ioannis Vergitsis (or, more properly, Vergikios), from a famous family of copyists, contracted with Lelio Torelli, Secretary of the Grand Duke of Tuscany, for the establishment of a Greek press in Florence. For reasons unknown, however, the agreement was never implemented (see Spyridon Lambros, "Συμβόλαιον περὶ ἱδρύσεως ἑλληνικοῦ τυπογραφείου ἐν Φλωρεντίᾳ τῷ 1551 [A Contract for the Establishment of a Greek Press in Florence in 1551]," NE, II [1905], 199–208). On Angelos Vergikios, librarian of Francis I, and his services both as copyist and creator of a most elegant Greek script, see Foucault, *Nicandre* (73), p. 185, and *cf.* Legrand, *Bibliographie hellénique* (2:55), I, clxxv–clxxxvi.

83. Nicholas Cartojan, *Cartile populare in literatura romaneasca. II: Epoca influentei greçesti* [*Popular Books in Rumanian Literature. II: The Period of Greek Influence*] (Bucharest, 1938), pp. 13–19.

84. Geanakoplos, *Greek Scholars in Venice* (3:36), pp. 223–255; and also his *Byzantine East and Latin West* (73), pp. 126, 148–149.

85. See Foucault, *Nicandre* (73), pp. 10–11, 12–13.

86. *Ibid.*, p. 21 and *passim.*

87. Crusius, *Turcograeciae* (1:53), pp. 494, 494–495. See Geanakoplos' views (*Greek Scholars in Venice* [3:36], p. 300) on the abatement of enthusiasm for Greek studies which became evident in Italy a few years before the death of Janus Lascaris in 1534.

88. See Crusius, *Turcograeciae* (1:53), p. 94.

89. Spyridon Lambros, "Τό ἐν Ρώμῃ ἑλληνικόν Γυμνάσιον (*Collegio Greco*) καὶ οἱ ἐν τῷ ἀρχείῳ αὐτοῦ ἑλληνικοί κώδικες [The Greek College in Rome (*Collegio Greco*) and the Greek Codices in Its Archives]," NE, X (1913), 3–32, which contains the relevant bibliography. See esp. p. 4, fn. 3, for material on the existence of unpublished archival sources. *Cf.* Kirillo Koralevskij, "Les Premiers Temps de l'histoire du Collège grec de Rome (1576–1622)," *Stoudion*, III (1926), 33–39, 80–89; IV (1927), 81–97, 137–151; VI (1929), 40–48. See also Koralevskij's "Italo-Greci e Italo-Albanesi nell'archivio di Propaganda Fide," *Archivio Storico per la Calabria e la Lucania*, XVI (1947), 113–153.

90. See Theodore Rentios' letter to Ioannis Zygomalas in Pericles G. Zerlentis,

Παραλειπόμενα τοῦ οἴκου Ζυγομαλᾶ. 'Επροστάτευσαν οἱ Πάπαι τούς "Ελληνας καί τά ἑλληνικά γράμματα; [Supplementary Notes on the House of Zygomalas. Were the Popes Protectors of the Greek People and Greek Letters?] (Athens, 1923), pp. 14–17. See pp. 6–7 for Zerlentis' critical comments; also Matthaios Paranikas, "Θεοδώρου Ρεντίου τοῦ Χίου Ποιητικῆς τοῦ 'Αριστοτέλους παράφρασις [A Free Translation of Aristotle's Poetics by Theodore Rentios of Chios]," 'Ελληνικός φιλολογικός σύλλογος Κωνσταντινουπόλεως, XII (1879), 75–100; and cf. Maximos Margounios' criticism of Rentios' work: "οὐδενός δεύτερος τῶν τά πρῶτα φερόντων ἐν τοῖς καθ᾽ ἡμᾶς χρόνοις ἕν γε ταῖς προπαιδείαις, μᾶλλον δέ καί τῶν πρωτείων τοῖς πᾶσιν ἀμφισβητῶν [he was in no wise the inferior of any of our contemporaries in the first rank of education; indeed, he might even be considered the best]" (Polychronis Enepekides, "Maximos Margounios an Deutsche und Italienische Humanisten, [Maximos Margounios' Letters to German and Italian Humanists]," JÖBG, X [1961], 137).

91. See Sauger, 'Η παροῦσα κατάστασις. (1:178), pp. 9–10.

92. Georgios Sotiriades, " 'Ελληνικά κολλέγια ἐν Πατανίῳ ἐπί Βενετοκρατίας [Greek Colleges in Padua at the Time of Venetian Rule in Greece]," HME (1926), pp. 431, 438, 439, 440, 442; and Giovanni Fabris, "Professori e scolari Greci" (14), p. 126; also, pp. 124–126, 133–134 (on students from Cyprus), and p. 126 (on students from Rhodes).

93. Sotiriades, " 'Ελληνικά κολλέγια" (92), pp. 443–444. See also Gerlach, Tagebuch (1:22), p. 200 (the approving comments of Symeon Kavasilas, who came from Padua, on the state of education there).

94. Fabris, "Professori e scolari Greci" (14), pp. 136–138; and Andreas Marmoras, 'Ιστορία τῆς νήσου Κερκύρας [History of the Island of Corfu] (Corfu, 1902), p. 337.

95. Georgios E. Tipaldos, "Οἱ ἐν τῷ πανεπιστημίῳ τοῦ Παταβίου "Ελληνες σπουδασταί [Greek Students of the University of Padua]," ΕΕΒΣ, VI (1929), 369–374. Cf. Kostas Kairophylas, "Σύμμεικτα (τά κρητικά στέμματα τοῦ Πανεπιστημίου τῆς Πάδοβας) [Miscellaneous (Greek Coats of Arms at the University of Padua)]," 'Ελληνικά, VI (1933), 328–332; it contains the relevant bibliography.

96. There are only three Cretan coats of arms at the University of Bologna (Fabris, "Professori e scolari Greci" [14], p. 135). In 1688 the engraving of coats of arms on the walls of the university was forbidden (p. 136).

97. See Crusius, Turcograeciae (1:53), pp. 205, 246, 494. As a general rule, most Europeans studied classical literature in Italy and Germany. Fewer did so in France (Dousae, De itinere [1:171], p. 6).

98. See the lecture by Cleovoulos Tsourkas, which surveys the contribution made by graduates from the University of Padua to the intellectual recovery of the Hellenic world (Gli scolari Greci di Padova nel Rinnovamento culturale dell'Oriente ortodosso [Greek Scholars from Padua and the Cultural Renewal of the Orthodox East] [Padua, 1957]).

99. On Symeon Kavasilas, see Gedeon, Χρονικά τῆς πατριαρχικῆς 'Ακαδημίας (32), pp. 64–66.

100. On these two scholars and their correspondence, see Nikolaos Tomadakis, "Μάξιμος Μαργούνιος πρός Συμεῶνα Καβάσιλαν (ἐν τῶν τοῦ Β. Α. Μυστακίδου) [Maximos Margounios to Symeon Kavasilas (from the posthumous papers of B. A. Mystakidis)]," ΕΕΒΣ, XIX (1949), 292–305, 393.

101. Crusius, Turcograeciae (1:53), pp. 494–495. Symeon the Deacon and Symeon Kavasilas were apparently one and the same person. On the man and his knowledge of Greek, see p. 500 (where Crusius' remarks are based on information supplied by Gerlach in a letter dated 1 February 1577).

102. Ibid., p. 537.

103. See Theophilos Voreas, " 'Ελληνική Φιλοσοφία κατά τούς μετά τήν ἅλωσιν

χρόνους [Greek Philosophy in the Years After the Fall of Constantinople]," ΠΑΑ, IV (1929), 78.

104. See Andreas Moustoxydis, "Νικόλαος Σοφιανός [Nicholas Sophianos]," 'Ελληνομνήμων, pp. 236–264; and Legrand, *Bibliographie hellénique* (2:55), I, clxxvii–cxciv.

105. On the life, letters, and other works of Eparchos, see Andreas M. Moustoxydis, 'Ιστορικά καί φιλολογικά ανάλεκτα εκδιδόμενα [*Edited Historical and Literary Analects*] (Corfu, 1872), I, 45–82. There is also the lengthy biographical treatment by Chrysostomos Papadopoulos, Πρώται σχέσεις τών ορθοδόξων πρός τούς διαμαρτυρομένους κατά τόν ΙΣΤ' αιώνα [*First Contacts between the Orthodox and the Protestants during the Sixteenth Century*] (Athens, 1924), pp. 8–12. For a supplementary bibliography of foreign sources, see Ernst Benz, *Wittenberg und Byzanz* (Marburg, Germany, 1949), p. 247. On the fate of Eparchos' manuscripts, see K. A. de Meyier, "Un Nouveau Catalogue des manuscrits grecs d'Antoine Eparque," *Scriptorium*, IX (1955), 99–104.

106. See Ioannis K. Vasdravellis, 'Ιωάννης Κωττούνιος, ό εκ Βεροίας σοφός [*Ioannis Kottounios, Sage of Veroia*] (Thessalonica, 1943), which contains the less recent bibliography. There is some additional material in Mertzios, Μνημεία μακεδονικής ιστορίας (2:59), pp. 471–504.

107. Fabris, "Professori e scolari Greci" (14), pp. 145 ff.

108. See Constantine Amantos, "Λέων 'Αλλάτιος; [Leo Allatios]," Εις μνήμην Σπ. Λάμπρου [*To the Memory of Spyridon Lambros*] (Athens, 1935), pp. 557–566; Carmela Jacono, *Bibliografia di Leone Allacci (1588–1669)* (Palermo, 1962).

109. Börje Knös, " 'Ο Λεονάρδος ό Φιλαράς [Leonardos Philaras]," Προσφορά εις Στίλπ. Π. Κυριακίδην [*Presented to Stilpon P. Kyriakidis*] (Thessalonica, 1953), pp. 345–357. For further information on Philaras, see the work by the traveller Magni, *Lettere* (1:142), pp. 26–28.

110. See Nikos A. Bees, "Μιχαήλ Κοντοπίδης Μάρκελλος σύνδικος καί αντιπρύτανις τού εν Παταβίω πανεπιστημίου [Michael Kontopidis Markellos, Syndic and Vice-Rector of the University of Padua]," 'Αρμονία, II (1901), 57–63. See also Zerlentis, 'Ιστορικά σημειώματα (4:116), pp. 21–22.

111. A few are mentioned by Andreas Moustoxydis in 'Ελληνομνήνων, I (1843), 288–294, 303–382.

112. Moustoxydis, 'Ιστορικών καί φιλολογικών αναλέκτων (105), I, 77–81. On Antonios Eparchos, see Legrand, *Bibliographie hellénique* (2:55), I, ccx–ccxxvii, and pp. 277–281 for a letter of Eparchos' to Dionysios.

113. The text is in Sathas, Μνημεία ελληνικής ιστορίας (4:218), VIII, 545–591.

114. Manoussacas, " 'Αρσενίου 'Αποστόλη επιστολαί (5:163), p. 28.

115. Amantos, "Λέων 'Αλλάτιος" (108), p. 565.

116. Crusius, *Turcograeciae* (1:53), pp. 94–95. The whole of the poem is in Moustoxydis, 'Ιστορικών καί φιλολογικών αναλέκτων (105), I, 67–73.

117. Crusius, *Turcograeciae* (1:53), pp. 543–545. Basileios Mystakidis found the date ζ' ελαφηβολιώνος αφμξ' [7 elaphivolionos (=7 March) 1547] in *Collectio Camerariana* (cod. lat. 10351–10478) (see Constantine Dyovouniotis, " 'Εκ τών καταλοίπων τού Β. Μυστακίδου τά υπ' αριθ. 16 καί 17 [Nos. 16 and 17 of Basileios Mystakidis' Posthumous Papers]," ΕΕΒΣ, XVII (1941), 276).

118. Crusius, *Turcograeciae* (1:53), p. 545. For comment on and explication of the ideas contained in Eparchos' letter, see Benz, *Wittenberg und Byzanz* (105), pp. 12–15; for Melancthon's indirect reply to Eparchos, in which he says that political problems must be solved before religious ones, see pp. 16 ff. There is further material on Eparchos in Crusius, *Turcograeciae* (1:53), p. 546; *cf.* Iakovos Diassorinos' letter to Melancthon on 23 November 1555 (p. 556). On Iakovos Diassorinos, and Iakovos

Vasilikos, Despot of Samos, see the bibliographical note in Dyovouniotis, " Ἐκ τῶν καταλοίπων" (117), p. 277, fn. 2. Regarding Diassorinos' letter and Melancthon's reply to it, see Benz, *Wittenberg und Byzanz* (105), pp. 34 ff. Matthaios Devaris, another Greek scholar and a contemporary of Eparchos', who was a convert to Roman Catholicism, expected the freedom of the "race" to flow from the reunion of the Churches. This was because religious reconciliation would provide the justification for liberating Greeks ("τὴν ἀφορμὴν ἐλευθερίας") (see Ioannis E. Kalitsounakis, Ματθαῖος Δεβαρῆς καί τό ἐν Ρώμη ἑλληνικόν Γυμνάσιον [Matthaios Devaris and the Greek College in Rome]," Ἀθηνᾶ, XXVI (1914), 99).

119. See Papamichael, Μάξιμος ὁ Γραικός (43), pp. 470–481.

120. See Basileios A. Mystakidis, "Excerpta Crusiana. Μαρτῖνος ὁ Κρούσιος καί Ἀνδρέας Δαρμάριος ὁ Ἐπιδαύριος ἐν Τυβίγγῃ ∶ 1584 [*Excerpta Crusiana.* Martinus Crusius and Andreas Darmarios from Epidaurus in Tübingen in 1584]," *Forschungen und Versuche zur Geschichte des Mittelalters und der Neuzeit* [*Research and on Contributions to Medieval and Modern History*] (Jena, 1915), p. 502. Mystakidis studied everything that Crusius wrote about Greece and the Greeks, but, instead of publishing his research in one major tome, he dispersed it in innumerable lesser studies, often repeating himself. Still, he is what we might call a "Crusiologist."

121. For details of the life of Franciscos Portos, see Crusius, *Turcograeciae* (1:53), p. 522 (*annotatio*). There is also the comprehensive study by Andreas Moustoxydis in Ἑλληνομνήμων, pp. 364–384. See also the work (which unfortunately I have not been able to consult) by J. Sturm, "Beiträge zur vita des Humanisten Franciscus Portus (1511–1581) [Contribution to the Life of the Humanist Francis Portus]," *Programm des k. Neuen Gymn. zu Würzburg für das Studienjahr 1902–1903* (Würzburg, 1903), pp. 3–30. *Cf.* Papadopoulos, Πρῶται σχέσεις τῶν ὀρθοδόξων (105), pp. 14 ff., which contains the bibliography. On Portos' posthumous works, see the letter written by his son, who was also a scholar, to Crusius (*Turcograeciae* [1:53], p. 534). And see Iorga, *Byzance après Byzance* (1:13), p. 43.

122. Crusius, *Turcograeciae* (1:53), p. 516.

123. *Ibid.*, p. 517.

124. See Papadopoulos, Πρῶται σχέσεις τῶν ὀρθοδόξων (105), p. 22. On Aimilios, see Crusius, *Turcograeciae* (1:53), pp. 520–521.

125. At this time Ioannis Zygomalas was successfully teaching ancient Greek to a few monks (see Gerlach, *Tagebuch* [1:22], pp. 270–271; and Legrand, *Zygomalas* (2:14), pp. 7 ff. See also Zerlentis, Παραλειπόμενα τοῦ οἴκου Ζυγομαλᾶ (90), pp. 3–6.

126. On Theodosios, see Zerlentis, Παραλειπόμενα τοῦ οἴκου Ζυγομαλᾶ (90), pp. 8–11, 17–18. Dyovouniotis has compiled a bibliography on him (Θεοδόσιος Ζυγομαλᾶς [39], pp. 18–40, 141–266).

127. Mystakidis, "Excerpta Crusiana" (120), pp. 503–504.

128. Crusius, *Turcograeciae* (1:53), p. 476. *Cf.* pp. 489–490, 499, 508; and Gerlach, *Tagebuch* (1:22), p. 451. See also Basileios S. Mystakidis, "Λασκάρεις, 1400–1869 [The Lascaris Family, 1400–1869]," ΕΕΒΣ, V (1923), 132.

129. Crusius, *Turcograeciae* (1:53), pp. 524–525.

130. See Mystakidis, "Λασκάρεις" (128), p. 137; Mystakidis, "Excerpta Crusiana" (120), pp. 508–509; Elias Zachariades, *Tübingen und Konstantinopel. Martin Crusius und seine Verhandlungen mit der Griechisch-Orthodoxen Kirche* [*Tübingen and Constantinople. Martin Crusius and His Discussions with the Greek Orthodox Church*], (Göttingen, 1941), p. 61.

131. Crusius, *Turcograeciae* (1:53), p. 527. *Cf.* his letter to Theodosios Zygomalas (Legrand, *Zygomalas* [2:14], pp. 175–176); and his letter to the monk Symeon Kavasilas on 27 May 1577 (Crusius, *Turcograeciae* [1:53], p. 457). See Iorga, *Byzance après*

Byzance (1:13), pp. 41–42, for a characteristic expression of his philhellenic sentiments, and Mystakidis, "Λασκάρεις" (128), pp. 134–136. On his relationship with Symeon Kavasilas, see Basileios Mystakidis, Βιβλιογραφικά μελετήματα ἐκ τῶν τοῦ Μ. Κρουσίου (Τυβίγγης) ἐκδόσεων [Bibliographical Studies on Works Edited by Martinus Crusius (Tübingen)]," Θεολογία, VIII (1930), 144–146, 148, 154–158.

132. See Crusius, *Turcograeciae* (1:53), p. 479: "Τῆς Ἑλλάδος φωνῆς καὶ τοῦ Ἑλληνικοῦ ἔθνους εἰμὶ φίλος τε καὶ θαυμαστὴς ὡς οὐδεὶς τῶν ὁμοεθνῶν [More than any other of my compatriots, I am a friend and admirer of the Greek language and the Greek nation]." For further expressions characteristic of Crusius' philhellenism see pp. 78–79.

133. Mystakidis, "Excerpta Crusiana" (120), pp. 503–504.

134. Zachariades, *Tübingen und Konstantinopel* (130), p. 76.

135. See Legrand, *Zygomalas* (2:14), pp. 178–179, and especially the material in Mystakidis, "Excerpta Crusiana" (120), pp. 507 ff.

136. See Wilhelm Göz and Ernst Conrad, *Diarium Martini Crusii 1598–1599* [*Diary of Martin Crusius, 1598–1599*], (Tübingen, 1931), p. 28; and Spyridon Lambros, Δύο Ἀθηναῖοι τοῦ δεκάτου ἕκτου αἰῶνος [Two Athenians of the Sixteenth Century]," NE, XV (1921), 29. On one of these visitors to Tübingen, Emmanuel Mouzikis, see also Mystakidis, "Δύο Ἕλληνες" (2:21), pp. 1–14. Also relevant is Polychronis Enepekides, "Aus Wiener und Pariser Handschriften. Beiträge zu den Griechisch-abendlandischer Beziehungen im 16 Jahrhundert [Texts from Manuscripts of Vienna and Paris. Contribution to Studies of Greek—Western Relations in the Sixteenth Century]," JÖBG, III (1954), 67 ff. There is more on Emmanuel Mouzikis in Joan Leonclavius, *Annales sultanorum othmanidarum* (Frankfurt, 1558), pp. 221–222. *Cf.* Zerlentis, Σημειώματα περὶ Ἑλλήνων (2:55), pp. 18–91, where there is a reference to Mouzikis as one of Crusius' students in ancient Greek at the University of Tübingen in August 1586; and on the same point, see Basileios A. Mystakidis, "Βιβλιογραφικά σημειώματα ἐκ τῶν τοῦ Μ. Κρουσίου (Τυβίγγης) [Bibliographical Notes on the Works of M. Crusius (Tübingen)]," ΕΕΒΣ, VI (1929), 216–232. See also Mystakidis' other articles, "Βιβλιογραφικά μελετήματα" (131), pp. 146–147; " Ἰωνᾶς Ταρίτζιος ἐκ Κυζίκου καὶ Μαρτῖνος ὁ Κρούσιος ἐν Τυβίγγῃ [Jonas Taritzios from Cyzicus and Martinus Crusius in Tübingen]," Θεολογία, VIII (1930), 193–197; "Λασκάρεις" (128), pp. 151 ff.; and "Βιβλιογραφικά σημειώματα [Bibliographical Notes]," Θεολογία, VIII (1930), 144–147. See also Zachariades, *Tübingen und Konstantinopel* (130), pp. 60–70; *cf.* pp. 80–100, and also pp. 100–106 (for his correspondence with Gerlach and Solomon Schweigger).

137. See Crusius, *Turcograeciae* (1:53), p. 532: "αὐτὴν ἐνθήσομαι τῇ σήμερον Ἑλλάδι, ἥν συγγράφω, ἱστορίᾳ [I shall put this (regarding Crete) in the history of modern Greece that I am now writing]." *Cf.* his letter of similar content to Maximos Margounios (Basileios A. Mystakidis, " Ὁ ἱερὸς κλῆρος κατὰ τὸν ΙΣΤ' αἰῶνα (Μάξιμος ὁ Μαργούνιος) [The Holy Clergy during the Sixteenth Century: Maximos Margounios]," Εἰκοσιπενταετηρὶς Κωνσταντίνου Κόντου [*The Twenty-fifth Jubilee of Constantine Kontos*] (Athens, 1893), pp. 170–171. On the Cretan scholar, Morzenos, see Constantine Dyovouniotis, " Ἰωάννης Μορζῆνος (βίος καὶ ἔργα του, ὧν ἐκδίδονται δύο ἀνέκδοτα ἐκ χειρογράφων Βιβλ. Βουλῆς) [Ioannis Morzenos: His Life and Works (Two of Which, from the Manuscripts of the Greek Parliamentary Library, Are Now Edited)]," Νέα Σιών, XVII (1922), pp. 654 ff.

138. See Mystakidis, "Excerpta Crusiana" (120), pp. 505–507. *Cf.* Zerlentis, Σημειώματα περὶ Ἑλλήνων (2:55), pp. 28, 31–32, 35, regarding the Greeks recommended to Crusius by Jeremiah II.

364 NOTES—CHAPTER 6

139. Zerlentis, Σημειώματα περί Ἑλλήνων (2:55), pp. 27–28. There is a reference to a school on Mykonos in 1639 in du Loir, *Voyages* (1:108), p. 6.

140. Crusius, *Turcograeciae* (1:53), pp. 205, 246. See also Pennas, Σερραϊκά χρονικά (1:176), p. 29.

141. See Basileios Laourdas, " ᾽Ισιδώρου ἀρχιεπισκόπου ὁμιλία περί τῆς ἁρπαγῆς τῶν παίδων καί περί τῆς μελλούσης κρίσεως [The Homily of Archbishop Isidore on the Seizure of Children, and on the Last Judgment]," Ἑλληνικά, appendix 4, presented to S. P. Kyriakidis (Thessalonica, 1953), p. 392.

142. Pennas, Σερραϊκά χρονικά (1:176), pp. 31–32. Andreas Darmarios the copyist also studied in Mistra under the priest Dorotheos, who came from Nauplia (Mystakidis, "Excerpta Crusiana" [120], p. 510).

143. Nikos A. Bees, "Darstellungen altheidnischer Denkern und Autoren in die Kirchenmalerei der Griechen [Ancient Pagan Thinkers and Authors in Greek Ecclesiastical Painting]," BNJ, IV (1923), 126–127.

144. See Athenagoras, " Ἡ Σχολή τῶν Φιλανθρωπηνῶν" (5:262), p. 40. See also Nitsos, Μονογραφία περί κώμης τοῦ Τσαμαντᾶ (3:111), pp. 77–83. The whole problem of the "crypto-school" is re-examined by Tasos A. Gritsopoulos, Σχολή Δημητσάνης [*The Dimitsana School*] (Athens, 1962), pp. 17–32, which also contains the relevant bibliography.

145. Bees, "Darstellungen altneidnischer Denkern" (143), pp. 126–127.

146. *Ibid.*, pp. 115 ff., 121–122; Bees gives a bibliography. See also Andreas Xyngopoulos, "Μεσσαιωνικά μνημεία ᾽Ιωαννίνων [Mediaeval Monuments of Ioannina]," HX, I (1926), 136–137. And *cf.* I. Dujčev, "Klassisches Altertum im mittelalterlichen Bulgarien [Classical Antiquity in Medieval Bulgaria]," *Renaissance und Humanismus im Mittel- und Ost Europa* (Berlin, 1962), I, 352–353.

147. Gerlach, *Tagebuch* (1:22), p. 184. For further details about this church, see pp. 201–202.

148. See Bees, "Darstellungen altneidnischer Denkern" (143), pp. 122–127. Constantine Spetsieris, on p. 446 of his study, "Εἰκόνες Ἑλλήνων φιλοσόφων εἰς ἐκκλησίας [Portraits of Greek Philosophers in the Church]," ΕΕΦΣΠΑ, XIV (1963–1964), 386–458, speaks emphatically about the importance of these pictures after 1204—a time of "the vigorous development of Greek nationalism."

149. Dujčev, "Klassisches Altertum" (146), pp. 355–356.

150. See Bees, "Darstellungen altneidnischer Denkern" (143), pp. 118–119, which provides the relevant bibliography.

151. Schweigger, *Constantinopel* (1:116), pp. 221–222.

152. *Ibid.*, p. 221.

153. See Sauger, Ἡ παροῦσα κατάστασια (1:178), p. 15.

154. Crusius, *Turcograeciae* (1:53), p. 246.

155. *Ibid.*, p. 495.

156. *Ibid.*, p. 216. We should search for certain schools, identifying them with those mentioned by Tryphon E. Evangelidis in his chronological study of specific areas, Ἡ παιδεία ἐπί τουρκοκρατίας [*Education under Turkish Rule*] (Athens, 1936), 2 vols.

157. Ninolakis, Μελέτιος ὁ Πηγᾶς (5:49), p. 27, fn.

158. Crusius, *Turcograeciae* (1:53), p. 537. On Daniel Phourlanos, see also Voreas, " Ἑλληνική Φιλοσοφία" (103), p. 79.

159. Crusius, *Turcograeciae* (1:53), p. 495.

160. See Listarchos' correspondence in Andreas Moustoxydis, "Μιχαήλ Λήσταρχος ἤ Ἑρμόδωρος Ζακύνθιος [Michael Listarchos or Hermodoros from Zacynthus]," Ἑλληνομνήμων, pp. 581–615. See also Phaedon K. Bouboulidis, Ἕλληνες λόγιοι μετά

τήν "Αλωσιν. Α. Μιχαήλ 'Ερμόδωρος Δήσταρχος [*Greek Scholars after the Fall of Constantinople: Michael Hermodoros Listarchos*] (Athens, 1959), which provides the relevant bibliography.

161. Bouboulidis, "Ελληνες λόγιοι (160), pp. 18–24. *Cf.* Constantine Amantos, Τά γράμματα εἰς τήν Χίον κατά τήν Τουρκοκρατίαν, 1566–1822 (Σχολεῖα καί λόγιοι) [*Education in Chios under Turkish Rule, 1566–1822 (Schools and Scholars)*] (Piraeus, 1946), pp. 43 ff.

162. Amantos, Τά γράμματα εἰς τήν Χίον, pp. 7–8, 54–56, 61–63. For a bibliography on the Koresios family, see Manoussos Manoussacas, "Στέφανος Κατράριος ὁ πρῶτος γνωστός "Ελληνας νοτάριος τῆς Χίου [Stephanos Katrarios, First Known Greek Notary on Chios]," Εἰς μνήμην 'Αμάντου (Athens, 1960), p. 268, fns. 5–8.

163. Amantos, Τά γράμματα εἰς τήν Χίον (161), p. 8.

164. Manuel I. Gedeon, "Πνευματική τῶν Χίων ἀνάπτυξις πρό ἐτῶν διακοσίων [Intellectual Development of the People of Chios Two Centuries Ago]," EMA, XII (1962), 42–44.

165. There is an enlightening survey by Manoussacas, 'Η Κρητική λογοτεχνιά (59), which also contains the appropriate bibliography. See also Manoussos Manoussacas, Κριτική βιβλιογραφία τοῦ "Κρητικοῦ Θεάτρου" [*A Critical Bibliography of the "Cretan Theater"*] (Athens, 1964). A selection of Cretan literary works, with extracts from them, is given in Phaedon Bouboulidis, Κρητική Λογοτεχνία [*Cretan Literature*] (Athens, 1955). *Cf.* Dimaras, 'Ιστορία τῆς νεοελληνικῆς λογοτεχνίας (59), pp. 81–92; and Alexandre Embiricos, *La Renaissance crétoise, XVIᵉ et XVIIᵉ siècles. Vol. I: La Littérature* (Paris, 1960).

166. Crusius, *Turcograeciae* (1:53), p. 366.

167. *Ibid.*, p. 74.

168. *Ibid.*, pp. 430, 431, 433; also p. 434: " 'Ημεῖς ὀνόματι "Ελληνες, αὐτοί δέ σοφίᾳ καί ἔργοις ἀρίστοις καί λαμπροῖς [We are Greeks by name, but they (the Germans) are Greek in their wisdom and in their excellent and peerless works]." *Cf.* Crusius' letter (p. 454): " 'Η 'Ελλάς τήν ἑαυτῆς γλῶσσαν καί καρδίαν ἐς τήν Γερμανίαν μετακεκομικέναι πως δοκεῖ [Greece's language and heart seem somehow to have moved to Germany," and the poem by Laurentius Rhodomanus at the very beginning of the work.

169. *Ibid.*, p. 434.

170. See Vacalopoulos, *Origins of the Greek Nation* (1:62), p. 176.

171. Crusius, *Turcograeciae* (1:53), p. 94.

172. *Ibid.*, p. 94.

173. *Ibid.*, p. 74.

174. *Ibid.*, p. 94.

175. *Ibid.*, p. 367.

176. Mystakidis, "Λασκάρεις" (128), p. 140, fn. 2.

177. See Michael Sophianos' letter to his teacher, Hermodoros Listarchos, written on his behalf by George the Corinthian (Bouboulidis, "Ελληνες λόγιοι [160], pp. 38–39).

178. On Noukios and his travels, see Moustoxydis, 'Ιστορικά καί φιλολογικά ἀνάλεκτα (105), I, 24–44. There is also Foucault's recent publication (*Nicandre* [73]).

179. Theodosios Zygomalas was so enamored of antiquity that he copied down every ancient inscription he found on his travels. He gave some to George Dousa (Legrand, Ζygomalas [2:14], pp. 70–71).

180. See Ioannis Kallitsounakis, " 'Η διέλευσις τοῦ περιηγητοῦ Arnold von Harff δι' 'Ελλάδος κατά τό 1477 [Arnold von Harff's Pilgrimage through Greece in 1477]," ΕΕΒΣ, XXIII (1953), 258–259.

181. Crusius, *Turcograeciae* (1:53), pp. 75, 99. On the geographical spread of the Greek language, see p. 489. On the dialects, see pp. 216, 426, 487, 489; and on the Pontus dialect, see Zerlentis, Σημειώματα περί 'Ελλήνων (2:55), p. 34. For some interesting dialectical characteristics of the period, see the speech by Pachomios Rousanos, "Περί τῆς ἐκ τῶν θείων Γραφῶν ὠφελείας; [On the Benefits of Holy Scripture]," PG, XCVIII, cols. 1345–1352. On the respective influences of the Greek and Turkish languages upon each other, see Belon, *Observations* (1:123), p. 5a.

182. Crusius, *Turcograeciae* (1:53), p. 496.

183. *Ibid.*, pp. 216, 461, 489.

184. *Ibid.*, pp. 485, 486, 496. *Cf.* p. 489. See also du Fresne-Canaye, *Voyage* (1:123), p. 81.

185. Belon, *Observations* (1:123), p. 4b.

186. Crusius, *Turcograeciae* (1:53), p. 489.

187. Sauger, 'Η παροῦσα κατάστασις (1:178), p. 15, is mistaken in his viewpoint: 'Η ποίησις σύγκειται παρ' αὐτοῖς ἔκ τινων βακχικῶν ἀσμάτων εἰς χυδαίαν γλῶσσαν, ὧν ὁ ρυθμός καί ἡ μουσική τραχύτατα [Their poetry consists of some Bacchic songs in a vulgar language; the rhythm and the music are crude]."

188. Crusius, *Turcograeciae* (1:53), p. 273.

189. Rousanos, "Περί τῆς ἐκ τῶν θείων Γραφῶν ὠφελείας" (181), cols. 1352–1353.

190. Gerlach, *Tagebuch* (1:22), p. 304. See Mystakidis on the language of the sermon (Basileios S. Mystakidis, " 'Ιωάννου Ζυγομαλᾶ λόγος ἐν τῇ Παμμακαρίστῳ [Ioannis Zygomalas' Sermon in Pammakaristos]," Θεολογία, VI [1928], 286 ff.).

191. Crusius, *Turcograeciae* (1:53), p. 205.

192. Dousae, *De itinere* (1:171), p. 41.

193. Belon, *Observations* (1:123), p. 4b.

194. *Ibid.*, p. 37b.

195. Zerlentis, Σημειώματα περί 'Ελλήνων (2:55) p. 28.

196. Crusius, *Turcograeciae* (1:53), p. 336. For a lengthy biography of Ioasaph II (1555–1565), see Manuel I. Gedeon, " 'Ο πατριάρχης 'Ιωάσαφ Β' ὁ Μεγαλοπρεπής [Patriarch Ioasaph II the Magnificent]," 'Ημερολόγιον τῆς 'Ανατολῆς, II (1883), 242–265. *Cf.* Gedeon's Χρονικά τῆς πατριαρχικῆς 'Ακαδημίας (32), pp. 53–56.

197. Matthaios Paranikas, " 'Ιωάννης ὁ Ζυγομαλᾶς καί Μιχαήλ 'Ερμόδωρος ὁ Λήσταρχος [Ioannis Zygomalas and Michael Hermodoros, Called Listarchos]," ΕΦΣΚ, II (1876–1877), 40–41. On the life of Listarchos, see Bouboulidis' study, Μιχαήλ ἤ 'Ερμόδωρος Λήσταρχος (160), which contains the relevant bibliography. Bouboulidis also identifies Listarchos' students.

198. Jeremiah II begged Crusius to send him from the West printed books "of spiritual value" ("ὡς τάς ἐξηγήσεις τάς περί ψυχῆς")—theological, historical, even philosophical if there were any of worth (Crusius, *Turcograeciae* [1:53], p. 467). During the patriarchate of Jeremiah II, that is, at the time discussions were in progress between the Orthodox and the Protestants concerning Church unity, Greek theologians expressed interest in having their works published in the West.

199. Sathas, Βιογραφικόν σχεδίασμα (5:337), p. 99; Mertzios, Θωμᾶς Φλαγγίνης (5:137), pp. 257–266. More recent than both of these, and with a more recent bibliography, is the biographical study by Polychronis Enepekides, "Der Briefwechsel des Maximos Margounios, Bischof von Kythera (1549–1602) [The Correspondence of Maximos Margounios, Bishop of Kythera (1549–1602)]," JÖBG, X (1961), 93–145. On Gabriel Severus and the effect of Roman Catholic proselytizing on the Orthodox East, see Apostolos Vacalopoulos, 'Ιστορία τοῦ Νέου 'Ελληνισμοῦ [History of Modern Hellenism] (Thessalonica, 1968), III, 434–435.

200. See M. Sicherl, "Manuel Glynzunios als Schreiber Griechischer Hand-

schriften [Manuel Glyzounios as a Scribe of Greek Manuscripts]," BZ, XLIX (1956), 34–54.

201. See Constantine Amantos, " Ἡ Λογαριαστική τοῦ Γλυτζούνη [The Arithmetic of Glytzounis]," HME (1934), pp. 179–184.

202. Sathas, Βιογραφικόν σχεδίασμα (5:337), pp. μγ' – μδ' [xliii–xliv]. On Glytzounis' affection for the Greek nation, see his letter addressed to Gabriel Severus (Bees, "Χειρόγραφα καί Παλαιότυπα;" (5:248), pp. 10–11).

203. Mystakidis, " Ὁ ἱερός κλῆρος" (137), pp. 167–168.

204. Ibid., pp. 166–167.

205. Moustoxydis, Ἱστορικά καί φιλολογικά ἀνάλεκτα (105), I, 73–76.

206. Manoussos I. Manoussacas, "Συμβολή εἰς τήν ἱστορίαν τῆς ἐν Κωνσταντινουπόλει Πατριαρχικῆς Σχολῆς [Contribution to the History of the Patriarchal School of Constantinople]," Ἀθηνᾶ, LIV (1950), 10.

207. See Evangelidis, Ἡ παιδεία ἐπί τουρκοκρατίας (156), I, 235. Sathas has some useful comments on the minutes of the synod (Βιογραφικόν σχεδίασμα [5:337], pp. 82–92), especially on the seventh canon (p. 91). Cf. p. πθ' [lxxxix].

208. See Demetrios M. Sarros, "Μαξίμου τοῦ Πελοποννησίου ἀπόκρισις πρός φιλομαθεῖς Ἄρτης ἐξ Ἰωαννίνων τῷ 1614 [The Reply of Maximos of the Peloponnese to the Learned Men of Arta, Made from Ioannina in 1614]," HX, XII (1937), 258. Ioannis K. Dyovouniotis provides some material on his life and work: "Μάξιμος ὁ Πελοποννήσιος [Maximos the Peloponnesian]," Ἐκκλησιαστικός Φάρος, XIII (1914), 451–463.

209. On his life, see Katramis, Φιλολογικά ἀνάλεκτα (4:214), pp. 231–238.

210. Moustoxydis, "Παχώμιος Ρουσάνος" (5:245), p. 647.

211. Sarros, "Μαξίμου τοῦ Πελοποννησίου" (208), p. 257.

212. Legrand, Bibliothèque grecque vulgaire (5:268), II, 315.

213. Crusius, Turcograeciae (1:53), p. 509. Cf. Gerlach, Tagebuch (1:22), pp. 483–484; Schweigger, Constantinopel (1:116), p. 70. However, the poverty of the monasteries of Mt. Athos led to the smuggling out of manuscripts as gifts for the Czar (for the relevant documentation, see Stilpon P. Kyriakidis, " Ἡ ἐξαγωγή χειρογράφων ἐξ Ἁγίου Ὄρους [The Commerce in Manuscripts from Mt. Athos]," Μακεδονικά, IV (1960), 532–533. Cf. Michael Lascaris, "Arsène Suhanov et les manuscrits de l'Athos," Byzantion, XXVIII (1958), 543–545. And see Christos G. Patrinelis, "Διονύσιος Ἰβηρίτης μεταφραστής τῆς "Χρονογραφίας τοῦ Δωροθέου" εἰς τήν ρωσικήν καί μητροπολίτης Οὑγγροβλαχίας [Dionysios of Iveron as Translator of the "Chronicle of Dorotheos" into Russian and as Metropolitan of Hungaro-Walachia]," ΕΕΒΣ, XXXII (1963), 315).

214. See Politis, " Ἁγιορεῖτες βιβλιογράφοι" (13), pp. 355–384.

215. Gerlach, Tagebuch (1:22), p. 360.

216. See du Fresne-Canaye, Voyage (1:123), p. 109. On the contents of the library, see the article by an anonymous writer, " Ἡ βιβλιοθήκη τοῦ οἰκουμενικοῦ πατριαρχείου κατά τά τέλη τοῦ 16 αἰ. [The Library of the Oecumenical Patriarchate Towards the End of the Sixteenth Century]," Ἐκκλησιαστική Ἀλήθεια, IV (1883), 566–567.

217. See, typically, Busbecq's remarks about the large number of coins and manuscripts that he sent to Vienna (Life and Letters [5:170], I, 416–418).

218. See Gerlach, Tagebuch (1:22), pp. 425, 428.

219. See Dositheos, Δωδεκάβιβλος [Twelve Books], Book XI, p. 1173 (cited by Spyridon Lambros, NE, II (1905), 156). See also Ypsilantis, Τά μετά τήν Ἅλωσιν (1:92), p. 166; and Manoussos I. Manoussacas, " Ἀνέκδοτα πατριαρχικά ἔγγραφα περί Ἀθανασίου τοῦ Ρήτορος [Unpublished Patriarchal Documents about Athanasios

the Orator]," EMA, II (1949), 134–135, where there is a basic bibliography on the man and his works.

220. See Collignon, *Le Consul Jean Giraud* (1:52), p. 48.

221. Petros Papageorgiou, "Αἱ Σέρραι καί τά προάστεια. Τά περί τάς Σέρρας καί ἡ μονή 'Ιωάννου τοῦ Προδρόμου [Serrai and Its Suburbs. On Serrai and the Monastery of St. John the Baptist]," BZ, III (1894), 286.

222. Spyridon Lambros, "Βιβλιογράφοι ἐκ τοῦ οἴκου Ζυγομαλᾶ [Bibliographers of the House of Zygomalas]," NE, IV (1907), 489–490.

223. Gerlach, *Tagebuch* (1:22), p. 448.

224. Crusius, *Turcograeciae* (1:53), p. 498. *Cf.* pp. 419–420. On the purchase of theological manuscripts, see p. 33. *Cf.* also Dousae, *De itinere* (1:171), pp. 70–71 (regarding educated monks and manuscripts in 1590). See Nikos A. Bees, " 'Ελληνίδες βιβλιογράφοι καί κυρίαι κωδίκων κατά τούς μέσους αἰῶνας καί ἐπί τουρκοκρατίας [Greek Women Bibliographers and Owners of Codices during the Middle Ages and under Turkish Rule]," Ποικίλον 'Ημερολόγιον (1905), pp. 54–63, which contains the early bibliography on the subject. See also Spyridon Lambros, " 'Ελληνίδες βιβλιογράφοι καί κυρίαι κωδίκων [Greek Women Bibliographers and Owners of Codices]," NE, IV (1907), 377–379, for the addition of two names unknown to Bees.

225. Crusius, *Turcograeciae* (1:53), p. 487. This unreliable information given by Gerlach (and that similarly offered by Belon [*Observations* (1:123), p. 38a] refers, as we saw at the beginning of the chapter, to the decline of philosophical studies as a consequence of the spread of mystical Hesychast ideas.

226. Crusius, *Turcograeciae* (1:53), p. 487.

227. *Ibid.*; also pp. 498, 511. See the works of the sixteenth-century theologian George Kalyvas, which Augerius de Busbecke procured in Constantinople (Dyovouniotis, "Γεώργιος Καλύβας" [62], pp. 80–99).

228. Dousae, *De itinere* (1:171), p. 9. Maximilian I of Bavaria donated the Palatine Library to the Vatican, and it was taken there by Leo Allatios (see Amantos' study, "Λέων 'Αλλάτιος" (108), p. 560.

229. For details, see Sathas, Μεσαιωνική βιβλιοθήκη (5:100), III, η' – ια' [viii–xi].

230. Crusius, *Turcograeciae* (1:53), pp. 94–95.

231. Gerlach, *Tagebuch* (1:22), p. 174.

232. See Manoussacas, "Συμβολή εἰς τήν ἱστορίαν τῆς ἐν Κωνσταντινουπόλει Πατριαρχικῆς Σχολῆς" (206), pp. 3–28, which provides the bibliography.

233. Spyridon Lambros, " 'Ενθυμήσεων συλλογή πρώτη [First Collection of Memoirs]," NE, VII (1910), 181.

234. Manuel I. Gedeon, "Θεσσαλονικέων παλαιαί κοινοτικαί διενέξεις [Past Communal Disputes in Thessalonica]," Μακεδονικά, II (1941–1952), 18.

235. Spyridon Lambros, "Περί τῆς παιδείας ἐν 'Ιωαννίνοις ἐπί Τουρκοκρατίας [On Education in Ioannina under Turkish Rule]," NE, XIII (1916), 273–317.

236. Athenagoras, " 'Η Σχολή τῶν Φιλανθρωπηνῶν" (5:262), pp. 55–72, where the evidence is critically examined. There is further material on the Epiphanios School in Phanis Michalopoulos, Τά Γιάννινα καί ἡ νεοελληνική ἀναγέννηση (1648–1820) [*Ioannina and the Modern Greek Renaissance (1648–1820)*] (Athens, 1930), pp. 29–31; Athenagoras, "Σχολή 'Επιφανίου 'Ηγουμένου [The School of Epiphanios Hegoumenos]," HX, IV (1929), 64–78; and especially Constantine Mertzios, "Τό ἐν Βενετίᾳ 'Ηπειρωτικόν ἀρχεῖον [The Archives of Epirus in Venice]," HX, XI (1956), 65 ff.

237. Mystakidis, "Δύο 'Έλληνες . . . ἐν Τυβίγγῃ" (2:21), pp. 6–7. On the seventeenth-century priest-monk Pringileus, who was a bibliographer, see Spyridon Lambros, " 'Επιστολαί Νικηφόρου τοῦ Πριγγιλέως [The Correspondence of Nicephorus Pringileus]," NE, IV (1907), 118–119.

238. Eustratiadis, " Ἐπιστολαί Εὐγενίου Ἰωαννουλίου τοῦ Αἰτωλοῦ" (5:164), p. 275.

239. Crusius, *Turcograeciae* (1:53), p. 205. *Cf.* Gerlach, *Tagebuch* (1:22), p. 211, regarding Symeon: "Der Mönch kan 3–4 Schüler haben, von denen er so viel habe, dass er kleiden könne: die Türken saugen sie eben gar auss [A monk named Symeon, with 3–4 students, might take in tuition fees just enough for his clothes; the Turks were appropriating all they could]." It would seem from one of Crusius' letters that Symeon was teaching in the Patriarchal School at this time, or later in 1585; the reference "τῶν ἐν τῷ πατριαρχείῳ διδασκαλείων ἄξιον καθηγητήν [a distinguished professor of the Patriarchal School]" is given by Mystakidis, "Βιβλιογραφικά μελετή-ματα" (131), pp. 145, 155 ff. See also Manuel I. Gedeon, Παιδεία καί πτωχεία παρ' ἡμῖν κατά τούς τελευταίους αἰῶνας [*Our Education and Our Poverty over the Last Few Centuries*] (Constantinople, 1893), pp. 16 ff.; also Gedeon's Χρονικά τῆς πατριαρχικῆς Ἀκαδημίας (32), p. 63. For evidence regarding the school's fees during the seventeenth century, see Lambros, " 'Ἀμοιβαί διδασκάλων" (27), pp. 195–198.

240. Sathas, Βιογραφικόν σχεδίασμα (5:337), p. μγ' [xliii].

241. Rousanos, "Περί τῆς ἐκ τῶν θείων Γραφῶν ὠφελείας (181), col. 1356. *Cf.* col. 1353: " 'Ἀπόδος τι μέρος (τῶν χρημάτων) καί τῇ ψυχῇ [Part with some (of your money) for the sake of your soul]." See also Moustoxydis, "Παχώμιος Ρουσάνος" (5:245), p. 646; and du Fresne-Canaye, *Voyage* (1:123), p. 81. On Pachomios Rousanos, see Börje Knös, *L'Histoire de la littérature néo-grecque. La période jusqu'en 1821* (Uppsala, 1962), pp. 281–283.

242. The bibliography on Manolakis is in Hasluck, "The First English Traveller's Account of Athos" (5:211), p. 103, fn. 3, and p. 105. See also Manoussacas, "Συμβολή εἰς τήν ἱστορίαν τῆς ἐν Κωνσταντινουπόλει Πατριαρχικῆς Σχολῆς" (206), p. 4, fn. 1 For a bibliography on the establishment of schools, see Georgios P. Kounoutos, "Σχολεῖα τῆς τουρκοκρατουμένης Καστοριᾶς [Schools in Kastoria under Turkish Rule]," Γέρας Α. Κεραμοπούλου (Athens, 1953), p. 429, fn. 1.

243. Pericles G. Zerlentis, "Περί τῶν ἐν Χίῳ φροντιστηρίων [On the Seminaries of Chios]," Ἀθηνᾶ, XXIX (1917), pp. 231 ff. (for details of the seminary in the Church of St. Anargyroi during the middle of the seventeenth century): "τοῦτο τό σχολεῖον δέν εἶναι μερικόν, ἀλλά τῆς κοινότητος [This is not a private school, but belongs to the community]." On the institution of seminaries, see p. 245, where there is also a reference to another, St. Victor, founded by Manolakis in 1660. On George Koressios, a Chian teacher of the beginning of the seventeenth century, see Pantelis Kontogiannis, "Γράμμα τῆς κοινότητος τῆς Βενετίας πρός Γεώργιον Κορέσσιον καί ἀπάντησις αὐτοῦ [A Letter from the Greek Community of Venice to George Koressios, and His Reply]," BNJ, V (1926–1927), 89–96; and also Constantine Amantos, Γεώργιος Κορέσσιος [George Koressios]," Ἀθηνᾶ, XLVI (1935), 191–204.

244. See Anna Morava-Chatzinikolaou, Πάτμος [*Patmos*] (Athens, 1957), pp. 42–45.

245. See Georg Hofmann, "Apostolato dei Gesuiti," OCP, I (1935), pp. 145, 146, 154–156; and Zerlentis, Ἱστορικά σημειώματα (4:116), pp. 20–23.

246. For details, see Valettas, " Ὁ Ἅγιος Ἰγνάτιος Ἀγαλλιανός" (4:15), pp. 290 ff., esp. pp. 303 ff. A letter from Pachomios Rousanos to Ignatios of Antissa contains some interesting information about teaching (see Moustoxydis, "Παχώμιος Ρουσάνος" (5:245), pp. 681–710.

247. Zerlentis, Ἱστορικά σημειώματα (4:116), p. 28.

248. See Mertzios, Θωμᾶς Φλαγγίνης (5:137), pp. 167–185, for material on the subsequent history of this school, which functioned intermittently until 1926.

249. In 1611 one such bequest was made by Mondanos of Trikkala, a merchant

in Ioannina. The amount specified in his will was the interest on 1,000 ducats: "νά δίδηται ἀενάως εἰς τό σχολεῖον ὁπού θέλει γενῆ διά τούς σπουδαίους εἰς τά 'Ιωάννινα [to be donated continuously to the school, which will be founded for educated men in Ioannina]" (see Mertzios, "Τό ἐν Βενετίᾳ 'Ηπειρωτικόν ἀρχεῖον" [236], pp. 18, 34–37.

250. Mertzios gives detailed evidence (Θωμᾶς Φλαγγίνης [5:137], pp. 5–165).

251. Athenagoras, " 'Η Σχολή τῶν Φιλανθρωπηνῶν" (5:262), p. 60.

252. See Nikolaos M. Panagiotakis, " 'Ιταλικές 'Ακαδημίες καί θέατρο. Οἱ Stravaganti τοῦ Χάνδακα [Italian Academies and Theater. The Stravaganti of Candia]," Θέατρο, XXVII–XXVIII (Athens, 1966), pp. 45–50, for details.

253. Moustoxydis, 'Ιστορικῶν καί φιλολογικῶν ἀναλέκτων (105), I, 2–3; and Marmoras, 'Ιστορία τῆς νήσου Κερκύρας (94), pp. 329–330. On education generally in Corfu during the sixteenth and seventeenth centuries, see Spyridon M. Theotokis, "Περί τῆς ἐκπαιδεύσεως ἐν 'Επτανήσῳ [On Education in the Ionian Islands]" Κερκυραϊκά Χρονικά, V (1956), 12–13.

254. Panagiotakis, " 'Ιταλικές 'Ακαδημίες καί Θέατρο" (252), pp. 39–45, 255. Cf. Nikolaos Panagiotakis and Alfred L. Vincent, "Νέα στοιχεῖα γιά τήν 'Ακαδημία τῶν Stravaganti [New Evidence Concerning the Stravaganti Academy]," Θησαυρίσματα, VII (1970), 52–81.

255. Cléobule Tsourkas, Les Débuts de l'enseignement philosophique et de la libre pensée dans les Balkans. La Vie et l'oeuvre de Théophile Corydalée, 1570–1646 (Thessalonica, 1967), pp. 34–35.

256. Ibid., pp. 179–195.

257. Constantine D. Mertzios, "Θεόφιλος Κορυδαλλεύς ὁ 'Αθηναῖος [Theophilos Corydalleus the Athenian]," 'Αθηναϊκά, XI (1958), pp. 3–5 of the reprint.

258. Tsourkas, Corydalée (255), pp. 46–48.

259. Mertzios, "Θεόφιλος Κορυδαλλεύς" (257), pp. 5–8.

260. Tsourkas, Corydalée (255), pp. 73–76. In 1620, on Zacynthus, Theophilus Corydalleus wrote a "canonical" sketch of St. Gerasimos (Chrysostomos Papadopoulos, " 'Ο ῞Αγιος Γεράσιμος [5:300], pp. 18–19).

261. See Samuel Baud-Bovy, "Antoine Léger, pasteur aux Vallées Vaudoises du Piédmont et son séjour à Constantinople. D'après une correspondance inédite, 1622–1631 [Antoine Léger, Pastor in the Valleys of Vaud in the Piedmont and His Stay in Constantinople. According to Unpublished Correspondence, 1622–1631]," Revue d'Histoire Suisse, XXIV, II (1944), 206.

262. See Gedeon, Χρονικά τῆς πατριαρχικῆς 'Ακαδημίας (32), p. 83: "ἀπό τῆς διδασκαλίας τούτου ἡ τῆς πατριαρχικῆς σχολῆς πρόοδος τῶν μαθητῶν ἤρξατο εὐμαθέστερον [through his teaching, the students of the Patriarchal School attained the peak of learning]."

263. Tsourkas, Corydalée (255), pp. 23, 87–88.

264. See Constantine Dyovouniotis, "Μελέτιος Συρῖγος [Meletios Syrigos]," in his 'Ιερόν Σύνδεσμον (Athens, 1914), p. 12 of the reprint. See also Manuel I. Gedeon's 'Επιστολή Γεωργίου Κορεσσίου πρός Θεόφιλον Κορυδαλλέα [A Letter from Georgios Koressios to Theophilos Corydalleus]," 'Εκκλησία, XIV (1936), 282–285, 298–300, 313–315.

265. Tsourkas, Corydalée (255), pp. 76–79.

266. Εἰς ἅπασαν τήν Λογικήν τοῦ 'Αριστοτέλους ὑπομνήματα καί ζητήματα [Notes and Problems Pertaining to Aristotle's Logic] (Venice, 1729); Εἴσοδος φυσικῆς ἀκροάσεως κατ' 'Αριστοτέλην [Introduction to Aristotle's Physics] (Venice, 1779); Περί γενέσεως καί φθορᾶς κατ' 'Αριστοτέλην [On Being and Nonbeing according to Aristotle] (Venice, 1780); Διαίρεσις τῆς ποιητικῆς καί τά εἴδη αὐτῆς [Forms and Divisions of the Poetics] (Venice, 1781) (see Tsourkas, Corydalée [255], pp. 95 ff.).

267. See Tsourkas, *Corydalée*, pp. 101–102.

268. Kostas Kyrris, " Ὁ Παναγιωτάκης καί δάσκαλος τοῦ Φαρμακᾶ στά 1789 ἦταν ὁ Παναγιωτατζῆς Λογιώτατος [Panagiotakis of Pharmakas on Cyprus in 1789, Called "The Teacher," Was Panagiotatzis Logiotatos]," Κυπριακαί Σπουδαί, ΚΘ′ [XXIX] (1965), 169–170.

269. Tsourkas, *Corydalée* (255), pp. 197–198.

270. *Ibid.*, pp. 204–205.

271. *Ibid.*, p. 203.

272. *Ibid.*, pp. 203–204.

273. *Ibid.*, pp. 197–205.

274. *Ibid.*, 207–208.

275. Anastasios Gordios, "Βίος Εὐγενίου Ἰωαννουλίου τοῦ Αἰτωλοῦ [The Life of Eugenius Giannoulis the Aetolian]," in Sathas, Μεσαιωνική βιβλιοθήκη (5:100), III, 475.

276. *Ibid.*, pp. 442–444.

277. *Ibid.*, p. 475.

278. Tsourkas, *Corydalée* (255), p. 100.

279. See Gedeon, Χρονικά τῆς πατριαρχικῆς Ἀκαδημίας (32), pp. 45–74; Tsourkas, *Corydalée* (255), pp. 23, 91, 169–175, 211–216; and Mihai Guboglu, "Dimitrie Cantemir Orientaliste," *Studia et acta orientalia*, III (1961), 130.

280. Gedeon, Χρονικά τῆς πατριαρχικῆς Ἀκαδημίας (32), pp. 86–92.

281. On his life, see Zacharias Tsirpanlis, "Μελέτιος Συρίγος, 1586–1664 [Meletios Syrigos, 1586–1664]," Γρηγόριος Παλαμᾶς, LIV (1971), 156–171.

282. See the biography by his student, Anastasios Gordios, "Βίος Εὐγενίου Ἰωαννουλίου τοῦ Αἰτωλοῦ [The Life of Eugenius Giannoulis the Aetolian]," in Sathas, Μεσαιωνική βιβλιοθήκη (5:100), III, 424–445. On the man himself, see p. 478. There is a newer and better edition of his life by Spyridon Lambros, "Βίος Εὐγενίου Ἰωαννουλίου τοῦ Αἰτωλοῦ [The Life of Eugenius Giannoulis the Aetolian]," NE, IV (1907), 27–82. *Cf.* Panos I. Vasileiou, Εὐγένιος Γιαννούλης ὁ Αἰτωλός [*Eugenius Giannoulis the Aetolian*] (Athens, 1957), I, 9–21, which contains the relevant bibliography; and Ioannis T. Kolitsaras, "Εὐγένιος ὁ Αἰτωλός [Eugenius the Aetolian]," ΑΕΑΣ, I (1958), 37–45.

283. Sathas, Μεσαιωνική βιβλιοθήκη (5:100), III, 445 ff.; and Vasileiou, Εὐγένιος Γιαννούλης ὁ Αἰτωλός (282), pp. 24–39 (there is a chronological table of the main events of his life on pp. 37–39). See also the study of Eugenius Giannoulis and the school at Vraniana in Agrafa in Georgios P. Pavlidis, " Ἐπίσκεψις εἰς τήν ἕδραν τῆς Σχολῆς τῶν Ἀγράφων [A Visit to the Seat of the Agrafa School]," ΘΧ, VII–VIII (1959), 221–227. On the schools of Agrafa after 1645, see Vasileiou, Ἡ ἐπισκοπή Λιτζᾶς καί Ἀγράφων (3:104), pp. 84 ff.; and pp. 148 ff. on education generally in western central Greece after 1657. See also Panos I. Vasileiou, "Οἱ σχολές τῶν Ἀγράφων στά χρόνια τῆς Τουρκοκρατίας [The Schools of Agrafa during the Years of Turkish Rule]," Ρουμελιώτικο Ἡμερολόγιο (1957), pp. 146–151.

284. See Basileios Georgiadis, " Ἐξ ἐπιστολαί Εὐγενίου Ἰωαννουλίου [Six Letters of Eugenius Giannoulis]," Ἐκκλησιαστική Ἀλήθεια, I (1885), 556.

285. Constantine N. Sathas, Νεοελληνική Φιλολογία. Βιογραφίαι τῶν ἐν τοῖς γράμμασι διαλαμψάντων Ἑλλήνων ἀπό τῆς καταλύσεως τῆς βυζαντινῆς αὐτοκρατορίας μέχρι τῆς ἑλληνικῆς ἐθνεγερσίας (1453–1821) [*Modern Greek Literature. Biographies of Distinguished Greek Literati from the Time of the Overthrow of the Byzantine Empire to the Greek National Revolution (1453–1821)*] (Athens, 1868), p. 329.

286. See Tasos A. Gritsopoulos, "Εὐγενίου Ἰωαννουλίου Αἰτωλοῦ ἐπιστολαί ἀνέκδοτοι [The Unpublished Letters of Eugenius Giannoulis the Aetolian]," Ἀθηνᾶ LVIII (1954), 29–34, which refers to the codices containing Eugenius' letters and

also provides the relevant bibliography. Some emendations have been given by Panos I. Vasileiou in one of his earlier studies, "Διορθώσεις ἐπί ἐπιστολῶν Εὐγενίου Γιαννούλη [Emendations on the Letters of Eugenius Giannoulis]," 'Αθηνᾶ, LXI (1957), 64; but a complete corpus of the letters has still to be collected and published. On the language of the letters, see Kolitsaras, "Εὐγένιος ὁ Αἰτωλός" (282), p. 54.

287. Eustratiadis, " 'Επιστολαί Εὐγενίου 'Ιωαννουλίου τοῦ Αἰτωλοῦ" (5:164), pp. 280–281. Cf. Eustratiadis in 'Ελληνικά, VII (1934), 93.

288. Eustratiadis, " 'Επιστολαί" (5:164), p. 280. Cf. Eustratiadis in Ελληνικά, VII (1934), 223.

289. Eustratiadis, " 'Επιστολαί" ('Ελληνικά, VIII [1935], 274).

290. Ibid., VII [1934], 243.

291. Ibid., VIII [1935], 128. Cf. the " 'Επιστολαί" in VII (1934), 243–244, where there is a letter dated 22 April 1661 to the inhabitants of Aetoliko.

292. On Gordios, see Kolitsaras, "Εὐγένιος ὁ Αἰτωλός" (282), p. 33. On the students of Eugenius, see Vasileiou, Εὐγένιος Γιαννούλης ὁ Αἰτωλός (282), pp. 72–92.

Chapter 7

1. See Aristotle Vrekosis, "Αἱ ἑλληνικαί κοινότητες τῶν ἑλευθέρων χωρικῶν [The Greek Communities of Free Peasants]," 'Επιθεώρησις τῆς Τοπικῆς Αὐτοδιοικήσεως IX (1930), 2nd series, p. 136, which contains the less recent bibliography. For a legal view of the problem of communities, see Nikolaos Pantazopoulos, 'Ελλήνων συσσωματώσεις κατά τήν τουρκοκρατίαν [Corporations of Greeks under Turkish Role] (Athens, 1958), pp. 5–9, where there is a splendid bibliography.

2. Cf. Iakovos Visvizis, " 'Η κοινοτική διοίκησις τῶν 'Ελλήνων κατά τήν τουρκοκρατίαν [Greek Community Government under Turkish Rule]," Hell. Contemp., commem. vol. 1453–1953 (1953), pp. 183–184, 187–188.

3. Demosthenes I. Danielidis, 'Η νεοελληνική κοινωνία καί οἰκονομία [Modern Greek Society and Economy] (Athens, 1934), takes a sociological view of the community. He describes it (pp. 126 ff.) as "geoeconomic—a single structure based on the complementary roles of town and countryside, production and manufacture." However, this is an imperfect definition, and Danielidis admits as much when he says that one "has not yet been formulated in any full or systematic way."

4. Paparrhegopoulos, 'Ιστορία τοῦ ἑλληνικοῦ ἔθνους (2:63), V, 115. Paparrhegopoulos gives a much more analytical view in 'Ιστορικαί πραγματεῖαι [Historical Essays] (Athens, 1858), pp. 219–220.

5. Vrekosis, "Αἱ ἑλληνικαί κοινότητες" (1), pp. 127–141.

6. David Urquhart, La Turquie. Ses Resources, son organization municipale, son commerce, traduit de l'anglais par X. Raymond (Paris, 1836), II, Part 1, pp. 37, 43.

7. Pericles Argyropoulos, Δημοτική διοίκησις ἐν 'Ελλάδι [Local Government in Greece] (Athens, 1859), I, 26 (n. a), 36–37.

8. Nikolaos Moschavakis, Τό ἐν 'Ελλάδι δημόσιον δίκαιον ἐπί τουρκοκρατίας [Municipal Law in Greece under Turkish Rule] (Athens, 1882), pp. 73–76.

9. Louis Bréhier, Les Institutions de l'empire byzantin (Paris, 1949), pp. 203–208.

10. Ibid., p. 203. Cf. Ch. Petit-Dutaillis, Les Communes françaises. Caractères et évolution des origines au XVIIIᵉ siècle (Paris, 1947), p. 18.

11. Bréhier, Les Institutions (9), pp. 208, 211.

12. Cf. Ioannis Voyatzidis, "Γλῶσσα καί λαογραφία "Ανδρου [Language and Folklore of Andros]," AX, IX (1960), 128–130. Cf. esp. p. 128: "If the institution of local self-government did not survive the stern decree of Leo the Wise, who died in 912 A.D., how is it that it was still found intact at the commencement of Frankish rule in 1204?"

NOTES—CHAPTER 7 373

13. Bréhier, *Les Institutions* (9), pp. 211–212.
14. Justinian was only legitimizing a *de facto* situation in Italy when he promulgated the so-called *Pragmatica sanctio* after Narses' victory at Capua in 554. According to this, bishops received the right to exercise a certain supervisory control over municipal government in concert with civic notables (*primores civitatis*) and wealthy citizens (*possessores*). Constantine Amantos comments on this in his Ἱστορία τοῦ Βυζαντινοῦ κράτους [*History of Byzantine Rule*] 2nd ed. (Athens, 1939), I, 35, 48–50, 193–194, 216.
15. Danielidis also believes that some elements of the institution of the community may have originated in classical antiquity but that the community "would hardly have survived, indeed would almost certainly have perished, both as an idea and as an institution transcending particular places and times, had it not become identified with local realities; for, small as Greece is, it has always been a land of great geoeconomic contrasts" (Νεοελληνική κοινωνία καί οἰκονομία [3], p. 131).
16. See Apostolos Vacalopoulos, "Συμβολή στήν ἱστορία τῆς Θεσσαλονίκης ἐπί Βενετοκρατίας (1423–1430) [A Contribution to the History of Thessalonica under Venetian Rule (1423–1430)]," in his Τόμος Ἀρμενοπούλου (Thessalonica, 1952), pp. 129–130.
17. See Voyatzidis, "Γλῶσσα καί λαογραφία Ἄνδρου" (12), pp. 126–130, 174.
18. See Anonymous, "Γεωγραφικά ὅρια τῆς Κυζίκου [Geographical Boundaries of Kyzikos]," Ξενοφάνης, I (1896), 215–216.
19. See Vacalopoulos, *Origins of the Greek Nation* (1:62), pp. 124–125, 146–148.
20. For the period 1666–1669, see Laourdas, "Βυζαντινά καί μεταβυζαντινά ἐγκώμια" (5:306), p. 114.
21. See Vacalopoulos, *Origins of the Greek Nation* (1:62), pp. 54–57. The appropriate chapter notes contain the bibliography.
22. See Denis Zakythinos, "La Commune grecque," *Hell. Contemp.* (1948), pp. 25–26 of the reprint.
23. Theodor Ouspenski, "Ζητήματα πρός μελέτην τῆς ἐσωτερικῆς ἱστορίας τοῦ βυζαντινοῦ κράτους [Questions concerning the Domestic History of the Byzantine State]," ΔΙΕΕ, II (1885–1886), 545. See also Vrekosis, "Αἱ ἑλληνικαί κοινότητες" (1), pp. 138–139.
24. See Darrouzès, "Lettres de 1453" (6:18), pp. 78, 80, 85, 87.
25. See Vacalopoulos, *Origins of the Greek Nation* (1:62), pp. 146–147.
26. Papageorgiou, "Αἱ Σέρραι" (6:221), p. 280.
27. Nitsos, Μονογραφία (3:111), pp. 72–76. It is interesting that Tsamanta, an isolated village in Epirus, preserved an older tradition.
28. Collignon, *Le Consul Jean Giraud* (1:52), p. 28.
29. *Ibid.*, p. 21.
30. Philippos P. Argentis and Stilpon P. Kyriakidis, Ἡ Χίος παρά τοῖς γεωγράφοις καί περιηγηταῖς ἀπό τοῦ ὀγδόου μέχρι τοῦ εἰκοστοῦ αἰῶνος [*Chios from the Eighth Century to the Twentieth according to Geographers and Travellers*] (Athens, 1946), I, 66.
31. Papageorgiou, "Αἱ Σέρραι" (6:221), p. 280. Papageorgiou goes no further than this (p. 12 of the codex of Serrai). Yet it is clear that the codex contains much that is germane to the history of Greek communities under Turkish rule.
32. Aravantinos, Χρονογραφία τῆς Ἠπείρου (2:50), II, 259–260.
33. See Apostolos Vacalopoulos, "Οἱ δημοσιευμένες ὁμιλίες τοῦ ἀρχιεπισκόπου Θεσσαλονίκης Ἰσιδώρου ὡς ἱστορική πηγή γιά τήν γνώση τῆς πρώτης τουρκοκρατίας στήν Θεσσαλονίκη (1387–1402) [The Published Homilies of Isidorus, Archbishop of Thessalonica, as an Historical Source for Knowledge of the First Turkish Dominion in Thessalonica (1387–1402)]," Μακεδονικά, IV (1960), 24–25.

34. For the relevant resolution on this matter, see Papageorgiou, "Αἱ Σέρραι" (6:221), p. 281.

35. *Ibid.*, p. 282.

36. *Ibid.*, p. 241.

37. Spyridon Lambros, "Ναυπλιακόν ἔγγραφον τοῦ οἴκου Πουλομμάτη ἐν ἔτει 1509 καὶ ὁ βιβλιογράφος Μιχαήλ Σουλιάρδος [A Document of Nauplia from the House of Poulommatis (1509), and the Copyist Michael Souliardos]," NE, VI (1909), 279.

38. Ricaut, *Histoire* (1:90), p. 326.

39. But disagreements did arise—for example, over the excessive cost of a community project. In 1665 the Athenians suspended work on an impressive but expensive project for the irrigation of olive trees even though 3,000 gold pieces had already been spent on it (see Collignon, *Le Consul Jean Giraud* [1:52], pp. 54–55).

40. For instance, in April and May each year the *epitropoi* ordered the people of Aegina to go out into the fields to destroy the nests and break the eggs of partridges, which would otherwise wreak havoc on the grain crop (*ibid.*, p. 23; and *cf.* Magni, *Relazione* [5:269], p. 34).

41. For extensive detail, see Eleutheriadis, Ἀνατολικαί μελέται (5:3), pp. 49 ff., and Fattal, Le Statut légal (1:1), pp. 344 ff.

42. On the animosity towards them, see Heuzey, "Discours historique" (5:255), p. 250.

43. The punishments he imposed were fines, imprisonment, or flogging, which could be avoided by means of a bribe (see Miller, "Lichtle's Description" [1:94], p. 449). *Cf.* what Georgieviz has to say about the punishments meted out generally by cadis (*De Turcarum moribus* [1:26], p. 58). See also Gerlach, *Tagebuch* (1:22), p. 484. De Tournefort has some interesting comments to make in relation to Melos (*Relation* [1:90], I, 59). Besides his judicial duties, the cadi also performed those of policeman and market inspector, as for example in Athens in 1675 (see Collignon, *Le Consul Jean Giraud* [1:52], pp. 35–36, where there are also other details about the office and jurisdiction of the cadi).

44. *Cf.* Dapper, *Description* (4:136), p. 208; de Tournefort, *Relation* (1:90), I, 59; and Chatzidakis, Ἡ ἱστορία τῆς Μήλου (4:4), pp. 163–164.

45. See Crusius, *Turcograeciae* (1:53), p. 316.

46. See Heuzey, "Discours historique" (5:255), p. 218.

47. See Charalambos Rempelis, Κονιτσιώτικα [*On Konitsa*] (Athens, 1953), p. 197.

48. For details, see Gerlach, *Tagebuch* (1:22), p. 413, and *cf.* p. 213. See the unpublished document no. 27 of the typed résumé of the codex issued by the *şeri* (Moslem ecclesiastical court) of Veroia for the years 1049 (1639–1640) and 1050 (1640–1641) (1:50).

49. The title of *kocabaşı* apparently appeared locally at different times during the later centuries of Ottoman rule (see Demetrios P. Paschalis, "Κοτζαπάσηδες [*Kocabaşıs*]," HME [1935], 301).

50. Rempelis, Κονιτσιώτικα (47), p. 47.

51. See Vacalopoulos, *Origins of the Greek Nation* (1:62), pp. 146–147.

52. See Collignon, *Le Consul Jean Giraud* (1:52), p. 44, where there is material concerning inheritance law within the jurisdiction of the Archbishop of Athens.

53. The so-called "Treaty of Droviani," which B. D. Zotos copied from the codex of the monastery of Douviani, may be an utterly suppositional event. If authentic, it was probably signed, not on 1 June 1456 as Evangelos Boggas would have us believe ("Δύο ἱστορικά ἐνθυμήματα τοῦ 15 αἱ. ἐκ Βορείου Ἠπείρου [Two Sixteenth-Century Historical Memoirs from Northern Epirus]," ΔΙΕΕ, XIII (1959), 427–429), but much later, perhaps in 1756.

54. Vacalopoulos, *Origins of the Greek Nation* (1:62), p. 180.

55. See Nikolaos K. Spyropoulos, "Τά "Αγραφα τῆς Θεσσαλίας. 'Ιστορικά καί Λαογραφικά [Agrafa, Thessaly: History and Folklore]," ΘΧ, II (1931), 172.

56. See Lambridis, 'Ηπειρωτικά Μελετήματα (3:154), Τεῦχος 8, Part 1, pp. 42–43. On Zagora, its Vlach villages, and other matters, see the critical comments by the poet Kostas Krystallis, "Απαντα [*Complete Works*], ed. Georgios Valetas (Athens, 1959), II, 507 ff. Krystallis discerns Slavic influences on the Vlachs of Zagora (see pp. 513–514, 517, 518).

57. See Lambridis, 'Ηπειρωτικά μελετήματα (1:82), Τεῦχος 9, Part 2, pp. 19–22. *Cf.* pp. 12–15.

58. *Ibid.*, p. 20.

59. *Ibid.*, pp. 10–11. For an analysis of the privileges based on certain notes, see pp. 33–37; also pp. 82–86; and Demetrios Sarros, "Ζαγοριακῶν θεσμίων ἔρευνα [Researches on the Institutions of Zagora]," ΗΧ, II (1927), 286–301, which refers mainly to the middle of the nineteenth century.

60. Lambridis, 'Ηπειρωτικά μελετήματα (1:82), Τεῦχος 9, Part 2, pp. 78–80. *Cf.* Ali Pasha's attempts to convert a number of the villages of Zagora into *çiftliks* (pp. 73–78).

61. See Ioannis Lambridis, "Πολιτική ἐξάρτησις καί διοίκησις Μαλακασίου [The Political Dependence of Malakasi and its Administration]," Παρνασσός, X (1886), 376–379. *Cf.* Krystallis, "Απαντα (56), pp. 595–601, who follows Lambridis.

62. Lambridis, "Πολιτική ἐξάρτησις" (61), pp. 379–384. *Cf.* Lambridis' 'Ηπειρωτικά Μελετήματα (1:82), Τεῦχος 5, Part 2, pp. 25 ff.; and Basileios Skaphidas, "Τά προνόμια τοῦ Μετσόβου [The Privileges of Metsovon]," HE, I (1952), 657–660, which contains the translation of a firman (its first publication), probably issued by Mustapha III (1757–1774), and which mentions that the inhabitants of Metsovon, who constituted the garrison of a mountain pass, paid a "lump sum" of 108,000 *akçes* (*aspra*) in tax, covering the *haraç*, the corn tithe, and the taxes on vineyards, bees, gardens, walnuts, fruit, wine, marriage, pastures, mills, and pigs (p. 660).

63. See Basileios K. Skaphidas, " 'Ιστορία τοῦ Μετσόβου [History of Metsovon]," HE, X (1961), 1055–1056.

64. Lambridis, "Πολιτική ἐξάρτησις" (61), p. 384.

65. In the firman of Mustapha III, there are references to Metsovon as comprising seven neighborhoods with a population of 437 raia vassal families (Skaphidas, "Τά προνόμια τοῦ Μετσόβου" [62], p. 660).

66. See Lambridis, "Πολιτική ἐξάρτησις" (61), pp. 385–388.

67. See Lambridis, 'Ηπειρωτικά μελετήματα (1:82), Τεῦχος 5, part 2, pp. 15–16.

68. See Drosos, 'Ιστορία τῆς νήσου Τήνου (4:117), pp. 3, 247 ff., 263: "διετάχθη ἡ ἀκριβής τήρησις τῶν ἐθίμων καί ἠθῶν τῆς πιστῆς ταύτης νήσου [It was ordered that there should be no interference in the customs and manners of this loyal island]." Even during the siege of Tenos the islanders displayed an amenable attitude towards the new conqueror, with the result that they were successful in preserving their traditional privileges (see pp. 393–394, also pp. 25–35).

69. This question is dealt with at length in the study by Zerlentis, Φεουδαλική πολιτεία (1:111).

70. See Christos V. Mavropoulos, Τουρκικά ἔγγραφα ἀφορῶντα τήν ἱστορίαν τῆς Χίου [*Turkish Documents concerning the History of Chios*] (Athens, 1920), pp. 69, 80–81, 83: "τό ἀποκαλεῖν τούς κοτζαμπασῆδες ποτεστάτους ἀποτελεῖ αὐτόχρημα συκοφαντίαν [To call the *kocabaşıs potestatoi* (governors) is a downright calumny]." However, in a Turkish document of 1715 it is possible that the word *potestatoi* comprehended the *kocabaşıs* (p. 107: "the inhabitants of the island of Chios and the raia *potestatoi* . . ."), who, in another document of 1756, were also referred to as *protomastoroi*, chief of crafts-

376 NOTES—CHAPTER 7

men (p. 88). We still await a systematic study of the regimes on Chios under Genoese and Turkish rule. The study by Aimilia K. Sarou ("Τό χιακόν πολίτευμα κατά τούς αἰῶνας [Government on Chios over the Centuries]," ΕΕΒΣ, XXII (1952), 150–158) is inadequate. Sarou says that there were twelve notables on Chios under Turkish rule and identifies each with the *kodespotai* or *syndespotai* or *protogeroi* (one in every district) of Genoese rule (p. 156). *Cf.* Argentis-Kyriakidis, 'Η Χίος (30), I, 66; and Philip Argenti, *Chius Vincta 1566–1912* (Cambridge, 1941), pp. clxxiv ff. (*q.v.* p. clxxix, regarding the *deputati*, and pp. clxxxii ff., regarding the Brotherhoods).

71. Miller, "Lichtle's Description" (1:94), p. 448.

72. See Zerlentis, Φεουδαλική πολιτεία (1:111), p. 4.

73. Sauger, Ἱστορία τῶν ἀρχαίων δουκῶν (4:9), p. 192. Regarding community organization on Melos, as well as the administration of justice, see D'Arvieux, *Mémoires* (Paris, 1735), IV, 335–337. On the two *epitropoi* on each of the islands of Tzia (Kea), Siphnos, and Andros in 1563, see Zerlentis, Γράμματα τῶν τελευταίων Φράγκων δουκῶν (1:124), p. 29. *Cf.* Gion, Ἱστορία τῆς Σίφνου (4:132), pp. 139–141, where he describes the customary basis of community government and the administration of justice. See also Psyllas, Ἱστορία τῆς νήσου Κέας (4:64), pp. 153–154. On Syros at the end of the eighteenth century and the beginning of the nineteenth century, the people usually elected one *epitropos* each year (see Antonios Sigalas, " 'Η πατέντα τῶν κοτζαμπάσηδων [The Patent of the *Kocabaşıs*]," HME, IX (1930), 403–421). *Cf.* Sigalas' " 'Ανέκδοτα ἔγγραφα ἀφορῶντα εἰς τήν ἐκλογήν τῶν κοτζαμπάσηδων [Unpublished Documents concerning the Election of *Kocabaşıs*]," Ἑλληνικά, III (1930), 69–88.

74. See Drosos, Ἱστορία τῆς νήσου Τήνου (4:117), pp. 8, 9, fn. a.

75. See Sathas, Μνημεῖα ἑλληνικῆς ἱστορίας (4:218), IV, 328, 329.

76. This is how the community notables of Thessalonica were designated (see Vacalopoulos, *Origins of the Greek Nation* [1:62], p. 124).

77. Sathas, Μνημεῖα ἑλληνικῆς ἱστορίας (4:218), p. 272, where the manner of their election is set forth in an illuminating way. For further details see pp. 275, 284, 291, 330–331, 334, 336, 339.

78. See Pericles G. Zerlentis, Σύστασις τοῦ κοινοῦ τῶν Μυκονίων [*Establishment of the Municipality of Mykonos*] (Hermopolis on Syros, 1924), pp. 6–9. For details on the municipality's governing body see pp. 9–13, 18 ff.

79. *Ibid.*, p. 8.

80. *Ibid.*, pp. 19–23.

81. *Ibid.*, pp. 23–24.

82. *Ibid.*, pp. 25 ff.

83. See Voyatzidis, 'Αμοργός (4:106), p. 66, esp. pp. 67–68. De Tournefort says that on Melos in 1700 there were three *epitropoi* elected triennially who were responsible for the apportionment and collection of the capitation tax, as well as the letting of salt marshes, millstones, and customs duties. At the end of their period of office, these *epitropoi* were called *primati* or *vechiardi*, that is, *prokritoi* or *dimogerontes* (see de Tournefort, *Relation* [1:90], I, 58). In 1722 the *kapudan* pasha, Ghazi Hussein, passed on an order to the community of the island of Melos: "the seal of the municipality shall be in three or four parts, each of which will remain in the hands of separate individuals. The names of these persons shall be written in the *divan chane* (council house), and each year two or three shall be elected from among the *proestoi* (community leaders) to supervise the affairs of the municipality without interference from anyone else" (Vallindas, Ἱστορία τῆς νήσου Κύθνου [4:92], p. 63). By the nineteenth century the duties of the *castellanos* had shrunk to those of a constable or town crier. The *castellanos* was also called a *protogeros* (p. 78).

84. Sauger, Ἱστορία τῶν ἀρχαίων δουκῶν (4:9), p. 127.
85. See Zerlentis, Γράμματα τῶν τελευταίων Φράγκων δουκῶν (1:124), p. 43. Regarding these and other offices on Naxos during the later years of Turkish rule, see Iakovos T. Visvizis, "Ναξιακά νοταριακά ἔγγραφα τῶν τελευταίων χρόνων τοῦ δουκάτου τοῦ Αἰγαίου (1538–1577) [Notarial Documents from Naxos Dating from the Final Years of the Duchy of the Aegean (1538–1577)]," Ἐπετηρίς Ἱστορίας τοῦ Ἑλληνικοῦ Δικαίου [Annual History of Greek Law], pub. Academy of Athens IV (1951), 120–122.
86. Zerlentis, Γράμματα τῶν τελευταίων Φράνκων δουκῶν (1:124), p. 44.
87. See Amantos, "Οἱ προνομιακοὶ ὁρισμοί" (5:41), pp. 127 ff.
88. Ibid., p. 132. Cf. Karl Hopf, "Venetobyzantinische Analekten [Miscellany]," Sitzungsberichte der Kaiserlichen Akademie Philosophische-Historischen Classe, XXXII (1959), no. 3, pp. 521–523, which set forth the ahtname of Sultan Ibrahim (1646). Cf. the Greek translation in Argyropoulos, Δημοτικὴ διοίκησις (7), I, 45–50; also Gion, Ἱστορία τῆς Σίφνου (4:132), pp. 144–148.
89. The ahtname of Murad III (1574–1595) is in Zerlentis, Γράμματα τῶν τελευταίων Φράγκων δουκῶν (1:124), pp. 101–105. Cf. the ahtname of Ibrahim (1640–1648) regarding Siphnos (Gion, Ἱστορία τῆς Σίφνου [4:132], pp. 144–148). Both texts are given by Demetrios P. Paschalis, "Προνόμια καὶ διοίκησις τῶν Κυκλάδων ἐπὶ τουρκοκρατίας [The Privileges of the Cyclades and Their Administration under Turkish Rule]," AX, I (1948), 130–138. See also pp. 138–149, for the earlier ahtname issued by Suleiman I to Iakovos IV Crispos (1565).
90. See Zerlentis, Γράμματα τῶν τελευταίων Φράγκων δουκῶν (1:124), pp. 101–105; also pp. 75–78; and cf. their renewal by Ibrahim (Argyropoulos, Δημοτικὴ διοίκησις [7], I, 48–50).
91. See Hasluck, "Depopulation" (4:1), pp. 165–166, which contains the relevant bibliography. When Belon, speaking about the islands, says "Les magistrats et chefs des villes sont communément Turcs [The magistrates and chiefs of the towns are generally Turks]," he is undoubtedly referring to the agents of Turkish authority, the cadi and the voivode (Belon, Observations [1:123], p. 89).
92. Chaviaras, "Φιρμάνια" (4:29), p. 329.
93. See Hasluck, "Depopulation" (4:1), p. 165.
94. Ibid., p. 164, which also provides the relevant bibliography.
95. Chaviaras, "Φιρμάνια" (4:29), p. 327. Jeanne Z. Stephanopoli's remarks about Syme before 1821 (Les Iles de l'Egée. Leurs Privilèges [Athens, 1912], pp. 33 ff.) are based on Chaviaras' study. However, neither of these writers examines the problem in a systematic way. The lawyer Miltiadis Karavokyros also takes a number of extracts from Stephanopoli in his study," Τῶν Σποράδων νήσων τὰ δίκαια καὶ προνόμια [The Rights and Privileges of the Sporades]," Ἐκκλησιαστικὴ Ἀλήθεια, XXXII (1912), 381–388, 397–406, 419–424, 427, 432, 467–468. On the Turkish and Greek Community authorities on Icaria, see Georgirenes, Description (I:45), p. 68.
96. Chaviaras, "Φιρμάνια" (4:29), p. 347.
97. See Ricaut, Histoire (1:90), pp. 362–363. On Melos particularly, see Chatzidakis, Ἡ ἱστορία τῆς Μήλου (4:4), pp. 162–165, 266, 267–268; see pp. 269–270, for a document relating to the election of an epitropos. The epitropoi of the islands had the authority to impose all punishments except death, which required confirmation by the Porte (Sauger, Ἱστορία τῶν ἀρχαίων δουκῶν [4:9], p. 192).
98. Regarding Naxos, see Miller, "Lichtle's Description" (1:94), p. 448. The Roman Catholics who lived in Kastro elected two syndics. There were about three hundred Roman Catholics, and they had extensive properties.
99. Gion, Ἱστορία τῆς Σίφνου (4:132), pp. 142–143. Gion says that there was one in the main town and in each of the smaller towns on the island.

100. On this point, see Iakovos K. Visvizis, "Οἱ κοινοί καγκελλάριοι τῆς Νάξου ἐπί τουρκοκρατίας [The Community *Cangellarioi* of Naxos under Turkish Rule]," Ἀρχεῖον Ἰδιωτικοῦ Δικαίου, XII (1945), p. 3 of the reprint. *Cf.* Visvizis' "Ναξιακά νοτιαρακά ἔγγραφα" (85), pp. 1–167, esp. pp. 110–149, which deal with the notarial system, the laws in force, the courts, and related matters.

101. Stephanos T. Kavvadas, Οἱ κώδικες τῆς Χίου [*The Codices of Chios*] (Chios, 1950), pp. 5 ff., and p. 37.

102. For details, see Visvizis, "Οἱ κοινοί καγκελλάριοι" (100), pp. 11–15.

103. See Zerlentis, Σύστασις τοῦ κοινοῦ τῶν Μυκονίων (78), pp. 56–57; and Chatzidakis, Ἡ ἱστορία τῆς Μήλου (4:4), pp. 165–166, 265. See also Psyllas, Ἱστορία τῆς νήσου Κέας (4:64), pp. 154–155; and *cf.* Visvizis, "Οἱ κοινοί καγκελλάριοι" (100), pp. 5–6, 8. The earliest mention of a Greek notary on Chios is of a certain Stephanos Katrarios in 1446 (see Manoussacas, "Στέφανος Κατράριος" [6:162], pp. 265–271). There is interesting material on the notaries of Andros under Frankish and Turkish rule in Demetrios P. Paschalis, " Ὁ Σπαρτιάτης Στρατηγόπουλος, δημόσιος ὑπό βασιλικήν ἐξουσίαν νοτάριος ἐν Ἄνδρῳ [The Spartan Strategopoulos, Notary of Andros by Royal Authority]," BNJ, VII (1930), 87–98, esp. pp. 95–98. See also Phaedon K. Bouboulidis, "Νοτάριοι Ζακύνθου [Notaries of Zacynthus]," Ἐπετηρίς Ἀρχείου Ἱστορίας Ἑλληνικοῦ Δικαίου, VI (1958), 112–113. We still await a monograph on this subject, which has not been studied in a systematic way.

104. On the variety of titles, which probably had their origins in Frankish times, see Visvizis, "Οἱ κοινοί καγκελλάριοι" (100), p. 8.

105. *Ibid.*, pp. 9–10.

106. *Ibid.*, p. 9.

107. For further details, see Vallindas, Κυθνιακά (1:111), pp. 82–83. See also (though reservedly) Vallindas' Ἱστορία τῆς νήσου Κύθνου (4:92), pp. 74 ff., esp. p. 74, for some interesting but undated evidence concerning the composition of the *dodekada* of lay notables and the corresponding body of ecclesiastical notables.

108. See Zerlentis, Σύστασις τοῦ κοινοῦ τῶν Μυκονίων (78), pp. 70–71, and elsewhere.

109. Visvizis, "Οἱ κοινοί καγκελλάριοι" (100), pp. 3–4, where the bibliography has been assembled. See pp. 10–11 on the method of election of the municipal *cangellarioi* of Naxos, and related matters.

110. Kritikidis, Πραγματεία (4:41), pp. 33–37.

111. See Stamatiadis, Σαμιακά (4:46), II, 21.

112. Georgirenes, *Description* (1:45), p. 28.

113. *Ibid.*, pp. 6–7. I do not agree with Sevastakis (Τό δημόσιον δίκαιον ἐν Σάμῳ [4:53], p. 17) that a detrimental change took place in 1619, curtailing the extent of self-government, when an aga and a cadi were appointed to the island. Sevastakis relies on Stamatiadis (Σαμιακά [4:46], II, 15, 22), who says that the earlier document appointing the aga dates from 1619.

114. Georgirenes, *Description* (1:45), pp. 27–28.

115. See Vacalopoulos, *Thasos* (1:59), pp. 50–51.

116. Georgirenes, *Description* (1:45), p. 8. On the administration of Samos at the end of the seventeenth century, the institution of the four "general" or "great" notables, and other matters, see Kritikidis, Πραγματεία (4:41), p. 38. *Cf.* Stamatiadis, Σαμιακά (4:46), II, 30 ff. Other revenue apart from the *haraç* was deemed *wakf* and went to the Mosque of Topchane in Galata (Georgirenes, *Description* [1:45], p. 9).

117. *Cf.* Dapper, *Description* (4:136), p. 208.

118. Miller, "Lichtle's Description" (1:94), p. 449.

119. Zerlentis, Σύστασις τοῦ κοινοῦ τῶν Μυκονίων (78), pp. 67–68.

120. See de Tournefort, *Relation* (1:90), I, 67.

121. Zerlentis, Σύστασις τοῦ κοινοῦ τῶν Μυκονίων (78), pp. 19–23.

122. Vrekosis believes that the Greeks acquired "many distinctive traits," but he is not specific; he only says in a general way that "the influence of the municipal laws of foreign peoples in no way changed the sense of communal ownership; rather, the laws of the invaders were beneficially merged with this." See Vrekosis, "Αἱ ἑλληνικαί κοινότητες" (1), pp. 129, 138.

123. See above, pp. 191–192.

124. See Vacalopoulos, "Συμβολή στήν ἱστορία τῆς Θεσσαλονίκης" (16), p. 147, which also contains the relevant bibliography. The volume in which this study appears has a number of studies relating to the legal work of Armenopoulos, particularly the *Hexabiblos*.

125. There is a need for much more research of a systematic kind on post-Byzantine law throughout the Hellenic world. We still await a history of the subject. However, see the praiseworthy effort to collate the relevant bibliography by Demetrios S. Ginis, Περίγραμμα ἱστορίας τοῦ Μεταβυζαντινοῦ Δικαίου [*An Outline History of Post-Byzantine Law*] (Athens, 1966). There are further additions in the journal EEBΣ, XXVIII (1958), 258–263. See also Nikolaos Pantazopoulos, "Community Laws and Customs of Western Macedonia under Ottoman Rule," *Balkan Studies*, II (1961), 1–22, which also provides a bibliography of other relevant works by this writer.

126. For relevant examples, see Iakovos T. Visvizis, "Τινά περί τῶν νομικῶν ἐθίμων ἀπό τῆς τουρκοκρατίας μέχρι καί τοῦ Β. διατάγματος τῆς 23 Φεβρουαρίου 1835 [Data Relating to Customary Law from the Period of Ottoman Rule in Greece up to the Royal Decree of 23 February 1835]," Ἀθηνᾶ, LIII (1949), 225–256.

127. See the useful historical survey by Demetrios A. Petropoulos, "Συνεταιριστική ὀργάνωση καί κοινωνικό καθεστώς [Co-operative Organization and Social Status]," Συνεταιριστής, CIV–CVI (1955), 80–82.

128. See Spyridon Lambros, "Ὑπόμνημα Βησσαρίωνος εἰς Παλαιολόγον [A Memorandum of Bessarion's to Palaeologus]," NE, III (1906), 42 ff.

129. An exception is the commendable effort made by Angeliki Chatzimichali in her numerous studies of Greek folk art.

130. On Byzantine guilds, see A. Stöckle, *Spätromische und byzantinische Zünfte* [*Late Roman and Byzantine Guilds*] (Leipzig, 1911).

131. On the pronounced moral and religious character of their guilds, see Sabri F. Ülgener, "La Morale des métiers depuis le XIVᵉ siècle et les critiques qui ont été adressées [Morale in the Crafts since the Fourteenth Century and Criticisms of Them]," *Revue de la Faculté des Sciences Economiques de l'Université d'Istanbul*, XI (1949–1950), nos. 1–4, pp. 59–66. *Cf.* Robert Mantran, *Istanbul dans la seconde moitié du XVIIᵉ siècle* (Paris, 1962), pp. 349 ff.

132. See the observations and opinions of Franz Taeschner, "Das bosnische Zunftwesen zur Türkenzeit (1463–1878) [Bosnian Guilds in the Turkish Period]," BZ, XLIV (19151), 551–559, esp. pp. 556–559.

133. Georgieviz, *De Turcarum moribus* (1:26), pp. 57–58.

134. Dernschwam, *Tagebuch* (1:20), pp. 112–113, where the writer stresses the influence of apostates. See Gerlach, *Tagebuch* (1:22), p. 19; and du Fresne-Canaye, *Voyage* (1:123), p. 120. *Cf.* Magni, *Lettere* (1:142), p. 193, and Mantran, *Istanbul* (131), p. 421.

135. See de Busbecq, *The Life and Letters* (5:170), I, 255.

136. See Gassot, *Le Discours du voyage* (1:141), p. 11a; and Mantran, *Istanbul* (131), p. 420.

137. See Mantran, *Istanbul*, pp. 357 ff., 448–452. But *cf.* the opinion of Eleni

Vourazeli-Marinakou, Αἱ ἐν Θράκῃ συντεχνίαι τῶν Ἑλλήνων κατά τήν τουρκοκρατίαν [*Greek Guilds in Thrace under Turkish Rule*] (Thessalonica, 1950), p. 83.
138. Quiclet, *Les Voyages à Constantinople par terre* (Paris, 1664), p. 151.
139. Ermannos Lountzis, Περί τῆς πολιτικῆς καταστάσεως τῆς Ἑπτανήσου ἐπί Ἑνετῶν [*On the Political Situation in the Ionian Islands under Venetian Rule*] (Athens, 1856), pp. 203–205; and Leonidas C. Zoïs, Αἱ ἐν Ζακύνθῳ συντεχνίαι [*The Guilds of Zacynthus*] (Zacynthus, 1893), pp. 22 ff.
140. See Nikos A. Bees, "Τό ρουφέτιον τῶν γυναικῶν στά Τρίκκαλα τῆς Θεσσαλίας [The Women's *Rufeti* of Trikkala in Thessaly]," Ὁ Συνεταιριστής, CIV–CVI (1955), p. 79.
141. See the general comments of Angeliki Chatzimichali, "Μορφές ἀπό τή σωματειακή ὀργάνωση τῶν Ἑλλήνων στήν Ὀθωμανική αὐτοκρατορία [Forms of Co-operative Organization among the Greeks of the Ottoman Empire]," *Hell. Contemp.* commem. vol. (1453–1953), pp. 297–303. *Cf.* the study by the same writer in which she covers virtually the same ground, "Οἱ συντεχνίες-τά ἰσνάφια [*Guilds-Isnafia*]," Ἐπετηρίς Ἀνωτάτης Σχολῆς Βιομηχανικῶν Σπουδῶν, II (1949–1959), pp. 1–22 of the reprint, which is also reproduced in Συνεταιριστή, CIV–CVI (1955), 83–87. See also Pantazopoulos, Ἑλλήνων συσσωματώσεις (1), pp. 18–19, esp. pp. 33–39 for the bibliography. See Mantran, *Istanbul* (131), pp. 367 ff., on the organization of Turkish guilds in Constantinople during the seventeenth century.
142. On the guilds of Thrace, see Vourazeli-Marinakou, Αἱ ἐν Θράκῃ συντεχνίαι (137), pp. 78 ff.
143. See, for example, the constitution or charter of the *rufeti* of tailors in Philippopolis, in Myrtilos Apostolidis, Ἡ τῆς Φιλιππουπόλεως ἱστορία ἀπό τῶν ἀρχαιοτάτων χρόνων μέχρι τῶν καθ' ἡμᾶς [*History of Philippopolis from Ancient Times to the Present*] (Athens, 1959), pp. 366–368. The oldest surviving charter, which is of this guild, is dated 15 May 1685 (p. 370: "ἔγεινεν σύνοδο τῶν μαστόρων τῶν ἀμπατζήδων, μικροί καί μεγάλοι, καί ἐκαινούργησαν τό παλιό κατάστιχο καί τό ἀφιέρωσαν ἐτοῦτο ὁ κύρ Δροσινός εἰς τό ρουφέτι [a meeting of the *mastoroi* (chiefs) of the tailors, young and old, was held, at which they reviewed the old constitution and inducted Mr. Drosinos into the *rufeti*])." The charters of Kozane in the eighteenth and nineteenth centuries are reproduced by Kalinderis, Αἱ συντεχνίαι τῆς Κοζάνης (3:99).
144. See Aravantinos, Χρονογραφία τῆς Ἠπείρου (2:50), II, 260; and Vourazeli-Marinakou, Αἱ ἐν Θράκῃ συντεχνίαι (137), pp. 111–114 (for details of the recreational pastimes of guild members). See also Sarou, "Τό χιακόν πολίτευμα" (70), p. 157. *Cf.* the religious patrons of the Turkish guilds of Constantinople (Mantran, *Istanbul* [131], p. 360).
145. See Gerlach, *Tagebuch* (1:22), p. 379.
146. On the survival of the wood-carving tradition here up to the present day, see Evripidis Sourlas, " Ἡ ξυλογλυπτική τέχνη στήν ἐπαρχία Κονίτσης [The Art of Wood Carving in the Konitsa District]," HE, VI (1957), 39–43.
147. Angeliki Chatzimichali, " Ἠπειρωτική λαϊκή τέχνη [Folk Art in Epirus]," HX, V (1930), 255 ff., where there is considerable detail about the various arts and crafts; and see Chatzimichali's "Ραπτάδες — Χρυσορράπτες καί καποτάδες [Tailors, Embroiderers and Capote Makers]," Ἀφιέρωμα στή μνήμη Μ. Τριανταφυλλίδη [*To the Memory of M. Triantaphyllidis*] (Thessalonica, 1960), pp. 445–474.
148. Apostolidis, Ἡ τῆς Φιλιππουπόλεως ἱστορία (143), pp. 366 ff., 369 ff.
149. Papageorgiou, "Αἱ Σέρραι καί τά προάστεια" (6:221), p. 280.
150. Aravantinos, Χρονογραφία τῆς Ἠπείρου(2:50), II, 259–260.
151. "Δ. Γρ. Κ." [Demetrios G. Kambouroglou], "Κρατεῖ ἀπ' τούς δώδεκα["He is cast in the same mold as the Twelve"]," Ἁρμονία, III (1922), 242.

152. Cited by Basileios A. Mystakidis, "Τά ἐσνάφια, ἤτοι ρουφέτια τῆς Θεσσαλονίκης [The *Isnafia* or *Rufetia* of Thessalonica]," Ἡμερολόγιον Θεσσαλονίκης, ed. Meropi Tsiomou (Thessalonica, 1932), pp. 269–270.

153. On the guilds of Constantinople and Thessalonica over the past few centuries, see the disconnected article by Mystakidis, "Τά ἐσνάφια" (152), pp. 266–282. Note the explanation of the Turkish derivations of the names of certain artisans and craftsmen, for example, *aktardes* (perfumers), *meïtantzides* (street-vendors), *machramatzides* (hatters), *basmatzides* (cloth merchants), *kepetzides* (drapers).

154. See the mid-eighteenth century patriarchal document in Herbert Hunger, "Ein griechischer Patriarchen-Geleitbrief des 18 Jahrhunderts [A Greek Patriarchal Letter of Recommendation of the Eighteenth Century]," JÖBG, VI (1957), 145–149.

155. Gedeon, Μνεία τῶν πρό ἐμοῦ (5:108), pp. 180–181. *Cf.* Ioannis Philimon, Δοκίμιον περί τῆς Φιλικῆς Ἐταιρείας [*Essay on the Philike Hetaireia*] (Nauplia, 1934).

156. Gedeon, Μνεία τῶν πρό ἐμοῦ (5:108), p. 182.

157. Philimon, Δοκίμιον (155), p. 31.

158. See Vacalopoulos, Δυτικομακεδόνες ἀπόδημοι ἐπί τουρκοκρατίας (3:96), pp. 18, 20, which also contains the relevant bibliography. For further details, see Chatzimichali, "Μορφές ἀπό τή σωματειακή ὀργάνωση τῶν Ἑλλήνων" (141), pp. 296–301. There were also furriers in Zagoria and Grammenochoria in Epirus (p. 298).

159. See Mystakidis, "Τα ἐσνάφια" (152), p. 280.

160. In the seventeenth century Ioannis Alatzios, a relative of the savant Leo Allatios, was a member of the Brotherhood of St. Anargyri. He was the "oldest and most prominent brother, and derived great joy from promoting the development of the *phrontistirion*, that is, the school" (see Zerlentis, "Περί τῶν ἐν Χίῳ φροντιστηρίων" (6:243), p. 247).

161. On this general question, see Ἐκκλησιαστική Ἀλήθεια, XXV (1905), 134–136; and also the article by Mystakidis, "Τα ἐσνάφια" (152), pp. 277–278. There is more interesting and specific evidence in Manuel I. Gedeon, "Γηραιᾶς ἀδελφότητος ἱστορία [History of an Old Brotherhood]," Ἐκκλησιαστική Ἀλήθεια, XXVII (1907), 154–156. See also Gedeon's Μνεία τῶν πρό ἐμοῦ (5:108), pp. 343 ff. And for material on the Brotherhoods of Tenos, see Drosos, Ἱστορία τῆς νήσου Τήνου (4:117), p. 9 (fn.), and also p. 15.

Chapter 8

1. See Vacalopoulos, Origins of the Greek Nation (1:62), pp. 157–158. To historians in the time of Mohammed II armatoles were Christians who, till then, had collaborated with the Turks. The word usually connoted informers or spies (see Robert Anhegger, "Martoloslar hakkında [About the Armatoles]," *Turkiyat Mecmuası*, VII–VIII [1942], no. 1, p. 286). My own conclusion as to the date when the institution was founded as an organized military force agrees with that of Leo Barbar, who deduces the year 1421 from the evidence of unnamed Turkish historians (Anhegger, "Martoloslar" p. 285). However, Anhegger thinks that the institution originated in the second half of the fifteenth century, that is, mainly in the time of Mohammed II (1451–1489) (p. 286).

2. *Cf.* Fauriel, *Chants populaires* (3:134), I, xlvj.

3. The 832,077 Christian families in the Balkans at the beginning of the sixteenth century included 7,581 families of voynuks and 82,692 of armatoles and Vlachs ("de Martolos et d'Eflac qui formaient des classes militaires, jouissant d'une organisation et d'un statu speciaux [Armatoles and Vlechs who formed military classes enjoyed an organization and a special status]" [see Barkan, "Essai" (3:50), p. 34; and *cf.* his "Déportations" (3:159), p. 63]).

4. See Fauriel, *Chants populaires* (3:134), I, xlviij.

5. In 1553 the traveller Hans Dernschwam observed that there were innumerable brigands in the Ottoman Empire and that the roads were unsafe for travellers (*Tagebuch* [1:20], p. 68).

6. As a reward for garrisoning narrow mountain defiles, a *kanunname* of 1496 bestowed privileges on the inhabitants of five villages of the clan of Klementi, calling them *derventzides* (see the entry "Arnawutluk," by Halil Inalcik in the English edition of the *Encyclopaedia of Islam*, p. 652).

7. See Néroulos, *Histoire moderne* (3:102), p. 95. *Cf.* Apostolos Vacalopoulos, Νεοελληνική παράδοσις διὰ τά ἐπί τουρκοκρατίας προνόμια τῶν Δερβενοχωριῶν Κορίνθου [*Modern Greek Tradition on the Privileges of the Dervenochoria of Corinth under Turkish Rule*] (Thessalonica, 1941). See also the case of Gjatovo, in Aleksandar Matkovski, Турски извори за ајдутството и арамиството во македонија [*Turkish Sources on Klephts and Armatoles in Macedonia*] (Skoplje, 1961), II (1650–1700), 31. *Cf.* I (1620–1650), 42–44. On the inhabitants of the village of Cochia, Serbia, see Gassot, *Le Discours du voyage* (1:141), p. 6b.

8. See Anhegger, "Martoloslar hakkında" (1), p. 308.

9. On the etymology of the word, see the article by Hans J. Kissling in ZDMG, XVII (1936), new series, p. 570; and the reply by Ettore Rossi in ZDMG, XCIII (1939), 305. I was not myself able to consult either of these articles.

10. Fauriel, *Chants populaires* (3:134), I, xlviij.

11. Constantine Koumas, Ἱστορίαι τῶν ἀνθρωπίνων πράξεων [*Histories of Human Deeds*] (Vienna, 1832), XII, 543.

12. Nikolaos Kasomoulis, Ἐνθυμήματα στρατιωτικά τῆς ἐπαναστάσεως τῶν Ἑλλήνων, 1821–1833 [*Military Reminiscences of the Greek Revolution, 1821–1833*] (Athens, 1942), III, 625.

13. Edouard Brown, *Relation de plusieurs voyages* (Paris, 1674), p. 91.

14. See Nikolaos G. Politis, Ἐκλογαί ἀπό τά τραγούδια τοῦ ἑλληνικοῦ λαοῦ [*Selections of Greek Folk Songs*] (Athens, 1925), p. 39.

15. Cousinéry, *Voyage* (3:94), I, 53.

16. *Ibid.*, p. 15.

17. *Ibid.*, p. 68.

18. Kasomoulis, Ἐνθυμήματα (12), I, 141 ff.

19. H. Lauvergne, *Souvenirs de la Grèce dans la campagne de 1825 ou Mémoires historiques et biographiques* (Paris, 1826), pp. 206–207.

20. See Heuzey, "Discours historique" (5:255), p. 236: "πολλοῦ ὄντος τοῦ φόβου κατ' ἀλήθειαν ἀπό τούς λῃστάς [there was indeed a great fear of brigands]." *Cf.* p. 244.

21. See Vacalopoulos, *Origins of the Greek Nation* (1:62), p. 158.

22. Néroulos, *Histoire moderne* (3:102), p. 50.

23. Fauriel, *Chants populaires* (3:134), I, xlvj–slvij. *Cf.* Demetrios Aenian, Ἀρματολοί καί κλέφτες [*Armatoles and Klephts*] (Athens, 1852), p. 275.

24. *Cf.* Fauriel, *Chants populaires* (3:134), I, xlvj.

25. Ἀκολουθία ὁσίου Διονυσίου (5:284), p. 23.

26. Heuzey, *Le Mont Olympe et l'Acarnanie* (3:95), p. 139.

27. Fauriel, *Chants populaires* (3:134), I, 32.

28. Aravantinos, Χρονογραφία τῆς Ἠπείρου (2:50), I, 194.

29. Gökbilgin, "Kanunı Sultan Süleiman" (1:134), p. 259.

30. *Ibid.*, pp. 251, 260.

31. *Ibid.*, p. 258.

32. *Ibid.*, p. 251.

33. Anhegger, "Martoloslar hakkında" (1), p. 282.

34. *Ibid.*, p. 293.

35. *Ibid.*, p. 295.

36. *Ibid.*, p. 293.

37. See document no. 13 in Vasdravellis, Ἀρματολοί καί κλέφτες (2:47), p. 59.

38. See *ibid.*, p. 51, for the commission of armatoles in the village of Ano Megalos Agiannis in Western Macedonia.

39. See Dernschwam, *Tagebuch* (1:20), p. 246. *Cf.* the murder of a Turk in a forest outside Edessa (Mertzios, Μνημεῖα μακεδονικῆς ἱστορίας [2:59], p. 130).

40. Zerlentis, Σημειώματα περί Ἑλλήνων (2:55), p. 10. The complete note is in Demetrios G. Kambouroglou, Μνημεῖα τῆς ἱστορίας τῶν Ἀθηναίων. Τουρκοκρατία [*Monuments of Athenian History. Turkish Rule*] (Athens, 1891), I, 87. *Cf.* the capture of two Turks in Chasiá, Attica, in the following century.

41. See du Loir, *Voyages* (1:108), pp. 303–308, where there is material on the Arvanito-Vlach villages, their women, and their way of life generally.

42. Deshayes, *Voyage* (1:26), p. 467.

43. There are many relevant documents on Macedonia in Vasdravellis, Ἀρματολοί καί κλέφτες (2:47), pp. 49–64.

44. See document no. 91 in the typed résumé of the codex issued by the şerî of Veroia (1:26). *Cf.* Spyropoulos, "Τά Ἄγραφα τῆς Θεσσαλίας" (7:55), p. 178, on the village of Tsatsa in the Agrafa in 1758.

45. See the relevant documents in Matkovski, Турски извори (7). Apart from a few general orders issued to the Turkish local authorities of various cities and towns, mainly in western Macedonia (Kastoria, Phlorina, Sarigöl, and others), the documents refer to districts in present-day Yugoslav Macedonia, particularly Monastir. The introduction to the book is notable for its prolixity and vague generalizations. On the way of life of these klephts, based on the same documentary material, see Aleksandar Matkofski, "Massnahmen der osmanischen Regierung zur Unterdrückung des Haiduckenwesens in Mazedonien in der ersten Hälfte des 17 Jahrhunderts [Measures Taken by the Ottoman Rulers to Control the *Chaïdout* (Bandits) of Macedonia during the First Half of the Seventeenth Century]," Südost-Forschungen, XXVI (1967), 46–71, which also contains the relevant bibliography.

46. See Vasdravellis, Ἀρματολοί καί κλέφτες (2:47), pp. 59–60 (for the year 1682), p. 61 (1683), pp. 61–62 (1684). See the relevant documents in Matkofski, Турски извори (7), II, 45 ff., *passim*.

47. See Braudel, *La Méditerranée* (1:63), pp. 643 ff., 658. *Cf. ibid.*, p. 660.

48. Brown, *Relation* (13), p. 109.

49. Dernschwam, *Tagebuch* (1:20), p. 246; Brown, *Relation* (13), pp. 103, 104. *Cf.* Giannis A. Tozis, "Πῶς εἶδε τήν σκλαβωμένη Θράκη στά 1634 ὁ ἄγγλος περιηγητής Sir Henry Blount [The English Traveller Sir Henry Blount's Impression of Thrace in 1634]," ΑΘΓΛΘ, XIX (1954), 216. Under Turkish rule, there was a sentry-box with a bell placed at each end of the narrow passes near the village of Avdimi, Thrace (see Maximos Maravelakis and Apostolos Vacalopoulos, Αἱ προσφυγικαί ἐγκαταστάσεις ἐν τῇ περιοχῇ Θεσσαλονίκης [*The Refugee Settlements in the Area of Thessalonica*] (Thessalonica, 1953), p. 450). Brown refers to the Gypsies of Greece as brigands (*Relation* [13], pp. 102–103), but these bore no relation to the real mountain klephts. On the punishment of klephts, see Gerlach, *Tagebuch* (1:22), p. 169, where there is a reference to the execution of two Greeks in Constantinople in 1576; in the company of other comrades, they had robbed and killed people outside the city.

50. See Vasdravellis, Ἀρματολοί καί κλέφτες (2:47), pp. 49 ff., *passim*. See also

the unpublished document no. 29 for the year 1639–1640, and nos. 429 and 493 for the year 1640, in the typed résumé of the codex issued by the şeri of Veroia (1:26).

51. Aravantinos, Χρονογραφία τῆς Ἠπείρου (2:50), I, 224–225. On Moslem armatoles in Sofia around the middle of the seventeenth century, see Anhegger, "Martoloslar hakkında" (1), p. 292.

52. See Anhegger, "Martolosar hakkında," p. 291.

53. See Vasdravellis, Ἀρματολοί καί κλέφτες (2:47), pp. 59–60.

54. Ibid., p. 61.

55. Lavriotis, Τό "Αγιον "Ορος (5:145), p. 46. Cf. pp. 47 ff.

56. See Ioannis K. Vasdravellis, Ἱστορικά Ἀρχεῖα Μακεδονίας. Β' Ἀρχεῖον Βεροίας-Ναούσης (1598–1886) [Historical Archives of Macedonia. II: The Archives of Veroia-Naoussa (1598–1886)] (Thessalonica, 1954), pp. 108–111, 115–116.

57. See Vasdravellis, Ἀρματολοί καί κλέφτες (2:47), pp. 65–67.

58. Vasdravellis, Ἀρχεῖον Βεροίας-Ναούσης (56), pp. 111–112. .

59. See Anhegger, "Martoloslar hakkında" (1), p. 292. Cf. p. 300.

60. See Fauriel, Chants populaires (3:134), I, I–Ij. There was an encounter between Albanians and the Varsami and Boukouvalaioi klephts on 13 April 1728 (see Nikos A. Bees, "Χρονογραφικά σημειώματα ἐκ τῶν κωδίκων τῆς Ἐθν. Βιβλιοθήκης τῆς Ἑλλάδος [Chronological Notes from the Codices of the National Library of Greece]," ΔΙΕΕ, VI (1902–1906), 98). It is not known exactly when the office of derven-başı was created (cf. Fauriel, Chants populaires I, xlix–l).

61. Fauriel, Chants populaires (3:134) I, xlix. Cf. the list in Thomas Gordon, History of the Greek Revolution (Edinburgh-London, 1844), I, 29 (fn.).

62. Fauriel, Chants populaires (3:134), I, xliij.

63. Ibid., I, xliv. Cf. Apostolos Vacalopoulos, Τά ἑλληνικά στρατεύματα τοῦ 1821 [The Greek Troops of 1821], (Thessalonica, 1948), pp. 63 ff.

64. Fauriel, Chants populaires (3:134), I, xlv.

65. Ibid., I, xlix.

66. Koumas, Ἱστορίαι (11), XII, 543. Cf. Philimon, Δοκίμιον (7:155), p. 41.

67. Armatoles and klephts became even more closely identified in foreign languages, for example, in Serbo-Croatian, Hungarian and Rumanian (see Anhegger, "Martoloslar hakkında" [1], p. 284).

68. Tertsetis, "Απαντα (5:126), III, 18.

69. See Fauriel, Chants populaires (3:134), I, lxviij.

70. Ibid., I, lviij.

71. Ibid., pp. lxix–lxx.

72. Ibid., p. liij.

73. Ibid., p. lix.

74. Ibid., pp. lviij–lix.

75. Ibid., pp. lvij–lviij.

76. Ibid., p. lx.

77. Ibid., pp. lxv–lxvj.

78. Ibid., p. lx.

79. Ibid., p. lxj.

80. Koumas, Ἱστορίαι (11), XII, 543.

81. See Vacalopoulos, Τά ἑλληνικά στρατεύματα (63), pp. 137–142, which provides the bibliography.

82. Fauriel, Chants populaires (3:134), I, lvj–lvij.

83. Ibid., p. lxij.

84. Giannis Vlachogiannis, Ἀπομνημονεύματα στρατηγοῦ Μακρυγιάννη [Memoirs of General Makrygiannis] (Athens, 1907), II, 350 (2nd ed. [1947], II, 108). Cf. Aenian,

'Αρματολοί καί κλέφτες (23), pp. 271–272. And see Philimon, Δοκίμιον (7:155), p. 41: "τό Σύστηνα τῶν Κλεπτῶν ἦτο . . . τό πρότυπον πολεμικόν σχολεῖον τῆς μελλούσης μεταβολῆς, σχηματίζον τήν πρώτην στρατιωτικήν δύναμιν τῆς Ἑλλάδος [the system of the klephts was a model, a school in which Greeks were tutored for war, the first military force in Greece]."

85. Fauriel, *Chants populaires* (3:134), I, lxx–lxxj.

86. For examples, see Philimon, Δοκίμιον (7:155), p. 39, fn. 1; and Christos Anargyrou, Σπετσιωτικά [*On Spetsai*] (Athens, 1861), I, 43–44.

87. On this point, see Vacalopoulos, Τά ἑλληνικά στρατεύματα (63), pp. 76–77, which also provides the relevant bibliography.

88. Demetrios Petropoulos, "'Ακριτικά τραγούδια στήν Πελοπόννησο [Akritic Songs in the Peloponnese]," Πελοποννησιακά, II (1957), 335.

89. For example, in Andros—undoubtedly as a hangover from the old feudal system—the first son received the entire inheritance, while his younger brothers became monks, priests, or teachers (see Miliarakis, "Ανδρος-Κέως [4:82], p. 52). *Cf.* adulterers who were publicly anathematized (du Loir, *Voyages* [1:108], pp. 180–181). On the customs of the people of the Aegean in particular, there is some material in Sauger, 'Η παροῦσα κατάστασις (1:178), pp. 16–18.

90. See Gerlach, *Tagebuch* (1:22), pp. 405–406. In Xanthe, among other places in Greece, newborn babies were sprinkled with salt in the manner of an ancient Christian tradition (see Lampsidis, " 'Ο Παχώμιος Ρουσᾶνος" (5:174), p. 389, which also contains the relevant bibliography).

91. Gerlach, *Tagebuch* (1:22), pp. 151, 155–157; and Grelot, *Relation* (1:90), pp. 201–203.

92. On the Aegean islands, see Sauger, 'Η παροῦσα κατάστασις (1:178), pp. 16–17.

93. Georgirenes, *Description* (1:45), pp. 31–32.

94. *Ibid.*, pp. 65–66.

95. See Crusius, *Turcograeciae* (1:53), p. 501, on the festivities of Greeks and Turks during the Feast of St. George. See also Lampsidis, " 'Ο Παχώμιος Ρουσᾶνος" (5:174), pp. 387–388. There is also material in Grelot, *Relation* (1:90), pp. 203 ff.

96. Voyatzidis, 'Αμοργός (4:106), pp. 128–134.

97. There is a beautiful description in Sauger, 'Η παροῦσα κατάστασις (1:178), p. 17. See also du Mont, *Voyages* (1:90), IV, 3 ff.; and Gerlach, *Tagebuch* (1:22), p. 499, for a great deal of material. On the sword dance of Crete, see Belon, *Observations* (1:123), p. 22a.

98. See Gerlach, *Tagebuch* (1:22), p. 220.

99. *Ibid.*, pp. 87, 356 ff.

100. On this custom, see Nikolaos Politis, "Τα κατά τήν τελευτήν [On Death]," Λαογραφικά Σύμμεικτα, III, 331, which also contains the relevant bibliography. *Cf.* Lampsidis, " 'Ο Παχώμιος Ρουσᾶνος" (5:174), p. 390.

101. Belon, *Observations* (1:123), pp. 6a, 6b; Gerlach, *Tagebuch* (1:22), pp. 119, 410 (on which is the remark: "und schreyen wie die heyden [and wail like pagans]"; Sauger, 'Η παροῦσα κατάστασις (1:178), pp. 17–18; and du Mont, *Voyages* (1:90), IV, 21–24.

102. Gerlach, *Tagebuch* (1:22), p. 274.

103. *Ibid.*, p. 94.

104. *Ibid.*, p. 331; Grelot, *Relation* (1:90), pp. 189–190.

105. Gerlach, *Tagebuch* (1:22), p. 368.

106. Crusius, *Turcograeciae* (1:53), p. 328.

107. *Ibid.*

108. On the sixteenth and seventeenth centuries, see Spyridon Lambros, " 'Ανέκδο-

τος λόγος Παχωμίου τοῦ Ρουσσάνου περί δεισιδαιμονιῶν καί προλήψεων κατά τόν ΙΣΤ' αἰῶνα [An Unpublished Speech of Pachomios Roussanos on Superstitions and Prejudices in the Sixteenth Century]," ΔΙΕΕ, I (1883–1884), 101–112; and Ioannis N. Karmiris, " Ἀνέκδοτος λόγος Παχωμίου Ρουσσάνου [An Unpublished Speech of Pachomios Roussanos]," Ἐκκλησία, XVI (1938), 232. See also Maximos the Peloponnesian's "Λόγος περί τῶν μαντευομένων καί τῶν ὁμοίων [A Speech on Prophecy and Similar Matters]," ed. D. M. Sarros, Ἠπειρωτικὴ Ἑστία, V (1956), 849–857, 983–988. The innumerable superstitions of Chios are listed in a work by Leon Allatios, "De templis Graecorum recentioribus" (cited by Amantos in "Λέων Ἀλλάτιος" [6:108], p. 564). Amantos refers to Allatios as "the first who can justifiably be called a folklorist."

Chapter 9

1. See Thevenot, *Relation* (4:81), p. 1: "il me semble que jamais cette passion de voyager ne les a pressez avec tant de force qu'en nos jours [it seems to me that this passion for travelling has never been so strong as in our day]." *Cf.* Dousae, *De itinere* (1:171), p. 5.

2. See Vacalopoulos, *Origins of the Greek Nation* (1:62), p. 198.

3. See Vera P. Mutavčieva, "откупуването на държавните приходи в османската империя през xv–xvii век и развитието на паричните отношения [The Letting of State Revenues in the Ottoman Empire from the Fifteenth Century to the Seventeenth and the Development of Financial Relations]," *Istoriceski Pregled*, XVI (1960), no. 1, pp. 54–56.

4. Regarding these men, see Nikolai Todorov, "по някой въпроси на балканския град xv–xvi век [Questions concerning the Balkan Town during the Fifteenth and Sixteenth Centuries]," *Istoriceski Pregled*, XVIII (1962), no. 1, pp. 52–54.

5. On the difficulties involved in carrying on trade, see Robert Walpole, *Memoirs Relating to European and Asiatic Turkey and Other Countries of the East* (London, 1818), p. 6, which treats the problem at length.

6. Vacalopoulos, *Origins of the Greek Nation* (1:62), *passim*.

7. There is material on population increase in the study by Todorov, "по някой въпроси" (4), pp. 32–58.

8. Ömer Lûtfi Barkan, *Quelques Observations sur l'organisation économique des villes ottomanes* (Brussels, 1955), pp. 290, 291.

9. See de Busbecq, *The Life and Letters* (5:170), I, 93 (Belgrade was one).

10. *Ibid.*, p. 107.

11. See Michael Lascaris, "Σημειώσεις περί τοῦ πληθυσμοῦ τῆς Πάργας κατά τόν ΙΖ' αἰῶνα [Notes on the Population of Parga in the Seventeenth Century]," HX, II (1927), 170–172. *Cf.* Aravantinos, Χρονογραφία τῆς Ἠπείρου (2:50), II, 199, fn. 1.

12. Georgios I. Phousaras, "Τά «Εὐβοϊκά» τοῦ Ἐβλιᾶ Τσελεμπῆ [Evliya Tschelebi's 'On Euboea']," Ἀρχεῖον Εὐβοϊκῶν Μελετῶν, VI (1959), 162–163; also Magni, *Relazione* (5:269), p. 104.

13. On the old suburb of Trebizond, which, at the beginning of the seventeenth century, was a commercial center inhabited by many foreigners, in contrast to Trebizond itself, which engaged in no trade, see Bordier, *Relation* (1:123), p. 119; and p. 121, where Bordier, having first remarked on the exquisite textiles of Trebizond, continued: "de ces toilles se faict merveilleux trafic en ce bourg, car dans la ville ne se voit marchant ny artisant [there is a marvellous traffic in this stuff in the castle, because one sees neither merchant nor artisan in the town]"; also pp. 128–129.

14. See Pero Tafur, *Travels and Adventures, 1435–1439* (New York-London, 1926), tr. and ed. Malcolm Letts, p. 50: "The people are very wealthy, for these places

(Modon-Coron) are the ports of discharge for Greece and the Black Sea for all classes of merchandise."

15. The relevant source is Georgios Soulis, "Notes on Venetian Modon," Πελοπον-νησιακά, III (1959), 267–275. For certain statistics relating to Modon and Coron at the beginning of Turkish rule, see Gökbilgin, "Kanunı Sultan Süleiman" (1:134), p. 280. On Coron in 1586, see Mystakidis, "Δύο Έλληνες" (2:21), p. 10. Regarding the Gypsies of these parts, see the study by Constantine Biris, Ρώμ καί Γύφτοι, ἐθνογραφία καί ἱστορία τῶν Τσιγγάνων [Romany and Gypht: Ethnology and History of the Gypsies] (Athens, 1954), pp. 12–13, where a distinction is made between two kinds of Gypsies. The first, according to Biris, were Egyptians; the second had Indian origins (pp. 43 ff.).

16. Maurand, Itinéraire (4:9), p. 153.

17. Gökbilgin, "Kanunı Sultan Süleiman" (1:134), p. 281. According to Greek sources, which naturally exaggerated, Mistra had 50,000 Greeks, among whom were many Jews, and the Turks lived in the citadel (Legrand, Zygomalas [2:14], p. 189). Cf. Zerlentis, Σημειώματα περί Ἑλλήνων (2:55), p. 11. On the Jews of Mistra and other cities of the Byzantine Empire, see the study by Andreas Andreadis, Έργα [Works] (Athens, 1938), I, 609–627, which also contains the relevant bibliography.

18. Legrand, Zygomalas (2:14), p. 190; and Zerlentis, Σημειώματα περί Ἑλλήνων (2:55), p. 12.

19. Gerlach, Tagebuch (1:22), p. 183.

20. Zerlentis, Σημειώματα περί Ἑλλήνων (2:55), p. 10. In the time of Mohammed II, Corinth had 328 families. It was classified as the governor's property [hassa mirliva (mirlivâ hası idi)] and produced revenues amounting to 27, 151 akçes (Gökbilgin, "Kanunı Sultan Süleiman" [1:134], p. 281).

21. Legrand, Zygomalas (2:14), p. 189.

22. Todorov, "по някой въпросн" (4), p. 49.

23. Nikos A. Bees, "'Η Τρίπολις πρό τοῦ ιζ' αἰῶνος [Tripolis before the Seventeenth Century]," 'Αθηνᾶ, XVIII (1906), 608–616.

24. Denis Zakythinos, "Εἰδήσεις περί τῆς ἐμπορικῆς κινήσεως τῶν λιμένων τῆς 'Αττικῆς κατά τά μέσα τοῦ IZ' αἰῶνος [Evidence on the Commerce of the Ports of Attica in the Middle of the Seventeenth Century]," 'Ελληνικά, VII (1934), 265.

25. See Collignon, Le Consul Jean Giraud (1:52), pp. 41–43, 50, for comments on the way of life, the weapons, and the dress of these Albanians.

26. The names of some of the Athenian merchants were Palaiologos (Christian and surname), Nikolos (his brother), Vourvis and his son Ioannis, Angelis Podaras, Theodoris Gialouris, Tomprotis, Ioannis Chrysis, Manoussos Kalapodas, Giannakis Kavallouris, Kastakalis Pieros (son of Mama), Kantylis, Gomenis, Vestarchis, Dimitris Zonos (see Zerlentis, Σημειώματα περί Ἑλλήνων [2:55], p. 19. The note appears in extenso in Legrand, Zygomalas [2:14], p. 189; and also in Mystakidis, "Δύο Έλληνες" [2:21], p. 8). The Palaiologos family is thought to have been a branch of the royal family (see Henri Omont, "Athènes au XVIIe siècle," REG, XIV (1901), pp. 271 ff.). The Kantylises may have been a branch of the Chalco-condyles family.

27. Barkan, "Essai sur les données statistiques" (3:50), p. 27. The Corinthian Gabriel Kallonas, a "priest in the district of Philippi in Macedonia," undoubtedly exaggerated when he told Crusius in 1583 that Athens had 6,000 houses (see Zerlentis, Σημειώματα περί Ἑλλήνων [2:55], p. 10). Contrast this with the more reliable evidence of the Athenian, Manuel Mouzikis, that it had about 1,000 houses (Mystakidis, "Δύο Έλληνες" [2:21], p. 6, fn. 3). In the middle of the seventeenth century Athens had thirty-two neighborhoods or precincts with an approximate total

of 2,050 houses—1,300 Greek, about 600 Turkish, and about 150 Albanian (see Collingnon, *Le Consul Jean Giraud* [1:52], pp. 27, 28, where Collignon says he believes the evidence of Giraud to be more reliable than that of other travellers). During this period the area of Athens was six times greatèr than it had been under Frankish rule (Travlos, Πολεοδομική ἐξέλιξις τῶν 'Αθηνῶν [5:340], p. 180).

28. Travlos, Πολεοδομική, pp. 174–176, where there are interesting sketches and drawings.

29. Magni, *Relazione* (5:269), pp. 35–36.

30. Legrand, *Zygomalas* (2:14), p. 189. *Cf.* Zerlentis, Σημειώματα περί 'Ελλήνων (2:55), p. 11; and Zosimas Esphigmenitis, "'Η Λαμία καί τά πέριξ [Lamia and its Environs]," Προμηθεύς, VI (1894), 581.

31. On the port of Piraeus (and a village named Peraia which was once situated near it), see Collignon, *Le Consul Jean Giraud* (1:52), p. 48. On the harbor and produce of Aegina, which came under the commercial control of Athens, see p. 24.

32. See Zakythinos, "Εἰδήσεις" (24), p. 254. *Cf.* Collignon, *Le Consul Jean Giraud* (1:52), pp. 44–45, 51, which tally with Zakythinos. See Collingnon's comments on pp. 8–9, especially on the arrival of French ships in Attica; and Magni, *Relazione* (5:269), pp. 33–34, 35. *Cf.* the general remarks about French consulates and French consuls in the Peloponnese, in Auguste Boppe, "Le Consulat général de Morée et ses dépendances," REG, XX (1907), 18–37.

33. See Biris, Τά 'Αττικά τοῦ 'Εβλιᾶ Τσελεμπῆ (4:168), p. 66. Note Evliya Tschelebi's description: "Its honey, perfumed and pure, has no equal anywhere else on earth, because it comes straight from the blossoms of wild vegetables and plants that grow on the mountain sides. It is a thick, sugary, clear syrup, fit for sending to kings as a gift." Tschelebi also speaks about the export of certain plants of pharmaceutical value (p. 55), and of Hymettus honeý (see also Collingnon, *Le Consul Jean Giraud* [1:52], p. 46).

34. Zakythinos, "Εἰδήσεις" (24), p. 255. *Cf.* Collignon, *Le Consul Jean Giraud* (1:52), p. 44.

35. Zakythinos, "Εἰδήσεις" (24), p. 254.

36. See Crusius, *Turcograeciae* (1:53), p. 95.

37. See Collignon, *Le Consul Jean Giraud* (1:52), p. 27.

38. Biris, Τά 'Αττικά τοῦ 'Εβλιᾶ Τσελεμπῆ (4:168), p. 46.

39. Deshayes, *Voyage* (1:26), p. 474.

40. Biris, Τά 'Αττικά τοῦ 'Εβλιᾶ Τσελεμπῆ(4:168), p. 44, fns. 67, 66.

41. *Ibid.*, p. 46. On dress generally, see Collignon, *Le Consul Jean Giraud* (1:52), pp. 40–41; and on the dress of women especially, see Magni, *Relazione* (5:269), pp. 21–30.

42. See Biris, Τά 'Αττικά τοῦ 'Εβλιᾶ Τσελεμπῆ (4:168), pp. 44–45; and Collignon, *Le Consul Jean Giraud* (1:52), pp. 27–28.

43. See Biris, Τά 'Αττικά τοῦ 'Εβλιᾶ Τσελεμπῆ (4:168), pp. 46, 64–65. There is a precise description of their dress in du Loir, *Voyages* (1:108), p. 311.

44. Magni, *Relazione* (5:269), pp. 24, 25–26. On their dress, see pp. 24–25; and *cf.* p. 28. See also Léon Emmanuel Laborde, *Athènes aux XVᵉ, XVIᵉ, et XVIIᵉ siècles* (Paris, 1854).

45. See Zerlentis, Σημειώματα περί 'Ελλήνων (2:55), p. 13.

46. Mertzios, Μνημεῖα μακεδονικῆς ἱστορίας (2:59), p. 199. On Angiolello, see Georgios I. Arvanitidis, "J.-M. Angiolello, περιηγητής καί ἱστορικός (1452–1525) [J.-M. Angiolello, Traveller and Historian (1452–1525)]," Βιβλιόφιλος, XII (1958), 1–6.

47. Zakythinos, "Εἰδήσεις" (24), p. 265.

48. *Ibid.*, p. 265.

49. Phousaras has translated the relevant part ("«Τὰ Εὐβοϊκά»" [12], pp. 150–171).

50. See Nikolaos I. Giannopoulos, " 'Υπάτη, Νέαι Πάτραι [Hypate, Nea Patras]," ΔΙΕΕ, VII (1910–1918), 453–457.

51. See Barkan, *Quelques Observations* (8), p. 294. *Cf.* p. 296.

52. See p. 60 above.

53. See Vacalopoulos, *Origins of the Greek Nation* (1:62), p. 165.

54. Mertzios, "Τὸ ἐν Βενετίᾳ 'Ηπειρωτικὸν ἀρχεῖον" (6:236), p. 41.

55. See Zerlentis, Σημειώματα περὶ 'Ελλήνων (2:55), p. 30.

56. See Gökbilgin, "Kanunı Sultan Süleiman" (1:134), p. 282, which also provides additional evidence.

57. Zerlentis, Σημειώματα περὶ 'Ελλήνων (2:55), p. 25.

58. See Mertzios, "Τὸ ἐν Βενετίᾳ 'Ηπειρωτικὸν ἀρχεῖον" (6:236), pp. 239–243; and also Mertzios' "Μικρὸς 'Ελληνομνήμων." (5:126), pp. 470–471. On the Jews of Ioannina, see Nikos A. Bees, "Übersicht über die Geschichte des Judentums von Janina [Survey of the History of the Jews in Ioannina]," BNJ, II (1921), 166–169.

59. See Spyridon Papageorgiou, " 'Οδοιπορικὸν 'Ιακώβου Μηλοΐτη [Travel Memoirs of Iakovos Miloïtis]," Παρνασσός, VI (1882), 641. There is some material on Miloïtis in Zerlentis, Σημειώματα περὶ 'Ελλήνων (2:55), pp. 25–28.

60. See Sarros, "Μαξίμου τοῦ Πελοποννησίου ἀπόκρισις" (6:208), p. 257.

61. Ioannis Anastasiou, " 'Ο Ἄγγλος περιηγητὴς Τζώρτζ Χουῆλερ (Χειμάρρα-Λευκάδα-''Αρτα-Γιάννινα) στὰ 1675 [The English Traveller George Wheeler (Cheimara-Leukas-Arta-Ioannina) in 1675]," 'Ηπειρωτικὴ 'Εστία, III (1954), 363.

62. Papageorgiou, " 'Οδοιπορικὸν 'Ιακώβου Μηλοΐτη" (59), p. 641.

63. See Barkan, "Essai sur les données statistiques" (3:50), p. 36. Barkan says that in 1478 there was not a single Jew in Thessalonica. What became of the Jews of Byzantine Thessalonica?

64. See Vacalopoulos, *A History of Thessaloniki* (1:133), pp. 78–80. The persecution of Jews continued after this date (see Gerlach, *Tagebuch* [1:22], p. 138).

65. Mertzios, Μνημεῖα μακεδονικῆς ἱστορίας (2:59), p. 113.

66. See I. S. Emmanuel, *Histoire de l'industrie des tissus des Israélites de Salonique* (Paris, 1935).

67. Nicolay, *Navigations* (1:140), p. 279.

68. Gökbilgin, "Kanunı Sultan Süleiman" (1:134), p. 266. See also the evidence adduced by Todorov, "по някой въпросн" (4), p. 50.

69. Basileios A. Mystakidis, "Μ. Κρούσιος καὶ Θεοδ. Ζυγομαλᾶς καί τά ὀφφίκια πρωτεκδίκου καί δικαιοφύλακος τοῦ ἱστορικοῦ Παχυμέρους [Martinus Crusius and Theodoros Zygomalas, and the Offices of Protekdikos and Dikaiophylax Spoken of by the Historian Pachymeres]," 'Ορθοδοξία, LX, p. 5 fn. 3, of the reprint. Zerlentis' estimates are incorrect (Σημειώματα περὶ 'Ελλήνων [2:55], p. 13). There is more about Thessalonica in Carlo Ranzo, *Relazione di un viaggio fatto da Venetia in Constantinopoli [Report of a Journey made from Venice to Constantinople]*, (Turin, 1616), p. 57.

70. See Laourdas, "Βυζαντινὰ καί μεταβυζαντινὰ ἐγκώμια" (5:306), p. 114.

71. Legrand, *Zygomalas* (2:14), p. 128.

72. Roberts, *Adventures* (4:155), p. 33.

73. On its location, see Georgios Bakalakis, "Τὸ παρὰ τὴν Χρυσούπολιν τείχισμα [The Wall near Chrysoupolis]," 'Ελληνικά, X (1938), 310, 314–318.

74. Belon, *Observations* (1:123), p. 57a. Ships from Ragusa, Chios (and other parts of Greece), Venice, and sometimes from Egypt entered the mouth of the River Strymon, sailed about a league up the river, and rode at anchor until their goods

were sold—up to two months in winter. They left in the spring after loading wheat, wool, and skins. At the mouth of the river were the ruins of a city, completely uninhabited, which the people of the region called Chrysoupolis (Belon, *Observations* [1:123], pp. 56b–57a). By 1470 the side of the mountain facing the sea was already known as Kavalla (see Mertzios, Μνημεῖα μακεδονικῆς ἱστορίας [2:59], p. 203́, for a full description of its strategic advantages). However, by 1519 the locality was deserted (p. 117). For a description of the place in 1591, see p. 139. *Cf.* Hadschi Chalfa, *Rumeli und Bosna*, German trans. by Joseph von Hammer (Vienna, 1812), p. 71.

75. Barkan, "Essai sur les données statistiques" (3:50), p. 27. *Cf.* Todorov, "по някой въпроси" (4), p. 50.

76. Hans Jakob Amman, *Reise ins Gelobte Land [Journey to the Promised Land]* (Zurich, 1919), p. 43.

77. For descriptions of Adrianople, see Dernschwam, *Tagebuch* (1:20), pp. 24–25; Gassot, *Le Discours du voyage* (1:141), p. 8; Tozis, "Sir Henry Blount" (8:49), pp. 219–221.

78. Chesneau, *Le Voyage* (2:57), p. 15. For the descriptions of other travellers, see "A.A.S." [Antonios A. Stamoulis], "Περιηγήσεις [Travels]," ΑΘΛΘ, VII (1940–1941), 337–340; Quiclet, *Les Voyages* (7:138), pp. 150–152; Ranzo, *Relazione* (69), pp. 18–20. *Cf.* the journeys of Dernschwam (*Tagebuch* [1:20], pp. 241–246) and Gerlach (*Tagebuch* [1:22], pp. 507–513), from Constantinople to Adrianople through Greek villages. Beyond Adrianople to the north they both encountered Bulgarian villages. For other material on the commerce and guilds of Adrianople, as well as other matters, see Vourazeli-Marinakou, Αἱ ἐν Θράκῃ συντεχνίαι (7:137), pp. 56–62.

79. Nicolay, *Navigations* (1:140), p. 265, where the reference is to a large commercial city in which the leaders were Jews.

80. Gassot, *Le Discours du voyage* (1:141), pp. 8a–8b.

81. Trajan Stoianovich is relevant here ("The Conquering Balkan Orthodox Merchant," *The Journal of Economic History*, XX [1960], 243, which also provides a bibliography of Barkan's works on the subject).

82. Heuzey, *Le Mont Olympe et l'Acarnanie* (3:95), p. 265: "La grande ville des Hellènes," *Cf.* a study by Demetrios S. Loukatos, " Ἡ «Πόλη» στή γλώσσα καί τά κείμενα τοῦ ἑλληνικοῦ λαοῦ [The 'City' in the Language and Texts of the Greek People]," Νέα Ἑστία, LIII (1953), 833–840.

83. See, for example, Todorov, "по някой въпроси" (4), p. 51, on the numbers and places of origin of the laborers and craftsmen who worked on the mosque and imaret of Suleimanye in Constantinople.

84. Alfons M. Schneider, "Die Bevölkerung Konstantinopels [The Population of Constantinople]," *Nachrichten der Akademie der Wissenschaften im Göttingen, Philologische-Historische Klasse*, IX (1949), 233 ff.

85. An office analogous to that of eparch in the Byzantine Empire.

86. See Abraham Papazoglou, "Μωάμεθ Β' ὁ Πορθητής [Mohammed II the Conqueror]," ΕΕΒΣ, XVI (1940), 221–222; Kritoboulos of Imbros, Συγγραφή ἱστοριῶν (1:7) I, 73 (14); Ducas, *Historia byzantina* (1:2), p. 313 (Bonn), p. 393 (Bucharest).

87. Kritoboulos of Imbros, Συγγραφή ἱστοριῶν (1:7), I, 67 (2).

88. Babinger, *Mehmed der Eroberer* (1:8), p. 122.

89. Kritoboulos of Imbros, Συγγραφή ἱστοριῶν (1:7), I, 73 (4).

90. *Ibid.*, 5–8. See also Nikolaos B. Tomadakis, " Ὁ μετά τήν ἅλωσιν τῆς Κωνσταντινουπόλεως (1453) ἀποικισμός αὐτῆς κατά τάς ἑλληνικάς πηγάς [After the Fall of Constantinople (1453): Repopulation of the City according to Greek Sources]," Πεπραγμένα Θ' διεθνοῦς βυζαντινολογικοῦ συνεδρίου (Athens, 1956), II, 614–615.

91. Kritoboulos of Imbros. Συγγραφή ἱστοριῶν (1:7), II, 1 (4).
92. Ducas, *Historia byzantina* (1:2), p. 313 (Bonn), p. 393 (Bucharest).
93. On the Armenians, see Kritoboulos of Imbros, Συγγραφή ἱστοριῶν (1:7), III, 11 (2). On the Serbs, Hungarians, and Bulgarians, see II, 22 (2).
94. *Ibid.*, II, i (1). See also the *Chronicle of Aşik paşa Zade*, tr. Richard Kreutel (Vienna, 1959), pp. 200, 201–202. Friedrich Giese maintains that it was Mohammed II's initial intention to recolonize Constantinople with Turks but that his Turkish subjects proved unwilling. It was only in the face of this unwillingness that he turned to Christians, a policy which became evident mainly during the period after Gennadius ascended the patriarchal throne, that is, after 6 January 1454 (see Friedrich Giese, "Die Stellung der christlichen Untertanen [The Status of Christian Subjects]," *Islam*, XIX [1931], 268 ff.). Gunnar Hering's recent attempt to bolster this theory is not at all convincing ("Das islamische Recht" [5:33], pp. 245–248).
95. Kritoboulos of Imbros, Συγγραφή ἱστοριῶν (1:7), III, 11 (1). *Cf.* Ἱστορία Πολιτική τῆς Κωνσταντινουπόλεως (1:3), p. 25. Professor Barkan estimates that Mohammed II colonized 180 villages around Constantinople with Christians from the Peloponnese, Albania, and Serbia ("Déportations" [3:159], p. 40). On the establishment of new settlers in the suburbs of Constantinople, see also (though reservedly) the testimony of Evliya Tschelebi in Alexandros A. Pallis, Σελίδες ἀπό τήν ζωή τῆς παλιᾶς γενιτσαρικῆς Τουρκίας κατά τήν περιγραφή τοῦ Τούρκου περιηγητῆ τοῦ 17 αἰ. Ἐβλιᾶ Τσελεμπῆ [Pages from the History of Old Janissary Turkey as Related by Evliya Tschelebi, the Seventeenth-Century Turkish Traveller] (Athens, 1941), pp. 78–79.
96. For details, see Barkan, "Les Formes" (1:21), pp. 20–22.
97. *Ibid.*, p. 38. On the village of Bosna, see Jean Chardin, *Voyage de Paris à Ispahan* (Paris, 1830), I, 81.
98. Kritoboulos of Imbros, Συγγραφή ἱστοριῶν (1:7), III, 9 (2); II 1 and 22.
99. *Ibid.*, III, 11 (2).
100. *Ibid.*, III 17 (4).
101. *Ibid.*, IV, 14 (1).
102. *Ibid.*, V, 2 (2–4).
103. Ἱστορία Πολιτική τῆς Κωνσταντινουπόλεως (1:3), p. 25.
104. *Ibid.*, p. 26.
105. See Phrantzes, Χρονικόν (5:1), p. 308.
106. See Tomadakis, " Ὁ μετά τήν ἅλωσιν τῆς Κωνσταντινουπόλεως" (90), p. 628.
107. Kritoboulos of Imbros, Συγγραφή ἱστοριῶν (1:7), Ι, 73 (4). On their resettlement, Tomadakis is relevant (" Ὁ μετά τήν ἅλωσιν τῆς Κωνσταντινουπόλεως [90], pp. 611–629). Turkish figures on the population of Constantinople in 1477 are given by Schneider, "Die Bevölkerung Konstantinopels" (84), p. 240; *Cf.* pp. 241–242.
108. Ducas, *Historia byzantina* (1:2), p. 318 (Bonn), p. 399 (Bucharest). *Cf.* Papazoglou, "Μωάμεθ Β' ὁ Πορθητής" (86), p. 222.
109. See Kritoboulos of Imbros, Συγγραφή ἱστοριῶν (1:7), I–II, *passim*, esp. II, 22 (1). See also Karolidis, Ἱστορία τῆς Ἑλλάδος, 1453–1862 (5:110), pp. 197–198. For a description of the metamorphosis of Constantinople into a Turkish city and various other aspects, see Iorga, *Byzance après Byzance* (1:13), pp. 45–59, where, however, certain evidence is unreliable and needs to be carefully examined. See also Babinger, *Mehmed der Eroberer* (1:8), pp. 115–116, 158.
110. Braudel, *La Méditerranée* (1:63), p. 271; Barkan, "Essai sur les données statistiques" (3:50), p. 21, fn. 1. *Cf.* Schneider, "Die Bevölkerung Konstantinopels"

(84), pp. 241–242. Stoianovich provides a bibliography on the organization of the city's food supply ("The Conquering Balkan Orthodox Merchant" [81], pp. 241–242). For further details, see Mantran, *Istanbul* (7:131), pp. 179 ff., 425 ff.

111. Braudel, *La Méditerranée* (1:63), p. 272. On the number of Jews in the middle of the sixteenth century, see Dernschwam, *Tagebuch* (1:20), p. 107.

112. Mantran, *Istanbul* (7:131), p. 47. For details of the different neighborhoods, as well as the people, in the city, see pp. 37 ff.

113. Gerlach, *Tagebuch* (1:22), pp. 21–22. *Cf.* the descriptions of various other travellers, for example, Deshayes in 1621 (*Voyage* [1:26], pp. 99 ff.). Many of their works contain beautiful gravures offering full or partial views of Constantinople. Some are also most objective (for example, Franz Babinger, *Eine unbemerkte holländische Grossansicht von Konstantinopel* [*An Unnoticed Dutch Picture of Constantinople*] (*um 1665*) [Göttingen, 1962], which also gives the full bibliography). See also Franz Babinger, "Drei Stadtansichten von Konstantinopel, Galata (Pera) und Scutari, aus dem Ende des 16 Jahrhunderts [Three Views of Constantinople, Galata (Pera), and Scutari at the End of the Sixteenth Century]," *Oesterreichische Akademie der Wissenschaften, Philologische-Historische Klasse* (Vienna, 1959), p. 77. And see Mantran, *Istanbul* (7:131), pp. 25–35.

114. Du Fresne-Canaye, *Le Voyage* (1:123), p. 120.

115. For details, see Carlier de Pinon, *Voyage en Orient* (1:89), pp. 71–73.

116. Du Fresne-Canaye, *Le Voyage* (1:123), p. 120.

117. Lubenau, *Beschreibung* (4:200), I, 157.

118. Gassot, *Le Discours du Voyage* (1:141), pp. 5a–5b.

119. Lubenau, *Beschreibung* (4:200), I, 150–151.

120. Du Mont, *Voyages* (1:90), II, 73–74.

121. Pacifique, *Relation* (4:121), p. 26. On the fires, see the article by Alfons M. Schneider, "Brände in Konstantinopel [Fires in Constantinople]," BZ, XLI (1941), 382–403. And see Mantran, *Istanbul* (7:131), p. 36.

122. *Recueil de voyages* (1:123), VIII, 47–48. See also Magni, *Lettere* (1:142), pp. 257–258.

123. Gerlach, *Tagebuch* (1:22), p. 405.

124. Beauvau, *Relation* (4:57), p. 52.

125. Gerlach, *Tagebuch* (1:22), p. 413. On shops, and the like, see du Fresne-Canaye, *Le Voyage* (1:123), pp. 96–97; Amman, *Reise* (76), pp. 45–46; and (in detail) Mantran, *Istanbul* (7:131), pp. 452 ff. On *wakf* tenements and their influence on the economy of the state, see Vera Mutafčieva, "за ролята на вакъфа в градската икономика на балканите под турска власт (XV–XVII B.) [On the Importance of *Wakf* in the Urban Economy of the Balkans under Turkish Rule (XV–XVII Centuries)]," известия на института за история, X (1962), 121–145.

126. See Maurand, *Itinéraires* (4:9), pp. 235–241; Gassot, *Le Discours du voyage* (1:141), pp. 11b–12b; du Fresne-Canaye, *Le Voyage* (1:123), p. 98; Dernschwam, *Tagebuch* (1:20), p. 113; Magni, *Lettere* (1:142), pp. 186 ff., 202–203.

127. Gerlach, *Tagebuch* (1:22), p. 393.

128. *Recueil de Voyages* (1:123), VIII, 35–36. 49–54, 103–105. Wild animals bred in a church close to the Hippodrome (du Fresne-Canaye, *Le Voyage* [1:123], p. 100, where there are also relevant extracts from other travellers). See also Gassot, *Le Discours du voyage* (1:141), pp. 12a–14a; de Busbecq, *The Life and Letters* (5:170), I, 127–128; Mitrović, Ἡ Κωνσταντινούπολις (1:123), p. 82.

129. Gassot, *Le Discours du voyage* (1:141), p. 11a; Amman, *Reise* (76), pp. 51–52; Deshayes, *Voyage* (1:26), pp. 116–117, and see p. 124, regarding Roman Catholics and their rights.

130. Maurand, *Itinéraires* (4:9), pp. 197–207; Gerlach, *Tagebuch* (1:22), p. 22: "und findet man darinnen allerhand lust und Kurzweil die melancholey und traurigkeit [one can find there every sort of amusement and reduce his melancholy and sorrow]." See also Mantran, *Istanbul* (7:131), pp. 73–79.

131. See Magni, *Lettere* (1:142), p. 99.

132. See Schweigger, *Constantinopel* (1:116), p. 132.

133. Crusius, *Turcograeciae* (1:53), p. 485. Their dress is described on p. 496.

134. There are some beautiful descriptions in Belon, *Observations* (1:123), p. 199a; and du Fresne-Canaye, *Le Voyage* (1:123), p. 79; see also the picture after p. 114 of the latter text. *Cf.* Gerlach, *Tagebuch* (1:22), pp. 31, 262, 279 ("wie ein gemahlet bild [like a printed picture]"), 368; and Nicolay, *Navigations* (1:140), pp. 120–121, where there are also drawings.

135. See Crusius, *Turcograeciae* (1:53), p. 487. On the arrival of prisoners in Constantinople, see pp. 501–502, 503, 504. *Cf.* Gerlach, *Tagebuch* (1:22), *passim.*

136. On the Greeks, Jews, and Armenians of the City in the latter half of the seventeenth century, see Mantran, *Istanbul* (7:131), pp. 48 ff.

137. On the composition of the bourgeois class, see *ibid.*, pp. 103–104.

138. *Ibid.*, pp. 60–61.

139. Gerlach, *Tagebuch* (1:22), pp. 21–22.

140. *Ibid.*, p. 192.

141. Albèri, *Le relazioni* (1:142), III, 389.

142. Deshayes, *Voyage* (1:26), p. 121; Magni, *Lettere* (1:142), p. 202; Febvre, *Théâtre* (1:152), p. 376.

143. Gerlach, *Tagebuch* (1:22), p. 397.

144. Crusius, *Turcograeciae* (1:53), p. 503; Dernschwam, *Tagebuch* (1:20), p. 113, where there is interesting material on their education. See also Gerlach, *Tagebuch* (1:22), p. 20; Nicolay, *Navigations* (1:140), pp. 168–169; and Ypsilantis, Τά μετά. τήν "Αλωσιν (1:92), pp. 26–27.

145. De Tournefort, *Relation* (1:90), I, 65–66, for comments on their primitive cures.

146. Skarlatos D. Vyzantios, 'Η Κωνσταντινούπολις [Constantinople] (Athens, 1862), II, 18, 29; and Gerlach, *Tagebuch* (1:22), pp. 99, 208. *Cf.* Melissinos Christodoulos, Τά Ταταῦλα ἤτοι ἱστορία τῶν Ταταούλων [*Tatavla, or, History of Tataoula*] (Constantinople, 1913), pp. 12–14.

147. Christodoulos, Τά Ταταῦλα (146), p. 14.

148. Beldiceanu, *Actes* (1:29), pp. 112–113. The relevant decree is given on pp. 146–148. In 1470 and afterwards a number of the lessors of state revenues possessing well-known Byzantine names were in fact Constantinopolitans descended from old families (see Mutafčieva, "откупуването на Държавните" [3], pp. 53–76, 71–72).

149. Zerlentis, Σημειώματα περί 'Ελλήνων (2:55), pp. 17–18, 19. There is mention of another Mouzalos, probably the same person, in Gedeon, Χρονικά τοῦ πατριαρχικοῦ οἴκου καί ναοῦ (5:49), pp. 137–138. On the match made between a daughter in the Ralles family and Andronicus, son of Michael Cantacuzenus, see Gerlach, *Tagebuch* (1:22), pp. 133, 200. On the family named Ralles descended from the Byzantine family of the same name, see Matthaios Paranikas, "Περί τῆς οἰκογενείας Ράλλη Καραβοκύρη ἐν Χαλκηδόνι [On the Ralles Karavokyres Family in Chalcedon]," 'Ελληνικὸς Φιλολογικὸς Σύλλογος Κωνσταντινουπόλεως, XII (1879), 159–161. *Cf.* the Palaeologinas family (up to 1914) in the Strandza area (Elpeniki Saranti, 'Από τήν 'Ανατολική Θράκη. 'Η Σηλυβρία καί τά γύρω χωριά της [*From Eastern Thrace. Selymbria and Neighboring Villages*] (Athens, 1956), I, 42, which also gives the

relevant tradition concerning the graves of the Palaeologi). On the scions of old Byzantine families who traded as merchants with Russia (Vatatzes, Chrysoloras, Azanaios, Chalcocondyles, and others), see Stoianovich, "The Conquering Balkan Orthodox Merchant" (81), p. 240, which also contains the relevant bibliography. Michael Cantacuzenus, the sultan's "μέγας πραγματευτής [grand peddler]," an avaricious and evil man, was put to death in 1578 (see Gerlach, *Tagebuch* [1:22], pp. 454, 463–467; and *cf.* Karolidis, Ἱστορία τῆς Ἑλλάδος, 1453–1862 [5:110], pp. 354–358).

150. Crusius, *Turcograeciae* (1:53), pp. 91–92. *Cf.* p. 497. Regarding a certain Raoul, who, at the beginning of the sixteenth century, left with all his belongings for Russia, where he died, see Gerlach, *Tagebuch* (1:22), p. 456. On other members of the Ralles family, see Mystakidis, "Οἱ Ράλλαι" (4:205), pp. 257–282, which also contains the relevant bibliography.

151. Crusius, *Turcograeciae* (1:53), p. 91. On the cities of the Black Sea at the end of the seventeenth century, see Magni, *Lettere* (1:142), pp. 311–325.

152. There is a rather good sketch of the descendants of the Byzantine nobility in Iorga, *Byzance après Byzance* (1:13), pp. 113–125, which also provides the relevant bibliography.

153. See Magni, *Lettere* (1:142), pp. 619–620. The new citizens included Manolakis the Kastorian, who had no heirs and planned to devote the whole of his huge estate to philanthropic works. See also Amman, *Reise* (76), p. 52.

154. Gedeon, Μνεία τῶν πρό ἐμοῦ (5:108), pp. 84–85. *Cf.* the other names of the archbishopric of Proikonnesos in Manuel I. Gedeon, Προικόννησος [*Proikonnesos*] (Constantinople, 1895), pp. 55–56, 216–217.

155. Nikolaos B. Phardys, Ὕλη καί σκαρίφημα ἱστορίας τῆς ἐν Κορσικῇ Ἑλληνικῆς ἀποικίας [*Data on, and an Historical Sketch of, the Greek Colony in Corsica*] (Athens, 1888), pp. 19–20.

156. Vacalopoulos, *Thasos* (1:59), p. 16, fn. 4.

157. Dernschwam, *Tagebuch* (1:20), p. 68; Febvre, *Théâtre* (1:152), pp. 254–266.

158. The commercial prosperity which generally prevailed throughout the whole of Europe in the 1600s was responsible for an increase in the mule population (see Braudel, *La Méditerranée* [1:63], pp. 244 ff., on the trade routes of the East).

159. For a description of a caravansary outside Ragusa, see du Fresne-Canaye, *Le Voyage* (1:123), pp. 23–24; *cf.* p. 40. This writer uses the word "*kirigi*" to refer to a muleteer (p. 20). Other descriptions are by Carlier de Pinon, *Voyage* (1:89), pp. 116–117 (in the year 1579); and Deshayes, *Voyage* (1:26), pp. 66–68, 84–85. See also the detailed description of the caravansary of Kavala, one of Ibrahim Pasha's establishments, where foreign guests received free board (Belon, *Observations* [1:123], pp. 60b–61b). On the caravansaries of Constantinople in 1573, *cf.* Gerlach, *Tagebuch* (1:22), pp. 15, 21; and Mitrović, Ἡ Κωνσταντινούπολις (1:123), pp. 43–46 (in 1599). On Constantinople's inns, caravansaries, and the like, in the following century, see du Mont, *Voyages* (1:90), II, 103–105. On the imarets, inns, and other Moslem benevolent institutions, see Gerlach, *Tagebuch* (1:22), p. 506; du Loir, *Voyages* (1:108), pp. 189–193; and de Dreux, *Voyage* (1:154), p. 35. On the fountains near the inns, see François-René de Chateaubriand, *Itinéraire de Paris à Jérusalem* (Paris, 1877), pp. 76–77; and Maxime Raybaud, *Mémoires sur la Grèce pour servir à l'histoire de la guerre de l'indépendance* [*Memories of Greece Useful for the History of the War of Independence*] (Paris, 1824), II, 174. For extensive details about caravans in European Turkey, see Ami Boué, *La Turquie d'Europe* (Paris, 1840), IV, appendix 1 ("Manière de voyager en Turquie"), pp. 442–469. Most travel books have so many descriptions of caravansaries and inns that it is unnecessary to acknowledge all the

relevant sources. However, there is one interesting reference to a deserted caravansary at Vigla, Attica, in the latter half of the seventeenth century, to which the community of the village of Chasia sent by turns one of the villagers to tend to the needs of travellers (Collignon, *Le Consul Jean Giraud* [1:52], p. 55).

160. See Gökbilgin, "Kanunı sultan Süleiman" (1:134), p. 279.

161. Pharmakidis, Ἡ Λάρισσα (3:103), p. 166.

162. P. N. Liouphis, Ἱστορία τῆς Κοζάνης [*History of Kozane*] (Athens, 1924), p. 43.

163. See Vasdravellis, Ἀρχεῖον Θεσσαλονίκης 1695–1912 (2:34), p. 4. *Cf.* p. 109, and *passim*. The people from Agrafa did not quit Thessalonica completely, as Pavlidis believes (" Ἐπίσκεψις εἰς τήν ἕδραν τῆς Σχολῆς τῶν Ἀγράφων" [6:283], p. 234). This writer was swayed too much by evidence to this effect in the archives of Thessalonica (see Vasdravellis, Ἀρχεῖον Θεσσαλονίκης, p. 193). *Cf.* references to people from the Agrafa in the letters of Eugenius the Aetolian (Eustratiadis, " Ἐπιστολαί Εὐγενίου Ἰωαννουλίου τοῦ Αἰτωλοῦ" [5:164], VII (1934), p. 250; and also Gritsopoulos, "Εὐγενίου Ἰωαννουλίου Αἰτωλοῦ ἐπιστολαί" [6:286], p. 43). People originally from the Agrafa were being settled in Thessalonica as late as the nineteenth century (see Apostolos Vacalopoulos, Ἡ Θεσσαλονίκη στά 1430, 1821 καί 1912–1918 [Thessalonica in 1430, 1821, and 1912–1918] (Thessalonica, 1947), pp. 32–33).

164. See Charilaos G. Tsekos, Ἱστορία τοῦ Ἀσβεστοχωρίου [*History of Asvestochorion*] (Thessalonica, 1957), pp. 38–41. It would appear that people from Agrafa came to Asvestochorion much earlier than 1821, not afterwards.

165. Tsoukalas, Ἱστοριογεωγραφική περιγραφή (5:127), p. 39. *Cf.* Apostolidis, Ἡ τῆς Φιλιππουπόλεως ἱστορία (7:143), p. 247.

166. See Pavlidis, Ἐπίσκεψις εἰς τήν ἕδραν τῆς Σχολῆς τῶν Ἀγράφων (6:283), pp. 234–237. *Cf.* Vasileiou, Ἡ ἐπισκοπή Λιτζᾶς καί Ἀγράφων (3:104), pp. 49–82, which contains the more recent bibliography on the subject. According to tradition, the houses in the most important villages of the Aspropotamos district were built in the middle of the sixteenth century (see Kasomoulis, Ἐνθυμήματα στρατιωτικά [8:12], I, 309; *cf.* p. 312). This was the time when the economic revival of the inhabitants began.

167. See Anastasios K. Orlandos, "Σταχυολογήματα ἐκ μονῶν τῆς Πίνδου [Gleanings from the Pindus Monasteries]," Ἀρχεῖον Βυζαντινῶν Μνημείων τῆς Ἑλλάδος, V (1939–1940), 167–197. See esp. pp. 178, 187.

168. Kritikidis, Τοπογραφία (4:45), p. 106.

169. Georgios A. Rigas, Σκιάθου λαϊκός πολιτισμός. Τεῦχος Α΄: Δημώδη ἄσματα [*The Folk Culture of Skiathos. Vol. I: Folk Songs*] (Thessalonica, 1958), pp. 264–265.

170. Charalambos Rempelis, "Δημοτικά τραγούδια Βούρμπιανης [Folk Songs of Vourbiani]," ΗΧ, I (1926), 191. *Cf.* the variations in Konitsa (Rempelis, Κονιτσιώτικα [7:47], p. 27) and in Nikete, Chalcidice (Triantaphyllos Anagnostaras, "50 δημοτικά τραγούδια Νικήτης [Fifty Folk Songs of Nikete]," Χρονικά Χαλκιδικῆς, IV (1962), 221). See also Rempelis, "Δημοτικά τραγούδια Βούρμπιανης,," p. 192, for the song of a girl who beseeched her loved one to return from abroad because she was about to be married off to a sixty-two-year-old man.

171. Nitsos, Μονογραφία (3:111), p. 26.

172. See Nikos B. Kosmas, "Οἱ δίοδοι τῆς Πίνδου [The Passes of the Pindus]," Ἠπειρωτική Ἑστία, IV (1955), 14–20, which provides the relevant bibliography.

173. See Vourazeli-Marinakou, Αἱ ἐν Θράκῃ συντεχνίαι (7:137), pp. 62 ff., for a discussion of the origins of the inhabitants, their commercial activities, their guilds, and other matters.

174. See G. Balastsev-Ikchiev, on the privileges of the raias settled in the lands

dedicated to the towns of Mecca and Medina, in *Minalo*, I (1909), 141–156; and
Dimitar Kostov, Арбанаси [*Arbanashi*] (Sofia, 1959). *Cf.* Amantos, "Σουλτανικός
προνομιακός ὁρισμός" (5:157), pp. 45–46.

175. Belon, *Observations* (1:123), pp. 62b–63b.

176. Myrtilos K. Apostolidis, Ὁ Στενίμαχος [*Stenimachos*] (Athens, 1929, p. 34
(fn.): "in Turkey the Epirotes used to be called Albanians because they knew the
Albanian language." If the Epirotes provoked other Greeks they might also be
called "Albanians" because, to the Greek, that was an expression of contempt.
Apparently, this confusion between the Epirotes and other Illyrian peoples also
existed in ancient times (*cf.* the view of Cousinéry, *Voyage* [3:94], I, 14: "des Albanais
amalgamés avec d'ancients Epirotes et avec des Illyriens" [some Albanians intermixed with ancient Epirotes and Illyrians],).

177. Belon, *Observations* (1:123), p. 65b. In 1621 Deshayes described the same
scene of Albanians journeying to the East (*Voyage* [1:26], pp. 92–93). Deshayes must
have been familiar with Belon's description, though he did not acknowledge it.
On the term "Anatolia" ("East"), see Belon, *Observations*, p. 68a. Belon thought
that the harvesting and winnowing implements of these workers were better than
those of his own country (pp. 65a–65b). On Greek, Albanian, and Bulgarian seasonal
workers, see also Anhegger, *Beitraege* (3:71), I, 93–94, which also provides the relevant
bibliography.

178. For these, see Antonios Keramopoullos, Τί εἶναι οἱ Κουτσόβλαχοι; [*Who Are
the Koutsovlachs?*] (Athens, 1939), p. 56 (fn.). See also Alexandros Letsas, " Ὁ γάμος
ἐν Βογατσικῷ [The Wedding Ceremony in Vogatsiko]," Μακεδονικά, I (1940),
124, 127.

179. There is material on these villages in Rempelis, Κονιτσιώτικα (7:47), p. 13.
On the masons' idiom, the *koudaritika*, see pp. 350–356.

180. See Keramopoullos, Τί εἶναι οἱ Κουτσόβλαχοι; (178), p. 56. On the Epirote
and Macedonian artisans, see Georgios Megas, " Ὁ λεγόμενος κοινός βαλκανικός
πολιτισμός. Ἡ δημώδης ποίησις [The So-called "Balkan" Culture: Folk Poetry],"
Ἐπετηρὶς τοῦ Λαογραφικοῦ Ἀρχείου, VI (1950–1951), 300.

181. On these large groups, see Chatzimichali, "Οἱ συντεχνίες — τά ἰσνάφια"
(7:141), p. 13 of the reprint. On itinerant laborers, see also Vourazeli-Marinakou,
Αἱ ἐν Θρᾴκῃ συντεχνίαι (7:137), pp. 21–22; *cf.* pp. 19–21. And see Nikolaos K.
Moutsopoulos, Καστοριά, Τά Ἀρχοντικά [*Kastoria. Mansions*] (Athens, 1962), p. 11,
which provides the relevant bibliography.

182. Asterios D. Gousios, Ἡ κατά τό Πάγγαιον χώρα. Λακκοβηκίων τοπογραφία,
ἤθη ἔθιμα καί γλῶσσα [*The Mt. Pangaion District. Topography, Customs and Language of
Lakkovikia*] (Leipzig, 1894), p. 34.

183. Nikolaos Oikonomou, "Πῶς Ἕλληνες ἐπιχειρηματίαι ἐμίσθωνον ὡς ἀνθρακεῖς σλαβοφώνους κατά τήν ἐποχήν τῆς τουρκοκρατίας δι' ἐργασίαν εἰς τήν Χαλκι-
δικήν [How Greek Employers in Chalcidice Hired Slavic-Speaking People to Work
as Coal Dealers during the Period of Turkish Rule]," Χρονικά Χαλκιδικῆς, II (1961),
194 (n. 2).

184. On the movement of Bulgarians into Macedonia (especially to the plains of
Serrai and Drama) and into Thrace as laborers, see the study by Petăr Koledarov,
"народно стният сьстав на драмско до средата на xix век [The Ethnological
Composition of the Drama Region up to the Nineteenth Century]," известия на
института за история, X (1962), 176 ff., which also contains the relevant bibliography. Unfortunately, this study is often vague and generalizes from insufficient
evidence. These tendencies are particularly marked in the conclusions drawn
pp. 183–186).

185. See Vacalopoulos, *Thasos* (1:59), p. 59.

186. See Oikonomou, "Πῶς Ἕλληνες ἐπιχειρηματίαι ἐμίσθωνον ὡς ἀνθρακεῖς σλαβοφώνους" (183), pp. 193–194.

187. Note, for example, the mistaken views of Conze and Perrot on the origin of the toponym Voulgaro on Thasos (Vacalopoulos, *Thasos* [1:59], p. 59).

188. Stilpon Kyriakidis, Θεσσαλονίκια μελετήματα [*Thessalonian Studies*] (Thessalonica, 1939), pp. 11, 13, 17.

189. Gökbilgin, "Kanunı sultan Süleiman" (1:134), p. 254. Spyridon Lambros mentions that in 1897 he saw the will of one Agatha "concerning the Siderokavsians of Mt. Athos, signed by Ierissos Nikandros in 6950 [1442]" in an eighteenth-century codex belonging to the student Georgios I. Kyvelos. I have not myself seen this and cannot say what light it would shed on Siderokavsia in the middle of the fifteenth century. See Lambros, "Κῶδιξ Νιφάκη καὶ ἁγιορειτικῶν γραμμάτων [The Codex of Niphakes and Haghiorite Documents]," NE, X (1913), 489.

190. See the demotic song concerning Isvoron in Stavros Papastavrou, " Ἔθιμα καὶ παραδόσεις τῆς Χαλκιδικῆς [Customs and Traditions of Chalcidice]," Χρονικά Χαλκιδικῆς, IV (1962), 179.

191. Fallmerayer (*Schriften und Tagebücher* [3:100], II, 155, fn. 1) rather surprisingly takes A. Grisebach to task—*Reise durch Rumelien und nach Brussa im Jahre 1893* [*Journey through Rumelia to Bussa in 1839*] (Göttingen, 1841), II, 13–14—for locating Siderokavsia in the wrong place; but Fallmerayer is the one who errs. On Mantemochoria and Chasikochoria in Chalcidice, see Grisebach, pp. 12–13.

192. See Moschopoulos, " Ἡ Ἑλλάς" (3:97), pp. 498–499. See also Hadschi Chalfa's description, which is almost contemporary (*Rumeli und Bosna* [74], pp. 82–83).

193. Belon, *Observations* (1:123), p. 45a.

194. See Babinger, *Sultanische Urkunden* (5:39), pp. 232–237. *Cf.* Beldiceanu, *Actes* (1:29), p. 138.

195. See Anhegger, *Beitraege* (3:71), I, part 1, pp. 11 ff.

196. Belon, *Observations* (1:123), pp. 45a ff. *Cf.* Anhegger, *Beitraege* (3:71), I, part 1, pp. 180–182. *Cf.* the designation of mine employees in Spyridon Lavriotis, " Ἀναγραφαί ἐγγράφων τῆς Μεγίστης Λαύρας τοῦ Ἁγίου Ἀθανασίου ἐν τῷ Ἄθῳ [Documentary Records of the Monastery of *Megiste Lavra* of St. Athanasius on Mt. Athos]," BNJ, VII (1930), 407. See also the Greek inscription, dated 1623, on the side of the fountain of the Monastery of St. Anastasia. This fountain had been constructed through the generosity of the daughter of Ioannis Panteugenios from Siderokavsia (Petros N. Papageorgiou, " Ἐκδρομή εἰς τήν βασιλικήν καὶ πατριαρχικήν μονήν τῆς Ἁγίας Ἀναστασίας, τῆς Φαρμακολυτρίας τήν ἐν τῇ Χαλκιδικῇ [Journey to the Royal and Patriarchal Monastery of St. Anastasia of Pharmakolytria in Chalcidice]," BZ, VII [1898], 82). On the influence of the German miners generally, see Anhegger, *Beitraege* (3:71), I, part 1, pp. 110–111, which provides a bibliography. The fact that most of the miners of Siderokavsia were Bulgarian does not make the village Bulgarian, as Professor Vsevolod Nicolaev asserts (характерьт на минните предприятия и режимьт на рударския труд в нашите зами през xvi, xvii и xviii в. [*The Character of Mineral Enterprise and the Position of Mineral Labor in our Country during the Sixteenth, Seventeenth and Eighteenth Centuries*] [Sofia, 1954], p. 13, fn. 4). *Cf.* the writings of Fallmerayer, which have a distinct pro-Slav bias (*Schriften und Tagebücher* [3:100], II, 152–155). Why do such writers stress the importance of Slav colonization yet nowhere mention that the people were Slavicized? Why, in attempting to account for the Greek character of these districts, do they point to the Hellenization of Slav inhabitants?

197. See Anhegger, *Beitraege* (3:71), I, part 1, pp. 182–183.

198. See Dušanka Šopova, македония во xvi и xvii век. документи од цариград-ските архиви (1557–1645) [*Macedonia in the Sixteenth and Seventeenth Centuries. Documents from the Archives in Constantinople (1557–1645)*], (Skoplje, 1955), p. 25 (document no. 14). For Pazarouda in Chalcidice and its Friday fair, which attracted 5,000–10,000 people, see Moschopoulos, " 'Η 'Ελλάς" (3:97), pp. 497–498; on the little town of Besikian and its thermal springs, see pp. 496, 497.

199. See Ahmed Refik, *Türkiye madenleri* [*Turkish Mines*] (Istanbul, 1931), p. 19 (document no. 32). *Cf.* Anhegger, *Beitraege* (3:71), I, part 1, p. 182; part 2, p. 307; on the silver coins (*aspra*) of Siderokavsia, see I, part 1, p. 183. See also Joannes Leunclavius, *Annales sultanorum othmanidarum* (Francofurd, 1588), pp. 221 ff.

200. See Moschopoulos, " 'Η 'Ελλάς" (3:97), pp. 498–500. On the mint's period of operation in the European regions of the Ottoman Empire, see Anhegger, *Beitraege* (3:71), I, part 1, pp. 80–81.

201. Refik, *Türkiye madenleri* (199), pp. 42–43.

202. See Anhegger, *Beitraege* (3:71), I, part 1, p. 184. There are some references to these mines at the end of the eighteenth century and the beginning of the nine-teenth century in Cousinéry, *Voyage* (3:94), II, 141.

203. Dernschwam, *Tagebuch* (1:20), p. 26.

204. Deshayes, *Voyage* (1:26), p. 93.

205. See Curipeschitz, *Itinerarium* (5:148), p. 55. See also Dernschwam, *Tagebuch* (1:20), pp. 247–248: "Und von Hadrianopol fecht sich Bulgaria an, haben in allen Dorffern bulgarisch geredt [Bulgaria extends beyond Adrianople into whatever villages Bulgarian is spoken]."

206. There is a moving account of these discussions with Greeks in Curipeschitz, *Itinerarium* (5:148), pp. 57–58.

207. Belon, *Observations* (1:123), p. 78b. On the seventeenth century, see Grelot, *Relation* (1:90), pp. 51–58.

208. Belon, *Observations* (1:123), pp. 68a–68b. *Cf.* Dernschwam, *Tagebuch* (1:20), pp. 27–28; and Lubenau, *Beschreibung* (4:200), I, 124–125. In 1621 Deshayes referred to Selymbria as having been almost totally destroyed (*Voyage* [1:26], p. 94).

209. Belon, *Observations* (1:123), p. 79a.

210. See Dernschwam, *Tagebuch* (1:20), p. 26; and Deshayes, *Voyage* (1:26), p. 92.

211. See Barkan, "Les Formes" (1:21), p. 299.

212. *Ibid.*, pp. 20–22.

213. See Lubenau, *Beschreibung* (4:200), I, 115.

214. Barkan, "Les Formes" (1:21), p. 299.

215. See Georgios Lampousiadis, " 'Οδοιπορικόν ἐπί τῶν ἡμερῶν τῆς ἑλληνικῆς κατοχῆς τῆς 'Ανατ. Θράκης [Travel in Eastern Thrace under Greek Occupation]," Θρακικά, II (1929), 91, where the villages are named.

216. Also under Mohammed II the suburb of Arnaoutkioï (Megalo Reuma) was colonized (see Gennadius, Metropolitan of Heliopolis, 'Ιστορία τοῦ Μεγάλου Ρεύμα-τος ('Αρναούτκιογι) [*History of Megalo Reuma (Arnaoutkioï)*] (Istanbul, 1949), pp. 8–9).

217. Maravelakis-Vacalopoulos, Αἱ προσφυγικαί ἐγκαταστάσεις (8:49), pp. 174, 295–296. *Cf.* the note by Socrates Liakos in the newspaper Μακεδονία, Thessa-lonica, 23 May 1955.

218. See Hasluck, "Albanian Settlements" (4:28), p. 227, which also provides the relevant bibliography. On Albanian colonization in various parts of the Ottoman Empire, see Georgirenes, *Description* (1:45), p. 16.

219. Christos Zachariadis, "Περί τῆς ἐπαρχίας Προικοννήσου [On the Province of Proikonnesos]," Ξενοφάνης, I (1896), 409. *Cf.* Gedeon, Μνεία τῶν πρό ἐμοῦ (5:108), p. 81.

220. M. Kleonymos and C. Papadopoulos, Βιθυνικά [On Bithynia] (Constantinople, 1867), pp. 93, 155.

221. F. W. Hasluck, "Bithynica," BSA, XIII (1906–1907), 304–305, is the source here.

222. Georgirenes, Description (1:45), p. 16.

223. For this tradition, see Eustratios I. Drakos, Διάκοσμος [Decoration] (Constantinople, 1890), p. 22.

224. Gerlach, Tagebuch (1:22), p. 379. Cf. the craft of the villagers of Konitsa (Athanasios Petridis, "Χρονικόν Δρυοπίδος [Chronicle of Dryopis]," in Νεοελληνικά Ἀνάλεκτα, I (1871), no. 2, p. 60.

225. Kritoboulos of Imbros, Ἱστοριῶν συγγραφή (1:7), II, 22 (2).

226. Bordier, Relation (1:123), p. 98.

227. Belon, Observations (1:123), p. 68b.

228. Ibid., p. 180a. The village of Bosnakioï is mentioned by D'Arvieux, Mémoires (7:73), IV, 378.

229. In 1578 there was a movement of 1,000 Bulgarians (see Gerlach, Tagebuch [1:22], p. 487).

230. At the end of the nineteenth century, a large number of these hostlers were living "in various villages and çiftliks (of the province of Vizye) and received wages" (see Savvas Ioannidis, Ἱστορία τῆς Βιζύης Ἀνατ. Θράκης [History of Vizye, Eastern Thrace] [Athens, 1954], p. 20). One writer says that the little town of Chaphsa in Thrace was also colonized by the Turkish-speaking Gagaouzoi from the plains of Dovroutsa in northeastern Bulgaria during the time of either Selim I or Suleiman I; see Georgios I. Lampousiadis, Θρακικῶν μελετῶν. τ. 1: Ἀπό Ἀδριανουπόλεως εἰς Λουλέ Βουργάζιον [Thracian Studies. I: From Adrianople to Loule Burgaz] (Adrianople, 1911), I, 26; cf. p. 45. Gerlach refers to it in 1578 as a small village, a timar of Mehmet Pasha. A few Greeks living there had to go to the neighboring village in order to attend Mass (Tagebuch [1:22], p. 511).

231. Zacharadis, "Περί τῆς ἐπαρχίας Προικοννήσου" (219), p. 405. Cf. the analogous evidence concerning the village of Voulgaro on Thasos (Vacalopoulos, Thasos [1:59], p. 59).

232. See A. Malkotsis, "Περί τῆς χερσονήσου Κυζίκου ἤ Ἀρκτονήσου ἤ (Τουρᾶ). Καπουδαγί [On the Peninsula of Cyzicus or (Toura). Kapoudagi]," Ξενοφάνης, I (1896), 159–260.

233. Barkan, "Essai sur les données statistiques" (3:50), p. 20.

234. Gerlach, Tagebuch (1:22), p. 99.

235. See Demetrios A. Petropoulos, Εἰσαγωγή στό βιβλίο τῆς Καλλιόπης Μουσαίου-Μπουγιούκου, Παροιμίες τῆς Μάκρης καί τοῦ Λιβισιοῦ [Introduction to the Book of Calliope Mousaiou-Bougioukou. The Proverbs sof Makri and Livision (Athens, 1961), pp. ια' - λα' [xi–xxxi] of the reprint; and also Nikolaos P. Andriotis, Τό ἰδίωμα τοῦ Λιβισιοῦ τῆς Λυκίας [The Dialect of Libisi, Lycea] (Athens, 1961), pp. 13, 14, 15.

236. Albert Wächter, Der Verfall des Griechentums in Kleinasien im XIV Jahrhundert [The Decline of Hellenism in Asia Minor in the Fourteenth Century] (Leipzig, 1903), p. 33. On Attalia, see Beauveau, Relation (4:57), p. 114: "elle garde la plus part des Grecs, les Turcs les ayant faict exempts de tribut, afin qu'ils vacassent à la conservation d'icelle [it is inhabited mostly by Greeks, whom the Turks have exempted from taxes in order to keep them in the Town]."

237. Wächter, Der Verfall (236), p. 34. On the dress of the women of Kastellorizo, see Achilleus Diamantaras, "Παράπλους Λυκίας ἀπό Μεγίστης (Καστελλορίζου) εἰς Μύρα [Sailing off Lycia from Megisti (Kastellorizo) to Myra]," Ξενοφάνης, IV

(1906–1907), 29–32. Lycia produced good robust wines (Gerlach, *Tagebuch* [1:22], p. 212).

238. Gerlach, *Tagebuch* (1:22), p. 99.

239. See Lykios, "Περί Λυκίας καί Λυκίων, περί Μάκρης καί Λειβισίου [On Lycea and Lyceans. On Makri and Libisi]," Ξενοφάνης, I (1896), 86–93.

240. See Anonymous, "Περιγραφή τῆς πόλεως 'Ατταλείας [Description of the City of Attalia]," Ξενοφάνης, V (1906–1908), 247.

241. Papageorgiou, " 'Οδοιπορικόν 'Ιακώβου Μηλοϊτη (59), p. 635.

242. Wächter, *Der Verfall* (236), p. 48.

243. Gerlach, *Tagebuch* (1:22), p. 372. *Cf.* Wächter, *Der Verfall* (236), pp. 38–39. Girls from the Cyclades also went to Smyrna and Constantinople as servants (see Evangelidis, 'Η νῆσος Σέριφος [4:154], pp. 100–101).

244. On Pergamon, see Georgios Chondronikis, 'Ιστορία τῆς Περγάμου [*History of Pergamon*] (Samos, 1910), p. 12, fn. 1. *Cf.* Wächter, *Der Verfall* (236), p. 44.

245. Barkan, Essai sur les données statistiques" (3:50), p. 30.

246. Carayon, *Relations* (2:31), p. 209.

247. The surplus population of Tenos, an acute problem at the beginning of the seventeenth century, went to Chios and Smyrna (see Hasluck, "Depopulation" [4:1], p. 126; and Thevenot, *Relation* [4:81], p. 196).

248. There is a vivid portrayal of the commerce of Smyrna during the third quarter of the seventeenth century in Magni, *Lettere* (1:142), pp. 44 ff.

249. For the year 1621, see Deshayes, *Voyage* (1:26), p. 126.

250. Magni, Lettere (1:142), p. 105. For details, see D'Arvieux, *Mémoires* (7:73), IV, 36–62, 77 ff.

251. Magni, *Lettere* (1:142), pp. 47–48. See the article by Halil Inalcik in the English edition of the *Encyclopaedia of Islam*, p. 214; and Fermanel-Fauvel-Baudouin-Stochove, *Observations curieuses sur le voyage du Levant* (Rouen, 1668), pp. 306–308. See also the graphic description by Philippos K. Phalbos, "Μπεζεστένια καί χάνια στή Σμύρνη [Bazaars and Inns in Smyrna]," MX, IX (1961), 130–195.

252. Magni, *Lettere* (1:142), pp. 46–47. *Cf.* Pacifique, *Relation* (4:121), p. 14.

253. See Phalbos, "Μπεζεστένια καί χάνια" (251), pp. 141 ff., 144.

254. Papageorgiou, " 'Οδοιπορικόν 'Ιακώβου Μηλοϊτη (59), p. 636. On Smyrna and the merchants of Smyrna, see Deshayes, *Voyage* (1:26), pp. 342–343. On Smyrna at the end of the seventeenth century, see Ricaut, *Histoire* (1:90), pp. 29 ff.; and also Chardin, *Voyage* (97), I, 14 ff. On the flourishing state of Smyrna's trade, see Braudel, *La Méditerranée* (1:63), p. 246.

255. Magni, *Lettere* (1:142), pp. 48–49.

256. There is a moving description by a refugee in Philippos Phalbos, " 'Ο φραγκομαχαλᾶς τῆς Σμύρνης καί τά φραγκοχιώτικα βιβλία [The Frankish Quarter of Smyrna and the Frankish-Chiote Books]," MX, VIII (1959), 173–226.

257. See Vallindas, Κυθνιακά (1:111), pp. 89–90. Perhaps these migrants and Christians living nearby were responsible for building the little Church of St. Theodore in the Greek quarter of Pergamon under the citadel (see Georgios Chondronikis and Arist. Thevaiopoulos, Πέργαμος (1300 π. Χρ.–1922) [*Pergamon (1300 B.C.–1922)*] Mytilene, 1929), p. 93).

258. See N. Tzolozoglou, "Μονογραφία περί Κασαμπᾶ [Monograph on Kasaba]," Ξενοφάνης, VI (1909), 522.

259. *Ibid.*, pp. 419–420. On the restrictions imposed on the Christians of Kasaba in the performance of their religious duties (before 1653), see Amantos, "Σουλτανικός προνομιακός ὁρισμός" (5:157), pp. 46–48. Besides the well-established outlets in Constantinople and Smyrna, emigrants from the Aegean islands also went to the

following places in the hinterland of Asia Minor: Vourla, Mainemeni, the two Phocaeas, Magnesia, Guiarkioï, Karagoulanian, Axari, Kelebon, Guiordes, Marmara, Kaïtziki. The people of Kythnos in particular went to these places as farmers and builders, many of them with their families, and stayed on permanently in the new lands. This stream of migration dried up only gradually after the establishment of the Greek nation (see Vallindas, Ἱστορία τῆς νήσου Κύθνου (4:92), pp. 44–45). Twenty-two builders from Rhodes and eleven from Euboea worked on the Suleimanye Mosque in Constantinople (see Todorov, "по нѧкой въпросн" (4), p. 51).

260. Gerlach, *Tagebuch* (1:22), p. 372.

261. Papageorgiou, " 'Ὁδοιπορικόν Ἰακώβου Μηλοΐτη" (59), p. 636.

262. See Charles Texier, *Asie Mineure* (Paris, 1862), pp. 425–426.

263. Zerlentis, Σημειώματα περί 'Ελλήνων (2:55), p. 19: " 'Η πόλις τοῦ Πριάμου (Τροία) ἤρξατο ἀνακαινίζεσθαι ὑπό τῶν χριστιανῶν· ἐν τῷ ἀκρωτηρίῳ Σιγείῳ, ὃ καλοῦσι Κεφαλήν γιανιτσάρου, ὑπάρχουσι δύο χωρία [Restoration of the city of Priam (Troy) was begun by Christians; on Cape Sigeion, which is called "Janissary's Head," there are two villages]."

264. Maravelakis-Vacalopoulos, Αἱ προσφυγικαί ἐγκαταστασάσεις (8:49), p. 208.

265. *Ibid.*, p. 211. Perhaps this is the place that the traveller Grelot called Guiaourkioï (*Relation* [1:90], pp. 3–4), and its inhabitants "Troyiaki" (that is, from "Little Troy").

266. See Grelot, *Relation* (1:90), pp. 38 ff.

267. Belon, *Observations* (1:123), p. 206a; and P. Vapheiadis, Τό Ρύσιον ('Αρετσοῦ). Σύντομος μονογραφία τῆς κωμοπόλεως 'Αρετσοῦς ἀπό ἀρχαιοτάτων χρόνων μέχρι τῆς ἀνταλλαγῆς τοῦ 1922 [*Rysion (Aretsou). A Brief Monograph on the Town of Aretsou from Ancient Times to the Population Exchange of 1922*] (Athens, 1924), p. 13: "Οἱ κάτοικοι τοῦ Ρυσίου εἰσίν αὐτόχθονες [the inhabitants of Rysion are indigenes]." These people were also fishermen and winegrowers (Vapheiadis, Τό Ρύσιον, pp. 15–16). There is material on fishing techniques in the Sea of Marmara in Belon, *Observations* (1:123), pp. 70b–74a. *Cf.* Maravelakis-Vacalopoulos, Αἱ προσφυγικαί ἐγκαταστασάσεις (8:49), pp. 48–49, on fishing among the people of Aretsou.

268. Barkan, "Les Formes" (1:21), p. 180. For a lengthier discussion, see pp. 242–244 of the Turkish text (see above, 1:9).

269. Gerlach, *Tagebuch* (1:22), p. 255. *Cf.* the contemporary testimony of du Fresne-Canaye, *Voyage* (1:123), pp. 153–154. See also Hippocrates K. Makris, "Οἱ κάτοικοι τῆς Κυζικηνῆς Χερσονήσου [The Inhabitants of the Cyzicus Peninsula]," MX, IX (1961), 211–226.

270. Makris, "Οἱ κάτοικοι τῆς Κυζικηνῆς Χερσονήσου" (269), p. 165. *Cf.* pp. 163–164.

271. Gerlach, *Tagebuch* (1:22), p. 256.

272. For details, see Barkan, "Les Formes" (1:21), pp. 177–178. The names of these villages are listed more fully in the Turkish text, pp. 225–227 (1:9). *Cf.* pp. 178–179, on the ill-defined characteristics of the *ellidjis*, both Moslem and Christian, who were in many ways similar to serfs.

273. See Ernest Charrière, *Négotiations de la France dans le Levant* (Paris, 1848), I, 374. Bugade is the same place as Biga.

274. On the settlements of Greeks from Thessaly-Macedonia, see Benediktos Adamantiadis, " 'Η ἐκκλησιαστική ἐπαρχία Προύσης [The Ecclesiastical Province of Prusa]," MX, VIII (1959), 114, 115; and also Hasluck, "Bithynica" (221), p. 301. Hasluck considers that the inhabitants of Kouvouklia and many other villages of the district were mainly Peloponnesians who, at least according to tradition, immigrated during the reign of Suleiman the Magnificent. However, some Greeks in a

402   NOTES—CHAPTER 9

number of villages, including Kouvouklia, were apparently descended from Byzantine families; others in the neighboring villages of Kopelia, Baloukli, Zographista, Anochori, and Kita were converts to Islam (see Deligiannis, "Τό ἐν τῇ περιφερείᾳ Προύσης χωρίον Κουβούκλια" [5:174], pp. 290–292).

275. Gerlach, *Tagebuch* (1:22), p. 256.
276. *Ibid.*, p. 257.
277. *Ibid.*
278. *Ibid.*
279. *Ibid.*, p. 259.
280. *Ibid.*, p. 94. About twenty years earlier, in 1555, Dernschwam wrote (*Tagebuch* [1:20], p. 235), the Greek population of Nicaea had all but disappeared (there were only eleven Christians and one illiterate priest left) and the city's once numerous churches had all been destroyed.
281. See Dernschwam, *Tagebuch* (1:20), pp. 235–236, 238.
282. *Cf.* Gregorios Ioséphidis, "Περί τινων πόλεων καί χωμῶν τῆς Βιθυνίας [On Some of the Cities and Towns of Bithynia]," Ξενοφάνης, II (1904–1905), 509–513.
283. Barkan, "Essai sur les données statistiques" (3:50), p. 30.
284. See Kleonymos-Papadopoulos, Βιθυνικά (220), p. 33.
285. *Ibid.*, pp. 67–68.
286. *Ibid.*, p. 88. The village of Kontze in Bithynia, for example, was settled by people from Lesbos. *Cf.* pp. 90, 91.
287. See Hasluck, "Albanian Settlements" (4:28), p. 227 and fn. 6. They were not settled after the revolution of 1770, as Thanasis Kostakis thought (Σύντομη γραμματική [3:151], pp. 147–155).
288. Maravelakis-Vacalopoulos, Αἱ προσφυγικαί ἐγκαταστάσεις (8:49), p. 294; *cf.* Kleonymos-Papadopoulos, Βιθυνικά (220), p. 152.
289. Kleonymos-Papadopoulos, Βιθυνικά (220), p. 77. *Cf.* Gregorios S. Iosephidis, "Βιθυνιακά [On Bithynia]," Ξενοφάνης, IV (1906–1907), 541.
290. On settlement there, see Maravelakis-Vacalopoulos, Αἱ προσφυγικαί ἐγκαταστάσεις (8:49), p. 394.
291. Kleonymos-Papadopoulos, Βιθυνικά (220), pp. 97–98. Some of these migrant villages are listed in the Turkish text of Barkan, Les Formes" (1:21), pp. 225–227. The name of the village of Boulgaratoi surely reveals that its inhabitants were of Bulgarian origin. On Bulgarian peasants in Gevze, Bithynia, see Dernschwam, *Tagebuch* (1:20), p. 152.
292. Kleonymos-Papadopoulos, Βιθυνικά (220), p. 88.
293. *Ibid.*, p. 90. *Cf.* Iosephidis, "Βιθυνιακά" (289), p. 543: "πρό 300 περίπου ἐτῶν ὑπό τινος 'Αλβανοῦ Βεζύρη τοῦ σουλτάνου Σουλεϊμάν ἐξ 'Ηπείρου καί Θεσσαλίας [about 300 years ago, under a certain Albanian vizier of Sultan Suleiman's, we emigrated from Epirus and Thessaly]."
294. Kleonymos-Papadopoulos, Βιθυνικά (220), pp. 147, 153. *Cf.* Entitzik of Panormus (Maravelakis-Vacalopoulos, Αἱ προσφυγικαί ἐγκαταστάσεις [8:49], p. 41).
295. Kleonymos-Papadopoulos, Βιθυνικά (220), p. 77. Armenochori on the peninsula of Cyzicus was founded in the nineteenth century (see Malkotsis, "Περί τῆς χερσονήσου Κυζίκου" [232], p. 260). *Cf.* Maravelakis-Vacalopoulos, Αἱ προσφυγικαί ἐγκαταστάσεις (8:49), p. 437. But see the opposing view of Hippocrates Makris, "Τά χωρία καί τά μοναστήρια τῆς Κυζικηνῆς χερσονήσου [The Villages and Monasteries of the Cyzicus Peninsula]," MX, VIII (1959), 162, who says that the inhabitants of Armenochori on the Cyzicus Peninsula came from Armenia in 1720.
296. Victor Cuinet, *La Turquie d'Asie* (Paris, 1894), IV, 310–311.
297. See Anthimos A. Papadopoulos, 'Ο ὑπόδουλος ἑλληνισμός τῆς 'Ασιατικῆς

Ἑλλάδος ἐθνικῶς καί γλωσσικῶς ἐξεταζόμενος [*An Ethnological and Linguistic Analysis of the Subject Greeks of Asiatic Greece*] (Athens, 1919), pp. 73–74. *Cf.* Cuinet's erroneous view (*La Turquie d'Asie* [296], IV, 73–74).

298. Kleonymos-Papadopoulos, Βιθυνικά (220), p. 96.

299. *Ibid.*, p. 93. One source says that Arvanitochori in Bithynia was settled around 1800 by people from Bitolj (Monastir) (see Adamantiadis, " Ἡ ἐκκλησιαστική ἐπαρχία Προύσης" [274], p. 125).

300. Ice was made by putting snow into large holes in the ground (Belon, *Observations* [1:123], pp. 188a–189a).

301. Belon, *Observations* (1:123), p. 203a. See also the entry "harir" by Halil Inalcik in the English edition of the *Encyclopaedia of Islam*, p. 215. There is a description of Prusa in Lubenau, *Beschreibung* (4:200), II, 76–78.

302. Barkan, "Essai sur les données statistiques" (3:50), p. 27.

303. *Ibid.*, p. 66b.

304. J. Sölch, "Historisch-geographische Studien über bithynische Siedlungen [Historical Geographical Studies on Settlements in Bithynia]," BNJ, I (1920), 296. On sericulture, see esp. pp. 302 ff. I have not been able to consult Basileios Kandis', Ἡ Προῦσα [*Prusa*] (Athens, 1883).

305. Du Loir, *Voyages* (1:108), p. 68. See also Mantran, *Istanbul* (7:131), p. 50, which provides the relevant bibliography.

306. There is some material in N.S. Rizos, Καππαδοκικά, ἤτοι δοκίμιον ἱστορικῆς περιγραφῆς τῆς ἀρχαίας Καππαδοκίας, καί ἰδίως τῶν ἐπαρχιῶν Καισαρείας καί Ἰκονίου [*Cappadocia, or, A Descriptive Historical Essay on Ancient Cappadocia, Especially the Provinces of Caesarea and Iconium*] (Constantinople, 1856), pp. 74–75, 89, 91, and elsewhere. See also N. Kechagiopoulos, " Ἀρχαῖος βίος τῶν ἐν τῷ ἐσωτερικῷ τῆς Μ. Ἀσίας Μικρασιατῶν [The Ancient Way of Life of the People of the Hinterland of Asia Minor]," Ξενοφάνης, VI (1909), 474; Valavanis, Μικρασιατικά (6:12), p. 45; Demetrios Makroas, " Ἡ Μαλακοπή [Malakope]," Ξενοφάνης, IV (1906–1907), 418–419, 421; Rizos Eleutheriadis, Συνασός [*Sinasos*] (Athens, 1879), pp. 23–24; Sophronos Sophroniadis, Ἡ Σινασός τῆς Καππαδοκίας καί τά δημοτικά τῆς τραγούδια [*Sinasos, Cappadocia, and Its Folk Songs*] (Athens, 1958), pp. 8, 17–21, 144–147, 223–234 (and see pp. 101, 183, for sketches of cave dwellings; and p. 127, for sketches of churches).

307. See Archelaos Sarantidis, Ἡ Σινασός [*Sinasos*] (Athens, 1899), pp. 17–21.

308. Pharasopoulos, Τά Σύλατα (6:12), pp. 18–19. *Cf.* Savvas B. Cholopoulos, Μονογραφική ἱστορία Ζήλης ἤ Σύλατας [Historical Monograph on Zile or Sylata]," Ξενοφάνης, II (1904–1905), 95–96.

309. Menas Christopoulos, "Πατριδογραφία [Description of My Homeland]," MX, III (1940), 283–284.

310. Papadopoulos, Ὁ ὑπόδουλος ἑλληνισμός (297), pp. 119–120. This is an interesting book, especially on Hellenism in the Pontus.

311. Barkan, "Essai sur les données statistiques" (3:50), p. 30.

312. Cuinet, *La Turquie d'Asie* (296), IV, 413.

313. Iosephidis, "Βιθυνιακά" (289), p. 206.

314. Ruy Gonzales de Clavijo, *Embassy to Tamerlane, 1403–1406*, tr. Guy Le Strange (London, 1928), p. 104. There were very few Turks.

315. Wächter, *Der Verfall* (236), p. 26.

316. *Ibid.*

317. Panagiotis G. Makris, Ἡράκλεια τοῦ Πόντου [*Herakleia of Pontus*] (Athens, 1903), p. 33.

318. See Iosephidis, "Βιθυνιακά" (289), p. 540. According to tradition, the Turks

had left one or two centuries before the time when Iosephidis wrote, following dissension between them and the Greeks.

319. Wächter, *Der Verfall* (236), p. 26. The seventeenth-century traveller Bordier mentions Eregli (Pontoherakleia) but says nothing about its inhabitants (*Relation* [1:123], pp. 92–93).

320. Bordier, *Relation* (1:123), p. 95.

321. Babinger, *Mehmed der Eroberer* (1:8), p. 203.

322. See Cuinet, *La Turquie d'Asie* (296), IV, 413. On Sinope and its inhabitants at the beginning of the seventeenth century, see Bordier, *Relation* (1:123), pp. 100 ff.; also p. 104: "les rues et maisons sont confuses et sens ordre ainsy que les habitants y sont meslés [the streets and houses are confused and without order even as the inhabitants there are mixed]."

323. Wächter, *Der Verfall* (236), p. 26.

324. See Triantaphyllidis, Οἱ φυγάδες (1:157), p. 65. On the shipyards and produce of Sinope, see Bordier, *Relation* (1:123), pp. 104–105. On the privileges granted to Greek woodcutters and sawyers from the south coast of the Pontus, see Deshayes, *Voyage* (1:26), p. 209.

325. See Triantaphyllidis, Οἱ φυγάδες (1:157), p. 73: "οἱ ἐν δὲ Ἀμισῷ καί τῇ ὑπερθαλαττίᾳ ἢ μετῴκησαν ἀπό ἄλλων μεσογειοτέρων χωρῶν, ἢ ὑπάγονται εἰς τό ἰθαγενές ἑλληνικόν στοιχεῖον [the Greek-speaking inhabitants of Amisus were descended from Byzantine families who lived there at the time of the Capture; the Turkish-speaking inhabitants (including those who lived inland) came from further inland or else sprang from indigenous Greek stock]." *Cf.* N. E. Lampadarios, "Περί Ἀμισοῦ καί περί τοῦ Πόντου ἐν γένει [On Amisus and on the Pontus in General]," Ξενοφάνης, I (1896), 266: "Κατακτηθεῖσα ὑπό τῶν Τούρκων οὐδέποτε ἀπώλεσε τήν σπουδαιότητα αὐτῆς, τό μέν ἕνεκα τῆς περί αὐτήν εὐφόρου χώρας, τό δέ διότι ἦτο πάντοτε τό ἐπίνειον τοῦ ἐσωτερικοῦ τῆς Μ. Ἀσίας [Though conquered by the Turks it never lost its importance, both because the country around it was fertile and because it remained the port for the interior of Asia Minor]." *Cf.* also Papadopoulos, Ὁ ὑπόδουλος ἑλληνισμός (297), p. 80: "Οἱ ἀρχαῖοι ἑλληνόφωνοι κάτοικοι τῆς πόλεως ἀποτελοῦν ἴδιον συνοικισμόν ὑπερκείμενον τῆς νέας πόλεως καί ὀνομαζόμενον Καδικιοΐν [the ancient Greek population of the city lived in the quarter known as Kadikioïn, which dominated the modern city]." A small Greek population also survived in Kerasous in the Pontus, which surrendered conditionally to Mohammed II after a siege of eight years. According to tradition, the treaty of surrender was still extant at the beginning of the nineteenth century, in the possession of the Photeinoglou family. Under the terms of the treaty, Greeks and Turks lived side by side in the citadel until the beginning of the twentieth century. The development of trade led to an increase in population and the expansion of the city towards the east, west, and south (see Kyrillos Elias Pavlidis, " Ὀλίγα τινά περί τῆς πόλεως Κερασοῦντος [Some Data on the City of Kerasous]," Ξενοφάνης, IV (1906–1907), 11). According to oral tradition among the inhabitants, which Bordier recorded at the beginning of the seventeenth century, a small island (two or three miles around) with a monastery, opposite Kerasous, held out against the Turks for seven years after the fall of Trebizond (Bordier, *Relation* [1:123], p. 115; for a description of Kerasous, see pp. 114–116).

326. Papadopoulos, Ὁ ὑπόδουλος ἑλληνισμός (297), p. 80.

327. See Joachim D. Saltsis, Χρονικά Κοτυώρων [*Chronicles of Cotyora*] (Thessalonica, 1955), pp. 14, 25–28. In 1652 Neocaesarea (Niksar) was inhabited by Turks and a small number of Turkish-speaking Greeks (see Zerlentis, Ἱστορικά σημειώματα [4:116], p. 29).

328. See Zinkeisen, *Geschichte* (2:40), II, 346.

329. Schneider, "Die Bevölkerung Konstantinopels" (84), pp. 240–241. However, this writer does not specify who the "people of Karaman" were. Obviously, they did not come to Constantinople during the reign of Selim I, as they told Dernschwam (*Tagebuch* [1:20], p. 52; for more about these people, see p. 107).

330. See M. Tayyîb Gökbilgin, *XV–XVI inci asırlarda Edirne ve Paşa livası vakıflar mülkler mukataalar* [Adrianople and the District of Paşa (in Rumelia) in the Fifteenth and Sixteenth Centuries. Religious Endowments, Properties, and Leases] (Istanbul, 1952), p. 88.

331. Nicolay, *Navigations* (1:140), pp. 239–240. The fact that many Karamanians were goldsmiths is corroborated by Gerlach (*Tagebuch* [1:22], p. 217).

332. See Gerlach, *Tagebuch* (1:22), pp. 173, 186, 217.

333. Dernschwam, *Tagebuch* (1:20), p. 52.

334. Nicolay, *Navigations* (1:140), pp. 239–240.

335. Gerlach, *Tagebuch* (1:22), p. 339. Crusius, whose main source of information was Gerlach, was apparently referring to these women in *Turcograeciae* (1:53), p. 485; cf. p. 496.

336. Athanasios Ioannidis, " Ὁδοιπορικαί σημειώσεις [Travel Notes]," Ξενο-φάνης, I (1896), 322–325. Among the Cappadocian merchants of Constantinople in the middle of the nineteenth century, a few were from Entorlouk (see Rizos, Καππαδοκικά [306], p. 78), a few from Urgüp (p. 85 of the same book), and considerably more from Sinasos (p. 87). There were merchants from Phertek in both Iconium and Constantinople (p. 103), and from Teneği in Amisos, Iconium and Constantinople (p. 106). Cf. Valavanis, Μικρασιατικά (6:12), p. 60, where there is a reference to the large number of immigrants into Iconium, Attalia (Antalya), Sparti (Pisidia), Smyrna, and Constantinople (and to a lesser extent into Odessa). Cf. also the emigration of the inhabitants of Sazala (Christopoulos, "Πατριδογραφία" [309], p. 292).

337. On this point, see Pharasopoulos, Τά Σύλατα (6:12), pp. 30 ff., for the tradition of a youth who migrated to Constantinople in order to seek his fortune. Cf. Makroas, " Ἡ Μαλακοπή" (306), p. 519; and Valavanis, Μικρασιατικά (6:12), p. 60.

338. Sarantidis, Ἡ Σινασός (307), p. 21.

339. *Ibid.*, p. 32.

340. *Ibid.*, pp. 33–34.

341. Triantaphyllidis, Οἱ φυγάδες (1:157), p. 54. Cf. Oikonomides, " Ἀργυρού-πολις" (3:72), pp. 187–188. On the dispersal of the people of Karamania and the Pontus, indeed Greeks generally, there are interesting inscriptions on religious vessels and vestments (see Eugenia Chatzidaki, "Χριστιανικές ἐπιγραφές Μ. Ἀσίας καί Πόντου στό Μουσεῖο Μπενάκη [Christian Inscriptions from Asia Minor and the Pontus in the Benaki Museum]," MX, VIII (1959), 24 ff.).

342. *Ibid.*, Triantaphyllidfs, Οἱ φυγάδες (1:157), p. 53.

343. *Ibid.*, p. 70.

344. Ypsilantis, Τά μετά τήν Ἅλωσιν (1:92), p. 117, where there is a reference to 30,000 Greek-speaking Christians who had their tongues cut out.

345. Gerlach, *Tagebuch* (1:22), p. 212.

346. Pacifique, *Relation* (4:121), p. 82.

347. Zerlentis, Σημειώματα περί Ἑλλήνων (2:55), p. 14. Regarding Cairo, see also Pacifique, *Relation* (4:121), p. 80. Trevisan says (*Relation* [3:130], p. 212) that there were many Orthodox churches and Greek monks in Cairo in 1512. See also Dyovouniotis, "Τό ὑπ' ἀρ. 21 χειρόγραφον" (2:50), pp. 273–274; and K. E. Para-syras, "Κρῆτες ἐν Καΐρῳ [Cretans in Cairo]," Ἐπετηρίς Ἑταιρείας Κρητικῶν Σπουδῶν, III (1940), 187–192.

Chapter 10

1. Stoianovich, "The Conquering Balkan Orthodox Merchant" (9:81), p. 237.

2. Barozzi-Berchet, *Relazioni* (1:146), p. 217.

3. Stoianovich, "The Conquering Balkan Orthodox Merchant" (9:81), p. 237.

4. Nikolaos B. Tomadakis, "Ναοί καί θεσμοί τῆς ἑλληνικῆς κοινότητος τοῦ Λιβόρνου [Churches and Institutions of the Greek Community in Leghorn]," XVI (1940), 81–127; and Braudel, *La Méditerranée* (1:63), pp. 107, 126.

5. Stoianovich, "The Conquering Balkan Orthodox Merchant" (9:81), p. 238.

6. See J. Cvijić, *La Péninsule balkanique. Géographie humaine* (Paris, 1918), pp. 26, 27.

7. For details, see Vacalopoulos, Δυτικομακεδόνες ἀπόδημοι (3:96), pp. 7 ff. Half of the inhabitants of the little town of Palanka, near Kola, which was part of the domain of Hassan Pasha, were Greeks; the other half were Turks (Deshayes, *Voyage* [1:26], p. 66).

8. De Busbecq, *The Life and Letters* (5:170), I, 93.

9. Theodoros M. Natsinas, Οἱ Μακεδόνες πραμματευτάδες εἰς τάς χώρας Αὐστρίας καί Οὑγγαρίας [*Macedonian Peddlers in Austria and Hungary*] (Thessalonica, 1939), pp. 11–12. This book is based largely on research carried out by the historian Spyridon Lambros.

10. Pantelis M. Kontogiannis, Ἱστορικαί διηγήσεις [*Historical Narratives*] (Athens, [n.d.]), p. 26.

11. See Gerlach, *Tagebuch* (1:22), p. 531.

12. I think this is the route taken by the philosopher, Ioannis Kottounios of Veroia, to join his brother Lampos in Walachia, where he learned Latin (see Basileios A. Mystakidis, "Οἱ Κοττούνιοι [The Kottounioses]," Ἑλληνικὸς Φιλολογικὸς Σύλλογος Κωνσταντινουπόλεως Fiftieth Jubilee number (Constantinople, 1913–1921), pp. 281, 285.

13. Henry Holland, *Travels in the Ionian Isles, Albania, Thessaly, Macedonia, etc., during the Years 1812 and 1813* (London, 1815), pp. 324–325; and Seraphim Maximos, Ἡ αὐγή τοῦ ἑλληνικοῦ καπιταλισμοῦ Τουρκοκρατία (1685–1789) [*The Dawn of Greek Capitalism (Turkish Rule 1685–1789)*] (Athens, 1945), p. 76.

14. For these and the movements of Orthodox merchants of the Balkans, see Stoianovich, "The Conquering Balkan Orthodox Merchant" (9:81), pp. 234–313.

15. Spyridon Lambros, "Σελίδες ἐκ τῆς ἱστορίας τοῦ ἐν Οὑγγαρίᾳ καί Αὐστρίᾳ Μακεδονικοῦ Ἑλληνισμοῦ [Pages from the History of Macedonian Hellenism in Hungary and Austria]," NE, VIII (1911), 272–273. However, Lambros errs in delineating the routes to central Europe.

16. Emanuel Turczynski, *Die deutsch-griechischen Kulturbeziehungen bis zur Berufung König Ottos* [*German-Greek Cultural Relations before the Reign of King Otto*] (Munich, 1959), p. 5.

17. *Ibid.*, p. 5, fn. 8, which provides the relevant bibliography.

18. Nestor Camariano, "L'Organisation et l'activité culturelle de la compagnie des marchands grecs de Sibiu," *Balcania*, VI (1943), 202.

19. *Ibid.*, p. 206.

20. *Ibid.*, pp. 206–207.

21. *Ibid.*, p. 208.

22. *Ibid.*, pp. 205, 208–209, 210.

23. See Lambros, "Σελίδες" (15), p. 267; and Georgios T. Lyritzis, Αἱ μακεδονικαί κοινότητες ἐπί τουρκοκρατίας [*The Macedonian Communities under Turkish Rule*] (Kozane, 1952), p. 16. See also Liouphis, Ἱστορία τῆς Κοζάνης (9:162), pp. 337–338; and Turczynski, *Die deutsch-griechischen Kulturbeziehungen* (16), pp. 8, 10.

24. See Armando Sapori, *Le Marchand italien au Moyen Age* (Paris, 1952), p. 15.

25. Camariano, "L'Organisation" (18), pp. 203–206, 210.

26. *Ibid.*, pp. 210–211.

27. *Ibid.*, pp. 210–213. As early as 1640 the Greeks had engaged a certain Seraphim, from the Monastery of Iveron, as their priest (p. 219). Before taking up his duties the priest was officially attached to the Orthodox bishopric of Transylvania (p. 219). In 1690 the Greeks built a small stone church in the village of Rungart outside the walls of Sibiu because they were forbidden to build it in the city (p. 222). Not until a century later were they permitted inside (pp. 222–226); even then, the authorities of Cluj frowned on the presence of Greek priests in Sibiu and strove to have them replaced by Rumanians (p. 220).

28. See Camariano, "L'Organisation" (18), pp. 215–218.

29. See also Spyridon Lambros, " Ἔρευναι ἐν ταῖς βιβλιοθήκαις καί ἀρχείοις Ῥώμης, Βενετίας, Βουδαπέστης καί Βιέννης [Research in the Libraries and Archives of Rome, Venice, Budapest and Vienna]," NE, XVIII (1924), 278, 279.

30. See Turczynski, *Die deutsch-griechischen Kulturbeziehungen* (16), pp. 31–32.

31. See Pennas, Τό χρονικόν τῶν Σερρῶν (1:176), I, 7.

32. Stoianovich, "The Conquering Balkan Merchant" (9:81), p. 241.

33. See Demostene Russo, *Studii istorice greco-române* (Bucharest, 1939), I, 103–109, 109–113; and Iorga, *Byzance après Byzance* (1:13), pp. 148–154.

34. See Turczynski, *Die deutsch-griechischen Kulturbeziehungen* (16), pp. 32–33, which contains the relevant bibliography.

35. *Ibid.*, p. 32, fn. 132, which provides a bibliography.

36. Anonymous, "Οἱ Ἕλληνες ἐν Πόζεν [Greeks in Poznan]," ΔΙΕΕ, IX (1926), 581.

37. See Stoianovich, "The Conquering Balkan Orthodox Merchant" (9:81), p. 240.

38. *Ibid.*, and Dousae, *De itinere* (1:171), pp. 13–14.

39. Zerlentis, Σημειώματα περί Ἑλλήνων (2:55), pp. 26–27.

40. See Turczynski, *Die deutsch-griechischen Kulturbeziehungen* (16), pp. 100 ff.

41. Asterios D. Gousios, Τά τραγούδια τῆς πατρίδος μου, ἤτοι συλλογή τερπνῶν δημωδῶν ἀσμάτων ἀδομένων ἐν τῇ κατά Πάγγαιον χώρᾳ [*The Songs of My Country, or, a Collection of Pleasant Folk Songs Sung in the Region of Mt. Pangaion*] (Athens, 1901), p. 104.

42. See Demetrios B. Oikonomides, "Τά βορειοηπειρωτικά δημοτικά τραγούδια. Τά τραγούδια τῆς ξενιτειᾶς [Folk Songs of Northern Epirus. Songs about Emigrants in Foreign Lands]," in Ἀφιέρωμα εἰς τήν Ἤπειρον, commem. vol., pp. 37–45. *Cf.* similar songs in Lambridis, Ἠπειρωτικά μελετήματα (1:82), Τεῦχος 8, part 1, p. 30, fn. 1.

43. Nitsos, Μονογραφία (3:111), p. 204.

44. Rempelis, Κονιτσιώτικα (7:47), p. 43.

45. There are so many poignant folk songs about emigrants and emigration that it is impossible to give a complete bibliography. Some useful material on the songs of Chalcidice will be found in the review, Χρονικά τῆς Χαλκιδικῆς, IV (1962), 182–185.

46. See, for example, Deshayes, *Voyage* (1:26), p. 358.

47. See Patselis, Τό Δελβινάκιον (3:111), pp. 32 ff., 50 ff.

48. See Vacalopoulos, Δυτικομακεδόνες ἀπόδημοι (3:96), pp. 9 ff.

49. Kalinderis, Αἱ συντεχνίαι τῆς Κοζάνης (3:99), pp. 4, 7–10.

50. See Georgios Chatzikyriakou, Σκέψεις καί ἐντυπώσεις, ἐκ περιοδείας μετά τοπογραφικῶν, ἱστορικῶν καί ἀρχαιολογικῶν σημειώσεων [*Thoughts and Impressions from a Journey, with Topographical, Historical and Archaeological Notes*] (Athens, 1906), p. 70.

Chapter 11

1. See Armand Delatte, *Les Portulans grecs* (Liège-Paris, 1947); and Stephanos I. Makrymichalos, " Ἑλληνικοί πορτολάνοι τοῦ 16, 17 καί 18 αἰῶνος [Greek Portolanos of the Sixteenth, Seventeenth, and Eighteenth Centuries]," Ἐρανιστής, I (1963), nos. 3–4, reprint (Athens, 1963).

2. Relevant here is a Viennese manuscript of the sixteenth century (see Armand Delatte, "L'Armement d'une caravelle grecque au XVIᵉ siècle d'après un manuscrit de Vienne [The Arming of a Greek Caravel in the Sixteenth Century according to a Viennese Manuscript]," *Miscellanea G. Mercati,* III (1946), 490–505).

3. Magni, *Lettere* (1:142), p. 20.

4. Belon, *Observations* (1:123), p. 156b.

5. Nicander Nucius of Corcyre, *The Second Book,* ed. J. A. Cramer (London, 1841), p. 12.

6. There is material in Partsch, Κεφαλληνία καί Ἰθάκη (4:32), pp. 256–272.

7. See *ibid.*, p. 256, for remarks in the reports of Venetian *provveditori* on the widespread demand for *uva passa.* See also Carlier de Pinon, *Voyage* (1:89), pp. 48–49; Dyovouniotis, "Τό ὑπ' ἀρ. 21 χειρόγραφον" (2:50), p. 275; and Buchon, *Voyage* (4:128), p. 91. On the fostering of viticulture on Zacynthus at the expense of wheat-growing, see Zoïs, Αἱ ἐν Ζακύνθῳ συντεχνίαι (7:139), pp. 132–148.

8. Deshayes, *Voyage* (1:26), p. 468; and Magni, *Lettere* (1:142), pp. 20–21.

9. Partsch, Κεφαλληνία καί Ἰθάκη (4:32), pp. 253–254.

10. Carlier de Pinon, *Voyage* (1:89), p. 49.

11. Partsch, Κεφαλληνία καί Ἰθάκη (4:32), pp. 256 ff., contains much material of interest. On the soil and produce of Cephalonia, as well as stock-raising on the island, at the end of the sixteenth century, see Albèri, *Le relazioni* (1:142), III, 2, p. 217.

12. Deshayes, *Voyage* (1:26), pp. 451–452.

13. There are interesting details in Partsch, Κεφαλληνία καί Ἰθάκη (4:32), pp. 229–234.

14. *Ibid.*, pp. 234 ff. On the increase in raisin production on Ithaca, see p. 261.

15. Bertrandon de la Brocquière, *Voyage d'outremer et retour de Jérusalem en France par la voie de terre, pendant le cours des années 1432 et 1433,* ed. Pierre Legrand D'Aussy, in Mémoires de l'Institut national des sciences et arts; sciences morales et politiques, (Paris, Fructidor an XII), v, 474.

16. See Freddy Thiriet, "Les Lettres commerciales des Bembo et le commerce vénitien dans l'empire ottoman à la fin du XVᵉ siècle," *Studi in onore di Armando Sapori,* p. 924.

17. See Spyridon Theotokis, " Ἡ Κρήτη τό 1570 [Crete in 1570]," HME (1933), p. 320.

18. Thiriet, "Les Lettres commerciales" (16), pp. 913–928. In 1512, 50,000 tons were exported (Trevisan, *Relation* [3:130], pp. 167–168).

19. Thiriet, "Les Lettres commerciales" (16), pp. 915–922; and also Voisins, *Voyage* (3:7), pp. 23, 29.

20. See Ioannis Kallitsounakis, " Ἡ διέλευσις τοῦ Arnold von Harff δι' Ἑλλάδος κατά τό 1477 [Arnold von Harff's Journey through Greece in 1477], ΕΕΒΣ, XXIII (1953), 252, and Denis Zakythinos, " Ἱστορικά σημειώματα [Historical Notes]," ΕΕΒΣ, IX (1932), 378. *Cf.* Nicolay, *Navigations* (1:140), p. 56.

21. Belon, *Observations* (1:123), p. 22a.

22. *Ibid.*, p. 8a.

23. *Ibid.*, pp. 8b–9a.

24. Grassetto, *Viaggio* (4:90), p. 23. On the fertility of the island, as well as its

varied agricultural produce in 1674, see Barres, *L'Estat présent* (4:2), II, 191–192. On its mineral wealth, see Kostas P. Kyrris, " Ὁ «Παναγιωτάκης καί δάσκαλος» τοῦ Φαρμακᾶ στά 1789 ἦταν ὁ «Παναγιωτατζῆς Λογιώτατος» ['Panagiotakis the teacher' of Pharmaka in 1489 and 'Panagiotatzis Logiotatos' were One and the Same Person]," Κυπριακαί Σπουδαί, XXIX (1965), 170–181.

25. Roberts, *Adventures* (4:155), p. 50.

26. Barres, *L'Estat présent* (4:2), II, 193: "il y a diverses nations mais plus de Grecs que de toute autre [there are various nations but more of the Greek than of any other]."

27. Deshayes, *Voyage* (1:26), p. 356.

28. Dapper, *Description* (4:136), pp. 163–164. *Cf.* also Deshayes, *Voyage* (1:26), p. 354.

29. Boschini, *L'Archipelago* (3:87), p. 12.

30. Papageorgiou, " Ὁδοιπορικόν Ἰακώβου Μηλοΐτη (9:59), p. 636. Sponges were also gathered by Euboean seamen (see Carlier de Pinon, *Voyage* [1:89], pp. 61–62, on the method of harvesting them).

31. See L. Spyridis, " Ἡ νῆσος Μεγίστη (Καστελλόριζον) [The Island of Megiste (Kastellorizo)]," Παρνασσός, IV (1880), 461–465.

32. Hasluck, "Depopulation" (4:1), p. 166.

33. Buondelmonti, *Description* (4:7), p. 69. *Cf.* the testimony of Lupazzolo in 1638 that their honey was exquisite (Hasluck, "Depopulation" [4:1], p. 168); and see Roberts, *Adventures* (4:155), p. 38.

34. Dapper, *Description* (4:136), p. 187.

35. Zerlentis, Σημειώματα περί Ἑλλήνων (2:55), p. 27.

36. Barres, *L'Estate présent* (4:2), I, 172–173.

37. See Zerlentis, Σημειώματα περί Ἑλλήνων (2:55), p. 27.

38. Hasluck, "Depopulation" (4:1), p. 166.

39. Barres, *L'Estat présent* (4:2), I, 182. See also Roberts, *Adventures* (4:155), p. 41.

40. Gassot, *Le Discours du voyage* (1:141), p. 11.

41. See Magni, *Lettere* (1:142), p. 46; and Hasluck, "Depopulation" (4:1), pp. 171–172, which contains the relevant bibliography. A bibliography on Chios has been compiled by Philip Argentis, *Bibliography of Chios from Classical Times to 1936* (Oxford, 1940).

42. See Deshayes, *Voyage* (1:26), p. 343.

43. Argentis-Kyriakidis, Ἡ Χίος (7:30), I, 58–59, where the views of the traveller Nicolay are given. *Cf.* du Loir, *Voyages* (1:108), pp. 18–19; and Barres, *L'Estat présent* (4:2), I, 84, 89–95.

44. Gerlach, *Tagebuch* (1:22), p. 50 (on the year 1574); Deshayes, *Voyage* (1:26), pp. 344–345; Monconys, *Journal* (5:174), Part 1, pp. 433–435.

45. Du Mont, *Voyages* (1:90), II, 169 ff. *Cf.* Barres, *L'Estat présent* (4:2), I, 85, 96.

46. Deshayes, *Voyage* (1:26), p. 347.

47. Barres, *L'Estat présent* (4:2), I, 99.

48. Sieur de la Croix, *Mémoires* (Paris, 1684), II, 6.

49. Barres, *L'Estat présent* (4:2), I, 99.

50. De la Croix, *Mémoires* (48), II, 6.

51. See Crusius, *Turcograeciae* (1:53), p. 512: "ad rationem italicam [according to the Italian way of life]." In reliving the past, and especially in recapturing the atmosphere of Frankish times, we are greatly helped by Aimilia K. Sarou's work, Τό κάστρον τῆς Χίου [*The Castle of Chios*] (Athens, 1916).

52. De la Croix, *Mémoires* (48), II, 6.

53. See M. G. Kephalas, "Λατινοϊταλικαί λέξεις ἐν τῇ χιακῇ διαλέκτῳ [Latino-

Italian Words in the Chian Dialect]," Ἑλληνικὸς Φιλολογικὸς Σύλλογος Κωνσταντινουπόλεως, Fiftieth Jubilee Number, 1861–1911 (Constantinople, 1913–1921), pp. 183–206.

54. On the architecture of Chios, see A. C. Smith, *The Architecture of Chios* (London, 1962), esp. pp. 18, 22, 23, 25. *Cf.* pp. 48 ff. And see Deshayes, *Voyage* (1:26), pp. 345, 346.

55. Beauvau, *Relation* (4:57), p. 19.

56. Barres, *L'Estat présent* (4:2), I, 96–97.

57. Du Mont, *Voyages* (1:90), II, 194–195. *Cf.* du Loir, *Voyages* (1:108), p. 19. On the composition of Chian society and the local nobility at this time, see "D.P." [Petrocochino], *Notice sur la famille de Pétrocochino de l'île de Chio* (Geneva, 1909).

58. Barres, *L'Estat présent* (4:2), I, 98.

59. Du Mont, *Voyages* (1:90), II, 193: "Scio est la seule ille du Levant, ou l'on ne s'habille pas à la longue [Chios is the only isle in the Levant where one does not wear a long dress]." On the dress of women, see Monconys, *Journal* (5:174), I, 434–435; also Barres, *L'Estat présent* (4:2), I, 100–108, where there is a discussion of the folk dances of the people.

60. Barres, *L'Estat présent* (4:2), I, 98–99.

61. See Sarou, "Περί μεικτῶν ναῶν" (3:3), p. 198.

62. De la Croix, *Mémoires* (48), II, 8.

63. Barres, *L'Estat présent* (4:2), I, 100.

64. Argentis-Kyriakidis, Ἡ Χίος (7:30), I, 58.

65. *Ibid.*, pp. 61–62. *Cf.* Gerlach, *Tagebuch* (1:22), p. 50; and Bordier, *Relation* (1:123), pp. 35–36 (regarding mastic); also Maurand, *Itinéraires* (4:9), pp. 165–167.

66. Barres, *L'Estat présent* (4:2), I, 100.

67. Du Loir, *Voyages* (1:108), p. 20.

68. Argentis-Kyriakidis, Ἡ Χίος (7:30), I, 58.

69. De Thevenot, *Relation* (4:81), pp. 26, 30.

70. *Ibid.*, p. 192. On Naxos in 1511, see Grassetto, *Viaggio* (4:90), p. 16. On the different names given to the island and its inhabitants, see Pericles G. Zerlentis, "Ναξία νῆσος καί πόλις [Naxos: Island and Town]," BZ, XI (1902), 491–499.

71. Sauger, Ἡ παροῦσα κατάστασις (1:178), p. 7.

72. *Ibid.*, p. 6. For a description of Naxos according to Lichtle, see Miller, "Lichtle's Description of Naxos" (1:94), pp. 432–450. On the translation of Lichtle's 'Description,' see Zerlentis, Φεουδαλική πολιτεία (1:111), p. 12, fn. 1.

73. Sauger, Ἡ παροῦσα κατάστασις (1:178), pp. 4, 5–6; and Miliarakis, Ὑπομνήματα περιγραφικά (4:82), pp. 26–27.

74. Sauger, Ἡ παροῦσα κατάστασις (1:178), pp. 4–5; and Barres, *L'Estat présent* (4:2), I, 137. On the present-day situation, see Miliarakis, Ὑπομνήματα περιγραφικά (4:82), pp. 28–29.

75. Barres, *L'Estat présent* (4:2), I, 138.

76. Voyatzidis, "Γλῶσσα καί Λαογραφία" (4:75), pp. 172–174.

77. Georg Hofmann, "Tinos nel secolo XVII [Tenos in the Seventeenth Century]," OCP, IV (1938), 593, where a figure of 12,000 *libbre grosse* is given as the estimated value of production in 1614. See also Zallony, *Voyage* (4:35), p. 47, and p. 46 on its other agricultural produce; see also Hofmann, "Tinos," p. 593.

78. See Miliarakis, Ὑπομνήματα περιγραφικά (4:82), p. 25; and Epameinondas Georgantopoulos, Τηνιακά [*On Tenos*] (Athens, 1889), p. 22.

79. De Thevenot, *Relation* (4:81), p. 198. On the vineyards of Santorini, viticulture, the varieties of grape, and different kinds of wine, see Abbé Pégues, *Histoire et phénomènes du volcan et des îles volcaniques de Santorin suivie d'un coup d'oeil sur l'état moral et réligieux de la Grèce moderne composé en 1837 [History and Phenomena of the Volcano and*

of the Volcanic Isles of Santorini Followed by a Glance at the Moral and Religious State of Modern Greece. Composed in 1837] (Paris, 1842), pp. 274–299.

80. Sauger, Ἡ παροῦσα κατάστασις (1:178), p. 6.

81. Sauger, Ἱστορία τῶν ἀρχαίων δουκῶν (4:9), pp. 208–209. On this monastery, see the monograph by H. H. Jewell and F. W. Hasluck, *The Church of Our Lady of the Hundred Gates (Panagia Hekatontapyliani) in Paros* (London, 1920).

82. De Thevenot, *Relation* (4:81), p. 203. *Cf.* Boschini, *L'Archipelago* (3:87), p. 34: "Abbonda di formento, vino e seta [It abounds in wheat, wine and silk]."

83. Gion, Ἱστορία τῆς Σίφνου (4:132), p. 153. The rich merchant Basil in particular was remembered by the people until the nineteenth century. There is a beautiful description of the island, as well as an analysis of its various products, especially cotton cloth, in de Tournefort, *Voyage* (1:90), I, 66.

84. Sauger, Ἡ παροῦσα κατάστασις (1:178), p. 7.

85. Sauger, Ἱστορία τῶν ἀρχαίων δουκῶν (4:9), p. 188; and Roberts, *Adventures* (4:155), p. 25. On the wines of Mykonos, see Magni, *Lettere* (1:142), p. 82. Amorgos sold the other islands honey, cotton, and a lot of wine (Boschini, *L'Archipelago* [3:87], p. 54).

86. See de Tournefort, *Voyage* (1:90), 59, 61. On the export of salt, see Zerlentis, Σημειώματα περὶ Ἑλλήνων (2:55), p. 27.

87. De Tournefort, *Voyage* (1:90), I, 61. In 1511 Grassetto spoke of Melos in these effusive terms: "insula digna, nobile e felice, como altra che in l'Egeo io habi trovà [an important island, noble and fortunate, the like of which I have not seen anywhere in the Aegean Sea]," (*Viaggio* [4:90], p. 15). See also Carlier de Pinon, *Voyage* (1:89), p. 57.

88. Sauger, Ἡ παροῦσα κατάστασις (1:178), p. 6. On the appearance of Melos, its produce, and its wealth, see D'Arvieux, *Mémoires* (7:73), IV, 322 ff., 334–336. *Cf.* de Tournefort, *Voyage* (1:90), I, 61 (and p. 62, on the island's wines and how they were made.)

89. De Tournefort, *Voyage* (1:90), I, 58.

90. *Ibid.*, I, 58.

91. On Siphnos, see Gion, Ἱστορία τῆς Σίφνου (4:132), p. 153.

92. *Barres, L'Estat présent* (4:2), I, 35.

93. Belon, *Observations* (1:123), p. 85a. *Cf.* Maurand, *Itinéraires* (4:9), p. 171; and Dernschwam, *Tagebuch* (1:20), p. 102 (also pp. 101–106, for material on wines, wine-bibbing, and the like in Turkey). See Gerlach, *Tagebuch* (1:22), p. 183, for the comment that the wines of Mytilene were the most highly regarded of all in Constantinople; and Boschini, *L'Archipelago* (3:87), p. 60: "ma il famoso è quello, che si fà in in luoco detto la Fontanella [but the famous one is that which is produced in a place called Fontanella]."

94. Sauger, Ἱστορία τῶν ἀρχαίων δουκῶν (4:9), p. 152.

95. Grelot, *Relation* (1:90), pp. 9–10.

96. Vacalopoulos, *Thasos* (1:59), p. 27. See also Boschini, *L'Archipelago* (3:87), p. 86: "al presente [the middle of the seventeenth century] benissimo habitata."

97. Belon, *Observations* (1:123), pp. 25b ff. *Cf.* Zerlentis, Σημειώματα περὶ Ἑλλήνων (2:55), p. 20: "It has a large town inhabited by Turks . . . with sixty suburbs, many ships, but not a single tree."

98. Carlier de Pinon, *Voyage* (1:89), pp. 64–65. There is material on this *terra*, including a tradition associated with it on p. 64, fn. 2. *Cf.* Gerlach, *Tagebuch* (1:22), p. 403; and du Loir, *Voyages* (1:108), pp. 295–296.

99. Zerlentis, Σημειώματα περὶ Ἑλλήνων (2:55), p. 20. For material on the other islands of the northern Sporades, see Roberts, *Adventures* (4:155), pp. 34–35.

100. As orally reported by K. D. Mertzios.

101. Sauger, Ἡ παροῦσα κατάστασις (1:178), pp. 5–6. Cf. della Rocca, Traité (1:178), I, 6–10.

102. Belon, Observations (1:123), p. 85a.

103. Zerlentis, Σημειώματα περί Ἑλλήνων (2:55), p. 25.

104. On the poverty of the Dodecanese, see, for example, Boschini, L'Archipelago (3:87), pp. 12, 14, 16, 20. On Anaphi, p. 22; on Melos, p. 28; and on Mykonos, p. 42. On Chiliodromia (Halonnesos), see Roberts, Adventures (4:155), p. 35; and p. 38 on Icaria.

105. Boschini, L'Archipelago (3:87), p. 52.

106. The poor of Santorini ate fresh bread only on three or four occasions throughout the year; for the rest of the time they could only afford stale bread (Sauger, Ἱστορία τῶν ἀρχαίων δουκῶν [4:9], p. 160).

107. Ricaut, Histoire (1:90), pp. 352–353.

108. Sauger, Ἱστορία τῶν ἀρχαίων δουκῶν (4:9), p. 162.

109. Ibid., p. 160. See Roberts, Adventures (4:155), p. 45.

110. Dapper, Description (4:136), p. 18.

111. See above p. 89.

112. See Chatzidakis, Ἡ ἱστορία τῆς Μήλου (4:4), pp. 174–177. For a list of the churches on Melos, see de Tournefort, Voyage (1:90), I, 59–60. See also D. Vasileiadis, "Συμβολή εἰς τούς τρουλλοκαμάρους ναούς τῆς Ἑλλάδος [Contribution to the Study of Greek Churches with Cupolas and Arches]," ΕΕΒΣ, XXX (1960–1961), 168–193.

113. Chatzidakis, Ἡ ἱστορία τῆς Μήλου (4:4), p. 176.

114. De Tournefort, Voyage (1:90), I, 59.

115. Note, for example, Kythnos (Vallindas, Κυθνιακά [1:111], p. 35).

116. Deshayes, Voyage (1:26), p. 350.

117. The monastery of Patmos (150 monks in 1587 [see Zerlentis, Σημειώματα περί Ἑλλήνων (2:55), p. 27]), which, except for that of Vatopediou, was the only one respected by Roman Catholics, found Turkish rule particularly onerous (Hasluck, "Depopulation" [4:1], p. 167 and fn.). As on certain other islands, Turkish authority was represented by a cadi and five or six other Turks (Deshayes, Voyage [1:26], p. 351). The people of Patmos were protected by the Knights of St. John of Malta and sailed under their flag. They also possessed written guarantees from both the King of France and the Duke of Tuscany that they would be protected from Roman Catholic corsairs and the Knights of St. Stephen (see Hasluck, "Depopulation," p. 167). According to de Thevenot (Relation [4:81], p. 192), pirates called at the island to replenish their supplies.

118. Zerlentis, Σημειώματα περί Ἑλλήνων (2:55), p. 27.

119. Hasluck, "Depopulation" (4:1), p. 167.

120. Deshayes, Voyage (1:26), p. 351.

121. Francesco Piacenza, L'Egeo redivivo, o sia chronographia dell'Archipelago [The Aegean Revived, or a History of the Archipelago] (Modena, 1688), p. 225.

122. See Morava-Chatzinikolaou, Πάτμος (6:244), p. 39.

123. Georgirenes, Description (1:45), p. 76; and Deshayes, Voyage (1:26), p. 351.

124. Georgirenes, Description (1:45), p. 76.

125. Kritikidis, Περίβασις (4:48), p. 108.

126. D. Kallimachos, " Ἡ σταυροπηγιακή μονή τῆς Ζωοδόχου Πηγῆς [The Patriarchal Monastery of Zoödochos Pege]," Ἐκκλησιαστικός Φάρος, XIII (1914), 292.

127. There is a lot of relevant data in Morava-Chatzinikolaou, Πάτμος (6:244), pp. 40–42.

128. See Franz Miklosich and Joseph Müller, Acta et diplomata graeca medii aevi sacra et profana [Greek Acts and Documents, Sacred and Secular, of the Middle Ages] (Vienna, 1860–1887), VI, 272, 278.

129. Georgirenes, *Description* (1:45), p. 76. At one time (though it is impossible to say exactly when), the people of Patmos were distributed fairly evenly all over the island; but in order to defend themselves as effectively as possible against piratical attacks they moved to the monastery of St. John and built their houses around it (p. 76).

130. See Epameinondas Alexakis, " "Ασμα Πατμιακόν εἴτε, ὡς κοινῶς τά τοιαῦτα ὀνομάζονται, ῥίμα [A Song of Patmos, or, as It Is Commonly Called, a *Rima*]," Παρνασσός, XII (1888), 324–329. See also Zerlentis, "Ρωμανοῦ Νικηφόρου καί Δανιήλ Καστρησίου ἐπιστολαί (5:234), p. 293. *Cf.* the testimonies of Girolamo Brusoni and Marinos Tzane Bounialis, in Agathangellos Xerouchakis, Ὁ Κρητικός πόλεμος (1645–1669) [*The Cretan War (1645–1669)*] (Trieste, 1908), pp. 412–414; and Ioannis Sakkelion, Πατμιακή Βιβλιοθήκη [*Library of Patmos*] (Athens, 1890), p. 63, fn. 1.

131. De Tournefort, *Voyage* (1:90), I, 169.

132. See Marava-Chatzinikolaou, Πάτμος (6:244), pp. 48–53, where the most noteworthy churches are listed; and Kanto Phatourou, Πατμιακή ἀρχιτεκτονική [*The Architecture of Patmos*] (Athens, 1962).

133. See Sauger, Ἡ παροῦσα κατάστασις (1:178), p. 15.

134. See the description by Paschalis, "Προνόμια καί διοίκησις" (7:89), pp. 126–127.

135. Miliarakis, Ὑπομνήματα περιγραφικά (4:82), pp. 52–53.

136. See Kasomoulis, Ἐνθυμήματα στρατιωτικά (8:12), I, 176–179.

137. See Miliarakis, Ὑπομνήματα περιγραφικά (4:82), pp. 52–53. On the social composition of Melos, see Chatzidakis, Ἡ ἱστορία τῆς Μήλου (4:4), pp. 166–168.

138. Vallindas, Ἱστορία τῆς νήσου Κύθνου (4:92), pp. 39–40.

139. Demetrios P. Paschalis, "Νομικά ἔθιμα τῆς νήσου Ἄνδρου [Customary Law on the Island of Andros]," Ἀρχεῖον Οἰκονομικῶν καί Κοινωνικῶν Ἐπιστημῶν, V (1925), 161.

140. On the art of navigation in the Mediterranean, see the contribution by Avelino Teixeira da Mota in the volume *Le Navire et l'économie maritime du moyen âge au XVIIIe siècle principalement en Méditerranée*, ed. Michel Mollat (Paris, 1958), pp. 127 ff.

141. The relevant work is by Domenico Sella, *Commercio e industrie a Venezia nel secolo XVII* (Venice-Rome, 1961), pp. 1–4.

142. Thiriet, "Les Lettres commerciales" (16), pp. 913–928. For a general treatment of Venice's commerce, travellers, and the ships of the period, see Jules Sottas, *Les Messageries maritimes de Venice aux XIVe et XVe siècles* (Paris, 1938). See especially the monograph by Frederic C. Lane, *Venetian Ships and Shipbuilders of the Renaissance* (Baltimore, 1934).

143. Thiriet, "Les Lettres commerciales" (16), pp. 928–932. On the internal grain trade of the Ottoman Empire, see Lütfi Güçer, "Le Commerce intérieur des céréales dans l'empire ottoman pendant la seconde moitié du XVIe siècle," *Istanbul Universitesi Iktisat Fakultesi Mecmuası*, XI (1949–1950), pp. 163–168.

144. Thiriet, "Les Lettres commerciales" (16), pp. 926, 932.

145. Belon, *Observations* (1:123), p. 79b. On the types of ships in Ragusa and other places at this time, see the contribution by Jorjo Tadić, "Le Port de Raguse et sa flotte au XVIe siècle," in *Le Navire et l'économie maritime* (140), pp. 9–26.

146. Albèri, *Le relazioni* (1:142), Series III, Vol. IV, pp. 36, 419.

147. See Carlier de Pinon, *Voyage* (1:89), pp. 93–94. For details on this paper, see p. 94 (also fn. 1). On the "Angora" goat, its wool, and the commerce in it, see Moyses V. Moyseidis, "Συμβολή εἰς τήν ἱστορίαν τῆς ἀνθυπατικῆς Γαλατίας. Μονογραφία περί Ἀγκύρας [Contribution to the History of Proconsular Galatia. Monograph about Ankara]," Ξενοφάνης, II (1904–1905), 433–435. There is a description of the sheep of Ankara in de Busbecq, *The Life and Letters* (5:170), I, 137–138.

148. Belon, *Observations* (1:123), p. 75b.

149. Carlier de Pinon, *Voyage* (1:89), p. 93. See also Albèri, *Le relazioni* (1:142), Series III, Vol. II, pp. 53, 54.

150. Dernschwam, *Tagebuch* (1:20), p. 109. On the activities of Jews in Smyrna, see Magni, *Lettere* (1:142), pp. 42–43.

151. Dernschwam, *Tagebuch* (1:20), pp. 109–110.

152. Magni comments on the organization of their work in *Lettere* (1:142), pp. 201–202.

153. *Ibid.*, p. 202.

154. Belon, *Observations* (1:123), p. 181a and *passim*. Christians, Greeks, Armenians, Maronites, Indians, and so on, all wore blue turbans.

155. Carlier de Pinon, *Voyage* (1:89), p. 109.

156. See Braudel, *La Méditerranée* (1:63), pp. 339, 341–343.

157. See Sella, *Commercio e industrie* (141), pp. 4–9.

158. The relevant work here is W. R. Lowder, "Candie Wyne. Some Documents on Trade between England and Crete during the Reign of King Henry VIII," Ἑλληνικά, XII (1952–1953), 97–102.

159. See Richard Hakluyt, *Voyages and Documents, Selected by J. Hampden* (London-New York-Toronto, 1958), pp. 13–14. *Cf.* Braudel, *La Méditerranée* (1:63), pp. 470–474.

160. See Hakluyt, *Voyages and Documents* (159), pp. 145–147.

161. *Ibid.*, pp. 225–226. For details, see Braudel, *La Méditerranée* (1:63), pp. 479–486. On the part played by Hoca Sadeddin Effendi in the cementing of Turkish-English relations, see the article by N. A. Kurat, "Hoca Sadeddin Efendinin Türk-Ingiliz münasebetlerinin tesisi ve gelismeşindeki rölu [Hoca Sadeddin's Role in Establishing and Developing Turkish-English Relations]," *Fuad Köprülü* (Istanbul, 1953), pp. 305–315.

162. See Braudel, *La Méditerranée* (1:63), p. 488.

163. See Magni, *Lettere* (1:142), pp. 51–54.

164. Du Mont, *Voyages* (1:90), II, 364. *Cf.* Magni, *Lettere* (1:142), pp. 49–50, on the consul and French merchants, as well as other matters.

165. Louis Bergasse and Gaston Rambert, *Histoire du commerce de Marseille* (Paris, 1954), IV (1599–1660) and V (1660–1789), pp. 5–6.

166. *Ibid.*, pp. 78 ff.

167. *Ibid.*, p. 74. Later, the French, on the initiative of Richelieu, took effective steps to protect their ships. Between 1637 and 1641 they instituted a system of marine patrols (pp. 76–77).

168. Biron, *Ambassade* (4:119), pp. 130, 136–137, 141–142, 143–144, 156, 160, 161, 166–167, 173, 178–179, and *passim*. See pp. 399–403. *Cf.* Barozzi-Berchet, *Relazioni* (1:146), I, 208–210.

169. The relevant documents are in Biron, *Ambassade* (4:119), pp. 416 ff.

170. See especially the unpublished letter of Th. Bendyshe, dated 14 January 1650, in the Public Records Office, London.

171. See Magni, *Lettere* (1:142), pp. 55–57.

172. See Bergasse-Rambert, *Histoire* (165), IV, 6–7, 149; and on pp. 48 and 50 on some of the obstacles to trade.

173. See D'Arvieux, *Mémoires* (7:73), IV, 112 ff., and Bergasse-Rambert, *Histoire* (165), IV, 63. On the Dutch, see Braudel, *La Méditerranée* (1:63), pp. 494–503.

174. See his unpublished letter in the Public Records Office, London.

175. Bergasse-Rambert, *Histoire* (165), IV, 63; and Braudel, *La Méditerranée* (1:63), pp. 101, 126.

176. Bergasse-Rambert, *Histoire* (165), IV, 63.

177. On the *prostateuomenoi*, see the monograph by Pantelis M. Kontogiannis, Οἱ προστατευόμενοι [*The Protected Persons*] (Athens, 1917).

178. They are characterized by Magni, *Lettere* (1:142), p. 48. *Cf.* p. 54.

179. Carayon, *Relations* (2:31), p. 193.

180. D'Arvieux, *Mémoires* (7:73), IV, 424; and Bergasse-Rambert, *Histoire* (165), IV, 64–65, which contains the memorandum of the "Consuls du Conseil de Ville" to the king, dated 14 July 1623.

181. Bergasse-Rambert, *Histoire* (165), IV, 63, 65–70. So that French goods would be carried only in their ships, the Marseilles merchants also secured a prohibition against the chartering of foreign ships in the ports of Provence if French ships were available (pp. 72–73).

182. *Ibid.*, p. 90.

183. *Ibid.*, pp. 90–92, 95–97. On the kinds of goods involved in this trade, see pp. 92–96, for much data. I have not myself seen G. Tongas' *Les Relations de la France avec l'empire ottoman durant la première moitié du XVIIe siècle et l'ambassade à Constantinople de Philippe de Harlay, comte de Cesy (1619–1640)* (Toulouse, 1942).

184. See Albert Vandal, *Une Ambassade française en Orient sous Louis XV: La Mission du marquis de Villeneuve, 1728–1741* (Paris, 1887), pp. 16–36, where there is a lot of material based on official correspondence, which is also cited.

185. Albert Vandal is interesting on this point. See his *Les Voyages du marquis de Nointel (1670–1680)* (Paris, 1900), pp. 274–280, which gives Charles Marie François Olier, Marquis de Nointel's instructions when he was sent to Constantinople.

186. Du Loir, *Voyages* (1:108), Prologue.

A SELECT BIBLIOGRAPHY OF RECENT PUBLICATIONS

Bees, Nikos A.   Τά χειρόγραφα τῶν Μετεώρων, Vol. 1 [*The Manuscripts of Meteora*]. Athens, 1967.

Bryer, A.   "The Tourkokratia." *Neo-Hellenika*, 1 (1970), 30–54.

Chatzidakis, Manolis.   Recherches sur le peintre Théophane le Crétois. *Dumbarton Oaks Papers*, 23–24 (1969–1970), 309–352.

Cook, M. A.   *Population Pressure in Rural Anatolia, 1450–1600*. London Oriental Series, Vol. 27. London, 1972.

Drakakis, Andreas T.   " 'Η Σῦρος ἐπί Τουρκοκρατίας [Syros under Turkish Domination]." Hermopoulis on Syros, 1948. Vol. 1.

————————.   " 'Η δικαιοσύνη καί τό δίκαιον [Justice and the Law]." *Epetiris Etairias Kykladikon Meleton*, 6 (1967), 63–492.

Fedalto, Giorgio.   *Ricerche storiche sulla posizione giuridica ed ecclesiastica dei Greci a Venezia nei secoli XV e XVI*. Florence, 1967.

Hassiotis, I. K.   'Ισπανικά ἔγγραφα τῆς κυπριακῆς ἱστορίας ΙΣΤ΄-ΙΖ΄αί. [*Spanish Documents on Cypriot History, XVIth–XVIIth Centuries*]. Nicosia, 1972.

Inalcik, Halil.   "Capital Formation in the Ottoman Empire." *The Journal of Economic History*," XXIX, No. 1 (March, 1969), 97–140.

————————.   "The Policy of Mehmed II toward the Greek Population of Istanbul and the Byzantine Buildings of the City." *Dumbarton Oaks Papers*, 23–24 (1969–1970), 229–249.

Karathanassis, Athanasios.   "Νεώτερες εἰδήσεις γιά τόν Ιωάννη Κοττούνιο [New Data on John Kottounios, 1572–1657]." *Makedonikà* 13 (1973), 267–273.

Karouzou, Semni.   Μαρτίνος Κρούσιος, ὁ πρῶτος φιλέλλην [*Martinus Crusius, the First Philhellene*]. Athens, 1973.

Kresten, Otto.   *Das Patriarchat von Konstantinopel in ausgehended 16. Jahrhundert*. Osterreichische Akademie der Wissenschaften ... Sitzungsberichte, 266. Band 5, Abhandlung. Vienna, 1970.

Manoussacas, Manoussos.   "Βιβλιογραφία τοῦ 'Ελληνσμοῦ τῆς Βενετίας. Μέρος Α΄ Γενικά [A Bibliography of Hellenism in Venice, Part I. General Publications]." *Thesaurismata* (1973), pp. 7–87.

————————. " "Ελληνες ζωγράφοι έν Βενετία μέλη τῆς 'Ελληνικῆς 'Αδελφότητος κατά τόν ΙΣΤ' αἰώνα [Greek Painters in Venice. Members of the Greek Brotherhood in the XVIth Century]." *Mnymosynon to Sophia Antoniadis*. Venice, 1974, pp. 212–226.

————————. Δανιήλ Φουρλάνος (1550 ci–1592). "Ενας λησμονημένος λόγιος τοῦ Ρεθέμνου [Daniel Fourlanos (1550 ci–1592), a Forgotten Scholar of Rethymnon]. Πεπραγμένα Γ' Διεθοῦς Κρητολογικοῦ Συνεδρίου. Athens, 1974. Vol. 2.

Noica, Constantin.   "La Signification historique de l'oeuvre de Théophile Corydalée." *Revue des Etudes Sud-Est Européennes*, 11 (1973), 285–306.

Patrinelis, Christos.   "The Exact Time of the First Attempt of the Turks to Seize the Churches and Convert the Christian People of Constantinople to Islam." *Actes du Premier Congrès International des Etudes Balkaniques et Sud-Est Européennes*, 3 (Sofia, 1969), 567–572.

Pfeiffer, Gerhard.   "Studien zur Fɪ ɪhphase Philhellenismus (1453–1750) [Studies on the Early Phase of Philhellenism (1453–1750)]." Dissertation, Erlangen, Germ., 1969.

Runciman, Steven.   *The Great Church in Captivity: A Study of the Patriarchate of Constantinople from the Eve of the Turkish Conquest to the Greek War of Independence*, Cambridge, Eng., 1968.

Russo, Francesco P.   "I monasteri Greci della Calabria nel secolo XV. Supplemento al 'Liber Visitationis' di Atanaṣio Calceopulo del 1457–58." *Bollettino della Badia Greca di Grottaferrata*, 16 (1962), 3–4.

Tomadakis, N. D.   " Οἱ νεομάρτυρες τοῦ Βυζαντίου καί ἡ ὁσιομάρτυς Φιλοθέη Μπενιζέλου ἡ 'Αθηναία (+19 Φεβρουρίου 1589) [The Byzantine Neo-Martyrs and the Athenian Philothea Benizelou (+February 19, 1589)]." *Epistimoniki Epetiris Philosophikis Scholis Panepistimiou Athenon* (1970–1971), pp. 9–25.

Vasić, Milan.   *Martolosi u jugoslovenskim zemljama pod turkom vladovinom* [Armotoloi in Yugoslavian Lands under Turkish Rule]. Serajevo, 1967.

Vryonis, Speros, Jr.   *The Decline of Medieval Hellenism in Asia Minor and the Process of Islamization from the Eleventh through the Fifteenth Century*. Berkeley-London, 1971.

INDEX

Abbas the Great, Shah of Persia, 256
Abraham's Sacrifice (Kornaros), 172
Abruzzo province, Italy, 47
Academy degli Assicurati, Corfu, 182
Academy of Bucharest, 183
Academy of Sterili, Canea, 182
Academy of Stravaganti, Canea, 182
Acarnania, 62–63, 64, 163, 186; armatolikia of, 216, 219, 220
acem oğlan, 37–38, 41, 42, 304n54
Achaia, Greece, 58
Achelous River, *see* Aspropotamos (Achelous) River
Achouria, Epirus, 60
Achtala, Archbishopric of, 52
Achtze Punar, Bithynia, 255
Achyrona, Lesbos, 339n158
Acronauplia, Nauplia, 322n95
Acropolis, The, 227
Adapazari, Bithynia, 255, 256
Adelphotis (Brotherhood), 51, 210, 223
Adrianople, Thrace, 9, 10, 23, 117, 219, 249, 304n54; Christian population (1520–30), 52, 230; education in, 153, 154, 175; Greek community government in, 191; Scholarios in, 103; seraglio, 40; trade, 226, 231, 239, 248, 249, 390n78
Adriatic Sea, 81

Aegean islands, 52, 70–99, 126, 170, 224, 253; community government in, 198–204; Frankish rule of, 20, 22, 45, 75, 82, 198; population (1470), 71; trade of, 270, 271, 272–84, 287, 289; Turkish colonization efforts in, 77, 79, 80–85, 89, 90, 92. *See also specific islands*
Aegean Sea, 284
Aegina island, 80, 92, 325n168, 388n31; community government in, 191, 374n40; population (1470), 71; tax laws of, 18; Turkish fleet service, 87, 89
Aetolia, 146, 185, 186; armatolikia of, 216, 219, 220
Aetoliko, Greece, 185
Aetos, Greece, 64
Africa, 75, 287
Agallianos, Ignatius, 140
Agallos, Manuel, 154
Agatha, will of, 397n189
Agatha, Italy, 48
aged, taxation of, 15
Agia, Greece, 61
Aginatoi, Bithynia, 255
Agousa, Paros, 92–93
Agoutmous, Pontus, 32
Agrafa, Pindus, 63, 64–65, 185, 348n293; armatoles in, 211, 212,

Meteora monastery group, 127, 132, 133–40, 153, 342*n*201, 345*nn*251, 255; klepht attack (1300's), 215; manuscript library of, 178; paintings at, 147
Methodios III, Patriarch of Constantinople, 340*n*177
Methone, Messenia, *see* Modon (Methone), Messenia
Methymna, Mytilene, 318*n*15, 339*nn*152, 158
Metron and Athyron, 126
Metrophanes of Veroia, cited, 345*n*245
Metsovon, Epirus, 195, 197, 375*n*65
Miaoulis, Antonios, *grandpère*, 82
Miaoulis, Antonios A., *grandfils*, cited, 82
Michael of Granitsa, Agrafa, 350*n*315
Mihalic, Asia Minor, 254
Milan, Italy, 157
Milia, 60, 195; armatoles of, 216
Milionis, Christos, 63
military, the: Christians in, 17, 20, 35–42, 44, 54, 211–24; guerrillas, 63, 218, 222–23, 384*n*84; island garrisoning, 77; land grants to, 6, 8, 11–12, 23, 54; looting, 68, 70; Peloponnese invasion, 57; Pindus troops, 197; Pontus invasion, 55, 56; revenues for, 15, 27
Military Memoirs (Kasomoulis), 215
millet başi, defined, 125
Milo, Antonio di, 321*n*68
Miloïtis, Jacob, cited, 80, 274, 331*n*49
Mindonios, Ioannis, 172
Miniatis, Elias, 136
mining, 23, 32, 55–57, 247–48, 261, 312*nn*70–71, 76, 314*n*115, 397*n*196, 398*nn*199–200. *See also specific minerals*
Minio, Marco, cited, 297*n*93
Mirafti (Mürefte), Thrace, 9
Misoripha, Italy, 48
Missolonghi, Aetolia, 185, 223
Mistra, Greece, 45, 62, 146, 226, 387*n*17; education in, 153, 154,

364*n*142
Mitrofanovič, Georgije, 149
Mitrovič, Baron Vegesla Vratislav von, quoted, 94–96
Modon (Methone), Messenia, 46, 159, 316*n*159; trade, 226, 227, 284, 386*n*14
Mohammed II (1451–1481), 4, 9, 100–101, 117, 253, 254, 258, 328*n*1, 329*n*5, 404*n*325; Albanian settlements and, 249, 398*n*216; armatoles and, 211, 212; census under, 10; Constantinople restoration by, 231, 233, 391*nn*94–95; Gennadius and, 101, 103, 104, 105, 106, 108, 112, 120, 121, 330*n*36; law codes, 14, 15, 31–32; mining and, 247
Mohammed IV (1648–1687), 195, 197
Moldavia, 120, 126, 149, 241, 264, 267; Mount Athos aid from, 131, 132, 344*n*236
Moluccas, islands of, 287
monasteries, 33, 46, 127–40, 143, 144, 274; in caves, 85; education and, 49, 101, 132–33, 140, 153, 177–78, 183, 345*nn*245, 250, 355*n*13, 367*n*213; fortified, 62, 129, 325*n*166, 327*n*216, 342*n*211; on invasion routes, 313*n*89, 324*n*154; in Italy, 49, 54, 307*n*12; regimens in, 129–31, 132, 342*nn*198, 211, 343*n*229; trade and, 274, 279, 281; Turkish land confiscations from, 121, 131, 292*n*18. *See also specific monasteries*
Monastir, Yugoslavia, 23, 217, 219, 231, 248, 264, 403*n*299
Mondanos, L., 369*n*249
Monemvasia, Greece, 157, 161, 273
money lending, 12, 28
Mongols, 44
Montacuto di Maremma, Tuscany, 47
Morava River, 263, 264
Morea, Despotate of, *see* Peloponnese, The

Parenzo, Italy, 46

Parga peninsula, 61, 83, 226

Parikia, Paros, 90

Parnes range, 217

Paros, island of, 71, 94, 181, 276, 317n9; community government, 201; pirates and, 85, 87, 89, 90, 92–93, 324n148

Parou, Pontus, 32

Partheni, 257

Parthenius I, Patriarch of Constantinople, 183

Parthenius II, Patriarch of Constantinople, 183

Paschalis, Demetrius, 81; quoted, 283–84

Pasha, Greece, 69(tab.)

Pasha-Liman, island of, 249, 250

Passavas, Greece, 62

pasture tax, 16–17

Patlaman, Asia Minor, 261

Patmos, island of, 71, 80, 170, 181; architecture in, 279, 281, 413n129; trade, 274

Patras, Peloponnesus, 227

Patratziki, Thessaly, 216

Patriarchal School (Great School of the Nation), Constantinople, 101–102, 151–52, 154–55, 171, 180, 181, 369n239; Corydalleus directorship of, 183, 185

Patroulas, 267

Paul (pirate), 92

Pausanias: Mousouros' Preface to, 359n79

Pazarouda, Macedonia, 248, 398n198

peasants, 6, 8, 9–12, 14–20, 22, 23, 83; community self-government of, 188, 190–91, 199; Constantinople importation of, 231, 233, 249, 250, 391n95; seasonal workers, 245–46, 396n177; trade and, 283. See also agriculture

Pec, Patriarchate of, 150

Peladatoi, Bithynia, 255

Peloponnese, The, 5, 45, 144, 211, 241, 271, 276, 277; bibliographic scholarship in, 154; Christian fiefdoms in, 17, 297n93; Dervenochorites of, 212; education in, 171; emigration from, 42, 46, 48, 49, 51, 57, 80, 81, 83–84, 157, 249, 255, 401n274; grain of, 272; painting in, 146, 148; piracy and, 75; population (1520–1538), 69(tab.). See also specific placenames

Peltos, Bithynia, 254

Pendedaktylon, Italy, 48

Pentecost, Feast of, 49

Pera, Constantinople, 237

Peraia, Attica, 388n31

Pergamon, Turkey, 251, 252, 400n257

Peribleptos, Mistra, 146

Peripatos, island of, 75

Peristereota monastery, 54

Perlepe (Prilep), Yugoslavia, 149, 217, 219, 248

Persia, 12, 252, 256, 285

Persian language, 40

Persio, Ascanio, cited, 48

Pest, Hungary, 230, 264

Petit, Louis, cited, 329nn6, 11

Petraveris (merchant), 258

Phalieros, Marinos, 159

Phanarion, Thessaly, 137, 194; as liva, 216

Phanariots, 131–32, 209, 241, 344n236

Pharanga, Lesbos, 140

Pharsala, Thessaly, 16, 60, 216, 248

Phatiri, Epirus, 60

Phertek, Cappadocia, 405n336

Philadelphia (Alasehir), Turkey, 251, 252

Philanthropenos School, Lake Ioannina, 180

Philaras, Leonardos, 163

philhellenism, 169, 363n132

Philintas, M., cited, 212

Philip II, King of Spain, 47

Philippi, Macedonia, 217, 387n27

Philippopolis (Plovdiv), Bulgaria, 68, 208, 244, 380n143

Philo, 171

St. Menas, Church of, Thessalonica, 121
St. Michael, Church of, Mantamados, 352n348
St. Nicholas, Chapel of, Lavra, 147
St. Nicholas, Church of, Naples, 308n23
St. Nicholas, Church of, Prusa, 254
St. Nicholas, Zagorion district, 57
St. Nicholas of Anapaphsas, Church of, Meteora, 147
St. Nicholas of Spanos, monastery of, Ioannina, 171, 180
St. Nikanor, monastery of, 139–40, 348nn296–98
St. Onoufrios, monastery, 62
St. Panton, monastery of, Meteora, 134
St. Paul, monastery of, Mount Athos, 4, 128
St. Peter and St. Paul, Church of, Naples, 47
St. Savvas, Church of, Cairo, 262
St. Theodore, Asia Minor, 254
St. Theodore, Church of, Nicaea, 254
St. Theodore, Church of, Pergamon, 400n257
St. Vlasius, Church of, Venice, 51
Salamis (Koulouri), 80, 83, 89, 92, 322n95
salt, 26, 273, 276
Samarina, Pindus, 60, 148
Samos, island of, 170, 224, 279; Agrafa emigrés in, 244; community government, 203; taxation in, 10, 18, 87; timber of, 274; Turkish repopulation of, 77, 79–80, 81
Samothrace, island of, 71
Samsun (Amisus), Asia Minor, 53, 258, 261, 404n325
Santa, Pontus, 54–56, 66, 312n76
Santa Maria, Damiano de, 161
Santa-Sourmena, Pontus, 56
Santorini, island of, 71, 276, 277, 295n53, 410n79; community government of, 201; poverty of, 412n106
Sarajevo, Yugoslavia, 231

Sarakinis, Nicholas, 80, 203
Sari Dogan, Bithynia, 255
Sarigöl, Macedonia, 217
Saronic Gulf, 80
Sarou, Aimilia K., cited, 375n70
Sathas, Constantine N., cited, 189–90
Sauger, cited, 81, 171, 199, 200; quoted, 30, 90, 162, 282–83, 319n44, 323n126; aesthetic attitudes of, 145, 366n187
Sava River, 264
Savoy, 245
Saxony, laws of, 56, 265
Scholarios, George, see Gennadius II
schools, 101–102, 151–52, 154–55, 157, 183, 251, 364n139; Church "narthex" schools, 170–71, 175, 176; community government and, 195; Constantinople numbers (non-Turkish, 1576), 179–80; financial provision for, 181–82, 369nn239, 249; guilds and, 209, 210; hostel endowments, 162; lecture methods in, 184
Schwarzerd, Philip (Philip Melancthon), 166, 167
Schweigger, Salomon, quoted, 22
Sclaverochori, Crete, 146
Scotto, 161
sculpture, 352n348
Scutari (Uskudar), Turkey, 257
Scyrus, island of, 71, 277
Sea of Marmara, 10, 244, 253; fishing in, 401n267; islands, 249
Séguier, Pierre, 178
Selim I (1512–1520), 4, 120, 250, 405n329; Egyptian expeditions (1517), 17, 261, 301n170; Sumela monastery and, 312n67
Selim II (1566–1574), 4, 70, 121, 249; quoted, 275
Selim III (1789–1807), 195
Selitsa, Greece, 58
Seljuk Turks, 4, 12, 206
Selymbria, Thrace, 249, 398n208
seraglios, 38, 40
Seraphim (priest), 407n27

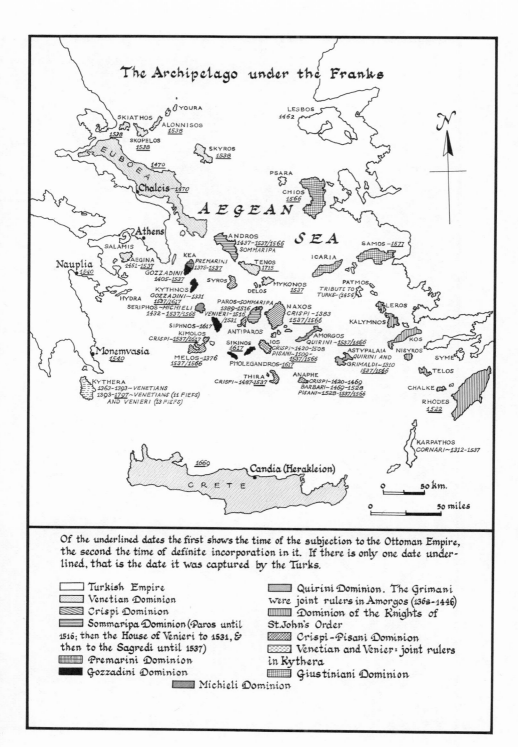

The Archipelago under the Franks

YOURA

SKIATHOS
_1538_

ALONNISOS
_1538_

SKOPELOS
_1538_

SKYROS
_1538_

LESBOS
_1462_

EUBOEA

_1470_

Chalcis – _1470_

PSARA

CHIOS
_1566_

AEGEAN   SEA

Athens

SALAMIS

ANDROS
_1437_–_1537_/_1566_
SOMMARIPA

SAMOS – _1571_

AEGINA
_1451_–_1537_

KEA
PREMARINI
_1375_–_1537_
GOZZADINI
_1405_–_1537_

TENOS
_1715_

ICARIA

Nauplia
_1540_

SYROS

DELOS

MYKONOS
_1537_

PATMOS
TRIBUTE TO
TURKS (_1454_)

HYDRA

KYTHNOS
GOZZADINI
_1537_/_1617_
SERIPHOS – MICHIELI
_1432_–_1537_/_1566_

PAROS – SOMMARIPA
_1389_–_1516_
VENIERI – _1516_
/_1531_

NAXOS
CRISPI – _1383_
_1537_/_1566_

LEROS

KALYMNOS

SIPHNOS – _1617_
KIMOLOS
CRISPI – _1537_/_1617_

ANTIPAROS

SIKINOS
_1617_

IOS
CRISPI – _1420_–_1508_
PISANI – _1509_–
_1537_/_1566_

AMORGOS
QUIRINI – _1537_/_1566_

ASTYPALAIA
QUIRINI AND
GRIMALDI – _1310_
_1537_/_1566_

KOS

NISYROS

SYME

Monemvasia
_1540_

MELOS – _1376_
_1537_/_1566_

PHOLEGANDROS – _1617_

ANAPHE
CRISPI – _1420_–_1469_
BARBARI – _1469_–_1528_
PISANI – _1528_–_1537_/_1566_

TELOS

CHALKE

THIRA
CRISPI – _1487_–_1537_

KYTHERA
_1363_–_1393_ ~ VENETIANS
_1393_–_1797_ ~ VENETIANS (11 FIEFS)
AND VENIERI (13 FIEFS)

RHODES
_1522_

KARPATHOS
CORNARI ~ _1312_–_1537_

_1669_

Candia (Herakleion)

CRETE

0   50 km.

0   50 miles

Of the underlined dates the first shows the time of the subjection to the Ottoman Empire,
the second the time of definite incorporation in it. If there is only one date underlined, that is the date it was captured by the Turks.

Turkish Empire
Venetian Dominion
Crispi Dominion
Sommaripa Dominion (Paros until
1516; then the House of Venieri to 1531, &
then to the Sagredi until 1537)
Premarini Dominion
Gozzadini Dominion
Michieli Dominion

Quirini Dominion. The Grimani
were joint rulers in Amorgos (1368–1446)
Dominion of the Knights of
St. John's Order
Crispi – Pisani Dominion
Venetian and Venier: joint rulers
in Kythera
Giustiniani Dominion

Movement of Greek Populations towards
BLACK
MEDITERRANEA
Pherrai
Chariopolis
Rhaedestos
Tsataltza
Constantinople
Chrysopolis
Nicomedia
Ada Pazar
Sapantza
L. Ascania
Nicaea Isnik
Eregli
Bartin
Amas
Saframboli
(Safranbolu)
Propontis
SAMOTHRACE
Bulair
Gallipoli
IMBROS
Artaki
Biga
Dardanelles
Mudanya
Kios
Prusa
Biletzik
Sangarios R.
TENEDOS
Gran
(Cank
Soyut
Eskisehir
Pursak R.
Ankara
Balia Maden
LESBOS
Adramyttion
Kydoniai (Ayvalik)
Kotyaeon
(Kütahya)
Pergamon
CHIOS
Phocaea
Magnesia (Manisa)
Menemen
Hermus R.
Kula
Usak
Afyon Karahissar
Lake Tu
Smyrna
Philadelphia
Ephesus
Theira
Ayasoluk
Maeander R.
ICARIA
Scalanova
Aydin
SAMOS
Soker
Denizli
Iconium
Sparta
Lake Bensehir
PATMOS
KOS
Attaleia (Antalya)
Makri
Leibesion
TELOS
Rhodes
RHODES
KASTELLORIZON
KARPATHOS
CYPR

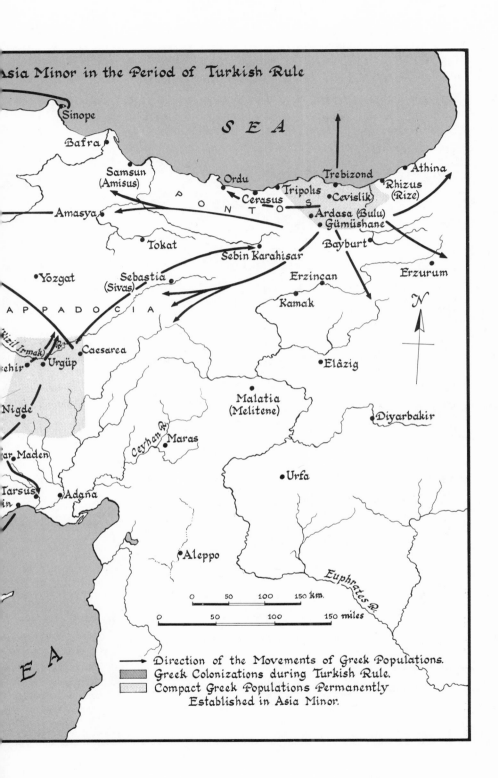

Asia Minor in the Period of Turkish Rule

Sinope
Bafra
SEA
Samsun (Amisus)
Ordu
Trebizond
Athina
PONTO
Tripolis
Cerasus
Cevislik
Rhizus (Rize)
S
Ardasa (Bulu)
Amasya
Gümüshane
Tokat
Sebin Karahisar
Bayburt
Yozgat
Sebastia (Sivas)
Erzincan
Erzurum
APPADOCIA
Kamak
Kizil Irmak
Caesarea
Urgüp
ehir
Elâzig
Nigde
Malatia (Melitene)
Diyarbakir
ar Maden
Ceyhan R.
Maras
Tarsus
Adana
in
Urfa

Aleppo

Euphrates R.

E A

| 0 | 50 | 100 | 150 km. |
| 0 | 50 | 100 | 150 miles |

⟶ Direction of the Movements of Greek Populations.
▨ Greek Colonizations during Turkish Rule.
▢ Compact Greek Populations Permanently
    Established in Asia Minor.

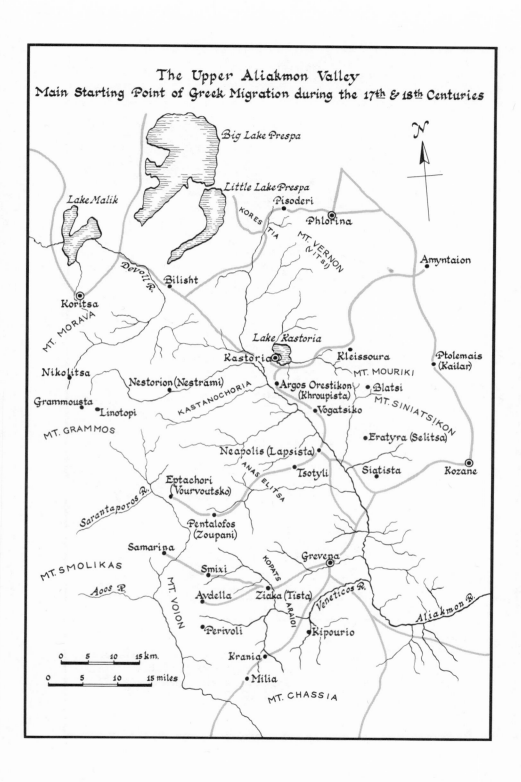

The Upper Aliakmon Valley
Main Starting Point of Greek Migration during the 17th & 18th Centuries

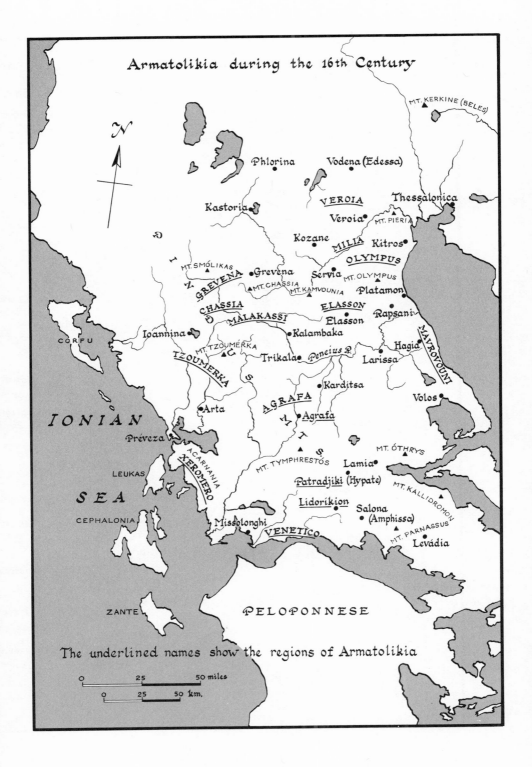

Armatolikia during the 16th Century

MT. KERKINE (BELES)

Phlorina

Vodena (Edessa)

VEROIA

Thessalonica

Kastoria

Veroia

MT. PIERIA

Kozane

MILIA

Kitros

OLYMPUS

MT. SMÓLIKAS

Grevena

Servia

MT. OLYMPUS

GREVENA

MT. CHASSIA

MT. KAMVOUNIA

Platamon

CHASSIA

ELASSON

Rapsani

MALAKASSI

Elasson

Ioannina

Kalambaka

MT. TZOUMÉRKA

Trikala

Peneius R.

Larissa

Hagia

CORFU

TZOUMERKA

MAVROVOUNI

AGRAFA

Karditsa

Volos

Arta

Agrafa

IONIAN

Préveza

MT. TYMPHRESTÓS

MT. ÓTHRYS

ACARNANIA

XEROMERO

Lamia

LEUKAS

Patradjiki (Hypate)

MT. KALLIDROMON

SEA

Lidorikion

Salona
(Amphissa)

CEPHALONIA

Missolonghi

VENETICO

MT. PARNASSUS

Levádia

ZANTE

PELOPONNESE

The underlined names show the regions of Armatolikia

0   25   50 miles

0   25   50 km.

Bártf

Kisszeben •

Eperje

Sajo R.

↓Besztercebánya

↓Radvány •

Rozsnyó

Kass

Jász

VIENNA
+ ⊚

Nagyszombat +

Losonc •

↓Rimaszombat

Tal

M.

•Pozsony

•Léva ▲ +

•Fülek▲

Szikszo •

Duna R.

Ipoly R.

•Moson

Balassagyarmat

+▲■↓ Miskolc •

Komárom

Esztergon

Vác

•Pásztó

•Eger ▲■↓

Sopron +

+▲■Győr

Ács•

Szentendre•

Gyöngyös ▲■↓ +

▲↓+Debrec

Tata•

•Hatvan

Továros

Romáz

+▲■↓BUDA⊚PEST

Nagykáta

Hajduszobos

Tétény•

•Soroksár

•Irsa

Szolnók

Ráckeve•

Sári

Cegléd

•Karcag

+ Székesfehérvár•

Szabadszállás•

Tas

Szabadszállás•

+▲■↓ Kecskemet

Nagykörös +

Kőrös R

Dunaföldvár•

•Solt

Csongrad •

Szarvas Bé

Dunapataj•

Ágasgyhaza•

Kunszéntmárton

•Nagykanizsa +

+▲■Szentes•

Cyula

▲■

•Kalocsa

▲■Hódmezővósárhely•

Makó

•Baja

+▲Szeged•

Pécska A

Szabadka•

Nagyszentmiki

Topolya•

Temesvá

▲■

Eszék ↓

Szenttamás•

Dráva R.

Szává R.

Péterrárad ↓

•Nagybecskérek

Ujvidék▲+■↓

Karlóca↓

Versec•

Fehértemlo

Zimony
+▲■ ↓

•Pancsova

T U R K E Y

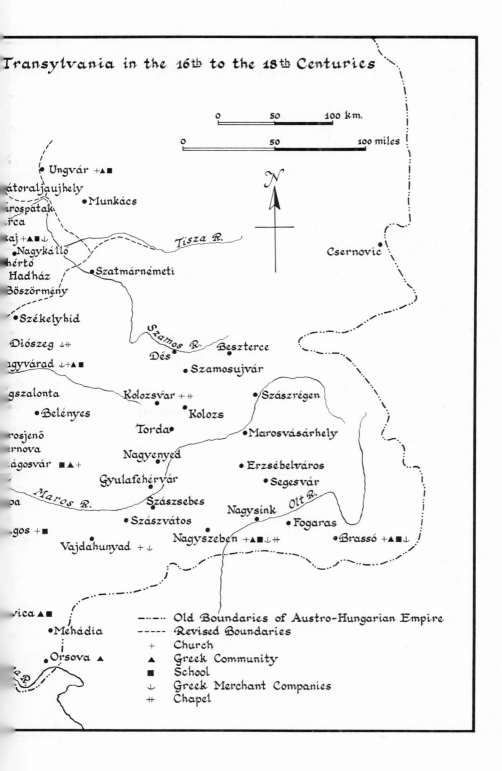

Transylvania in the 16th to the 18th Centuries

0   50   100 km.

0   50   100 miles

N

Ungvár +▲■

átoraljaujhely

rospatak

rea

aj +▲■↓

Nagykálló

hértó

Hadház

Böszörmény

Székelyhid

Diószeg ↓+

gyvárad ↓+▲■

gszalonta

Belényes

rosjenő

ernova

ágosvár ■▲+

pa

gos +■

Vajdahunyad +↓

Munkács

Tisza R.

Szatmárnémeti

Szamos R.

Dés

Beszterce

Szamosujvár

Kolozsvár ++

Kolozs

Torda

Nagyenyed

Gyulafehérvár

Maros R.

Szászsebes

Szászvátos

Szászrégen

Marosvásárhely

Erzsébelváros

Segesvár

Nagysink

Olt R.

Fogaras

Nagyszeben +▲■↓+

Brassó +▲■↓

Csernovic

vica ▲■

Mehádia

Orsova ▲

—··— Old Boundaries of Austro-Hungarian Empire
----- Revised Boundaries
  +   Church
  ▲   Greek Community
  ■   School
  ↓   Greek Merchant Companies
  +   Chapel

Greek Emigration mainly 1600-1800 to the Southern and Northern Balkans and towards Central Europe

Vienna ⊚ (A)
Bratislava • (3) (A)
Hemnitz •
to Breslau
to Lvov • Santagora
Chernovtsy •
BUKOVINA
Suceava • (3)
Kishinev •
Dniester R.

Győr • (3) (A)
(Raab)
Budapest ⊚
Miskolc •
Tokaj •
Egger (Erlau) •

HUNGARY
SIEBENBÜRGEN
Bistritsa • Jassy •
MOLDAVIA
Prut R.

Kecskemét • (3)
Szentes •

Szegedin •
Mokrin • (A)
Rekas •
Maros R.
Sibiu •
Brașov •
Galali •
Braila • (3)

Temesvar •
Caransebes •
Neusatz •
VANAT
Peterwardein •
Mehadia •
Semlin • Belgrade ⊚ (A) Orșova • (3)
Semendria •
Požarevac • (A)

BOSNIA
Kraiova •
Bucharest ⊚

Serajevo •
HERZEGOVINA (1)
Vidin •
WALACHIA
Danube R.

Ruschuk •
Lom Palanka •
Nis • (4)
Berkovitsa • (3)
Tyrnovo •

MONTENEGRO
Pirot •
Vranje •
Sofia ⊚
(2)

Adriatic
Sea
ALBANIA
Skoplje •
Kumanovo •
(3)
BULGARIA
Philippopolis (Plovdiv) •

Axios R.
EASTERN RUMELIA
Adrianople •

Veles •
Meleniko •
Constantinople ⊚

Durazzo •
(B)
Ochrid • Demir Hissar • Drama • Xanthe •
Komotine •
(C)

Kavaje •
Berat • (B)
Monastir •
Serrai •
Kavala •

Valona •
(B)
Biglista •
(C)
Thessalonica •

Koritsa •
Kleissoura •
Kastoria •
Kozane •

Samarina •
Grevena •

Bouthroto •
(B)
Metsovon •

Black
Sea

Ioannina •
Larissa •
Aegean
Sea

Parga •
Trikala • Volos •
Zagora •

Preveza •
Vonitsa •
Missolonghi •

Adrac
Sea

N

0   100 km.

100 miles

A Main emigration routes to Hungary and Austria
1 Through Bosnia
2 Through the Aliakmon and Axios valleys to Belgrade
3 Through Thessalonica or Serrai to Sofia-Vidin then branching off to Walachia-
   Moldavia or to Hungary-Austria
4 An extention of the same route from Sofia to Belgrade
B Trade routes to ports of Epirus and Albania, communicating with Trieste
   Venice and other ports of Italy
C Emigration current from Western Macedonia to Thessalonica - Serrai -
   Drama - Kavala - Constantinople

DATE DUE

JAN	2 1986		
GAYLORD			PRINTED IN U S A